PORTLAND COMMUNITY COLLEGE
LEARNING RESOURCE CENTERS

WITHDRAWN

D0573697

PORTLAND COMMUNITY COLLEGE
LEARNING RESOURCE CENTERS

The Archaeological
Encyclopedia of the
HOLY LAND

The Archaeological Encyclopedia of the
HOLY LAND

THIRD EDITION

Edited by AVRAHAM NEGEV

Introduction by Neil Asher Silberman

PRENTICE
HALL
PRESS

New York   London   Toronto   Sydney   Tokyo   Singapore

PRENTICE HALL PRESS
15 Columbus Circle
New York, NY 10023

Copyright © 1986, 1990 by G.G. The Jerusalem
Publishing House Limited, Jerusalem
Introduction copyright © 1990 by Neil Asher
Silberman

All rights reserved
including the right of reproduction
in whole or in part in any form

PRENTICE HALL PRESS and colophon are registered
trade marks of Simon & Schuster, Inc.

Library of Congress Cataloguing-in-Publication Data

The Archaeological encyclopedia of the Holy Land / edited by Avraham
    Negev. — 3rd ed., 1st Prentice Hall Press ed.
        p.   cm.
     Includes bibliographical reference and index.
     ISBN 0-13-044090-6 : $29.95
    1. Palestine—Antiquities—Encyclopedias.   2. Bible—Antiquities—
    Encyclopedias.   3. Excavations (Archaeology)—Palestine—
    Encyclopedias.   I. Negev, Avraham.
    DS111.A2A73   1990
    220.9′3—dc20   90-7782
                          CIP
Designed by Yael Gafni
Manufactured in Israel

Third Edition

Contents

Preface

This encyclopedia lists the majority of the geographical names mentioned in the Bible, both places in the Holy Land and countries and cities in other parts of the Middle East, identifying them as far as possible, describing the excavations that have been carried out at or near them, and analyzing the importance of the finds they have yielded. As well as tracing their history in biblical times, the encyclopedia discusses historical references to them in later periods up to the Arab conquest.

Three of the articles — Archaeology of the Holy Land, Archaeology: methods of research, and Prehistory — are a valuable introduction to the encyclopedia. In addition there are several general articles which provide a survey of specific aspects of the life and customs of the peoples of the Holy Land and the surrounding areas in pre-biblical, biblical and post-biblical times, and thus complement the information provided in the geographical entries. The following articles, which appear in their correct alphabetical position in the encyclopedia, will be particularly useful background reading for anyone who is unfamiliar with these periods: Agriculture, Baths and bathing, Burial, Cult objects, Embalming, Flint tools, Fortifications, Houses, Hunting and fishing, Inscriptions, Metals, Monasteries, Money, Musical instruments, Palaces, Precious stones, Roads, Seals, Stone implements, Stores, Synagogues, Trade, Water supply, Weapons and warfare, Weights and measures, and Writing materials.

Additional aids to the reader are to be found at the end of the book: they include an extensive glossary, a chronological chart of prehistory and of historical events in biblical and post-biblical times, and some information about the ancient sources which are frequently referred to in the text.

An asterisk (*) has been used throughout this encyclopedia for cross-references and to draw the reader's attention to other entries in which related subjects are discussed.

Foreword

There's something remarkable about that small stretch of territory hemmed in between the great Syrian Desert and the eastern shore of the Mediterranean Sea. In its unexpected variety of climate and landscape — ranging from the rugged, snowcapped mountains of Lebanon in the north to the arid Wilderness of Zin in the south, from the fertile plains of Philistia and Sharon on the west to the silent, salty Dead Sea on the east — it has been the scene of thousands of years of civilization, bitter warfare, intellectual and religious achievement, political wrangling, accommodation, and tragic inflexibility. And at the heart of the world's fascination with this small country is its greatest literacy production — the Bible — a timeless collection of wisdom, law, chronicle, prophecy, and poetry that is central to the faith of Jews and Christians and to the historical traditions of Islam.

The names that have been used over the centuries to describe this land are many: Retenu, Canaan, Zion, the Land of Israel, Palaestina, Filastin, the Holy Land, the Land of the Bible, Palestine, and Israel. And over the centuries, Egyptians, Philistines, Israelites, Assyrians, Babylonians, Greeks, Romans, Arabs, European Crusaders, Egyptian Mamluks, Ottomans, British, Jordanians, and Israelis have all attempted, with varying levels of justification and effectiveness, to take possession of the land, its people, and its history. That history is to be found not only in scripture and tradition, but also in the plentiful remains of ancient cities, fortresses, temples, tombs, and farmhouses scattered across the landscape. And for the past 200 years, western scholars have been engaged in a concerted effort to retrieve, catalogue, study, and analyze this wealth of archaeological evidence — as a means of better understanding biblical history.

That isn't to say that the aim of Biblical Archaeology has been merely to confirm the "truth" of the Bible. From the first, the careful excavation of its ancient sites and artifacts represented a dramatic departure from traditional western veneration of the Holy Land. Although countless European pilgrims and penitents, in search of saints' bones and other wonder-working relics, continued to visit the country through the Middle Ages, the founders of Biblical Archaeology — the small group of curious and skeptical western travelers who began to arrive in the Holy Land in the late 1700s — were not content merely to accept at face value the authenticity of the many icon-laden biblical shrines. In the spirit of the European Enlightenment, these early explorers demanded that the ancient legends be verified by systematic historical study. They insisted that the location of ancient sites be confirmed by the discovery of authentic antiquities. And beginning with the pioneering 1838 researches of a dogged New England Congregationalist minister named Edward Robinson, faith in the Bible was firmly joined with the scientific spirit. The landscape of the Land of the Bible slowly emerged from the realm of idealized tradition to be explored thoroughly, mapped accurately, and described in modern archaeological terms.

This newly revised *Archaeological Encyclopedia of the Holy Land* presents both general and more specialized readers with a convenient and useful source of information on the fundamental findings of Biblical Archaeology. In its pages, readers will find concise descriptions of hundreds of individual archaeological sites and discoveries as well as special articles on more general aspects of ancient daily life, culture, geography, and technology. The descriptions of specific sites include information on the date and circumstances of discovery, a listing of citations in biblical and classical literature, and a brief presentation of the most important finds. Review articles provide descriptions of the major archaeological periods and the most important finds from

Egypt, Phoenica, Cyprus, Asia Minor, Mesopotamia, Arabia, and Iran. In addition, a detailed chronological table, glossary of technical terms, and descriptive index of ancient sources offer useful points of reference for further study of the richness and complexity of the cultures of the ancient Near East.

The archaeological discoveries described in this book span more than 10,000 years of human history, and it's important to recognize how dramatically those finds have transformed our understanding of biblical history. Despite the Holy Land's lack of the monumental architecture, extensive archives of ancient tablets, and hoards of precious burial offerings found in neighboring Egypt and Mesopotamia, generations of Biblical archaeologists have nevertheless constructed a scheme of the development of civilization in the country that extends back as far as the Stone Age and as far forward as the Islamic period.

In few other regions of the world has the pace of exploration been so constant; every year, dozens of expeditions fan out across the rugged landscape of the area of modern Israel and Jordan, discovering and documenting previously unknown archaeological sites, uncovering ancient city levels, architecture, inscriptions, and artifacts. In recent years, clear indications of the emergence of early modern humans have been unearthed in the prehistoric cave sites of the country; evidence of the earliest use of agriculture as a means of survival has been found at rich Neolithic sites like Munhata, Ain Ghazal, and Jericho. The superimposed layers of the *tells*, or ancient city mounds of the country, have revealed abundant evidence for the rise of Bronze Age Canaanite civilization. Architecture, artifacts of daily life, inscriptions and seals from the Iron Age have shed new light on the culture and economies of the Israelite kingdoms. Finds from urban centers like Jerusalem, Samaria, Caesarea, and Acco have revealed the extent of Greco-Roman cultural influence in the country in New Testament times. And outside the Holy Land, archaeological excavations in neighboring countries have widened our understanding of the larger cultural landscape of the ancient Near East.

One word of caution: despite the popular Hollywood images of swashbuckling explorers quickly stumbling upon Lost Arks and other ancient treasures, the work of modern biblical archaeologists is, for the most part, a slow and painstaking process of discovery. Scholars routinely work at a single site for years with their colleagues, team members, and students, slowly uncovering the super-imposed layers of soil and crumbled buildings, analyzing architecture, pottery, and fragments of bone. Soil composition and plant and animal remains often provide important information on ancient daily life, diet, and environmental conditions. And the most important archaeological discoveries are usually not readily-recognizable buried treasure, but new insights on how ancient social systems worked, how changes in material life affected the course of history.

The main editors and contributors to this encyclopedia are among the most prominent Israeli and American biblical archaeologists. They represent a wide range of theoretical and historical perspectives, ranging from political, to economic, to environmental explanations of biblical history. Some, like the late professors Michael Avi-Yonah and Nelson Glueck, first rose to prominence in the 1930s for their excavations and explorations throughout the country during the period of the British Mandate. Others directed large-scale excavations of important biblical, Hellenistic, and Roman cities in more recent decades. Among the most notable of these projects were the excavations of Gezer led by William Dever, of Ai led by Joseph Callaway, of Beer Sheva by Yohanan Aharoni, of Ashdod and Acco by Moshe Dothan, of Dan by Avraham Biran, and of the Nabatean cities of Oboda and Mampsis by the encyclopedia's chief editor, Avraham Negev.

Through their study of material culture, these modern scholars and their many colleagues have greatly expanded the modern knowledge of biblical civilization. Their excavations have provided the raw material for writing the ancient social history of the region — by presenting the basic evidence of daily life, technology, warfare, and cult. Even in the Land of the Bible, where the detailed historical information preserved in the Old and New Testaments is richly supplemented by the chronicles of ancient Egypt, Anatolia, Mesopotamia, and Greece, archaeology has a unique contribution to make. Historical questions about the nature of the Israelite Conquest, the later wars and destruction suffered by the Israelite Kingdoms, and the spread of Christianity throughout the Mediterranean world cannot be answered by written sources alone. Newly discovered archaeological evidence on the vital economic, cultural, and social facets of the various ancient societies must also be taken into account.

Biblical Archaeology has been able to reveal an essential correlation, if not complete correspondence, between the spiritual and the material — between the text and the artifact. While a passage of ancient Hebrew poetry is by its nature quite different from an ancient oil jar or city level, their juxtaposition may have great historical significance. The timelessness of biblical literature may be at least partly derived from its endless capacity for reinterpretation. In a similar way, the physical remains of antiquity offer a complex focus for historical reflection. And as archaeologists continue to uncover unexpected finds and gain new historical insights in the Land of the Bible, this wide-ranging encyclopedia will serve its readers as a useful introduction to the richness of the archaeological record — and to the ancient Near Eastern cultures from which the Bible emerged.

Neil Asher Silberman

Contributors

The Late AHARONI, YOHANAN
Professor of Biblical Archaeology, Director of Institute of
Archaeology, Tel Aviv University

APPELBAUM, SHIMON
Professor Emeritus of Classical Archaeology, Tel Aviv
University

The Late AVI-YONAH, MICHAEL
Professor of Archaeology and History of Art, Hebrew University, Jerusalem

BARAG, DAN
Professor of Classical Archaeology, Hebrew University,
Jerusalem

BAR-YOSEF, OFER
Professor of Archaeology, Harvard University

BEN-TOR, AMNON
Professor of Biblical Archaeology, Hebrew University,
Jerusalem

BIRAN, AVRAHAM
Professor of Biblibal Archaeology, Director of the Nelson
Glueck School of Biblical Archaeology, Hebrew Union
College, Jerusalem

CALLAWAY, JOSEPHA A.
Professor Emeritus of Biblical Studies, Southern Baptist
Theological Seminary, Louisville, Kentucky

COHEN, RUDOLPH
Israel Department of Antiquities and Museums,
Jerusalem

DEVER, WILLIAM G.
Professor of Near Eastern Studies, University of Arizona,
Tucson

DOTHAN, MOSHE
Professor of Archaeology, Haifa University

DOTHAN, TRUDE
Lauterman Professor of Archaeology, Hebrew University,
Jerusalem

GEVA, SHULAMIT
Researcher, Van Leer Institute, Jerusalem

GEVA, HILLEL
Archaeologist

GICHON, MORDECHAI
Professor, The Department of Classics,
Hebrew University, Jerusalem

The Late GLUECK, NELSON
Professor of Biblical Archaeology, President of the Hebrew
Union College, Jewish Institute of Religion, Jerusalem-
Cincinnati, Ohio

GONEN, RIVKA
Senior Lecturer in Archaeology and Ancient Cultures,
Bezalel Academy of Art and Design, Jerusalem

GOREN-INBAR, NAAMA
Senior Lecturer in Archaeology,
Hebrew University, Jerusalem

HUMBER, JEAN-BAPTISTE O.P.
Professor of Archaeology, Ecole Biblique, Jerusalem

JAKOBY, RUTH
Teacher, Rothberg School for Overseas' Students,
Hebrew University, Jerusalem

KOCHAVI, MOSHE
Professor of Biblical Archaeology, Director of Institute of
Archaeology, Tel Aviv University

MAZAR, AMICHAI
Associate Professor of Archaeology,
Hebrew University, Jerusalem

MESHEL, ZEEV
Senior Lecturer in Archaeology, Tel Aviv University

MESHORER, YA'AKOV
Associate Professor of Classical Archaeology, Hebrew
University, Jerusalem, Curator, Israel Museum

NAVEH, JOSEPH
Professor of Semitic languages, Hebrew University,
Jerusalem

NEGEV, AVRAHAM
Professor of Classical Archaeology, Hebrew University,
Jerusalem

NETZER, EHUD
Senior Lecturer in Archaeology,
Hebrew University, Jerusalem

ROTHENBERG, BENO
Professor of Archaeology, University of London

ROSENTHAL, RENATE
University of Göttingen

The Late SHILOH, YIGAL
Head of the Institute of Archaeology and Chairperson of
the Department of Archaeology,
Hebrew University, Jerusalem

STERN, EPHRAIM
Lauterman Professor of Biblical Archaeology, Hebrew
University, Jerusalem

YEIVIN, ZEEV
Deputy Director of the Israel Department of Antiquities
and Museums, Jerusalem

A

ABARIM *See* *NEBO

ABEL-BETH-MAACHAH A fortified town in the north of Palestine (2 Sam. 20:14-18), also called Abel (2 Sam. 20:18) and Abel-Maim (2 Chr. 16:4). Joab, son of Zeruiah, laid siege to it in order to capture Sheba, son of Bichri (2 Sam. 20:13). In the days of Baasha, King of Israel, it was taken by Ben-Hadad, King of *Aram (1 Kgs. 15:20), while in the time of Pekah, son of Remaliah, it fell to Tiglath-Pileser III, King of Assyria (2 Kgs. 15:29). In the Hellenistic-Roman period it was known as *Abila. Eusebius (*Onom.* 32:16) and Stephen of Byzantium (*Abila) mention it as a city of Phoenicia. Identified with Tell Abil, within the limits of the Christian village of Abil el-Qamh.

ABEL-MEHOLAH A town in the territory of Issachar, in the *Jordan Valley. After their defeat the Midianites fled to the region of Abel-Meholah (Judg. 7:22), in the fifth district of the kingdom of Solomon (1 Kgs. 4:12). The birthplace of the prophet Elisha (1 Kgs. 19:16), it has been identified with a village called Abelmea, or Abelmain, with hot springs, that was known in the Roman period. Eusebius (*Onom.* 34:23) identified the site with Bethmaela, 10 miles south of Beth-Shean.

ABEL-SHITTIM; SHITTIM The last station on the route of the Exodus, east of the *Jordan, in the plains of *Moab (Num. 33:49). From there Joshua sent out spies to the land of *Canaan (Josh. 2:1), and there the Israelites gathered to cross the *Jordan (Josh. 3:1). Known as Abila, it also flourished in the Hellenistic-Roman period, when it was the capital of a toparchy in the *Perea and famous for its palm plantations (Josephus, *War* IV, 438). Identified with Tell el-Harman, west of *Heshbon.

ABILA A city of the *Decapolis, mentioned by Eusebius (*Onom.* 32, 14) as lying 12 miles east of *Gadara. Pliny does not include it among the cities of the *Decapolis, but an inscription from the time of Hadrian, found near Palmyra, confirms that it was part of the league. In addition, city coins starting from 64 BC followed the dating of the era of Pompey, which indicated that Abila was an important city in Hellenistic-Roman-Byzantine times. Antiochus III seized it from the Ptolemies (Polybius V, 71; XVI, 39; Josephus, *Antiq.* XII, 136). Conquered by Alexander Jannaeus,

it was subsequently taken by Pompey and granted independence. In the New Testament Lysanias is mentioned as tetrarch of Abilene (Luke 3:1). On city coins from the time of Caracalla it appears as Seleuciae Abila. (*See also* *ABEL-BETH-MAACHAH.)

The archaeological remains cover two hillocks (Tell Abil and Tell umm el-Amad) linked by a paved Roman road and a bridge across the valley. A temple, a large theater and a basilica are discernible on the surface.

ABU GOSH The modern village of Abu Gosh is situated 9 miles to the west of *Jerusalem. Within the limits of the village remains of prehistoric times, and of the Roman, Byzantine and later periods have been found. The earlier remains were excavated by J. Perrot in 1950, on behalf of the French Commission for Excavations. Three occupation levels were unearthed. Level A contained mixed deposits of late historic periods as well as flint tools. Level B was a mixed-occupation level, containing a lithic assemblage parallel to the pre-Pottery Neolithic B era in *Jericho and rectangular houses with plastered floors. It also contained some potsherds of the 4th millennium BC. Excavation of the site was resumed by Perrot in 1967-8 on behalf of the French National Center for Scientific Research. Two main occupation levels were now unearthed. In the upper level foundations of rectangular houses built of roughly squared blocks of stone were discovered, while the houses of the lower level were built of unworked field stones. The lithic industry of both levels was similar to that found in the 1950 excavations.

The remains of the later periods were excavated in 1923 and 1944 by the community of the local Benedictine monastery. To the Roman period belong a tomb and the remains of a large reservoir, part of which is still to be seen in the crypt of the Crusader church. This reservoir is ascribed to the Legio X Fretensis, a unit of which was stationed on the site. The remains of the Arab and Crusader periods are more extensive.

ABU HAWAM (TELL) A fortified harbor city near the mouth of the Kishon River. Excavations were undertaken by R.W. Hamilton of the Palestine Department of Antiquities in 1932-3 and soundings were carried out by E. Anati of the Israel Department of Antiquities in 1952 and 1963. The site was settled

PORTLAND COMMUNITY COLLEGE
LEARNING RESOURCE CENTERS

during part of the Late Bronze Age and Iron Age, between the 14th and 10th centuries BC, and reoccupied from the late 6th to the early 4th centuries. Discussions about the dating of the early layers, labelled V-VIII, have not yet reached any conclusion. Scholarly opinion is further divided on the date of destruction of Level III; while some attribute this to Pharaoh Sheshonq, in the last third of the 10th century BC, others favor the *Arameans as conquerors and a date in the last third of the 9th century BC.

The city of level V was surrounded by a solid stone wall. Two public buildings have been identified, a citadel and a temple. Of level IV several private dwellings — small square houses and a larger rectangular one — have been unearthed. This Iron Age settlement was apparently unwalled. No Philistine pottery has been found. Level III was again fortified, this time with a bastion of two parallel and heavily built walls. Private houses show uniform planning. The architectural remains of level II are unimpressive, apart from some Corinthian and Attic vases that point to trade connections with the Aegean world.

ABU MATAR (TELL) A site of the Chalcolithic period, about a mile southeast of *Beer-Sheba and less than a mile from *Bir el-Safadi, excavated in 1952-4 by J. Perrot on behalf of the French National Center for Scientific Research.

The settlement consisted of underground houses entered by shafts, which were excavated from the surface. These shafts led into underground rooms which were oval or circular in shape and were connected by tunnels, with numerous pits and silos sunk into the floors (*Stores). The entrance shafts were 4-7 feet deep, with handholds and footholds to facilitate climbing. The average size of the rooms was 9 feet by 14 feet, but some were larger. On the surface, above the underground habitations, were fireplaces, basins and additional silos. Flint was still used to some extent for household utensils and agricultural implements, as well as for scraping tools. There were considerable

Basalt bowl from Tell Abu Matar,
Chalcolithic period

quantities of malachite and ovens in which traces of copper smelting and casting were found. Some implements were made of bone. Basalt, brought from far away, was used for making bowls with very thin walls. The pottery was handmade, the necks alone being fashioned on a slow potter's wheel. The agricultural implements and the large number of silos found on the site indicate that the economy was based mainly on farming. The bones of domestic animals suggest that herding was also practised.

Interesting among the small finds are large quantities of pebbles painted with crosses and other marks. It is not known what purpose they served. Art objects found include pendants and beads made of mother-of-pearl, precious stones, ivory and copper.

Because of the close similarities between the local culture and that found in numerous other sites in the northern *Negev, it is known as the *'Beer-Sheba culture'. It is estimated to have lasted about two or three centuries and has some affinities with the later phase of the culture of *Tuleilat Ghassul. Carbon 14 tests have dated the *Beer-Sheba culture to the second half of the 4th millennium BC. Its origin is not known, although it has some similarities with the pre- and proto-dynastic cultures of *Egypt.

ABU SIF (CAVE) Paleolithic site on the right bank of Wadi Abu Sif in the *Judean Desert, excavated by R. Neuville. A few handaxes found above bedrock in layer E were considered by the excavator to be Micoquian. An empty layer of gravels (D) separated layer E from the earlier layers (B and C); these included an assemblage characterized by numerous Mousterian tools with elongated points, often in the form of a knife and flaked from elongated cores, which sometimes reveal a prepared striking platform. Similar points were found in the Mount Carmel caves but a closer comparison may be made with the tools found in the neighboring *Sahba Cave and in Hazar Merd Cave in Kurdistan. (*See also* *PREHISTORY; *FLINT TOOLS.

ABYDOS A city in Upper *Egypt. Important as a religious center from early times, it was the center of the Osiris cult in the days of the Middle Kingdom. The numerous mortuary monuments found testify to its significance as a city of the dead and a center of pilgrimage for the living. Apart from the mortuary chapels built by private persons, it also has numerous royal temples. Of great importance are those of Sethos I and Rameses II, whose reliefs include important data relating to *Canaan. Royal tombs of the first two Egyptian dynasties were discovered not far from Abydos. The pottery finds are of great importance for dating Early Bronze Age pottery of the same type found in Palestine. (*See also* *POTTERY.)

ACCAD A town in Shinar, or *Mesopotamia, listed in the table of nations among the cities of the kingdom of Nimrod (Gen 10:10) and frequently mentioned in Babylonian inscriptions. It should probably be sought north of the city of *Babylon, near Sippar. From the time of Sargon I it was the first capital of the kings of the Accadian Dynasty, who ruled Babylon for about 200 years. In the days of the 3rd Dynasty of *Ur (c. 2200-2100 BC) the name Accad was applied to the northern part of the kingdom of *Babylon.

Stele of Naram-Sin, King of Accad

ACCO Extensive excavations were begun at Tell Acco in 1973 on behalf of the University of Haifa and a number of universities in Germany, Denmark and the USA, under the direction of M. Dothan.

Remains of the earliest city, dating to the Early Bronze Age I, were discovered directly on *kurkar* bedrock in a small section of the mound. They consisted of pottery, foundations of walls, floors and several pits dug into the rock, and indicate that a settlement of farmers lived at the site at the end of the transitional period from the Chalcolithic period to the Early Bronze Age I. This settlement existed for about 200 years. It is possible that at the end of this time the sea level rose and inundated part of the mound over a long period of time. In any case, settlement on the mound was not resumed until the urbanization of the Canaanite coast in the Middle Bronze Age I. The fortifications of the town in this period consisted mainly of earthen ramparts built one above the other, which extended the area of the mound towards the

north. The earliest rampart was made of solid clay earth above which was a wall built of very large stones. This wall was subsequently strengthened by an additional rampart, topped by a brick wall containing a series of offsets. As only 60 feet of this wall was exposed, it is not known whether it defended the entire city, or was part of a citadel. The wall and stone steps that were added to it were later covered by a third rampart and above it a two story brick citadel was erected which was designated Citadel A. In its last phase, apparently in the Late Bronze Age, another rampart, dated to Late Bronze Age I, was erected above the remains of this citadel. These ramparts protected the mound on all sides except for the south, where Acco was defended by the swamps of the Naaman River. Another possibility is that a lagoon afforded anchorage on this side for light craft.

In the southwestern part of the mound a gate was found called by the excavator the 'Sea Gate', which belonged to the earliest rampart. It is almost 60 feet long, and consisted of two chambers and three pairs of asymmetric pilasters. One of the chambers contained a stone bench, perhaps for the city elders, for trade or for passing judgment. Pottery found in the gate attests to its use in three phases of Middle Bronze Age IIA. In the earliest rampart, within the city, *burials of children in jars were found.

In Middle Bronze Age IIB the earlier citadel formed a solid building (46 feet by 30 feet), originally of two stories, with walls 6 feet wide, still standing to a height of 14 feet. The destruction of this citadel is dated to the end of the 18th century BC. In a room in the lower story of the citadel was found a large tomb with its inner walls faced with thin stone slabs. In the tomb were three skeletons, of a woman with a child on either side of her; they apparently belonged to the local nobility. It contained numerous pottery vessels, silver ornaments and a Hyksos type of *pottery juglet. The tomb was apparently robbed still in antiquity. Numerous burials of this period were also found on the slope of the mound, with many pottery vessels, weapons, scarabs, and a rare jug of the chocolate-on-white type, of northern Syria or Anatolian origin. A unique type of tomb has a vaulted roof.

Remains of the Late Bronze Age I-II were discovered all over the mound. These consisted of massive walls, attesting to large buildings (only partly investigated). Among the *pottery were numerous Cypriote vessels of various types. One pit was found full of crushed murex shells, attesting to a purple dye industry. Some of the rooms, especially those built above the rampart, were connected with agriculture, and contained silos and various stone implements. In one small area were discovered, alongside Cypriote and Mycenaean pottery of the latest phase of the Late Bronze Age, bronze figurines of the 'Resheph' type and moulds for casting Astarte figurines. In the light of these finds, it appears that Late Bronze Age Acco was a well planned city, though no traces of its fortifications have as yet been found. The location of the gate destroyed by Pharaoh Rameses II, which is depicted in the reliefs in his palace at Karnak has also not yet been solved.

END OF THE LATE BRONZE AGE AND BEGINNING OF THE IRON AGE In several places on the mound, and especially above the citadel, were found remains of buildings covered with a layer of ashes of varying depth. These ashes came from an industrial quarter, mainly from pottery kilns and metal foundries. The pottery associated with these industries is Mycenaean-III-C of the end of the Late Bronze Age. The crushed murex shells also indicate that wool was dyed in this quarter. An Egyptian scarab dates this level after 1200 BC. It is possible that Acco was occupied in this period by some of the Sea Peoples.

IRON AGE I-II Little has survived of the 11th-9th centuries BC. The decline of Acco at this period may possibly be connected with the rise of Tyre. Acco witnessed a revival in the 9th century BC, reaching its peak in the 8th and 7th centuries BC. Ashlar construction, possibly of public buildings, occurs here for the first time. One of these buildings which was still in use in the Assyrian period contained a solid brick wall still standing to a height of seven courses. This building was destroyed in a conflagration during one of the Assyrian conquests, apparently by Sennacherib. To this level belongs a cache of small geometrically-shaped silver ingots. In another building were several rooms, whose destruction is ascribed to Asurbanipal. Here too there were traces of a metal industry.

PERSIAN PERIOD This was a crucial period in the history of Acco. The city now moved closer to Acco Bay, as a result of the transformation of Acco into an administrative and commercial center, mainly in the time of Cambyses. From that time Acco became an important naval center of importance both to Egypt and Persia. In addition to Phoenician elements, Greek finds also appear in the new city of Acco. Following the Babylonian decline a revival is also noted on the mound itself, where a well-planned city was built. One public building, constructed of ashlars, apparently served as the Persian administrative center. Numerous cult objects, including zoomorphic and anthropomorphic figurines, were found in a pit. Two ostracons were found inscribed in Phoenician characters. Also discovered were buildings displaying the Phoenician method of construction in which the walls featured a combination of alternating ashlar and fieldstone sections. In the part of the town containing these buildings, the finds are mostly Greek, notably Attic pottery of the late 6th-5th centuries BC. From the following century there are Attic Red-Figured vases and Cypriote vessels. This was apparently a Greek merchants' quarter, and it thus seems that Phoenician and Greek cultures existed side by side in Acco.

HELLENISTIC PERIOD The center of the city, now known as Akke and later as Ptolemais, moved to the bay, although the inland mound still retained its administrative functions. In the earlier phase buildings were still constructed in the Phoenician fashion. The many stamped jar handles point to an extensive import of wine from Rhodes, Cos and Thasos. However, the population now intermingled and there was no ethnic separation as in the previous period.

In later times, and especially in the last century, agricultural activities caused the destruction of several of the Hellenistic levels of occupation. Coins found on the surface of the mound attest to its strategic importance from the Roman period to Turkish times.

ACHMETHA The capital of the Medes (*Madai) (Ezra 6:2), also named Ecbatana, and the summer capital of the Achaemenid Empire; today Hamadhan, in Iran. The city was conquered by Alexander the Great in 331 BC and remained a royal city under the Parthians and Sassanids. No systematic excavations have been conducted but the surface remains and the evidence of ancient writers (mainly Herodotus and Polybius) give a fairly good idea of its former splendor.

Gold drinking horn from Achmetha

ACHOR (VALLEY OF) A valley northwest of *Jericho, close to *Ai, where the Israelites stoned Achan (Josh. 7:24-6). Identified with el-Buqeia.

ACHSHAPH A Canaanite city-state on the border of the territory of Asher (Josh. 19:25). Achshaph was a member of the league led by Jabin, King of Hazor, against Israel, and was among the cities that were vanquished (Josh. 11:1; 12:20). One of the earliest Canaanite cities, it is mentioned for the first time in the later group of *Execration Texts. It is also listed among the cities conquered by Tuthmosis III in the middle of the 15th century BC. According to the *El Amarna letters, its king sent 50 chariots to the aid of the King of *Jerusalem. It also appears in the Egyptian papyrus Anastasi I of the 13th century BC. The location of Achshaph is not certain, but it should perhaps be identified with Khirbet el-Harbaj, at the southern end of the Plain of *Acre. Some identify it with Tel-Kisan, southeast of Acre, where remains from the Bronze and Early Iron Ages were found.

Horse's head
from the Phoenician cemetery,
Achzib, 6th-5th centuries BC

ACHZIB *a)* A town in Judah (Josh. 15:44) whose destruction was foretold by Micah (Mic. 1:14). Tentatively identified with Tell el-Beide, northeast of *Mareshah.

b) A Canaanite city on the Mediterranean coast, in the territory of Asher (Josh. 19:29). The inhabitants were not driven out by Joshua, so the Asherites lived among them (Judg. 1:31-2). According to the annals of Sennacherib Achzib was among the cities that he conquered. It is also possibly mentioned in the list of Scylax (5th century BC), and was an important place in the Roman period. Pliny (*Nat. Hist.* V, 75) refers to the town of Ecdippe on the Phoenician coast, and it appears under the same name in Josephus' account of the Parthian invasion in 40 BC (*Antiq.* XIV, 343, *War* VII, 257). Eusebius (*Onom.* 30:13) knew it as a station on the road to *Tyre, 9 miles from *Acre, while the Pilgrim of Bordeaux, who visited the Holy Land in AD 333, gives a distance of 8 miles. In the Jewish sources it is referred to frequently as the northern border of the Holy Land and a synagogue is mentioned there.

Achzib is identified with ez-Zib, 11 miles north of *Acre. The site was excavated in the years 1958, 1960 and 1963-4 by S. Moscati, on behalf of the University of Rome, and by M. Prausnitz on behalf of the Israel Department of Antiquities and Museums. In a series of trial trenches the remains of fortifications were discovered. The earliest fortifications go back to the Middle Bronze Age II B, and include a rampart system, consisting of a fosse and stone revetment some 15 feet high. These fortifications were violently destroyed at the beginning of the Late Bronze Age. In the course of this period the city was resettled. The earliest town wall dates from the Iron Age II. (10th to 9th centuries BC), during which time the city attained its greatest expanse, occupying an area of some 20 acres. Within the wall six occupation levels were observed, ranging from the 9th to the 3rd centuries BC. Outside it, an occupation level of the Persian period was noted. The remains of this period consisted of a series of pavements and pits. Below this level four Phoenician tombs of the 10th-9th centuries BC were discovered. The tombs were built in the form of cists 4 feet by 7 feet, made of slabs of stone dressed in the typical Phoenician manner (*Burial). The tombs of that period contained Phoenician pottery, scarabs, ivories, seals and jewelry, all of excellent workmanship. To the east of the town another cemetery of the Phoenician and Persian periods was discovered. Part of the mound also yielded remains of the Hellenistic and Roman periods. In the fill of a Hellenistic building was found a stele in late Phoenician style of a type known from Punic colonies in the Mediterranean region.

ACRE *See* *ACCO

ADAM A town in the *Jordan Valley, close to the point where the Israelites crossed the river (Josh. 3:16). It was in this region, between *Succoth and *Zarethan, that Solomon cast the copper vessels for the Temple (1 Kgs. 7:46, 2 Chr. 4:17). The town is mentioned, as Adama, in Pharaoh Sheshonq's list of conquests in the temple of Karnak. It is identified with Tell ed-Damiyeh, on the eastern bank of the *Jordan, where remains of ancient times, as well as of the Roman and Byzantine periods, were discovered.

ADMAH A Canaanite border city in the *Jordan Valley (Gen. 10:19), whose king, Shinab, was beaten by Chedorlaomer, King of *Elam (Gen. 14:1-10). Together with Sodom and Gomorrah it was consumed by brimstone and salt (Deut. 29:23).

ADORAIM; ADORA One of the fortress cities built by Rehoboam, the first King of Judah (2 Chr. 11:9). In the Hellenistic-Roman period it was a large village named Adora or Adoreos. By the latter name it is mentioned in one of the Zenon papyri of 259 BC. It was the center of the eastern district of *Idumea in the early Hellenistic period, and was later conquered by Alexander Jannaeus (1 Macc. 13:20). Identified with Dura, south of *Hebron.

ADULLAM A Canaanite city-state, situated in the territory of Judah (Josh. 15:35), whose ruler was one of the 31 Canaanite kings vanquished by Joshua (Josh. 12:15). David hid in a cave near Adullam when fleeing from Saul (1 Sam. 22:1). The city was fortified by Rehoboam (2 Chr. 11:7) and was resettled by the Judeans after the Exile (Neh. 11:30). Judas Maccabaeus encamped there after the Battle of *Mareshah (2 Macc. 12:38). Called Odollam, it is mentioned by Eusebius (*Onom.* 24:21; 172:7) as a large village, 10 miles west of Eleutheropolis (*Beth-Gubrin). The biblical site is identified with Khirbet esh-Sheikh Madhkur, whereas the site of the later periods is identified with nearby Khirbet Id el-Ma, which has possibly retained the ancient name of the site.

ADUMMIM A mountain ridge traversed by the border between the territoties of Judah and Benjamin (Josh. 15:7), probably so called because of the reddish color of the rock (*adom* means 'red' in Hebrew). The place was also known in the days of the Mishna (1st century BC to 2nd century AD, and contained a fortress at that time. Eusebius (*Onom.* 24:10) refers to it as Maledomnei, which preserved the full Hebrew name: Maale Adummim, 'the ascent of Adummim'. In the fourth century AD it was garrisoned by Cohors I Flavia.

AENON A place on the River *Jordan near *Salim, where John baptized (John 3:23). According to Eusebius (*Onom.* 40:1) the site of Aenon was shown in his time 8 miles south of *Beth-Shean, in the vicinity of Salim and the Jordan River. *See also* *SALIM. The *Medaba map shows another Aenon, on the left bank of the river, opposite *Beth-Abara, where, according to a 6th-century Christian tradition, there was a cave known as Safsafas, in which Jesus dwelt while he was visiting John the Baptist.

AFFULEH An ancient mound situated within the limits of the modern town of this name. It has been almost completely obliterated, but some remains, mostly burials, are still being discovered over a large area around the site. In 1926 and 1931 trial digs were made on the site by E.L. Sukenik on behalf of the Hebrew University, in the course of which 19 burials were found, of the Early Bronze Age III, Middle Bronze Age II, Late Bronze Age II, and the Hellenistic and Roman periods. The earliest settlement remains on the mound are late Chalcolithic or from one of the first phases of the Early Bronze Age. This occupation level was represented by pottery typical of the *Tuleilat Ghassul culture. There were also gray burnished vessels. The houses were of convex mud brick. Early Bronze Age II and III were also represented, both by pottery and the latter by the Khirbet el-Kerak (*Beth-Yerah) type of ware. An olive press was also found belonging to the Byzantine period. In 1951 and 1952 I. Ben-Dor and M. Dothan excavated at the southern part of the mound on behalf of the Israel Department of Antiquities and Museums. Ten occupation levels were discovered. The earliest stratum (X) was of the late Chalcolithic period or an early phase of the Early Bronze Age, and was represented by two silos in which numerous gray burnished pottery vessels were found. The next stratum (IX) was of the Early Bronze Age I, to which scanty building remains belonged. Strata VIII and VII were of the Early Bronze Age III and IV. The earlier contained extensive remains of a house with numerous rooms, one of which was at least 16 feet long.

After the destruction of the latest Early Bronze Age settlement the succeeding one (stratum VI) was of the Middle Bronze Age I, to which a large oval pottery kiln belonged. In one pit of this period numerous pig bones were found. Stratum V is of the Middle Bronze Age IIB period, when the *Hyksos ruled the country. At this time Affuleh was a city of some importance. A section of two streets with some houses was unearthed. Nearby, a pit with unfired pottery was discovered, indicating that pottery was locally pro-

duced at that time. Among the local pottery, vessels of the well-known Tell el-Yehudiyeh type, typical of the Hyksos period, were also found. Within the town a large number of burials of this period were discovered. The Late Bronze Age II was represented on the mound by burials which contained typical pottery only. Stratum III was of Iron Age IA-B; to this period belongs a four-room house and a pottery kiln; noteworthy among the small finds is a stone game board. This settlement suffered destruction in the middle of the 11th century BC, possibly in the time of Saul. In the later phases of the Iron Age the site was sparsely settled. Affuleh is tentatively identified with *Ophrah.

AGRICULTURE Agriculture in the ancient Near East and its hinterland began when the climate turned cooler, between the 10th and 5th millennia BC. Southwestern Asia seems to have been the main point of origin of the earliest cultivated cereals and other food crops. The wild forerunners of many grain crops and pulses, the pear, grapevines and cabbage are found in *Egypt, *Mesopotamia, Syria, Palestine, Turkestan and Asia Minor, and traces of many of them have been revealed and dated to between 8000 and 5500 BC in archaeological excavations in the area. The Asiatic steppe was the point of origin of wild sheep and cattle.

Agriculture, involving the domestication of animals and the deliberate sowing and cultivation of food-plants, particularly cereals, succeeded the hunting and food-gathering stage. It was preceded by a phase of harvesting non-cultivated grasses, represented in Palestine by the Neolithic Natufian culture (*Prehistory). In the excavations this period is characterized by grindstones, mortars and sickles, and by evidence of the domestication of the dog on sites occupying alluvial soils (Mount *Carmel, *Eynan, *Yokneam). It is not certain whether actual cultivation was reached in this phase.

The origin of animal domestication has been attributed to the symbiosis of man and beast at points of water supply in times of drought, but it is disputed whether sedentary agriculture originated with cattle-keeping groups or with nomadic shepherds. The fact that rainfall was limited to the winter months and fluctuated annually tended to force cultivating and pastoral groups, in so far as these were distinct, into contact and competition over pasture and water in summer, while favorable years extended the limits of pasture and cultivation. Agriculture developed initially around perennial streams and springs, and as population growth resulted in settlement spreading to the uplands semi-nomadic shifting agriculture appeared in the south and east on the margins of these areas. Evidence of domestic animals multiplies in the Neolithic settlements (7th-5th millennia BC), which concentrated increasingly along perennial streams (*Sorek, *Yarkon, *Kishon and *Jordan), where the remains have been found of homes of single families or kinship groups. Remains of domestic cattle and swine have been claimed as early as the 9th millennium BC at such Neolithic sites as el *Khiam and *Eynan, and also at Kilweh (Transjordan, *c.* 6500-4500 BC). Figurines of cattle, goats, sheep and dogs

Egyptian model
of plowmen with oxen

from pre-Pottery Neolithic *Jericho show that the population of this walled oasis was at least partly engaged in agriculture in the 7th and 6th millennia BC. The tools of the period were the pick, the axe and the digging-stick, while the Yarmukian culture (*Shaar-Hagolan) used the spindle-whorl.

The Chalcolithic culture (4th millennium BC) was characterized by a shifting 'garden' cultivation, as at Wadi Shallal, evolving to something of a more continuous nature. Among animal remains, 84 per cent were of domesticated stock at Khirbet el-Bitar, 95 per cent at Tell *Abu Matar where sheep and goats preponderated and oxen and dogs were poorly represented. Wheat, some einkorn and barley were grown, also lentils; olive stones have been found at *Tuleilat Ghassul. Other Chalcolithic sites have yielded bones of dogs, donkeys and the half-ass (*hemionus*).

Later in the 4th millennium BC an urban civilization emerged, focused chiefly on the alluvial and clay soils of the lowlands. This development was made possible by increased food production, the use of bronze and the growth of population, the urban communities being surrounded by satellite farmsteads. Early Bronze Age strata at *Lachish yielded grains, grapes and pulses. Egyptian records during the 2nd millennium BC show that the area was rich in barley, wheat, honey and wine, figs and other fruits, together with sheep and cattle. In the 14th century BC Tuthmosis III of Egypt took over 2,000 horses, 1,900 cattle, 2,000 goats, 296 oxen and 20,000 sheep from *Megiddo. The excavations there have also revealed the presence of pigs and small specimens of the horse family. Cattle preponderated, however, at Bronze Age *Gezer. One of the major technical advances contributing to Bronze Age agricultural development was the invention of the bronze ploughshare (*Beth-Shemesh). Ploughs were small and were drawn by animals, throwing the soil equally to left and right. Nothing was known of crop rotation, but legumes might have raised soil fertility, as well as providing fodder for livestock, while the short sickle of the Bronze Age would leave stubble, possibly for grazing and manuring.

The Hebrew patriarchs owned large flocks of sheep and goats, but they were not fully nomadic because they did sow seasonally, sometimes with success (Isaac at *Gerar). Genuine camel nomadism appears

in the 13th-11th centuries BC, with peoples such as the *Midianites. The camel in fact occurs at Gezer in the Middle Bronze Age and sporadically in Egypt from the pre-Dynastic period. From the clash between an agricultural urban society and immigrant semi-nomadic landless groups (15th-13th centuries BC) the Hebrews emerged as the dominant force. They were able to consolidate their hold on the hill country because they had already developed techniques for conserving water in plastered cisterns and for terrace cultivation (*Water supply). Initially their fields were cultivated from the towns (Tell *Beit Mirsim), but with improved security in the later royal period (9th-6th centuries BC) livestock were kept outside and the towns became the centers of agricultural industries (Tell *Beit Mirsim, *Weaving and *Dyes and dyeing; *Beth-Shemesh, *Oil production). Settlement was by kinship within the framework of the tribe. Kinship bore responsibility for keeping the family lots within the group. By the end of the 11th century iron had been introduced, probably by the *Philistines, with consequent improved facilities for plowing and cultivation. The Gezer calendar (*Inscriptions) regulated a mixed-farming pattern, composed of early and later-sown cereals, flax, olives, vines and undefined summer crops. Plant finds from *Lachish in the Early Iron Age comprised olives, grapes, wheat, barley and other cereals and pulses.

Hebrew biblical agriculture was self-sufficient mixed farming based mainly on the small family unit. In the course of time it became highly diversified: the farmers of Transjordan brought cereals, lentils, butter, sheep and cattle to David. Later sources (Proverbs; Ecclesiastes) describe the large self-supporting household with orchards, vineyards and livestock, producing woollen, linen and leather goods for sale. Mishnaic references indicate manuring by the folding of stock or by farmyard manure. Unsown arable land was plowed three or four times, suggesting biennial fallow, but the Hebrew sabbatical (seventh) year fallow was also important to soil fertility. Some 30lbs of seed were used to the half-acre, about half the quantity normally used today, possibly planted by dibbling. Summer crops, such as cumin and flax, were sown before barley and wheat. Irrigation was known, particularly in the Jordan Rift. Weeding was by hoe and harvesting by sickle, the stalk apparently being

Oldest deep mortar and its pestle, made of basalt, 15,000 years old

cut high. Grain was threshed by oxen, threshing sled or stone threshing roller. Legumes and barley were fed to stock, along with chopped straw and hay. While the vegetables recorded in the Bible are few — leeks, onions, garlic — a number of herbs and several plants (hyssop, myrtle, camphor, crocus, rose, etc.) were used for perfumes and incense as far back as the period of the United Monarchy (*Spices and perfumes; *En-Gedi). Among orchard and plantation produce were nuts, pomegranates, figs, dates, grapes, olives, the fruits of the sycamore and carob trees, *ethrogs* (a citrus fruit) and apples.

The foundation of the United Monarchy by David in 1020 BC led to the growth of larger estates held by the king and his nobles; the prophets provide evidence of land accumulation at the expense of the small peasant and the emergence of a royal tenantry. State control of production and systematic royal taxation began under David, who appointed stewards in charge of cattle-rearing, vineyards, olive and sycamore groves and granaries (*Stores). Stamped jar-handles (*Seals) and the ostraca found at *Samaria provide evidence of systematic taxation of oil and

wine. Solomon's chariotry also implies a well-organized supply of grain and fodder; indeed Solomon also exported large quantities of wheat to Tyre annually, while the establishment of the Temple cult testifies to a well-developed animal husbandry, especially cattle. It seems that geese were fattened for the royal court, but other poultry does not appear before the 6th century BC.

After the return from the Babylonian exile, enslavement of small peasants for debt (*Slavery and work) and land-grabbing by the aristocracy increased the number of large estates, though the process was checked by the efforts of Nehemiah. Judea remained a country of preponderantly peasant holdings until it fell within the Hellenistic orbit in 332 BC. In western Samaria field-towers of the Hellenistic and earlier Roman periods, each representing a family holding, have been found to be connected with wine production, but were also associated with oil presses and threshing floors, the units varying from 5 to 25 dunams. In southwest Samaria, four-roomed Early Iron Age II farmhouses, each inhabited by 40-50 souls, continued to be occupied into the Hellenistic age.

Hellenization accelerated technical progress and initiated gruelling taxation, only temporarily alleviated by the Hasmoneans. Ptolemaic control led to the expansion of state-owned lands worked by tied peasants. In the 3rd century BC the country was exporting summer wheat, olive oil, wine, meat and cheese. Some new introductions such as fenugreek *(Trigonella graecum L.)* probably preceded the arrival of the Greeks, who acclimatized Egyptian beans, lentils and gourds. Apricots, peaches, cherries, oranges and lemons reached the area from Asia via Italy. Cotton and rice also entered the country in this period. Mishnaic and Talmudic sources list numerous plants first imported in the Hellenistic and Roman periods, including lupins, asparagus, marrows and turnips. The agriculture of the times was mixed and intensive, chiefly for home consumption and based primarily on grain, olives and vines. But it also included industrial crops (cotton, flax, hemp and perfume plants), fruit and market gardening. Oil production reached industrial proportions, perhaps associated with a cooperative system of distribution. Manuring was careful and intensive; though there were rabbinical reservations with regard to goat rearing, this denotes a close relationship between cattle rearing and arable farming. Fallow was biennial, but summer crops must sometimes have resulted in a triennial rotation. The plow of the Mishna was a heavy beam plow to which mould-boards could be fitted. It had no iron blade, but could cut to a depth of about a foot. Iron plow-points are found from the early 1st millennium BC — e.g. Tell el-Ful, stratum II. Irrigation machinery was also much elaborated, resulting in greatly increased grain yields. Farm units tended to shrink, owing to population growth and Gentile pressure. Tenancy, on the other hand, increased again after AD 70 with the growth of Roman state domains, parts of which were leased to the Jewish patriarchs in the 3rd century AD. Judea's prime

(Right) Plowing and sowing, in an Egyptian wall-painting

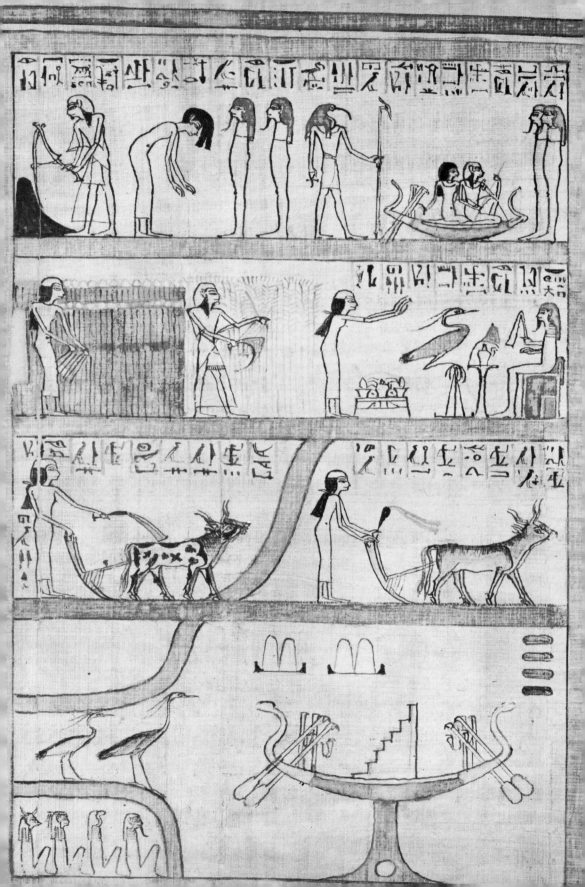

exports were wine, dates and incense. Linen became a speciality in the 4th century AD (*Beth-Shean, *Arbel) and a very fine wool, identified in the *Dead Sea scrolls, may be related to the fine Eastern Mediterranean wools mentioned in the ancient sources.

The Hellenistic, Roman and Byzantine periods saw the growth of the isolated farm as opposed to farming focused on village centers. In Byzantine times such farms, associated with olive and vine growing, were densely distributed in the coastal plain. Greco-Roman terminology and the use of the Roman mile to determine the limits of cattle ranging denote Greco-Roman influences in the country.

The Mishna states that fields were customarily open in the lowlands and enclosed in the hills. Small square fields (possibly market gardens) have been noted near *Ashkelon, and in the northern *Negev. The earliest traces of arid zone run-off farming in the central Negev date from the period of the Divided Monarchy (931 BC). Three successive phases, probably further developed by the *Nabateans, may be noted through an expansion of the cultivated stream-bed areas to a year-round cultivation of enclosed summer and winter crops, combined with manuring, stock grazing and the benefits of a wider drainage area by means of canals. There is evidence of vines and figs being cultivated at *Nessana.

Trial sections against ancient dams in the Negev suggested a sharp rise in rainfall in the 9th century BC. It is now thought that in the Middle East between the 4th century BC and the end of Byzantine rule a slow but steady decline towards increased aridity occurred.

Excavations at Heshbon (1968-76) showed that sheep and goats were 75 percent of the bone finds from Early Iron Age I to the early Arab period. The domestic pig was most numerous in the Hellenistic period. Generally the number of livestock fell off in the Hellenistic and Roman periods and recovered in the Byzantine period. At Jericho cattle increased in the Hellenistic, Roman, Byzantine and Arab strata, but goats were more prominent. At Tell Hepher the domestic pig appeared when Byzantine settlers replaced the Samaritan population.

AI; HAI An ancient Canaanite city-state situated near Beth-Aven, east of *Beth-El. The name Hai, or Haai in Hebrew, means 'ruin', and it is possible that the Israelites took this name over from their predecessors, the *Canaanites, in whose time the site was already in ruins. Abraham pitched his tent between *Beth-El and Hai and built an altar to the Lord there (Gen. 12:8), going back to the same spot on his return from *Egypt (Gen. 13:3). After the conquest of *Jericho Joshua sent spies to Ai (Josh. 7:2). Later 'Joshua burnt Ai, and made it a heap for ever, even a desolation unto this day' (Josh. 8:1-24, 28). The King of Ai is in the list of those vanquished by Joshua (Josh. 12:9). In the period of the kingdom of Judah Ai is mentioned in the form of Aiath (Isa. 10:28). After the Restoration in 538 BC, 223 men of Ai and *Beth-El returned from exile with Zerubbabel (Ezra 2:28; Neh. 7:32). The town is mentioned once in the form of Aija (Neh. 11:31).

Ai is identified by most scholars with et-Tell, i.e. 'the mound', about a mile southeast of Beitin, which is identified with *Beth-El. As no remains of the Middle and Late Bronze Ages were found at et-Tell, some

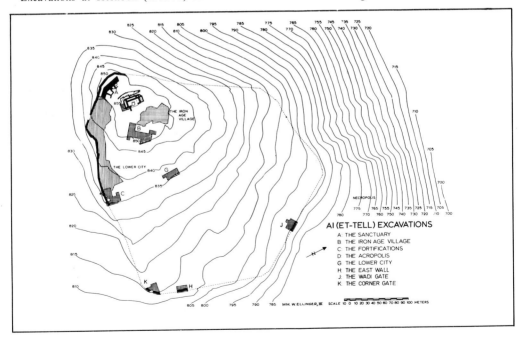

AI (ET-TELL) EXCAVATIONS

A: THE SANCTUARY
B: THE IRON AGE VILLAGE
C: THE FORTIFICATIONS
D: THE ACROPOLIS
G: THE LOWER CITY
H: THE EAST WALL
J: THE WADI GATE
K: THE CORNER GATE

WM. W. ELLINGER, III   SCALE 10 0 10 20 30 40 50 60 70 80 90 100 METERS

Plan of the excavations at et-Tell (Ai)

scholars have tried to identify Ai with one of the other ancient sites in its vicinity, but none have yet been proved. The Rothschild excavations at et-Tell in 1933-5, directed by Mme. J. Marquet-Krause, began on the acropolis to the southwest of the mound. During the first campaign a large structure, termed a palace, was exposed and a number of Early Bronze Age tombs were found on the northeastern slope of the site. On a terraced level under the acropolis to the northeast an Iron Age city was excavated. The lower city, which consisted primarily of Early Bronze Age architecture and fortifications, was also excavated across the southern point of the mound on a terrace under the acropolis. The well-known Early Bronze Age sanctuary was found against the city wall southwest of the acropolis.

To complete the work begun by Mme. Marquet-Krause the Joint Archaeological Expedition to Ai was organized and began excavations in 1964. This expedition was sponsored by the American School of Oriental Research in co-operation with a consortium of American institutions and the Palestine Exploration Fund and was directed by J.A. Callaway. Sites have been excavated in the upper city, to check the archaeological history reconstructed by Mme. Marquet-Krause, and on the lower eastern side of the mound along the city wall. Her conclusion that the site was unoccupied between Early Bronze Age III and Iron Age I was confirmed by sections obtained in several places. The Iron Age village covered not more than about $21^1/_2$ acres and was unfortified, while the Early Bronze Age city enclosed $27^1/_2$ acres within its walls. Minor modifications in her reconstruction of the cultural history of the Early Bronze Age on the site seem to be warranted. The results of the various excavations can be briefly summarized.

EARLY BRONZE AGE I A number of tombs excavated in 1933-5 contained linear-decorated and plain pottery similar to that found in corresponding levels at *Jericho. The assemblages from tombs at Ai suggest settlement of the site later than the initial Early Bronze Age settlement at *Jericho. On the mound itself almost no linear-decorated pottery has been found. It is probable that remnants of small walls found on bedrock under the first city-building phase at et-Tell should be associated with the people who buried their dead in the tombs on the northeastern slopes.

EARLY BRONZE AGE II A new walled city of $27^1/_2$ acres in area was constructed on the site in about 2900 BC. The walls of this city were 18 feet wide and they have been traced on several sites (see plan). Considerable planning and organizational work are reflected in the completeness and siting of the first city, which had a sanctuary at Site A, a walled citadel on the acropolis at Site D and what appeared to be an industrial area at Site C. Narrow entrances through the city wall are indicated at Sites J and K. Pottery found in Site C indicates at least a trade relationship with *Egypt during this period. The city seems to have been terminated by a major earthquake which toppled the mudbrick walls. The city wall, of field stones, leaned outward from the rebuilt inner wall of acropolis structures. It was buttressed by a second outer wall and

repaired, preserving the tilt in the reconstructed wall. In every place excavated there was evidence of a fierce conflagration, reaching temperatures sufficient to reduce stone to powdered lime.

EARLY BRONZE AGE IIIA A massive rebuilding of the entire city took place at the beginning of Early Bronze Age III. The city wall was strengthened with a second wall that encircled the original one. Debris from the destruction of the earlier city had accumulated as high as the inner top of the Early Bronze Age II wall. Consequently houses were built over the ruined top of the old city wall and the new walls, almost touching the original ones at the base, extended the fortifications outward. A 24 feet-wide section of the east wall at Site H remained to a height of 21 feet. Both the sanctuary and the acropolis buildings were reconstructed during this period. The sanctuary was a rather crude structure of field stones, built against a tower integral with the city wall. The tower was 24 feet wide and 9 feet long. The finds in the sanctuary, such as an alabaster figurine of a hippopotamus, may suggest the presence of an Egyptian cult. It is not unlikely that the Early

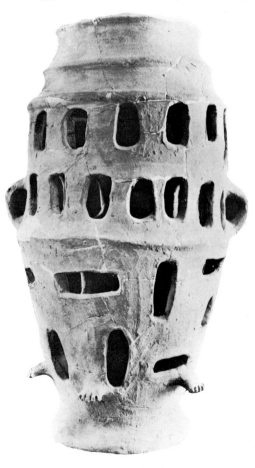

Incense stand, clay, Iron Age, found at Ai

Bronze Age IIIA city at et-Tell was much more under Egyptian control than the Early Bronze Age II city, and could indeed have been Egypt's vassal.

A few pieces of Khirbet Kerak ware (*Pottery) have been found in the last phase of Early Bronze Age III occupation. The city seems to have been destroyed by military action after the Khirbet Kerak culture appeared in the north and presumably penetrated to *Jericho. The excavator believes that the city fell during the disintegration of the Pyramid Age dynasties in *Egypt, before the end of Early Bronze Age III in Palestine.

IRON AGE I Et-Tell lay in ruins until it was resettled at the beginning of Iron Age I. When the neighboring Iron Age I villages of *Beth-El, Tell en-*Nasbeh, *Gibeah and *Gibeon were built, a small, unfortified village was established at et-Tell on the acropolis, covering about 2½ acres. Cisterns in almost every house excavated indicate a dependence upon stored water. The houses were unsophisticated, although one house excavated in Site B, Area XV, did have a central court with a long room on either side. The partitions between the court and rooms were built of standing pillars with field stones laid between the pillars (*Houses). Pottery and other objects from the Iron Age village indicate that it was built at the beginning of the period. There was a major phase of occupation, after which the village seems to have suffered some damage to its original structure and was abandoned for a short time. When it was reoccupied a smaller area of the acropolis was rebuilt with flimsy structures. This phase ended with the emergence of the Davidic monarchy. The Iron Age I village at et-Tell was probably biblical Ai. The 'men of Ai' whom Joshua defeated in the wadi north of the site (Josh. 8:1-29) were probably the first inhabitants of the Iron Age I site. They would have been contemporaries of the Iron Age I inhabitants of *Gibeon, with whom Joshua negotiated a treaty which led to the war with the *Amorites. *Gibeon had no Late Bronze Age city that has been found, although one major Late Bronze Age tomb was excavated there. But there was a significant Iron Age I village. The statement in Joshua (10:2) that *Gibeon was greater than Ai reflects a comparison between the Iron Age I villages, not the earlier ruins. This conclusion is supported by excavations at *Dibon and *Arad, where the Children of Israel found settlements before they entered the hill country from the east. Neither *Dibon nor *Arad was occupied between Early Bronze Age and Iron Age I, which gives the same archaeological picture as at et-Tell. The settlements encountered were Iron Age I, unless the accounts are historically faulty, a suggestion that is not warranted by the evidence. To transfer the conquest of Ai to *Beth-El became the evidence at Ai does not fit a Late Bronze Age dating of the conquest also seems unwarranted.

AIJALON a) It is mentioned by the name Aialuna in the *El-Amarna letters of the 14th century BC. A town in the northwestern part of the *Plain of Judah (Josh. 19:42), inhabited by *Amorites who became tributaries of the "house of Joseph" (Judg. 1:35). Saul and Jonathan won a great victory over the *Philistines in

the valley of the same name (1 Sam. 14:31). It was inhabited by the tribe of Ephraim (1 Chr. 6:69) and then by Benjaminites (1 Chr. 8:13). It belong to the kingdom of Judah and was one of the cities fortified by Rehoboam (1 Chr. 11:10). In the times of Ahaz it was conquered by the Philistines (2 Chr. 28:18). Eusebius (*Onom.* 18:14) mentions it by the name of Ailon, a village 3 miles west of *Bethel. It has been located (doubtfully) at Khirbet Haiyan or Tell el-Qoqa in the vicinity of Yalo, which possibly preserves the ancient form of the name.

b) A site in the territory of Zebulun, the birthplace of the judge Elon (Judg. 12:12). Not identified.

AJALON (VALLEY OF) The valley in which the city of *Ajalon was situated, and where, during the war between the Israelites and the five kings of the *Amorites, the moon stood still (Josh. 10:12-13). The valley is mentioned in one of the *El-Amarna letters, in which the king of *Jerusalem complains to Pharaoh about the plundering of a caravan on its way across the valley to *Egypt. In the time of the Hasmonean uprising (*c.* 167 BC) the Valley of Ajalon is referred to as 'by Emmaus in the plain country' (1 Macc. 3:40 ff.). It is identified with Merj Ibn Omar, which is intersected by the main highway from *Tel Aviv to *Jerusalem, some 15 miles from the latter.

AJJUL (TELL EL-) A site at the mouth of Wadi Ghazzeh, some 6 miles south of modern Gaza. Excavations undertaken between 1930 and 1934 by the British School of Archaelogy under the direction of W.M.F. Petrie brought to light rich finds. He concluded that the tell was the site of ancient Gaza in the

Gold pendant, Tell el-Ajjul, Late Bronze Age

Gold pendant in the shape of a flying hawk from Tell el-Ajjul

Middle Bronze Age and part of the Late Bronze Age. It is probably to be identified with Beth Eglaim, mentioned by Eusebius at a distance of 8 miles from Gaza. The excavation results were published with many illustrations but without precise data as to the location of these finds in terms of occupation levels. All of the absolute dates fixed by Petrie proved to be too high, and have been rectified by W.F. Albright. The ceramic evidence drawn from the large number of excavated tombs is of great significance for the dating of Palestinian pottery.

The earliest remains on the mound consisted of a cemetery. Copper weapons were found in many of the tombs. Dated by Petrie to 3300-3100 BC, it has proved to be 1,000 years later, belonging to the Early Bronze Age III and corresponding to the earliest stratum (J) at Tell *Beit Mirsim. To the succeeding period, the Middle Bronze Age, belong the cemetery, numbered by the excavators 100-200, the area to the east of the mound and cemetery 1500 to the north, each of which had distinct burial customs. In cemetery 100-200 tombs contained mainly disarticulated skeletons, plus a few intact burials, and the tomb shafts were circular. In cemetery 1500 the majority of tombs contained intact skeletons and their shafts were nearly rectangular in shape. These features, as well as the offerings, pottery and weapons, can be compared with the tombs at *Jericho.

A large building, termed a 'palace' by Petrie, is attributed to the Middle Bronze Age IIB and C. This building was succeeded by four reconstructions. In Albright's opinion the first palace (of the Middle

Bronze Age) and the second one (of the beginning of the Late Bronze Age) were residences, while the three later structures (the last belonging to the Early Iron Age) were fortresses.

In the Middle Bronze Age, the *Hyksos period, the site was one of the prosperous city-states of which Canaanite Palestine was made up. Covering an area of about 5 acres, it was surrounded by the typical fortifications of that period, a huge ditch at the foot of the mound and a sloping rampart of beaten earth. The great wealth of the city in this and the succeeding Late Bronze Age is indicated by finds of gold and silver jewelry, comprising bracelets, torques, earrings and nose-rings, pendants and fillets for the hair. One of the most interesting finds is the rich tomb of a *Hyksos noble which contained chariots and horses. The painted pottery found abundantly on this site is characteristic of the last phase of the Middle Bronze Age II and of the Late Bronze Age I. It appears along the coast and in the low hill country before the end of Middle Bronze Age IIC, its dominant feature being its bichrome painted decoration, divided like a Doric frieze, with geometric patterns and bird and fish motifs. Some of the pottery finds suggest Philistine occupation.

AKRABBIM (ASCENT OF) A place on the southern border of the territory of Judah, probably somewhere south of the *Dead Sea, in the vicinity of the Wilderness of Zin (Num. 34:4; Josh. 15:3; Judg. 1:36). Eusebius (*Onom.* 14:8) knew a place of this name in the eastern part of Judah, where there was a very large village called Akrabettene, 9 miles east of Neapolis.

This, however, does not fit the biblical references. On the *Medaba map it figures on the eastern border of Judah, "named today Akrabitte". Some scholars prefer to identify it with the pass made by the Romans in the 2nd century AD, now Naqb Sfai, in the central *Negev, south of *Mampsis.

ALABASTER The garden of the king's palace at *Shushan was paved with red, blue, white and black marble (Authorized Version: Esther 1:6). The Hebrew Bible uses the word *bahat* instead of marble. (It is not really known what this Hebrew word meant in antiquity, but today it is used for alabaster.) Chemically, alabaster is a crystalline calcium carbonate or calcite. In Egypt it was used for making small bowls, juglets and scent bottles as early as the 3rd Dynasty. There are alabaster mines in Upper *Egypt and *Sinai and alabaster of inferior quality is also found in Palestine.

Alabaster head of a bull from Mesopotamia, between the 4th and 3rd millennia BC

High-grade alabaster is white, with delicate reddish-yellow veining, while the inferior category is yellow. Imported vessels made of alabaster were found in Palestine from as early as the Early Bronze Age. Local imitations of Egyptian vessels, probably produced at *Beth-Shean, began in Palestine in the Middle Bronze Age. Alabaster containers for perfumes and other costly substances were also made in the Roman and later periods in Palestine.

ALALAKH An ancient site in the plain of Amuq in northern Syria, identified with Tell Atchana, excavated in 1936-49 by C. L. Woolley. Its importance lies in its situation in one of the most fertile plains of the Fertile Crescent, and on the road junction connecting northern Syria with the Hittite empire and *Mesopotamia.

The earliest remains of human habitation were found on two smaller mounds nearby. The occupational history of Alalakh begins in the late Chalcolithic and early phases of the Early Bronze Age. The earliest level, XVII, is dated by the pottery. To level XVI belongs a temple, which was rebuilt no less than 17 times during the subsequent periods. The earliest building, a brick construction, was erected upon a platform 13 feet square and 16 feet high. This was rebuilt in level XV (3200-3100 BC), when the site had close trade relations with Mesopotamia. The earliest houses discovered were at level XIII (2900-2700 BC) and were of the courtyard type.

Level XII (2700-2350 BC) marks a new phase in the history of Alalakh. To this period belongs a palace, of which a row of huge brick columns and a vast platform, which raised the building above those surrounding it, have been preserved. This level was dated by cylinder seals to the Early Dynastic period of *Mesopotamia (*Seals). The temple of this phase was also rebuilt to a new plan, consisting of a forecourt and a small room, from which a staircase led to the shrine on the upper level. In level XI (2350-2200 BC) both temple and palace were rebuilt. The palace, of which six rooms were excavated, extended at this period over an area formerly occupied by private houses. Some of the rooms were vaulted. The prosperity of Alalakh at this period derived from its trade in hard wood from the rich forests in the surrounding mountains. The destruction of this city is attributed to Sargon of *Accad. In levels X and IX both buildings were rebuilt again. Level IX (2050-1900 BC) is of the same period as the 3rd Dynasty of *Ur. The same process of rebuilding was repeated in level VIII (1900-1780 BC). The excavator suggests that this city was vanquished by the kings of the 12th Dynasty of *Egypt when the rest of Syria was conquered.

The excavations from level VIII to XVII were made in quite a narrow pit, at a depth of 50 feet, while level VII and those above it were excavated over a wider area. In level VII the palace, a temple and the city gate were revealed. The dating here was easier, because numerous inscribed clay tablets, mentioning Hammurabi and two contemporary rulers, were discovered. At this period Alalakh was an independent state under the leadership of Yarim-Lim. To this level belongs also a large citadel, built above a plateau and protected by a brick glacis (*Fortifications) faced with clay. The city gate was a huge construction, of the direct-approach type, flanked by two towers. The gate was built of bricks set in a frame of wooden beams, a feature common among the *Hittites. The palace was a large complex of several courts, with the halls and rooms arranged around them. The temple, which was nearby, had extremely thick walls and consisted of a forecourt with a large rectangular shrine. In these buildings evidence of contact with the Mycenaean world and other countries came to light.

After the destruction of the city of level VII the citadel was rebuilt in levels VI (1750-1595 BC) and V (1595-1447 BC), both to the plan of a thickly walled castle set upon a high platform and protected by a steep glacis. As no inscribed material was discovered in these levels, the dating was by finds of pottery imported from Cyprus and Palestine. During this period Alalakh knew a short period of direct Egyptian rule, at the time when Tuthmosis I moved through the upper *Euphrates Valley after elephant (*Ivory) and Tuthmosis III imposed tribute on the city.

Level IV (1447-1370 BC, the period in which northern Syria was under Egyptian control) disclosed a rebuilt royal palace, in which numerous tablets were found, mostly of the reign of Niqmepa, to whom the building is attributed. It had 30 rooms in two separate complexes of buildings at least two stories high, a large gate and a spacious courtyard. The new temple had a tripartite plan, consisting of a forecourt with stairs in the wall leading to an upper level, an antechamber and a shrine with a niche in its rear wall. The citadel of this period was a large barracks with numerous rooms built around a court. The end of the city of level IV came with the Hittite conquest.

Levels III (1370-1347 BC) and II (1347-1283 BC) represent the Hittite domination of Alalakh. The citadel of this period was a rectangular building, with very thick walls and numerous rooms of unequal size. The new temple also differed in plan from its predecessors. Built on a high brick platform, it consisted of an outer court and an inner one, in which stood an altar. A portico and a staircase led to the temple proper. In level II the temple was rebuilt again, to a plan similar to those of earlier times. The whole city of level III was surrounded by a massive double wall protected by a glacis. The inner wall was 15 feet thick and the outer one 10 feet thick, the two separated by a passageway $4^{1}/_{2}$ feet wide. In level II a 40 feet-wide triple wall was built. Private houses were of the courtyard type, two stories high, and were provided with sanitary installations. The destruction of level II was attributed to the *Hittites, who crushed a revolt of the pro-Egyptian party in the city.

In level I two phases were distinguished, A (1283-1241 BC), under Assyrian rule, and B (1241-1194 BC), a city whose destruction was probably caused by the Sea Peoples (*Philistines). The temples of this period were built according to the old plan. In the latest a pair of lions, one on each side, faced the entrance from the court to the shrine.

Alalakh's harbor was discovered on the coast to the west of the site. This is identified with el-Mina ('the Port' in Arabic). It was founded in about the 12th century BC and the Greeks knew it by the name of Poseidon. Warehouses of different periods were found here. From the time of its foundation until its destruction in 301 BC it handled a very lively trade with Greece and the Mediterranean islands.

ALEXANDRIA A city in Egypt, founded by Alexander the Great in 332-331 BC after the conquest of *Egypt. The city was built on the site of a small Egyptian village, Rhakotis, in which the pharaohs of *Egypt settled Greek mercenaries and merchants. It is situated to the west of the Canopic arm of the *Nile, between the Mediterranean and Lake Marceotis. The island of Pharos was connected with the mainland by means of a mole 1,200yd long, and thus an excellent double harbor was formed. In the western harbor the

war-ships of the Ptolemies were stationed.

The city itself was built as a rectangle with streets intersecting at right angles. It consisted of five divisions and numerous suburbs. On the coast of the island of Pharos the world-famous lighthouse, one of the 'Seven Wonders of the World', was built by Sostratos the Cnidian in 297 BC. The most important buildings in the city were the Temple of Poseidon, situated by the eastern harbor, close to which Antony built his palace; the Caesarium of Cleopatra, which was begun by Antony and finished by Augustus; the Museion and close to it the Bibliotheca (library), the temples of Pan and Sarapis. The tomb of Alexander the Great is mentioned by the ancient writers but has not yet been discovered.

According to the Greek historian Diodorus Siculus (XVII, 52, 6), the city had 300,000 inhabitants in his time (first half of the 1st century BC). During the struggle between Caesar and Antony in 47 BC the great library of Alexandria was burnt down and the 900,000 volumes which it contained were lost. Antony rebuilt the library and brought books to it from Pergamon.

The city had a large and prosperous Jewish quarter, with a synagogue of vast and legendary size. This quarter was burnt down by Hadrian. Other parts of the city were severely damaged when it was conquered by Zenobia, Queen of Palmyra (*Tadmor), in AD 269. In AD 389 the temple of Sarapis was closed and the library plundered. In AD 618 the Persians conquered Alexandria. It was regained in 629 by Emperor Heraclius of Constantinople and was finally lost to the west when it was conquered by the Arabs in 642.

At first Alexandria was an autonomous Greek *polis* with limited rights (e.g. it did not have a *boule* or city council). After the Roman conquest Roman citizenship was conferred upon its inhabitants. In addition to the Greeks, a considerable number of Egyptians and Jews lived there. The economy was based on factories producing linen, paper (papyrus) (*Writing materials), gold and silver objects and large potteries. The main source of income, however, was the Indian and Arab spice trade, which reached *Egypt via the *Red Sea. Commerce declined after the Arab conquest.

Alexandria was a world center of science and letters. In the pre-Roman period the huge library was the most important center of learning in the world and many of the most famous Greek scholars served as its directors. One of the outstanding undertakings of this institution was the translation of the Bible into Greek. Known as the *Septuagint,* 'the translation of the seventy', it was the work of Jewish scholars. Alexandrian art exerted a great influence on Roman painting and mosaics and its most characteristic features can be detected in Jewish synagogal art (*Dura Europos), as well as in early Christian art. Early Roman and Nabatean pottery also owe much in their techniques and their stylistic repertoire to the art of the potters of Alexandria.

ALEXANDRION; SARTABA A fortress built by the Hasmonean king, Alexander Jannaeus, on the northwestern border of Judea, west of the *Jordan (Josephus, *Antiq.* XIII, 417). In 63 BC his widow, Alexandra, sought refuge at Alexandrion with her son Aristobulus, who fought Pompey there (Josephus, *War* I, 134). In 57 BC her grandson Alexander held out there against Gabinius and Antony (Josephus, *Antiq.* XIV, 86-91), who razed the fortress to the ground after it had fallen. In 38 BC it was rebuilt by Herod, who buried his mother-in-law and his wife Mariamne (30 BC) there, as well as his two children by this marriage, Alexander and Aristobulus (7 BC). Herod used the fortress to guard his treasures (Josephus, *Antiq.* XIV, 413-19, etc.). The site is identified with Qarn Sartaba, about 15 miles southeast of *Shechem, a lofty hill on the top of which the remains of the fortress are still to be seen. Sartaba is mentioned in the Mishna and the Talmud in connection with the beacons which were lit there to announce the new moon. Remains of the town of Alexandrion and of an aqueduct were found at the foot of the hill.

Excavations were conducted at the site in 1981 and 1983 by Y. Tzafrir, on behalf of the Hebrew University and Y. Magen, Archaeology Officer. Due to the ruinous state of the huge fortress, which had been shattered by a severe earthquake, no excavations were possible without resorting to specialized equipment, which was not available, and the excavations were therefore limited to the upper slope. There, part of a structure, apparently a two-story *palace decorated with Corinthian and Ionic capitals, was cleared. It contained a 60 feet square hall, with heart-shaped corner columns, surrounded by columns on all sides. The walls and ceiling of the building were decorated with frescoes. The capitals of this peristyle hall were of the Corinthian order. The floor was paved with *mosaics. It is dated to the time of Herod. In the debris of this building were discovered remains of an earlier palace, of the Doric order, which was apparently constructed by Alexander Jannaeus. Among the small finds were fragments of Italian wine jars inscribed with Hebrew, Aramaic and Greek inscriptions. Also found was a mould for casting Hasmonean coins. During the war against the Romans a Roman garrison was stationed at Alexandrion.

ALLON TO ZAANANNIM; ZAANAIM (PLAIN OF) A place on the southern border of the territory of *Naphtali, between *Mount Tabor and the River *Jordan (Josh. 19:33). Heber the Kenite pitched his tent 'unto the plain of Zaanaim, which is by Kedesh' (Judg. 4:11). The identification is not clear; some experts identify it with a site in the vicinity of *Kedesh (*Naphtali), but others suggest the fertile plain southwest of the Sea of *Galilee.

AMALEKITES; AMALEK The son of Timna, concubine of Eliphaz, Esau's son (Gen. 36:12), the youngest of the dukes of Edom (Gen. 36:16). It is possible that at an early stage in their history the Amalekites formed part of the Edomite tribal organization. They were an ancient nomadic tribe in northern *Sinai and the *Negev. While they were in *Rephidim the Israelites were attacked by the Amalekites (Exod. 17:8 ff.), and because of what happened then they were instructed to 'remember what Amalek did unto thee' (Deut. 25:17-19). Ehud, son of Gerah, vanquished a coalition of *Moab, *Ammon and Amalek (Judg. 3:12 ff.). Gideon fought the Amalekites, who joined

*Midian and all the children of the east (Judg. 6-7). They were beaten again by Saul (1 Sam. 15:2-33), but only David succeeded in annihilating them completely (1 Sam. 27:8-9; 30:1-17).

AMANAH *a)* A mountain range in southern Syria, mentioned in the Bible together with Shenir and *Hermon (S. of S. 4:8). The name occurs frequently in Mesopotamian inscriptions of the 21st century BC as a place from which the Sumerian and Assyrian kings brought high-quality marble and timber for building. Identified with Jebel Zebedani, source of the River Amanah.
b) The name of a river mentioned in the Bible, together with the *Pharpar (2 Kgs. 5:12; Authorized Version: 'Abana'), as irrigating the *Damascus region. Amanah is identified with the River Barada, which rises on the slopes of Jebel Zebedani.

AMMON; AMMONITES The land east of the River *Jordan, on the north bank of the River *Jabbok, called after the Ammonites. According to archaeological evidence, they settled there at the beginning of the 13th century BC together with the Moabites (*Moab) and the Edomites (*Edom), who settled more to the south. The Ammonites are mentioned as descendants of Lot (Gen. 19:38) and it seems that they originated from the *Amorites (cf. Num. 21:25 ff.).

At first Ammon extended as far as the *Jordan, but after the penetration of the Gadites and Manassites its border was pushed back towards the desert (Josh. 13:8-10). There was enmity between the Israelites and the Ammonites from early times (Deut. 23:3-4) and open war broke out when the Ammonites attempted to encroach on Israelite territory (Judg. 11). In the time of Saul they attempted to capture *Jabesh-Gilead but were driven back (1 Sam. 11). David sought refuge with Nahash the Ammonite and after the death of the Ammonite king sent men to comfort his son Hannun. But they were mocked, and this act of humiliation started a long war, at the end of which Ammon was defeated (2 Sam. 11:1). During Solomon's reign peace was established, and the ties became even stronger after his marriage with Naamah the Ammonite (1 Kgs. 14:21, 31). In the period of the divided kingdom Ammon took part in the rebellion against the Assyrians, but according to Assyrian documents the Ammonites had to pay tribute to Sennacherib. They suffered the same fate at the hands of Esarhaddon and Ashurbanipal.

When the Jews returned from exile Nehemiah forbade them to marry Ammonites and Edomites (Neh. 13:23 ff.). Ammon was then ruled by the Tobiads, Tobiah the Ammonite possibly being governor of Ammon on behalf of the Persian king (Neh. 2:19; 4:7; 6:10). By that time many Jews had settled in this area. Under the Ptolemies it became a Jewish political entity, called Ammanitis. Its capital was now Birta, or Tyros (*Araq el-Emir), the other important city being *Rabbath-Ammon, renamed Philadelphia. At the end of the Seleucid period the whole region became exclusively Jewish, under the name of *Perea.

According to recent archaeological discoveries the land of the Ammonites was sparsely inhabited during the periods of the *Hyksos and the New Kingdom of

Egypt. The discovery of a *temple in the region of Amman, and Cypriote and Mycenaean *pottery found in the temple and in contemporary tombs indicates that the country supported a permanent population during the first half of the Late Bronze Age. After a long gap in the history of settlement the land of Ammon was inhabited again at the end of the 14th century BC, and it was in this period that the kingdoms of the Ammonites, Moabites (*Moab) and the Edomites (*Edom) were created.

AMORITES One of the peoples found in northern Syria and *Mesopotamia from about 3000 BC, who also inhabited the land of *Canaan before the Israelite conquest. The name derives from *Martu,* meaning 'west' in Sumerian, and some believe that the *Martu* mentioned in Mesopotamian sources is the same as Amu in contemporary Egyptian sources, where the reference is to wanderers who overran Syria and Palestine and reached the borders of *Egypt. Somewhat later they are referred to in the Accadian documents as *Amurru,* which is very close to the biblical name. During the 2nd millennium BC the Amorites spread over large areas in *Mesopotamia and east of the Jordan, pressing southwards and westwards. They reached their zenith in the middle of the same millennium, but declined rapidly and merged with the newly arriving elements, the *Horites, *Hittites, *Canaanites, Hebrews, *Arameans and other peoples.

From the 15th century BC onwards the name Amurru appears as a geographical designation and refers to the area of the *Lebanon, central and southern Syria. This kingdom was sponsored by *Egypt as a buffer state between the Egyptian-held territories in the south and the Hittite menace to the north. The Amorite kingdom was conquered from time to time by each of the struggling parties, until it was finally taken by the *Hittites after the battle of *Kedesh-on-the-Orontes in 1297 BC. This state of affairs is well described in the *El Amarna letters. While the Hittites were pressing southwards the Amorite kingdom had to withstand growing pressure from the rising Assyrian kingdom. When contacts were established between them for the first time, in the days of the Patriarchs, the Amorites possessed a culture that was greatly influenced by that of *Mesopotamia, with strong local *Canaanite affinities.

The common cultural background of the Amorites and the early Hebrews may be seen in the documents of *Mari, of the 18th-17th centuries BC. In that period the Amorites dwelt in several places in Palestine (Gen. 14:7; 48:22), alongside the *Hittites (Gen. 23; Authorized Version: 'Heth'). According to Deuteronomy (1:7, 20) the Amorites occupied the mountains. In the period of the Israelite conquest the kings of *Jerusalem, *Hebron, *Jarmuth, *Lachish and *Eglon were Amorites (Josh. 10). The Gibeonites were the remnant of the Amorites (2 Sam. 21:2). The Amorites also dwelt far to the south, as far as *Akrabbim (Judg. 1:36), but paid tribute to the house of Joseph (Judg. 1:35). To the east the realm of Sihon, King of the Amorites, extended from *Arnon to the *Jabbok (Num. 21:21-31; Josh. 12:2, etc.). Another Amorite kingdom, farther to the north, was that of Og, king of

the *Bashan (Deut. 3:8; 4:47) which was also conquered by the Israelites (Josh. 12:4-5). In the period of the United Monarchy, when there was peace between Israel and the Amorites (1 Sam. 7:14), they paid tribute to Solomon (1 Kgs. 9:20 ff.). There is no later mention of them in the Bible.

ANAFA, (TEL) This mound is situated in Upper Galilee, on the western slopes of the Golan Heights. It extends over an area of 44 acres, rising some 45 feet above the plain. In the Hellenistic period the small mound served as an acropolis of a much larger lower town. The site has been excavated since 1968 by an expedition on behalf of the Museum of Art and Archaeology of the University of Missouri, under the direction of S. Weinberg in the years 1968-70, of S. Weinberg and S. Herbert in 1978 and of S. Herbert in 1980 and 1981. Aerial photographs indicate that the mound was surrounded by an enclosure wall in which there are several complexes of large buildings.

The northeastern part of the mound is occupied by a large building surrounded by a peribolos wall 6 feet wide. The building is dated to the end of the 2nd century BC. By the end of this century the building was dismantled down to the lowest foundation courses and above its remains a new building of a residential character was erected at that time. This building existed for about 30 years only, until not later than 75 BC. Within this short time five sub-phases were distinguished in this building. It was constructed of solid stone walls covered with stucco and had good clay floors (the courts were paved with flagstones). On the floor of the earliest court a stylobate supported a colonnade.

Another building, discovered in the central sector, represents another architectural phase. Its walls were preserved to a height of 9 feet. The outer walls were built of ashlar headers with a fill of large fieldstones, reminiscent of the Phoenician method of construction. The interior walls were built of mud brick on a substantial stone foundation. The upper story of the building was decorated with elaborately painted and gilded stucco, found in the debris. The building measures 124 feet by 124 feet; one of its rooms was 26 feet by 11 feet. This building included a hot bath consisting of three rooms, one of which was the stuccoed room. The heating and the sewage systems were located in the western part of the building which contained remains of mosaic floors along the walls. In one room (17 feet by $7\frac{1}{2}$ feet) the mosaic floor consisted of black diorite stones and white marble and was decorated with black lines and geometric designs. The bathhouse and the mosaic floors belong to the late Hellenistic phase. This is one of the earliest heated baths in the Middle East and its mosaic is the earliest found in Palestine.

In the northwestern part of the mound another building was excavated. Its upper phase was considerably damaged by an Arab cemetery, but the second phase was better preserved. In a courtyard a sequence of double ovens was discovered. The latest double oven was covered with cobblestones, instead of the usual cover of large potsherds embedded in a heavy coat of mud. Each oven was provided with a flue made of the neck of a Rhodian wine jar, which lay on the court floor outside the oven and was connected with a hole in the oven wall. The building to which these ovens belong is provisionally dated to the first half of the 2nd century BC.

The fourth area of excavations was a trench dug in the southern slope of the mound, outside the acropolis enclosure wall. Here a street with houses along its sides, part of a domestic quarter, was discovered. The later Hellenistic phase was more poorly represented. The remains of the earlier Hellenistic phase were much more substantial; they were built above an area which had suffered destruction by conflagration, apparently at the end of the Persian period.

The dating of the three Hellenistic phases was based on the large number of coins and stamped amphora handles. Most of the coins, dating not later than 85-84 BC, are of Seleucid kings or are city coins of Tyre and Sidon, dating between 150 and 85-84 BC. Only a few are earlier than 150 BC. It thus appears that the earliest Hellenistic phase dates to the first half of the 2nd century BC, the second phase to the second half of the century, and the third to the first quarter of the 1st century BC. The settlement was abandoned by 75 BC.

The finds from Tell Anafa portray the life of an extremely wealthy town. Especially impressive is the stucco coated with gold leaf and the richly painted and paneled walls, decorated with columns and pilasters, niches and windows. The floors were covered with mosaics made of very small glass and stone tesserae. Unusually large quantities of moulded glass vessels were found. The excavators estimate the number of glass vessels used in the acropolis area and the lower town in the many tens of thousands, and this in an age when glass was still a rare commodity. It is suggested that the glass vessels were produced in the region of Tel Anafa already in 150 BC. The same also applies to the Hellenistic red-slipped (or red-glazed) *pottery found in very large quantities, more than at any other site of the Hellenistic period in the country. There were also rich finds of gold, silver, bronze and iron implements and weapons. A small cache of excellently-cut semiprecious stones was also uncovered. The Greek influence at Tel Anafa is evident in the imports from Greek lands and in the numerous graffiti in Greek appearing on the red pottery. Only one seal had one line in a Semitic alphabet.

Also found were remains of the Persian period, Iron Age, Late Bronze Age, Middle Bronze Age and Early Bronze Age II. The uppermost level of occupation was attributed to the Roman and early Arab periods. It is however the occupation levels of the Hellenistic period which were most thoroughly investigated.

ANANIAH *See* *BETHANY

ANATHOTH A Levitical city in the territory of Benjamin (Josh. 21:18), the birthplace of two of David's mighty men (2 Sam. 23:27; 1 Chr. 12:3). Abiathar the priest was banished to his own fields at Anathoth by Solomon (1 Kgs. 2:26). The prophet Jeremiah was born there (Jer. 1:1) and the city is also mentioned in the prophecies of Isaiah (10:30). It was reinhabited after the Jews returned from exile (Ezra 2:23; Neh. 7:27). It was also known by Eusebius (*Onom.* 26:27)

who places it at a distance of about 3 miles from Jerusalem. The ancient name of the site has been preserved in the name of the modern village of Anatha; the biblical site is identified with Ras el-Kharrubeh, $^2/_3$ of a mile from this village.

ANTHEDON A Greek city between *Gaza and *Ashkelon (Theodosius, P. 138), located by Sozomenos (*Hist. Eccl.* 5,9) on the coast about 2 miles from Gaza, identified with Khirbet Teda. Pliny (*Nat.Hist.* v, 14) seems to have made a mistake when he placed it inland. The city was conquered by the Hasmonean king, Alexander Jannaeus (Josephus, *Antiq.* XIII, 395), and then by Pompey, and rebuilt by the proconsul Gabinus in 55 BC (Josephus, *Antiq.* XIV, 88). It was one of the cities given by Augustus to Herod as a reward for his loyalty in the war against Antony and Cleopatra (Josephus, *Antiq.* XV, 217). Herod renamed it Agrippias or Agrippeion (Josephus, *Antiq.* XIII, 357; *War* I, 416) in honor of Augustus' general and son-in-law, Marcus Vispanius Agrippa, but the new name did not last; imperial coins from the time of Elagabalus to Severus Alexander, and the Byzantine sources, all have the old name.

ANTIOCH-ON-THE-ORONTES The capital of Seleucid Syria, modern Antakija, about 16 miles from the sea. The city was built almost entirely on the left bank of the Orontes, on an island in the river, and

Tyche, goddess of Antioch, with the river god at her feet, Roman copy of Hellenistic original

extended along the foot of Mount Silpius, roughly parallel to the river. Daphne, a suburb 5 miles to the south overlooking the city in a garden area with numerous springs, was as famous as the city itself, and as a result Antioch was sometimes called 'Antioch near Daphne'.

The city was founded in 300 BC by Seleucus I Nicator, who brought there the 5,300 Athenian and Macedonian veterans whom Antigonus had settled at Antigonia in 307 BC. It was constructed according to the Hippodamian plan and originally consisted of two districts, a larger one for the European settlers and a smaller one for the native Syrians. A third district was added by Seleucus II. After the defeat of Antiochus III by the Romans in the Battle of Magnesia in 190 BC, the city's population expanded thanks to the enrollment of Aetolians and Euboeans who had supported Antiochus in Greece. They were accommodated in the new district begun by Seleucus II. Antiochus IV Epiphanes (175-163 BC) added a fourth district, named Epiphania. The population also included a large Jewish community, claiming privileges that went back to Seleucus I. As citizens of its capital, the inhabitants took an active part in the dynastic struggle of the later Seleucid Empire.

After a short period of Armenian rule under Tigranes (83-69 BC), the city was annexed by Pompey and became the capital of Syria. In AD 194 Septimius Severus reduced the city to the status of a village under the city of Laodicea, because it had sided with Piscennius Niger. In 201 Caracalla restored its former rank and added the title *colonia*. The glory of the ancient capital was finally destroyed when a series of disasters befell it between AD 525 and 540, including a great fire, two earthquakes, a sack by the Persians in 540 and an outbreak of the plague. Although it was rebuilt by Justinian it was little more than a frontier fortress when the Arabs conquered it in AD 637.

Antioch was a *polis*, with a council of 1,200 members. Its inhabitants were divided into 18 tribes, which indicates how large an area was governed. In the Roman Empire it ranked as the third city after Rome and *Alexandria, maintaining this status until the 4th century AD, when it was superseded by Constantinople. At the beginning of the 5th century the inhabitants, excluding those in the suburbs, numbered about 200,000, not counting children and slaves. Christianity came to the city in about AD 40, the earliest community being founded by Jews from the Diaspora (Acts 13 ff.) and led by Barnabas and Saul. It was at Antioch that members of this movement which had originated as a sect among the Jews became known by the Greek name, *Christianoi*. It was from here that the mission to the pagans began and the city rivalled *Jerusalem as the center of Christianity.

From historical sources and from the extensive excavations it is possible to obtain an idea of the city's former architectural splendor and wealth. The Seleucid rulers and the Roman emperors surpassed each other in the erection of public buildings. Seleucus I began the construction of the Temple of Zeus Bottiaios and an agora. The public library is referred to for the first time during the reign of Antiochus III,

though it was most probably built earlier. Antiochus IV erected a *bouleuterion*, or council chamber, within a second agora. Several statues were set up, the most famous being the Tyche of Antioch by Butychides, between 296 and 293 BC.

The Roman emperors continued these building activities: sources record a forum called the *Caesarium* (in honor of Julius Caesar); the restoration of the Temple of Artemis and also of the Temples of Ares and Herakles, which had suffered in an earthquake (during the rule of Claudius); the building of a public bath and the restoration of the Temples of Athene and of Zeus Olympos (during the rule of Commodus); the construction of the *Plethion* for Olympic Games (during the rule of Didius Julianus); and a forum on the site of the old Caesarium (Valens). The remains of two circuses or stadia were also found in the excavations (*Stadium). The first is dated to the 1st century BC and the other to the late 5th or early 6th century AD. Both were situated on the island. At Daphne, where the Seleucids held Olympic Games, there must have been a third stadium. These games and other public festivals were re-established under Augustus and Claudius, and Antioch was renowned for them in the Roman period. The residence of the Seleucids was probably at Daphne, while the Roman palace was located on the island. The greatest revelation in the excavations was the large number of private houses with beautiful mosaic floors found all over the city. They date from the time of the early empire to the beginning of the 6th century AD.

The wealth of Antioch must have derived from its position as an administrative center and from extensive trade between east and west. No industries are known except the imperial mint and jewelry. Coins of the Seleucid kings were minted there from the time of Antiochus IV onwards. These show motifs common to other Seleucid mints, such as Tyche and Zeus. In the Roman period there was also an imperial mint at Antioch, with coinage extending from Augustus to Valerian. A special motif was the Tyche of Antioch, which appeared for the first time on the coins of Tigranes, King of Armenia, who ruled over Syria from 83-69 BC, and seems to have been an exact copy of the Eutychides statue. The robed goddess is seated on a rock, representing Mount Silpius; in her right hand she holds a sheaf of wheat, and on her head is placed a turreted crown representing the city wall, with the river god Orontes at her feet. This representation of Tyche became popular among many other cities of the Hellenized East.

APHEK; ANTIPATRIS *a)* An important station on the ancient Via Maris (*Roads), mentioned in the list of Pharaoh Tuthmosis III. The King of Aphek was one of the 31 rulers of *Canaan vanquished by Joshua (Josh. 12:18). The *Philistines gathered their armies there to go into battle against Israel (1 Sam. 4:1; 29:1). Scholars believe that in both cases Aphek in the *Sharon is referred to. In a later period the place is mentioned in one of the inscriptions of Esarhaddon, and also in a letter written in Aramaic that was sent to Pharaoh before the Babylonian conquest of Palestine.

Early in the Hellenistic period a fort on the border

between the districts of *Samaria and the *Sharon was built at this place, then known as Pegai. John Hyrcanus I conquered it in about 132 BC. At that period it was also known as Arethusa, both names implying that it was built near rich sources of water, as indeed it was. After the conquest by Pompey in 63 BC the town of Arethusa was rebuilt. When Herod the Great ascended to the throne he built a new city at Arethusa, renaming it Antipatris, after his father Antipater. This new city became the center of a district with many prosperous villages. In the later Roman period it was named Antipatris Antoniniana, probably after Elagabalus. The Mishna mentions it under the name of Mei Piga, the Waters of Piga.

Aphek-Antipatris is identified with Tell Ras el-Ain, which is rich in springs and vegetation. The sizeable mound is now occupied by a large Turkish citadel, built on the remains of a Crusader castle. Trial digs unearthed remains from the Bronze Age to the Roman period, including a large Roman mausoleum.

Extensive excavations were carried out on the site in the years 1974-84 by M. Kochavi on behalf of Tel Aviv University and American archaeological institutions. The earliest remains on the site are those of a city wall of the Early Bronze Age found in the northern part of the mound. On the acropolis on the western part of the mound were discovered a series of *palaces. The earliest of these palaces belongs to the Middle Bronze Age IIA. Its walls are 4 feet thick, and are still standing to a height of 5 feet. The palace consists of a central hall with a roof supported by two columns. Numerous rooms are grouped around this spacious hall. It was destroyed by a fierce fire in the middle of the 16th century BC. Two city walls also belong to this period. Above this palace another, larger palace was built in the Late Bronze Age. This spacious building contained numerous rooms; a staircase tower gave access to the rooms on the upper story, where the princes of Aphek lived. North of the palace was a spacious court, and another service building east of it. Wine presses discovered nearby and numerous grape pips uncovered in the ruins of the palace attest to the existence of a *wine industry. In the ruins of the palace were discovered Egyptian, Hittite and Accadian documents, among them a cuneiform bilingual, Sumerian-Accadian dictionary, and a fragment of a trilingual Sumerian-Accadian-Canaanite dictionary. This is the only known multilingual dictionary which includes the Canaanite language. Most of these documents date from the 14th-13th centuries BC. The acropolis was destroyed at the end of the 13th century BC. Scanty occupation remains are found from the end of the Late Bronze Age. A small faience plaque discovered in the Early Iron Age level bears the names of Pharaoh Rameses II written in ink and a dedication to the goddess Isis, indicating the possible existence of a temple dedicated to this goddess. In the 12th century BC Aphek was occupied by the *Philistines. The new city consisted of various quarters each built according to a different plan and different standard of construction, and each apparently inhabited by a different class of citizens. The houses were almost square and consisted of a large front hall with smaller rooms in

the rear. The poorer houses were oblong structures, set closely together, and built with thin walls. In this quarter were discovered fishing-net weights, copper fishing hooks and tortoise shells. Numerous storage bins from the 10th century BC, the Israelite period, testify to the conquest of the site by David. Two levels containing dwellings were found from the time of the United Kingdom. Above the ruins of the Middle Bronze Age II palace were discovered two Israelite houses of the four-room type (See*HOUSES), from the 10th and 8th centuries BC.

In the higher levels of the mound Ptolemaic, Seleucid, Hasmonean and Herodian levels were encountered. In the Herodian period the city was laid out along a new plan. At the junction of the main streets was the forum; it was rebuilt in the Late Roman period. One of the streets leading to the forum was lined with shops. In the time of Herod Agrippa I the street was repaved and workshops were built along it. The city declined after the fall of the Second Temple and was not rebuilt before the 2nd century AD. From the Roman period large sections of the cardo, the main street, were discovered. A *theater stood at the southern end of the street. From this period a market and a quarter for the wealthier citizens were also found. In AD 363 the entire city was destroyed in an earthquake.

b) A Canaanite town in the territory of Asher (Josh. 19:30) which was not conquered by the Israelites (Judg. 1:31). Identified with Tell Kurdaneh, near the mouth of the River Naaman, southeast of *Acre.

c) A town in the *Golan, east of the Sea of *Galilee, on the Via Maris between *Beth-Shean and *Damascus. A great battle took place there between the armies of Ben-Hadad, King of *Aram (Authorized Version: 'Syrians') and Ahab, King of Israel (1 Kgs. 20:26-30; 2 Kgs. 13:17). The biblical site is tentatively identified with Khirbet el-Asheq, near modern En Gev, on the eastern shore of the Sea of *Galilee, where remains of an Israelite town have been unearthed in recent excavations. In the Roman period Apheka was a large village. Remains of buildings, architectural fragments and inscriptions which may have belonged to a synagogue have been found. The village of the late Roman period is identified with Fiq, on the plateau rising above the lake, in the vicinity of the ruins of Hippos (*Susita).

APOLLONIA A city on the coast between Jaffa and *Caesarea, 22 miles south of the latter, as shown in the Peutinger map (a Roman road map of the 4th century AD). According to Appian it was founded by Seleucus I Nicator (c. 358-280 BC) or at any rate named after him. It was one of the cities conquered by the Hasmonean Alexander Jannaeus (Josephus, *Antiq.* XIII, 395) and was later captured by Pompey, then rebuilt by the tribune Gabinius (Josephus, *War* I, 166). In the 6th century AD the city appears under a new name. Sozusa, 'City of the Savior'. It seems likely that it gradually declined in the Roman period and that when the Christians started a new settlement there in the Byzantine period they objected to the pagan name. The Arab name is Arsuf, showing that the pre-Hellenistic name was related to the Semitic god

Reshef, later equated with Apollo. This is an interesting example of the survival of an ancient name among the indigenous population.

AR; AR MOAB A town on the northern border of *Moab (Num. 21:15), on the western bank of the *Arnon (Num. 22:36; Authorized Version: 'a city of *Moab'). An important town in the Roman period, when it was named *Rabbathmoba, or Acropolis. It was a fortified town and remains of a Roman temple were found there. Identified with er-Rabbah.

ARABIA A peninsula 2,000 miles long and 600 miles wide between Africa and Asia, the most westerly of the three large peninsulas of southern Asia. Most of the central part is desert, with large scattered oases. The more fertile parts lie along its fringes, especially on the west, facing the *Red Sea. The major trade routes connecting Arabia with the outside world led to *Babylon and Assyria, to *Egypt and northwards along the coast to Palestine and Syria:

Arabia and the Arabs are mentioned frequently in the Bible. These Arabs were mostly the nomadic tent-dwellers who occupied the northwestern part of the peninsula, where they grazed their flocks (Isa. 13:20). When the scanty rains failed to produce the meager pasturage they needed they would push northwards to the cultivated lands and menace the civilized world. This culminated in the conquest of a great part of the Roman Empire by the Arabs in AD 636. The fact that all the great empires of the ancient world tried to check the depredations of the nomadic tribes is confirmed by the Bible. Close relations were maintained between the Israelite kingdom and the Arabi-

ans, especially with the richer southern kingdoms, from the time of Solomon onwards. Gold and silver were brought from there (2 Chr. 9:14). Jehoshaphat received flocks of rams and goats as tribute from the nomads (2 Chr. 17:11), as did *Tyre (Ezek. 27.11), while spices, precious stones and gold were brought from Sheba and Raamah (Ezek. 27:22). There is evidence that Arabs tried to settle in Judea after the destruction of the First Temple. It was those Arabs who attempted to prevent Nehemiah rebuilding the fallen walls of *Jerusalem (Neh. 2:19).

Arabia and the Arabs are also frequently mentioned in Assyrian sources. During the days of Shalmaneser III 1,000 Arab camel-riders took part in the Battle of Qarqar (854 BC). Zabiba, Queen of Arabia, paid tribute to Tiglath-Pileser III. Sargon II recorded how he subdued the Arabs 'who live far away', exiling some to distant *Samaria and imposing on the others a tax of gold powder, precious stones, ebony seeds, spices, horses and camels. Under his successor, Sennacherib, Arabs invaded the Assyrian kingdom and caused much havoc before they were finally defeated by Sennacherib's son, Esarhaddon. Ashurbanipal conducted a campaign in order to subdue the Arab tribes who overran *Edom and *Moab. The last Assyrian king, Nabonidus, spent the last eight years of his life in the oasis of Teima in northwestern Arabia.

The Greeks came to know Arabia mainly after the campaigns of Alexander the Great in the east, but they never explored beyond the coastal strip. The fabulous riches of Arabia, whose products Greece and Rome acquired by trade, earned it the name of Arabia Felix

Part of a relief from the palace of Ashurbanipal, depicting Assyrians fighting Arabs mounted on camels

*Seal impression from Mampsis
showing the goddess of Provincia Arabia*

or Arabia Eudaimon, meaning 'Arabia the Happy' or 'Arabia the Blessed', in contrast with the arid north, known as Arabia Deserta (deserted) or Petraea (stony).

After the conquest of *Egypt by Augustus several expeditions were sent out with the aim of conquering the spice-producing countries, but they all failed. Better shipbuilding helped the Romans to overcome these difficulties and to take over the greater part of the Arabian trade. This, coupled with the destruction of the ancient dams, brought to an end the great prosperity of the Arabian peninsula and turned it into the desert which it has remained down to the present day.

It is only in the last two or three decades that archaeological and topographical research has penetrated this unhospitable area. Settlement in Arabia began as early as the Paleolithic and Neolithic periods. In 1951-2 an expedition from the American School of Oriental Research, led by W.F. Albright, surveyed the southwestern part of the peninsula, where the Sabean kingdom flourished in the late 2nd and early 1st millennium BC, and discovered there the Temple of the Moon in the city of Marib. This expedition, and others which followed, also discovered remains of the large dams which diverted into the fields the flood waters streaming down the dry river beds, thus providing the basis for the prosperity of the ancient kingdoms of southern Arabia. The largest dam of this kind was that of Wadi Adhamat in the kingdom of Sheba. The Sabean kingdom occupied the southwestern part of Arabia (now the Yemen). Dominating the most fertile part of the peninsula, it concentrated into its hands the greater part of the trade in spices and incense, some of which were produced locally while others came from India and the Far East. The Sabean kingdom flourished during the greater part of the 1st millennium BC. Towards the last centuries BC it dominated the greater part of the peninsula, incorporating the lesser-known kingdoms of Qataban and Hadramaut.

ARAD An important city in the eastern *Negev, on the border of Judah, situated on the main road to *Edom. In the biblical tradition its king, 'Arad the Canaanite, which dwelt in the south', withstood the assault of the Israelites on their approach from *Kadesh-Barnea by way of Atharim (Num. 21:1; 33:40), defeating them at neighboring *Hormah (Num. 14:44-5; Deut. 1:44). But there is another tradition of the defeat at *Hormah of the King of Arad in a second Israelite assault (Num. 21:2-3). Both cities are mentioned in the list of the defeated Canaanite kings (Josh. 12:14). According to Judges (1:16) the *Negev of Arad (Authorized Version: 'wilderness of Judah') was settled by *Kenites, a people related to the family of Moses. Pharaoh Sheshonq mentions in his list of conquered cities (c. 920 BC) Arad the Great and Arad of the House of Yrhm (perhaps Jerahmeel; cf. 1 Sam. 27:10; 30:29). The last biblical reference to Arad lists the city in the *Negev district of Judah (Josh. 15:21, corrupted to Eder), but Eusebius (*Onom.* 14, 2) mentions a village called Arad 20 Roman miles from *Hebron and 3 from Malaatha (Moleatha), distances which exactly fit modern Tell Arad, situated about 20 modern miles east-northeast of *Beer-Sheba.

Excavations of the mound were carried out between 1962 and 1967 on behalf of the Hebrew University of Jerusalem, the Israel Department of Antiquities and the Israel Exploration Society. The excavations in the two different settlements discovered at the site were directed by R. Amiran (the Early Bronze Age city) and Y. Aharoni (the Iron Age and later fortresses). Up to 1980 14 seasons of excavations had been directed by R. Amiran.

EARLY BRONZE AGE CITY (2900-2700 BC) A large fortified city existed here during the Early Bronze Age II, preceded by an open settlement of the late Chalcolithic period. It was surrounded by a stone wall about 8 feet thick supported by projecting semicircular towers (*Fortifications). The city was divided into separate districts and the houses were built according to a fixed architectural concept of a distinct 'broadhouse', i.e. with an entrance in one of the longer sides. A unique find is a clay model of one of these houses. Other remarkable finds are vessels imported from *Egypt and an abundance of painted and well-burnished local pottery, known hitherto mainly from Egyptian tombs of the 1st Dynasty (*Abydos). These provide evidence of a lively trade with *Egypt and are of great importance for the dating of the different strata. After a last unfortified level the city was completely destroyed and deserted before the end of the Early Bronze Age II, i.e. not later than 2700 BC. Several of the buildings at Arad were of a public nature, notably a twin temple. It consisted of two large halls with a short wall in common. Both opened onto courtyards and faced east. In the courtyard of the northern temple there is a platform (bamah) and a laver close to it. In a subsequent phase of the same period the hall was subdivided, forming a small cella and a covered hall. The southern hall had two bases for posts, one in the form of a large stele. This hall was full of non-domestic *pottery and other objects. In the vicinity of the twin temple was another building of a public nature, with benches along its walls and bases for posts. A remarkable find in this building was a small stone stele on which were carved two men, one standing and the other lying within a frame. Both have their arms raised and fingers outstretched, and both have an ear of grain instead of a human head. They seem to represent the same being, perhaps Dumuzi of the Grain, one of the aspects of the god Tammuz.

Between the lower city and the upper mound excavations were made in a sunken area which was found to contain the water-supply system of the town. In the upper level there were channels coated with Hellenistic-Roman plaster, testifying to its use in the Roman period. Below these was found Israelite *pottery. The total depth of the large water hole must have been more than 50 feet, but the water level has not yet been reached. The walls of the round hole are stone lined; around it buildings of the Early Bronze Age were discovered, attesting that the water-supply system had already at this time formed the nucleus of the early city. Some of these buildings were of a public nature. In the last seasons of excavation evidence was found that the area of the water hole which in the beginning had the form of a natural storage container for rain water, was already inhabited in the Chalcolithic period. On the other hand, it was also occupied in Roman and Byzantine times. In these later periods there were also pools for watering flocks.

IRON AGE FORTRESSES A new settlement was founded, on the southeastern ridge of the ancient city only, during the 11th century BC. It was a small open village and in its center was a paved *temenos* (enclosure) with a raised crescent-shaped platform and a square altar. Probably this was the high place where the venerated Kenite family served (Judg. 1:16). A temple was erected on its site in the middle of the 10th century BC. This now became part of a strongly fortified royal citadel, founded probably by Solomon. During the period of the monarchy it was destroyed and burnt six times (the first time evidently by Pharaoh Sheshonq), but it was always quickly rebuilt and served until the end of the First Temple as the royal, military and administrative center of the border area. Fortresses also stood here later, in the Persian, Hellenistic, Roman and early Arab periods until the fall of the Nabatean kingdom in AD 106. (*See also* *LIMES.)

TEMPLE The most remarkable discovery at Arad is the temple which occupied the northwestern corner of the citadel. It is the earliest Israelite temple to be discovered in any excavation. Its orientation, general plan and contents, especially the tabernacle, are similar to the Temple of Solomon. The temple consists of one main room, the *hekal,* and to the west of it is a raised shrine, the Holy of Holies, or *debir.* This contained a small *bamah* (high place) and a *massebah* (*Massebah). Flanking the entrance to it were two incense altars. East of the building was a relatively large courtyard, divided into a large outer area and a smaller inner area. Flanking the entrance to the *hekal* were two stone slabs, probably bases of pillars, similar to the pillars of Jachin and Boaz in the temple at *Jerusalem (1 Kgs. 7:21; 2 Chr. 4:17). In the outer court there was an altar for burnt offerings, built of earth and

Model of the Israelite fortress at Arad; the temple is at the top left-hand corner

unhewn stone (cf. Exod. 20:25, etc.). It was 5 cubits square and 3 cubits high, like the altar in the tabernacle (Exod. 27:1; cf. 2 Chr. 6:13). The altar was not used from the end of the 8th century BC and the temple was finally destroyed with the erection of the last Israelite citadel in the second half of the 7th century BC. Among some Hebrew ostraca found in the temple are two which contain names of priestly families known from the Bible, Meremoth and Pashhur.

OSTRACA More than 200 inscribed potsherds or ostraca (*Inscriptions) were found in the various strata. Nearly half were Aramiac (c. 400 BC) and the rest were Hebrew, from the period of the kingdom of Israel. The Aramaic ostraca are mainly dockets of the Persian garrison, containing lists of names, troops and quantities of various commodities such as wine, oil, flour and silver. The Hebrew ostraca derive from different Iron Age strata (a fact which increases their paleographic importance). Most of them are letters and dockets from the royal archives of the various citadels; some contain lists of private names, occasionally with the addition of numerals and an indication of a commodity, such as wheat. On a fragment of a large bowl names of families and numerals were written, among them the 'sons of Korach'. This may be a list of donations for the temple. Most illuminating is a group of letters from the archives of a man called Eliashib, son of Eshyahu, who was a high official, possibly the commander of the last citadel (c. 600 BC). They mainly consist of orders to provide certain persons with rations of wine and bread, particularly the Kittim, who were probably mercenaries of Aegean stock in the service of Judah. In one there is a reference to *Beer-Sheba and in another to the 'House of Yahweh', probably the Temple at Jerusalem. This is the first and only instance of a direct reference to the Temple in a Hebrew inscription. A letter from the same period contains a strict order to dispatch reinforcements of men from Arad and Kinah (Josh. 15:22) to Ramath-Negev (Josh. 19:8; 1 Sam. 30:27; Authorized Version: 'South Ramoth') against the threat of an Edomite attack.

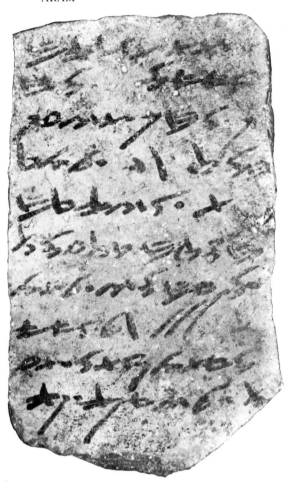

An ostracon from Arad. Early 6th century BC

ARAM; ARAMEANS A group of tribes spread over a wide area at the end of the 2nd millennium and in the first half of the 1st millennium BC, from the Persian Gulf and *Elam in the south and east and the Amanus mountains in the north to southern Syria and northern Transjordan in the west.

The origin of the Arameans is obscure. Some scholars claim they originated in the Syro-Arabian desert, while others believe that they may have arrived with some movement of the Horite tribes which migrated from the north. A city named Aram in the region of the upper Tigris (*Hiddekel) is mentioned around 2000 BC. In the 2nd millennium BC the Arameans are frequently mentioned in the documents of *Mari and *Ugarit. According to the Bible, Aram was one of the descendants of Shem (Gen. 10:22-3; 1 Chr. 1:17). It is not until the end of the 2nd millennium that Aram is mentioned frequently in the Assyrian sources. In the documents of the 14th-13th centuries BC they are referred to as invaders coming from the desert and penetrating the inhabited land. Tiglath-Pileser I of Assyria relates that in the fourth year of his reign (1112 BC) the Arameans came from the Arabian desert to invade the regions of *Tadmor, Mount *Lebanon and *Babylon. At the same time they were already settling on the west bank of the *Euphrates, where they founded cities. By the 11th century BC the Arameans had conquered the spacious plains of *Mesopotamia and constituted a menace to Assyria. In the regions which they conquered they founded strong political units. A ruler of Aramean descent even succeeded in ruling the kingdom of *Babylon. By the 10th century BC their expansion to the west was checked by the kings of Israel, while in the east they were pushed back by the Assyrians until, in the 8th century BC, they were finally defeated by Tiglath-Pileser III, who turned their kingdoms in Syria into Assyrian satrapies. The frequent rebellions of the Arameans were cruelly put down by Sargon and Sennacherib, who deported many of them to distant lands.

The Bible mentions several small Aramean kingdoms which sprang up to the north of the kingdom of Israel. Among them were Aram Beth-Rehov and Aram Maachah, the one being centered around the town of Beth-Rehob, close to *Dan (Judg. 18:28), and the other in the upper *Jordan Valley, around *Abel-Beth-Maachah. Together with Aram Zobah and Aram Maachah, the Arameans of Beth-Rehob participated in the war of the *Ammonites against David (2 Sam. 10:6; Authorized Version: 'Syrians', instead of the Hebrew 'Aram'). After their defeat the two petty kingdoms came under Israelite rule. In later generations they were ruled either by the Israelites or by the Arameans of *Damascus.

Aram Damascus, usually referred to simply as Aram, was the most important of the Aramean kingdoms in the 9th-8th centuries BC. It was bordered by the kingdom of Israel on the south, *Hamath on the north and the Phoenician cities on the west. David defeated the Arameans of *Damascus (2 Sam. 8:5; Authorized Version: 'Syrians of Damascus'). In the days of the Divided Kingdom there was a constant state of war between Aram and Israel. Aided by Asa,

IDENTIFICATION The results of the excavations contradict the accepted identification of the Canaanite city with Tell Arad, which lacks remains of the Middle and Late Bronze Ages. On the other hand its identification with the Israelite city has been confirmed by the appearance of the name Arad on two Hebrew ostraca. Two possible solutions have been suggested: *(a)* that no city of Arad existed in the Canaanite period, and that the name described a whole region, the *Negev of Arad, or *(b)* that Canaanite Arad was located at modern Tell Malhata, 8 miles southwest of Tell Arad, where strong *Hyksos fortifications have been discovered. This suggestion is strengthened by the duplication of the name in Pharaoh Sheshonq's list of conquered cities: it may be assumed that the fortress 'Arad of the House of Yrhm' is the early city which was settled by Jerahmeelite families; 'Great Arad' is then the strong citadel on the hill dominating the *Negev of Arad, which was founded by Solomon on the site of the venerated Kenite high place.

Hazael King of Aram-Damascus, from Arslan Tash, ivory

King of Judah, the Arameans under Ben-Hadad I conquered the land of Naphtali (1 Kgs. 15:18-20). Omri, King of Israel, was forced to cede cities in *Samaria to the Arameans (1 Kgs. 20:34), but Ahab succeeded in beating them back (1 Kgs. 20:1-34).

The rise of Assyria brought about a coalition between the kings of Syria and Israel. The great battle between Assyria and this coalition, in which thousands of chariots and myriads of infantry fought, took place in 853 BC near *Qarqar in the land of *Hamath. Neither this battle nor those which followed could bring a final settlement. When Assyrian pressure diminished temporarily, Hazael, King of *Damascus, conquered the whole of eastern Transjordan and penetrated into Israel, reaching the northern border of Judah (2 Kgs. 10:32-3; 12; 18-19; 13:7). Renewed Assyrian pressure forced Ben-Hadad III to pay tribute to Assyria, while Jehoash and Jeroboam II freed the conquered parts of their kingdom and even captured *Damascus (2 Kgs. 13:25; 14:25, 28). In 733-732

BC Tiglath-Pileser III conquered *Damascus and put an end to the independence of both Israel and *Damascus, turning them into Assyrian satrapies and deporting many of their inhabitants. The Aramaic script and language survived the Arameans for many centuries. (*See also* *INSCRIPTIONS.)

Aram Zobah was the largest and strongest of the Aramean kingdoms of Syria in the days of David. Its nucleus was in the Anti-Libanus, from whence it spread over the plain of *Lebanon, and the *Bashan, reaching eastwards as far as the *Euphrates (2 Sam. 10:16). Enmity between Zobah and Israel started as early as the days of Saul (1 Sam. 14:47). By the time Hadadezer of Aram Zobah had subdued all the other kings (2 Sam. 19:19; Authorized Version: 'Hadarezer'), he in turn was defeated by David in a series of battles, at the end of which David conquered Maachah, the land of *Tob (Authorized Version: 'Ish-Tob'), and other regions (2 Sam. 8:3 ff.; 10:6-14, 16-19). In 733 BC Zobah was conquered by the Assyrians and was turned into an Assyrian satrapy under the name of Subatu.

ARARAT The name of a mountainous region in Armenia, north of Lake Van. It is referred to in the Assyrian documents as Uruatri, Uratri and Urartu. During the first half of the 8th century BC palaces, temples and elaborate sewage systems were constructed in its important cities, mainly in Tushka, the capital; in the second half of that century a decline set in and it was incorporated in the Median and Persian empires.

According to Genesis (8:4), Noah's Ark rested on the mountains of Ararat. A similar story is found in the Greek version by the historian Berosus (*c.* 290 BC) of the Babylonian epic of the Flood. Berosus states that in his time the remains of a ship were to be seen on top of the Kurdish mountains. The Jewish, Christian and Moslem traditions sought the ark on the highest peak of these mountains, south of the town of Erivan, or on a mountain near the town of Calaenae in Phrygia.

ARBEL; ARBELA A village of the Roman period, to the northwest of Tiberias, west of *Magdala. In the plain of Arbel (today, Wadi el-Hammam) a battle was fought between the Hasmoneans and Bacchides (1 Macc. 9:2), and Herod fought the Zealots who hid in the caves above the plain (Josephus, *Antiq.* XIV, 445). After the destruction of the Second Temple it was the seat of the priestly family of Jeshua. It is identified with Khirbet Irbid. Jewish sources mention a synagogue there. A trial dig on the site in 1968 unearthed remains of a synagogue of the Galilean type.

ARCHAEOLOGY (METHODS OF RESEARCH) 'Excavation is both art and science' (W.F. Albright). 'There is no correct method of excavation, but many wrong ones' (M. Wheeler). The words of these two great archaeologists underline the main feature of archaeological technique: a continuous striving for perfection in excavation and in the publication of the results. Following the unearthing of archaeological remains of ancient Greece and the Near East in the first decades of the 19th century, nearly a hundred years were to elapse before excavators began to pay attention to the technical aspects of their work. Sir Flinders Petrie was clearly aware of the need for planning and method in all aspects of archaeological work, as is shown by his book *Methods and Aims in Archaeology* (1904). His precepts were put into practice during his excavations at Tell el-*Hesi (begun in 1890 and later continued by F.J. Bliss). It was here that the stratigraphy of a mound was understood and correctly interpreted for the first time (*Tell). At *Samaria, during excavations directed by G. Reisner in 1908, a trained staff was engaged for the first time to carry out all phases of the archaeological work.

The importance of a qualified team is obvious if one realizes that each excavation involves the destruction of archaeological evidence. Each stage of the work must therefore proceed with the utmost care, under the eyes of a trained excavator, and be recorded in great detail by surveys, drawings, photographs and word notes. The disastrous results of an excavation handled by a single archaeologist relying solely on unskilled labor are well illustrated by the work of R.A.S. Macalister at *Gezer and G. Schumacher at *Megiddo, both before the First World War.

Just as the technical aspects of archaeological work have become more important and been more refined, so the dependence of archaeologists upon information from specialists in the natural sciences has been more clearly recognized. Their contributions will open up new fields of study.

Archaeological research comprises three aspects: discovery and surface survey of the site; the technique of excavation; and the technique of interpretation.

DISCOVERY AND SURFACE SURVEY OF THE SITE Many factors may contribute to the choice of a site for excavation, including its historical importance, chance finds of great consequence, the impressiveness or accessibility of the site and, very often, the need to check findings from previous excavations. The preparation of a new site for digging must be thorough and should include a study of existing surface remains and of surveys already carried out in a large part of the Holy Land. The survey of western Palestine led by C.R. Condor and H.H. Kitchener (1872-8); Schumacher's survey of the Hauran and northern Transjordan (from 1884 on); the survey of C.L. Woolley and T.E. Lawrence in the *Negev (1913-4); and N. Glueck's survey of Transjordan (begun in 1933) all deserve special mention here.

Valuable information can also be obtained from aerial photographs. In a tell it is mainly the fortifications and the architectural remains of the most recent stratum that will be revealed, while on a Hellenistic-Roman-Byzantine site the layout of a city and its main buildings can be discerned. In all cases photographs taken from the air help to locate remains by revealing changes in surface contours that are not visible at ground level. The first aerial photographs for archaeological purposes were taken of Stonehenge, in England, from a military balloon in 1906. In the Holy Land this technique was first used during the First World War.

TECHNIQUES OF EXCAVATION First the excavator selects a number of areas on the site and appoints a junior archaeologist to be responsible for each. An area is generally allotted to each excavator to fit in with his special field of interest. A picture of the life of the inhabitants can be obtained only by combining the results of all concerned, which will cover such aspects as the town's acropolis, its royal or administrative quarter, its living quarters, its industrial installations, its fortification system and its cemeteries. Within each area the excavation is carried out according to the grid-system, in which squares or rectangles, 5 or 10 meters square or 5 meters by 10 meters respectively, are exposed. The grid, which is marked on the surface, is left untouched, thus forming a bank about 1 meter wide between each section. This enables the excavator to relate every structural detail or small find to a fixed point of reference. The most difficult problem posed by excavating is that of correctly distinguishing the superimposed layers remaining from all the different occupation levels.

There are two types of site — those with mud brick buildings and those with stone buildings — each giving rise to different problems and methods of approach. In sites of the later periods (Hellenistic, Roman and Byzantine) the length of time during which a building or town existed is much shorter, the construction is always of stone and the excavator knows from the outset at least the nature of what he is going to excavate.

The Neolithic tower at *Jericho is a good example of the first type of site; it is the earliest fortification in the world and was discovered at the bottom of a deep trench. The excavators of the theater at *Caesarea, on the other hand, knew from the beginning the nature of the building they would find. On sites of the later type excavators can choose between single monuments, such as temples, churches, theaters, colonnaded streets or the living quarters of a town. In the houses no stratigraphy (i.e. indications of layers, or strata, of remains from preceding habitations) can be expected until the floor of the most recent occupation level has been reached. Excavations will proceed along the walls of the building. The interior of a room will have to be excavated in the same way as a tell; only part of it will be cleared at a time, so that the different living floors in section can be seen. Excavation has to proceed slowly and carefully so that no important evidence or find, however small, can be overlooked. Scarabs, seals and coins can be discovered only by sifting the soil.

Adequate recording is an important part of the field work. The person responsible for each area must keep a diary, describing both in diagrams and in words the progress of the excavation and recording every object found in terms of its vertical and horizontal position on the grid. Pottery sherds are collected in numbered buckets and are also recorded in the diary. After the sherds have been washed and dried they are sorted by a specialist in the pottery of the period. Pieces which are important for chronological evidence are drawn and recorded in a special pottery file. Where possible, vessels are reconstructed. Lastly, the whole excavated area is drawn by an architect, in plan and in section, and numerous photographs are taken.

TECHNIQUES OF INTERPRETATION The preparation of the report involves much work and much time, but ultimately it is the most important element in the whole procedure. Without it an excavation has no value for general archaeological research. The preliminary work for the report includes assessing the value of all finds and need not be carried out by the excavator himself. The plans and sections must be drawn; the drawings of pottery must be compared with pottery finds on other sites so that an accurate dating can be arrived at; and various objects must be photographed.

As has been indicated, archaeology has become increasingly dependent on the natural sciences: the geologist can analyse rocks; the metallurgist bronzes; the botanist and the zoologist the fauna and flora remains; the paleontologist the skeletal remains. Evidence for purposes of dating can be obtained by several methods. Although none of them is completely reliable they are indispensable. First there is absolute dating, by the radio-carbon method, in which the degree of disintegration of the carbon 14 content, one of the essential elements of all organic matter, is measured. Secondly there is the method of dating bone by measuring its fluorine and uranium content. This increases with time, while the protein content, measured as nitrogen, decreases. This method is a way of obtaining a relative dating, the contents of associated bones being measured and compared. These tests can be carried out only in special laboratories and are used exclusively for early human settlements where no historical evidence is available, such as the Neolithic remains at *Jericho or those of the Chalcolithic culture.

The examination of ceramic materials is also very useful. The source of the clay can often be identified and information can be obtained about the various techniques of firing and washing and about slip and glaze and other means of decoration.

When writing his final report the excavator has all the data arrived at in the preliminary studies. Very often such a report will be the collective work of several scholars, each dealing with his specific field of research. All aspects of the excavations have to be presented in such a way that the reader will be able to reconstruct in his mind the way the field work progressed. The report should include the history of previous research on the site, a short summary of the aims of the current research and the methods employed and a description of the remains found. As many illustrations as possible should be added, comprising plans and sections, photographs of the site and of special objects, scale drawings of pottery, glass and other small finds. Very often pictorial reconstructions are used to bring life to the ground-plan and elevations or isometric drawings are needed to show all the architectural elements.

Finally, the excavator has to present the relative and the absolute chronology worked out on the basis of his finds. The first, which establishes the sequence of the finds is based on such elements as stratigraphy, typology (comparison with similar articles of known date or provenance), an examination of closed finds (such as burials) and a study of distribution and dating by reference to similar finds elsewhere. Absolute dating can be obtained by correlation with historical dates and events, by means of coins or by one of the scientific methods referred to above.

Many excavators feel that publication of the report should be delayed until they are able to produce comprehensive studies. In this context it is still valid and relevant to quote a comment by F. Cumont in 1926. When publishing with remarkable speed the report of his excavations at *Dura Europos he wrote that he preferred to expose himself to critics 'rather than to resemble the dragon in the fable, jealously guarding a sterile treasure in its lair'.

ARCHAEOLOGY OF THE HOLY LAND

EARLY RESEARCHES (1800-1914) Although interest in the Holy Land has never subsided, archaeological, historical and geographical research did not begin in Palestine until the beginning of the 19th century. One of the most important among the early arrivals was the British biblical scholar E. Robinson, who travelled across the country in 1824 and 1852 and opened the way for the study of the historical geography of the Holy Land. As early as 1815 Lady Hester Stanhope made an unsuccessful attempt to unearth statues at *Ashkelon, and in the middle of the 19th century F. de Saulcy cleared a site known as 'Tombs of the Kings' in Jerusalem, which later proved to be the royal tombs of the kings of Adiabene.

The foundation of the Palestine Exploration Fund (PEF) in Britain in 1865 accelerated archaeological research in the area. Its major aim was to explore the ancient remains in *Jerusalem, but between 1871 and 1878 the PEF surveyed most of western Palestine, recording on maps and describing in accompanying volumes all the data collected. This monumental work has since provided a sound basis for all archaeological research in the country. Before the turn of the century more archaeological societies were founded: the German Palestinian Society (1877), the French School of Biblical and Archaeological Studies (1890) and the American School of Oriental Research (1900). Each of these institutions founded periodicals in which the results of their surveys and excavations were published.

Having completed the first surface surveys of the country the PEF embarked upon actual digging. The first tell that they excavated was Tell el-*Hesi in the Shephelah (*Plain). The work was directed by W.M.F. Petrie in 1890. Petrie, who had already done much digging in *Egypt, developed scientific methods of excavating, digging and recording archaeological remains. He also demonstrated the great importance of pottery sherds, which were found on every ancient site in large quantities, for the dating of archaeological occupation levels. Although archaeology in the Holy Land has made great progress since Petrie's beginnings he has rightly been acclaimed as the 'Father of Palestinian Archaeology'.

Two of Petrie's students, R.A.S. Macalister and F.J. Bliss, excavated four sites in the Shephelah from 1898 to 1900. According to the Turkish Law of Antiquities a licence for digging was granted not for a single site but for a piece of land 10 kilometers square. Their choice therefore fell on a square which included four sites: Tell es-*Safi, Tell Zakariyeh (*Azekah), Tell el-*Judeideh and Tell Sandahanna (*Mareshah). Most of the work, however, was done on the last site, which they correctly identified as biblical *Mareshah, or Hellenistic Marissa. They intended to uncover the whole site, layer after layer, but this proved to be impracticable and only the upper (Hellenistic) layer was exposed. Having completed their work on the site they covered everything over again in order to return it to its owners for further use, as was required by Turkish law. Encouraged by the results of their excavations, Macalister dedicated most of the first decade of the 20th century to the excavation of the large and important tell of biblical *Gezer (1902-3, 1907-9). To comply with Turkish law, he employed a new system of excavation known as the 'strip method', in which an area is excavated strip by strip, the rubble from succeeding strips being dumped into the previous ones. Although economical, this does not offer a satisfactory picture of the history of the site and prevents further research. It is therefore no longer used.

While the PEF expedition was digging in the Shephelah German and Austrian biblical scholars and architects were excavating other sites: E. Sellin at Tell Taanach, biblical *Taanach (1902-4); G. Schumacher at *Megiddo (1903-5); Sellin and C. Watzinger at *Shechem (1907-9). Although the choice of sites could not have been a happier one, the results obtained were poor because the excavators lacked training in excavating archaeological mounds and were not competent in Palestinian archaeology. Of much greater importance was the survey of the ancient synagogues in Galilee made in 1905-7 by H. Kohl, Sellin and Watzinger. This survey is still a basic work for the study of the ancient synagogues in the Holy Land.

An expedition sent by Harvard University and directed by D.G. Lyon, C.S. Fisher and G.A. Reisner brought about great changes. During the years 1908 and 1910-11 they excavated at *Samaria, where an Israelite royal city and remains of subsequent periods were unearthed. More careful methods of excavating and of handling finds made this excavation a turning-point in the archaeology of Palestine.

RESEARCH DURING THE BRITISH MANDATE The conquest of Palestine by the British (1917-18) and the foundation of the Palestine Department of Antiquities inaugurated the opening of the golden age in Palestinian archaeology. Its beginning is marked by the work of W.F. Albright, who in his excavations at *Gibeah (1922-3) and Tell *Beit-Mirsim (1926-36) made great contributions to our knowledge of Bronze Age and Iron Age pottery. Albright showed if good results are to be obtained the extent of the area excavated is less important than the care taken in digging. (*See also* *ARCHAEOLOGY, METHODS OF RESEARCH*.)

Some of the most important archaeological excavations were made in the 1920s and 1930s. For instance, an expedition headed by C.S. Fisher, A. Rowe and G.M. FitzGerald on behalf of the University of Pennsylvania excavated at *Beth-Shean (1921-3, 1925-8, 1930-3), where a sequence of 5,000 years of history was traced. Fisher, P.L.O. Guy and G. Loud exca-

vated at *Megiddo (1925-39) on behalf of the Oriental Institute of the University of Chicago. A joint expedition of American and British institutions, together with the Hebrew University, re-excavated *Samaria (1931-3, 1935). J. Garstang, director of the Palestine Department of Antiquities, carried out excavations at *Jericho (1930-6) on behalf of the British School of Archaeology in Jerusalem. J. L. Starkey excavated at *Lachish (1932-6) on behalf of the Wellcome Expedition. These major excavations added a great deal to existing knowledge of the pre-biblical and biblical periods. Finds were placed in the Palestine Archaeological Museum in Jerusalem and the results were published in scores of volumes. Much work was also accomplished concerning the later periods: Hellenistic, Roman, Byzantine, Arab and Crusader. The murder of Starkey by an Arab gang in 1936 while he was on his way to *Lachish and the outbreak of the Second World War brought this great age in the archaeology of Palestine to a close. Only one remarkable excavation took place during this period: that of the large Jewish town and necropolis of *Beth-Shearim (1936-40), under the direction of B. Mazar on behalf of the Hebrew University (HU) and the Israel Exploration Society (IES).

RESEARCH IN THE STATE OF ISRAEL The turbulent years preceding the foundation of the State of Israel in 1948 brought archaeology almost to a standstill, but in the month before the proclamation of the new state a remarkable discovery was made, that of the *Dead Sea Scrolls.

Archaeological activities during the first decade after the foundation of the State of Israel were concentrated around the Department of Antiquities and Museums. These were all minor digs, mostly of single monuments discovered during the course of development works, and nearly all required prompt treatment. Some important excavations also took place, however, including the excavations at Tell *Qasileh, near Tel Aviv (1948-9), directed by B. Mazar on behalf of the IES and the Tel Aviv Museum; the excavations at the ancient tell of *Joppa (1948-50, 1952, 1955) by J. Kaplan on behalf of the Jaffa Museum of Antiquities; and at *Ramat Rahel (1954, 1959, 1960, 1963) by Y. Aharoni on behalf of the HU, the IES and the University of Rome.

The excavation of *Hazor (1955-8, 1968) by Y. Yadin on behalf of the HU opened up a new era of archaeological activity in Israel. In this excavation the younger generation of Israeli archaeologists, all of whom received their training at the Hebrew University, took part, and the site also served as a training ground for scores of new students. This was followed by excavations at *Arad (1962-7) by Aharoni and R. Amiran on behalf of the HU and the IES; and at *Ashdod by M. Dothan on behalf of the Department of Antiquities and Museums (DAM).

During these years much work was also done by foreign expeditions, the most important being the excavations of *Jericho and *Jerusalem by Miss Kathleen Kenyon on behalf of the British School of Archaeology in Jerusalem; of *Jerusalem (1961-8) by the same excavator; and of *Gezer by the Hebrew

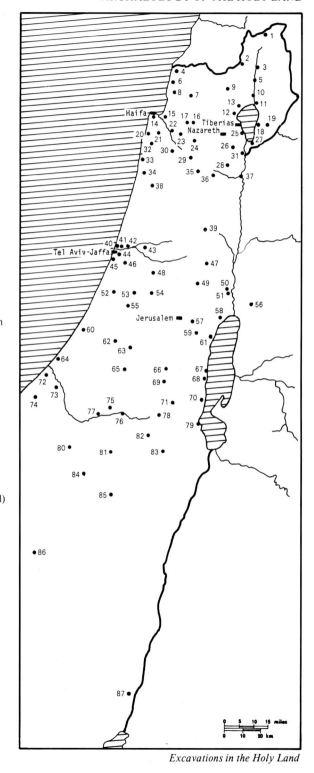

KEY TO NUMERALS ON MAP

1. Dan	44. Tel Aviv
2. Kedesh	45. Jaffa
3. Eynan	46. Azor
4. Achzib	47. Shiloh (Tel)
5. Hazor	48. Modiim
6. Nahariya	49. Ai
7. Hayonim Cave	50. Jericho Herodian
8. Acco	51. Jericho
9. Safad	52. Yavneh
10. Chorazin	53. Gezer
11. Capernaum	54. Sha'alabim
12. Wadi Amud	55. Batash (Tel)
13. Tabgha	56. Tuleilat Ghassul
(Heptapegon)	57. Ramat Rahel
14. Shikmona	58. Qumran Khirbet
15. Abu Hawam (Tell)	59. Herodian
16. Shema Khirbet	60. Ashkelon
17. Sepphoris	61. Murabba'at
18. En Gev	62. Gath (Tell)
19. Sussita (Hippos)	63. Lachish
20. Megadim (Tel)	64. Gaza
21. Wadi Oren	65. Beit Mirsim (Tell)
22. Beth Shearim	66. Susiya
23. Japhia	67. En-Gedi
24. Qedumin Cave	68. Nahal Hever
25. Beth Yerah	69. Eshtemoa
26. Ubeidiya	70. Masada
27. Shaar Hagolan	71. Arad
28. Kokhav ha-Yarden	72. Deir el-Balah
29. Meggido	73. Maon
30. Jokneam	74. Rafiah
31. Munhata	75. Beer-Sheba
32. Athlit	76. Beer-Sheba (Tel)
33. Dor	77. Bir es-Safadi
34. Caesarea	78. Malhata (Tell)
35. Taanach	79. En Boqeq
36. Beth Hashita	80. Rehoboth
37. Beth Shean	81. Elusa
38. Zeror (Tel)	82. Aroer (Tell)
39. Shechem	83. Mampsis
40. Qasileh (Tell)	84. Sobota
41. Grisa (Tell)	85. Oboda
42. Bene Berak	86. Kadesh-Barnea
43. Aphek (Tel)	87. Timnah

Excavations in the Holy Land

Union College under the direction of W.G. Dever.

At the same time much was done in the field of post-biblical archaeology. One outstanding example was the survey of the *Judean Desert Caves (1960-1), made on behalf of all Israeli institutions, which yielded some most important finds. The same institutions, under the direction of Yadin, excavated at *Masada (1963-5), while A. Negev, on behalf of the HU and the National Parks Authority, excavated at Avdat-*Oboda (1958-60), *Caesarea (1960-2) and Mamshit-Mampsis (1965-8). In 1968 B. Mazar began the excavation of the south wall of the Temple Mount in *Jerusalem on behalf of the three Israeli institutions, while in 1969 N. Avigad began excavation in the Jewish quarter of the Old City of Jerusalem, where remains of a magnificent Hellenistic villa with mural paintings have been revealed. Also in 1969, excavations were begun at Tel Anafa in the Hula Valley under the direction of S. Weinberg on behalf of the Museum of Art and Archaeology of the University of Missouri.

ARCHELAIS Village in the *Jordan Valley, founded in 4 BC by Herod's son Archelaus and named after himself (Josephus, *Antiq.* XVII, 340). According to the Peutinger map it was situated on the road from *Jericho to Scythopolis (*Beth-Shean), 12 miles north of *Jericho. It was famous for its palm groves and dates (Pliny, *Nat.Hist.* XIII, 44). The identification is not clear, but most scholars locate it at Khirbet Auja et-Tahtani, about 7 miles north of *Jericho.

ARGOB A region in the *Bashan, in Transjordan, conquered by the Israelites before they crossed the River *Jordan (Deut. 3:4). Jair, son of Manasseh, who conquered the region, called it after himself, Bashan-Havoth-Jair (Deut. 3:14). Under Solomon the region Argov and the towns of Jair were two separate districts under Ben-Geber (1 Kgs. 4:13; Authorized Version: 'son of Geber').

ARIMATHEA *See* *RAMAH

ARNON A stream in Transjordan, identified with the River Mogib, rising in the Syro-Arabian desert and flowing into the *Dead Sea. In its 30-mile course the river descends about 3,500 feet, the last part through a deep, narrow gorge. Sihon, King of the *Amorites, conquered the land north of this river, which had previously been held by the first Moabite king, so that the river then formed the border between the kingdoms of Amorites and Moabites (Num. 21:13-26). After the Israelite conquest by Saul the Arnon served as the border between the territories of Gad, Reuben and half of the tribe of Manasseh to the north and *Moab to the south (Deut. 3:8-16). After the conquest of *Moab by David the Arnon formed the limit of Israelite expansion to the south (2 Sam. 24:5; Authorized Version: 'the river of Gad'). After the death of Ahab, King of Israel, the people of *Moab conquered the land to the north of the Arnon (Judg. 11.18). Mesha, King of *Moab, boasted (in the Mesha stele) of making the highway which crossed the river (*Inscriptions). This is very possibly the road referred to in Isaiah (16:2) as 'the fords of Arnon'.

AROER *a)* A town on the bank of the *Arnon (Deut. 2:36, etc.), on the border of the kingdom of Sihon,

King of the *Amorites (Josh. 12:2). It was conquered by the Reubenites, and formed part of their territory (Josh. 13:16), but Numbers (32:34) states that it was built by the Gadites. It was fortified by Mesha, King of *Moab (*Inscriptions), but was soon afterwards conquered by Hazael, King of *Aram (2 Kgs. 10:32-3). In the time of Jeremiah it was a Moabite town once more (Jer. 48:19). Eusebius mentions it in his day. Identified with Khirbet Arair on the River Mogib (*Arnon), where remains of Bronze Age and Iron Age settlements, and of a Nabatean settlement, have been found.

Excavations at the site were conducted in the years 1964-6 by the Spanish Center in Jerusalem, under the direction of E. Olavarri. The site was first occupied by a semi-nomadic population in the early stages of the Middle Bronze Age. After a long gap it was resettled at the end of the Late Bronze Age and beginning of the Iron Age. To this stage belong dwellings and an Israelite fortress which was subsequently conquered by King Mesha of *Moab. The new fortress which was built by Mesha was a 150 square feet building, fortified by three circumvallating walls. The king also constructed a reservoir to store rainwater. It was deserted until the Hellenistic period when it was again inhabited by a semi-nomadic population of *Arabian stock. The *Nabateans occupied the site from the 1st century BC to the 1st century AD. Four houses and a large number of cisterns built around the deserted fortress belong to this period. The settlement declined in the 2nd and 3rd centuries AD, after the annexation of the Nabatean kingdom to the Roman empire.

b) A town in the south of the territory of Gad, named Aroer before Rabbah (*Rabbath-Ammon) (Josh. 13:25). Jephthah smote the *Ammonites from Aroer to *Minnith (Judg. 11.13). Tentatively located northwest of Amman.

c) Because the stream bordering the mound was called Wadi Aroer E. Robinson identified the site in 1838 with biblical Aroer. Extensive excavations were conducted there in the years 1975-81 by the Nelson Glueck School of Biblical Archaeology under the direction of A. Biran and R. Cohen. Four levels of occupation were distinguished: three Iron Age levels (7th/6th centuries BC) and one occupation level of the Roman period (1st century AD). In the Iron Age the site was fortified by a massive wall, within which typical Israelite four-room *houses were unearthed. The foundation of the fortified town is ascribed to Hezekiah and Josiah as a precaution against the *Edomite threat. At the highest part of the mound a fortress (*c.* 40 feet by 35 feet) was built of ashlars with projecting bosses. It was destroyed in the second year of the War against the Romans. This fortress guarded the border between the Herodian and *Nabatean kingdoms.

ARUBOTH (TELL EL-ASAWIR) The seat of the overseer of the third district in Solomon's kingdom (1 Kgs. 4:10). It is mentioned in the *Taanach tablets (*Inscriptions) and in the list of conquest of Pharaoh Sheshonq at the temple at Karnak. Its identification is not certain; it should possibly be identified with Tell el-*Asawir, an ancient mound at the southern outlet of the pass of Wadi Ara (*Roads). In 1953 a tomb was excavated on this site by M. Dothan, on behalf of the Israel Department of Antiquities and Museums, and was found to contain burials of two distinct periods. The one at the lower level dated from the end of the Chalcolithic period or the beginning of the Early Bronze Age, while the one at the upper level was of the *Hyksos period. Both burials contained much pottery, which helped to date the tombs. The later tomb dates from the late 17th or first half of the 16th century BC. In both periods mass burial was practised.

ARVAD; ARVADITES A Phoenician city built on an island some 2 miles from the coast, between Tripoli and Lattakiyeh. The name Arvad occurs in the table of nations (Gen. 10:18). Ezekiel refers to it as the place to which the Tyrian 'mariners' and 'army' came (Ezek. 27:8, 11). In the inscriptions of the *El Amarna period the Arvadites are referred to as seafarers, who had close contacts with the ports of the eastern Mediterranean and *Egypt. In about 1100 BC Arvad was conquered by Tiglath-Pileser I and from that time it is frequently mentioned in the Assyrian documents. The King of Arvad took part in the Battle of Qarqar (853 BC). Tiglath-Pileser III conquered the town in 737 BC and during the days of Nebuchadnezzar it was a tributary to *Babylon. It was an important harbor in the Persian and Hellenistic periods but later declined.

ASAWIR (TELL EL-) *See* *ARUBOTH

ASHDOD One of the main Philistine cities (Josh. 13:3), situated in the Judean Plain, 3 miles from the coast. It is not mentioned in any of the early historical sources, but the Anakims (giants in Hebrew) who dwelt at Gaza, Gath and Ashdod (Josh. 11:22) are perhaps remnants of the ancient population of that region, who were subdued by the Philistines.

In the 11th century BC Ashdod was already an important Philistine center, and the Ashdodites belonged to one of the five cities of the Philistine lords (Josh. 13:3). The ark of God was brought from Ebenezer to the house of Dagon at Ashdod (1 Sam. 5:1 ff). This important Philistine temple still existed in the Hellenistic period, when it was destroyed by Jonathan Maccabeus who set it on fire (1 Macc. 20:84). In the time of the Kingdom of Judah Ashdod was a Philistine royal city, and Amos mentions its palaces (Amos 3:9). Uzziah fought the Philistines and broke down the walls of Ashdod and built cities about that city (2 Chr. 26:6). In the times of Ahaz Ashdod experienced a revival, invaded Judah and conquered several Judean cities (2 Chr. 28:18).

In the period of Assyrian supremacy Ashdod paid tribute to Sargon II. In 714 BC the King of Ashdod refused to pay tribute, and was deposed. At this time the city revolted against Assyria, and a certain Yamani (i.e. Greek) usurped the throne, siding with the Egyptians, the enemies of the Assyrians. In 711 BC Sargon reconquered Ashdod, deported many of its inhabitants, and made it an Assyrian satrapy. By the end of the 8th century BC Ashdod was ruled by a local king, an Assyrian vassal. Sennacherib annexed portions of Judah to Ashdod. With the downfall of Assyria and the ensuing wars between Babylon and Egypt Ashdod, situated on the main road to Egypt, suffered

General view of excavations at Ashdod

greatly. These events are mentioned by Zephaniah (2:4) and Zechariah (9:6), and Jeremiah (25:20) speaks of the remnant of Ashdod. It is apparently in this period that Pharaoh Psamtik besieged Ashdod for a period of 29 years and conquered it (Herodotus II, 157). Under Nebuchadnezzar II Ashdod was a small kingdom subject to Babylon. In the Persian period Ashdod became the capital city of a satrapy which included parts of Judah in the Shephelah and Ekron. Jews married Ashdodite women, and the Ashdodite dialect was heard in the streets of Jerusalem (Neh. 13:23-24). The Ashdodites were among those opposing Nehemiah's building activities in Jerusalem (Neh. 4:1 ff). In the Hellenistic sources the city is named Azotos. It was a flourishing town when it was conquered by John Hyrcanus (1 Macc. 15:10). Pompey granted it autonomy and it was rebuilt by Pompey. It was still a prosperous city in the time of Herod and in the Roman period. It was inhabited by gentiles and Jews. It then consisted of the twin towns, Azotus Paralus, i.e. coastal Azotus, which was also the ancient harbor, and Azotus Mesogeius, inland Ashdod.

The mound of Ashdod consists of two parts, an acropolis extending over an area of some 20 acres, and a lower city, of at least 70 acres. The site was extensively excavated in the years 1962, 1963 and 1965 as a joint project of the Pittsburgh Theological Seminary, the Pittsburgh Carnegie Museum and the Israel Department of Antiquities, and in the years 1965-72 on behalf of the Pittsburgh Carnegie Museum and the Department of Antiquities, under the direction of M. Dothan.

The earliest traces of occupation on the mound are sherds of the Chalcolithic period and of the Early Bronze Age. In the Middle Bronze Age IIC the first fortified city was built on bedrock. To this period belongs a fragment of a massive mud brick gate of a direct approach type (*Fortifications). It is dated by finds to the second half of the 17th century BC. The acropolis was apparently enclosed in this period (Stratum 18) by a brick wall, of which only the foundation trench has survived. The wall was apparently surrounded by a fosse.

The next four occupation levels (Strata 17-14) belong to the Late Bronze Age (c. 1450-1230 BC). Stratum 17 is dated by painted Cypriote *pottery to the 15th century BC. To this period belong brick buildings and stone pavements of courtyards or streets. From the following phase (Stratum 15) there are houses of the same type, and perhaps also a public building with thick walls. The lower city south of the acropolis also contained houses dating to the same four phases. It was apparently fortified by a brick wall, placed on a high stone foundation. In a plastered cistern in one of the courts of the buildings rainwater was collected from the roofs, and a conduit led to another larger cistern. The finds of the latest phase (Stratum 14) include imported Mycenaean *pottery and local ware of the 13th century BC. The city was destroyed by fire, apparently at the end of the century.

The transition between the Late Bronze Age and Iron Age I is marked by a thick layer of ashes. Stratum 13-B is a transitional phase. The following phase, Stratum 13-A, marks the beginning of the Philistine occupation of Ashdod. The Philistines first arrived in small numbers in about 1200 BC, destroying only part of the earlier Canaanite city. The second, and larger wave of the Sea Peoples arrived at Ashdod in the first quarter of the 12th century BC. This Philistine city flourished mainly in Strata 12 and 11. The Philistines built a well-planned city at Ashdod. Two complexes of buildings separated by a street were investigated in one section of the city. One building terminates in a small apsidal structure. To its north is a row of rooms and a large hall with two stone bases, apparently of columns supporting the roof. Among the finds were large quantities of Philistine *pottery as well as jewelry. An outstanding find is a figurine of a seated woman which formed part of a throne. It apparently represents a Philistine goddess, rendered as the Mycenaean Great Mother. Two seals uncovered had characters in the Cypro-Minoan script used in Cyprus in the 13th-early 12th century BC. These seals are the earliest written records found in a Philistine context. In the middle of the 11th century BC the Philistine city spread outside the acropolis area. At the beginning (Stratum 10-B) several kilns were built in an area which was enclosed by a wall in the following phase (Stratum 10-B). This formed a potters' quarter which was in use for many centuries. The fortifications consisted of a brick wall (15 feet wide), strengthened at places with stone, and a gate (45 feet by 53 feet) defended by two solid towers. The gate was destroyed in the first half of the 10th century BC, perhaps at the end of the reign of David, or during the expedition of Pharaoh Siamon, about 960 BC. For some time Ashdod was an unfortified town. The rebuilding of the fortifications belong to Iron Age II.

In the city of Stratum 9 a new city gate was built south of the earlier gate. It, too, was constructed of bricks on a stone foundation. It consists of two towers, each with three rooms. The corners of the gate were strengthened with dressed and undressed stones. The gate measures 67 feet by 60 feet and the gateway is 15 feet wide. In plan it is similar but not identical with the gates found at Solomonic *Hazor, *Megiddo and *Gezer. The wall adjoining the gate on the north is 28 feet wide. This system of fortifications was used throughout Iron Age I (Strata 10-6). The earliest gate is dated to the last third of the 10th century BC, and its destruction is ascribed to Uzziah, King of Judah. The lower city, too, was fortified by a wall. In one building a new type of pottery was found, named Ashdod ware. The vessels are red burnished and decorated with black bands, replacing the typical Philistine pottery. Stratum 8 contained a small temple, consisting of several rooms. In the main room was a brick-made structure, apparently an altar. Near the altar were a large number of *cult objects, including figurines of domestic animals and miniature clay offering tables. This temple is dated to the 8th century BC, and its destruction is ascribed to the end of the century. In the temple and its vicinity skeletons and bones of some 3,000 individuals were found in secondary burial; they were apparently killed during the conquest of Ashdod by Sargon II. In the acropolis area were uncovered three fragments of a basalt stele in Assyrian cuneiform script that is similar to a victory stele found at the Assyrian capital of Dur Sharrukin (Khorsabad), supporting the date of destruction of this level of occupation. In Stratum 7 (first half of the 7th century) the potters' quarter was still in its original site in the lower city. Streets, houses and courtyards which contained numerous kilns and were used as workshops were discovered here. The destruction of this city is ascribed to Psamtik I of Egypt. On the acropolis a Hebrew inscription reading 'the potter' was found engraved on a jar of the 8th century BC. To this period also belong Hebrew inscribed *weights. During the 7th century BC Ashdod had close relations with Judah, and it may even have been conquered by Judah in the days of Josiah and remained in the kingdom until his death in 609 BC.

There are scanty remains of the Persian period (Stratum 5); the destruction of this phase is ascribed to the Hellenistic period. There are remains of stone foundations of a large building, which was perhaps an administrative center. Aside from typical pottery of the Persian period, there was also much Attic *pottery of the black-figured type. An ostracon in Aramaic mentions a quantity of wine delivered to a man by the name of Zebadiah.

The city in the Hellenistic period (Stratum 4) was carefully planned. The main building apparently belonged to the agora of the city. Numerous Rhodian-type wine jars were found in this building. In one corner of a room were found a stone altar and two miniature stone altars nearby. This corner apparently served as a cult place. On a lead plaque was a representation of a deity with a fish tail. These finds were uncovered in a layer of ashes attributed to the destruction of the city by the Hasmoneans at the end of the 2nd century BC. The latest coin found in this level was of Antiochus VII and was dated to 114 BC.

In the Roman period (Stratum 3) the general plan of

the Hellenistic city was retained. This city, of the time of the dynasty of Herod, was apparently destroyed during the First Revolt in AD 67. The glory of Ashdod passed. Little remains of the town of the late Roman and Byzantine periods (Stratum 2). Several small houses belong to the end of the Byzantine and the Umayyad periods (Stratum 1). A marble slab with Jewish symbols and a Samaritan inscription attest to a mixed population in this period.

ASHKELON; ASKELON; ASCALON One of the oldest, largest and most important cities in the Holy Land, on the southern part of the Mediterranean seaboard, where the earliest remains of human occupation date back to the Neolithic period. The earliest mention of Ashkelon, in the form Ascanu, is found in the *Execration Texts of the 19th century BC. In the period of the 18th-20th Dynasties it was one of the Canaanite city-states under Egyptian influence. The city rebelled against *Egypt a number of times during the 13th century BC. The capture of Ashkelon by Rameses II is depicted in the reliefs at the temple of Karnak in *Egypt, where the city appears as a fortified tower. Ashkelon is mentioned several times in the *El Amarna letters and another document, an Egyptian panegyric, refers to the conquest of the city in 1229 BC by Pharaoh Merneptah.

The history of Ashkelon in the period of the Israelite occupation of *Canaan is not at all clear. Only in Judges (1:18) is its capture mentioned, and in the Septuagint the same verse states that the city was not taken. There is also no mention in the Bible of its conquest by the *Philistines, which must have taken place early in the 12th century BC. During the period of the Judges it was one of the five cities of the *Philistines (Josh. 13:3), and it also features in the story of Samson (Judg. 14:19). The Assyrian sources refer to Iskaluna (or Askaluna) as a kingdom extending over a large area towards *Joppa and *Ono in the north and northeast, an area greatly reduced under strong Assyrian pressure in the 8th century BC. A little later it was one of the states paying tribute to Tiglath-Pileser III.

In his day Rezin, King of *Aram, Pekah, son of Remaliah, King of Israel, and the King of Ashkelon revolted against Assyria. Ashkelon was severely punished (732 BC), but rebelled again in the days of Sennacherib and was suppressed in 701 BC when its king, Sidka, was deported to Assyria. During the campaigns of Esarhaddon and Ashurbanipal against *Egypt, at the end of the 7th and early 6th centuries BC, Ashkelon was used as a base for their armies, and the prophets refer to the hardships which the city endured at this period (Zeph. 2:4; Jer. 25:20, etc.). During Nebuchadnezzar's campaigns many of the inhabitants of Ashkelon were deported. Before the end of the Babylonian period, or early in the Persian period, Ashkelon became a Tyrian emporium. It is still mentioned as such at the end of the same period. In the early Hellenistic period, under the Ptolemies, Ascalon, as it was then known, became a free port and an autonomous city. In 111 BC it minted silver coins and in 104 BC became independent, with coins being minted which were dated from the year of independence. All attempts by the Hasmoneans to conquer Ascalon failed. Herod was a native of Ascalon, and in later years he adorned the city with palaces, temples and a large stoa.

As *Colonia Ascalon liberata et foederata,* the city flourished throughout the Roman period. Greek philosophers and grammarians abounded. Although Hellenistic in culture, the city was cosmopolitan and had a large Jewish community as well. The cults were those of the local Atargatis or Derketo (a goddess with the face of a woman and the body of a fish), Isis, Apollon and Heracles. The city was one of the three largest commercial centers in the country. Ascalon continued to flourish in the Byzantine period, to which remains of a synagogue belong.

The city covered some 160 acres. The more ancient part, with an area of 15 acres, lay in the center of the ruins, at Tell el-Hader. Limited excavations in 1920-1 by W.J. Phythian-Adams and J. Garstang on behalf of the Palestine Exploration Fund brought to light remains mainly of the Hellenistic and Roman period.

Menorah relief from Ashkelon, Byzantine period

On the mound remains of typical *Hyksos fortification were discovered. Above this a 10 feet layer represents the period of Egyptian rule over Palestine. The finds in this stratum indicate strong relations with the Aegean and Cypriot cultures. Since 1920–1 very little archaeological research has been carried out at Ashkelon. In the vicinity of the of the city, however, a painted tomb of the late Roman period has been discovered. Remains of a building identified as the council-house (bouleuterion) also belongs to the Roman period. It is a 335 feet long building with a theater-shaped structure at its southern end. The council chamber was entered through a large forecourt, surrounded by colonnades on all sides. The columns, of the Corinthian order, were 25 feet high. The walls of the hall were decorated with winged victories holding a wreath in the raised right hand and a palm branch in the left hand. In 1937 a painted tomb was excavated at Ashkelon by J. Ory on behalf of the Department of Antiquities. It consists of one vaulted room covered with painted stucco. Within medallions formed by vine trellises are portrayed a bust of a woman, a dog chasing a gazelle, a Gorgon mask, harvest scenes, Pan playing a syrinx. On the back wall are painted two seated nymphs against a background of Nilotic landscape. A semicircular city wall and a church of the 7th–8th centuries AD belong to the Byzantine period. To the same period are dated remains of a *synagogue with a pedestal and a chancel screen decorated with menorahs.

In 1985 Professor L. Stager resumed excavations at Ashkelon on behalf of the Oriental Institute of the University of Chicago. Remains of occupation from the transition Late Bronze–Iron Age of the 12 century BC to the Muslim period of the 10th century AD have been uncovered. Two areas were investigated. In one area remains of the Middle Ages were uncovered; in the other area the old excavation of W.J. Phythian-Adams

was cleared and remains of the Philistine period were discovered.

ASHNAH The name of two towns in Judah, one of them mentioned in Joshua (15:33) after *Zoreah, among the cities in the territory of Judah. Ashnah's identification is not certain; some suggest Khirbet el-Assalin, more than a mile to the northwest of *Zorah, while others propose Khirbet Ashainah, over 4 miles to the southeast of Khirbet el-Assalin. The other Ashnah is also in Judah, in the district of *Libnah (Josh. 15:43).

ASHTAROTH; ASHTEROTH KARNAIM The capital of the kingdom of Og, King of the *Bashan (Josh. 9:10, etc.). After his defeat it was given to Machir, son of Manasseh (Josh. 13:31). The town is of great antiquity and is mentioned in the *Execration Texts, in the list of Thutmosis III and in the *El Amarna letters. In the form of Ashteroth Karnaim it is referred to as one of the cities of the Rephaim (Gen. 14:5). The site was also inhabited in the Hellenistic period (1 Macc. 5:26, as Carnaim; 2 Macc. 12:26, as Carnion) and was known in the Roman period. It is identified by most scholars with Tell Ashtarah, north of the River *Yarmuk.

ASPHALT; BITUMEN A blackish mineral referred to several times in the Bible. Of the bituminous substances, asphalt was known as *homer* in Hebrew (Gen. 14:10; Authorized Version: 'slime'). There were pits of it in the valley of Siddim, in which lay the cities of *Sodom and *Gomorrah. According to the Bible the same substance was used in the land of Shinar when building the Tower of Babel for mortar in buildings made of brick (Gen. 11:3). The ark of the infant Moses was daubed with it (Exod. 2:3; Authorized Version: 'slime'). Two other substances, also bituminous but belonging to the pitches, were *kopher*, which was used to caulk Noah's Ark inside and out (Gen. 6:14) and *zephet*, which was used for a similar purpose (Exod. 2:3; Isa. 34:9; Authorized Version: 'pitch').

Conquest of the city of Ashtaroth by the Assyrians, depicted in reliefs from the palace of Tiglath-Pileser III

There is archaeological evidence that these bitumi-
nous substances were used in Palestine as early as the
Early Bronze Age, as some lumps of it were found in
*Jericho. Asphalt has been found at Tell *Beit-
Mirsim and Ophel (*Jerusalem), and recently a few
pots containing this material have been discovered at
*Arad. It dates from the Iron Age on both sites.

The richest bituminous deposits in the ancient Near
East were in *Mesopotamia, but there were also some
in Syria, *Phoenicia and Palestine, where the main
source of asphalt is near the *Dead Sea. Although
some of the rocks in the vicinity contain a high percentage of rock asphalt it is certain that this was not
exploited in antiquity; it seems that instead the large
patches of asphalt that floated on the surface of the sea
were collected. Greek and Roman authors referred to
the *Dead Sea as the 'Asphalt Lake' (e.g. Josephus,
Antiq. I, 174, 203; *War* IV, 476-85) and the substance
extracted was known as *bitumen iudaicum* (Vegetius I,
20, 1; III, 56, 3; etc.). Vitruvius (*De Architectura* VIII, 3,
2) says that there were large lakes in *Arabia producing much bitumen, which was collected by the neighboring tribes. Pliny (*Nat. Hist.* XXXV, 178) describes
the viscous semi-liquid asphaltic bitumen of the
*Dead Sea. Diodorus Siculus (XIX, 98, 2) writes:
'Every year a large quantity of asphalt in pieces more
than three *plethra* [a *plethron* being 100 feet] float in
the middle of the sea, but most of them are only two
plethra in length.' Diodorus also knew of this as a lake
situated in the land of the *Nabateans (II, 48, 6).

There is no direct evidence that the asphalt of the
*Dead Sea was exported to *Egypt, but as she needed
much bitumen for embalming and for shipbuilding
and had no sources of her own this seems highly
probable. The only other source of bitumen in that
part of the world was in *Phoenicia, whence *Egypt
imported cedar wood and cedar pitch, both used in
embalming.

Another bituminous substance was petroleum. It is
not mentioned in the Bible but appears as *nepht* (or
nathpic) in the Mishna and the Talmud. The only
place where crude petroleum came to the surface in
open wells was *Mesopotamia. It seems that petroleum was not used in Palestine until the Roman
period.

ASTARTE; ASHTORETH Fertility goddess of the
*Canaanites, the Sidonians (*Sidon) (1 Kgs. 11.5) and
the *Philistines (1 Sam. 31:10, where the name
appears in the plural form, Ashtaroth). Ashtoreth is
the counterpart of Baal, god of storm and fertilizing
rain. The Babylonians and the Assyrians knew her by
the name of Ashtar, goddess of fertility and love. In
the Bible she is referred to as the Queen of Heaven
(Jer. 7:18). The cult of Astarte was universal in Palestine in the Canaanite period and was also much
favored, especially by women, in the Judean and
Israelite kingdoms. Thousands of Astarte figurines
made of clay have been found at most of the excavated
sites of the Canaanite and Israelite periods. Some of
these reveal the influence of *Egypt, while others bear
a resemblance to Phoenician goddesses. Astarte is
usually represented as a woman, naked, holding her
breasts with her hands, with her hair long; she has

*Astarte figurine,
silver,
Bronze Age,
Nahariya*

horns on her forehead. In a temple of the *Hyksos period found at *Nahariya a stone mould for casting Astarte figurines in bronze was discovered. In the Hellenistic and Roman periods Astarte was identified with Venus-Aphrodite in the Near East.

ASTROLOGY Astrology is an ancient system of divination based on the belief that the stars can influence the fate and behavior of men and the general course of human events. A belief in the supernatural powers of

*Astarte figurine,
clay,
Late Bronze Age*

the celestial bodies was common to the *Babylonians, Egyptians, Assyrians and Chaldeans. In the 4th century BC it reached the Greeks and somewhat later the Romans.

Isaiah (47:13) lists three classes of astrological practitioners common among the Babylonians: 'Let now the astrologers, the stargazers, the monthly prognosticators, stand up...' The astrologers foretold the future by the movements of stars in different quarters of the sky, from which they were able to deduce omens. The earliest division of the sky was based on the four cardinal points of the compass. Many tables based on these divisions have been discovered in *Mesopotamia, one of which contains a list of eclipses from the beginning to the middle of the month of Tammuz, the tenth month. The implications of each eclipse depended on the quarter of the sky in which it was observed. Many other tables were drawn up for divination by the constellations of the planets and used by the star-gazers. One prediction reads: 'When Venus draws near to Scorpion the prince will die of a scorpion's sting and his son will ascend to the throne in his stead.' As time went on systems of star-gazing and divination developed and became more and more complicated.

The monthly prognosticators referred to in Isaiah based their divinations on observations made at the appearance of the new moon. An astrological treatise compiled by Sargon, King of *Accad (mid-3rd millennium BC) listed signs and portents connected with the new moon: 'If the moon of the 1st of the month be like that of the 27th, mischief will befall the land of *Elam; and if the moon of the 1st of the month be like that of the 28th, mischief will befall the land of Amurru.' The variations in the rays of the moon were also helpful in divination.

Astrology originated in *Mesopotamia, where the celestial bodies were worshipped as deities. In the library of Ashurbanipal, King of Assyria, there were large numbers of clay tablets relating to astrology. These contained about 7,000 omens, based on observations of the sun, moon and the five planets.

The Egyptians made use of astronomy in their calculations of time. They believed in 'good' and 'bad' days, but otherwise they had little use for astrology.

To the Greeks astrology was hardly known before the conquest of *Babylon byAlexander the Great. Greek scholars created a new form of astrology and from being an eastern religion it began to acquire the semblance of a science. Whereas in *Babylon astrology was at the service of the court, in Greece and the countries within its sphere of influence it was put at the service of the ordinary man, who believed that by studying his horoscope he could ascertain his future and his fate. To build up such a large number of horoscopic tables required a greater knowledge than that possessed by the Babylonians, and the Greeks were helped by their knowledge of mathematics. The culmination of Greek astrology is to be found in the works of Ptolemy (Claudius Ptolemaeus, died c. AD 150), which also form the basis of modern astrology.

Astrology reached Rome in the 2nd century BC. It was banned in 139 BC by a decree of the Senate but nevertheless flourished and became an accepted Roman institution. Augustus even put Capricorn, the zodiacal sign under which he was born, on his coins. The zodiacal circle, or separate signs of the zodiac, are very common on the coins of many Roman provinces.

Astrology was deeply rooted in Palestine by the 2nd century BC. A zodiacal circle supported by a goddess was found in the Nabatean temple at Khirbet et-*Tannur and it also appears on seal impressions found at *Mampsis. The extent to which astrology was accepted in the late Roman and Byzantine periods in Palestine is indicated by the numerous representations of the zodiac in the synagogues.

ASTRONOMY Stars and planets are mentioned quite frequently in the Bible, where the word 'star' is used to denote every radiant celestial body except the sun and the moon. The limitless numbers of stars in the sky are said to testify to the greatness of God, their maker (Exod. 32:13; Deut. 1:10, etc.). The stars symbolize the difference between God and man: God is the creator of the stars; it is he who guides them in their celestial paths, and only he can know their number; it is the vanity of man that makes him attempt to trespass beyond the limits set for him by God (Gen. 1:14, 18; Ps. 8:3-4; 136:7-9; 147:4; Amos 5:8; Job 9:7; Isa. 14:13; Obad. 4). Men have always felt an urge to worship the stars, but according to the biblical view they have no significance when compared with the might of God, their maker (Deut. 4:19; Neh. 3:16-17). The vision of doomsday is associated with unusual astronomical phenomena: the light of the stars will cease to shine (Isa. 13:10; Ezek. 32:7; Joel 2:10) and stars will fall to the ground (Dan 8:10).

The Bible 'as names for different stars and groups of stars: 1) *Ash* (Job 9:9; 38:32). It is translated as Arcturus in the Authorized Version, but modern astronomers believe it should be identified with the brightest star of *Ursa Major* (the Great Bear), which is why Job (38:22) mentions 'his sons', which are probably the seven main stars of this group.

2) *Mazzaroth* (Job 38:32). The meaning of this term is not known with certainty. It should perhaps be identified with the mazaloth of 2 Kings 23:5 (Authorized Version, 'planets'). In Babylonian mythology *mazzaroth* were transformed into stars and planets, all of which took the form of animals, as did the *Ursa Major* constellation.

3) *Pleiades* (Job 9:9; Amos 5:8). A group of seven stars in *Taurus* (the Bull), the light of which is dim. They are seen in the spring before sunrise and the renewal of plant growth in spring was attributed to them.

4) *Orion* (Job 9:9; 38:31; Amos 5:8), the Hunter. This is the most conspicuous constellation in the southern quarter of the sky, some of whose stars shine with an exceptionally bright light, such as the Betelguese (upper left, reddish light), and Rigel (lower right, blue light).

5) *The chambers of the south* (Job 9:9). This is an unidentified group of stars, perhaps a constellation, which would be visible above the southern horizon if one were along a caravan route leading from Israel to *Arabia. Astronomical observations were made by the *Babylonians from as early as the 4th millennium

Tyche (city goddess) surrounded by signs of the zodiac

BC. They could plot the exact courses of the five planets which were known to them and could predict the arrival of the new moon, the eclipses of the sun and moon and other astronomical phenomena. Unlike the Babylonian belief, which was based solely on mythology, the Old Testament concept of the universe does not conflict with modern astronomy. The universe is immense — frighteningly so (Ps. 104) — and is entirely dependent on rules established by God. The size of the universe is well expressed in God's promise to Abraham: 'I will multiply thy seed as the stars of the heaven, and as the sand which is upon the seashore' (Gen. 22:17, etc.). Man with his human limitations can see only a few thousand stars but God, who is their creator, can count and name them all. In contrast the other ancient peoples believed that the universe was limited to what man could perceive with his senses.

In the New Testament we find an inclination towards the star worship (Acts 7:43). The Last Judgement is also associated with supernatural astronomical events (Rev. 6:12-13; and cf. also Matt. 24:29; Mark 13:25; Luke 21:25; Rev. 9:1). References to the sun, the moon and the stars are also used metaphorically (Rev. 1:16, 20; 2:1; 3:1; 12:1; 22:16).

The star of *Bethlehem which announced the birth of Jesus is mentioned in Matthew 2:9 only. There are three possible explanations for the appearance of this star. It may have been Halley's comet, which was seen in 11 BC, or a similar one of 4 BC. A comet of this kind may move against the direction of the course of the planets and the astrologers might have attached special significance to it. This is doubtful, however, because it is not known whether the comet was visible long enough for its course to be observed. Alternatively, it may have resulted from the formation of an unusual conjunction of planets, such as was observed in 7 BC, when Jupiter, Saturn and Venus came close to each other. But such a phenomenon does not last long and could hardly be classified under the term 'star'. A rare appearance of a supernova is a third possibility. Novae, stars whose light is normally dim but becomes temporarily strong, occur quite often. A supernova, on the other hand, is very rare, and since the invention of the telescope no such phenomenon has been observed. A nova cannot be seen by the naked eye but the light of a supernova is so strong that it can momentarily light up the sky very brightly. Novae and supernovae cannot be predicted.

ATARIM (WAY OF) An important road in the central Negev by which the Israelites went from *Kadesh-Barnea to Mount *Hor (Num. 20:22; 21:1). The Hebrew term *derech hatarim* is difficult to explain, and some prefer the reading *tarim*, interpreting it as 'the road of the scouts'. Other scholars, however, believe that the name refers to a road much frequented in all periods leading from Ain el-Qudeirat (*Kadesh-Barnea) to the northeast, toward *Arad. Along this road were found remains of settlements of the Middle Bronze and Iron Ages.

ATAROTH A town built by the Gadites after the conquest of the kingdom of the *Amorites in the 13th century BC (Num. 32:3, 34). Mesha, King of *Moab, recounts in his stele (*Inscriptions) that Omri, King of Israel, fortified Ataroth but that he, Mesha, recaptured it. Identified with Khirbet Atarus, on a hill half a mile north of the *Arnon. Another Ataroth, not identified, is mentioned in the territory of Ephraim (Josh. 16:7).

AZEKAH A town in the northwest of Judah. Between here and Sochoh (*Socoh) the *Philistines gathered to fight Israel in the days of Saul (1 Sam. 17). Azekah was one of the cities fortified by Rehoboam for the defence of Judah (2 Chr. 11:5, 9) and was one of the last two cities to withstand Nebuchadnezzar (Jer. 34:7), the other being *Lachish. Azekah is mentioned among the towns of Judah which were settled at the time of the Restoration (Neh. 11:30). It was situated on one of the western passes leading from the coast to the Judean Hills and near it passed the road to *Bethlehem via the Valley of *Elah. It seems that Azekah should be identified with Tell Zakariyeh.

The site was excavated in the years 1898-9 by F.J. Bliss and R.A.S. Macalister on behalf of the Palestine Exploration Fund. The top of the hill had been levelled, and on it stood a small town surrounded by a wall, strengthened with massive towers. This town was probably built in the 10th century BC, in the days of the United Monarchy, and was one of a string of fortresses built along the boundaries of Judah to guard the major roads and other strategic points. It is

mentioned in one of the *Lachish letters (*Inscriptions), which indicates its importance at the end of the Judean kingdom. Very few remains of the Persian and Hellenistic periods were brought to light.

AZOR An ancient mound 4 miles north of Jaffa. The place is not specifically mentioned in the Bible, but the Septuagint (Josh. 15:45) enumerates it among the cities of *Dan. An Assyrian document mentions its conquest by Sennacherib. Excavations conducted by J. Perrot (1958-9), and M. Dothan (1958, 1960) were mainly carried out in the local cemeteries, which represent all periods of occupation. Perrot excavated a cave 20 feet by 35 feet and 12 feet high, hewn in the local sandstone and dated by the finds to the Chalcolithic period. In the earliest level burial was in ossuaries. Most of these measure about 24in by 10in and are of crudely baked clay, shaped like houses. Some take the form of oval jars with an opening at the shoulder. Others are zoomorphic in shape. All the ossuaries have openings large enough for a skull to be inserted and are decorated with a schematic figure, probably the guardian of the dead. There were also small ossuaries, probably miniatures to serve as offerings. More than 120 ossuaries of all kinds were found. Pottery vessels which had contained funerary offerings included bowls on high stands, deep bowls, spherical vessels and miniature churns. Above the earliest burials were found later ones of the same period. These were plain burials, consisting of cooking ovens, which indicate the presence of human dwellings.

In the area excavated by Dothan evidence of settlements of the Chalcolithic period and the transition to the Early Bronze Age, Middle Bronze Age II and the Iron Age was discovered. The Middle Bronze Age II is represented by burials of men together with horses, a practice typical of the *Hyksos. The other cemetery excavated by Dothan belongs to the Iron Age. Five methods of inhumation were observed here. The first three were in pits, dated to the 12th-11th centuries BC by the typical Philistine pottery; burials in large clay jars, of the 11th-10th centuries BC; and in coffins made of unbaked mud bricks, dated by pottery to the 11th century BC; the fourth, cremation burials, with the bones of the cremated placed in a large pottery jar (the jars contained offerings in pottery vessels and metal objects, dated to the second half of the 11th century BC); and the last was collective burials, which consist of tombs surrounded by a stone wall 6 feet by 9 feet and about 3 feet high in which bodies were positioned in layers one on top of another, representing several generations. The pottery found with these burials is of the 10th-9th centuries BC.

B

BAALAH; BAALE *See* *KIRJATH-JEARIM

BAALBEK *See* *HELIOPOLIS

BAAL-HAZOR The place in Ephraim where Amnon was killed by the servants of Absalom (2 Sam. 13:23ff.); it is mentioned in 1 Macc. 9:15 by the name of Azoros oros (emended from Azotos oros) as a place to which Judas Maccabaeus pursued Bacchides; also known in the Roman period. Identified with Tell Asur, 5 miles northeast of *Beth-El, the highest point in the mountains of Ephraim.

BAAL-SHALISHA; LAND OF SHALISHA A place in Mount Ephraim where Saul sought his father's asses (1 Sam. 9:4). Also mentioned in connection with Elisha (2 Kgs. 4:42). Eusebius (*Onom.* 56:21) follows the Septuagint and calls it Baitsarisa, but mistakenly locates it 15 miles north of *Lod, in the territory of Thimnah. Not identified.

BAAL-ZEPHON A place in *Egypt close to the spot where the *Red Sea was divided (Exod. 14:2, 9, 16; Num. 33:7-8). Identification of this site depends upon the actual route taken by the Israelites on their journey from *Egypt to the land of *Canaan According to those who favor a northerly route, Baal-Zephon should be sought somewhere near Lake Sirbonis (identified with Sabkhat Bardawil), possibly Mons Cassius, which was a cult place in the Hellenistic-Roman periods and might have perpetuated the sanctity already ascribed to it in more ancient times. Others point to sites nearer to the eastern estuary of the *Nile delta, where temples to Baal-Zephon have been found. Those who maintain that a southerly route was taken suggest that it should be sought farther south, just north of Suez.

BAB EDH-DHRA A site on the *Dead Sea, whose ancient name remains unidentified. In 1965-7 extensive excavations were carried out here under the direction of P.W. Lapp, on behalf of the American School of Oriental Research. The site is situated on the road from el-Kerak (Kir-Moab) to es-Safi (*Zoar). It has remains of a fortified town and two cemeteries.

The town was surrounded by an irregularly shaped wall strengthened by towers, one of which was unearthed. But the excavators concentrated mainly on the two cemeteries, where three types of burial were found. The latest type, of about 2300 BC, is attributed to the people who conquered the site and set it on fire, and the excavators termed it the 'tumulus tomb'. It consists of a narrow, shallow pit in which the body was laid with pottery vessels and a dagger alongside it. On top of the pit stones were piled in a rounded heap (hence the use of the word 'tumulus').

To the preceding period, Early Bronze Age III, belong the 'ossuary' type of burials, These are rectangular mud-brick constructions, varying from 53 feet by 17 feet to 20 feet by 15 feet. The tombs had an entrance in one of their long sides and their floors were paved with pebbles. Each of the tombs contained heaps of bones of many individuals, which is why they are described as 'ossuary' (*Burial). The tombs also contained pottery vessels and weapons. In one of them more than 800 vessels were counted.

Tombs of the third type are called 'pit graves'. These are round pits, 2-3 feet in diameter and about 3 feet deep, with one step leading to the interior. In these tombs skulls, or fragments of skulls, were placed on one side of the pit, while the rest of the bones were heaped in the center. Pottery vessels, some containing beads, were stacked along the walls. Female figurines were deposited with the bones. The excavators estimate that the cemetery of Bab edh-Dhra contained not less than 20,000 burials of the pit-grave type. These graves belong to a pre-urban period of the settlement, and are dated by the finds to about 3150-3000 BC.

The excavations at Bab edh-Dhra have still left unanswered the problem of the origin of the inhabitants of the site, the source of the burial customs and of the related cults, and especially the existence of its huge cemetery which was much too large for the needs of the small ancient town.

BABYLON (CITY OF); BABYLONIANS One of the most important cities of *Mesopotamia, whose ancient name probably meant 'the gate of the gods'. The ancient Hebrews understood the name differently: 'Therefore is the name of it called Babel; because the Lord did there confound the language of all the earth' (Gen. 11:9). Babylon is the Greek form of the name. The greatness of Babylon began during its 1st Dynasty, especially in the reign of Hammurabi, the sixth king of that line. During his reign and that of his son numerous temples were built there and irrigation channels were excavated, but then the city

Reconstruction of the Gate of Ishtar at Babylon

mounds scattered over the area concealed some of the more important monuments. A huge bridge over the river connected old Babylon with the new city, built under Nebuchadnezzar II. In the excavations of Tell Babil extensive remains of his palace were discovered. It consisted of several large courts around which were grouped countless halls, rooms, stores and so on. The same palace was still further enlarged by subsequent rulers, especially Artaxerxes III Ochus. A monumental passageway led to the palace from the east, terminating in the third court, adjoining which was the 50 feet square throne hall. The walls of his vast hall were lined with bricks enamelled in white, light blue, yellow and red, on a dark blue ground. Another huge palace was discovered in a mound in the northeastern quarter of the city. It consisted of a narrow passage, along which were grouped two lines of rooms, seven in each group. The excavators believed that these were the gardens of Queen Semiramis — the 'Hanging Gardens of Babylon' famous in classical literature. Inscribed clay tablets were found here on which were written the portions of food allotted to foreign artisans and important captives, among them Jehoiakim, King of Judah.

Along the eastern side of the two palaces ran a ceremonial street connected with the inner city by the famous Ishtar Gate, decorated with enamelled bricks on which wild oxen and legendary animals were depicted. The street led into the most sacred part of the city, where the most venerated shrines were situated. In the center of a huge court (1,200 feet by 1,500 feet) stood the temple of Marduk, named E Sag Ila, and the 'Tower of Babel'. Owing to the rise in the level of the ground water the excavators were unable to penetrate the strata pertaining to the Babylon of Hammurabi, but remains of the Persian, Hellenistic and Roman periods did come to light.

BABYLON IN THE BIBLE The story of the Tower of Babel is told in Genesis (11:1-9). This building is generally identified with the ziggurat, the tower which rises in the center of the court of the Temple of Marduk. Babylon is referred to as the first city which was built by man and Jeremiah (51:7) describes it as 'a golden cup in the Lord's hand'. Isaiah also referred to the glories of the city (13:19) and prophesied its downfall (13:20-2; 14:7-21).

BAHURIM A place in the territory of Benjamin, on the Mount of *Olives, the home of Shimei, son of Gera, of the house of Saul (2 Sam. 16:5, etc.), and of Azmaveth the Barhumite, one of David's mighty men (2 Sam. 23:31). David's men found refuge here from Saul (2 Sam. 17:17-18). Identification is not certain, but possibly modern Ras et-Tmim, near et-Tur.

BASHAN (THE); BATANEA Region northeast of the River *Jordan. Most of the area is a fertile plain, with plenty of water. It borders on Mount *Hermon on the north and the *Gilead in the south (Deut. 3:8-10; Josh. 12:1-5). The River *Yarmuk forms the boundary between the Bashan and *Gilead. On the east the Bashan extends as far as *Salchah, on the slopes of Jebel ed-Druz (Deut. 3:10), which was once covered by oak forests (Isa. 2:13; Ezek. 27:6). It thus included the region later known as Trachonitis.

suffered a rapid decline. It revived again in the 13th century BC but continued to suffer frequent onslaughts, resulting in destruction, at the hands of the rising Assyrian Empire. It was not until the downfall of Assyria that Babylon, in the time of Nebuchadnezzar II, rose again to the status of the most important city in *Mesopotamia. Cyrus, King of Persia, conquered the city, which then became part of the Persian Empire. In 331 BC Babylon was conquered by Alexander the Great, who attempted to rebuild the venerated but decaying city. With his untimely death its long decline set in and in the Roman period it was no more than a famous heap of ruins. Early in the 17th century the Italian explorer Pietro Della Valle brought back from Babylon the first cuneiform tablets. These soon attracted the attention of numerous scholars, the most famous among whom were H. Layard and R. Koldewey.

The ruins of Babylon form a vast triangle and extend over an area of more than $3^1/_2$ square miles. The whole area was surrounded by walls, while on the west the city was defended by the *Euphrates. Tell Babil, which has preserved the ancient name, rises in the northern part of this triangle. Several additional

The land of Bashan was famous for its rich pasture, on which grazed large herds of cattle and sheep (Deut. 32:14; Jer. 50:19, etc.). Before the Israelite conquest Og was King of the Bashan (Josh. 9:10) and the Israelites defeated him at *Edrei (Num. 21:33-5). Then the region was allotted to the families of Jair (Deut. 3:14) and Nobah of the sons of Manasseh, who received *Kanath in the Bashan (Num. 32:42). After the division of the kingdom of Judah the Bashan became part of the kingdom of Israel, but the kings of Syria soon conquered Ramoth-*Gilead (*Mizpah) in the Bashan (1 Kgs. 22:3 ff.; 2 Kgs. 8:28). The remaining part of the Bashan fell to Syria in the days of Jehu (2 Kgs. 10:32-3). During the reigns of Jehoash and his son Jeroboam it returned to Israel (2 Kgs. 13:25; 14:25, 28). In 732 BC Tiglath-Pileser III conquered it and deported many of its inhabitants (2 Kgs. 15:29, supplemented by the lists of Tiglath-Pileser).

In the Persian period a district named *Karnaim was formed which included the Bashan and the *Golan. In the early Hellenistic period the area was named Batanea, and formed a separate administrative unit. Judas Maccabaeus conquered part of the region (1 Macc. 15:17-45). In 63 BC Pompey annexed the Bashan to the kingdom of the Itureans. When Herod the Great ascended the throne the Bashan was given to him and after his death it was ruled by his son Philip. In AD 37 it formed part of Agrippa I's kingdom, and it belonged to the kingdom of Agrippa II until his death. It was then annexed to the Roman province of Syria. With the new administrative division in the days of Diocletian (c. AD 300), the Bashan became part of *Arabia.

BATASH (TEL) (TIMNAH) Tel Batash is situated in the Sorek Plain, 4 miles west of Beth-Shemesh and 5 miles south of Gezer. The identification of the site with the biblical town of Timnah is well established thanks to the clear identification of Ekron with Tel Miqne. In the description of the northern border of Judah (Josh. 15:10-11) Timnah is mentioned between Beth-Shemesh and Ekron, along the Sorek Valley and Tel Batash is the only possible candidate for this location. Timnah is also mentioned elsewhere in the Bible, most prominently in Judges 14-16, where it plays an important role in the Samson stories. In this narrative Timnah appears as a Philistine town, located close to the Israelite area of settlement around Beth-Shemesh and Zorah. Timnah is also included in the list of cities of Dan (Josh. 19:43) which probably dates to the period of the United Monarchy. In 2 Chronicles 28:18 Timnah is one of the cities captured by the Philistines from the Israelites in the time of Ahaz. Outside the Bible, Timnah is mentioned in the Assyrian annals as a city seized by Sennacherib during his invasion of Judah in 701 BC.

Excavations at Tel Batash have been carried out since 1977 under the direction of G.L.Kelm and A.Mazar, and sponsored by South Western Baptist Theological Seminary in Forth Worth, Texas in collaboration with the Hebrew University of Jerusalem. They have revealed the history of the mound from the Middle Bronze Age until the Persian period. The mound is square in shape, each side 600 feet long. Its

peculiar shape was created when a huge earth rampart was constructed in the Middle Bronze Age. A massive mud-brick city wall was erected at the top of this rampart. During the Late Bronze Age (strata X-VI) a Canaanite town flourished at Tel Batash. Large buildings of this period were exposed in the northeastern corner of the mound. There was no city wall at this time, the outer walls of the buildings forming a defense line. The town suffered continuous attacks; each of the five Canaanite levels was heavily burnt. The destruction levels contained numerous finds, including seals, scarabs, metal objects and various local and imported pottery vessels. A large building of stratum VII (mid-14th century BC) is of particular importance because its ground floor was roofed with the support of two rows of pillars. This is a unique example of the use of pillars in Canaanite architecture and may be considered the forerunner of the later Iron Age pillared buildings.

The Philistine town of Timnah was uncovered in the excavations (stratum V). Brick and stone structures from this period as well as open areas containing baking ovens and silos were excavated. Among the finds in this level was typical Philistine pottery as well as seals and seal impressions. During the period of the United Kingdom (10th century BC) the town was rebuilt after being abandoned. The 10th-century town was probably not completely built up, since buildings were uncovered only in part of the areas excavated so far. A large public building of this period partly excavated in the southern part of the mound may have been a palace. Two massive square towers in the city gate area (Area C) may have been erected in this phase.

The 10th-century town may have been destroyed during the Egyptian invasion of the country by Sheshonq, five years after the division of the kingdom. After an occupational gap which probably lasted most of the 9th century BC, the town was again rebuilt during the 8th century BC (stratum III), perhaps when the region was part of the kingdom of Judah in the time of Uzziah. The newly planned city was surrounded by a massive stone city wall and was entered through a large gate, which was composed of outer and inner gates. The city suffered a violent destruction which can be safely attributed to the Assyrian conquest in 701 BC. One of the most important discoveries in this city was a storehouse containing over thirty jars of the type known as *lamelek* jars. These are typical Judean vessels, some of whose handles are stamped with the royal Judean seal. On one handle there was a private seal impression. These jars are evidence of Judean activity in Timnah, probably during Hezekiah's preparations for his war against Sennacherib. It is possible that in the years prior to 701 BC the outer gate of the town was strengthened by the addition of a huge outer bastion, which defended the approach to the town.

During the 7th century BC the city was rebuilt on a large scale (stratum II). The city wall and gate were rebuilt, and new buildings were erected in the town. The use of monolithic pillars to divide courtyards of buildings is characteristic of this phase, though it probably already started in the previous level. The buildings are well planned and arranged in blocks. A large fort or public building was found in the northeastern corner of the mound, and a series of houses was excavated to its west. One of these contained a typical Iron Age oil press. Several other oil presses unearthed in this area indicate that this was an industrial quarter. The houses were severely damaged by fire in c. 600 BC, probably during the Babylonian conquest of this region. Rich pottery assemblages and other finds throw light on the material culture of Timnah during that period which is characterized by a combination of coastal (late 'Philistine') and Judean cultural traditions. In the Persian period there was a small, very poor settlement at Tel Batash, as is attested by pits and some poor structures.

BATHS AND BATHING BIBLICAL PERIOD Washing, bathing and immersion were common in ancient religious practice (cf. Lev. 14:18, etc.; John 1:28, etc.). A new-born baby would be bathed before being dressed for the first time (Ezek. 16:4). The primitive conditions of life in the biblical period would hardly have permitted bathing in the sense understood in the Roman period, however, so this would usually have taken place in a natural source of water such as a river (cf. Exod. 2:5; 2 Kgs. 5:9–14). The normal dwelling rarely had bathing facilities, and only in the better houses, such as that found at Tell el-*Ajjul, could one expect to find a spe-

Phoenician figurine of a woman bathing, Achzib

cial chamber, with a tub used as a bath. This was built on a plan common in *Egypt, where the practice seems to have originated. Such installations were also discovered in the great palaces in the neighboring countries. More common was a shallow clay bowl with a raised ridge in the middle, which was probably used for washing the feet. These have been found mainly in Iron Age strata.

HELLENISTIC-ROMAN PERIODS Public baths were not built until the late Hellenistic and early Roman periods. The earliest baths in Palestine are those built by Herod at *Masada and at *Herodium, which were constructed on the regular Roman plan and comprised: 1) the *apodyterium*, a room in which discarded clothes were kept in built-in cupboards; 2) a *frigidarium*, a cold bath in which the bather was expected to cleanse himself before passing into the other parts of the bath (the *frigidarium* was in the form of a basin, with a bench to sit on; some were faced with marble and they sometimes took the form of a small pool); 3) the *tepidarium*, a tepid bath, usually in the form of a shallow pool faced with water-resistant plaster where the bather would warm himself before proceeding; 4) the *caldarium*, a hot bath, which sometimes consisted of more than one room, one of which contained tubs for bathing built of bricks and faced with plaster or marble, and another in which a steam-bath was taken.

The heating of this part of the bath-house was by means of a *hypocaust*, which consisted of a furnace built of bricks outside the house. The heat from this was conveyed to the rooms containing the *caldarium* through a brick tunnel or clay pipes. The floors of the *caldarium* were supported on numerous small brick pillars, creating cavities into which hot air passed from the furnace. Water poured on to the heated surface filled one room with steam, while clay pipes built along the walls heated the other in which bathing took place. Flues built into the wall took the smoke out. The floors of the more luxurious bath-houses were paved with mosaics and the walls were decorated with frescoes. The public bath became a social institution and baths built in this way have been found throughout Palestine, even in regions where water was precious (*Oboda, *Mampsis). They are mentioned in the Talmud under the name *demosion* ('public') and there is also a reference to a 'Bath of Aphrodie' at Acre in the Roman period (Sboda Zara 1, 7; 3–4).

There was also another kind of bath, built near or above hot springs thought to have medicinal properties. The most celebrated were those of *Tiberias (Josephus, *Antiq.* XVIII, 36), and of *Callirrhoe, where Herod was recommended to bathe when mortally ill (Josephus, *Antiq.* XVII, 17).

BEER-LAHAI-ROI A place in the *Negev, between *Kadesh-Barnea and Bered, where God appeared before Hagar in the guise of an angel (Gen. 16:7–14), and where Isaac met Rebekah (Gen. 24:62; Authorized Version: 'the well Lahai-Roi'). Not identified.

BEEROTH One of the towns of the Gibeonites (Josh. 9:17), listed among the towns of Benjamin (Josh. 18:25). The home of Baanah and Rechab, who killed Ish-Bosheth (2 Sam. 4:2–8), and of Naharai, one of David's mighty men (2 Sam. 23:37). Beeroth was resettled after the Restoration (Ezek. 2:25). Eusebius (*Onom.* 48:9) mentioned a village by this name 7 miles from Jerusalem, on the way to *Neapolis. Identification not certain; possibly Nebi Samwil, north of *Jerusalem.

BEER-SHEBA A town in the *Negev, prominent in the history of the Patriarchs. The servants of Abimelech, King of *Gerar, had seized a well which belonged to Abraham, but a covenant was made between the contestants on oath (*shebuah* in Hebrew), and because of this the place was called Beer-Sheba, 'the well of the oath' (Gen. 21:22-32). Abraham planted a tamarisk (Authorized Version: 'grove') there, called on the name of the Lord (Gen. 21:33) and lived there (Gen. 22:19). Isaac went to live at Beer-Sheba, concluded a covenant with Abimelech, and dug a well there which he named Sheba (Gen. 26:13-33). Later Jacob offered sacrifices there (Gen. 46:1-4). After its conquest by Joshua Beer-Sheba was in the territory of Simeon within the territory of Judah (Josh. 19:2). In the time of the Judges Beer-Sheba was already a city, perhaps even the center of a district (1 Sam. 8:2). It seems that the saying 'from Dan to Beer-Sheba' reflects its religious and administrative importance (Judg. 20:1; 1 Sam. 3:20; 2 Sam. 3:10, etc.).

Beer-Sheba is also mentioned, together with *Dan, *Beth-El and *Gilgal, as a religious center in the later days of the kingdom of Israel, when all four towns were reproached because of their rivalry with *Jerusalem (Amos 5:5; 8:14). Josiah defiled all the high places from *Geba to Beer-Sheba (2 Kgs. 23:8). The recent discoveries of Israelite temples at *Lachish and *Arad testify to the presence of such local cult places. The town of Beer-Sheba was resettled after the Restoration (Neh. 11:27). Later it was probably the southern limit of *Idumea.

Although Beer-Sheba must have been an important place in the Roman and Byzantine period it does not appear very frequently in the sources. Eusebius (*Onom.* 50:1) states that in his time Bersabe was a large village 20 miles south of *Hebron, where a garrison of soldiers was stationed. It is also mentioned among military posts in the somewhat later Notitia Dignitatum (73:22). The *Medaba map shows it under the name of Berossabe. In the Byzantine period Beer-Sheba was part of Palestina Tertia.

Biblical Beer-Sheba is identified with Tell es-Seba, 3 miles to the east of modern Beer-Sheba. However, Iron Age tombs have been discovered within the limits of the modern city, which is built on the site of the Byzantine town. To this period belong numerous inscriptions, houses, churches and tombs discovered during sporadic excavations carried out on the site during the 1960s by Y. Israeli and R. Cohen on behalf of the Israel Department of Antiquities and Museums.

In the years 1969-75 Y. Aharoni conducted extensive archaeological excavations at Tel Sheva on behalf of Tel-Aviv University. The earliest traces of settlement on the mound date from the Chalcolithic period (3400-3100 BC). Nine occupation levels were identified from the 13th-11th centuries BC to the 7th-8th centuries AD. The earliest levels of occupation (IX-VIII) represent unfortified settlements containing scattered dwellings and silos. A well about 7 feet wide was dug at the northeastern edge of the mound at this time. It was cleared to a depth of 73 feet, but no water was reached. In the second half of the 11th century BC (VII) the earliest *fortifications were built. For a short time at the end of the same century (VI) Beer-Sheba was a peaceful, unfortified town containing several solidly built houses. A massive city wall was erected on the site during the course of the 10th century BC (V). It is a solid construction, 12 feet wide, strengthened by a series of insets and offsets. It was erected above an artificial ramp 18-20 feet high, protected by a moat in front of it. It continued in use in the following occupation level (end of the 10th and early 9th century BC [IV]). This wall was destroyed and a new wall built in the following stage of occupation, mid-9th to beginning of the 8th century BC (III). At this stage the solid wall was replaced by a casemate wall (*Fortifications), protected by a glacis, which was also in use in

Churn from Beer-Sheba, Chalcolithic period

the 8th century BC (II). The destruction of this system of fortifications at the end of the 8th century BC is ascribed to Sennacherib. After this calamity attempts were made to partly reconstruct the wall, but this new settlement is characterized mainly by an isolated fortress at the top of the mound (I).

In the southeastern part of the mound a series of city gates was discovered. The earliest, in strata V-IV, is a 63 sq feet structure. The gate is flanked on either side by two guardrooms and a tower. Inside the gate was a small cult installation with an incense altar. Its similarity to the gate of *Dan recalls the biblical phrase "from Dan to Beer-Sheba". The later gate, associated with the casemate wall, is narrower and lacks the flanking towers.

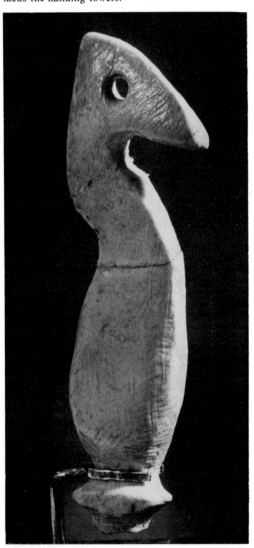

Figurine of a bird, Chalcolithic culture of Beer-Sheba

The city of stratum II has been excavated almost completely and offers a fine example of a royal store-city. Adjoining the gate inside the city is a square surrounded by several rooms, apparently an inn used by passers-by. The western quarter of the city contained three *houses of the "four-room" type. An ashlar building close by the gate was possibly the governor's residence. Three adjoining storehouses to the east of the gate contained an abundance of pottery vessels, different types in each store house, indicating that different products were stored in each one. A Hebrew ostracon found in a storehouse mentions two towns in the Beer-Sheba district, Eltolad (Josh. 15:30) and Amam (Josh. 15:26). A wide stairway discovered in the northeastern corner of the mound possibly led to the city's main *water-supply system. The city contained a sophisticated drainage system, emptying outside the gate. An unexpected find were large ashlars reused in the construction of the storehouses. When assembled these formed a large horned altar, which probably belonged to an Israelite *temple, which may have been destroyed in the course of Hezekiah's reforms (2 Kgs. 18:4, 22). The excavations at Beer-Sheba revealed one of the most complete plans of a small Israelite city.

BEIT MIRSIM (TELL) On the assumption that biblical *Debir (*Kirjath-Sepher) should be identified with Tell Beit Mirsim, excavations were made on this site on behalf of the Xenia Theological Seminary, Pittsburgh, and the American School of Oriental Research in Jerusalem in 1926, 1928, 1930 and 1931 under the direction of W.F. Albright. Situated on the border between the Judean Hills and the *Plain, 12 miles southwest of *Hebron and 16 miles north-northeast of *Beer-Sheba. The site is about 1,500 feet above sea level and some 8 acres in area.

In the excavations ten occupation levels were discovered and labelled A-J. The earliest stratum (J) is of the Early Bronze Age III (22nd century BC). Hardly any building remains are extant and it was dated by its pottery, some of which was imported from *Egypt, as well as by comparison with local pottery exported to *Egypt in the time of the 6th Dynasty. After it had been abandoned for about four hundred years a new settlement (stratum I) was built on the site in the Middle Bronze Age period (about 20th or early 19th centuries BC). A layer of ashes shows that this town was destroyed by fire. The town of stratum H was fortified, as we can infer from its topographical setting. The destruction of this stratum is dated to about 1800 BC. The cities of strata F and G are of Middle Bronze Age IIA (about 18th century BC). They were separated by a layer of ashes but no difference was noted in the pottery, which means that they were almost contemporaneous. In these strata remains of houses were discovered.

Strata E and D were of the *Hyksos period. To the earlier phase belongs an embankment of beaten earth (*Fortifications). Three well-built houses, one of which had a large number of rooms adjoining a court, belong to these strata. In an inner room was a built-in bench, probably a bed, while in the court there were storage facilities. These cities flourished at about

1700-1540/30 BC, a period of great prosperity at Tell Beit Mirsim, judging by the buildings and small finds.

City D was destroyed in a large conflagration and was abandoned for about a hundred years. City C is of the Late Bronze Age and in it were observed two phases, C1 and C2. It was smaller than the previous cities but still fortified, with a gate on the east where the Middle Bronze Age gate was built. The wall was about 7 feet thick. The destruction of stratum C2 is dated by pottery to about 1235 BC and may possibly be attributed to the Israelites who conquered the country at that time.

The city of stratum B is of the Early Iron Age. The building remains are scanty and the excavators had to go by pottery found in some storage pits when they divided them into three occupation phases. The three phases are represented by pre-Philistine, Philistine and post-Philistine pottery. The destruction of the city of the last phase is dated to the campaign of Pharaoh Sheshonq in 918 BC. The uppermost stratum (A) belongs to the 9th-6th centuries BC. The city was surrounded by a casemate wall (*Fortifications). There were two gates, one on the east and one on the west. The houses, of the four-room type, were well built of stone, the upper stories being supported by massive stone pillars. In one of these houses a dyeing installation was discovered. Of the numerous finds, an important one is the seal of 'Elyakim the servant of Yochan', found on the handles of two jars. Similar seals were found at *Beth-Shemesh and *Ramat Rachel (*Seals). This would date the destruction of the last phase of city A to the campaign of the Babylonians in 589-587 BC.

The importance of the excavations at Tell Beit Mirsim lies not so much in the remains of the buildings or in the small finds, but rather in the fact that this site afforded the possibility of differentiating accurately between the pottery of the different phases for the first time.

In recent years doubt has been cast on its identification with *Debir. Some scholars suggest locating Debir at Khirbet er-Rabud higher in the mountains to the east and identifying Tell Beit Mirsim with *Eglon (Josh. 15:39).

BENE-BERAK A town in the territory of *Dan (Josh. 19:45). Although not mentioned in the later biblical sources it is referred to as one of the cities of Sidka, King of *Ashkelon, which were conquered by Sennacherib (701 BC). In the Roman period it was the seat of numerous Jewish scholars, the most famous of whom was Rabbi Akiba. Identified with Kheiriyeh; also known as Ibn Ibrak, east of Jaffa. Excavations in the vicinity revealed a cemetery of the Chalcolithic period, including burials in ossuaries.

BETH-ABARA A place on the River *Jordan where Jesus was baptized (John 1:28). Eusebius (*Onom.* 58:18) locates it on the right bank of the river, east of *Jericho, and states that in his time many of the brothers tried to bathe there. It is similarly located on the *Medaba map: 'Bethabara, the place where St John baptized'. Although early Christian scholars place Bethabara east of the *Jordan, as implied in the New Testament, the Emperor Anasthasius (AD 491-518) built the church of St John the Baptist to the west of it. There is some justification for this. The normal route for a Jew to take when travelling from *Galilee to *Jerusalem, as Jesus did, was to cross the *Jordan and go through an area populated by Jews, thus avoiding the region of *Samaria, occupied by hostile Samaritans, and then to cross the *Jordan again opposite *Jericho. The site is identified with a place called by the Arabs Qasr el-Yahud, the Fort of the Jews. (*See also* *AENON.)

BETH-ALPHA A Jewish settlement in the Valley of *Jezreel that took its name, which is not otherwise known, from the Arab village of Khirbet Beit Ilfa. A synagogue was discovered there in 1928 and E.L. Sukenik excavated the building in 1929 on behalf of the Hebrew University. The *synagogue belongs to the late type, and was the first of its kind to be found. The building measures 85 feet by 55 feet and is of hammer-dressed blocks of basalt set in mortar. It consists of a spacious atrium containing a reservoir, a narthex and a basilica, with an apse facing south, towards *Jerusalem. The atrium was paved with coarse white mosaics, while the nave of the synagogue had a multicolored pavement. In comparison with the beautiful mosaic floor of *Hammath (*Tiberias), the one at Beth-Alpha is quite amateurish, and it may possibly be an example of contemporary popular art. At the entrance to the nave there are two dedicatory inscriptions, in Aramaic and in Greek, one mentioning the names of the artisans who laid the floor, Marianos and Haninah, and the other with the names of donors and the date of the dedication of the synagogue, in the time of Justinian (early 6th century AD). The dedicatory inscriptions are flanked by a buffalo and a lion. Next comes the first panel, in which is a biblical scene: Abraham preparing to sacrifice Isaac. The central panel shows Helios in his heavenly chariot drawn by four horses, with the twelve signs of the zodiac, each with the appropriate name in Hebrew. In the corners the four seasons are depicted as young maidens, each with the fruits of the season. The third panel, close to the pulpit and the apse where the Torah Shrine stood, has a representation of a Torah Shrine flanked by the seven-branched candlestick (*Menorah), with a *shofar* (ram's horn), *lulab* (palm branch) and *ethrog* (a citrus fruit), an incense

Sacrifice of Isaac, mosaic, Beth-Alpha synagogue

shovel and a pair of fierce-looking lions, one on each side. The spaces between the columns are decorated with small rectangular panels in which animals, birds and fruits are depicted against a background with a geometric design.

BETHANY; BETH-HANANIA A village on the eastern slope of the Mount of *Olives (Mark 11:1), identified by some with biblical *Ananiah (Neh. 11:32) and prominent in the events of the New Testament. Jesus left *Jerusalem after his triumphal entry and spent the night here (Matt. 21:17). The last halt on the pilgrims' road from *Jericho to *Jerusalem (Mark 11:1; Luke 24:50-1), 15 furlongs from *Jerusalem (John 11:18). It was the home of the sisters Mary and Martha and their brother Lazarus (John 11:1), and also of Simon the Leper (Matt. 26:6; Mark 14:3). The place of the Ascension (Luke 24:50-1).

Bethany was known to early Christian tradition. In the 4th century a sanctuary of Lazarus was already in existence there; its name, Lazarium, is still preserved in the name of the Arab village with which it is identified, el-Azariyeh. The church built above the cave where Jesus resurrected Lazarus from the dead was already known to Eusebius (*Onom.* 58:15) and was still extant in the 12th century.

Bethany was excavated by S.J. Saller in 1949-53. In the course of the excavations remains of four superimposed churches built to the east of Lazarus' tomb came to light. All had mosaics. The earliest is dated to the 4th or 5th century. The second is of the Byzantine period, while the remaining two are medieval. Associated with the churches are a large number of rock-cut tombs, some of which are within the precincts of the churches. Apart from these, remains of the ancient village of Bethany came to light, among them remains of houses, wine-presses, cisterns, silos and the like. The earliest pottery finds are of the Persian and Hellenistic periods, indicating an occupation of the site after the Restoration. Numerous finds date to the Roman, Byzantine and later periods.

BETHAR A fortress in Judea, 7 miles southwest of *Jerusalem and 2,150 feet above sea level, identified with Khirbet el-Yahud, 'the ruin of the Jews', where Bar-Kochba fought his last battle against the Romans in the Second Jewish Revolt. The site is not mentioned in the Bible, but in the Greek translation it is listed among the cities of Judah, and in archaeological surveys sherds of the Israelite period have in fact been found. The site is also mentioned by Eusebius (*Hist. Eccl.* 4,6). It was mainly inhabited in the Roman period and only sporadically in the Byzantine and early Arab periods.

The site has not been excavated, but remains of the fortress built by Bar-Kochba have been observed in surveys. The fortress was set on a lofty hill, surrounded on three sides by deep gorges. The fortress itself was encircled by a dry ditch, about 15 feet deep and 45 feet wide. The walls were fortified by rectangular towers and half-rounded bastions, and sections of them could be traced among the garden walls of the modern village of Batir. There were two, or possibly three, gates in the wall. Within the enclosed area remains of one building only, about 30 feet by 26 feet,

could be seen. This has been tentatively identified as an arsenal, or as the headquarters of Bar-Kochba. The fortress is nicely suited to its topographical setting but hastily planned and built. Of special interest were some iron tools found on the site, probably implements of a local mint, in which some of the coins (*Money) of the Revolt were minted.

BETH-BAAL-MEON; BAAL-MEON A town in *Moab, in the vicinity of *Medaba, in the territory of Reuben (Josh. 13:17), also named Baal-Meon (Num. 32:38) and Beth-Meon (Jer. 48:23). It was conquered in the middle of the 9th century BC by Mesha, King of *Moab, who subsequently rebuilt it (*Inscriptions). The name Baal-Meon is later mentioned in the Talmud. In the Roman period it was a large fortified village. Eusebius knew it under the name of Beelmaous, 9 miles from *Heshbon (*Onom.* 46:1). Identified with Main, 4 miles southwest of Medaba.

BETH-DAGON *a)* A town in the territory of Judah (Josh. 15:41). The name is Canaanite, probably deriving from the god Dagon, for whom there might have been a temple at this site. In Eusebius' time it was a very large village, between *Lod and *Jabneh, known by the name of Kaparadagon (*Onom.* 50:15-16).
b) A place on the eastern border of the territory of Asher (Josh. 19:27). Not identified.

BETH-EL A town on the border of the territory of Ephraim (Josh. 16:1-4), identified with Beitin at an important road junction 11 miles north of *Jerusalem. Abraham built an altar there and at Hai (*Ai) and Jacob had his dream there (Gen.28:10-22), naming the place 'House of God', which is the meaning of the Hebrew name. The place featured in Joshua's conquest of the *Canaanites in connection with the battle of *Ai and was captured by the tribe of Joseph (Judg. 1:22-6). In the period of the Judges there was a place of worship in Beth-El (Judg. 20:26; Authorized Version: 'house of God'), probably connected with an ancient tradition from the time of the Patriarchs. The prophetess Deborah sat under her palm tree nearby (Judg. 4:5) and Samuel came there each year to judge the people (1 Sam 7:16). The building of Solomon's Temple in *Jerusalem greatly reduced the importance of Beth-El, but its power was restored with the split of the United Monarchy. Jeroboam, King of Israel, built two temples, one at *Dan near the northern border of Israel and the other at Beth-El on the southern border (1 Kgs. 12:29). Beth-El was captured by Abijah, King of Judah (2 Chr. 13:19), but was probably retaken shortly afterwards by Baasha, King of Israel. It was partly destroyed in 721 BC when the kingdom of Israel fell to the Assyrians, and completely destroyed in 587 BC when Judah was laid waste by the *Babylonians, to be resettled only after the Restoration (Neh. 11:31).

Beth-El is mentioned twice in literary sources of the time of the Second Temple: it was fortified by Bacchides, military commander of Ptolemy Soter of *Egypt (1 Macc. 9:50) and destroyed by Vespasian during the First Jewish Revolt against the Romans (Josephus, *War* IV, 551).

The site was excavated in 1934, 1954, 1957 and 1960 by W.F. Albright and J.L. Kelso on behalf of the American School of Oriental Research. A few potsherds were the only remains from the oldest settlement, dating from the 21st century BC, the end of the Early Bronze Age. Traces of houses were uncovered from Middle Bronze Age I and a high place built on the hilltop also belongs to this period. The first city wall dates to the Middle Bronze Age II, the time of the Patriarchs. The Late Bronze Age layers have yielded many well-built private houses containing much local and imported pottery. The last Late Bronze Age stratum is covered by a very thick layer of ashes and charred and fallen bricks, possibly remnants of the destruction of Beth-El by the Israelites. At the beginning of the Iron Age houses were poor, but building improved in the 10th century BC, when it became a strongly fortified town. The fortifications were rebuilt several times during the 8th and 7th centuries BC before it was finally destroyed in 587 BC. The site was resettled in the Hellenistic period and conquered by the Hasmoneans, and was still inhabited in the early Roman period. After the destruction of the Second Temple its importance diminished, but a church was built there in the 4th century AD to commemorate Jacob's dream, and there are some remains of a small fortified town of the Byzantine period.

BETH-GUBRIN; ELEUTHEROPOLIS A city 25 miles southwest of *Jerusalem, in the center of *Idumea, which owed its growth and importance to the destruction of *Mareshah by the Parthians in 40 BC. Josephus (*War* IV, 447) records that it was conquered by Vespasian, who stationed troops in the area. In AD 200 Septimius Severus made it a city and gave the *ius italicum* to its inhabitants, renaming it Eleutheropolis, City of the Free. It began minting at that time, with coinage dated by its own era.

The city was very prosperous until the Arab conquest. It is marked on the Peutinger map and also appears in the itinerary of the pilgrim Antoninus (6th century AD). Its first bishop participated in the Council of Nicaea in AD 325. The city territory was large, comprising most of Idumea and extending to the *Dead Sea at *En-Gedi. In the southern part, called Daroma, several Jewish settlements survived until the late 4th century AD.

After the Arab conquest settlement of the city, known then as Jibrin, continued. Mukkadasi records that there were marble quarries there, that it was rich in goods which were sent to the capital (Ramla), but that there was a decline in population. The Crusaders conquered Beit Jibrin, and in 1134 King Fulk built a fortress, which later became the property of the Order of the Hospitalers.

Archaeological discoveries include beautiful mosaics from the Roman-Byzantine period and ornamental fragments from a synagogue.

BETH-HACCEREM A place near *Jerusalem in the territory of Judah. The name does not occur in the early books of the Bible but the Septuagint includes it in addition to the names given in Joshua (15:59). Jeremiah (6:1) mentions Beth-Haccerem as the place where fire signals were set up in time of war. After the Restoration Malachiah, son of Rechab, ruler of part of Beth-Haccerem, repaired the Dung Gate of *Jerusalem (Neh. 3:14). It has been tentatively identified

Mosaic from a wealthy Roman villa, Beth-Gubrin

with Ain Karim, but this would not fit a place from which fire signals could be seen. Another possibility is Khirbet Salih, modern *Ramat Rahel, south of *Jerusalem, where extensive excavations have been made. A site by the name of Beth Ha-Cerem is mentioned in the Copper Scroll (*Dead Sea Scrolls).

BETH-HORON A town in the territory of Ephraim, on the border of Benjamin (Josh. 16:5, 18:13-14). There were in fact two places, adjacent to each other and distinguished by the descriptions 'upper' and 'lower'. The upper town was a key point on one of the main roads leading from the *Plain to the Judean Hills. After Joshua defeated the five kings of the *Amorites he pursued them to upper Beth-Horon (Josh. 10:10; Authorized Version: 'the way that goes up to Beth-Horon'), and on the descent from there God cast down large stones from heaven on the fugitives (Josh. 10:11). Beth-Horon was given to the Levites of the family of Kohath (Josh. 21:22) and one of the companies of the *Philistines passed through it (1 Sam. 13:18).

Solomon built 'Beth-Horon the nether' (1 Kgs. 9:17) and 'Beth-Horon the upper' (2 Chr. 8:5). The place is mentioned in the list of conquests of Pharaoh Sheshonq. On the ascent of Beth-Horon Judas Maccabaeus defeated the Syrian army (1 Macc. 3:16). In the Roman period a fort was built there to guard the road. Lower Beth-Horon is identified with Beit Ur et-Tahta; upper Beth-Horon with Beit Ur el-Foqa, northwest of *Gibeon. The site is mentioned in the Copper Scroll (*Dead Sea Scrolls). Two villages by this name existed in Eusebius' time on the 12th mile from Jerusalem on the way to Lod (*Onom.* 46:21).

BETHLEHEM *a)* A city in the territory of Judah, 6 miles south of *Jerusalem, possibly mentioned in the *El Amarna letters. In the Bible it appears first in connection with Rachel's death and her burial 'in the way to Ephrath, which is Bethlehem' (Gen. 35:19). It was also the scene of the story of Ruth (Ruth 4:13, 22) in the period of the Judges, Bethlehem was the birthplace of David, and the place of his anointing by Samuel (1 Sam. 1 ff.). It thus became the symbol of David's Dynasty and the center of Messianic belief, for the Messiah would be a descendant of the house of David (Micah 5:2). Bethlehem was of strategic importance from early times. It was on the caravan route from *Jerusalem via *Hebron to *Egypt. Before the time of David the *Philistines kept a garrison there in order to protect it against attacks from the north (2 Sam. 23:14). Later it was part of the fortifications built by Rehoboam (2 Chr. 11:6) to guard *Jerusalem from the south and southeast, but by the time of Micah (second half of 8th century BC) it had already lost its strategic importance.

As the birth-place of Jesus (Luke 2:1-7) it is one of the most sacred Christian sites. According to Hieronymus, a Christian scholar of the 4th century, the cult of Adonis was practised in the time of the Romans near the cave where Jesus was born, but Origines, another Christian scholar of the same period, makes

Church of the Nativity, Bethlehem

no mention of the fact. However, St Jerome relates that from the time of Hadrian to the reign of Constantine, Jupiter and Adonis were worshipped there. In about AD 330, after the pilgrimage of his mother Queen Helena, Constantine began to erect the Church of the Nativity. The Pilgrim of Bordeaux, who visited the country in about AD 330, records that a basilica had been built there by order of Constantine. Many pilgrims describe its beautiful interior, ornamented with gold and silver, embroideries, marble, wall paintings and mosaics.

For unknown reasons, but possibly because it had been damaged, the church was demolished in the reign of Justinian (AD 527-65) and a new one was built. The floor level was raised and a stone pavement laid. In 1099 Bethlehem was conquered by the Crusaders, who restored the church in the middle of the 12th century. The main structure as it stands today can be attributed to Justinian, but apart from the columns and the continuous line of carved wooden architraves above the capitals nothing remains of the original decoration. The church is a five-aisled basilica with a spacious atrium. In the east, the Constantinian sanctuary consisted of an octagonal memorial structure above the sacred grotto. Justinian's architect changed this part by adding a transept with an apse at its southern and northern ends as well as a presbytery with an apse in the east.

b) A town in the territory of Zebulun, (Josh. 19:15), the birth-place of the judge Ibzan and the place where he was buried (Judg. 12:8-10). In the days after the destruction of the Second Temple the place was known under the name of Bethlehem Zoriah — Bethlehem of Tyre — and was the seat of the priestly order of the family of Malchiah. Identified with Beit Lahm in Lower *Galilee.

BETH-PEOR; BETFOGOR A town in the territory of Reuben, east of the *Jordan (Josh. 13:20), where the Israelites camped (Deut. 3:29). It was in the valley close to Beth-Peor that Moses revealed the laws to the children of Israel (Deut. 4:46), and that he was buried (Deut. 34:6). Eusebius knew it under the name of Betfogor, a place situated at a distance of 6 miles from Livias (*Onom.* 58:13). The site of the Roman period is identified with Khirbet esh-Sheikh Jail, in the territory of *Heshbon.

BETHPHAGE; BETH-PAGE A village on the Mount of *Olives, close to *Jerusalem (Matt. 21:1) and near *Bethany (Mark 11:1; Luke 19:29). Eusebius (*Onom.* 58:13) locates it on the Mount of Olives. Early Christian tradition identified it with et-Tur, east of *Jerusalem on a mountain overlooking the city, where the modern Church of the Resurrection was built. Beth-Page is well known also from later Jewish sources, from which it is clear that it lay very close to the city.

BETHSAIDA; BETH-RAMTHA; LIVIAS-IULIAS A town on the northeastern shore of the Sea of *Galilee. It was a small fishermen's village, known under the name of Beth-Ramtha, and formed part of the *Perea. In the early Roman period Herod Agrippa conferred on the place the rights of a *polis*, naming it Livias in honor of Livia, wife of Augustus (Josephus, *Antiq.* XVIII, 27). When Livia changed her name to Iulia the city was also sometimes called Iulias (Josephus, *War* II, 168). It was later annexed by Nero to the kingdom of Agrippa II. In the New Testament it is named Bethsaida. It was the home of Philip, Andrew and Peter (John 1:44; 12:21). Jesus healed the blind there (Mark 8:22) and it was one of the cities which he reproached (Matt. 11:21; Luke 10:13). Eusebius (*Onom.* 58:11) locates it in Galilee, near Lake Genezareth. Bethsaida is identified with et-Tell, east of the River *Jordan.

Stele of Sethos I, 14th century BC, found at Beth-Shean

BETH-SHEAN; SCYTHOPOLIS A mound in the valley of the Harod, a rivulet which flows into the *Jordan at the eastern end of the *Jezreel Valley. Although 350 feet below sea level the mound (Tell el-Husn) is imposing and is situated on highways that were important in all periods, giving access in all four directions. The ruins of the Hellenistic-Roman and Byzantine town cover a wide area to the south and southwest of the mound. Excavations were begun in 1921 under the direction of A.Rowe on behalf of the University of Pennsylvania.

In the Late Bronze Age the city was an important stronghold of the Egyptian empire, especially in the period from Sethos I to Rameses III. It seems that the latter, after defeating the invading Sea Peoples (Philistines) early in the 12th century BC, posted a garrison of mercenaries from among the vanquished armies in the city. In the biblical period it was one of the Canaanite towns that resisted the attack of the Israelites. After the defeat of the Israelites by the *Philistines the bodies of Saul and his sons were displayed on the walls of Beth-Shean (1 Sam. 31:10, 12); but David conquered the city, with *Megiddo and *Taanach, during the expansion of his kingdom northwards and with these two cities it belonged to the fifth administrative district of Solomon, under Baana, one of the twelve officers of the kingdom of Israel (1 Kgs. 4:12). In about 700 BC the site was deserted and was not reoccupied until the Hellenistic period, when it became known as Scythopolis, 'City of the Scythians', a name which most probably originated from a unit of Scythian cavalry in the army of Ptolemy II. Under the Seleucids in the 2nd century BC the city received an additional name, Nysa, to commemorate the nurse of Dionysus who, according to legend, had been born there. Having been conquered by John Hyrcanus (135-104 BC) (Josephus, *Antiq.* XIII,, 280), it was taken by Pompey in 63 BC and became the capital of the *Decapolis. (Josephus, *Antiq.* XIV, 75). During that time it enjoyed great prosperity. Later it became a Christian city and the seat of a bishop. With the Arab conquest in AD 636 the city gradually lost its importance.

EXCAVATIONS Altogether 18 levels of occupation were unearthed and virgin soil was reached at a depth of 70 feet. Of the earliest levels, which were reached in a restricted area only, levels XVIII-XVII belong to the Chalcolithic period, and remains of plano-convex brick walls (i.e. with one surface plane and the other convex) of houses were found. Levels XVI—XI are of the Early Bronze Age. Level XVI has remains of apsidal houses built of flat bricks. In levels XV-XIV were houses built of bricks standing on stone foundations. All these levels contained pottery typical of the period and a large number of flint tools. Level X dates to the Middle Bronze Age IIB and C, the period of *Hyksos domination. Levels IX-V represent the Late Bronze Age and the beginning of the Iron Age. The excavators dated these levels by the names of Egyptian rulers, but failed to attribute them correctly. W.F. Albright proposed a corrected scheme with the following dates: level IX ('Tuthmosis III'), late 14th century BC; level VIII ('pre-Amenophis'), 14th-13th century BC; level VII ('Amenophis III'), 13th century BC; level VI ('Sethos I'), 12th century BC; level V ('Rameses II or III'), 12th-10th centuries BC. To level IX belongs the sacred precinct with a shrine dedicated to Mekal, who is named as Lord of Beth-Shean on a votive stele. To level VIII, which includes the reign of Sethos I, two stelae must be attributed, although they were found in later layers, where they had been reused: the first records military operations while the second, which is in a poor state, mentions the 'Apiru' or *Habiru. Two temples of similar plan were found in levels VII and VI, the latter being the better preserved. Built of sun-dried bricks, the sanctuary was nearly 50 feet long from north to south and almost as wide at the north, but narrower at the southern end. The temple was entered through two antechambers on the south. In the sanctuary stood an altar behind which a flight of seven steps gave access to the Holy of Holies. This contained another altar and was flanked by two storerooms. Its floor was colored blue and on it was found a life-size model of a hawk, wearing the crown of Upper and Lower *Egypt. The earlier temple of level VII can be reconstructed on similar lines. It was protected by a strong gate-tower, a rectangular building of five rooms and a staircase, further strengthened by bastions at the entrance. The building adjoining it was probably the governor's residence. There were two temples in level V. The southern temple, built over the temple of Rameses III of level VI, had a different orientation. It was about 50 feet long with a large hall (26 feet wide) and row of rooms on either side. Although the entrance (from the west) remained, the eastern part, which was where the altar stood, was destroyed by later building activities. Separated by a corridor stood the northern temple, a nearly rectangular building of about 47 feet by 27 feet.

Levels IX-V were extremely rich in finds such as scarabs, clay figurines of Astarte, cult objects of pottery, house-like shrines, gold and silver jewelry, faience and glass objects and inscribed material. Of special significance are tombs with anthropoid sarcophagi, associated with the *Philistines, though hardly any typical Philistine pottery was found (*Burial). The cult objects of pottery are believed to be connected with a cult of doves and snakes. They are cylindrical in shape, widening at the bottom and open at both ends. In the apertures birds are perched, while serpents are coiled around the outer surface.

Level IV, dating from about 815-700 BC, was a poor town, with insignificant buildings. Level III is attributed to the Hellenistic and Roman period, while levels II and I represent the Byzantine and Arab periods. Of the city plan in Hellenistic and Roman times little is known. A colonnaded street can be traced, and remains were found of a Hellenistic temple dedicated to Dionysus, which was rebuilt in the Roman period. A hippodrome has been identified and the theater has been completely excavated. To the Byzantine period belong a circular cathedral (*Churches) and a monastery. In one of the private houses mosaics, dating to the 6th century AD, have been found. Inscriptions name two Jews, Kyrios Leontis and his brother Jonathan. The mosaic pavements are of great interest,

depicting the River *Nile, its river-god, a Nilotic landscape and a Nilometer, the term given to a graduated pillar or the like showing the height to which the *Nile rises. The city of *Alexandria is mentioned in an inscription. Another building, found to the north of the mound, is a 6th century AD synagogue with a mosaic pavement depicting the Torah Shrine and other ritual objects.

ROMAN THEATER The theater of Scythopolis lies about 250yd south of Tell Husn. It was excavated by S. Appelbaum (1959-61) and A. Negev (1962) under the auspices of the Israel National Parks Authority and the Israel Department of Antiquities and Museums. It is among the larger of the medium group of Roman theaters, measuring 270 feet along the line of the *scaenae frons*[1] and 190 feet from the *scaenae frons* to the outer periphery of the *cavea*. (*See* *CAESAREA; *THEATERS.) Its seating capacity is estimated at some 8,000. The *cavea*, cut into the marl slope, is surrounded on the south by an outer masonry wall pierced opposite the *vomitoria*; from it access was obtained by steps to the *summa cavea*. The *cavea* was divided into upper and lower parts by the *praecinctio*; this gave access to the nine *vomitoria*, which took the form of double vaults. In each case one of the *vomitorium* passages communicated with a vaulted elliptical chamber impinging on the *praecinctio* in the body of the *cavea*. Behind the *pulpitum* ran a subterranean vaulted tunnel (*hyposcaenium*).

The *scaenae frons* had two stories and both colonnades appear to have had Corinthian columns. The *porta regalis*, set in an apse, was fronted by a propylon supported on two pairs of granite columns, each pair standing on a flanking podium. The *hospitalia* opened into flanking halls opposite the ends of the *cavea*; clearly the theater had been planned to a larger scale and reduced in diameter during the actual building. On each flank of the stage was a circular tower containing a spiral staircase to the upper story. There was no *scaenae*. The *scaenae frons* was sumptuously encrusted with multicolored *opus sectile* (*Mosaics) and the friezes were adorned in relief with acanthus leaves containing symbolic human and animal figures. A complete but dismembered statue, probably Hermes Psychopompus (1st century BC), was found in the western hall.

The theater dates from the Severan period but had fallen into disuse by the late 3rd century AD. It was rehabilitated in the 6th century, probably under Justin I (AD 518-27). The *hyposcaenium* was then rebuilt in its present form and water introduced, presumably for the performance of water-ballet.

The theater's *scaenae frons* is of the 'western' type. Its *valva regalis* is analogous to that of Palmyra (*Tadmor), and its sculpture has affinities with work at *Gadara and *Kedesh (Naphtali), though it also shows traces of the Nabatean tradition.

Archaeological excavations were renewed in 1986, in a major attempt to reveal large sections of the Hellenistic, Roman and Byzantine cities. This is a joint venture of the Institute of Archaeology, the Hebrew University,

---

[1] Italicized terms are defined in THEATERS section.

Jerusalem, with teams working in the Roman amphitheater and the center of town, and the Department of Antiquities with teams working in the theater, the public bath and several structures south of the theater. In these periods the city expanded south and north of the ancient mound, bisected from east to west by the *Harod River, and extended over an area of about 400 acres. Remains of the Hellenistic city were found on the slope of Tell Istaba. These include remains of houses and numerous stamped wine jar handles from Rhodes and Cnidus, dating from the end of the 3rd to the beginning of the 1st century BC. Of the Roman period one of the main streets of the city was discovered, extending for a distance of about 100yd from east to west, and crossing the Harod River over a bridge. The street, 18 feet wide, was paved with basalt flagstones. Traces of colonnaded streets were found north and east of the mound, one crossing a second bridge. At a distance of 600yd south of the *theater the western half of an amphitheater was found. It is a rectangle, 180 feet wide, with the long sides rounded. The rows of seats excavated were made of white limestone quarried at Mt *Gilboa. Above these rose 7–10 rows of wooden seats. To protect the spectators from wild beasts, the entire arena was surrounded by a limestone wall built on a basalt substructure, 12 feet high. The walls of the arena were covered with plaster decorated with frescoes. Between the theater and the mound the intersection of two main streets was discovered, on which stood a large imposing structure — possibly a triumphal arch. Two marble heads, of Athena and Aphrodite, belong to this structure. At the foot of the tell stood a temple with a circular naos, perhaps dedicated to Dionisos. It was built on a podium, and ascended by a flight of wide steps. The temple had enormous columns, 31 feet high. In the temple was found the base of a statue, carrying an inscription indicating that it was erected by the city in honor of the emperor Marcus Aurelius (AD 161–189). Near the temple stood an elaborately decorated nymphaeon, and, next to it, a large basilica.

Little change in town planning occurred in the Byzantine period, though the city expanded in all directions, and was enclosed by a strong wall. It is not known exactly when this city was founded, but by the first quarter of the 6th century AD it had already been repaired under the supervision of Arsenius, a Samaritan and high-ranking official in the imperial administration. East and west of the mound were discovered sumptuous houses. One, a private building with about 25 rooms on the ground floor, and additional rooms on the upper floor, contained extremely rich and varied small finds. Two other houses, mentioned above, belonged to Jews. Other private buildings, also in use in the Arab period, were discovered between the theater and amphitheater, which was an open area in the Roman period. A huge public bath, extending over an area of 1.2 acres, was built in the Byzantine period over remains of a Roman period bath. It is lcoated north of the theater. Built in basalt stones, the state of preservation of both structure and bath-house installations is good. Many inscriptions, mostly commemorating private donors, were inbedded in the mosaic pavings of the bath-house halls.

The semi-circular odeum in the northeastern corner of the bath-house belongs to the earlier, Roman period. Over it, and dating to the Byzantine period, is a structure with a delicate multi-colored mosaic floor, in the center of which is a representation of the goddess Tyche. Two large public buildings of unknown function, were connected in this period by a 16½ feet wide street lined with houses and shops.

BETH-SHEARIM Situated on the southern slopes of the mountains of Lower *Galilee, facing the western extremity of the *Jezreel Valley, the Jewish city of Beth-Shearim extended over more than 10 acres and was surrounded by a vast, famous and hallowed necropolis where Rabbi Judah I was buried. The place is first mentioned by Josephus (*Life* 24, 188–9), under the name Besara, as the center of the domains of Queen Berenice in the *Jezreel Valley. This name is given to the city in an epigram found in the excavation, a further confirmation of the identification of the place with Beth-Shearim. During the 2nd century AD Beth-Shearim was the seat of the Sanhedrin; the Talmud recounts the deeds and sayings of the sages and rabbis who lived there and describes the beauty of the buildings.

Systematic excavations at the necropolis of Beth-Shearim, and in the town itself, began in 1936 and extended over ten seasons, until 1959, directed by B. Mazar (1936–40 and 1956–9) and N. Avigad (1953–5). These excavations, especially in the necropolis, brought to light a wealth of architectural elements, inscriptions and — an as yet unparalleled phenomenon in Jewish sepulchers — tombs and sarcophagi decorated with human and animal figures. A short season of excavations was held in 1986, after a bulldozer hit the foot of yet another burial cave.

The importance of the inscriptions of Beth-Shearim for the study of the history and culture of the Jews in Palestine at that period is self-evident. They are found in great number on coffins, walls, ceilings and doors and are written in Greek, Hebrew, Aramaic and Tadmorian. Beth-Shearim served as the central necropolis for Jews from Palestine and from neighboring countries, the obvious reason being that it was the city where the venerated Rabbi Judah I had lived and where he was interred. Pious Jewis wished to be laid to rest close to the tomb of the great sage. When Gallus Caesar destroyed the city in AD 352 burials diminished, eventually ceasing altogether in the Byzantine era.

THE EXCAVATIONS IN THE CITY AREA In the northeastern section five building periods can be discerned. The first extends from the end of the 1st century BC to the middle of the 2nd century AD. The second period, extending from the end of the 2nd century to the beginning of the 3rd century AD, is remarkable for the high standard of its architecture, as seen in a large public building whose basement and ground floor were uncovered. This represents the period when the city was flourishing and when the construction of its great catacombs began. During the third period, from the second quarter of the 3rd century to the middle of the 4th century AD, a synagogue was built. This comprises a three-nave basilica preceded by an open court, the facade of which faced *Jerusalem and was composed of three monumental gates. At the end of the central nave is an elevated platform. At a later stage the walls of this synagogue were covered with colored plaster and marble slabs, the decoration of which included inscriptions in Greek and in Hebrew. This city was destroyed by a fire which apparently occurred in the middle of the 4th century AD, as indicated by hoard of 1,200 coins found there. This corresponds to the time when the legions of Gallus Caesar destroyed many Jewish communities in Palestine. The fourth period (from the middle of the 4th century AD to the end of the Byzantine era) and the fifth (from the early Arab and Mameluk periods) are very poorly represented and of no great interest.

THE EXCAVATIONS AT THE NECROPOLIS In the huge necropolis of the 2nd, 3rd and 4th centuries AD many catacombs were found hewn in the rock. Some of them were apparently private while others, where the density is greater, were evidently public. In one instance (catacomb 1) 400 burials were counted. The catacombs consists of corridors and courts. Built-in gates with stone doors moving on hinges give access from these courts to the burial halls, some arranged on several levels and some leading into others. Branching off from these halls are the chambers containing the actual graves. These were of different types, but were mainly *arcosolia* or *loculi* (*Burials). There were also pits sunk in the ground.

In all these graves coffins made of wood, lead, stone or clay were placed. The custom of secondary burials in small ossuaries was also practised at Beth-Shearim. The catacombs were mostly uniform in style but some are unusual in shape or decoration. Among these are catacombs 1–4, which are carved with a great variety of reliefs, drawings and engravings of typical Jewish symbols such as the seven-branched menorah and other ritual objects; and catacombs 14 and 20 with their ample courts whose façades were composed of three gates decorated with arches. Catacomb 20 is the largest and most important in Beth-Shearim, with more than 130 limestone coffins and an as yet unknown number of marble sacrophagi. Although these served as graves for Jews they have many pagan images among the Jewish symbols. Above ground, mausolea and courtyards were constructed for memorial ceremonies.

Catacomb No. 20, Beth-Shearim

BETH-SHEMESH A town on the border of the territory of Judah, in the northeastern part of the *Plain (Josh. 15:10). As Ir-Shemesh it is included among the cities of *Dan (Josh. 19–41), and it is listed elsewhere as one of the cities of Judah that was given to the Levites (Josh. 21:16). It is also identified with Mount Heres, which was not conquered by the *Danites and remained in the hands of the *Amorites (Judg. 1:34–5). It seems that later, in the time of the Judges, it was already in Israelite hands, as the ark was transferred there from the land of the *Philistines (1 Sam. 6:12–21). It was in the second district of Solomon (1 Kgs. 4:9). Amaziah fought Jehoash there (2 Kgs. 14:11), and according to 2 Chronicles (28:18) the *Philistines conquered it in the time of Ahaz, King of Judah. The site is not referred to again until the Roman and Byzantine periods, when it was a small town. Eusebius (*Onom.* 54:11–13) mentions Bethsames, 10 miles from Eleutheropolis (*Beth-Gubrin) on the way to Nicopolis (*Emmaus).

The site of Beth-Shemesh is identified with Tell er-Rumeileh, near the ruins of the Arab village of Ain Shams, which has preserved the ancient name. It was excavated in 1911–2 by D. Mackenzie on behalf of the Palestine Exploration Fund, and in 1928–33 by E. Grant on behalf of Haverford College. Six levels of occupation, the combined results of both expeditions, were discovered. The earliest stratum, VI, of which very little remains, is of the Early Bronze Age IV (about 2200 BC). Stratum V is of Middle Bronze Age II, the *Hyksos period. The town was surrounded by a wall enclosing an area of 8 acres. The wall consisted of a series of salients and recesses, with rectangular towers (*Fortifications). The lower part was built of large boulders, above which was a brick superstructure. On the south a large gate of the direct-approach type, flanked by two massive towers with small rooms in them, was found. One of the houses, which backs on to the city wall, is of the courtyard type (*Houses).

In the second half of the 16th century BC the town was completely destroyed, probably during the campaign of the Egyptians against the *Hyksos. It was rebuilt in the Late Bronze Age (stratum IV). The houses of this town were well built, the better ones being of ashlar, and contained numerous storage bins (*Stores). Two potter's kilns show that pottery was produced locally. Aegean, Cypriot and Egyptian articles indicate the town's wide commercial connections. Some short inscriptions in Ugaritic cuneiform and Hebrew-Phoenician were also found. The identity of the destroyers of this city is not certain.

Stratum III is dated to Iron Age I. Most of the pottery at this level is Philistine, and it is here that this type of pottery was first fully studied by Mackenzie. Metal was also smelted here. The old city wall had been repaired. The houses were of the courtyard type. The city was probably destroyed in the time of Saul and its rebuilding is attributed to David.

The city of stratum II is of the period of the kingdom of Judah (10th–8th centuries BC). The city wall is of the casemate type (*Fortifications). Houses were built against the wall, their entrances facing the street which ran parallel to it; some were of the four-room

*A jewelry hoard from the early Israelite period —
Beth-Shemesh*

type (*Houses). The prosperity of this city derived from the agricultural hinterland. Numerous olive-and wine-presses and a large storage bin provide evidence of its prosperity (cf. 1 Kgs. 4:9). Important among the single finds are *lamelek* *seals and the seal of 'Elyakim servant of Yochan', which is similar to that found at Tell *Beit Mirsim. The destruction of this city is attributed to the Babylonians in 586 BC.

There were scanty traces of the Persian and Hellenistic periods. A small settlement appeared in the 4th century AD, and in the following century a monastery was built there.

BETH-YERAH; KHIRBET EL-KERAK One of the largest ancient mounds in Palestine, about 50 acres in area, situated at the southwestern end of the Sea of *Galilee, between the ancient and new courses of the River *Jordan. Khirbet el-Kerak had already been identified with talmudic Beth-Yaah in the 19th century. It is also identified with Philoteria, a city built by Ptolemy II. Others add an identification with Sennabris, mentioned by Josephus as forming the northern limit of the *Jordan Valley where Vespasian camped, 30 stadia from *Tiberias (*War* III, 447; V, 455). Between 1944 and 1955 the site was extensively excavated by various Israeli scholars, and in 1952-3 and 1963-4 by P.Delougaz on behalf of the Oriental Institute of the University of Chicago.

Phase I is of the Early Bronze Age. The settlers lived in pits roofed with twigs. In phase II there were already rectangular houses built of mud bricks. The pottery of this phase is of the red-burnished band slip type (*Pottery). In the settlement of phase III the mud-brick walls were built over a low base of basalt stones. A city wall built of bricks is attributed to this settlement. The settlement of phase IV was of long duration. Most of the houses were built of basalt and one measured 20 feet by 25 feet. The typical Khirbet el-Kerak type of pottery, first identified on this site, belongs to this phase. It is dated to the Early Bonze Age III.

In a section cut in a different part of the mound twenty-three occupation levels were discovered. The first four were of the Early Bronze Age I, to which an apsidal house belongs. Five levels were of Early Bronze Age II, six of Early Bronze Age III and three of Middle Bronze Age I, in which were found a paved street, a potter's workshop and other remains. Middle Bronze Age II was represented by a tomb. The uppermost level was of the Persian period.

On the east and north of the mound the town was protected by the lake, so that walls were built on the west and south. The earliest wall was of the early phases of the Early Bronze Age. It consisted of three connected parallel walls, forming a massive wall 25 feet thick. The gate was on the south and was built of basalt. Remains of other walls are dated to the later phases of the same period and to the Middle Bronze Age. (*See also* *FORTIFICATIONS.)

To Early Bronze Age III belong remains of a large building (90 feet by 120 feet) at the northern end of the site. Of this building only the basalt foundations of the walls remain, in the form of a pavement 30 feet wide. In this pavement ten large circles, sunk 4in below the pavement itself, were found. Each circle is intersected by two partition walls to form four compartments. Inside the court of the house were ovens in which Khirbet el-Kerak ware was found. The building is identified as a public granary (*Stores), but this is not certain.

After being abandoned for a long time the city was inhabited again in the Hellenistic period. To this time belongs a wall a mile long, built on a huge substructure of basalt 15-20 feet wide and 11 feet high. Little remains of the brick superstructure. The wall was strengthened by alternating rectangular and rounded towers. On the southern part of the mound a section of the Hellenistic town was discovered. It included a street along which houses were built, one of which had a paved court around which were eleven rooms. Some of the houses facing the lake have survived to the height of the window-sills.

North of the granary a Roman fort was discovered. It is 180 feet square with rectangular towers at the corners. The gate is on the south and is flanked by two towers. Within the courtyard of the fort a synagogue 65 feet by 110 feet was found. It was basilical, with an apse on its southern wall facing *Jerusalem. The nave was decorated with mosaics depicting plants, birds and lions. A menorah, a *lulab*, an *ethrog* and an incense shovel were engraved on a column base.

In this part of the mound a bath of the Roman period was found. The *frigidarium*[1] was faced with marble and in the center was a small pool with a covered roof. The ceiling of the room was faced with multicolored and gilded mosaics. The *hypocaust* was L-shaped. Above the arms of the hypocaust were the *caldarium* and *tepidarium*. The water was brought to the bath by means of an aqueduct.

[1] Italicized terms are defined in BATHS AND BATHING section.

Clay vessel, Early Bronze Age, Beth-Yerah

On the same northern part of the mound, a basilical church was discovered, 35 feet by 37 feet, with three apses and decorated with mosaics in geometric patterns. The church had been rebuilt several times. First built in the 5th century AD, its last phase is of 528-9. It was destroyed early in the 7th century and Arab houses were built on top of the ruins.

BETH-ZUR; BETHSURA A town in the mountains of *Hebron, in the territory of Judah (Josh. 15:58), later inhabited by the sons of Caleb (1 Chr. 2:45) and fortified by Rehoboam (2 Chr. 11:7). At the time of the Restoration it was an administrative center (Neh. 3:16). In the Hellenistic period it was also known by the Greek form of the name, Betsoura. Lysias was defeated there by Judas Maccabaeus. It was then fortified by Bacchides and was finally recaptured by Simon Maccabaeus, who strengthened it in 140 BC to form one of the important fortresses on the borders of Judea and *Idumea (1 Macc. 4:29, 61; 6:7, 26, 31, 49 ff.; 9:52; 10:14; 11:65; 14:7, 33). The fortress of Beth-Zur was still standing throughout the Roman period. Eusebius (*Onom.* 52:2) refers to it as a village by the name of Bethsoro, on the 20th milestone on the way from Jerusalem to *Hebron, which contained the spring in which Philip baptized Kandake's eunuch. The site is identified with Khirbet et-Tubeiqeh, about 15 miles southwest of *Jerusalem.

Trial excavations were carried out at Beth-Zur in 1931, and more extensively in 1957, by O.R. Sellers on behalf of the Presbyterian Theological Seminary. These revealed that it was first settled at the end of the 3rd millennium BC and fortified for the first time by the *Hyksos in the 18th-17th centuries BC. The early Israelite settlement followed. The numerous coins found there have helped to clarify the later history of the site. Notable is a coin of the Yahud type, one of the very few known examples. It bears the inscription "the governor Hezekiah" Beth-Zur flourished in the Hellenistic period. In the 3rd century BC a citadel was erected on the site. Under Antiochus Epiphanes (175-165 BC), Beth-Zur is described as a peaceful, prosperous town. Its houses included numerous bathing facilities and an inn, a butcher's shop, a tavern and other shops were discovered in the market place. After his victory in 165 BC Judas Maccabaeus reconstructed the old Middle Bronze Age wall and the citadel. In the years 163-161 BC it was again held by the Seleucids; the strengthening of the citadel is ascribed to Bacchides. It was recaptured by Simon, and under John Hyrcanus became once again a peaceful town, houses being built outside the city wall. By 100 BC Beth-Zur was deserted.

BEZEK The city of Adoni-Zedek, where the tribes of Judah and Simeon fought the Canaanites and the Perizzites (Judg. 1:4-7). According to the biblical account Bezek is north of Jerusalem and is possibly identical with the Bezek of 1 Samuel (11:8) where Saul conducted a census of the children of Israel. Eusebius (*Onom.* 54:6) mentions two neighboring villages called Bezek, one 17 miles from *Shechem on the way to *Beth-Shean. Identified with Khirbet Ibzik, northeast of *Tirzah.

BIR ES-SAFADI A site of the Chalcolithic period, about a mile southeast of *Beer-Sheba and the same distance from Tell *Abu Matar. The site was excavated in 1954-9 by J. Perrot on behalf of the French Archaeological Mission. The peculiar feature of this Chalcolithic settlement is the type of dwelling found there. While some of the houses, of crude mud brick, were built on the ground in the normal fashion, others were hollowed out below ground and consisted of irregularly shaped rooms connected by tunnels. One such house had six rooms and a total length of about 100 feet. Access to it was by two pits. Another type of underground house had a large circular courtyard 25 feet in diameter and 7 feet deep. Silos (*Stores) and numerous basins were excavated in the floor of the courtyard, which was open to the sky and had a tunnel leading from it to the subterranean rooms. Small bowls which served as lamps were used to light the rooms, some of which had fireplaces.

The utensils and weapons found on the site were of stone, bone, clay and copper. There were also most elaborate bone and ivory figurines of men, women and animals. The presence of ivory on the site indicated trade relations with Africa or Asia, because there were no elephants in Palestine at that time. The burials were either single or collective. Infants were buried in the floors of the houses.

Three strata indicating different phases of occupation were observed. To the latest belong oblong subterranean dwellings. To the preceding phase are attributed round or oval houses built of mud brick on stone foundations. To the earliest phase belong rectangular houses. These changes occurred over a very short period of time.

The settlement of Bir es-Safadi belongs to a culture which developed in the northern *Negev and which, because of its very close affinities with the cultures of the other contemporary sites in the northern *Negev, is termed the '*Beer-Sheba culture'. It is also closely related to the culture of the later phases of *Tuleilat Ghassul and has some affinities with pre-Dynastic and proto-Dynastic *Egypt. The local economy was based mainly on the cultivation of wheat, barley and lentils, on herding, on copper smelting and on trade with neighboring countries.

'Pinocchio',
ivory relief
from Bir es-Safadi,
Chalcolithic period

BOZRAH; BOSTRA *a)* An important city in northern
*Edom (Gen. 36:33; Amos 1:12), a symbol for the
whole country of *Edom (Isa. 34:6; 63:1, etc.); identified with Buseira, 30 miles south of the *Dead Sea.
b) A town in *Moab (Jer. 48:24), probably the same as
Bezer.

c) A city in the *Bashan, identified with Busra Eski-
Sham, about 73 miles south of *Damascus, its name
coming from the western Semitic *bosra*, meaning fortress. It was important from early times, being mentioned in the list of cities conquered by Tuthmosis III
and probably in the *El Amarna letters. In Greek and
Latin the city appears as Bostra; in 1 Maccabees (5:26)
the form Bosora is found. An Arab fortress in Hellenistic times, Bozrah was conquered by the *Nabateans and became almost as important as *Petra.
After the annexation of the Nabatean kingdom in AD
105-6, Trajan made it the capital of the newly created
province of *Arabia. He refounded the city, its era
beginning with the province, and it is described on
coins as the *'Nea Traiana Bostra'*. Some time afterwards the *Legio III Cyrenaica* was transferred to Bostra from *Egypt. Philip the Arabian gave it the title
'metropolis'.

The Romans used and enlarged the ancient high-
ways from the *Nile Delta to Bostra via the *Red Sea,
*Petra and *Philadelphia, and *Caesarea Maritime to
Bostra via Scythopolis (*Beth-Shean) and Adraa
(*Edrei) continuing on into northern Syria and
*Mesopotamia. Thus, in the 2nd and 3rd centuries AD
Bostra was a flourishing caravan city as well as a
cultural center. After the enlargement and division of
the *Provincia Arabia* in the times of Diocletian-
Constantine, Bostra remained the capital of the
northern part. In AD 632 it was conquered by the
Arabs and became an important city of Islam, as the
pilgrim route to Mecca passed through it for many
centuries.

The archeological remains are impressive. The eastern part of the site contains the old Nabatean acropolis and the remains of *Nabatean *temples. In the
center of the southern part of this quarter stood a
triumphal arch adorned with typical Nabatean capitals. South and east of this quarter rain water was
stored in two large public reservoirs. New Bostra,
built after the annexation of the Nabatean kindgom in
AD 106, was surrounded by a wall. Two colonnaded
streets connected the new and old towns, the *decumanus* ran from the new West Gate to the Nabatean arch
on the east. At the junction with the southern colonnaded street stood another triumphal arch. A short
colonnaded street led from this arch to the *theater. A
*hippodrome, with a capacity of 30,000 spectators
was built outside the city walls. Within the city wall
were a large market building and two public *baths. It
is noteworthy that the cathedral and other churches of
Bostra were all built within the limits of the eastern
Nabatean town.

BREAD AND BAKING The cultivation of corn in the
ancient Near East dates back to Neolithic times. In the
biblical period bread made of barley or wheat was a
staple food. Wheaten bread was used in religious
ceremonials (Exod. 29:2) and at the king's court (1

Kgs. 4:22). Although this is not clearly borne out by the text, it seems that only the really poor ate barley bread (cf. Ezek. 4:12). Both barley (John 6:9, 13) and wheat were used in the preparation of bread in the Roman period. On eating bread a special benediction was said (Matt. 14:19, etc., and Jewish daily prayers). Bread was taken on long journeys (Mark 6:8; Luke 9:3) and was eaten at the Last Supper (Matt. 26:26, etc.).

The method of preparing and baking bread did not change much through the ages. The flour was mixed with water to make dough, which could be baked immediately after kneading to produce unleavened bread, or left for some time to rise with the addition of yeast. Both in pre-biblical and in biblical times loaves were baked by placing them on flat stones previously heated in an open fire, or in ovens made of clay. The ovens took the form of a truncated cone, with an opening at the bottom for stoking the fire. The prepared dough was stuck to the insides of the heated

*Clay figurine of
a woman kneading dough,
from the Phoenician cemetery
at Achzib,
Iron Age*

walls. Baking by either method would result in very flat loaves, not more than an inch thick, which are frequently referred to in the Bible as cakes. Yet another method was the use of a flat bowl heated on an open fire. The flat loaves were placed on the upper (convex) side, which had small projections and cavities to facilitate their removal when ready.

In the Hellenistic and Roman periods, as in more ancient times, bread was generally prepared by each housewife in the courtyard of her house, as is still is in the East today. In the cities a new type of baking oven came into being in this period. The baking space was now separated from the heating device, which allowed the baking of thicker loaves more closely resembling those of the present day. In the Byzantine period some of the churches were provided with bakeries in which the bread used in the Mass was baked. These loaves, or rather cakes, were marked with a special seal made of clay or wood. A bakery of this type was discovered near the Byzantine church of Dominus Flevit on the Mount of *Olives, and a seal used for the marking was found at *Oboda.

BUILDING MATERIALS The earliest human dwellings were made of simple materials (i.e. reeds and branches), stone and mud. A hole in the ground, or in the rock, would be surrounded by a low wall of rubble or mud, above which reeds or branches would be placed to make the roof. This primitive type of home preceded cave dwellings.

woop Before the last forests were destroyed by the Turks in the 19th century AD Palestine was quite a heavily forested country (cf. Josh. 17:15; 2 Kgs. 19:23, etc.) The ordinary people used the cheap local sycamore (1 Kgs. 10:27; Isa. 9:10), while palaces and the houses of the rich were built of timber brought from the *Lebanon and Syria, areas rich in cedar and fir trees (1 Kgs. 5:8), or almug trees (a type of sandalwood, correctly called 'algum') brought from *Ophir

Making bricks and building, wall-painting in an Egyptian tomb

(1 Kgs. 10:11). Timber was in fact relatively little used in Palestine and even in the Byzantine period, when transport became much cheaper, other materials would be used for construction, timber being used only in public buildings, synagogues and churches, for roofs and doors. An analysis of wood found in ancient buildings in the drier regions of Palestine, where there was hardly any timber suitable for building, has shown that apart from a little of the local palm imported cedar, pine and fir trees were mostly used.

STONE As a great part of Palestine consists of rocky hills, stone was the most common building material. In *Galilee basalt predominated, while on the coastal plain sandstone *(kurkar)* was much in use. Even a city as great and as important as *Caesarea was built almost exclusively of this not very beautiful stone. In the hilly regions a harder limestone was available, of a quality which permitted the rough-hewn blocks to be polished and smoothed. Until the time of Solomon little ashlar was used; walls and houses, even temples and palaces, were built of rubble or roughly dressed stones.

The introduction of iron tools made stone-dressing easier. A good example of a wall built of dressed stones was found in Israelite *Samaria. The stones were smoothed on three or four sides, leaving nicely polished margins and a projecting boss. At Israelite *Megiddo a different system was employed. Ashlar pillars were incorporated at regular intervals in a rubble wall to give strength to the structure. The use of ashlar became more common from the Hellenistic period onwards.

In the Hellenistic period comparatively small stones were used for building, while in the early Roman period, especially in Herod's time, large blocks of up to 30 feet in length were employed. The stone were highly polished along the edges, leaving either a very shallow boss or a projecting boss in the center. Nabatean stone-dressing is distinctive. The stones were still polished round the edges, but the low boss was decorated with a fine oblique combing, crossing in one stroke from edge to edge.

In the Byzantine period some changes were introduced. The outer walls of the buildings were mostly of hammer-dressed stones and rarely of ashlar, while the inner faces of the walls were built of rubble, filled in with chips and later coated with several layers of plaster. With the invention of the arch in the early Roman period stone was also used in roofing. From this time, also, granite and porphyry were imported from *Egypt for columns and for facing floors and walls. It seems that marble was not imported into Palestine for building purposes until the 2nd century AD.

BRICK This was the most common and the cheapest building material in the valleys and plains, which occupy quite a large part of the country. In the earliest periods mud was formed into irregularly shaped chunks, dried in the sun and used as a primitive form of brick. In the Chalcolithic period bricks were made that were more uniform in size and shape, which permitted building in even courses.

Bricks were produced by a simple method. A hole was dug in the ground and filled with water. The mud thus produced was then mixed with straw (cf. Exod. 5:7-13) and trodden until it became a thick pliable substance. At first this was shaped with the hands into bricks but later a wooden mould was used, which gave greater uniformity. The newly made bricks were then laid out to dry in the sun (*Houses). This quite primitive method was in use until the Roman period. The enormous building activity that began at that time necessitated a speedier method and the production of a much more durable brick suitable for the construction of bridges, aqueducts (*Water supply), large vaults and the like. It was then that the fired brick was invented, though it is possible that these were also known in the Iron Age. The Roman brick was considerably thinner than earlier ones and was square, rectangular, round or polygonal. Roof tiles were

produced in the same manner, which made roofing cheaper. A factory for the production of roof tiles and bricks has been discovered near Jerusalem. Its operations were conducted by the Legio X Fretensis and its products were stamped with the seal of the legion.

MORTAR A mixture of lime, sand, ashes and water was known in the Israelite period and was used for plastering cisterns and reservoirs to make them water-resistant. In the Roman period the quality of the mortar was greatly improved and it was used as a binding material in the construction of bridges, aqueducts, substructures of theaters, stadia, hippodromes, vaults, domes and so on. Plaster was also made more durable and indeed reservoirs built and plastered in the Roman period still hold water today.

BURIAL It seems that belief in an after-life is almost as old as man. For this there is ample evidence in the careful attention paid, from very early times, to the burial of a dead person, to the position in which he was placed in the grave, to the offerings with which he was supplied and to the marking of the site of the tomb.

PREHISTORY The earliest burials found in Palestine are of the Middle Paleolithic period. The men of the Mousterian culture buried their dead in pits, sometimes covering the body with a few stones. Burials of this period were discovered in the es-*Skhul Cave on Mount *Carmel. The body was placed in a contracted

Roman sarcophagus depicting the war of the Amazons, found near Caesarea

position, with the knees drawn up and the hands near the breast. Sometimes funerary objects were placed near the body. The same grave might be used over and over again.

Hundreds of burials of the Natufian Mesolithic culture have been found. The interments of this period fall into two types: in one the whole body was placed in the grave in a contracted position, lying on its side, while in the other the skull alone was interred. Burials were either single or collective. Women, and sometimes men as well, wore pendants, necklaces and anklets of shell, bone and stones. The skeletons were sometimes painted with red pigment. The best-known cemeteries of the Natufian culture are those of el-Wad Cave, *Irq el-Ahmar, Nahal Oren and *Eynan. In the latter a pit 16 feet across was excavated; its walls were plastered and surrounded on the surface by a stone circle 21 feet in diameter. At the bottom of the pit were the bones, covered with flat stones. On top of the grave three large stones and some smaller ones formed the earliest known funerary monument.

New burial customs emerged in the Neolithic period. Beneath the floors of several houses in *Jericho a large number of skulls were discovered. During the same period megalithic monuments were also erected. To this class belongs the dolmen, the name given to several stones arranged in the form of a table. The tomb itself would be covered with a small mound of earth or small stones. The megalithic monuments of Palestine are generally confined to the semi-arid zones of the region, and numerous monuments of this class were discovered in the upper *Jordan and in the *Negev. In the tombs associated with them single or double burials have been found. The dating of these monuments is not at all certain, but it is known that they continued into the 4th millennium BC. (*See* also *PREHISTORY*.)

CHALCOLITHIC PERIOD During the 4th millennium BC, in the Chalcolithic period, entirely new burial customs emerged. On numerous sites in the coastal plain, such as *Azor, *Bene-Berak and Hedera, clay ossuaries have been found. These objects, which do not generally exceed 2 feet in length, contained detached human bones. The ossuaries were stored in artificial caves, dug into the soft sandstone. Most of them were made in the form of houses with gabled roofs, which are believed to represent the actual dwellings of the deceased whose bones they contained. Each was provided with an opening large enough to insert a skull and the doors which closed these openings were sometimes decorated with representations of human faces painted or in relief. Other ossuaries were shaped like animals. Sometimes offerings in the form of miniature ossuaries were placed inside the larger ones. Along with burials in ossuaries, cist (pit) graves are also common. A cemetery with graves of this type was discovered at *Tuleilat Ghassul, where burials in jars under the floors of the houses are also common.

EARLY BONZE AGE Funerary rites and cults developed still further in the Early Bronze Age. Graves were sometimes made more carefully than houses. The burials were either single or collective. Common in this period were shaft graves, with a deep shaft leading

Coffin-lid shaped like a man, Philistine, Beth-Shean

into a square or oval burial chamber. Each tomb was provided with a large number of pottery vessels, many of which were jugs of the 'teapot' type, as well as plates, bowls and cups (*Pottery). In some of the vessels remains of food were found.

A unique cemetery dating from this period was discovered at *Bab edh-Dhra, in which there were no less than 20,000 tombs. Here too a large number of well-supplied shaft graves were found. Some of the burial chambers were stone-lined and also had stone roofs. In some cases openings in one shaft led to a number of burial chambers. The bones were sometimes placed in a heap in the center of the chamber while the pots were arranged round the walls. The unique feature was the charnel house found there, a mud-brick building 35 feet by 17 feet, with a small antechamber. The threshold was paved with skulls. Inside were mixed layers of bones and pottery.

The latest form of interment observed on this site involved cairn burials. These consisted of a shallow pit in which a single skeleton was placed, together with pots and in one case with a dagger. The pit was then filled with stones, which also formed a heap above the ground.

THE MIDDLE BRONZE AGE Various different types of burial were now practised. In some places the dead were buried within the limits of the town, sometimes close to the houses. The tombs were built of stone and were reopened whenever a new burial took place. Tombs of this type have been found at *Megiddo. On other sites,

Clay sarcophagus from Azor, Chalcolithic period

such as *Lachish and *Jericho, collective burial was practised. Tombs of this type consisted of a vertical shaft excavated into the rock, opening at the base into the burial chamber. The number of individuals interred in such a tomb did not generally exceed 40, each being supplied with offerings and food. The body was placed on its back, sometimes with the knees raised. With each new burial the earlier corpses were moved to one side, so that in the end skeletons and offerings formed a pile at the side of the tomb. The body was generally placed on a mat and in one instance a wooden bed was found. Some wore toggle pins but jewelry was quite rare. On the other hand each adult had toilet equipment, which consisted of a oil juglet, combs and a basket with boxes decorated with bone carvings, and so on.

To the early phase of the Middle Bronze Age belong numerous tumuli, scattered over the hills of the central *Negev. The only one so far excavated are those of *Har Yeruham. A stone cist measuring 3 feet by 5 feet by $2^1/_2$ feet was built on the ground. The body was laid in the cist on a bed of flat stones and a jar and several grinding stones were placed nearby for the deceased's

use in the after-life. The tumulus, consisting of stones and earth, was raised over the grave to a height of about 10-15 feet, with approximately the same diameter.

In the latter part of the Middle Bronze Age, when Palestine was ruled by the *Hyksos, a new type of burial is observed. At Tell el-*Ajjul and *Jericho dead warriors were interred together with their mounts. A large number of pottery vessels and weapons were also placed in the tombs.

LATE BRONZE AGE The usual tomb consisted of a shaft, sometimes sloping towards the grave, which led to a rounded, square or irregularly shaped burial chamber. The chamber was continuously used and over 200 pottery vessels were found in one such tomb.

IRON AGE There was some development in this period, although the burial caves and chambers of earlier times were reused on many sites. The simplest innovation was a tomb consisting of a narrow oval pit with a ledge to carry the stone cover. Another new form had a shaft of the same length as the actual grave, which formed a recess in the wall of the shaft. After the interment the grave was blocked with stones.

But these were developments of existing types. An entirely new form of burial was the multiple-chamber tomb. This had an open court from which steps led into an underground antechamber, along the walls of which was a high ledge. From this ledge openings led to additional chambers with benches along the walls on which the dead were placed. In this period, too, offerings were common and many tombs had repositories at the back of the chambers in which the offerings were placed. Some tombs have *loculi* (cavities) hollowed out of the walls instead of benches. It is this type which becomes most common in the period of the Second Temple.

PHILISTINE BURIALS These form a class of their own. Philistine cemeteries have been discovered at *Beth-Shean, Tell el-*Farah (south) and *Lachish. The tombs were approached by a stepped corridor in its center. In one case there was an additional chamber leading off the rear wall of the main chamber. Each of these tombs contained at least one burial and an extremely large number of jars, jugs, juglets, bowls and lamps. The deceased was placed in a clay anthropoid coffin, about the size of an adult. Part of the top of the coffin was removable, so that the body could be inserted through the opening. On the lid is a human face in high relief, with realistic or primitively schematic features. It is in this second class that headdresses similar to those worn by the Sea Peoples (as portrayed on the relief at Medinet Habu) were found. Clay coffins of this type were also found in *Egypt, where they are considered to be imitations of coffins in vogue during the rule of the 18th Dynasty. In Palestine these burials are dated to the 13th century BC.

PERSIAN, HELLENISTIC AND ROMAN PERIODS To the Persian period belong tombs found at Tell el-*Farah (south) and at Athlit. The tomb of this period at Tell el-Farah is a rectangular chamber with a wide door, found blocked with large bricks. In the tombs the bronze fittings of a bed, a stool and a silver bowl and ladle were found. At Athlit cremation burials attributed to the *Phoenicians were discovered. A shallow pit was hollowed out in which the body was placed on a pyre. Some pots placed with the body had been warped by the fire. These cremation burials are dated to the 6th century BC. Both types of tomb are most unusual. Otherwise the well-known Iron Age types of burial were most commonly used.

In the Hellenistic period hollowed-out tombs attained a high degree of perfection. The best that have survived are those of Marissa (*Mareshah), in some of which unique wall paintings have been preserved. The most elaborate in this group is Tomb I, hollowed out like the rest in the soft local limestone. A stepped *dromos* led into a square chamber from which a short corridor led to an antechamber. This gave access to two halls, one on each side, in the walls of which gabled *loculi* were hollowed out. To prevent water seepage these were above a high ledge which ran along the walls. An opening in the same antechamber gave access to the main hall, with additional *loculi* in its walls. At the end of this hall were three small chambers, with burials in sarcophagi. There were forty-four burial places in this catacomb. The walls of the main hall were decorated with an animal frieze depicting hunting scenes featuring naturalistic and imaginary animals, birds and fishes.

Burial caves of the Roman period, similar to those of Mareshah, have been found elsewhere in Palestine. They range from small and simple family tombs to large catacombs with scores of *loculi*. The tombs of the Roman period usually have an open forecourt from which a corridor leads into a chamber, or series of chambers, in the walls of which were *loculi*. The more elaborate ones, such as the tomb of Helena, Queen of Adiabene, and those popularly known as 'Tombs of the Kings', the 'Tombs of the Judges', and so on, had porticoes resting on two or four columns with a frieze and a gable decorated with foliate motifs. Some tombs, such as that of the family of King Herod or the recently discovered 'Jason's Tomb' in *Jerusalem, had a mortuary monument *(nephesh)* in the form of a large pyramid above or near the cave. Normally the outer door would be blocked by a heavy slab of stone, but the more elaborate ones had a large rolling stone *(golal)* which moved in a narrow slot and could be opened mechanically.

Because of the great cost of hewing a burial cave in the hard Judean rock, a new method of interment now developed. In most of the burial caves, in addition to the normal *loculi, arcosolia* (benches with an arched roof) were dug in the walls. The body would first be placed on these; then after some time, when new burial space was needed, the bones would be collected into an ossuary made of wood, clay, metal or stone (mostly the latter). The ossuaries did not exceed 2 feet in length and had flat, arched or gabled covers. Some were plain but most were decorated. The most common motif was the compass-made rosette, from which evolved rich floral designs. Architectural decoration and geometric patterns were also common. Many ossuaries are inscribed with the names of the deceased. This form of interment, known as 'second burial', was in vogue during the last centuries BC and the first two centuries AD. Alongside these ossuaries full-sized coffins (sarcophagi) made of various materials were also common.

Limestone coffin from catacomb No. 20 at Beth-Shearim

'Absalom's Tomb', Early Roman period, Jerusalem

In a class of their own are the funerary monuments in the *Kidron Valley. The earliest of this group, the 'Tomb of — yahu who is over the house' and the 'Tomb of Pharaoh's daughter', date from the time of the First Temple. The first of these is a simple rock-cut chamber with a dedicatory inscription engraved on the lintel in the ancient Hebrew script. The other is a free-standing monument hewn out of the living rock and consists of a cube crowned with an Egyptian cornice surmounted in its turn by a pyramid. Both elements are common in Egyptian mortuary chapels. The most elaborate monuments of this group, however, date from the time of the Second Temple. The earliest one, of the late 2nd century BC, is the Tomb of Bene Hezir, members of a priestly family. It consists

Stone door of a catacomb, Beth-Shearim

of a complex of underground chambers and has a façade with a Doric entabulature resting on two columns. In the dedicatory inscription, written in the square Hebrew script, the tomb and the *nephesh* are both mentioned. To the north of this tomb is an additional façade consisting of simple door which leads nowhere. This, scholars believe, is the *nephesh* referred to in the inscription. According to their reconstruction it was once crowned with a pyramid.

Nearby, connected with the Tomb of Bene Hezir by a steep stepped corridor, is the 'Tomb of Zechariah'. This is a solid, free-standing monument carved out of the rock. Like the 'Tomb of Pharaoh's daughter', it consists of a cube standing on a stepped base, decorated with Ionic columns and crowned with a pyramid. Recent excavations have shown that a hewn chamber was begun at some time on the western face of the monument but never finished. The most elaborate monument in this group is that known as 'Absalom's Tomb'; this comprises a cube standing on a stepped base and is decorated on all sides with Ionic columns and corner pilasters. Above it is a smaller square base on which stands a round drum supporting a steeply sloping cone. While the lower part of the monument is carved from the living rock, the upper parts are built of beautifully polished ashlar. The whole monument is about 70 feet high. An opening in the square above the entabulature leads into a burial chamber in which are two *arcosolia*. This large monument must thus have been made for the burial of two men only.

To the late Roman period belongs the large Jewish necropolis of *Beth-Shearim. Here all the previously known forms of burial are found, ranging from simply constructed cists in the ground in which lead coffins were placed to burial caves of different shapes and sizes. The larger catacombs have an open court with a triple-arched façade at the back, from which one or two doors lead into a complex of halls. Bodies were interred in *loculi, arcosolia* or pits. The coffins were made of wood, clay and stone; ossuaries were very rare. Hundreds of inscriptions, in Hebrew, Aramaic, Palmyrene and Greek, identify the deceased, sometimes stating their origins and occupations.

The large number of images found in this necropolis are an important feature. Most common are paintings and engravings of the menorah in various forms. Other motifs include human figures, lions, bulls, eagles and even pagan deities. In fact the decoration repeats motifs already known from contemporary synagogues. Christian burial caves are not much different, save for the cross which identified their owners. In some of the Palestinian churches burials were found under the floor. These were in nicely built cists, sometimes in two or more tiers, covered with a slab, usually of imported marble, and inscribed with an epitaph. Cist graves were also discovered in the cemeteries of many towns in Palestine. These were normally marked by a square of stones with one large one indicating the place of the head.

To the Roman period belong also the large Nabatean necropoli of *Petra and el-Hegr in northern *Arabia. The burial places, mostly rock-cut, range from simple pylon tombs decorated with crenellations to the more elaborate proto-Hegr and Hegr types. The latter are decorated with multiple entabulatures, supported by pillars with typical Nabatean capitals and culminating in flights of from four to six steps on either side. To the late 1st and 2nd centuries AD belong the tomb façades made in the style of a Roman temple, the most famous example being that of el-Hazneh.

The Nabatean cemetery at *Mampsis has a shaft 15-20 feet deep. The lower part of this shaft was lined with nicely dressed stones and contained the wooden coffin. Above this the shaft was filled with stones up to ground level. Above ground a stepped pyramid marked the place of the tomb. In one tomb that was similar in other respects an ossuary was found, containing remains of bones wrapped in linen. At Mampsis and *Elusa other forms of secondary burial were also encountered. Much evidence for this practice also comes from Egra and Petra. The dead were buried with their personal jewelry and a coin was placed in the mouth; otherwise grave offerings were not common, though quantities of discarded bowls and cooking pots indicate that funerary meals were customary among the *Nabateans. There are many indications that their funerary customs did not differ much, in this and other respects, from those of the Jews.

BYBLOS A city about 25 miles north of Beirut, with an acropolis and a small but adequate harbor on the coast nearest to the timber-bearing mountains of the *Lebanon. In the 3rd millennium BC the Pharaohs,

who needed timber, had already established commercial ties with Byblos. Its Egyptian name was Gubla, the Gebal of the Bible (Ezek. 27:9), and this name is preserved in the modern name, Jebeil. During the 1st millennium BC Byblos was the intermediary in an extensive papyrus trade from *Egypt to the Greek world. This is reflected in the Greek name for the city, Byblos, which in Greek also meant papyrus. It later signified a book written on papyrus and, through the Latin *biblia*, entered the European languages as the Book of Books, the Bible.

From the Early Bronze Age until the arrival of Alexander the Great Byblos was ruled by local kings; the names of twenty-nine of them are known from inscriptions covering a period from c. 2350 to 333 BC. The city-state was nominally subject to the kings of the large empires — at first the Egyptian and later the Assyrian, Babylonian and Persian empires — whose rulers extorted tribute in the form of cedar wood and other commodities. It was in this way that the forests of the *Lebanon were exploited until their final disappearance. After Crusader occupation the site sank into obscurity and was forgotten until AD 1860, when Ernest Renan came to Jebeil and identified the ancient city. Excavations were undertaken by Pierre Montet in 1921-4 and continued by Maurice Dunand from 1925 until the present time.

The earliest remains on the site belong to the Paleolithic and Neolithic periods. From the Chalcolithic period two successive settlements and a necropolis

The Ahiram Sarcophagus from Byblos

were unearthed. The Early Bronze Age settlement, the first, is characterized by solidly built houses, some with several rooms surrounding a courtyard. The city was surrounded by a massive wall with two gates, the Sea Gate and the Land Gate. The Temple of Baalat-Gebal, constructed c. 2800 BC, was the first example of monumental architecture in Phoenicia. It underwent several stages of construction and was finally incorporated in the Roman temple. Another temple, called by the excavator the L-shaped Temple, was built facing the earlier one in c. 2600 BC. This consisted of two separate units and a courtyard, arranged roughly in the shape of an L.

Small objects and inscribed tablets testify to contacts with Egypt during the time of the 1st to the 6th Dynasties. The most important document from Byblos of that time is the Palermo Stone, which records that a shipment of cedar wood was transported by ship under Snerferu (4th Dynasty). The pharaohs needed the wood for shipbuilding, tomb construction and funerary ritual (cedar oil was used for embalming). For about two hundred years, during the 1st Intermediate period in Egypt, contacts with Byblos ceased and there are signs that the city was destroyed by fire. It is during this time that, according to G. Schaeffer, a new people arrived from Anatolia. They were called the Torque Wearers because of the metal necklaces which they wore and introduced to Byblos the art of metal-working, which began to play an important part in city's economy.

In the Middle Bronze Age a new temple called the Temple of the Obelisks was built over the L-shaped Temple. The main sanctuary was erected over a podium and its chief element was a stone pedestal, possibly intended for a cult object, on a masonry substructure. In the necropolis four royal tombs of the Middle Bronze Age were found intact, two containing stone sarcophagi. In all of them were rich funerary offerings of gold jewelry, bronze objects, pottery vessels, knives of precious metal, ivory plaques, silver and bronze cups and alabaster vases. In another tomb

a richly carved sarcophagus was found, with the famous Phoenician funerary inscription of the Sidonian king, Ahiram, on the lid. This tomb was reused, however, and the inscription is dated to the beginning of the 10th century BC, although some scholars prefer to date the sarcophagus to the 12th century.

For the Late Bronze Age and the first phase of the Iron Age (1600-900 BC) the archaeological material is meager, but there is much information about Byblos in inscriptions and papyri. An inscription from *Thebes, for instance, records that under Tuthmosis III an official was sent on a mission to Byblos to secure cedar wood. The inscription implies either that timber was exacted as tribute or that the pharaohs had forest preserves or royal domains near Byblos. The situation had changed completely by the 11th century BC, when we learn from the Wen-Amon papyri that Wen-Amon had been sent to obtain cedar but secured this only with great difficulty and after payment to the King of Byblos.

This was a time of prosperity and intense commercial activity, when the city-states of the Phoenician coast were members of the greatest seafaring nation and dominated the trade of the Mediterranean world. This period of prosperity continued until the arrival of Alexander the Great in 333 BC, when a commercial decline set in. Byblos surrendered to Alexander without a fight and in the following century became completely Hellenized. Inscriptions mention the establishment of a gymnasium and the existence of a council of elders.

The Roman period was a time of great building activity. Two temples were set up — Byblos was the center of the Adonis cult — and remains of a theater, a bath, a basilica and a colonnade have been unearthed. The city was famous for its wine and its linen trade.

In the 4th century AD the temples were destroyed. The Byzantine period is poorly represented in archaeological finds. The city was conquered by the Arabs in AD 636 and, after an Arab and a Crusader settlement, the site was abandoned.

C

CABUL A town in the territory of Asher (Josh. 19:27), which gave its name to the surrounding region. Solomon gave Hiram, King of *Tyre, 20 towns in the land of Cabul in return for timber and as payment for the skilled workers from Tyre who were employed in the building of the Temple (1 Kgs. 9:11-13). In the time of the Second Temple it was a town on the border of the district of *Galilee (Josephus, *War* III, 38). After the destruction of the Temple a priestly clan of the family of Shechaniah dwelt there. According to ancient Hebrew sources a synagogue was built there. Identified with Kabul, about 10 miles east of *Acre.

CAESAREA Named by its founder, Herod the Great, in honor of Caesar Augustus, the city was the capital of the Roman province of Judea for about 600 years. The name was preserved in its Arabic form as Qaisa-riyeh. To distinguish it from other cities of the same name and founded at the same time it was also called Caesarea Maritima, Caesarea Palaestina and so on. The port of Caesarea was given the name of Limen Sebastos by Herod, Sebastos being the Greek equivalent of Augustus.

In the middle of the 3rd century BC, during the Hellenistic period, the sandy hills along the shores of the Eastern Mediterranean were given by the Persians to the *Phoenicians, who built a small fortified anchorage there which they named Strato's Tower, Straton being the Greek form of Abdashtart, the name of a Sidonian king. At the end of the 2nd century BC Zoilos, the tyrant of Dora (*Dor), conquered Caesarea, but it soon fell to the Hasmonean Alexander Jannaeus. It seems that the first Jewish community was founded there at this time. In 66 BC Pompey conquered Palestine and Strato's Tower became a non-Jewish city. Early in Herod's reign it was given to him by Augustus, and between the years 22 and 10 BC Herod built an entirely new city. Josephus, who must have known Caesarea in all its grandeur, left a detailed description of the city and its port. Quite early in the Roman period Caesarea became the seat of the Roman procurators of the province of Judea, and it also served as the headquarters of the Roman legions stationed in the province. Most of the inhabitants of Caesarea were Syrian Greeks, but there was also a considerable and economically strong Jewish community. Constant tension between the communi-

ties ended in AD 66, during the rule of Gesius Florus, in the outbreak of the First Jewish Revolt. During Vespasian's stay in Caesarea the legions stationed there proclaimed him emperor, and as a token of gratitude he conferred the status of *colonia* on the city. Christianity penetrated rather early, and at the end of the 2nd century the town already had a bishop. In the 3rd and 4th centuries Origen and Eusebius, two of the Early Fathers, taught in the Christian school, which had a world-famous library. Out of this library came the famous translation of the Bible known as the Hexapla. There was also a considerable Jewish community in Caesarea at this period, with many synagogues and houses for the study of the Law; one of the tractates of the Talmud of Jerusalem, *Zeraim*, was completed here. In AD 639 Caesarea was conquered by the Moslems, who held it for 460 years until 1101, when it was conquered by the Crusaders. In 1265 it was completely destroyed by Sultan Baybars to prevent a Christian resettlement.

Although Caesarea was one of the most important cities in Palestine from the Roman period onwards its investigation was much delayed. The first useful survey was made by C.R. Conder and H.H. Kitchener on behalf of the Palestine Exploration Fund in 1873, during their survey of western Palestine. They drew a valuable map of the ruins of the city and also the ground-plans of some of the important structures. It was not until 1945, towards the end of the British Mandate, that the Department of Antiquities made a small excavation on a site where many years earlier winter rains had uncovered remains of a mosaic floor belonging to a synagogue. Some casual finds led the Israel Department of Antiquities and Museums to undertake excavations in 1951, in the course of which a Byzantine street and church were uncovered. In 1956 and 1962 M. Avi-Yonah, on behalf of the Hebrew University, excavated remains of synagogues in the Jewish quarter. The year 1959 marks the beginning of research on a larger scale. An Italian expedition launched its excavations of the Roman theater (1959-63). In 1960 the E. Link underwater research team made soundings in the Roman port, and at the same time (1960-3) A. Negev excavated on behalf of the National Parks Authority in the Crusader town, where remains of Roman, Byzantine, Arab and Crusader periods came to light. In the years 1971-84 R. Bull, on behalf of the American School of Oriental Research, directed extensive excavations in the Roman city between the *theater and the Crusader town. Soundings were also made in the northern outskirts of the city, to locate remains of the Hellenistic town and the northern fortifications of the city.

HELLENISTIC PERIOD While the excavations of the Jewish quarter, which occupied the northern part of the city, were in progress, a very shallow mound was observed at a small distance to the east. A trial trench brought to light great quantities of typical Hellenistic pottery of the 3rd-2nd centuries BC. Under the large heap of pottery the corner of a building was discovered. This represented the remains of a large structure, the only one which could with certainty be attributed to the Phoenician Strato's Tower. It had probably been dismantled by Herod's builders in search of building material. More building remains were found beneath the Jewish buildings, which also confirms the close relationship between the old Hellenistic town and the somewhat later Jewish quarter of the 1st century BC. A short distance to the north of the Jewish quarter a wall with round towers, similar in construction to those of Hellenistic *Samaria, was discovered. Its excavators have dated it to Herodian times but it is more probable that this was the wall of Strato's Tower.

ROMAN PERIOD Remains of this period were found in many parts of the city. At a short distance to the west of the ancient port, within the Crusader *enceinte*, the team of the Palestine Exploration Fund had already marked on their plan what they thought to be remains of the Temple of Augustus, which was known from the writings of Josephus. During the 1960 excavations this area was checked and it became obvious that the small elevation to the west of the port, where the remains of the temple were observed, represented an artificial hillock. The whole area facing the port was made up of a series of substructures built of local sandstone and filled with crushed quarry refuse. The southern half of this artificial mound was different; here a series of vaulted chambers 65 feet long, 21 feet wide and 45 feet high was constructed. The two parts of the substructure formed a podium 50 feet higher than the surrounding ground. Above this podium the Temple of Augustus and the palaces were built. To the

Inscription of the Legio X Fretensis on the aqueduct at Caesarea

west of the podium, between it and the seashore, remains of the port were discovered. Exploration of the port was conducted from the sea and on land. The divers of the underwater research team followed the two breakwaters, the northern one measuring 250yd and the southern 600yd, enclosing a sheltered area of about 40 acres. At the same time excavations in front of the podium revealed no building remains earlier than the 5th-4th centuries BC. Further excavations brought to light a massive wall 30 feet wide, running out from the podium westward towards the sea. On this wall were found sea shells which could have formed only if the wall was under water for a considerable time. It thus seems that the construction of the port was begun by excavating an inner harbor and the piers, and only when this was completed were the outer breakwaters built. When both parts were complete the narrow strip of land separating them was removed, allowing the water to enter the inner basins. Deposits containing sea shells and sea-corroded potsherds were found at a distance of 100-150 feet from the podium, at a depth of about 10 feet, confirming the theory of the existence of an inner harbor. In AD 130 the port was severely damaged by an earthquake, and from the 4th or 5th century AD it became unusable.

South of the Crusader town the American expedition revealed remains of a public building of the Byzantine period. This building overlay a series of vaulted structures, similar to those unearthed by A. Negev within the Crusader town. The presence of numerous 1st century AD storage jars confirms that these structures had served as storehouses, apparently facilities for the harbor. These storehouses were still in use in the late Roman and Byzantine periods. In the late Roman period one of the vaulted chambers served as a Mithraeum. It was decorated with painted symbolic scenes and contained a small plaque with the god's effigy and symbols. This late Mithraic sanctuary was preceded by an earlier one. East of these structures were discovered sections of streets of the Byzantine period, one of which may have been the cardo. In this area a large public building of the Byzantine period, possibly an archive, was found lavishly decorated with mosaics. Another public building in this area contained Latin inscriptions honoring a procurator and two governors of Syria. A third public building which was partly excavated by A.Negev, had an apse on the west side and bore traces of wall mosaics.

Theater The theater, an innovation introduced in the Near East by Herod, was built at the southern extremity of the city facing the sea. Its base was a solid concrete construction above which rose the seats and the vaulted entrances. Of the superstructure very little remains, but the floor of the early theater is of special interest, consisting as it does of very fine plaster painted with vivid colors. The floor was renewed in this way not less than 14 times. In the 3rd century a large half-rounded square was added at the back of the stage building. In the next century the theater was adapted for water games and a large reservoir was built nearby. In one of the reconstructions of the theater a stone bearing an inscription mentioning Pontius Pilate was reused as an ordinary building stone. Very little of the beautiful marble decoration remained, most of it having been burnt to lime when a Byzantine citadel was built on top of the theater. Between the theater and the seacoast were the remains of a *palace, probably one of Herod's.

Hippodrome Soundings were also made in the *hippodrome where an obelisk made of Aswan granite was found, its original length more than 80 feet. With an overall length of 1400 feet and a width of 290 feet, this hippodrome is one of the largest installations of its kind in the Roman world. In the area of the high-level aqueduct a villa and a fish-pond of the Byzantine period were discovered.

Water supply The whole area of Caesarea is lacking in springs and there are no rivers close to the city. Storage of rainwater would not have provided an adequate supply for a city of this size. Two aqueducts were therefore built. One, carried on arches, drew its water from springs on the southern slope of Mount Carmel, 8 miles from Caesarea. Near its source the water was conveyed in clay pipes; then, over a large swamp, the water conduit was supported on high arches; a sandstone ridge running parallel to the coast was traversed in a tunnel, and finally the conduit was brought down the coast on arches to the city. When the volume of water was not large enough to meet the demand the capacity of the aqueduct was doubled by the addition of a parallel duct. This drew its water from the Crocodile River, 6 miles to the north of Caesarea, and brought water for irrigation. Here a dam was constructed across the river in order to raise the level of the water and create a large reservoir. From the dam the water was carried to the city by means of a conduit at ground level, protected by a vaulted roof. The high-level aqueduct is dated to the time of Herod; the date of the other is not exactly known. From inscriptions found on the aqueducts it is clear that both had to be repaired from time to time. One of these repairs was carried out during the Bar-Kochba rebellion, when thousands of soldiers were rushed in to quell the revolt. (*See also* *WATER SUPPLY.)

BYZANTINE PERIOD Many fragmentary remains of the late Roman period are scattered over the whole area but no building could be attributed to that period. On the other hand, the Byzantine period is represented by the remains of many buildings. The city of this period was fortified by a circular wall 1½ miles long. On top of the Herodian podium a huge building with marble floors and marble capitals decorated with crosses was found. The plan of the building is that of a large court around which halls and rooms are grouped. Another such building was discovered to the south of the Crusader *enceinte*, not far from the one just described. Half of its length was destroyed when the Crusaders built their moat, but the remaining half gives a fairly good idea of how it looked. The entrance was on the east via a porch supported by columns; then followed a series of small anterooms leading to a large hall, possibly in the form of a basilica and paved with multicolored mosaics. There were four such floors, superimposed one upon another, indicating that the building must have been in use for a considerable length of time. At the western end was a half-rounded

Podium of the temple of Augustus from the time of Herod, Caesarea

apse, the walls and dome of which were covered with glass-gilded mosaics (*Mosaics). A quotation from St Paul's Epistle to the Romans (Rom. 13:3) was found in the mosaic of one of the side rooms. In the debris of this building a statue of the Good Shepherd was discovered. There is no doubt that this was also an important Christian public building, but certainly not a church. It might have been connected with the ecclesiastical school of Caesarea, though definite proof of this is lacking.

In the years 1976 and 1977 L.I. Levine and E. Netzer made soundings on behalf of the Hebrew University in the southeastern part of the Crusader town. They uncovered occupation levels of the early Arab period (9th-10th centuries AD) and a large public building of the Byzantine period bearing the word *shalom* inscribed in Hebrew on one of its columns. Below these were remains of the early and late Roman period. Trial digs beneath the Crusader *fortifications revealed that the Crusader wall was built above a wall of the early Arab period; beneath the northeastern corner of these fortifications was a gate of the Byzantine period. These excavations were resumed in 1979 by E. Netzer who, in three soundings in the central part of the Crusader town, encountered occupation levels of the Crusader (10-11th centuries AD), early Arab (8th-9th centuries AD) and Byzantine periods.

To the east of the Crusader *enceinte* a section of a Byzantine street 130yd long was discovered. Part is paved with large marble slabs taken from Roman palaces, part with large white mosaics. The two sections of this street are at different levels, a broad flight of steps leading from the marble-paved to the mosaic-paved section. In front of the steps a triple gateway at the sides of which stood two over-lifesize statues, one of red porphyry and the other of white marble. Both were taken from Roman buildings of the 2nd and 3rd centuries AD. Along the street were workshops and shops. Outside the Byzantine city wall to the east, where the main cemetery of the city is situated, were discovered the remains of a large church paved with mosaics. As no trace of bases for columns was found this church was obviously of the unroofed type. The mosaic pavement is decorated with medallions depicting birds of different kinds, while the border has fruit trees and animals, both wild and domestic.

Mention has already been made of a citadel which was built on top of the Roman theater. Part of the theater structure was used for this, while on the west an additional heavy wall was built and fortified with round towers. A tomb containing beautiful gold crosses inlaid with precious stones dated the citadel to the Byzantine period. Above the remains of the Hellenistic walls a large building of the early Roman period was discovered. From the 4th century onwards a series of synagogues was built on this base, the latest of which was of the 7th century AD. Capitals with Jewish symbols and dedicatory inscriptions helped to identify the buildings, but the excavated area was too small for complete plans of them to be made.

CALAH A city in the land of Asher. According to Genesis (10:11) it was built by Nimrod, who also built *Nineveh and the city of *Rehoboth. Called Kalhu in Assyrian, the city was already in existence in the time of Hammurabi (second half of 18th century BC). Ashurnasirpal attributes its 'making' to Shalmaneser I (c. 1300 BC), which probably means that he rebuilt it and made it his capital. From that time onwards it served as one of the capitals of the kingdom, along with the cities of Ashur (*Mesopotamia) and *Nineveh.

Calah is situated in the stretch of land at the junction of the River Great Zab and the River Tigris (*Hiddekel) and is identified with Nimrod. The largest of the buildings was the ziggurat, which was built of bricks and lined with stone and stood about 130 feet high. In the course of the excavations made at Nimrod the palace of Ashurbanipal was discovered. Its walls were decorated with reliefs and paintings. Other important monuments found were the palace of Esarhaddon and the obelisk of Shalmaneser III. The city was surrounded by a wall strengthened with 108 towers, enclosing an area of more than 60 acres.

CALENDAR The Gregorian calendar used in our own era takes its origin from the Roman calendar established by Julius Caesar and is based on the solar year. In the ancient world the Egyptians were alone in reckoning by solar time; the other nations of the ancient Near East all based their calendars on the cycles of the moon. At first the length of the month and of the year was fixed empirically, by the appearance of the new moon and its orbit during the month. To avoid the resultant irregularities months of a fixed length were ordained, with either 29 or 30 days each. The lunar year, with 354 days, lags behind the solar year, so that over a period the months shifted through all the seasons of the year. This system had a number of disadvantages which affected economic life as well as religious practice. In order to adjust the lunar to the solar year a system whereby an intercalary month was added was introduced in Babylonia in the 6th century BC. On this basis there were three leap years in a cycle of eight years. The Babylonian calendar was later adopted as the official calendar of the Persian Empire and by the Jews in Palestine and Egypt.

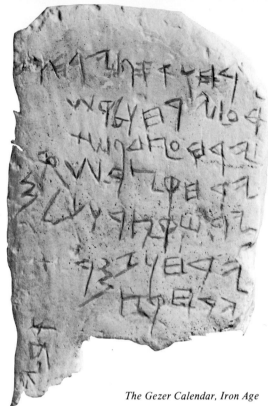

The Gezer Calendar, Iron Age

In biblical times the Hebrew calendar was based on the lunar year and it may therefore be inferred that the Flood (cf. Gen. 7:11; 8:14) lasted 365 days (354-11). The Hebrew calendar, although based on the lunar year, was greatly influenced by the positions of the sun, as may be seen from the arrangement of the religious festivals. These fall on specific days of specific months of the lunar year, but they always fall in the same seasons of the solar year. The method by which this coordination between the lunar and the solar year was arrived at is still unknown. There is no direct reference in the Bible to a 13th (intercalary) month, the only possible hint of intercalation being the reference to a second Passover (Num. 9:10 ff.). In fact we do not even know how the intercalation was effected in Babylon — whether by the addition of a fixed intercalary month or by the addition of days in a more haphazard way whenever the difference between the lunar and the solar years became too great. However, it seems that both in Babylon and in Palestine the adjustments were made quite arbitrarily. Intercalation was effected by the priests until after the destruction of the Second Temple, when it became the privilege of certain scholarly families such as that of Raban Gammaliel. From the middle of the 2nd century AD preparations were made to form a calendar based entirely on mathematical calculations, but this was not finally settled until the 4th century AD. Throughout the whole period of the Second Temple and in the centuries following its destruction the beginning of a new month was announced by beacons being lit on certain high mountains.

THE NEW YEAR The year of the ancient Hebrews began in the autumn. According to 1 Kings (12:32) it was celebrated in the kingdom of Israel one month later than in the kingdom of Judah. In Babylon, also, the civic New Year was celebrated in the autumn, but alongside it was another, celebrated in the spring, which originated in Babylon and marked the beginning of the religious year. In Israel the religious calendar followed the cycle of the annual festivals, the first of the religious year being the Passover; the New Year therefore fell on the day of the new moon in the month of Nissan. It seems that a year which begins in the autumn is based on the needs of an agricultural society. Thus: 'and the feast of ingathering, which is in the end of the year, when thou hast gathered in thy labors out of the field' (Exod. 23:16). The jubilee, which is clearly an economic institution, also began in the autumn, in the seventh month, when the New Year was celebrated (Lev. 25:9). On the other hand, there is much evidence in the Bible to show that the Passover was considered to be the first feast in a cycle which terminated with the Feast of Tabernacles (cf. Lev. 23:5—36; Deut. 16:1—16).

In the time of the Babylonian exile the order of the months was fixed, Nissan, the month of spring, coming first, though the New Year was — as it still is today — celebrated in Tishrei, the seventh month, which falls in the autumn. (*See also* *INSCRIPTIONS.)

CALENDARS IN ARCHAEOLOGICAL FINDS In the excavations of Tell el-*Farah (south), *Gezer and *Lachish small flat bone plaques were found, each heavy and with 30 small perforations arranged in three rows, ten to a row. These plaques belong to Iron Age strata and are believed to have been monthly calendars. At *Gezer another stone plaque was discovered on which names of months and certain agricultural activities are listed. This is variously explained. (*See also* *INSCRIPTIONS.)

In the Roman period the official reckoning of time in Judea followed the Julian calendar (devised in 47 BC). Caesar instituted a new solar calendar of 365 1/4 days, beginning on 1 January 47 BC. Although most of the former inconveniences were overcome in this new calendar it was still not accurate enough and by AD 325 there was a difference of four days between the Julian and the true solar year, so that the vernal equinox fell on 21 March instead of 25 March. The Julian system was revised by Pope Gregory XIII in 1582. Ten days were omitted from that year and the new leap year rules prevented further errors.

CALLIRRHOE A group of hot springs on the northeast shore of the *Dead Sea, identified with modern Uyun es-Sara, to which Herod went in search of a cure shortly before his death (Josephus, *War* I, 657; *Antiq.* XVII, 171). References are also found by other ancient writers, such as Pliny (*Nat. Hist.* v, 16), and in the Talmud. On the *Medaba map three buildings are shown: a spring house, a *nymphaeum* and another construction through which a stream flows from the foot of the mountains and passes through a pool into the *Dead Sea. A survey has confirmed the existence of several buildings on the shore, with pools into which the water was channelled from the hot springs and the remains of a *nymphaeum* with an *exedra*.

CALNEH One of the four original cities of Nimrod's kingdom, mentioned together with Babel, *Erech and *Accad in Genesis (10:10). Its identification is not certain. Some suggest Nippur (modern Nifr), basing their theory on the Babylonian creation myth in which it is related that Marduk was the founder of Babylon, *Erech and Nippur. Nippur was the most important city in that group and the kings of *Babylon conferred benefits on it from time to time in order to gain the favor of its gods Enlil and Ninlil, who dwelt in the large ziggurat called e-Kura. In the excavations made at Nippur about 50,000 clay tablets were found, dealing with literary and commercial matters. Calneh is identified by others with Kunulua or Kulani (now Chatal Huyuk) in northern Syria, which was conquered by Tiglath-Pileser III in 738 BC. This is possibly the same as the Calneh of Amos (6:2), and the Calno of Isaiah (10:9), which are mentioned together with *Carchemish, *Hamath and Arpad, all cities in northern Syria.

CANA A village in *Galilee 5 miles south of *Sepphoris. Scene of the first miracle of Jesus, the turning of water into wine during the course of the wedding at Cana (John 2:1, 11). The place was little known but for the part it played in the early ministry of Jesus. When Josephus was preparing *Galilee for the war against the Romans Cana served for some time as his headquarters (Josephus, *Life* 86). After the destruction of the Temple it was the seat of the priestly family of Eljashib. In Byzantine and medieval times the place of the miracle was shown to pilgrims. Identified with Khirbet Qana.

CANAAN; CANAANITES A name found in the Bible in the table of nations (Gen. 10:6), as well as in the cuneiform, Egyptian and Phoenician texts, and later also in Greek and Roman historical texts. In all of these sources Canaan is used both as a geographical term and as an ethnic appellation. According to Genesis (9:20—3; 10:6), Canaan was the son of Ham,

Decorations on the war chariot of Tuthmosis IV, showing Canaanite warriors

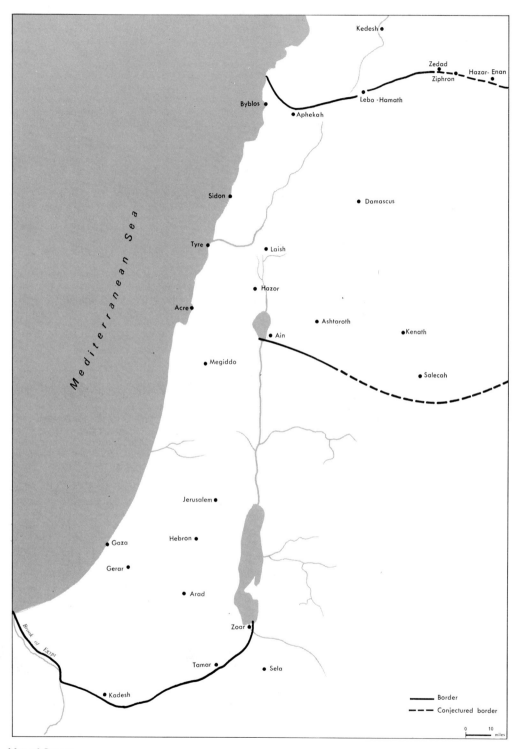

Map of Canaan

Noah's second son. Canaan was the father of Sidon, Heth, the Jebusite, Amorite, Girgasite, Hivite, Arkite, Sinite, Arvadite, Zamarite and the Hamathite. Most of these 'sons' may be identified as nations, kingdoms or cities in Palestine, *Syria and *Phoenicia which were prominent in the biblical story.

Based on this list an attempt may be made to drawn the boundaries of Canaan as reflected in the Bible. To the north it reached as far as northern *Phoenicia and southern *Syria, and also included the whole of Palestine and the territory east of the River *Jordan. According to other references in the Bible Canaan coincided with the land later conquered by the Israelites (cf. Gen. 15:19—21; Exod. 3:8; 34:11; Deut. 7:1; Josh. 3:10, etc.). The term Canaan as it appears in the Bible is vague and was applied at different times to different parts of the country. The Bible forbade any contact with the Canaanites; thus it was specifically forbidden to bow to their gods (Exod. 23:24), to make a covenant with them and to intermarry with them (Gen. 24:3). In the later biblical literature Canaan is synonymous with a merchant (Isa. 23:8; Authorized Version: 'merchants').

A study of the placenames in Palestine and Syria in the external sources shows that as early as the Neolithic and Chalcolithic periods these countries were inhabited by Semites. The names of early settlements, such as *Jericho, *Megiddo and numerous others, are certainly Semitic and may be taken as evidence that most, if not all, of their inhabitants in that early period were Canaanites. This is further verified by Egyptian and cuneiform documents of the 2nd millennium BC, such as the *Execration Texts, the documents of *Mari and *Ugarit and the *El Amarna letters. In the early part of the 2nd millennium BC the north of Canaan was under Mesopotamian influence, but towards the middle of the same millennium the influence of Egypt increased. The foundation of the *Hyksos kingdom did not affect the Canaanite city-states, although they did become part of it politically. Only after the overthrow of the *Hyksos in the middle of the 16th century BC did some of the Canaanite cities attempt rebellion, and this was soon suppressed. They remained under Egyptian rule until early in the 13th century BC, when the Israelite conquest took place.

The *El Amarna letters provide a good picture of the Canaanite way of life before the Israelite conquest. Their names indicate a very mixed stock speaking a dialect close to biblical Hebrew (cf. Isa. 19:18). At the base of their religion were the gods of the Canaanite epic literature, but many cities also had local deities. As with the other nations of the ancient Near East, religious syncretism was common. The Canaanite cult involved female and male prostitution as well as human sacrifice.

In about 1220 BC the Israelites conquered great parts of the land of Canaan and by the end of the same century most of the large and prosperous Canaanite cities already lay in ruins. The destruction of the coastal cities was completed by the Sea Peoples (*Philistines), who invaded them at the beginning of the 12th century BC. Shortly afterwards the cities on the Phoenician coast were destroyed as well. In the same turbulent period the *Arameans, coming from the Syrian desert, conquered the northern parts of the Canaanite kingdom. In the late 12th and early 11th centuries BC a small Canaanite kingdom crystallized around *Sidon and *Byblos, basing its economy on maritime trading. Although it did pay tribute to the Assyrians this small kingdom maintained its independence. An Egyptian account of the early 11th century BC mentions *Sidon and *Byblos as traders in cedar wood. By the 10th century BC the Sidonian kingdom, whose capital at that time was *Tyre, had taken the place of the Canaanite kingdom of *Byblos.

CAPERNAUM A town on the western shore of the Sea of *Galilee, on the highway from the Mediterranean coast to *Damascus, with a small port for its population of fishermen. The town is known from the early Roman period onwards and Josephus describes it as very fertile and its people as having taken an active part in the war against the Romans (Josephus, *War* III, 516-21; *Life* 72).

Capernaum is one of the places most frequently mentioned in the Gospels. Jesus went there, on the borders of the territories of Zebulon and Naphtali, from Nazareth (Matt. 4:13) and there found his first disciples, Peter, Andrew and the two sons of Zebedee (Matt. 4:18-22). He taught there in the synagogue (John 6:24-59) and directed Peter to find a coin in the mouth of a fish with which to pay the tax-gatherers (Matt. 17:24-7). He also lodged there in Peter's house, healing the sick and teaching (Mark 1:29-34; 2:1-12; Luke 4:38-48). Leaving Capernaum he condemned it along with other cities that had not heeded his calls to repentance (Matt. 11:23; Luke 10:15).

In later Jewish sources Capernaum is referred to as a seat of *minim*, or sectarians, perhaps referring to the time of Jesus. In the 4th century AD the city had an almost exclusively Jewish population. The first Christian community gathered there c. AD 352 around the convert Joseph, and built a church on the site of Peter's house.

The latest evidence of a living community at Capernaum is a 5th-century inscription in Aramaic in the synagogue of el-Hamma (*Hammath-Gader). From that time onwards nothing remains but ruins. The most impressive are those of the synagogue, first mentioned by E. Robinson in 1838 and identified as Capernaum by C. Wilson in 1865. In 1894 the Franciscans bought the site and fenced it off to prevent the theft of masonry. It was explored in 1905 by H. Kohl and C. Watzinger, excavated in 1921 by G. Orfali and partly reconstructed in 1925. The excavations by the Franciscans were renewed in 1968.

The synagogue is the most elaborate of the synagogues in the Galilee. It was formerly considered an example of an early type of synagogue, but it is now designated merely a Galilean type, without assigning it to a specific date. The building is orientated north-south, stands on a podium and is built of nicely cut limestone, in contrast to the black basalt houes round about. Built to a height of two stories, it is 65 feet long and has an atrium on the east. The façade is decorated with arched gables. Three doors lead into the synagogue proper, which is divided into a broad nave and

two narrow aisles by rows of columns. Another row of columns facing the entrance connects the two longitudinal rows and its plan thus differs from the basilical type. Along the aisles are stone benches and there is no fixed position for the Torah Shrine. The synagogue is distinguished for its richly carved stone ornamentation, which depicts stylized plants, fruits, geometric motifs, animals and even mythological figures. Of special interest is a fragment of a cornice bearing an image of an Ionic temple on wheels, which may represent the Ark of the Covenant or a Torah Shrine. The style of architecture and the decoration point to a general dating between the end of the 2nd and the beginning of the 3rd century AD. The Fransciscan excavators, however, on the basis of stratified small finds, mainly coins, unearthed in the latest excavations (1969-70), date the synagogue to the mid-4th century AD.

To the Byzantine period belongs an octagonal church with a multicolored mosaic floor, supposedly standing on the site of Peter's house. Further excavations beneath this church in 1968 revealed houses dating to the 1st century AD which were used as a cult place in the 2nd and 3rd centuries. The excavators believe that one of these houses was that of Peter, above which the first Jewish synagogue, mentioned in the Gospels, was built.

CAPHTOR The place where the *Philistines came from (Jer. 47:4; Amos 9:7). According to Genesis (10:14), the Caphtorim were the descendants of Ham, son of Noah, and they destroyed the Avim and lived in their place (Deut. 2:23). There is clear evidence connecting the culture of *Crete with that of the *Philistines. Indeed in the Bible the *Philistines are sometimes mentioned in conjunction with the Cheretim. Caphtor is also mentioned in the documents of *Mari and *Ugarit and many scholars tend for these reasons to identify Caphtor with *Crete. Others prefer to identify it with the Keptiu of the Egyptian sources, a people who dwelt in Cilicia (Asia Minor).

CAPITOLIAS One of the cities of the *Decapolis, whose era, according to coins, began in AD 98-9 (Nerva or Trajan). Extant coins from Aurelius to Macrinus indicate that the city was autonomous and not founded as a Roman colony. The Peutinger map gives its position as halfway between Adraa and *Gadara, 16 miles from each. The itinerary of the pilgrim Antoninus (6th century AD) places it between Gadara and Neve (*Naveh) on the road to *Damascus, 36 miles from Neve and 16 from *Gadara. Capitolias has been identified with Beit Ras in the Ajlun. In the Talmud it is called Beth-Resha, with a reference to cattle pastures in its vicinity. From Latin inscriptions we know that several natives of Capitolias served in the Roman army. In the Byzantine period it was part of Palestina Secunda and its bishops participated in the councils from AD 325 to 536. Arab sources mention a fortress and record that the village was famous for its vineyards.

Archaeological remains include a city wall enclosing 51 acres, a paved street with a double-arched gateway, a Roman cemetery and the remains of a church and a mosque. Of special interest are the elaborate water cisterns all over the city. Remains of a

Roman road leading eastwards from Capitolias to the *Hauran have been identified. This road most probably continued northwest to Gadara, though no traces have been found.

CARCHEMISH An important Hittite city on the right bank of the *Euphrates in northern Syria, identified with Jarablus. It is mentioned among the cities conquered by Tuthmosis III. In the days of Rameses II it took part in the battle of *Kedesh-on-the-Orontes. Tiglath-Pileser I devastated the city and was later conquered by Ashurbanipal, who imposed a heavy tribute on it, as did Shalmaneser II. In the days of Sargon II the city attempted to free itself, but failed. Its citizens were deported and others were brought in to replace them (717 BC). Despite its subjection to Assyria Carchemish was an important trading center and its *maneh* (*Weights and measures) was the official monetary unit of *Nineveh. The Assyrians turned Carchemish into an Assyrian province. In the days of Josiah, King of Judah, Pharaoh Necho attacked Carchemish (2 Chr. 35:20 ff.), but four years later (605 BC) he was defeated by Nebuchadnezzar near the walls of the city (Jer. 46:2), in a battle which decided the fate of the whole of western Asia.

In the excavations of the site remains of the mixed Aramean and Hittite culture were discovered, including many inscriptions in the Hittite hieroglyphic script. Other finds included reliefs of Hittite gods and other works of art in which an Assyrian influence could be detected.

CARMEL A town in the hills of Judah (Josh. 15:55) where Saul set up a monument after his victory over *Amalek (1 Sam. 15:12). Nabal was shearing his sheep in Carmel when David's messengers arrived and his wife Abigail, a native of the town, went out from there to appease David (1 Sam. 25:2 ff.; 27:3). It was also the birth-place of Hezrai, one of David's mighty men (2 Sam. 23:35). Eusebius mentions Carmel three times (*Onom.* 92:19-22; 118:5; 172:20), twice as Chermala, and refers both to the biblical narrative and to the fact that in his time a Roman garrison was stationed there. Once, however (118:5), he calls it Karmelos, omits the mention of the Roman garrison and states that it was a large Jewish village in his time. In the 4th century it still contained a Roman garrison and the *Nessana papyri relate that it paid more taxes than any other town on the *Limes, proof of its superior economic position. The Roman (and Byzantine) armies chose this site both for its excellent strategic location and mainly because of the presence of two springs whose

Carmel in the hilly region of Hebron

(Left) The synagogue at Capernaum (Kefar Nahum), with Byzantine remains in the foreground

Caves of Wadi Mughara, in the Mount Carmel Range

Relief of carpenters at work, Egyptian

waters were collected in a large reservoir. Three large churches of the Byzantine period have also been found there (*See also* *KHIRBET SUSIYA).

CARMEL (MOUNT) A mountain range, the northwestern continuation of the hills of Samaria, rising to 1,650 feet above sea level. The Carmel formed the southern limit of the territory of Asher (Josh. 19:26) and the southwestern border of the Valley of Esdraelon (*Jezreel) (1 Kgs. 18:42-6). The River *Kishon flows at its foot (1 Kgs. 18:40). Falling steeply to the Mediterranean, it leaves only a narrow coastal plain (Jer. 46:18) and its canyon-like cliffs are dotted with numerous caves, some of which served as dwellings in prehistoric times (*Prehistory). Most of the Carmel is covered with a thick deposit of good soil and abundant vegetation. It was noted as a symbol of beauty (Isa. 33:9; S. of S. 7:5) and compared with the *Lebanon and the *Bashan (Isa. 29:17; 32:15; Authorized Version: 'fruitful field'; Jer. 50:19). An altar to Baal was set at the top of the mountain; it was here Elijah confounded the prophets of Baal (1 Kgs. 18:17-46). Elisha dwelt there for some time (2 Kgs. 4:25).

Some scholars believe that Mount Carmel is referred to by Veni, a general of Phiops I, King of Egypt, who describes the 'gazelle's nose' on reaching the coast of Palestine. As 'Holy Head', or 'Holy', it is mentioned in the list of conquests of Tuthmosis III. In the Persian period the Carmel formed the northern limit of the satrapy of Dora (*Dor), but from the Hellenistic period onwards it formed part of the eparchy of *Acco (*Acre). The Carmel range was taken by the Hasmonean Alexander Jannaeus (Josephus, *Antiq.* XIII, 396, where it is referred to as the mountain of the Tyrians). Pompey returned it to *Acco in 64 BC (Josephus, *War* III, 35).

The sanctity of Mount Carmel was still preserved in the Hellenistic period when, according to Scylax, a temple of Zeus stood on the mountain. There was also an altar and an oracle there (Tacitus, *Histories* II, 78), and a fragmentary inscription found on the mountain mentions a cult of Zeus Heiopolitanus. Christian tradition places the site of the altar of Baal on the southeastern end of the mountain. A Jewish village called Husifa existed in the Byzantine period on one of the peaks of Mount Carmel, where remains of a synagogue have been discovered.

CARPENTRY Wood was employed in certain forms of construction in prehistoric times. The walls and roofs of some early dwellings, and also the roof beams of larger houses, were made of wood and twigs. In fact

before the introduction of the arch in the Roman period wood was used universally for roofing. In the Byzantine period most *Churches were roofed with wood imported from *Lebanon and Syria. Furthermore, among the finds of *Jericho and in the *Judean Desert Caves, where climatic conditions have been favorable to their survival, furniture and various utensils made of wood have been found (*Building materials).

That the carpenter's craft was known in biblical times is indicated by several references to the carpenter's tools and descriptions of this work. One such description concerns the making of a wooden image (Isa. 44:13 ff.; and cf. Jer. 10:3-4). A tool referred to in Isaiah (44:12), called *maasad* in Hebrew, is translated as 'tongs' in the Authorized Version. However, talmudic literature refers to it as a carpenter's plane used for smoothing wood. Another tool used by the carpenter is the 'workmen's hammer' (Judg. 5:26) or wooden mallet, used for knocking in tent pegs but also in the carpenter's craft. Timber was felled with an axe (Deut. 19:5) and the saw, not specifically mentioned in the Bible though it appears in later literature, was most probably used in biblical times also. Numerous iron tools have been found on Iron Age sites, some of which must have formed part of a carpenter's kit.

The ability of the *Phoenicians and some other nations to build ships suggests that the carpenter's skill attained a high degree of refinement in ancient times. Similarly, the very elaborate furniture found in *Egypt and depicted on *Mesopotamian reliefs reached a standard not inferior to the best handmade furniture of more modern periods, as did the furniture of the Greeks and Romans.

CARTHA A place on the border of *Phoenicia and Palestine and a halt on the coastal road. Mentioned in the itinerary of the Pilgrim of Bordeaux as Mutatio Certha. It was in the territory of *Dor and is identified with Khirbet Dustrei, within the walls of the Crusader castle of Athlit.

In 1930-3 a section of the mound was excavated by C.N. Johns on behalf of the Palestine Department of Antiquities. Remains of the Middle and Late Bronze Ages, of the Iron Age and of the Persian, Hellenistic and Roman periods came to light. In excavations carried out in 1969 at Tel *Megadim, to the north of Athlit, by M. Broshi on behalf of the Israel Exploration Society, remains of a large road station were discovered, which the excavator identified with Mutatio Certha.

CHEBAR The name of a river near which Ezekiel was a captive (Ezek. 1:1, etc.) and where he had one of his visions (Ezek. 10:15). Some believe it is identical with *Habor (2 Kgs. 17:6), the variation representing a different dialect. But a tablet of the 5th century BC has *nar-kabaru*, i.e. the 'Great Channel' (a channel which draws water from the *Euphrates near the city of *Babylon) inscribed on it. Identified with Shat en-Nil.

CHERUB; CHERUBIM Cherubim are mentioned in the Bible in the story of Adam and Eve (Gen. 3:24), where they are referred to as the guardians of the way to the tree of life. Golden cherubim were placed at either end of the mercy seat above the Ark of the Covenant (Exod. 25:18-22, 37:7-9). They were also embroidered on the veil (2 Chr. 3:14) and used in the adornment of various other parts of the Temple (cf. 1 Kgs. 6-7, etc.). In the description of Ezekiel's chariot (Ezek. 1:5-14) the four living creatures, usually interpreted as cherubim, are described as bearing the chariot of God.

The cherub is equivalent to the griffin, a name found almost in the same form in Persian and in Greek. In ancient Near-Eastern mythology griffins were intermediaries between men and gods, carrying men's prayers up to the higher beings. Cherubim are not described in detail in the Bible and it is known only that they had faces and wings. Some scholars believe that they are analogous with the beings depicted in Egyptian paintings as having the bodies of

Cherub, ivory engraving from Megiddo, Iron Age

young winged boys and girls, or that they were similar to the Mesopotamian winged bulls, guardians of the temples. But it is now thought that they were represented as sphinxes, i.e. lions with human faces and outspread wings touching at the back. There are numerous representations of sphinxes in the art of Palestine during the Bronze and Iron Ages.

The griffin (lion-bodied, eagle-faced) and the sphinx (lion-bodied, human- mostly female-faced) were borrowed from the Near East by western religion and art. At first the griffin was thought to be hostile to human beings but gradually this idea changed. It was then consecrated to Apollo and guarded the wine of Dionysus. Both griffin and sphinx are frequently represented in Greek, Roman and Hellenistic art, and to a much lesser extent also in Byzantine religious art.

CHINNERETH a) One of the fenced cities of *Naphtali (Josh. 19:35), which gave its name to the Plain of Chinneroth (Josh. 11:2; 1 Kgs. 15:20, 'Cinneroth'). Mentioned in the list of cities conquered by Tuthmosis III in 1468 BC, it is identified with Khirbet el-Oreimeh, 6 miles north of *Tiberias. This mound rises above a fertile plain rich in springs, known as the Plain of Gennessar in the Roman period. It guards a stretch of the Via Maris (*Roads) between Hattin and *Hazor. Trial excavations were conducted at the site in 1940 by B. Mazar in a rock-cut tomb which was discovered less than a mile from *Beth-Yerah. Three phases of burial were distinguished, all from a late stage of the Early Bronze Age II, and containing pottery types known from *Abydos which attest to relations with Egypt. Ornaments of gold, semi-precious stones, bone and mother-of-pearl were also found.

b) See *GALILEE, SEA OF.

CHINNEROTH *See* *GALILEE, SEA OF

CHORAZIN A Jewish town in Upper *Galilee, 3 miles north of *Capernaum, named with *Bethsaida as one of the cities reproached by Jesus (Matt. 11:20-4) and in Jewish literature in connection with the supply of grain to the Temple for ritual use. Eusebius (*Onom.* 174, 23 ff.) knew it as a deserted site.

The synagogue of Chorazin was discovered as early as 1869 in the survey of the Palestine Exploration Fund. It was excavated in 1905-7 by H. Kohl and C. Watzinger on behalf of the German Oriental Society. The synagogue was completely cleared in 1926 by N. Makhouly and J. Ory on behalf of the Department of Antiquities. Further exploration of the site was made for the department by Z. Yeivin in 1962/3 and 1980-4.

The synagogue, of the Galilean type, is situated in the center of the town, at its highest point, in the midst of some large buildings. The building, of local black basalt, is about 70 feet by 50 feet and its walls are largely preserved. The three monumental entrances face south, towards *Jerusalem. There was a courtyard on the west of the building and a small room on the north. On the outer wall of this room was a staircase leading to the upper floor. In front of the building was a large open courtyard from which a broad flight of steps probably led up to the synagogue, which would be on higher ground. The interior of the building was divided by three rows of columns into a nave (20 feet wide) and three aisles (each 6 feet wide);

'Throne of Moses', the synagogue at Chorazin, 3rd-4th centuries AD

benches were built along the walls. There were capitals of two orders in the synagogue, one quasi-Ionic, the other quasi-Doric. The outer walls of the building were decorated with pilasters with Ionic bases and Corinthian capitals. Above the pilasters, and probably also along the walls of the upper story, were carved friezes. The decoration consists of rich floral designs encircling human and animal figures, among them men pressing grapes, a lion attacking a centaur, an animal suckling a cub, a lion devouring another animal and so on. Most of these images, except for a Medusa which was preserved intact, were damaged in antiquity, probably by Jewish iconoclasts. Among the finds in the synagogue was a basalt throne, decorated with a rosette on the back support. This is the 'Throne of Moses', which was used during the reading of the Torah.

East of the synagogue two large public buildings (90 feet x 90 feet each), built of ashlars laid dry, were partly excavated. West of the synagogue a residential quarter was examined. The houses were not placed close together; among them were two oil-presses. Architectural fragments of the synagogue were used in the construction of these houses. Several houses were also found north of the synagogue, and to their north were three underground chambers, one of them a ritual bath (*mikveh*), connected by a channel to a cistern. This unit of *mikveh* and cistern was enclosed by a wall, forming a court, and was partly roofed for greater comfort. The ritual bath apparently formed part of a larger complex of public buildings. At a later stage, possibly in the 6th or 7th century AD, an oilpress was added. A sewage channel north of the synagogue yielded a hoard of hundreds of coins, the latest of which date to the time of Constantine the Great, and according to the excavators, mark the end of the existence of the synagogue (*Synagogues). The residential quarter of the Jewish town was tentatively dated to the 2nd-4th centuries AD.

The new excavations in 1980 uncovered remains of the earliest phases of occupation, of the 1st and 2nd centuries AD. It was also established that some of the buildings which reused earlier architectural stones date to the 12th and 13th century AD, and not earlier, as was previously thought. This also applies to the two public buildings near the synagogue, which were in continuous use from the late 3rd-early 4th to the 13th century AD. Four trial pits were made in the area of the synagogue. The building was apparently repaired during the course of the 6th century AD. Near the main entrance to the prayer hall was found a hoard of about 1000 coins, most of them of the late 6th-early 7th century AD. Trial pits were also dug inside the synagogue. In its earliest phase it was paved with stone slabs laid on a layer of earth above virgin rock. The stone benches also belong to this early phase. In a later phase the stone pavement was replaced by a plastered floor. The benches were repaired with small uncut stones. Underneath the stone pavement were two early 4th century AD coins, which assist in dating the construction of the synagogue to the late 3rd-early 4th century AD.

CHURCHES Literary evidence (Acts 1:13-14; 2:46) shows that the earliest congregational meetings of the disciples of Jesus, for prayer, the eucharist and the agape (a love-feast held in connection with the Lord's supper) took place in private houses. The first archaeological evidence is the community house at *Dura Europos, dated to the first half of the 3rd century AD. Built as a peristyle house (*Houses) with a courtyard, several rooms on three sides and a portico on the fourth, it was altered in AD 231 to serve as a meeting-place for the city's Christian community. The reception room with benches on three sides was connected with the adjacent room, providing space for 50-60 people. In another room a baptistery was installed.

Church construction on larger scale began under the Emperor Constantine, when sanctuaries were erected to commemorate holy places. Thus we find a church at *Bethlehem built over the Grotto of the Nativity and a church at *Jerusalem over and around Mount Calvary and the Holy Sepulcher. At *Ramat el-Khalil, near Mamreh, a small church was built near the enclosure of the oak of Abraham, venerated by Jews and Christians. Churches at this time do not follow a standard plan.

The Church of the Nativity at *Bethlehem consisted of a forecourt (100 feet long) which opened into an atrium (148 feet by 92 feet) enclosed by a colonnade. The nave and its four aisles, separated by two colonnades on each side, formed an almost square enclosure (93 feet by 95 feet). To the east of the basilica an octagon was attached, raised by seven steps and flanked by rooms. From the center of the octagon it was possible to look through the floor into the cave where tradition places the birth of Jesus. Each part of the church had its function: the forecourt served as a place for the pilgrims to rest, the atrium was open to everybody, and in the basilica the congregation attended services. The location of the altar is unknown. The octagon was reserved for the clergy, being essentially the shrine commemorating the site of the birth.

In *Jerusalem the association of a basilica with a martyrium occurs in the original church of the Holy Sepulcher. Little of the early church has remained but Eusebius gives a fair idea of the layout. The traditional site of the sepulcher, a rock-cut tomb, was hewn into a conical shape and surrounded by 12 columns supporting a canopy. The ground from the sepulcher to the Roman main street to the east, a distance of some 400 feet, was levelled. Mount Calvary, about 90 feet southeast of the tomb, was cut into a cube, and together with the tomb was enclosed by a courtyard with a portico which was probably curved at its west end. To the east this courtyard was attached to the basilica and an atrium. The basilica was shallow and wide. The nave was flanked by double aisles on each side. To the west, near the courtyard of the rock and the sepulcher, a structure of 12 columns, forming a nearly full circle, supported a dome. As at *Bethlehem, it was attached to the nave. The octagonal structure at *Bethlehem and the circular one at *Jerusalem recall the mausolea of the late Roman empire.

The 5th century AD saw an increase in church building, which reached its peak in the 6th century. More than 200 churches have been surveyed or excavated in Palestine and Syria. They were mainly of the basilical type, deriving from the Greek and Roman courts of justice with the tribunal in the apse. Further types are the centralized church, the cruciform church and the chapel. Churches were usually placed in the center of towns or villages. A large city like *Gerasa had a dozen churches, all beautifully constructed.

THE BASILICA This type has several subdivisions. The standard basilica has a tripartite hall with a nave and two or sometimes four aisles. (*Nessana, the Church of Mary, mother of God; *Mampsis, the eastern and western churches; *Gerasa, the Cathedral, the Church of St Theodore, the Church of Sts. Peter and Paul, among others.) The aisles and the nave terminated in the east, to which the churches were always orientated, sometimes in three apses, the central one being larger (*Nessana, Church of St Mary). Or else the nave would have a central apse flanked by two rooms, one the *prothasis*, where the eucharist was prepared, the other the *disconicon*, where the priests dressed (cathedral at *Gerasa).

Recent studies on the churches of the Negev have shown that contrary to the accepted view, which maintained that the typical church of this region was the triapsidal type, it was rather the church with one apse which was dominant. Moreover, some churches which originally had a single apse were converted into triapsidal buildings in a later stage of their history (e.g. the North and South Church at *Sobata and the East Church at *Elusa) because of changes in the performance of the cult of saints and martyrs. Almost all churches in the Negev were dedicated to saints, two or more in each church. Some of these churches attracted great numbers of pilgrims, who came to pay their respects to the saints on certain days of the year, commemorating their martyrdom. In the beginning the relics of the saints were placed in a reliquary above or below a small altar, in the rear walls of the rectan-

The church in the central quarter, Sobata

gular rooms flanking the single apse. This caused inconvenience when large numbers of pilgrims wished to come in close contact with the box containing the relic. By constructing shallow apses, in the form of large semicircular niches, the relics were brought closer to the public. This change occurred in about AD 500. The main altar stood in front of the central apse on a dais, separated from the church by chancel screens. These were slabs of marble joined by screen posts, all decorated with geometric and floral designs, more rarely with crosses or animals. In the west of the church there was a square or rectangular atrium surrounded by a portico.In the center was a cistern (as in the churches of the *Negev, where water had to be stored) or a basin, known as the *cantharus* (*Mampsis, both churches; church at Ras Siyagha on Mount *Nebo). Sometimes church and atrium were separated by a narthex, an antechamber (*Sobata, the North Church; *Heptapegon, the Church of the Multiplication of Loaves and Fishes; Shavei Zion; Evron).

Another important feature of the church is the baptistery. This was usually a rectangular chapel attached to the church, with a basin, mostly cruciform in plan, below floor level with steps descending into it. Such was the baptistery in a church at *Beth-Yerah. At *Sobata the baptistery of the South Church is found within the church complex, but as a separate chapel with an apse. At *Susita the baptistery was a separate church with three aisles, the font in the central one. A quatrefoil baptistery was found in an apsidal chapel to the south of the church at Ras Siyagha on Mount *Nebo.

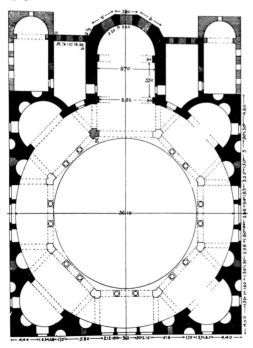

The cathedral at Bostra (Bozrah), Byzantine period

An extension of the basilica-type church is the church with an apsidal or rectangular transept. Churches of this type are quite rare in Palestine and Syria. An apsidal transept appears in the Church of the Nativity at *Bethlehem, while a rectangular transept is found in the church at *Heptapegon. The last group is the unroofed basilica, or *basilica discoperta*, where the nave is open to the sky while the aisles are covered. A single example has been found so far, at *Caesarea, near the Byzantine cemetery.

THE CENTRALIZED CHURCH The earliest of this type is the octagonal Church of the Theotokos on Mount *Gerizim. It is also one of the few free-standing churches with no buildings attached to it. Built in AD 484 by the Emperor Zeno, it has a central octagonal room covered by a dome resting on eight corner piers and seven pairs of columns. The room is surrounded by an octagonal ambulatory which has three entrance porticos and a chancel with an apse on the main axis and four chapels in the diagonals. The round church found at *Beth-Shean belongs to this type, consisting as it does of two circles with a chancel and an apse attached to the outer circle on the east and several rooms on the west. The cathedral at Bostra (*Bozrah), built in 512, has a square plan with an apsidal chancel to the east flanked by two rooms on each side. The interior is circular and decorated with four large and several smaller niches. Above the center a dome rested on four corner piers and 16 pairs of columns. The church of St George at Ezra, about 30 miles from Bostra, and the Church of St John the Baptist at *Gerasa had the same general plan.

THE CRUCIFORM CHURCH The earliest example of this type is a church at *Gaza, built in 401. The Church of the Prophets, Apostles and Martyrs at *Gerasa, built in 645, is square with a small projecting apse. In the corner of the cross are four rooms. The four arms are divided into a nave and aisles by 30 columns.

THE CHAPEL The usual chapel is a single-naved building with an apse. It is found attached to large churches (*Mampsis, *Gerasa, *Sobata) or included in monasteries (*Beth-Shean). A more complex type is the chapel with an apsidal transept, three apses arranged in a trefoil pattern. Such chapels were found at Khan el-Ahmar in the Judean Hills and at Deir Dossy in the *Judean Desert.

DECORATION While the façades of the churches were simple and external ornamentation was restricted to doorjambs, lintels and the cornice, the interior was lavishly decorated with mosaic floors, carved columns, doorjambs, lintels and arches, marble chancel screens, plastered and painted walls, marble paving and facing. Such decoration was found in churches of all types and sizes. Remains of wall paintings are rare, as most walls have not survived. The best example comes from the baptistery of the community house at *Dura Europos. The evidence from churches in the Judean Desert and in the Negev shows that religious scenes from the life of Jesus and the saints seem to have been represented. Groups of glass tesserae found during excavation suggest that the walls were also decorated with glass mosaics (Church of the Nativity in *Bethlehem and of the Theotokos on

Chancel screen, limestone, Oboda

Mount *Gerizim). The mosaic pavements are very colorful, the designs being generally geometric and floral, with amphorae, animals, hunting scenes and crosses. Human figures are depicted in the funerary chapel at *Beth-Shean and in the church on Mount *Nebo. The houses and towns with trees in the churches of Sts Peter and Paul and St John the Baptist at *Gerasa are unique, as is a map of the Holy Land in a church at *Medaba.

Mosaic ornamentation in churches develops from the aniconic style (without human or animal figures) to an iconic style, in contrast to the mosaics in synagogues, where the opposite development occurred. In AD 427 an edict forbade the use of crosses and other religious symbols on pavements, so that they might not be trodden upon. The church at Evron, where the first mosaic floor, with crosses and the letters X P arranged in the shape of a cross, was overlaid by a new pavement free of such symbols, suggests that the edict was obeyed. It is not clear, however, whether it was taken into consideration everywhere, so it cannot be used with certainty for dating purposes. Inscriptions were frequently included in mosaic floors; they were mostly written in Greek, but sometimes in Aramaic, Coptic, Syriac and Latin. They include dedications with or without dates, blessings and quotations from the Bible.

CLOTHING AND FOOTWEAR
THE BIBLICAL PERIOD The Authorized Version uses several terms for clothing: apparel (1 Kgs. 10:5; 2 Chr. 9:4; Zeph. 1:8); vestments (2 Kgs. 10:22); garments (Isa. 63:3); raiment (Ezek. 16:13: Job. 27:16), etc. As no clothing has survived from the pre-biblical periods we must turn to the neighboring countries, in which statues, reliefs and wall paintings have been preserved, to obtain an idea of how the ancient Israelite may have covered his body. An Egyptian wall painting of the 12th Dynasty shows merchants coming

from the east. They are wearing some kind of long tunic, covering the whole body from neck to ankles, while others wear something resembling a kilt that reaches from the hips to the thighs. These garments appear to have been made of plain white linen, but others were of multicolored wool, arranged in stripes. The longer garment is probably of the kind worn by Joseph (Gen. 37:3).

The Bible offers little information about clothing in the early Israelite period. Achan took 'a goodly Babylonian garment' (Josh. 7:21); the Gibeonites wore 'old garments' (Josh. 9:13); Deborah speaks of a prey of 'divers colors of needlework' (Judg. 5:30); in the story of Samson's marriage and his riddle 30 sheets and 30 changes of garment are mentioned (Judg. 14:12). There is a little more information about clothing in the period of the Israelite kingdom. The poor had one garment only, referred to as 'raiment' (Exod. 22:26; Deut. 24:13), a fact which is also borne out by the letter of the poor farmer (*Inscriptions). The richer people had more and better garments (Isa. 3:22; Zech. 3:3-4). From the Hebrew text we may conclude that the clothing of that time consisted of some king of undergarment covering the lower part of the body, with a garment of 'divers colors' worn on top (2 Sam. 13:18-9) to cover the entire body and part of the arms. In addition to these women wore hoods, veils and other items of clothing which cannot be identified (cf. Isa. 3:18-23).

THE ROMAN PERIOD We have much more evidence about the clothing of this period, both literary (from the Mishna and the Talmud) and from actual garments discovered in recent years in the *Judean Desert Caves. These garments do not differ basically from those worn along the whole Mediterranean coast at that time but the observance of the Mosaic Law, which forbade the mixing of wool and linen in the same garment, can be noted. The basic garment, according to these finds, was a tunic made of two identical lengths of woollen material joined at the top, with a slit so that it could be passed over the head. The tunic was decorated with two vertical stripes. The average size of each part of the tunic was about $2^{1}/_{2}$ feet by $3^{1}/_{2}$ feet, though smaller and larger ones were also found. The tunics were red, yellow or black, with contrasting stripes in this color range, or multicolored. This garment is called *haluq* in the Mishna. The other garment found was a mantle (*talith* in Hebrew, *pallium* in Latin and *himation* in Greek). This was also made of wool, consisted of one piece of cloth and was worn over a tunic. The mantles were yellow or brown and decorated with gammas or checkerboard patterns. Some of them had weavers' marks woven into them. There were also woollen kerchiefs decorated with fringes and made in a large range of colors. There were some garments made of linen and of leather, but their exact shape could not be determined.

A large number of leather sandals were also found in the *Judean Desert Caves. These consisted of several pieces of leather stitched together. Strips of leather were attached at the heel and toe to ensure a firm grip on the foot. These tally exactly with the description of sandals in the Mishna.

COAL; CHARCOAL There is no evidence that the coal mentioned in the Bible was of mineral origin. Anthracite, a form of hard coal, is found in some places in the Middle East in upper geological strata, but it is not known whether it was exploited. It seems that in Palestine in ancient times the reference is to charcoal, which was much used in metal foundries (Isa. 44:12). Charcoal for household and industrial purposes was produced by piling up wood in beehive formation, with a funnel in the center, and covering the whole with leaves and earth. After the fire had been kindled the funnel was blocked to prevent complete combustion; slow burning for several days, in an atmosphere poor in oxygen, produced good charcoal. Charcoal was made in the same way by the Arabs in the area until recently, and a great part of the natural forest of the country was destroyed in the process.

COLUMBARIUM (plural COLUMBARIA) Meaning dovecot in Latin, the word was used in antiquity to denote a niche in a sepulchral chamber. In modern usage it refers to the monument itself, probably because of its resemblance to a dovecot. These monuments were found all around Rome and Pompeii and take the form of large rectangular chambers, partly above and partly below ground. The walls are lined with niches in symmetrical rows for the urns containing the ashes of the deceased. They were erected by people who could not afford separate burial places and who formed themselves into *collegia* (clubs) in order to raise the necessary sum by subscription. The size of the monuments varies considerably; one of the largest and most elaborately decorated was built by Livia for her slaves and freedmen and has 3,000 niches. The earliest *columbarium* found is in the Etruscan region, near Veii, which was destroyed in 396 BC and contained exclusively Etruscan objects. In Rome *columbaria* were used from the late Republic down to the Antonine period, when cremation went out of favor.

In Palestine traces of *columbaria* have been discovered in many places, but none has been found undisturbed. As their niches are usually too small to accommodate an urn most recent scholars connect

The columbarium at Marissa (Mareshah)
(Hellenistic period)

them with a cult for which doves were required, but this conclusion is mere speculation so long as no decisive archaeological, literary or epigraphical evidence can be adduced. In the course of a survey of the *Beth-Gubrin area carried out by A. Oren on behalf of the Israel Department of Antiquities and Museums more than 200 *columbaria* were located, no less than 132 cut into the soft limestone of the area round *Mareshah. Two-thirds of these *columbaria* are round or symmetrical, with a pillar in the center or near the wall. Some reach a height of 12 feet. The niches are of various shapes, cut into walls and pillars in rows. Pottery from the Hellenistic period to the 4th century AD was found in them. The remaining one-third were built to a plan resembling a symmetrical cross: a long hall intersected by another. Near the main opening there is often a cistern. In any one cave there may be anything from 500 to 200 niches arranged in rows, the average size of each being 8in square and 8in deep. From a study of their carving A. Oren concludes that most of them were cut in the 3rd century BC and the pottery associated with them shows that they were in use until the 1st century BC.

Comparison with the *columbaria* of Rome indicates that the niches could not have held urns, since they were only a quarter the size of the Roman ones. Yet the great care taken to preserve symmetry when cutting the caves, and their considerable number, with hundreds and sometimes thousands of niches, suggest that they could not have been ordinary dovecots. The same consideration, and the lack of positive evidence, militate against Oren's theory that these *columbaria* were used for breeding sacred doves for the cult of Ashtoreth-Atargatis, to whom he also attributes the temple at *Mareshah.

Y. Yadin unearthed a *columbarium* in the excavations at *Masada. The almost circular room is divided by two attached pilasters, with a passage running down the center. Niches are found along the interior wall and along the pilasters. The building has not been preserved to its full height. Again there are no indications of the original function of this *columbarium*. After an attempt to induce a dove to nest in one of the niches had failed, Yadin came to the conclusion that it was after all a burial place, built by Herod to take the ashes of his deceased slaves and servants. The *columbarium* found at *Ramat Rahel has been interpreted by M. Kochavi as being connected with some form of necrolaty (death worship). Further *columbaria* have been found at *Gezer and *Samaria, but no indication of their function has been preserved. Many more have been noted during surveys in most parts of the country.

It must be stressed that none has ever been found in its original state, as they were all pillaged in antiquity. There is still the possibility that ashes were collected, put into the niches and closed with a stone plaque, with or without an inscription commemorating the deceased. The excavation of tombs of Roman soldiers at *Mampsis has shown how little remained after cremation. The corpse was burnt on a pyre and the remains of the bones were laid in a small cavity made in the rock near the pyre.

An indication that *columbaria* were after all burial places is provided by examples from *Petra. They are among the many rock-cut tombs with beautifully carved façades situated in the lateral wadis into which the necropolis of *Petra extends. Some were cut high up in the rock and inaccessible. A traveller at the end of the last century noted that some of the niches were still closed. Another *columbarium*, consisting of three floors with a carved façade and an inner chamber with a pillar in the center, has been discovered near *Araq el-Emir, in the rocks of Wadi es-Sir. A definite solution to the question of the function of the Palestinian *columbaria* will be reached only when excavations at *Petra, or some other site, reveal one that has remained undisturbed.

A new possible solution to this intriguing problem was recently suggested by A. Negev. The majority of these installations were discovered in the *Shephelah or other rural regions which were rich in wild flowers and fruit trees ("I also think that olives are wrongly excepted, as it is certain that the largest number of swarms are produced where olive-trees are growing" (Pliny, *Nat. Hist.* XI, 8,18). Palestine is a country of the olive-tree, especially in the region in which these *columbaria* were found. Since the Holy Land was basically a land which derived its wealth from agriculture and agricultural industries, he proposed that the *columbaria* were bee-hives of a very elaborate type, which originated in the Hellenistic period, and the bees actually made their honeycombs inside the quite shallow niches. The large number of niches appearing in some of the installations — one had almost 3000 — though they averaged 300-500, can be explained because of the lack of artificial food, half of the honeycombs were left in the bee-hive as food for the bees in the dry seasons. Most of the *columbaria* are bell-shaped with a opening in the roof. By burning the dry vegetation, which covers the floors, the extraction of the honey would be made easier. Pliny (*Nat. Hist.* XI, 19, 59) wrote: "in the neighborhood of Thermodon there are two kinds (of bees), one that makes honey in trees and the other that makes it underground in a threefold arrangement of combs, and is most lavishly productive". The importance of honey in all aspects of life cannot be overestimated. The presence of the very small *columbarium* at *Masada can thus be easily explained. It is inconceivable that Herod, who erected sumptuous palaces on the site and provided it with a great abundance of water, would have left it a barren, shadeless rock, but in all probability, he planted flower gardens and probably also fruit trees, and above all palm trees which are native to this region. It is not certain whether the ancients were aware of the role of the bee in plant life, but a bee-hive or two would not have been beyond the imagination of a king like Herod.

CRETE; CHERETIM The largest and southernmost of the Greek islands in the Mediterranean. According to Ezekiel (25:16) and Zephaniah (2:5), the *Philistines originated in Crete (Authorized Version: 'Cheretim, Cherethites'). Some scholars identify the Cherethites of the Bible with *Caphtor.

Until half a century ago very little was known of the culture of Crete, and that little was drawn mainly from the ancient Greek writers, who mention Minos, the mighty ruler of Crete. The excavations by Sir Arthur Evans at Knossos and other excavators elsewhere revealed remains of the Cretans' rich culture, illustrating their great achievements in architecture, pottery, metal-work and painting. These finds shed much light on the strong influence of Crete on the history and culture of the Mediterranean countries from as early as the beginning of the 3rd millennium to the end of the 2nd millennium BC. Traces of this influence may be observed on the Greek mainland and the Aegean islands, while numerous finds attest to Crete's close cultural and commercial contancts with Asia Minor, *Egypt, *Phoenicia and Palestine, where objects have been found which were either direct imports from Crete or local imitations.

Cretan material culture may be divided into three main periods: Early Minoan (*c.* 3000-2000 BC), Middle Minoan (2000-1500 BC) and Late Minoan (1500-1200 BC). The appearance of the hieroglyphic script of Crete is attributed to the beginning of the Middle Minoan period. At first its use was limited to seals, but as time went on it was applied also to clay tablets, where it assumed a more cursive form. Later in the same period this script was replaced by what is known as Linear A script. Near the beginning of the Late Minoan period Linear B script made its appearance. Only Linear B has so far been deciphered; it proved to be an early form of the Greek language. In addition to this evidence of the highly developed Minoan culture, prehistoric remains and remains of the Iron Age and later periods have also been discovered in Crete.

CULT OBJECTS The Bible contains detailed descriptions of the objects used in the ritual of the *Tabernacle and the *Temple of Solomon, while the later Jewish literature adds information concerning the Second Temple. These sources are supplemented by archaeological finds, which help in forming a clearer picture of some of the items.

THE TABERNACLE This was taken by the Israelites on their Exodus, so the cult objects must have been comparatively small and provided with rings so that they could be carried easily. Among the items associated with the Tabernacle was the Ark of the Covenant (Exod. 37:1-5), which was made of *shittim* wood (most probably acacia which is plentiful in *Sinai and the *Negev) and plated with gold. It had rings at the corners into which staves could be inserted. Another item was the mercy seat (Exod. 37:6-9), made of gold and decorated with two cherubim. It is probably a seat of this king that is depicted on one of the ivories of *Megiddo. The table for the shewbread (Exod. 37:10-15), made of the same *shittim* wood and plated with gold, also had rings for staves. The vessels placed on this table included dishes, spoons and bowls, all made of gold (Exod. 37:16). The candlestick (*Menorah) is described in more detail (Exod. 37:17-22). It was of gold a consisted of a central shaft with six branches, three on each side, each with knops and flowers. In addition there were seven lamps (Exod. 37:23) all made of gold, as were the snuffers and snuffdishes to be used with them. There were two altars in the Tabernacle. One, the incense altar (Exod. 37:25-8), was made of gold-plated wood and measured 1 cubit square by 2 cubits high. (A cubit is thought to measure 18-22in.) It had horns at the corners and 'a crown of gold round about'. The other altar, for burnt offerings (Exod. 38:1-7), was made of wood overlaid with brass, measured 5 cubits by 5 cubits by 4 cubits and also had four horns. The vessels for use with this altar were also made of brass and included pots, shovels, basins, fleshhooks and firepans. The last object mentioned is the laver (Exod. 38:8); this was a large brass vessel for the priests' ablutions. The position of the various items is specified in Exodus (40).

THE TEMPLE OF SOLOMON The objects in the Tabernacle were the same as those used in the Temple, but as this was a permanent structure some of them were considerably larger. There were two altars in the service of the Temple. The smaller, of cedar wood covered with gold, stood before the entrance to the *debir* (Holy of Holies) (1 Kgs. 6:20; 7:48-50; Authorized Version: 'oracle') and measured 20 cubits by 20 cubits high. It probably served the same purpose as the altars in the ancient Canaanite temples, on which offerings were placed and incense burnt. The other altar, a larger one, was of brass and its place was in the court, before the porch (1 Kgs. 8:64; 2 Chr. 8:12). This altar is described in detail in Ezekiel (40:47; 41:22; 43:14-17). It had horns at the corners, like the ones found on the small portable Canaanite altars, and like those depicted in the later Nabatean rock carvings. An altar corresponding to the measurements given in the Bible,

but made of ashlars, was found at *Beer-sheba. Inside the court there was also the 'brazen sea' (1 Kgs. 7:23-6, 29, 44; 2 Chr. 4:2-5, 15; Authorized Version: 'molten'), a huge bowl-like vessel which contained 2,000 (1 Kgs. 7:26) or 3,000 (2 Chr. 4:5) 'baths', the equivalent of 1,700 or 2,800 cubic feet of water. The weight of this vessel is estimated at about 30 tons. The huge bowl rested on 12 oxen, arranged in four groups of three. Two pillars were set up in the porch of the Temple, the pillars of Jachin and Boaz (1 Kgs. 7:15-24, 41-2; 2 Chr. 3:15-17, 4:12-13). The pillars either supported the roof of the porch or were free-standing, both forms having been observed in Canaanite temples and recently also in the Israelite temple at *Arad. The purpose of these pillars remains obscure, although some experts believe that they were used for burning incense. In the Temple there were also ten bases of brass (1 Kgs. 7:27-37), each 4 cubits by 4 cubits by 3 cubits. Attempts have been made to visualize these bases by comparison with certain complicated cult objects found in some Canaanite temples, which took the form of metal basins resting on rectangular supports that could be moved on four wheels.

Among the other vessels of the Temple were brass pots, lavers, shovels and basins (1 Kgs. 7:40, 43, 45), the table of gold on which the shewbread was placed (1 Kgs. 7:48) and 10 candlesticks of gold (1 Kgs. 7:49) served with bowls, snuffers, basins, spoons and censers, all of gold (1 Kgs. 7:50). A few comparable vessels have been uncovered by archaeological excavations in strata of the Bronze and Iron Ages.

Part of the mosaic in the synagogue at Beth-Shean, depicting the Torah Shrine, the Menorah and other ritual objects

THE SECOND TEMPLE Here too similar vessels were in use, though the altars were considerably larger to match the proportions of Herod's building. The main sources of information about these are the Mishna, the writings of Josephus (*War* xv, 184-237) and the reliefs on the triumphal arch of Titus in Rome. According to Josephus there were a lampstand (*Menorah), a table and an alter for incense in the inner sanctuary (*War* v, 217). The altar of burnt offerings (*War* v, 225) was considerably larger than the one in the First Temple, being 50 cubits square and 15 cubits high. It also had horns at its four corners and was approached from the south up a gentle slope.

CULT OBJECTS FOUND IN EXCAVATIONS Many vessels, mainly of stone or clay, to which a cultic significance is ascribed have been found in and around numerous Canaanite temples as well as in private dwellings of the Bronze and Iron Ages. Among these are a large number of censers, of three kinds. Cylindrical pottery censers, about 2 feet high, are common; they are pierced with small openings and ornamented with reliefs, frequently of snakes, or with incised decoration. A pieced bowl in which the incense was burnt was placed on top. Another group consisted of stone or clay bowls decorated with the head of an animal in relief. There were also ladles made of bone or clay, with an aperture in the side to which a pipe was attached. The incense was placed in the bowl and kept burning by air being blown through the pipe. Bowls with tiny cups attached to their rims or with seven small cups in the center were found on many sites. These were probably for offerings of precious oils or aromatics. In private houses there were numerous figurines of goddesses, depicted naked and supporting their breasts; they are believed to have been connected with a popular fertility cult. Many are of the Israelite period and probably belong to the popular cults against which the prophets so frequently inveighed.

Small menorahs made of bronze and silver were recently found in the *synagogues of *Beth-Shean, Khirbet *Susiya and *En-Gedi.

CULT OBJECTS IN SYNAGOGUE AND CHURCH Little if anything of the cultic furniture of the synagogues has come to light, so that present knowledge depends upon artistic representations, mainly on mosaic floors, showing the Torah Shrine, menorah, *shofar* (ram's horn), incense shovel, *lulab* (palm branch), and *ethrog* (citrus fruit), which were used in the ritual for specific festivals. Small menorahs made of bronze and silver were recently found in the *synagogues of *Beth-Shean, Khirbet *Susiya and *en-Gedi. In numerous churches both artistic representations and actual objects have been found, including crosses, incense burners and other vessels used in the ritual, not much unlike those still in use in churches today.

CUSH *See* *ETHIOPIA

CUTHAH; CUTH One of the cities from which the Assyrians brought settlers to replace the Israelites deported from *Samaria in 722 BC (2 Kgs. 17:24, 30). It seems that the men of Cuthah formed the majority of the settlers of *Samaria, as the name Cuthite was applied to the inhabitants of the city from that time onwards. Documents found at Tell Ibrahim, 16 miles north of *Babylon, mention the city of Gudha, or Cutha, with which biblical Cuthah is identified by some scholars. This town in the Babylonian kingdom attained great importance after the decline of the city of *Babylon. A great temple dedicated to Nergal, a god venerated also by the Cuthites (2 Kgs. 17:30), stood there.

CYPRUS The third-largest island in the Mediterranean, in the northeastern reaches, south of Cilicia in Asia Minor, with an area of 3,584 square miles. Excavations and intensive research were begun there in the 1920s by the Swedish Cyprus Expedition under E. Gjersted, continued independently in the 1930s by P. Dikaios and, more recently, by V. Karageorghis.

The earliest remains of human settlement cover the Neolithic and Chalcolithic periods and are dated by carbon 14 tests to the period from 5800-2300 BC (*Archaeology, Methods of Research). During excavations two phases of the Neolithic culture plus an intermediary phase and two phases of the Chalcolithic culture have been identified. The sequence of these cultures on the island is not known with certainty, but it seems that during these $3^1/_2$ millennia there were substantial periods when the island was uninhabited. The first pottery was made in Cyprus only in the second phase of the Neolithic period. The majority, which is of excellent quality, was the monochrome red lustrous ware though a small proportion was combed

Jug from Cyprus, Late Bronze Age

ware (*Pottery). In the Chalcolithic period pottery developed still further, Cypriot examples being distinguished by their high-quality clay and firing and their beautiful shapes and ornamentation. On the whole Cypriot culture developed on essentially local lines for about 3,000 years between 5800 and 2300 BC. But during the Early Bronze Age, called here Early Cypriot, pottery shows Anatolian influences, the first indication of foreign trade contacts.

In the Middle Bronze Age Cyprus's connections with her powerful continental neighbors became stronger. The culture of the time is known mainly from cemeteries and only in the last phase were two settlements investigated in addition to tombs. Remains of fortifications were also found. Here people from the villages could gather in time of danger and this, together with the large number of weapons buried with the deceased, indicates a period of internal strife. It seems that the biblical reference to Chittim (Jer. 2:10), a name preserved in the city of Citium (modern Lacarna), should be attributed to this period.

In the Late Bronze Age the island became closely involved with her neighbors and was influenced by their culture and their material prosperity, but she also suffered in their wars. Cyprus became an important factor in the mercantile trade from the eastern shore of the Mediterranean and *Egypt to Greece and the islands of the Aegean. It was at this time (c. 1400 BC) that Greek settlers reached Cyprus and introduced Mycenaean culture into the island. The main Mycenaean influence is noted in pottery, which now began to be made on the wheel, and was decorated with naturalistic designs.

The wealth of the island at this period is indicated by the growing use of gold, ivory, enamel and glass. For the first time in her history Cyprus now begins to be referred to in the ancient sources. In about 1450 BC it was seized by Tuthmosis III, who lists it among his conquests. It remained under Mycenaean influence during the whole of this phase. The main Mycenaean city was Salamis. That Cyprus had close contacts with Syria and Palestine is indicated by Cypriot pottery found at *Ugarit and on numerous sites in the Holy Land. The Mycenaean colonists brought with them a variant of the Minoan script, which survived down to the Classical period when it was used for writing in the Greek language. At this period Cyprus was known as Alashia; it is referred to by this name in the *El Amarna letters, in other Egyptian texts, in Hittite documents and in the epics of *Ugarit. This is probably the Elisha of the Bible (1 Chr. 1:7). At the end of the Late Bronze Age, when both the Egyptian and the Mycenaean sea powers declined, Cyprus was left alone.

The introduction of iron into Cyprus occurred during the Iron Age and, as elsewhere in the Eastern Mediterranean area, its appearance was accompanied by a strong cultural, economic and political upheaval. There is evidence of a great cultural decline in Cyprus at this time. The pottery of the period is decorated with simple designs, and gold and silver are rare.

In about 800 BC the *Phoenicians reached Cyprus and settled in its cities, mainly Citium and Idalium (modern Dali). They used the ports of Cyprus as halts on their long trade route to Cornwall, from which they imported tin, which is essential in the production of bronze. A change in the island's status occurred in 709 BC, when it was conquered by Sargon II of Assyria. Somewhat later, in 670 BC, it came under direct Assyrian rule.

In the 6th century BC, after the fall of Assyria, Cyprus became an Egyptian possession, ruled by a local prince who acted as governor. At this period the island was subdivided into a large number of city-states ruled by petty kings. In 525 BC, after the rise of Persia, Cyprus became part of the Persian empire. The Greek settlers, together with the Ionians, rose against Persia but were crushed. In 480 BC 150 ships built of timber from Cyprus took part in Xerxes' expedition against the Greeks. In the following century there was a struggle between the Greek settlers and the *Phoenicians for control of Cyprus. When Persia was conquered by Alexander the Great Cyprus welcomed Alexander and supplied him with timber to build ships for his siege of *Tyre. After the death of Alexander the island was held by Antigonus, but it was soon seized by the Ptolemies, who held it until the Roman conquest. Because of its natural riches Cyprus was considered to be a jewel in the crown of Egypt.

In 58 BC Cyprus was conquered by the Romans and became a Roman province, a status which she retained until AD 395. With the conquest of the island Rome laid her hand on an immense treasure, collected there by pirates who had made the island their base. Early in the Roman period, and perhaps even in the time of the Ptolemies, Cyprus had a large Jewish community. Stephen travelled all the way there to preach to the Jews (Acts 11.19-20). Barnabas, a native of the island, revisited it twice and was finally martyred at his birth-place, Salamis. In AD 117, just before the accession of Hadrian, the Jews of Cyprus revolted against Rome and large numbers of the insurgents lost their lives. The rest were expelled from the island by a decree of the Roman Senate. After the division of the Roman Empire (AD 395) Cyprus became part of the Byzantine realm and the capital of the island was transferred from Paphos to Salamis, now renamed Constantia. At the beginning of the 7th century AD Cyprus was conquered by the Arabs.

D

DABERATH A Levitical city in the territory of Issachar (Josh. 21:28; Authorized Version: 'Dabareh'; 1 Chr. 6:72), mentioned in the description of the boundary of the territory of Zebulun, between Chisloth-Tabor and *Japhia (Josh. 19:12). Josephus (*Life* 126; 318; *War* II, 595) writes about the village under the name Dabaritta. In the Mishnaic period Daberath was an administrative center and Eusebius (*Onom.* 78:5) describes it in the 4th century AD as a Jewish village in the territory of Diocaesarea (*Sepphoris). Identified with Daburiyeh, on the northern slopes of Mount *Tabor.

DAMASCUS City at the foot of the Anti-Lebanon, within an oasis richly supplied with water (2 Kgs. 5:12). It is situated at the crossroads of the two main international highways of the ancient Near East, the Via Maris, connecting *Mesopotamia, the Mediterranean and *Egypt, and the King's Highway, connecting *Arabia and the *Red Sea to northern Syria (*Roads). It was an important commercial city in early times and appears in descriptions of military campaigns. The earliest written sources to mention it are the *Execration Texts, where it appears as Apum, and possibly the *Mari Tablets. In Egyptian sources it is mentioned frequently, especially in the list of Canaanite cities conquered by Tuthmosis III (15th century BC) and in the *El Amarna letters. A Hittite source records an invasion of the Damascus region *(Upi)*, which took place in consequence of the Egyptian failure against the Hittite Empire in the battle of *Kedesh-on-the-Orontes (1286 BC).

At the end of the 1st millennium BC Damascus was the center of an Aramean state conquered by David and incorporated in his empire (2 Sam. 8:5-6; Authorized Version: 'Syria of Damascus'). However, it regained independence in the time of Solomon (1 Kgs. 11:23-5) and rose to be the most important kingdom in Syria, being referred to both as *Aram and as Damascus. In this period Damascus appeared as a rival of *Hamath in central and northern Syria. Conflict between the Jewish kingdoms and the Aramean state continued from the time of Solomon throughout the 9th century BC, though none of the military campaigns was ultimately decisive.

A new enemy arose for *Aram-Damascus in the Assyrian Empire, which now sought to penetrate into Syria. After the first clash in the battle of *Qarqar in 853 BC, the Assyrians attacked several times under Shalmaneser III and Adadnirari III. About 700 BC Damascus lost a large area to Jeroboam II (2 Kgs. 14:25; Amos 6:13-14). Although Damascus entered into a coalition with Israel it was conquered by Tiglath-Pileser III in 732 BC and became the capital of an Assyrian province. Sargon II quelled an uprising in Damascus, *Samaria, *Hamath and elsewhere.

In the Persian period Damascus was an important and flourishing city (Strabo XVI, 2,20). After Alexander's conquest of Syria in 332 BC the city became Macedonian and afterwards Seleucid, gradually losing its importance in favor of the newly founded Antiochia (*Antioch-on-the-Orontes). In the 2nd and 1st centuries BC it issued bronze coins dated by the Seleucid era. At the beginning of the 1st century BC it was the capital of Demetrius III and Antiochus XII and coins struck under the name of Demetrias with the effigies of these kings are generally attributed to Damascus. In 85 BC it asked the Nabatean king, Aretas III, for help against the Itureans and was subsequently ruled by the *Nabateans (Josephus, *Antiq.* XIII, 392; *War* I 103). It was annexed by Pompey (64 BC) and added to the Province of Syria (Josephus, *Antiq.* XIV, 29; *War* I, 127). Antony granted it to Cleopatra, then Octavian recovered it for Rome. Gaius Tiberius gave it back to the Nabatean king and 2 Corinthians (11:32) attetts to a Nabatean governor and garrison under Aretas IV in AD 39. In about AD 62 it was taken over again by the Romans. For some time it was a member of the Decapolis, and most probably the capital of the league in the 2nd century AD.

Damascus is known to have had a large Jewish population. Josephus (*War* II, 561) gives an account of a persecution in the course of which about ten thousand Jews were killed and Acts 9:2 refers to the existence of several synagogues. From the Damascus Document, found in 1896 among ancient texts preserved in the Cairo synagogue, it is also known that there was a community there affiliated to the *Qumran sect and with the same way of life (*Dead Sea Scrolls). It was before the gates of Damascus that Saul of Tarsus was converted (Acts 9:1 ff.).

From the 2nd century AD onwards Damascus again became a flourishing city, receiving the title *metropolis* from Hadrian and the status of *colonia* from Septimius Severus. From the 4th century it was the seat of a bishop. It was conquered by the Arabs in 636 and the Umayyads made it their capital; it now became one of the centers of Islam.

In every city with a long history of occupation archaeological finds are rare and mainly of later periods. In the Hellenistic period there was a temple containing cult statues of Baal and Atargartis. This temple appeared on coins of Demetrius III. In Acts (9:11) a street 'which is called straight' is mentioned and this must refer either to the *decumanus* or to the *cardo*, the two main streets of a Roman town, which cross at right angles. Two theaters are known to have stood near the street 'called straight' and in the north there was a hippodrome. In the 3rd century the ancient temple was rebuilt and dedicated to Jupiter Damascenus. In about AD 338 Constantine built a covered market, the *gamma*, to the north and west of the temple area. After AD 400 the temple was converted into a Christian church, dedicated to St John the Baptist. In 705 the church was rebuilt and became a famous Umayyad mosque.

DAN (TELL); DANITES Formerly known as Tell el-Qadi, the mound of the Judge, Tel Dan, source of one of the main tributaries of the Jordan, is situated at the foot of Mount Hermon in Upper Galilee. The mound is about 50 acres in area and rises to a height of some 65 feet. It is rectangular, sloping gently inwards. The city was originally called Laish and is mentioned in the Execration Texts and the Mari documents. The identification of Laish with Dan is referred to in the Bible, notably in Judges 18:29: 'And they called the name of the city Dan, after the name of Dan their father, who was born unto Israel; howbeit the name of the city was Laish at the first.'

Archaeological excavations directed by A. Biran began in 1966 on behalf of the Department of Antiqui-

Head of a woman figurine, possibly Astarte, discovered at the high place at Dan; 9th century BC

ties and Museums, and since 1974 for the Hebrew Union College-Jewish Institute of Religion and are still in process (1985). Results thus far obtained indicate that Dan, or Laish as it was first called, was already occupied in the first half of the 5th millennium BC. It was then deserted, and re-occupied at the end of the Early Bronze Age II and prospered during the Early Bronze Age III. A number of phases were discovered representing a rich material culture. Following a gap, it was reoccupied in the Middle Bronze Age IIA. Towards the end of this period the sloping earthen ramparts similar to the fortifications of other major Near Eastern sites were built which gave the site its shape. A central supporting structure served as a core for sloping earthen ramparts built on either side of it. In one excavated section the core is built of stone and preserved to a height of 34 feet. In other sections the core was built of mudbricks. The ramparts sloped about 45° to provide a formidable defensive system. A triple arch gate of mudbrick was built in the southeastern corner of the ramparts. Stone steps led from the plain on the east to the gate and down from the gate to the street inside the city. The ramparts and the gate were constructed in the mid-eighteenth century BC.

Soon after completion the inner slope was apparently used by the inhabitants for dwellings; a number of child burials were found as well as remains of floors and walls. The city prospered and trade flourished between Laish (Dan) and the neighboring countries. In a tomb of the Late Bronze Age was found Mycenean imported ware, including a Charioteer vase dated to the 14th century BC and vessels, bronze weapons, and ivory boxes of the 13th century BC.

Towards the end of the 13th-beginning of the 12th century BC Laish was conquered by the tribe of Dan. Settlements pits were found which contained a large number of vessels including collar-rim jars. The Danites, like their predecessors, relied on the earthen ramparts for defence. During that period, and even earlier, there was a metal industry at Dan. Around the middle of the 11th century BC, the city was destroyed in a fierce conflagration. Jars, juglets, cooking pots, oil lamps and other household utensils were found in an 2-3 feet deep accumulation of ashes and burnt brick. The city was soon rebuilt and a century later Dan became the religious and administrative center of the region. Jeroboam I set up the golden calf at Dan. Remains of the temenos with an installation for water libation ceremonies, large pithoi with snake decorations, faience figurines, decorated incense stands and many vessels were uncovered. During the reign of Ahab the temenos was enlarged and a stone structure, 62 feet by 62 feet, and surrounded by an earthen courtyard, was built. Ahab also built a city wall 13 feet thick which was probably 50 feet high, an outer and inner gate with benches and a canopied structure and flagstone pavement. A four-horned altar was also discovered. From the 8th-7th centuries BC were found an upper gate with four chambers, a large flagstone square, a Hebrew inscription לאמצ written on a sherd from the shoulder of a jug, a Phoenician inscription לבעלפלט also written on a sherd and numerous vessles. In the area of the temenos was built a *lishkah* or chamber.

Head of an Ammonite king; 9th century BC

Ammonite Ashtoreth figurine; 9th century BC

Aerial view of Aroer in the Beersheba Valley

Cuneiform tablet found at Aphek at the site of the Late Canaan period palace

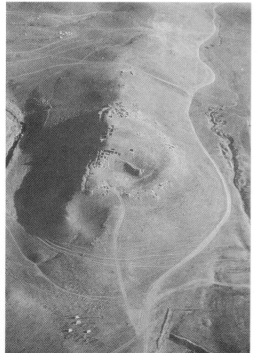

Tell Beth-Shean; general view from the south

Aerial view of Caesarea showing southwestern part and theater

The synagogue at Capernaum

Excavations at the village of the Roman and Byzantine periods east of the synagogue at Capernaum

Reconstructed synagogue at Chorazin

The "Throne of Minos" at Knossos, Crete

The Church of the Nativity at Bethlehem

Aerial view of Tell Dor: Area B; Gates area; levels from 11th century BC to Roman period

Top left: Roman period lamp depicting a satyr with Heracles headdress found at Tell Dor
Top right: Pregnant Ashtoreth from Achzib; 5th-4th century BC

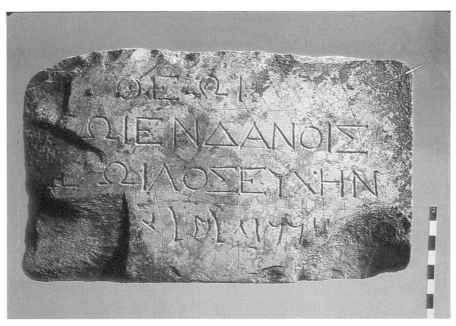

Top: High place (bamah) at Tell Dan; Iron Age to Hellenistic period
Below: Bilingual (Greek and Aramaic) inscription mentioning the god of Dan; Hellenistic period

Narthex of the synagogue at Eshtemoa

Central mosaic at the synagogue of En-Gedi

Main street at Gerasa lined with columns

Neolithic tower at Jericho

Stoa at Herod's palace, Jericho

Pottery heads from the City of David excavations; the three on the left are of the Late Bronze II; the one on the right is of the Byzantine period

Pottery vessels found in the "Bullae house", Area G of the City of David; 586 BC

Left page: General air view of the City of David, looking north

Graffito on the wall of a tomb chamber of the early 6th century BC. This is the only known inscription from the First Temple period mentioning Jerusalem by name

Excavations at the southern part of the walls of Jerusalem

The so-called burnt house recently excavated in the Old City of Jerusalem; Second Temple period

Lachish: Late Bronze Age temple at the summit of the tell, looking east

One of the "Lachish Letters" written in the last days — *of the Judean monarchy, ca. 586 BC*

Gold sheet with depiction of Ashtoreth standing on a horse, from Lachish; Late Canaanite period

Model of reconstructed city of Megiddo showing mainly Iron Age levels

Above: Aerial view of Megiddo

Stone weights and scale pans used in weighing ingots; Israelite period

Roman period temple at Philadelphia

The theater at Philadelphia

Chariot vase from the Mycenean period, discovered in tomb 387 at Tell Dan; 14th century BC

The city was probably destroyed during the Babylonian conquest but was reoccupied at the end of the Persian-beginning of the Hellenistic period. Figurines of Osiris and Bes, oil lamps and coins from this time were found. Around the 3rd century BC the temenos was enclosed by a stone wall and a basin plastered on the inside and outside added. A bilingual inscription in Greek and Aramaic 'To the God who is in Dan' confirms the identification of the site with Dan. The site continued to be occupied in the Roman and Byzantine periods. A fountain house, water pools with mosaic floors, coins and vessels were found from these periods.

DEAD SEA; SALT SEA The large lake in the lower part of the *Jordan Valley (Gen. 14:3, etc.) between the hills of *Moab on the east and the Judean Hills on the west. First name derives from the high proportion of minerals present in the water (28-33 per cent of potassium, natron, chlorine, and compounds of manganese, calcium and bromide). It is also referred to as the 'east sea' (Ezek. 47:18).

The Salt Sea, or Dead Sea as it became known in the later periods, is the earth's lowest point, lying about 1,200 feet below the level of the Mediterranean. At the north end its bottom is about 2,400 feet below sea level. About 48 miles long, its maximum width is about 11 miles. Most of the water of the lake comes from the Rivers *Jordan, *Arnon, Zered and *Kidron and from numerous other streams, most of which are dry in the summer. Because of the exceedingly high rate of evaporation the volume of water stays more or less stable. The southern part is no more than 18 feet deep and was dry in some historical periods. In Herodian times a road to *Moab passed through a part of it which is today under water. Of the natural resources of the Dead Sea only bitumen (*Asphalt), used for embalming in *Egypt, was exploited in ancient times. This was extracted and shipped to *Egypt by the *Nabateans. From the mountains on its southwestern shore salt was obtained.

DEAD SEA SCROLLS The Dead Sea Scrolls are perhaps the greatest archaeological discovery of the present century. The seven scrolls were found by a Bedouin in a cave near the northwestern shore of the Dead Sea, in 1947. Some of these were acquired by E.L. Sukenik for the Hebrew University while the rest were sold in the United States and later bought by the Government of Israel; all are now kept in the Shrine of the Book in Jerusalem. Shortly after the first discovery several scholars, and larger numbers of Bedouins, began the hunt for more scrolls. Numerous additional ones were found in the vicinity of *Khirbet Qumran, and some in four other caves to the north of that site.

The scrolls were mostly written on parchment (*Leather); only a few were on papyrus (*Writing materials). The writing was mostly in ink made of

Thanksgiving Scroll of Eulogies before being opened, from the Qumran Caves

powdered charcoal, though a metallic ink was also used. One scroll was engraved on copper sheets. In the main the scrolls were written in the Hebrew square script (*Inscriptions). Paleographic analysis has divided this script into three chronological periods: pre-Hasmonean, Hasmonean and Herodian. Certain words, such as the names for God, were sometimes written in the ancient Hebrew script.

The importance of the discovery of these scrolls is that some of them are copies of certain books of the Bible made between the 2nd century BC and the 2nd century AD, and are thus earlier by about a thousand years than any previously known copy of the Bible. They are of great value in tracing the process of codification of the books of the Bible. The scrolls fall into two main classes: manuscripts of the Bible and the Apocrypha; and the special writings of the Dead Sea sect.

THE BIBLICAL AND APOCRYPHAL LITERATURE Except for the book of Esther, complete scrolls or fragments of all the books of the Old Testament were found. The most complete texts were in cave 1, which yielded one complete scroll of Isaiah, another containing chapters 53-60 and fragments of others. One of the Isaiah scrolls differs from the current Hebrew text in the use of the full script (i.e. with all vowels, which were later partly replaced by dots below and above the letters) and also in certain grammatical forms. Other fragments of Isaiah are much closer to the present Masoretic (traditional) text. Cave 4 yielded numerous fragments of scrolls representing fourteen copies of Deuteronomy, twelve of Isaiah, ten of Psalms and eight of the twelve minor prophets. Of the Book of Exodus two copies, one of which is close to the Samaritan codex, were in the ancient Hebrew script, while six others were in the square Hebrew script, one being close to the text of the Septuagint. One copy of Numbers was written in red ink and is more detailed than the current text. Differences of this kind are found in other books from this and the other caves.

The Apocrypha includes fragments of the Hebrew or Aramaic texts of Jubilees, Enoch, Tobit, Testament of Levi, Testaments of the Twelve Patriarchs, the Wisdom of Ben-Sirah, etc. It is not known whether these books were considered by the Dead Sea sect to be as sacred as the books of the Bible. What is certain is that, unlike the copies of the books of the Bible, they were not written by the sect's own scribes. The texts of the Apocrypha found in the *Judean Desert Caves settle once and for all some doubts concerning the original language of some of the books that were previously known only from late translations; they were found at *Khirbet Qumran for the first time written in their original language. Still other books, such as the Genesis Apocryphon (written in Aramaic), were not known at all.

THE WRITINGS OF THE DEAD SEA SECT These scrolls include a large number of books peculiar to the Qumran community and other sects which dwelt in the *Judean Desert. They fall into several groups.

The Commentaries Each of these scrolls begins with a biblical passage, followed by a commentary. The commentaries include allusions to contemporary events and provide a glimpse into the history of the sect and the actions of its leader. Most complete are the commentaries on the Book of Habakkuk. Other fragments concern the Psalms, Isaiah, Micah, Zephaniah and Nahum. One scroll book, entitled 4Q Florilegium, is a compilation of commentaries on verses from Genesis (49), 2 Samuel (7) and the Psalms (2-3).

The Scrolls of Manuals In this scroll three main works are assembled. The largest and most important is the Manual of Discipline, which contains prescriptions for the annual ceremony at which the covenant between the sect and God was renewed; the ideology of the sect; its laws and regulations; the principles of religion and law; and the rules of conduct for sectarians. This part concludes with a hymn of praise to God. The other work in the Manual is the Rule for all the Congregation of Israel in the Last Days. This contains an ideal constitution for the future Israelite congregation, which will carry out the precepts of the sect. The scroll concludes with the Psalms of Thanksgiving, to be included in a certain ritual in the Last Days.

The Scroll of the War of the Children of Light against the Children of Darkness This scroll describes a future war between the people of Israel and the nations which rule the world (called Kittim in the scroll). Israel is referred to as the Children of Light, representing the righteousness of the world, while Kittim represent evil. The scroll contains a prophecy of the coming war, followed by regulations for the enrollment of the people, the ritual and the strategy of the war, including a time-table according to which the Children of Light will conquer the world. It specifies the trumpet calls and signals to be used by the warriors and describes their arms; it also lays down the tactics to be employed. The extant part of the scroll concludes with the prayers to be said before, during and after the battle. The end of the scroll is missing.

The Thanksgiving Scroll This is a collection of hymns of praise to God, usually opening with the words 'I thank thee, O Lord'. In these hymns the poet expresses his belief that all his spiritual qualities, as well as his right to be a member of the sect, are due to the grace of the Lord. Man is lowly and cannot achieve real righteousness, but God has chosen the poet and his friends, giving them unusual spiritual qualities. The poet has also been endowed with the qualities of leadership and the ability to enlighten others with the true belief. It is for this reason that he is being hunted by his adversaries.

The Damascus Document This book was already known from a later copy found in 1896 among the ancient texts preserved in the Cairo synagogue (*Damascus). Fragments of several copies were found to supplement the known text. The Damascus Document contains certain exhortations whose aim is to make the people return to the true faith. It is interwoven with the history of Israel and there are some allusions to the history of the sect as well. The second part contains rulings which differ to a lesser or greater degree from the standard regulations of the Mishnaic authorities.

The Copper Scroll This scroll consists of two rolls of copper found in cave 3. Written in Hebrew, it contains a list of hiding-places in Palestine containing fabulous treasures, with instructions for reaching them. Whether these were real treasures of the Temple or the sect or purely imaginary is still a matter of dispute. In any case, attempts to locate some of the treasures listed have ended in complete failure. Nor is it known whether this scroll originally belonged to the Dead Sea sect or whether it dates from one or two generations later.

In addition to the foregoing, numerous small fragments of many other sectarian writings were discovered. That the sources have not yet been exhausted is proved by two new finds, of a complete phylactery which differs in some details from those now in use, and of the 'Temple Scroll', which is perhaps one of the most exciting so far revealed.

The Temple Scroll. This scroll appeared on the antiquities market in 1960 and was acquired in 1968. Apart from being one of the most important documents found in the *Dead Sea Caves, it is also the largest; its overall length is about 26.5 feet and it is 9.5-10in high. It deals with the following subjects: *a)* the festivals; *b)* offerings and holy gifts; *c)* the Temple and its courts; *d)* the Temple City and the laws of uncleanness and purity; *e)* the statutes of the king; *f)* miscellaneous laws. The ordinances on all these matters are known only in part from *halakhic* sources; many are unique to the Dead Sea sect and are meant to clarify the *halakhic* meaning of the commands. The festivals begin with the First day of the month of Nissan, the days of ordination, and the Passover and the Feast of Unleavened Bread - in each case the number and quality of sacrifices are specified, as is the case with the other festivals. This is followed by the feasts of First Fruits. Many of these festivals and the ritual connected with them are unknown from other sources. The festivals include: the Feast of First Fruits of Barley - the Day of Waving the Sheaf (celebrated on Sunday, the 26th of the 1st month of the sectarian calendar); the Feast of First Fruits of Wheat (Sunday, the 15th of the 3rd month); The Feast of First Fruits of Wine (Sunday, the 3rd of the 5th month); the Feast of First Fruits of Oil (Sunday, the 22nd of the 6th month). Next comes the Feast of Wood Offering (beginning on Monday, the 23rd of the 6th month), for which there is only scanty evidence from other sources. This cycle of festivals terminates with the Day of Memorial (Wednesday, the 1st of the 7th month), the Day of Atonement (Friday, the 10th of the 7th month), the Feast of Booths (Wednesday, the 15th of the 7th month), and the Eight Days of Assembly (Wednesday, the 22nd of the 7th month). The section on offerings and holy gifts deals with Sin Offerings, the Cereal and the Drink Offerings, dues from the Peace Offering and Profane Slaughtering, Levitical tithes, the Holy Fruit Offering of Praise and the Tribute Offering. The most detailed sections deal with the Temple. They begin with a detailed plan of the Temple, its dependencies, courts and furniture and clarify hitherto obscure points. This is followed by ordinances concerning uncleanness and purity in conjunction with entry into the Temple, the Temple City and other cities and laws concerning uncleanness contracted from the dead and from carcasses. Next are given the statutes of the king, dealing with matters such as the organization of the army, the royal guard, the judicial court, the wife of the king and the laws of marriage and divorce, and the laws of war and booty. The scroll terminates with miscellaneous laws dealing with the beautiful woman captive, the "seduced" woman and the "seized" woman, laws of incest, laws concerning hanging on a tree, laws concerning evidence, capital offences, matters of property and the death penalty for one who takes a bribe or perverts righteous judgement. The Temple Scroll is tentatively dated to the beginning of the 2nd century BC.

THE BAR-KOCHBA PERIOD In addition to the manuscripts found in the vicinity of *Khirbet Qumran, documents of the Roman, Byzantine and Arab periods were discovered in the locality. Many of the caves in which these were found are still known only to the Bedouins who discovered them. The most important date from the time of the Bar-Kochba rebellion (AD 132-5) and the period immediately preceding it. They belonged to fugitives who found shelter in the caves of the wadis running down to the *Dead Sea (*Judean Desert Caves), mainly in Wadi Murabbaat, Wadi Khabra and Wadi Seiyal. Among them were fragments of biblical literature, in Hebrew and in Greek translations, phylacteries, legal and administrative documents (including copies of lists of taxpayers) and a scroll on which copies of contracts were written, according to which the people of the town of Irnahash leased land from 'Simon Bar Koseba Nasi of Israel'. There were also letters written by Bar-Kochba himself, or on his instructions, to his subordinates. Some of these documents were found by the Bedouins in caves in Israeli territory and were subsequently published by foreign scholars as documents 'of unknown provenance'. This group of documents is most important for the study of a period in Jewish history of which very little is known. They offer a glimpse into

Bar-Kochba's administration, the military and police organization, the system of supplies for his soldiers, leases of public lands, marriage contracts, the Roman administration in the years preceding the revolt and relations between the Jews and their Nabatean neighbors. Of great importance also are the fragments of biblical texts (Genesis, Exodus, Numbers, Deuteronomy, Isaiah, Amos, Obadiah, Jonah and Micah), which are very close to the Masoretic text now in use. This means that the editing of the books of the Bible must have been done by the generations following the destruction of the Second Temple.

DEBIR An ancient Canaanite city whose former name was *Kiriath-Sepher (Josh. 15:15; Judg. 1:11). The city was conquered by Othniel, the son of Kenaz (Judg. 1:13), and its ruler was one of the Canaanite kings vanquished by Joshua (Josh. 12:13). It was later one of the cities of Judah (Josh. 15:49). and of the Levites (Josh. 21:15; 1 Chr. 6:58). Debir was identified by W.F. Albright with Tell *Beit Mirsim, though others have suggested different sites. It has recently been identified with Khirbet er-Rabud.

DECAPOLIS A league of ten Hellenistic cities (Josephus, *Life* 342; 410) with a Jewish minority, all (with the exception of Scythopolis) situated in Transjordan. The membership of the league, originally ten as indicated by its name, was never constant. Pliny (*Nat. Hist.* v, 74) enumerates *Damascus, *Philadelphia (*Rabbath-Ammon), Raphana, Scythopolis (*Beth-Shean), *Gadara, Hippos (*Susita), *Dium, Pella (*Pehel), *Gerasa and Canatha (*Kanath) but admits that other writers give a different list. Ptolemy (*Geography* v, 14, 18) lists different cities, omiting Raphana but adding *Abila, Lysianae and *Capitolias. Stephan of Byzantium (*Gerasa) mentions fourteen cities instead of the original ten.

The earliest mentions of the Decapolis are in the New Testament (Matt. 4:25; Mark 5:20). As most of the cities date their era from 64/62 BC it is evident that the foundation of the Decapolis was part of Pompey's settlement in the East, though the exact date is obscure. During the reign of the Hasmoneans many of the Hellenistic cities on the coast and nearly all the cities in Transjordan had lost their independence, which was restored by Pompey (Josephus, *Antiq.* XIV, 74 ff.; *War* I, 155 ff., 164 ff.). Most of the cities of the Decapolis were ancient towns which had been resettled and rebuilt by the Seleucids or the Ptolomies. They enjoyed autonomy, except for the military supremacy of the Hellenistic monarchs and the obligations to pay various taxes. Pompey placed the cities under the authority of the governor of Syria but most of them enjoyed municipal autonomy, having their own courts and their own finance, with authority to strike coins and to reckon according to local eras.

*Gadara was the first capital of the league but *Damascus took over later. According to Josephus (*War* III, 446) *Scythopolis was the largest of the cities; thus *Damascus cannot have been a member in his time. The main area of the Decapolis was to the southeast of the Sea of *Galilee, where the city territories of *Hippos, *Gadara and *Pella formed a broad strip between the *Perea and the Tetrarchy of Philippus. On the other side of the Jordan was the territory of *Scythopolis, which guarded the road to the Mediterranean and was thus an essential member of the league.

The changing history of single cities did not affect the unity of the league, which continued in existence until late into the 2nd century AD. *Hippos and *Gadara were given to Herod as a present by Augustus, while *Abila went to Agrippa II. The transfer of *Philadelphia and *Dium to the province of Arabia after AD 106, and of *Gerasa at a later date, seems to have brought about the dissolution of the league.

DEIR ALLA (TELL) One of the most prominent ancient mounds in the Jordan Valley, situated $7^1/_2$ miles north-northeast of the junction of the Jabbok and the Jordan Rivers. It is identified by many scholars with biblical Succoth (Gen. 33:17; Josh. 13:27; Judg. 8:5; 1 Kgs. 7:46). In the Palestinian Talmud a place by the name of Tarela, or Derela, is mentioned, which already at that time was identified with Succoth. The Arab name has preserved the talmudic form.

The site was excavated in 1960 by H.J. Franken, on behalf of the University of Leyden. The earliest remains on the site are of a village of the Chalcolithic period. From the Late Bronze Age there is a sanctuary complex. In the beginning a holy of holies was built on a small artificial mound, and pillars (*massebot*) were placed around it. This was apparently an open air sanctuary; it was destroyed in the early 12th century BC. In the Iron Age I (12th to 10th century BC) a metal workers' village existed on the site. In the later stages of the Iron Age settlers identified as Arameans, with a completely different ceramic tradition typical of the 8th to 7th century BC, inhabited the site. The most spectacular discovery here was an early Aramaic inscription, the longest early Aramaic inscription ever found. It mentions Balaam, a non-Israelite biblical prophet.

DEIR EL-BALAH A site situated about 1 mile east of the Mediterranean coast and 7 miles southwest of Gaza. The ancient name of the site is unknown. In the years 1972-82 extensive excavations were carried out on the site on behalf of the Hebrew University, directed by T. Dothan. Beneath 45 feet of an accumulation of sand dunes were unearthed levels of occupation ranging from the Late Bronze Age to the Byzantine period. The main effort of the excavation was concentrated on the investigation of the extensive Late Bronze Age settlement and cemetery.

The earliest settlement on the site goes back to the second half of the 14th century BC, the *El Amarna period. To this period belongs a residence built alongside a man-made pond, measuring 60 feet by 60 feet. This pond, originally used as a quarry for brick material subsequently served as a water reservoir. There is a similarity between the construction and plan of the residence and buildings of the same period at El Amarna in Egypt. The residence was composed of three buildings, two constructed on a single axis and the third extending to the east. The longer unit contained 15 rooms and the smaller one, four-five. The large quantity of animal bones found in the debris filling the pond indicates that the occupants lived on animal husbandry. A large amount of pottery of the El Amarna period was discovered. In one of the loci were found cylindrical pieces of jaspar and blue frit with traces of gold. These were reconstructed as a staff or a flail, of a type found, inter alia, in the tomb of Tutankhamun. Above the remains of this settlement were traces of another, short-lived settlement, and above these was a fort or tower complex which was built near the pond, which was still in use. The fortress, 60 square feet, has corner towers and contains 15 rooms. It is dated to the beginning of the 13th century BC. It is not known how long it was in use. The following settlement contained an artisan's quarter and an industrial area. The new structures, in which two phases were distinguished, were built above the filled-in pond. Kilns and a water installation which were apparently connected with the preparation of clay for the coffins used in the cemetery and their firing were also discovered. The artisans also produced many of the offerings deposited with the dead. Both phases of settlement date to the 13th century BC and overlap with most of the 19th dynasty. Five pits containing *Philistine *pottery were dug into the levels of the Late Bronze Age. The settlement of this period apparently extended southwest of the excavated area, and is now concealed under the heavy sand dunes. The pottery found in the pits is dated to the second half of the 12th and early 11th century BC. Only few remains of the Iron Age (10th-early 9th century BC) were uncovered. There are extensive remains of the Byzantine period, at which time, according to the historical sources, a monastery was built at the site.

THE CEMETERY The cemetery was in continuous use during the 14th and 13th centuries BC. Its main feature is the burial in clay coffins. Two to four bodies were deposited in each coffin which were laid in graves excavated in the *kurkar* stone or red sand. Between the coffins were simple burials. The coffins, cylindrical in shape, are 5-6 feet long. The upper part is closed by a removable lid, on which the facial features, wig, arms and hands of a man are modelled in high relief. The coffin lids vary greatly in style, but this difference does not necessarily indicate a chronological difference. Among the funerary offerings were stelae with hieroglypic inscriptions, scarabs — some, royal scarabs of the 19th and 20th Dynasties — *alabaster vessels, and a great quantity of local and imported pottery vessels (Mycenaean, Cypriote and Egyptian).

DIBON a) A town in the *Negev of Judah, mentioned only since the time of the Restoration (Neh. 11:25). Not identified.
b) A city of *Moab, known also as Dibon-Gad, north of the River *Arnon, conquered by Sihon, King of the *Amorites (Num. 21:30). One of the stations on the route of the Exodus (Num. 33:45-6). According to Numbers (32:34) it was built by the children of Gad, but in Joshua (13:17) it is listed among the towns of Reuben. A fort named Dibon is depicted on one of the reliefs of Rameses II at Luxor. The famous stele of Mesha, King of *Moab, was found at Dibon (*Inscriptions).

It was also known in the Roman period, and the Jewish sources mention a large Jewish village there. Eusebius (*Onom.* 16:18) refers to it as a large town near the *Arnon. Excavations at Dibon were conducted on behalf of the American School of Oriental Research in Jerusalem under the direction of F.V. Winnett (1950-1), W.L. Reed (1952), A.D. Tushingham (1952-3) and W.H. Morton (1955). The earliest traces of occupation on the mound go back to the Early Bronze Age. After a very long gap the summit of the mound of Dibon was inhabited by the *Moabites in the Iron Age I, who built a sanctuary and a number of public buildings. In the Iron Age II (mid.-9th century BC) a royal quarter was established in the southeast part of the site, presumably by Mesha King of Moab, centered around a citadel. This area was still occupied in the last quarter of the 8th century BC. By the end of the 7th or beginning of the 6th century BC, in the period preceding the destruction of the city in 582 BC, the walls of the citadel were strengthened by great buttressed walls.

The *Nabateans built a *temple on the site of the citadel, on the traditional Canaanite-Israelite plan (*Temples). The temple was erected under Aretas IV (9 BC-AD 40) and renovated under Rabel II (AD 70-106) (*Nabateans). No remains of Nabatean dwellings or other structures were discovered on the site. To the 3rd century AD is attributed a building tentatively identified as a *bath-house and a section of a wall, possibly a fort. In the Byzantine period two churches were constructed on the site, one above the remains of the Nabatean temple. The site was still sparsely settled in the 8th and 12th-13th centuries AD.

DIONYSIAS Identified with modern Suweida, the main city of the Jebel ed-Druz area, its ancient name was Soada, as mentioned in inscriptions found on the site. From the middle of the 3rd century AD it was known as Dionysias, a center of the cult of Dushara-Dionysus. It also appears by this name in the episcopal lists. It was one of the earliest Nabatean cities and an important city throughout the Roman and Byzantine periods. In the Byzantine period it was part of Palestine Tertia. The Nabatean remains include a temple, a funerary monument from the 1st century BC and a dedicatory inscription of Dushara from AD 147. Further architectural remains are a *nymphaeum*, a theater, a bridge and a basilica.

DIUM; DION A city of the *Decapolis, founded by Alexander the Great or by Perdiccas, or in the course of the Ptolemaic consolidation of the territory won from the Seleucids. Named after a Macedonian city. Alexander Jannaeus conquered it in his second compaign (Josephus, *Antiq.* XIII, 393) and Pompey restored its autonomy (Josephus, *Antiq.* XIV, 75; Ptolemy, *Geography* V, 14, 18). Coins from the time of Caracalla and Geta use the Pompeian era and show a draped male divinity that occurs on other Syrian coins and is identified with Zeus-Hadad. The identification of Dium is still disputed, though most scholars place it at Tell Ashari, 9 miles northwest of *Edrei.

DIVINATION See *WITCHCRAFT AND DIVINATION.

DOLMEN Meaning 'stone table' in Breton (*dol*, 'table', plus *men*, 'stone'), this is a prehistoric megali-

Dolmen, east of the Jordan, south of the Yabbok River

thic funerary monument made of one or more blocks of stone placed horizontally over a few vertical ones to form a table-like structure, sometimes surrounded by one or two circles of smaller stones. Monuments of this type have been found in many places in Europe, notably in France. Many dolmens have also been found in Palestine, concentrated mainly in Upper *Galilee and northern Transjordan. They are mostly built on four large vertical stones, measuring about 9 feet by 12 feet, covered by another large stone. In most cases they are surrounded by one or two circles of small stones.

Originally dolmens were completely covered with small stones and earth, which has since been washed away. Each served as a burial place for one or more people. In Upper *Galilee more than two hundred dolmens have been counted, mostly in the vicinity of *Chorazin, while in Transjordan they total about twenty thousand, found in groups of three hundred to a thousand each. Some dolmens have been excavated and dated by their contents to the Chalcolithic period and Early Bronze Age. (*See also* *PREHISTORY.)

DOPHKAH One of the stations on the route of the Exodus, between the wilderness of Zin and Alush (Num. 33:12). Some see a connection between this name and the Egyptian word *mafkat*, 'turquoise', and for this reason locate it in the region of *Serabit el-Khadem in the *Sinai Peninsula, where the Egyptian mined this mineral.

DOR; DORA One of the important Canaanite city-states in the league of Jabin, King of *Hazor (Josh. 11:2). It was among the cities of Manasseh in the territory of Asher, but according to Judges (1:27) it was not conquered by them. Solomon appointed the son of Abinadab as overseer of the region of Dor, which was the fourth district of his kingdom (1 Kgs. 4:11). According to the Egyptian documents it fell into the hands of the Zakkala, one of the Sea Peoples (*Philistines), early in the 12th century BC. Under the name of Du'ru it belonged to the Assyrian province of the same name.

In the Persian period, when the cities on the coast were granted autonomy, Dor became a Sidonian colony. In the early Hellenistic period it was a Ptolemaic royal fortress. At the end of the 2nd century BC Dora was in the hands of the tyrant Zoilus, who also ruled Strato's Tower (*Caesarea). Alexander Jannaeus acquired the two cities by negotiation. After conquering the country (63 BC) Pompey restored Dora to its former owners, as was his policy with all cities that had formerly been autonomous. The city retained its freedom during the reign of Herod and his successors. A change in status came about early in the 2nd century AD, when it was annexed to the province of *Phoenicia. In the late Roman period it became part of Palestina Prima. Eusebius (*Onom.* 78:9; 136:16) states that it is 9 miles from Caesarea.

The excavations at Dor, which is identified with Tantura, have shown that it was founded by the Egyptians in the 15th or 14th century BC. It was already an important harbor, which, as is indicated by the finds, had close connections with Cyprus and the Aegean countries. The most important remains, however, belong to the Hellenistic-Roman period. At that time the harbor was divided by a cliff into two parts, on one of which a large tower was built. In the city itself temples to Zeus and Astarte were discovered, as well as a theater. According to Josephus (*Antiq.* XIX, 300) a synagogue existed there before the destruction of the Second Temple. The Byzantine period is represented by a church.

The first excavations at Dor were conducted by the British School of Archaeology in Jerusalem in 1920 and 1923-4. Roman Dora was excavated in 1950 and 1952 by J. Leibowitz on behalf of the Department of Antiquities.

Large scale excavations were begun at Dor in 1980 on behalf of the Hebrew University, under the direction of E. Stern. Several areas of the large 30-acre mound are being examined, all in the central part of the mound. In the upper level are remains of the Byzantine period. Below these lie remains of a city wall of the Hellenistic period, which was apparently built in the latter part of the reign of Ptolemy II Philadelphus, and was still in use in the early Roman period. The wall, built of large ashlars, is still standing to a height of 7 feet, and it has a tower with a projection of 45 feet. It is built over the remains of a city wall of the Persian period, which is composed of large uncut stones and encloses a somewhat larger city. Beneath the Persian wall were sections of a brick Israelite city wall, at least 8 feet wide. Buildings remains were found within the wall. Whereas the buildings of the Persian and early Hellenistic period followed the Phoenician method of ashlar pillars alternating with a fill of undressed stones, the later Hellenistic walls were built of headers only. A dyeing installation of the Hellenistic period yielded large quantities of murex shells. Another monumental building of the Hellenistic period contained several plastered pools. The sections of the Hellenistic city examined revealed that it had been laid out according to the Hippodamian principles of town-planning, consisting of parallel intersecting streets, which

Residential quarter of the Hellenistic period at Dor

formed a checkerboard pattern. What is surprising, however, is that at Dor this method of town planning originated in the Persian period. In the interior, adjacent to the wall, were shops opening on to a street. Little remained of the underlying Persian level, except for pottery found in pits sunk into late Israelite levels. Inside the city were uncovered channels of an elaborate sewage system and of an aqueduct (*Water-supply). From the city gate a 30 feet wide street led into the city, into an area which contained workshops of the Byzantine period. The gate of the Roman period has not been preserved. In deeper levels the gates of the Hellenistic and Persian periods were found, and beneath them an Israelite city gate, made of cyclopean boulders brought from Mt. *Carmel. In plan this gate resembles the gate of *Meggido IV-A. It consists of two guardrooms with paved squares at the front and back of the gate. Beneath this gate was a very solid gate of the four-chamber type, which is a unique example of Phoenician-Iron Age construction methods. One pilaster of the gate, facing the town, was made of polished orthostats. This gate is dated to the 9th–8th centuries BC and its destruction is ascribed to the Assyrians in 734 BC. The earliest remains of occupation of the site discovered until now belong to the Middle Bronze II period, when the site was surrounded by a glacis. Several walls were dated to the 11th century BC. Thousands of pottery vessels and other locally made and imported objects were uncovered from all levels of occupation.

DOTHAN Dothan is mentioned in the Bible in the story of Joseph and his brothers. They threw him into the pit when he went there in search of them (Gen. 37:17 ff.). It is mentioned again in connection with the *Arameans' search for Elisha (2 Kgs. 6:13; Authorized Version: 'Syrians'). It was also known in the Hellenistic

and Roman periods, in the form of Dothain. The site was known to Eusebius (*Onom.* 76:13) at a distance of 12 miles north of *Samaria. It is identified with Tell Dothan, 5 miles north of *Shechem, on the main road northwards across the hills. C.W.H. Van de Velde also identified the site in 1851.

Excavations on the site were carried out by J.P. Free on behalf of Wheaton College, Illinois, in the years 1953–60. Potsherds of the late Chalcolithic period were unearthed there. In the Early Bronze Age Dothan was a large walled town. The wall, 10 feet wide and built of undressed stones, still rises to a height of 15 feet. Seven occupation levels, all of this period, belong to this *fortification system. Dothan was again inhabited in the Late Bronze Age IIB-Iron Age I, when the site was still fortified by the old wall. The prosperity of the town is well attested by a large tomb dug into the slope which contained about one hundred bodies and one thousand complete vessels. However, most of the finds on the site belong to the Iron Age II. One street excavated was more than 90 feet long; along it were houses containing storerooms, ovens, pottery and other household utensils. One of the occupation levels of this period was destroyed by fire. It was dated by a carbon 14 test to 804 (±80) BC. A house with very solid walls from this period is believed to have been several stories high. One of its rooms contained about one hundred storage bins of identical shape and volume. The destruction of the building is attributed to the *Aramean invasion in the 9th century BC. By the end of that century it was rebuilt and enlarged and additional storerooms were added. It was still inhabited in the 8th century BC and its destruction is attributed to Tiglath-Pileser III in 782 BC, or to the fall of the Israelite kingdom in 712 BC. For a short time Dothan still flourished under Assyrian domination. The site was very sparsely settled in the Hellenistic and Roman periods.

DUR SHARRUKIN A city in northern *Mesopotamia, about 10 miles to the north of *Nineveh, built by Sargon II of Assyria as his northern capital, on the site of a small village (713 BC). Its ground plan is square and measures about 5,300 feet by 5,100 feet. It was oriented to the cardinal points of the compass and completely surrounded by a double wall. There were two gates on each side, each named after one of the chief deities of Assyria. The palace of Sargon, erected on a platform 45 feet high in the northwestern quarter of the city, consisted of a very large number of halls and chambers arranged round two large and numerous smaller courts. The façade and the walls of the more important halls were richly decorated with wall paintings. To the southwest, separated from the palace by a thick wall, stood one of the largest temples in the city. It was approached through a long, stepped hall, decorated with the Tree of Life, demons and other images. The temple itself consisted of three aisles: there may originally have been more, each dedicated to a different deity. The main entrance was decorated with enamelled panels depicting gods, the king and various symbols.

Dur Sharrukin is modern Khorsabad. It was excavated by E. Botta (1842-4), V. Place (1852-5) and others. Excavation was resumed in 1936 by the University of Chicago.

The Tent of Covenant, from painting in the synagogue at dura Europos

DURA EUROPOS One of the cities guarding the Syro-Mesopotamian frontier along the *Euphrates, founded by Macedonian settlers in about 312 BC shortly after the conquest of Syria by Alexander the Great. The name Dura is of Semitic origin, probably meaning 'wall', while Europos was added by the new settlers. At the time of its foundation it served as a fortress on the frontier of the Seleucid kingdom, and as a key point on the caravan route leading to the east. At that period it had the status of a *polis*, in which the Semitic inhabitants did not have full rights of citizenship. In the 3rd century BC it formed part of the Seleucid kingdom. In the following century the war with the Parthians took place close to its walls and it was conquered by them.

After the conquest of *Mesopotamia by Trajan in AD 116 and the foundation of a Roman province there Dura became part of the Roman Empire, serving as a frontier fortress and an important caravan halt on the route connecting the Mediterranean with the East. In the 3rd century AD, when the Romans fought the Sassanids, the city was already diminishing in importance. In AD 253 it was temporarily and voluntarily abandoned by its inhabitants, and in 272 it was finally deserted for good. The underlying reasons were the conquest of *Antioch-on-the-Orontes by Shapur I, King of Parthia, and the change in the course of the *Euphrates, which left the city too far away from this important artery. When the Emperor Julian attacked the Parthians in AD 363 he found Dura deserted.

Identified with Qalat es-Salihiya, Dura Europos has been extensively excavated, by F. Cumont on behalf of the French Academy in 1922-3, and in the years 1928-36 by M. Rostovtzeff and others on behalf of Yale University. It was founded by the Greeks and built according to the Hippodamian plan, in which the streets are laid in straight lines intersecting at right angles. It was surrounded by a wall strengthened by rectangular towers, with a gate on the south, in the direction of Palmyra (*Tadmor). Built in a bend of the *Euphrates, the city was surrounded by the river on three sides, which made access to it more difficult. In the center were the agora and numerous temples, the oldest being the temple of Artemis. Some of these were built by communities of foreign traders who lived in the city. In a residential quarter close to the northern wall was the synagogue of the large, rich Jewish community. In another quarter a very early church (dating from AD 232) was discovered. In the temples, synagogue and church there were numerous wall paintings. Those of the synagogue and church are of a special importance for the study of early Jewish and Christian art.

In the synagogue two phases of building were observed. To the first, of the first half of the 3rd century AD, belongs a rather small prayer house, hidden among private houses. This early synagogue already has paintings of biblical scenes. Of greater interest, however, is the synagogue of the second phase, of the mid-3rd century AD. This building included a large court with three colonnades and a spacious prayer room with a niche for the Torah Shrine in its southern wall, facing *Jerusalem. After AD 257 the building was partly destroyed when the Romans built fortifications on it to prepare the city against the Parthian menace. Fortunately the damage was mostly to the courtyard and only a part of the walls of the synagogue was affected. The reconstructed building stands today in the museum of Damascus. On the four inner walls of the prayer room numerous representations of biblical and allegorical scenes were depicted, many of them explained by short biblical quotations in Greek. The paintings in the synagogue of Dura Europos show affinities with Alexandrian Hellenistic art, with strong Parthian and Sassanid influences.

DYES AND DYEING Most of the earliest dyes were natural products, mainly obtained from colored earth or from certain plants and animals. It seems linen and wool were dyed in quite early times.

The curtains of the tabernacle were dyed blue, among other colors. Blue, or rather purple, was extracted from a secretion of the murex shellfish. To obtain the pigment the shellfish were crushed, cooked in salt and left in the sun for some time, so that the secretion would turn purple. This dye was used for coloring precious cloths (Esther 8:15), as well as for the fringes of garments (Num. 15:38). Purple, which is the color of the cloth cover of the altar (Num. 4:13) is often mentioned together with blue (Exod. 25:4). This pigment was made from the same shellfish but with the addition of another substance. Scarlet (Exod. 25:4) was extracted from the eggs of certain lice (*Cocus vermilio* or *Cocus ilicis L.*). The eggs were collected with the female lice, dried and pounded into a red powder, which was then ready for use. Scarlet is mentioned together with precious cloths of other colors (Exod. 28:5; Num. 4:8).

In order to make these dyes ready for use a solution of water, potash and lime was prepared. Pots which contained potash and lime were discovered in a dyeing installation at Tell *Beit Mirsim. After two days the pigments were added. The actual dyeing was done in earthenware vessels or stone basins. Remains of such installations, of both biblical and later periods, have been found in Palestine. The Arabs in the East still use the same methods for preparing pigments and dyeing.

Vermilion was used for staining wood (Jer. 22:14; Ezek. 23:14). This was probably made from red and yellow ocher, the natural iron oxide ($Fe_2 O_3$) found in Palestine and used as early as the Chalcolithic period. From the Roman period onwards red oxide of lead ($Pb_3 O_4$) was used in addition to the ochers to produce the red color.

In the realm of cosmetics, kohl was used for painting the eyelids (cf. Ezek. 28:40). This was basic carbonate of copper ($2 CuCO_3 . Cu(HO_2)$) in the Roman period galena, a sulphide of lead (PbS) with the addition of other metallic substances, was also used.

Many other artificial dyes were known in the ancient world. Dye production reached a high degree of refinement in *Egypt, where numerous specimens of painted linen, papyrus, wood, plastered and painted walls and so on have been preserved thanks to the dry climate. It has therefore been possible to analyze the pigments used. Red and yellow pigments were extracted from the safflower *(Carthanus tinctorius L.v. inermis)* and in the Roman period a yellow dye was also made from the flowers of the crocus *(Crocus L.)*. Blue was produced from isatis leaves *(Isatis tinctoria L.)*, and in the Roman period indigo *(Indigofera tinctoria L.)* was used. Black was obtained either by painting red on blue or with the use of powdered charcoal. A green pigment was produced from powdered malachite, a hydrous carbonate of copper, which was also used in cosmetics. The same substance was used to produce a blue dye. White was made from chalk, carbonate of calcium ($CaCO_3$), of gypsum ($CaSO_4$), a sulphate of calcium. For painting pottery ochers and other earth pigments were mostly used — it was only in the Roman period that lead oxides and other metallic oxides were employed to a very limited extent.

E

EBAL (MOUNT) A hill rising 2,900 feet above sea level, north of *Shechem and opposite Mount *Gerizim. Joshua built an altar of unhewn stones on its summit, as he had been commanded by Moses (Josh. 8:30-2). The tribes of Israel then assembled on the slopes of Mount Ebal and Mount Gerizim, half on each, to hear the curses and blessings connected with the observance of the Law (Deut. 11:29; 27:11-13; Josh. 8:33-4). In ancient times there was some confusion about the location of both hills. In Deuteronomy (11:30) they are placed at *Gilgal, 'beside the plains of Moreh'. Eusebius (*Onom.* 65,9 ff.) disagrees with the Samaritans, who claimed that they were situated near Neapolis, ancient *Shechem. On the *Medaba map they are marked near Neapolis and later chroniclers accept this as correct.

Excavations carried out since 1980 revealed sizeable remains of a large altar, built of unhewn stones. The altar was ascended by a sloping ramp. Numerous animal bones were scattered on the pavement of the courtyard that surrounded the altar. This sacred enclosure had two phases, both dating to the 12th century BC. This date helps identify the structure with the altar built by the Israelites upon entering the Land of Canaan.

EBEN-EZER The place where the Isrelites pitched camp before their battle with the *Philistines (1 Sam. 4:1). It was from here that the *Philistines took the Ark of God (1 Sam. 5:1). The identification of this site depends on that of *Aphek. If the identification of *Aphek with Ras el-Ain is accepted, then Eben-Ezer lies east of it, closer to the mountains.

Eusebius (*Onom* 33:25) erroneously located the site between Jerusalem and *Ashkelon, near the village of *Beth-Shemeh.

EDEN A place in the East, that gave its name to the Garden of Eden (Gen. 2:8). From it flowed four rivers: the *Pison, the *Gihon, the *Hiddekel and the *Euphrates (Gen. 2:11-14). It is also called 'the garden of the Lord' (Gen. 13:10; Isa. 51:3) and 'the garden of God' (Ezek. 28:13). Tentatively identified in various places, from Armenia in the north to *Egypt and *Ethiopia in the south.

EDOM; EDOMITES The name of a country and a people to the east of the Arabah, bordered by *Ammon on the north, the *Dead Sea and the Arabah on the west and the desert on the south and east. In the early 4th

millennium BC the land was inhabited by semi-nomadic peoples who practised primitive forms of agriculture. These early cultures came to an end in about 1900 BC. In the Middle and Late Bronze Ages, when Palestine and northern Transjordan were densely populated, the south was almost uninhabited and none of its sites is mentioned in Egyptian documents. The country emerges from obscurity again in the 13th century BC, when Edom is specifically mentioned in a list of Sethos I of about 1215BC. Together with *Moab and the *Negev it is also mentioned in the records of a punitive campaign organized by Rameses III.

The Edomites were of Semitic stock and must have penetrated the area as early as the 14th century BC. Archaeological surveys have shown that the country flourished mainly from the 13th to the 8th centuries BC, declined, and was finally destroyed in the 6th century BC. In the surveys remains of fortified towns and of numerous villages have been found. Agriculture was highly developed and so was the local pottery. The inscription of Mesha, King of *Moab, Edom's neighbor, shows that literature also flourished there (*Inscriptions). From the list of tribute which Edom paid to Esarhaddon it may also be deduced that it was richer than the other countries in the vicinity. It seems that, in part, it owed its wealth to the exploitation of copper (*Metals). The country was clearly strongly fortified at an early stage, since the Israelites could not use the roads passing through Edom on their way to *Canaan (Num. 20:17-21).

The first Israelite king to conquer Edom was David, who stationed garrisons all over the country (2 Sam. 8:14; 1 Kgs. 11:15-16). Edom revolted in the days of Jehoram and the Edomites put up a king of their own (2 Kgs. 8:20-2), who probably also conquered *Ezion-Geber. About a hundred years later Amaziah took Selah in Edom and renamed it Joktheel (2 Kgs. 14:7). The reconquest of Edom was later completed by Uzziah, King of Judah (2 Kgs. 14:22; 2 Chr. 26:1-2). It was not until the days of Ahaz that the country finally regained its independence (2 Kgs 16:6). In the 6th century BC Edom was conquered by the Babylonians, and in the centuries following its downfall new nomadic tribes penetrated the country, pressing the Edomites westwards into Judea, where they settled south of *Hebron. Among the newcomers were the *Nabateans, who are not heard of before the late 4th century BC but who had established their kingdom in the former territory of Edom by the first half of the 2nd century BC.

EDREI; ADRAA *a)* A city in the *Bashan, where Og, King of the Bashan, was vanquished by Moses (Num. 21:33). It was inhabited in the Roman priod. In the 3rd century AD it became a *polis.* It is mentioned as a prominent city by Eusebius (*Onom.* 12:14; 84:8) who states that Adraa is a famous city of *Arabia, 24 miles from *Bostra, and in later Roman sources. Identified with Dera, halfway between *Damascus and *Amman.
b) A city in the territory of Naphtali to the east of *Chinnereth (Josh. 19:37), which appears in the list of conquests by Pharaoh Tuthmosis III. Not identified.

EGLON A Canaanite town in the *Plain of Judah. Debir, King of Eglon, was one of the five kings who fought *Gibeon (Josh. 10:3). Eglon was later conquered by Joshua (Josh. 12:12) and became part of the territory of Judah (Josh. 15:39). Identified with Tell el-*Hesi. Eusebius (*Onom.* 48:19) also knew this place by the name of Odolam (*Adullam), in his time a very large village, 10 miles east of *Beth-Gubrin.

EGYPT A land situated along the southeastern shores of the Mediterranean, bordered by the *Red Sea on the east and Lybia on the west. Its southern boundary changed in different periods. The territory falls naturally into two parts: Lower Egypt, the *Nile Delta, and Upper Egypt, from Cairo southwards.

The whole economy of the country depended on the *Nile, which was the sole source of water for drinking and irrigation. Ancient Egyptian civilization was therefore confined to the *Nile Valley. The river swells at the end of June, after the rainy seasons, in the lands where it rises and overflows and floods the valley in August and September. The annual floods bring much silt, replenishing the fertility of the soil. The water was distributed over the fields by an intricate system of dams and channels. The main crops were barley and spelt, from which the staple food and drink — bread and beer — were made, beans, lentils, cucumbers and onions. Among the fruits grown were grapes and figs; the names of others have not yet been deciphered. Clothing was made of flax and writing material of papyrus, of which Egypt had the monopoly. Pigs, lambs and cows were slaughtered for meat. Fowl, wild and domesticated, completed the diet. The most common beast of burden in Egypt was the ass, the camel being unknown until late; horses were used only to draw war chariots (*Weapons and warfare). Egypt abounds in stone of different kinds and qualities for building. Copper (*Metals) and turquoise were mined in *Sinai, while gold was found in the hills in the east and southeast of the country, though both copper and gold had also to be imported from abroad. All timber, tin for the production of bronze, and iron had to be imported also.

EARLY HISTORY The *Nile Valley was populated from the Lower Paleolithic period. In the proto-Dynastic period (4th and 3rd millennia BC) three cultures flour-

*Tutankhamun's war against the Nubians,
depicted on a wooden box from the Valley of the Kings at Thebes*

ished in Egypt: Badarian, Amrathian and Gerzean. In the first of the three copper was used in the production of jewelry, and in the last weapons and tools were made from it.

The valley of the *Nile, with the basins of the Tigris and the Euphrates, forms one of the most ancient cradles of civilization. Its unification goes back to the remote times of the 1st Dynasty when, in about 3000 BC, Upper and Lower Egypt were unified by the semi-legendary King Menes, to whom is also attributed the foundation of *Memphis. In this early period Egypt already took an interest in Asia, and the rulers of the 2nd Dynasty established relations with *Byblos, which supplied Egypt with timber from Lebanon. The Egyptian presence in Palestine is attested by finds at *Ai and *Lachish, where vessels made of *alabaster, *jewelry and other artifacts of Egyptian origin were found. Egypt attained great prosperity in the times of the Old Kingdom, notably under Pharaoh Djoser of the 3rd Dynasty, who dispatched peaceful expeditions to the mines of *Sinai. Sahu-re continued this policy, but also sent military expeditions to Asia, as can be learned from the wall paintings in his tomb, in which ships laden with a wealth of goods are depicted. At the end of the Old Kingdom the frontiers of Egypt were threatened by nomads. In order to repel the menace Phiops I (c. 2400-2370 BC) conducted military campaigns against Asia and Canaan. But these were short-lived victories and the end of the Old Kingdom was close at hand. Egypt entered a period of anarchy, the First Intermediate Period, during which the central authority of the pharaohs deteriorated and the country was ruled by a large number of local princes. Foreign enemies invaded the Delta and disorder reigned in the country for about a century. The Middle Kingdom came into existence with the rise of the 11th Dynasty, whose founders unified the country and restored order in Egypt. This was continued by Ammenemes I and Sesostris of the 12th Dynasty, whose rule forms one of the peaks of Egyptian history. In order to pacify the turbulent populations of the desert and Canaan, Ammenemes I built a chain of fortresses, blocking the road from Asia to Egypt. Prosperity was attained during the rule of Sesostris III (1878-1843 BC). He marched at the head of his armies against the cities of Palestine, culminating in the conquest of *Shechem in Mt. Ephraim. Egyptian cultural influence is noted now in the cities along the Syrian coast, in cities extending from *Byblos to *Ugarit. The wealth of the country attracted strangers, such as the group of Semites seen in the paintings of the tomb at Bani-Hassan. The period of prosperity of the Middle Kingdom terminated with the pressure exerted by new invaders who established their hold over the whole of the ancient Near East. Nothing portrays this period of unrest better than the famous *Execration Texts, in which numerous Palestinian cities are mentioned. The invation of the *Hyksos in about 1730-1700 BC marked the end of the Middle Kingdom and opened the Second Intermediate Period which lasted for about 550 years, a troubled time in which Egypt was ruled by foreigners. The Hyksos established themselves in the Delta, making Avaris their capital;

from there they spread their rule over Upper Egypt. It is generally accepted today that the Hebrews migrated to Egypt in the later part of this period, in about 1600 BC. At the time when Jacob migrated to Egypt, Palestine and Egypt formed a political entity, and the roads leading from one to the other were constantly being travelled. Amosis, the founder of the 18th Dynasty, defeated the Hyksos in two battles, one fought at Avaris, the Hyksos capital, and the other at *Sharuhen (Tell el-*Farah, south) in southern Palestine.In a period of half a century he and Amenophis I, his heir, established their rule over the country whose wealth is reflected in the magnificent monuments of *Thebes, now raised to the rank of a capital. Under the pharaohs who bore the names of Tuthmosis and Amenophis the 18th Dynasty Egypt attained new prosperity. The borders of Egypt were pushed up to the borders of Syria and Mesopotamia. At *Megiddo Tuthmosis III vanquished in 1468 BC a coalition of some 300 Canaanite and Syrian princes. The booty taken in this battle, as recorded in the kings' annals, speaks for itself: 2,238 horses, 924 chariots, arms without number, 1,929 heads of cattle, 2,000 goats, 20,000 sheep, etc. This victory, which assured Egyptian supremacy, turned Palestine into a vassal state, leaving the local rulers autonomy in ruling their city states, under close Egyptian supervision. For a short while an equilibrium reigned between the Egyptians and the newly-rising *Hittite empire, which extended its rule over central Syria as far as *Kedesh-on-the Orontes. The situation did not change much under Amenophis III (1379-1362 BC), who by the name of Akhenaton attempted to revolutionize the Egyptian religion, centering it on the worship of the sun, and built his new capital, Akhetaton, in the region of *El Amarna. It was there that the important royal archive was discovered, from which one may learn how the faithful Canaanite princes one after the other revolted against Egypt. This grave situation was momentarily saved by Horemheb, a general who usurped the throne, founded the 19th Dynasty (1348-1320 BC), and reconquered the land of Canaan. Sethos I (1318-1304 BC), whose triumphal stele was found at *Beth-Shean, followed by Rameses II (1304-1237 BC) attempted to restore Egyptian rule over Asia. Sethos I and Rameses II fought the Hittites but without bringing about any substantial change. The signing of a treaty with the Hittites, on the basis of the status quo, was followed by a comparatively long period of tranquility, enabling Rameses II to undertake the immense construction works at Karnak and Luxor. In the Delta he founded his new capital, which bore his name (*Rameses), where the Hebrew slaves toiled (Exod. 1:11). It was from this city that the Exodus began (Exod. 12:39; Num. 33:3). The date of the Exodus is disputed. Some place it in the rule of Rameses II, or at the beginning of the reign of Merneptah (1236-1223 BC). During the reign of Merneptah the Lybians revolted, and together with their allies, the *'Sea Peoples' (*Philistines), attacked Egypt. In a series of naval and land battles the invaders were beaten back by Rameses III (1198-1166 BC) of the 19th Dynasty, the last of the great pharaohs of Egypt.

The years which elapsed between the end of the 20th Dynasty and the conquest of Egypt by Cambyses in 525 BC were a period of decline for Egypt. Under Rameses XI the 20th Dynasty collapsed and the north of Egypt came under the rule of priests. At *Tanis a new Dynasty rose, the 21st (*c.* 1085-935 BC), whose members were of no great importance. With the rise of the 22nd Dynasty (935-720 BC) Egypt came under the rule of pharaohs of Lybian descent, who dwelt in Bubastis (Pi-Beseth). The first ruler, Sheshonq I (935-914 BC), biblical Shishak, attacked Palestine in the fifth year of the reign of Rehoboam and destroyed numerous cities there. The chronology of the later kings of this dynasty is not clear, nor is much known of the history of the 23rd and 24th Dynasties (*c.* 817-709 BC). In about 715 BC Re Piankhi, the ruler of the kingdom of Nubia (*Cush), attacked Egypt. Its conquest was completed by his son Shabaka (716-695 BC). Of the kings of this dynasty, Teharga (689-664 BC) is known in the Bible by the name of Tirhaka. At that time Egypt assisted Palestine and Syria against Assyria, which led to the Assyrian onslaught against Egypt. In 671 BC Esarhaddon attacked *Memphis, and in 667 BC Ashurbanipal reached *Thebes. In 663 BC Ashurbanipal completed the conquest of all Egypt. Esarhaddon appointed Necho as ruler over Egypt, and with his reign the 24th Dynasty begins. Under Psametichus I (695-689 BC) Egypt revolted and became independent. Necho II (610-595 BC) attempted to restore Egyptian rule over Palestine and Syria, but was defeated in 605 BC by Nebuchadnezzar at *Carchemish, and Egyptian influence over these countries ended. The attempts of Apries (598-570 BC) to restore Palestine and Syria to Egypt failed. After the end of the reign of Amasis (570-526 BC) Cambyses defeated Egypt in the battle of Pelusium (525 BC).

PERSIAN RULE On the death of Darius I (521-486 BC) Egypt rebelled against Persia but was put down by Xerxes (486-464 BC). The rulers of Persia are listed as the kings of the 27th Dynasty. Disturbances in Egypt broke out again under Artaxerxes I (464-423 BC).

From 404 to 399 BC Egypt was ruled by Amurthis of Sais, the only king of the 28th Dynasty whose name is known. From 399 to 380 BC he was followed by four kings of a family from Mendes, which is known as the 29th Dynasty. The kings of the 30th Dynasty attempted to free Egypt from Persian rule, but in 343 BC Artaxerxes III recovered it, until in 332 BC it was conquered by Alexander the Great.

THE HELLENISTIC AND ROMAN PERIODS Even before the conquest of Egypt by Alexander the Great there was a Greek colony in Naukratis where Egyptian corn was exchanged for silver. Greek mercenaries served in the Egyptian army but did not settle in Egypt. After the conquest Alexander founded *Alexandria, which he intended to be a center from which Greek culture would be disseminated throughout Egypt. Greek rule over Egypt began with Ptolemy I Soter, who founded Ptolemais in Upper Egypt. There was little interference in the internal affairs of the Egyptians in this period. His successor, Ptolemy Philadelphus, encouraged Greek literature and art. Under Ptolemy Epiphanes Egypt lost all its extra-territorial possessions except *Cyprus. In 25 BC it was conquered by Augustus, who made it his personal domain. This brought about the rapid deterioration of the Egyptian economy, since Egypt was forced to supply Rome with corn but received little in return. It remained a Roman province until its conquest by the Arabs in AD 638.

EGYPT (RIVER OF) The southern limit of the Promised Land (Gen. 15:18). Probably the eastern branch of the *Nile Delta, since the Brook of Egypt is identified with Wadi el-Arish.

EKRON One of the lordships of the *Philistines (Josh. 13:3), listed in one place as within the lot of Judah (Josh. 15:11, 45-6) but in another as within that of *Dan (Josh. 19:43). Despite the reference in Judges (1:18-19) it seems that the Israelites did not take Ekron in the early stages of the conquest. According to the Bible it was held by the Israelites in the time of Samuel (1 Sam. 7:14), but after the defeat of Goliath the *Philistines fled to the gates of Ekron (1 Sam.

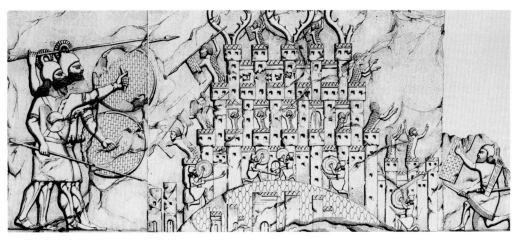

Relief from the palace of Sargon II showing the siege of Ekron by the Assyrians

17:52). According to 2 Kings (1:2) there was a temple there, dedicated to Baal-Zebub. In 712 BC Ekron was captured by Shalmaneser V of Assyria and in 701 BC by Sennacherib. It is not mentioned again until the Hellenistic period, when Alexander Balas granted Ekron and the villages around it to Jonathan the Hasmonean. From that time onwards it was in the Judean kingdom. It continued to be mentioned in sources of the late Roman period. Eusebius (*Onom.* 22:9) called Akaron 'a very large Jewish village', east of the road from *Ashdod to *Jabneh. The biblical and post-biblical towns are also portrayed on the *Medaba map.

Ekron has been identified with several sites. Despite the similarity of its name to that of the Arab village of Agir, this identification has definitely been ruled out. Today it is identified with Tel Miqneh (Khirbet el-Muqanna), northeast of *Ashdod.

Excavations carried out since 1981 at Tel Miqneh on behalf of the Albright Institute, the Hebrew University and Brandeis University, under the direction of T. Dothan and S. Gittin. In the excavations 13 occupation levels were distinguished. The four earliest levels (13–10) are represented by *flint tools and *pottery of the Chalcolithic period, Early Bronze Age I–II, Middle Bronze Age IIA–B, and Late Bronze Age I–II. Level 9, of the Iron Age I (12th century BC), contained a 13 feet wide city wall with a stone base, supported by bricks on the outside. The *pottery of this level is Mycenaean and *Philistine. The following Levels 8 (12th–11th century BC) and 7 (11th century BC) are represented by brick walls and pottery similar to that of Level 9. In Level 6 (end of 11th century BC) a two-room structure built of brick and paved with pebbles was discovered. Another structure probably had a cultic function. The site was abandoned and resettled in the 10th–9th centuries BC (Levels 5–3). The main feature of this period is a stone city wall and a gate with two rooms on each side, built in the 8th century BC. Its foundations penetrate down to the earlier Iron Age II occupation level. Inside the city were numerous oil presses, attesting that Iron Age Ekron was a major olive oil producing center. The last two levels contain burials of a late period. The destruction of Ekron is attributed to Sennacherib in 701 BC.

ELAH (VALLEY OF) A valley southwest of *Jerusalem, extending towards the land of the *Philistines, through which passed the important road from Phislistia to the Judean Hills and *Jerusalem. It was there that David slew Goliath (1 Sam. 17:2, 21:9). Identified with Wadi es-Samt.

ELAM *a)* The biblical name of a hilly country, 'Elamtu' in Accadian, east of the River *Tigris (*Hiddekel) bordered by Assyria (*Mesopotamia) and *Madai on the north, the Persian Gulf on the south and Persia on the east and southeast. Its capital was Susa (*Shushan). Most of our knowledge of it derives from Sumerian, Babylonian and Assyrian sources. There was a constant state of war between Elam and the kingdoms of *Lagash and Assyria. By the end of the 2nd millennium BC the Elamites had succeeded in deposing the Sumerian Dynasty of *Ur. According to Genesis (14) Chedorlaomer, King of Elam, ruled over all the countries which were formerly under the yoke of *Babylon, and the countries on the *Jordan were his tributaries.

At the beginning of the 12th century BC the Elamits invaded *Babylon, and the stone on which Hammurabi wrote his code of laws was captured by them and taken to Susa, where it was indeed found in 1902. The rise of Assyria in the 8th–7th centuries BC led to clashes between the two kingdoms. Sargon II, Sennacherib and Ashurbanipal conducted continuous military campaigns against Elam. Susa fell in 645 BC. Elamites then took part in the Assyrian campaigns against Judah (Isa. 22.6), and after the fall of *Nineveh Elam regained its freedom. Isaiah prophesied the unification of Elam and Media, which was to bring about the conquest of *Babylon (Isa. 21.2,9). The fall of Elam was foretold by Jeremiah (49:34–9) and by Ezekiel (32:24–5). During the period of the Persian Empire Elam was one of the satrapies, with Susa as its capital. Elamites who had been settled in Samaria impeded the Jews who returned from the Babylonia exile (Ezra 4:8–9).

b) A town in Judah which was settled after the Restoration, known as 'the other Elam' (Ezra 2:7, 31; Neh. 7:34) to distinguish it from the land of Elam. Not identified.

EL AMARNA Pharaoh Amenophis IV (1379–1362 BC) built a new capital in the sixth year of his reign,

King Akhenaton and Queen Nefertiti,
relief in the temple of the god Aton at El Amarna

naming it Akhetaton, 'the horizon of the god Aton'. About 160 miles from the *Nile Delta and 300 miles from *Thebes, it is known today as El Amarna. The ancient city was a mile wide and 4 miles long and the whole of it, with certain regions in its vicinity, was consecrated to the worship of Aton, as is set out in fourteen large inscriptions set up on the rocks around the city. The king, the nobles, landowners and warriors occupied the acropolis, while the populace lived in the lower city and the surrounding villages; in a class of their own were the *Habiru, nomads who wandered in the desert and the borderlands.

In 1887 clay tablets began to come to light in this area. Now totalling 540, these have become known as the El Amarna letters. They belong to the royal archives of Amenophis III and his son Amenophis IV and were written by the kings of *Babylon, Assyria, Mittani, Arauwa, the *Hittites, *Cyprus and numerous petty kings of the city-states of Syria and *Canaan. Most of them are written in Accadian, the official diplomatic language of that time (known as the El Amarna period), in cuneiform script. The letters tell us that *Canaan was inhabited by mixed elements of West Semites and Horians and divided into a large number of feudal states whose kings were subject to *Egypt. In a period of slackening Egyptian authority there were constant quarrels between these petty kings.

The El Amarna letters are a highly important source from which a great deal of knowledge has been gleaned concerning events in *Canaan in the 15th and 14th centuries BC. If the identification of the *Habiru referred to in the letters with the Hebrew is correct, they provide the first evidence of the penetration of Hebrew tribes into the land of *Canaan.

ELATH; ELOTH; EL-PARAN; BERENIKE; AILA A coastal town at the northern end of the northeastern arm of the *Red Sea, mentioned frequently in conjuction with *Ezion-Geber; both were stations on the route of the Exodus (Deut. 2:8). In the days of the United Monarchy Elath became an important harbor through which the trade with *Arabia and *Ophir flowed (1 Kgs. 9:26-8), but it may be inferred that in the days of Jehoram son of Jehoshaphat, it was taken by the *Edomites (2 Kgs. 8:20-2). Amaziah, King of Judah, subdued *Edom, and his son Azariah rebuilt Elath (2 Kgs. 14:22). In the days of Ahaz, Rezin, King of *Aram (Authorized Version: 'Syria'), took it once more; according to the Bible it was never in Israelite hands again (2 Kgs. 16:6).

Early in the Hellenistic period a port named Berenike was built here by the Ptolemies of *Egypt. Later, in the 3rd or 2nd century BC, Elath, together with most of the *Negev, was taken over by the *Nabateans, who used it as one of their main ports in the Arabian spice trade. The conquest of *Gaza by the Hasmonean Alexander Jannaeus (c. 100 BC) temporarily disrupted the flow of Nabatean trade through Elath and the *Negev. It was a prominent port throughout the Roman period, under the name of Aila. Early in the 2nd century AD a highway through the Arabah was constructed, leading from Aila northwards. According to Eusebius (*Onom.* 8:1): 'Ailam (a mistake for

Ailat) — a place at the end of Palestine, close to the desert on the south, and to the *Red Sea on the south, and it is a transit place for those who sail from Egypt to India. And there is stationed the 10th Roman legion. Named today Aila'. It seems that detachments of the Legio III Cyrenaica were stationed at Aila at this time, to be replaced later, in the late 3rd or early 4th century, by the Legio X Fretensis whose headquarters were at Elath. It was again an important city in the Byzantine period and its bishops participated in some of the early church councils. The Arabs used it as a base for their invasion of Palestine in AD 634.

Elath is identified with modern Aqabah. (*See also* *EZION-GEBER.)

ELEPHANTINE The southernmost city of *Egypt, situated on an island in the River *Nile. Recorded for the first time in the 3rd Dynasty, it was a military stronghold and trade center, the seat of the royal officials responsible for the trade with Nubia (*Ethiopia), whose most important export was ivory. The name of the city probably reflects this trade. From this region granite, used in building and sculpture, was transported to the south. On the east bank of the *Nile large quarries were found. Excavations revealed two temples from the time of Tuthmosis III and Amenophis III; a large number of tombs of royal officials; the settlement of a Jewish military colony from Persian times; and a temple dedicated to Chnum, the city god, from the period of Alexander the Great. Of outstanding importance was a find of Aramaic papyri, which give the colony's name as Yeb. The great majority are letters and legal documents reflecting the everyday life of the colony. Most of the documents are dated and relate to the 5th century BC. They deal with the transfer of property, inheritance, marriage and the lending and borrowing of money. A few come into the category of diplomatic correspondence and relate to governmental affairs. The most interesting information concerns the religious life of the community. The documents refer to a temple which was not an ordinary synagogue but a building of considerable size, with an altar, called *aguda* (meeting place) and *misgada* (place of worship).

The colony, established at the latest in the middle of the 6th century BC, had been destroyed by the 4th century BC. In the Roman period the place was again garrisoned by a military unit. An interesting find was a Roman Nilometer.

ELEALEH A city of *Moab, among those conquered by the Israelites (Num. 32:3) and given to Reuben (Num. 32:37). A large village in the Roman period in the district of *Heshbon, it is identified with El-Al, 2 miles northeast of Hesban. Eusebius (*Onom.* 84:10) mentioned it as a large village, not more than a mile from *Heshbon.

ELON A town in the territory of *Dan, in the northwestern part of the *Plain (Josh. 19:43). Thought by some to be identical with the *Ajalon of Joshua (19:42), Elon was in that case the Elon-Beth-Hanan of 1 Kings (4:9), a city in the second district of Solomon's division, tentatively identified with Khirbet Wadi Alin, southeast of *Beth-Shemesh, where remains of an Israelite settlement were found.

ELUSA A city in the northwestern part of the central *Negev. The modern Arabic name of the site, el-Khalasa, has preserved its ancient Arabic form, which is known to us from the *Nessana papyri as al-Khalus. Elusa was the principal city of the central *Negev, and is mentioned in many of the ancient sources. Ptolemy (died c. AD 150) enumerates it in his Geography among the towns of *Idumea west of the *Jordan. The Peutinger map situates it 71 Roman miles from *Jerusalem. In the *Medaba map it appears as a large town.

It seems that Elusa belongs to the group of early Nabatean foundations of the late 4th or early 3rd century BC. Evidence of this is provided by Hellenistic pottery found on the site and by a Nabatean inscription of the first half of the 2nd century BC in which Aretas, King of the *Nabateans, is mentioned. At that time Elusa and *Oboda were important stations on the main trade route running from *Petra to the emporium of *Gaza. The conquest of *Gaza by the Hasmonean Alexander Jannaeus at the beginning of the 1st century BC terminates the first chapter of the history of the *Nabateans at Elusa. Typical Nabatean pottery, early Roman sherds and a great number of coins attest to a renewed Nabatean settlement in the 1st century AD.

Elusa reached its greatest eminence in the late Roman period, when it became the most important city in the central *Negev and of that part of the Provincia Arabia. It was the birth-place of Libanius, the famous teacher of rhetoric, who went to teach in *Antioch and mentioned Elusa in his letters between AD 356 and 359. Christianity penetrated Elusa earlier than the other towns of the central *Negev, and there is literary evidence of pagan and Christian communities living side by side. Bishops of Elusa participated in the councils of the church in AD 431 and 451. But tomb-stones found in the local cemetery indicate that there were pagans at Elusa as late as the early 5th century. In this period the city belonged to Palestina Tertia. The city was visited c. AD 530 by Theodosius and in 570 by Antoninus of Placentia, who made a pilgrimage to Mount *Sinai. Elusa is frequently mentioned in the papyri of *Nessana, in which it is referred to as a *polis. According to the same sources Elusa was still an administrative center in the early Arab period, at least up to the end of the 7th century AD. No archaeological remains that can be attributed with certainty to the early Arab period have been found at Elusa.

The ruins of Elusa were first visited by E. Robinson in 1838, who identified it correctly on account of its Arabic name. He deplored the poor condition of the ruins, which he attributed to the poor quality of the local soft chalk of which the houses were built. The site was later visited by E.H. Palmer (1870), who could only see one street, but on a visit in 1897 A. Musil observed the remains of a city wall, two gates and two streets. Musil also confirmed Palmer's report that the stones of Elusa were being taken to Gaza, where construction was then in full swing. A. Jaussen, R. Savignac and H. Vincent (1905) discovered the cemetery of Elusa, where they found pagan and Christian tombstones. C.L. Woolley and T.E. Lawrence (1914) attempted to draw a plan of the remains, on which they could mark only the traces of a wall and two gates. As well as some additional Greek inscriptions they found an important archaic Nabatean text. J.H. Iliffe (1933) found Nabatean and Hellenistic pottery. T.J. Colin-Baly, on behalf of the Colt Expedition (1938), made some trial digs in some of the city's dumps in order to establish the chronology of the site.

The state of the ruins at Elusa is indeed deplorable. As the ancient site closest to both *Gaza and *Beer-Sheba it was an easy prey for stone robbers. Their depredations went on throughout the Turkish period and did not cease after the British conquest of Palestine, when the small village of el-Khalasa was built on the ruins, near the ancient wells.

A. Negev surveyed the site several times during his work at *Oboda and *Mampsis. His impressions were different: 'although Elusa presents a deplorable sight on the surface, it lies in the middle of a huge sea of sand which is still active and moving today, and constantly threatening the modern road leading from Beer-Sheba to Nitzana which touches only the fringe of these dunes.' In his view it was reasonable to assume that it was only the upper stories of the houses that were robbed of their stones, while the rest was still waiting under the sand for the archaeologist's shovel.

This view has now been fully confirmed in excavations conducted by Negev at Elusa in 1973 on behalf of the Hebrew University, in 1979 on behalf of the same institution and Ben-Gurion University, and in 1980 on behalf of the Hebrew University and the Mississippi State University. In the first season trial

The earliest Nabatean inscription found at Elusa

trenches were dug to examine whether the disappearance of Elusa was caused by the robbing of its stones. And, indeed, a tower, forming part of the city's defences was preserved to the level of its second story. Among the other finds were a reservoir (15 feet by 30 feet by 7 feet), which belonged to the *water supply system, and was in use over a long period of time; a Late *Nabatean quarter was discovered in the northeastern part of the site, and a house partly excavated there, was preserved to a height of 7 feet. In the ruins of this house were found two 'classic' *Nabatean capitals. This building was enlarged in the Byzantine period; among its ruins was a capital decorated with a cross and two doves. Its form is a late development of the Nabatean capital, and it continues a long tradition. On the southeasten side of the site was a Nabatean *theater. Excavations in the theater in 1979 and 1980 exposed a double semicircular corridor which, instead of containing the regular *vomitoria*, served as a filled-in retaining wall against which the *cavea* was built. The pottery in the fill was of the Middle Nabatean period, of the first half of the 1st century AD. In the *cavea* was found the donor's box. In the following season the stone-paved orchestra was reached; the vaulted side entrances-serving in this theater as the main entrances-were cleared and the *scaenae frons* was exposed. The door-posts of the central entrance were decorated with 'classic': Nabatean capitals. In the ruins of a side entrance was a Greek inscription mentioning Flavius Demarchus, an unknown governor of the province. The inscription, dating to AD 454/5, speaks of a new floor made for the "old theater" by a citizen named Abraham son of Zenobius. The sandaled feet of a Nabatean life-size marble statue were found in the debris.

In 1980 excavations were begun in the cathedral (210 feet by 90 feet), the largest church in the Negev. Two phases were distinguished in the use of the building. In the beginning it was a single apse basilica with rectangular rooms at the sides. In the second phase the side rooms were blocked by apses, and the church was turned into a triapsidal building. These alterations were due to changes in the practice of the cult of saints and martyrs. In the central apse there were unusually large and high marble-paved steps leading to the bishop's throne. For this reason the altar had to be moved from its regular place onto the bema. The floor of the church, bases, columns and the Corinthian capitals were all made of Proconesian marble. The walls and some of the side chapels had gold-plated glass mosaics. The church was entered by monumental stairs from an huge atrium containing four porticos. This atrium may have formed part of an earlier Nabatean *temple. In surveys made in 1979 and 1980 another large church was found in the southwest side of the site, and two smaller churches apparently stood north of the cathedral. Cemeteries of the Byzantine, late Roman and Middle Nabaten period were discovered east of the city. One tomb in the Nabatean cemetery contained a coffin in which individual bones had been collected (*Burial). On the cemetery grounds were discovered—as at *Mampsis—tables for funerary meals and a kitchen for the preparation of the food. At a distance of about a mile east of the site were traces of an encampment of the Middle Nabatean period.

EMBALMING The Egyptians believed that the soul leaves the body of a dying person but returns to it at a later time. They therefore thought it appropriate to preserve the body — the eternal resting-place of the soul — by embalming it. The art of preserving a dead body from decay by means of aromatics or by desiccation did in fact originate in Egypt and was mainly practised there. It was not restricted to human beings but was also applied to sacred birds and animals. From the Bible it is known that embalming was also practised by the ancient Hebrews; for instance, Joseph ordered the slave doctors to embalm his

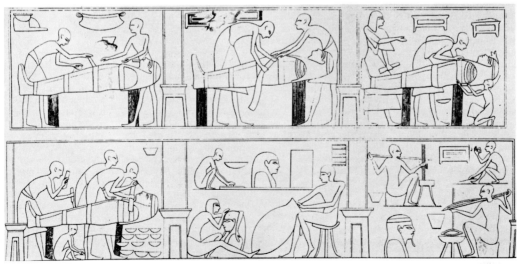

Embalming; the process depicted in a wall-painting in an Egyptian Tomb

father, Jacob (Gen. 50:2-3). The Bible refers to the period of mourning for Jacob as lasting seventy days, and this was in fact the period required for the completion of the embalming process. After his death Joseph's body was also embalmed and then put into a coffin (Gen. 50:26).

The art of the embalmer developed gradually. The process began with the 2nd Dynasty. The limbs were detached from the body, which was tightly swathed, the limbs being wrapped separately and placed alongside it. In the period of the 4th Dynasty the body was embalmed whole and the intestines kept separately in a container with natron (native sesquicarbonate of soda). A change occurred during the period of the 11th Dynasty; now the skin was preserved by being smeared with natron and oil and the body was swathed in wrappings soaked in resins, while the natural orifices and the incisions made in order to extract the intestines were smeared with beeswax. The complete removal of the intestines began with the 12th Dynasty, when the emptied body was filled with linen.

According to Diodorus of Sicily (II, 48, 6) the *Nabateans in the late 4th century BC exploited the *asphalt from the *Dead Sea, and apparently sold it to Egypt for use in embalming.

Herodotus (II, 86), one of the more detailed sources on these matters, mentions three methods of embalming. The first, and most expensive, necessitated extracting the brains by means of an iron hook. The emptied skull was subsequently filled with spices. The intestines were removed through an incision in the side of the body, and the emptied parts were cleansed and also filled with spices. Afterwards the body was packed in dry natron for a period of seventy days. The last stage of embalming by this method consisted of washing the body and wrapping it tightly in cloths soaked in resins. In this state the embalmed body was delivered to the relatives, who would put it in a wooden coffin made in the shape of a human body; this was then placed in an upright position in the burial chamber. The second method, a cheaper one, consisted of dissolving the intestines by infusing cedar oil through the anus. As with the previous method, the body was packed in dry natron and after seventy days the oil, together with the dissolved intestines, would emerge, so that all that remained of the body were the bones and the skin. The third and cheapest method of embalming involved cleansing the body by means of an enema before packing it in natron for seventy days. The embalmed body was then ready for burial. The secrets of the art of embalming were forgotten early in the Roman period.

EMMAUS; NICOPOLIS A town in Judea, on the border of Judea in the Persian period, when it was also known as Hamthan, a name which means 'hot springs'; this is a reference to the springs near the city which are mentioned in the Jewish sources. At the beginning of the Hasmonean revolt it was one of the places fortified by Bacchides in order to block the western passes to Judea. Judas Maccabaeus won a great victory over the Seleucid army of Gorgias and Nikanor near here in 166 BC. After the middle of the 1st century BC it became the capital of a district

(Josephus, *Antiq.* XIV, 275). In AD 68, following the destruction of *Jerusalem, Vespasian settled soldiers of the Legio V. Macedonica there. In AD 221 Elagabalus conferred the status of a *polis* on Emmaus, renaming it Nicopolis, 'the City of Victory'.

After the Crucifixion two of the disciples, who were on their way from *Jerusalem, met the risen Christ there without recognizing him (Luke 24:13ff). Remains of a Samaritan synagogue that have been identified there point to the presence of a Samaritan community at Emmaus in the late Roman period.

In 1873, 1887-90, 1900-2 and 1940-4 the Franciscans carried out excavations on the site, unearthing remains of the Hellenistic, Roman, Byzantine and later periods. To the Byzantine period belong ruins of a basilical mono-apsidal church built on the foundations of a more ancient house, identified as the house of Cleophas. On the ruins of this church a Crusader church was built that is still standing. Emmaus is identified with Imwas, about 18 miles northwest of *Jerusalem.

Excavations were renewed at the site in 1978 by Tel Aviv University, under the direction of M. Gichon. The excavations included the southern bath-house of Emmaus, Horvat Eked (the fort of Emmaus?) and Horvat Mesad, which was examined by M. Fisher.

The bath-house was constructed in the 3rd century AD and was built of a number of successive rooms on a single axis. The building originally consisted of at least six rooms. Following an earthquake, it was renovated in the Byzantine period (possibly in the 5th-6th century AD) when it assumed its present form.

The building, 45 feet wide, is composed of four rooms. The first room (from north to south) was the cold room (*frigadarium*) (in its original form the warm room [*tepidarium*]) with a stone cupola made up of four tapering segments with a central opening for a mechanical device for regulating the air which has not survived. The floor of the court was paved with marble tiles. A hot-water channel ran through the middle of the room; it fell into disuse when the room was turned into a *frigadarium*. This channel also extended up to a recess in the wall to heat a basin containing water for ablutions.

In the second room, originally the hot room (*caldarium*), a double floor was found as well as clay piping in the walls. When the barrel vault in this room collapsed and smashed the upper floor, it became a *tepidarium*, and the hypocaust which was attached to it went out of use. The room has two round recesses. Its present ceiling is a brick barrel vault.

The third room was the original *caldarium* and remained so throughout. The upper floor was preserved on a series of arches made of bricks and pipes for heating still lined the walls. The shape of the room and of the ceiling are similar to those of the *tepidarium*, both of which were illuminated by large glass-paned windows.

It is possible that Horvat Eked should be identified with the fort built by the Seleucid commander Bacchides at Emmaus (1 Macc. 9:40), although its distance from the city (1 mile) casts some doubt on this identification.

The well fortified site at the top of the steep hill suggests both by its large dimensions and by the numerous well-cut stones in a variety of styles found strewn over the ground that it was more than just a fort. Thus far the southern gate built of smooth ashlars has been excavated. It has a single entrance which was blocked by stones of the collapsed barrel vault, two narrow guardrooms and two watchtowers with rounded facades flanking it. The gate was constructed at the end of the Seleucid period and continued in existence until the Bar Kochba period.

The same date is assigned to the wall, 6-9 feet wide, which was built of roughly hewn stones. Two towers were uncovered, both of which protrude inside and outside the city, each with a square inner face and a rounded outer face. Up to their preserved height of c. 11 feet, both towers, 16 feet by 16 feet, were solid constructions with no inner spaces. Great care was taken in laying the foundations on the bedrock and reinforcing them with retaining walls to ensure the wall's stability and to prevent landslides.

The walls were breached either during the war with Varus (4 BC) or the war with Rome and were rebuilt in the time of Bar Kochba.

In the hill of Eked, Bar Kochba's soldiers built a network of subterranean halls and chambers which were conected by tunnels and which could be traversed only by crawling. Each branch had several concealed entrances. These were secret assault bases from which Bar Kochba's warriors rose up in arms at the outbreak of the Revolt. When the first phase of the uprising was successful, they advanced to the top of the hill, but when the Romans gained the upper hand they once again retreated underground.

In the excavation at the summit of the hill and in the caves the reverberations of the final battle have been preserved in the thick burnt destruction level which seals the period of Bar Kochba and the settlement at the site.

Horvat Mesad is a well fortified road station situated in the heart of *Har Hamelech* ('the king's mountain') and consists of a strongly built structure of large ashlar stones which guarded the road leading from Emmaus to Jerusalem. The square building was set in a courtyard enclosed by a stout ashlar wall, 4 feet wide. The building was substantially enlarged in the time of Herod when it was surrounded by a thicker wall (80 feet by 160 feet). Houses and storerooms were built against the inner face of the wall. Cisterns and other installations were also found on the site. After the destruction of the road station during the Jewish War, it was restored in the Byzantine period as a small fortress (32 feet by 16 feet) which was demolished during the Moslem conquest.

The relatively large number of coins discovered at the site, which included about 100 coins of Alexander Jannaeus, point to the importance of this route which later became a Roman road. A fragment of a milestone of Marcus Aurelius attests that the road was travelled even after the road station fell into disuse.

EN BOQEQ A small oasis on the southwestern shore of the Dead Sea formed by two springs gushing out of the eastern slopes of the escarpment and falling to the Dead Sea. The site was known by its Arab name Qasr Umm Baghgheq. It was first discovered by the French scholar F. de Saulcy in 1853, and was examined by F. Frank in 1931. After a preliminary survey by S. Appelbaum in 1966, the site was excavated by M. Gichon in the years 1967-72 on behalf of Tel Aviv University.

The main remains on the site consist of a probable industrial installation (now located in the vicinity of the En Boqeq Hotel), and a fort higher up on the slope. Remains of an aqueduct conveying water from the springs were also discovered.

The industrial installation, which measures 60 feet by 60 feet and is made of rather thick walls, $2^1/_2$ feet wide, is composed of two faces of roughly dressed stones with a rubble fill. It consists of a spacious central court surrounded by several halls and rooms. Some of the rooms contained installations which were apparently connected with drying, crushing, pressing and boiling. The excavator observed three phases in the use of this facility, ranging from the time of Herod to about the middle of the first century AD. Aside from standard early Roman pottery, there was also typical Nabatean pottery and coins of the Nabatean king Aretas IV (9 BC-AD 40). The excavator believed that this installation was designed for extracting odiferous substances, and that it was founded by Herod. For reasons connected with the history of this region, A. Negev suggested that the installation belonged to the Nabateans, who from the 4th century BC collected the asphalt gushing out of the Dead Sea for export to Egypt.

The fort (60 feet by 60 feet) defended by towers at its corners, still rises to a height of 18 feet. Inside the inner court were five rooms. This small fort was built in the second half of the 4th century AD, and was in use till about the beginning of the 7th century. It is not known what system of fortifications it belonged to. It may have guarded the roads leading from the western to the eastern part of *Palestina Tertia*.

EN-DOR; ENDOR One of the towns of Manasseh in the territory of Issachar (Josh. 17:11), where the 'woman that hath a familiar spirit' lived (1 Sam. 28:7). The place was also known in the Roman period. Eusebius (*Onom.* 34:9; 34:11; 94:22; 140:5) states that it is a very large village, 4 miles from Mt *Tabor, near the village *Nain. Identified with Khirbet es-Safsafah, in the *Jezreel Valley. The ancient name has been preserved in the Arab village of Indur.

EN-GANNIM *a)* A town in the *Plain (Josh. 15:34). Not Identified.

b) A Levitical city in the territory of Issachar (Josh. 19:21; 21:29). In the parallel passage in 1 Chronicles (6:73) the name *Aenon (Authorized Version: 'Anem') appears instead of En-Gannim. Tentatively identified with Khirbet Beit Jann, southwest of Tiberias.

EN-GEDI; ENGEDDI An oasis on the western shores of the *Dead Sea, named after the copious spring which waters it and mentioned together with the 'city of Salt' as part of the territory of Judah (Josh. 15:62). On his flight from Saul David dwelt in the strongholds of En-Gedi (1 Sam. 23:29), also referred to as the wilderness of En-Gedi (1 Sam. 24:1). The battle between Jehoshaphat, King of Judah, and the *Ammonites and Moabites began at '*Hazezon-Tamar which is En-Gedi' (2 Chr. 20:1 ff.). In antiquity En-Gedi was already known for its aromatic plants: 'the camphire in the vineyards of En-Gedi' is mentioned in the Song of Solomon (1:14). The site became still more renowned in the period of the Second Temple. Josephus relates that the finest palm trees and the opobalsamum (balsam) grew there (*Antiq.* IX, 7). At that time it was the capital of a district (*War* III, 55). During the Revolt it was a small town. It was raided by the Sicarii after they conquered *Masada in AD 68 (*War* IV, 402). Pliny (*Nat.Hist.* V, 73), who wrote somewhat later, says: 'Lying below the Essenes was formerly the town of Engedi, second only to Jerusalem in fertility of its groves of palm trees, and now like Jerusalem a heap of ashes.' In the time of Eusebius (*Onom.* 86, 16) it was a very large village, and it is still frequently referred to in sources of the Byzantine period.

In 1949 and in the following years surveys were made at En-Gedi, with a trial dig at Tell el-Jurn, the ancient mound near the spring. In 1961-2 and 1964 the site was excavated by B. Mazar and I. Dunayevski on behalf of the Hebrew University and the Israel Exploration Society. The small mound could denote only a very limited area of settlement. The earliest, period V, is attributed to the time of Josiah, King of Judah, and his successors, and its destruction and desertion are dated to about 582 BC. To this period belong several houses in which large rough storage jars were found, as well as other pottery vessels of a non-domestic nature. There were also metal utensils. The excavators believe that these houses were connected with the perfume industry and that the pottery and metal objects were probably used in the extraction of essence from balm. Several Hebrew seals, as well as inscribed weights, belong to this period.

On top of the burnt ashes of the settlement of period V a new settlement was built at the beginning of the Persian period. To this settlement, period IV, belongs a very large building, the full extent of which has not been ascertained. Here, too, large quantities of pottery were found. Among the finds were seals of the *Yahud* type (*Seals). There were also vessels imported from Attica, dating from the 6th-5th centuries BC. The destruction of this settlement is dated to the middle of the 4th century BC. The settlement of period III was a fortress founded in about the 4th century BC, this was most probably in existence during the reigns of John Hyrcanus (135-104 BC), who probably annexed En-Gedi to the Hasmonean kingdom, and of Alexander Jannaeus (104-76 BC). This settlement was destroyed before Herod's accession to the throne, probably during the Persian invasion of 40 BC.

A new strong fortress was built on the mound in the 1st century AD, when En-Gedi was the capital of a district (Josephus, *War* III, 55), but this was destroyed by the Romans in AD 68. There are no traces on the site of a settlement during the period of the Bar-Kochba rebellion, although En-Gedi is frequently mentioned in the letters of its leader found in the *Judean Desert Caves. The latest settlement, quite a poor one (period

I), was of the Byzantine period. Close to the mound a large public bath of the Roman period was discovered. This is thought to be part of a larger installation which has not yet come to light. The bath was probably built between AD 60 and AD 70, when a Roman garrison was stationed on the site, and was in use until early in the 2nd century AD. To the Byzantine period belong remains of a synagogue, discovered in 1970, which include a mosaic floor with animal, bird and floral motifs of the type found in the synagogue at *Maon (Menois). Among the single finds, the most important is a metal (probably silver) *menorah, unique of its kind in this period.

The earliest remains at En-Gedi, however, lie to the west of the mound, above the spring. Here a large complex of buildings of a late phase of the Chalcolithic period was discovered and dated to about 3300-3200 BC. The buildings were set inside a large walled enclosure with two gates, one on the north and one on the south. In the center was a small round structure which may have had a cultic significance. The main building, about 60 feet long, lies in the northern part of the enclosure and was identified by the excavators as a shrine. One object found in the building was tentatively identified as an altar and other finds which tend to support this identification included animal bones, pottery and ashes. The local pottery has affinities with the cultures of *Tuleilat Ghassul and *Beer-Sheba, which helped in the dating. The excavators believe that the shrine was used by shepherds and villagers of the *Judean Desert and its oases.

In 1966 remains of a *synagogue of the late Roman-Byzantine period were discovered and were excavated in the years 1970-2 by D. Barag and others on behalf of the Hebrew University. Two phases in the use of the building were distinguished, a later phase dating to the second half of the 5th and first half of the 6th century AD and an earlier to the late 2nd-early 3rd century AD. The later synagogue (40 feet by 48 feet) contained a semicircular niche for the Ark of the Law in the northern wall, facing Jerusalem. To its right was a seat for the head of the community. A bema in front of the Ark of the Law was surrounded by a chancel. The floor of the prayer hall is paved with mosaics which contained geometric designs, birds and menorahs. The mosaic pavement of the western aisle is unusual. It bears five *inscriptions in Hebrew and Aramaic. The first inscription quotes I Chronicles 1:1-4; the second lists the names of the twelve signs of the zodiac, the twelve months of the year, the three patriarchs, and the three companions of Daniel, ending with 'Peace on Israel'. The third inscription, in Aramaic, mentions names of donors and contains curses on those who commit certain sins against the community. The fourth inscription, also in Aramaic, mentions a donor who contributed toward the building of 'the great steps'. The fifth inscription is a blessing on all the people of the town who renovated the synagogue. The earlier synagogue was a smaller building with two entrances in the northern wall. It was paved with simple white mosaics and a swastika. This early synagogue underwent extensive alterations. A door in the northern wall was blocked and turned into a niche for the Ark of the Law. Entrances were opened in the western wall and a portico was constructed in front of them. North of the synagogue a two room building was constructed, possibly the community guest house.

EN GEV The sites of En Gev are situated on a sandy hill south of Kibbutz En Gev, about a mile east of the Sea of *Galilee. Four sites were found during excavations made at intervals between 1963 and 1968 and conducted by M. Stekelis and O. Bar-Yosef. Each site is the foundation of a hut dug into the slope of a hill, the dwelling of a hunting and food-gathering group.

En Gev I and II are huts dating from the same period. Six layers were found in En Gev I. These revealed the same types of tools, among which were a pestle and mortar (*Stone implements), several blades which showed signs of constant use, microliths (especially backed-bladelets obliquely truncated), burins and scrapers. Rich animal remains, including roe deer, gazelle and large and small wild oxen, indicate that the area was at that time forested. In addition to hunting these people augmented their diet by gathering wild cereals. A burial of a semi-flexed adult skeleton was found in layer 3 of En Gev I (*Burials).

En Gev III, only partly excavated, included microliths with a tendency to geometrization which is much more accentuated in En Gev IV (*Flint tools). In the latter, minute triangles executed with a microburin technique were found, as well as scrapers and blades which showed signs of frequent use. Fishbones indicate that the occupants of En Gev IV had a knowledge of fishing (*Hunting and fishing). Three of these lithic assemblages date in general from the same period as the Kebaran culture, while the fourth is contemporaneous with the Natufian. Remains of a fossilized spring, numerous shells of land snails typical of humid environments and the many concretions in Sites III and IV indicate that this period was then more humid than at present. (*See also* *PREHISTORY; *FLINT TOOLS.)

EN KEREM; AIN KARIM A village to the southwest of *Jerusalem. Its former identification with biblical *Beth-Haccerem of Jeremiah (6:1) has long been rejected. Late Christian tradition had placed the home of Zacharias and Elisabeth, the parents of John the Baptist, at this site (Luke 1:39-40). There are few remains of the Byzantine period; most date from Crusader times.

ERECH A city in the Land of Shinar, mentioned in the table of nations as one of the cities of Nimrod (Gen. 10:10). In the Babylonian sources it is known by the name of Uruk. The city was in existence as early as the 4th millennium BC. At this time, according to the Epic of Gilgamesh, he was its fifth king, and 'all the countries were sea'. To the earlier levels of occupation belong a ziggurat, temples and a city wall which was strengthened with hundreds of towers. The city endured for thousands of years until its decay in the Hellenistic period.

ESHTAOL; ESTAOL A town in the *Plain, mentioned together with *Zoreah and *Asnah in the territory of Judah (Josh. 15:33). In Joshua (19:41) it is listed together with *Zorah and Ir-Shemesh in the territory of *Dan (cf. also Judg. 13:25), but later the

*Danites went out from Eshtaol to look for better lands in the north (Judg. 18:2). In the Roman period a village called Estaol was known to Eusebius (*Onom.* 88:12) who states that a village by this name still existed in his time, 10 miles north of *Beth-Gubrin, on the way to *Emmaus. It is also mentioned in the Talmud. Identified with Ishwa, north-northeast of *Beth-Shemesh.

ESHTEMOA One of the cities of the priests of the sons of Aaron in the Judean Hills (Josh. 21:14, etc.), and one of those to which David sent presents after the defeat of the *Amalekites (1 Sam. 30:28). In the Roman and Byzantine periods it was a large Jewish village called Eshtemoa, or Astemo. Eusebius (*Onom.* 26:11; 88:20) states that it was a very large Jewish village in the Daroma, on the border of Beth-Gubrin. To this period belongs a synagogue built in the 4th or 5th century AD.

In 1934 L.A. Mayer and A. Reifenberg located the ruins of a synagogue on the site and in the year 1935-6 they conducted trial excavations on behalf of the Hebrew University. In 1969-70 the site was fully excavated by Z. Yeivin, Archaeological Officer, Judea and Samaria, and the synagogue was more extensively surveyed. Unlike most Palestinian synagogues it is of the broadhouse type (*Synagogues). The building occupied the most conspicuous site in the small town. It measures 40 feet by 65 feet and its masonry is of excellent quality. Entry is by three doors on the long, eastern side. A large niche, with two smaller ones on either side, in the wall facing north (towards *Jerusalem) housed the Torah Shrine and possibly two seven-branched candle-sticks (Menorah). The building had a mosaic floor and rich external architectural decoration. During clearance and reconstruction of the synagogue in 1970, Iron Age remains were found under the floor. These included a large hoard of silver jewelry and ingots, possibly indicating that it was once a silversmith's workshop. Identified with es-Semu, south of *Hebron.

Capital with menorah relief from Eshtemoa

ETHIOPIA; CUSH Named Cush in the Hebrew Bible and Cash in the Egyptian sources, Ethiopia is first mentioned in Genesis (2:13) as the land encompassed by the River *Gihon, which flowed from the Garden of *Eden. Situated in the *Nile Valley between the second and the fourth cataracts, it was identified from early times as Nubia. During the Old Kingdom many campaigns were directed against the Nubians, who supplied *Egypt at that period with ivory, ebony, spices and slaves, mostly pygmies. In about 2200 BC the *Egyptians met with resistance from Nubia, possibly because of the arrival there of a new ethnic element, but during the time of the Middle Kingdom they conquered the Nubians and began to exploit the gold mines. At that time the boundary of *Egypt reached as far as the second cataract, but during the period of the 18th Dynasty it was pushed farther south and the land was then divided into the two districts of Wawat and Cush. At this time numerous temples dedicated to Egyptian gods were erected and the influence of *Egypt over Nubia grew stronger. After the death of Rameses III (1150 BC) Nubia became an independent state again, and by 730 BC the Nubians had conquered part of Upper *Egypt. Shabako the Nubian (710-686 BC) founded the 25th Dynasty of *Egypt and his successor, Tirhakah (685-663 BC), sent an army to the aid of Hezekiah, King of Judah, in his war against the Assyrian king, Sennacherib (2 Kgs. 19:9; Isa. 37:9). The following decades saw a struggle between Nubia and Assyria, which lasted until the Nubians were defeated by Ashurbanipal in 663 BC. Psammetichus II conducted a campaign against Nubia in 551 BC.

In later centuries little is heard of Nubia, which the Greeks knew as Aithiopia. The Romans conducted a number of campaigns against Aithiopia and in AD 320 it was conquered by the King of Axum.

EUPHRATES One of the largest rivers of western Asia, about 2,000 miles long; known as Purattu in Accadian. The Persians called it Uprattu, meaning 'the good' — hence the Greek form, Euphrates. In the Bible it is referred to by several names, among them the 'great river' or just 'the river'.

The Euphrates is formed by the confluence of two rivers, the Murad-su, which comes down from Armenia, and the Karasu, flowing from the Anti-Taurus. At first the river runs through a deep narrow gorge, but as they descend towards *Babylon the Euphrates and the *Tigris (*Hiddekel) form the broad plain of *Mesopotamia. The rivers join at the head of the Persian Gulf to form the Shat al-Arab, though this union is quite recent. The Euphrates has a very strong current and for this reason was navigable only in its lower reaches. Along it flourished some of the important cities of *Mesopotamia, the greatest of which was *Babylon. Another, *Carchemish, was an important road junction and a river-crossing for the caravans coming from the Far East. Some of the great battles of history took place on the Euphrates, notably the battle between Nebuchadnezzar II and Pharaoh Necho II of *Egypt, in 605 BC (Jer. 46:2).

In the Bible the Euphrates is named among the four rivers which flow from the Garden of *Eden (Gen. 2:14), and it formed the northeastern limit of the Promised Land (Gen. 15:18). Throughout all periods it was the boundary between east and west, between the spheres of influence of Assyria and Egypt, and each of the great empires attempted the conquest of the borderland of Syria and Palestine. This is also true of the Persian period (Ezra 4:10, etc.). In the Hellenistic and Roman periods the Euphrates was crossed by a series of bridges. It then served as the boundary between the kingdoms of Armenia and Cappadocia, Sophene and Commagene. In the early Roman period it separated Rome from Parthia. Fortresses were built along its banks to protect Rome from the Sassanids. During the Roman period the people of *Palmyra (*Tadmor) built commercial colonies along its banks on the great trade route leading from *India to Syria.

EXECRATION TEXTS In modern literature denotes a special group of Egyptian documents of the Middle Kingdom (20th-18th centuries BC). The documents take the form of potsherds, or clay figurines, on which are written the names of rulers, various cities and ethnic groups, accompanied by a curse (or 'execration') directed against the owner of the inscribed name. If the object was broken and given a ritual burial it was believed that damage would be done to the party involved, who was considered to be an enemy of Pharaoh. The placenames inscribed on these objects provide one of the earliest and most important sources for the study of the historical geography of the land of *Canaan.

There are two groups of Execration Texts. The earlier one, of the late 20th and early 19th centuries BC, consists of potsherds that were broken and buried in a holy place. It included the names of more than thirty rulers and of about twenty towns or regions in Palestine and Syria, including *Jerusalem, *Ashkelon, *Beth-Shean, *Aphek, *Acre, *Misheal, *Achshaph and *Tyre. The later group is of the late 19th to early 18th centuries BC and consists of clay figurines in the form of crouching prisoners with their hands bound behind their backs. It includes sixty-four placenames, most of which represent cities which became important in the biblical period.

EYNAN A site in the Hula Valley, extending over an area of 1 acre, in which remains of the Natufian culture (*Prehistory) were discovered. Excavations on the site, made by J. Perrot on behalf of the French National Center for Scientific Research in the years 1955-6, 1959 and 1961, revealed three occupation levels. In the earlier one, labelled II-III, remains of human habitations were discovered. These consisted of round pits, the sides of which were reinforced with stone walls. In the center of each pit was a hearth lined with stones. One of the larger pits was 25 feet in diameter, with a plastered lining wall 3 feet high. The floor had a basic diameter of 4 feet and was 2 feet 6in deep. Another construction in these levels was a circular pit 16 feet in diameter and 1 feet 4in deep. Its walls were plastered and showed traces of nicely burnished red paint. The floor was paved with flat stones. In a later phase a grave had been dug into the floor of this pit. The habitations of the upper level, level I, were of the same nature but considerably smaller.

Numerous burials were discovered on the site.

These were of two types: collective secondary and single (*Burials). The collective burials were in pits in the ground, in which the skulls and dismembered bodies had been placed. The pits were covered with large flat stones to protect the bones. The single burials had the bodies placed in various ways: flexed, lying on the back or sitting on the haunches.

The lithic industry was abundant and included a small proportion of microliths (*Flint tools), among them points and scrapers. There were also burins, picks and so on, but no arrowheads. The local art was represented by a man's head made of flint, a headless stone figurine of a man, and pestles and mortars of basalt (*Stone implements) decorated with incised or pointed geometrical designs. Fauna included bones of horses, oxen, deer, gazelle, goats, pigs, hyenas, foxes and hares. There were also numerous bones of birds and fishes, but no traces of domestic animals.

The economy of the inhabitants of Eynan was that of a food-gathering, hunting and fishing society. Owing to the richness of the flora and fauna of the Hula Valley the settlement developed into a semi-permanent one. The number of dwellings is estimated at about fifty, giving a total of about two to three hundred inhabitants. The culture is identified as epi-Paleolithic rather than Mesolithic. (*See also* *PREHISTORY).

EZION-GEBER; EZION-GABER An Ezion-Geber and an *Elath of the time of the Exodus are mentioned in the Bible (Num. 33:35; Deut. 2:8), but no archaeological traces of that period have been discovered. Ezion-Geber re-emerges in history in the time of Solomon, and is to be identified with the small low mound of Tell el-Kheleifeh, which lies at about the center of the north shore of the Gulf of *Elath. Its position corresponds in general terms to the description in 1 Kings (9:26), where it is said to lie 'beside Eloth, on the shore of the Red Sea, in the land of Edom'. Ezion-Geber could have existed on one of the hills overlooking the oasis and town of Aqabah, or it could be buried under the modern city. In that case, Tell el-Kheleifeh would represent only a fortified outpost of the original site. There is, however, no evidence to disprove the present identification of Ezion-Geber with Tell el-Kheleifeh.

Ezion-Geber, according to the Bible, was Israel's southern gateway to *Arabia, Africa and *India. It was the home port for Solomon's fleet of ships of Tarshish voyaging to *Ophir and back (1 Kgs. 10:11, 22). Later on, Jehoshaphat's newly rebuilt fleet came to grief nearby, shattering his hopes of renewing the *Red Sea maritime trade instituted by Solomon (1 Kgs. 22:48; 2 Chr. 20:36, 37). The fortunes of Ezion-Geber/*Elath rose or fell depending upon whether or not Israel and/or Judah controlled the *Negev.

The excavations of Tell el-Kheleifeh, conducted by N. Glueck, revealed five periods of occupation, extending from the 10th to the 5th-4th centuries BC. *1)* Some sherds of 'Midianite' pottery, similiar to finds from Timna where they were dated to the 13th-12th centuries BC, were also uncovered. This time-span covers the history of Ezion-Geber. Period I dates to the time of Solomon, in the 10th century BC. Its main,

square, mud-brick building, with a glacis against all four sides, had three long rectangular and three small square rooms whose walls were pierced with two horizontal rows of apertures. These resulted from the ultimate decay and/or burning of wooden cross-beams laid across the mud-brick walls for anchoring or bonding purposes — a form of construction much used in the ancient Near East (*Houses). This building stood not quite in the center of a 135 feet square, enclosed by a casemate wall, each side of which was divided into three salients and two slight recesses. Much of the pottery found was handmade and crude ('Negebite'). The whole of this small fortified center was very similiar to the Negeb sites known as Israelite fortresses. It was also the seaport of Solomon, and may have been destroyed by Sheshonq, biblical Shishak, in the 5th year of Rehoboam (1 Kgs. 14:25, 26; 2 Chr. 12:2-3).

Period II represents a reconstruction, perhaps by Jehoshaphat (*c.* 870-848 BC), or a later king of Judah, with a massive double fortification wall strengthened with a glacis, and an elaborate city gateway with three pairs of doors between two opposite sets of guard rooms. This enlarged settlement may have been destroyed by the *Edomites in the middle of the 9th century BC, during their successful rebellion against Jehoram, son of Jehoshaphat. The name of Ezion-Geber is no longer mentioned in the Bible after the time of Jehoshaphat.

Period III may be attributed to Uzziah, who 'built Elath and restored it to Judah' (2 Kgs. 14:22; 2 Chr. 26:1, 10), probably shortly after the first quarter of the 8th century BC. A seal signet-ring was found with an inscription that reads, 'belonging to YTM'. (Below it is a representation of bellows or possibly an ingot of copper in front of a horned ram.)

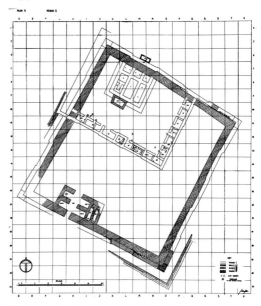

Plan of the Israelite fortress at Ezion-Geber

Seal of Yotam, Iron Age

Period IV belonged to the *Edomites, who regained control of *Elath from Uzziah's grandson, Ahaz (2 Kgs. 16:1, 6). With its various subperiods it lasted approximately from the end of the 8th century to the end of the 6th century BC. In addition to various Edomite lapidary and cursive inscriptions, one Edomite seal impression on pottery occurred frequently; this reads 'belonging to Qausanal' and bears part of a theophoric name to be found in biblical, cuneiform and Nabatean writings, among others. Incised on a large jar were two Minaean letters, indicative of trade with Arabia.

Period V has few remains but Aramaic (5th-4th centuries BC) and late Phoenician ostraca and black, glazed Greek pottery were found. The site was abandoned after this, but was succeeded (on a new location near the western side of modern Aqabah) by the settlement of Aila, which lasted from the Nabatean to Byzantine periods. *Elath is reflected, in the name Aila.

FARAH, TELL EL-(NORTH) This fairly large mound rises above a fertile plain of the same name about 6 miles north of *Shechem. It is situated on an important road leading from the *Jordan Valley into the mountains of *Samaria. Two springs provided the ancient site with a permanent water supply. The mound was excavated (1946-60) by R. de Vaux on behalf of the French School of Archaeology in Jerusalem (Ecole Biblique). It has been identified with various biblical sites, but the current identification with *Tirzah is accepted by all experts and seems to be supported by the results of the excavations.

NEOLITHIC PERIOD The site was occupied for the first time in the pre-Pottery phase of this period (*Prehistory). The remains of human occupation are scanty and consist chiefly of flint implements.

CHALCOLITHIC PERIOD Remains of the 4th millennium BC are more plentiful, consisting mainly of handmade pottery which has affinities with the Ghassulian culture (*Tuleilat Ghassul). Implements were of flint and basalt; bone is rare. No houses were found and the settlers lived in pits. Above the pits rose walls made of earth and pebbles. The few tombs which were found nearby indicate that collective burials were practised.

EARLY BRONZE AGE To this period belong the earliest building remains. The houses were of mud brick and the roofs were supported by wooden posts. This period is represented by five occupation levels, and by the remains of a temple. Local industry is represented by two pottery kilns. The town was comparatively well planned and had streets, some 7 feet wide, with sewers. The city was surrounded by a mud-brick wall strengthened by towers. Later in the same period this wall was replaced by a stone one. To the earlier wall belongs a city gate consisting of two towers, still standing to a height of 12 feet, which protected a passage 12 feet wide, narrowing to 7 feet. The gate was rebuilt in the later phases. The city was abandoned c. 2500 BC.

MIDDLE BRONZE AGE At the beginning of this period a small settlement was built from the remains of the earlier fortifications. Not until about 1700 BC was a larger, fortified town built; the remains of the Early Bronze Age fortifications were again used. A new gate, consisting of an oblong hall divided into a series of chambers (*Fortifications), was also built. At a later phase of the same period an earth rampart was used to strengthen the wall from without. In the town itself remains of store-houses and of a temple were uncovered. Under the floors of the houses child burials in clay jars were found. Adults were buried outside the inhabited area.

LATE BRONZE AGE The city of this period is badly preserved. The Middle Bronze Age city wall had been reused. A larger building, which may have been a temple with a shrine with steps leading up to it, was also discovered. The burials, both of children and of adults, were the same as those of the preceding period and distinguishable only by their pottery. This settlement must have been abandoned either at the end of the 14th century or early in the 13th century BC.

IRON AGE This period is represented by three separate layers. In the lowest, layer III, remains of the walls of the Late Bronze Age settlement were used, but the houses were built on a completely different plan, representing the four-room type of house (*Houses). The old city gate was still in use, but close to it a small temple was constructed. The excavators assume that the Canaanite cult still prevailed in the Israelite period. This layer is dated by pottery to the 10th and early 9th centuries BC. To it belong houses whose construction was interrupted, and they were therefore never completed. They are thought to have been abandoned when Omri chose *Samaria as his new capital instead of *Tirzah. The next layer (II), of the 8th century BC, represents a fortified town with a large administrative building near the gate. One of its rooms, a store-house, contained numerous jars. The private houses are of the four-room type seen in the previous layer, but are of superior workmanship. The destruction of this city is attributed to the Assyrians, by whom *Samaria was laid waste in 732 BC. The latest town (I) is a poor settlement, probably of the Assyrian garrison.

FARAH, TELL EL-(SOUTH); SHARUHEN The site is some 14 miles south of *Gaza and 16 miles west of *Beer-Sheba, near the ancient Via Maris (*Roads) connecting *Egypt and *Mesopotamia. W.M.F. Petrie identified Tell el-Farah with Beth-Pelet (Josh. 15-27; Authorized Version: 'Beth-Palet'), but W.F. Albright's identification with Sharuhen (Josh. 19:6) is now accepted by most scholars. Apart from the bibli-

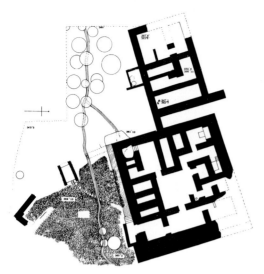

Plan of the Egyptian palace from the beginning of the Iron Age at Tell el-Farah (south)

cal reference, Sharuhen appears three times in Egyptian sources of the New Empire: in the description of the *Hyksos expulsion from Egypt, when Amosis besieged the *Hyksos for three years at Sharuhen; in the records of the first campaign of Tuthmosis III; and in those of the campaign of Pharaoh Sheshonq.

Two seasons of excavations were conducted in 1928-9 by the British School of Archaeology in Egypt under the direction of Petrie. The excavated areas of the mound revealed little in comparison with the many tombs that were investigated in the cemeteries round the city, but both give a picture of nearly continuous settlement from the Middle Bronze Age IIB (*c.* 1750 BC) to the Roman period.

From the Middle Bronze Age II the outstanding finds are the fortifications and the city gate; remains of living quarters are of little interest. In the southeast, built entirely of bricks on foundations of hard-beaten

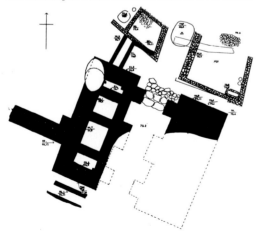

Plan of the gate at Tell el-Farah (south), Late Bronze Age

sand, is a typical *Hyksos gate with three pairs of attached pilasters. On each side of the corridor stood massive towers with rooms. Except for the west side and part of the south and north sides, the mound has natural fortifications in the slopes of the hill above the wadi. The south and west sides were protected by the typical *Hyksos fortification of a moat at the foot of the mound, a sloping glacis of beaten earth and a wall above it. On the north side remains of a huge bank of beaten earth have been found.

After the Egyptian conquest of Sharuhen at the beginning of the Late Bronze Age, it was occupied by an Egyptian garrison. The gate continued to be used throughout this period, though the moat and the glacis were neglected. The 'Governor's Residence' is attributed to the Late Bronze Age. This is a large almost square building (75 feet by 66 feet) with a central court surrounded by rooms. On its south side was a large paved court; on the west a building was attached which could not be entered from the residence and probably housed the servants. The building continued in use until Iron Age I (*c.* 1050 BC). The quantity of Philistine pottery in the upper occupation layers and its absence in earlier ones leads one to the conclusion that a Philistine conquest took place, after which the building continued to be used with certain modifications and additions, such as the paved court.

To the Iron Age belong several building layers, but the excavated area is too small to permit a reconstruction of houses or living quarters. The most interesting layer of the Iron Age is the one labelled layer S-R. In the northern part of the city part of a brick wall was excavated. Near the wall was a building 30 feet by 66 feet, with a long court and rooms on three sides. The date of this layer is not quite clear. Petrie attributed it to Pharaoh Sheshonq on historical grounds, as it is likely that he fortified the site. Further remains can be attributed to the Persian period, while several private buildings and a fort belong to the Hellenistic-Roman period. As no coins and no pottery later than the 1st century AD were found, it is evident that the site was not settled after that time.

THE CEMETERIES More than 350 tombs from all periods were excavated in the large burial area around the city. Most interesting are the Philistine tombs with anthropoid coffins and a Persian tomb with remains of furniture (*Burial). A rich collection of small finds from the tombs includes a great quantity of pottery, scarabs, weapons and jewelry. As no tombs can be attributed to the time between the middle of the 9th century and the 7th century BC, there seems to have been a gap in settlement.

FIELD OF BLOOD; ACELDAMA The field bought with the 30 pieces of silver which Judas cast down in the Temple (Matt. 27:3-8; Acts 1:19). A 4th-century tradition places this field opposite the hill of the Upper City (*Jerusalem), on the south side of the Valley of *Hinnom.

FLAVIA NEAPOLIS A town founded by Vespasian after the destruction of the Second Temple, on the site of a place named Maabartha, between Mount *Gerizim and Mount *Ebal (Josephus, *War* IV, 449; Pliny, *Nat. Hist.* V, 69). From AD 72 until the middle of the

3rd century the city had an era of its own, by which its coins were dated. It was raised to the status of a colony in AD 244 by Philip the Arab, with the title Colonia Iulia (or Sergia) Neapolis. The site has not been excavated but later sources refer to its fortifications and other monuments. The place continued to be mentioned frequently in Byzantine sources. Bishops of Neapolis participated in the church councils of Ancyra (AD 314) and Nycaea (AD 325). The Samaritan synagogue was built there in the 4th century AD, and the local Christian community was oppressed by the *Samaritans (*Samaria) who formed the majority of the population.

Neapolis figures on the *Medaba map as a large city surrounded by a wall, with a gate on the east opening onto the large marketplace. From the market a colonnaded street runs through the center of the city, where it is intersected by another running north-south. Located at this intersection is a circular building with a dome supported by columns. At the southern end of the north-south street a *Nymphaeum is depicted. A large church, possibly the episcopal basilica, stands in the southeastern quarter of the city. Neapolis is identified with the modern town of Nablus, which has preserved the ancient name.

In the last decade discoveries of great importance have been made at Neapolis, shedding new light on the archaeological history of the city. On the eastern slopes of Mt *Gerizim were discovered the remains of a very large Roman *theater, which is shown on the *Medaba map. Within the modern city of Nablus were discovered a *hippodrome, an amphiteater and several monumental tombs. The theater was excavated by Y. Magen, Archaeology Officer, in 1979. A very large structure with a diameter of 330 feet, it could accomodated 6,000-7,000 spectators. The surrounding wall was built of ashlars with drafted margins. Three of the *vomitoria* built of exquisite ashlars were uncovered. There was a triple *cavea*. Some of the seats were labelled in Greek with the names of the persons and families to whom they belonged. One family owned no fewer than 21 seats. The seats in the lowest row, made of blocks of fine white limestone, were provided with foot-stools. The orchestra was paved with colored marble. Sculptured remains, apparently of the *scaenae frons*, were also found. The theater was constructed in the 2nd century and was in use until the 6th century AD.

FLINT TOOLS Many raw materials were available in Israel during the prehistoric periods for making prehistoric tools (*Prehistory). Those made from organic material have, with rare exceptions, decayed and left no trace. Tools found in excavations are therefore made of the hard materials indigenous to the area: flint, chert, limestone, quartz, basalt, granite and obsidian, the most common being flint. This appears in various forms and qualities, either as blocks or small chunks on the surface and in wadi pebbles and boulders, or as a ground cover in arid areas, where it forms a type of 'desert pavement' called *hamada*. The flint may have a uniform texture that makes it easier to remove flakes, but sometimes its uneven and coarse texture results in irregular fractures.

Rock-piercing instrument from Ubeidiya, Lower Paleolithic period

The process of making flint tools was developed during the Pleistocene period. While various different techniques emerged from different cultural traditions the basic preparatory methods were uniform: a block of hard material was modified so that it could be used separately as a tool, or so that flakes could be chipped off and used. In the first stage of modification flakes were trimmed from the primary block (referred to as the 'core') in order to remove its natural outer surface, or 'cortex'. On the ventral surface of these flakes the point of percussion, called the 'bulb', may be observed; it sometimes shows a scar and concentric waves from the force of the blow. The area that received the initial blow is known as the 'striking platform'. Part of this is detached with the flake, while the other portion remains intact on the core. If flakes were to be removed for use as implements the process was repeated and suitable flakes were collected for the second stage of modification, which involved a process known as retouch.

All the processes of flaking and retouching were effected by striking the core with a hard stone hammer or a soft one made of wood, antler or bone. Three basic techniques were employed: 'direct percussion', in which the core was held in the hand or against an anvil and struck with a hammer at the correct angle to detach the flake (or against a fixed hammer); 'indirect percussion', in which the hammer blow was delivered by means of a chisel made of antler, bone or wood; and 'pressure flaking', where an intermediary tool was applied to the core in order to detach the flake under pressure. The latter technique was not used in Israel until the pre-Pottery Neolithic era; it requires obsidian or 'cooked' flint (i.e. which has undergone heating), as satisfactory results can be obtained only with a brittle material.

Flakes removed from the core are divided into three categories: flakes; blades (long narrow flakes, at least twice as long as they are wide); and bladelets (blades with a width of $^1/_2$ in or less). Cores are divided into categories according to the technique of flaking used, their shape, and the number of striking platforms observed on them.

The process known as secondary retouch involved direct percussion (with the flake held in the hand or laid on an anvil) or pressure flaking. The various types of retouch are classified as fine; semi-abrupt or bipolar (in relation to the ventral surface of the piece); 'racloir retouch'; 'pressure retouch' and Helwan retouch.

During the Neolithic period polishing was introduced as a further means of modifying the tools. During the Lower Paleolithic period in Israel direct percussion was the principal method used for facturing flint to produce tools. In the Acheulian culture of *Ubeidiya chopping tools were formed by bifacial flaking of a pebble, and spheroids were obtained by flaking around the entire circumference. From cores with one or more striking platforms flakes were detached and altered into points, notches or denticulated tools by means of the secondary retouch process.

Typical of the Lower Acheulian industries are bifacially flaked hand-axes, generally pointed, with a sinuous cutting edge and portions of the natural cortex remaining on the base. An element of the Acheulian tradition, especially that of the Upper Acheulian era, was the introduction of a soft hammer to improve the edge formation and the over-all regularity of the hand-axe. Common handaxe types of the Upper Acheulian era are classified as cordiform, oval, triangle or Micoquian. The terms are based on the ratio of the length to the width at different points in the tool, the thickness and the flaking techniques used. The names assigned to them describe geometric forms or suggest visual images (fish, leaf, etc.).

Cutting implement from Ubeidiya,
Paleolithic period

The direct percussion technique for flakes and chopping tools continued during the Middle Paleolithic era, in the Yabrudian culture. At this time discoidal and spherical cores appeared. In many cases the secondary modification involved an overlapping, step-like retouch. The classification of these tools is based on the axis of the piece, measured in the same direction as the main blow, with the striking platform considered as the proximal end. The tool is labelled according to the position of the retouch in relation to this axis. The typical Yabrudian forms (racloirs) are categorized according to the variance of the central blow axis to the axis of symmetry of the tool. Other types of racloirs are classified, according the position and form of the retouch, as convergent, convex, concave, straight or double.

Although some retouched blades, scrapers and burins have been found in small quantities in Acheulian industries, they are more common in Yabrudian assemblages. When they appear as an independent industry they are termed 'pre-Aurignacian' and date from the same period as the Yabrudian ones.

References to Mousterian industry are sometimes accompanied by the term 'Levallois facies'. The Levallois technique involved the preliminary shaping of the tool to be detached on a core specially prepared by centrally directed flaking, which removed the cortex of the core. Later the striking platform was prepared by one or more blows. The required tool was then detached by a single, direct percussion blow. When a point was to be manufactured the core had to be given a preliminary triangular shape. For many years the prepared faceted striking platform was considered to be the conventional indication of the Levallois technique, but it is now clear that the difference between Levallois and non-Levallois techniques lies in the method of preparing the core and not in the differences between the striking platforms.

These differences in technique constitute the criteria according to which assemblages are differentiated on both technological and typological grounds. Technological distinctions are made by reference to the techniques of flaking and the processes of shaping the basic piece (such as flake, blade or point), as well as the type of secondary work which completes the design of the tool. Typological comparisons are based on the general characteristics of the tools, as expressed in a list which sorts the finished tools into various categories: scraper, burin, handaxe and so on.

The transition to the Upper Paleolithic period is distinguished by the introduction of the punch (or chisel). Indirect percussion now became a major technique in fracturing flints. In the early stages the same type of core was used, with prepared striking platform. On this the chisel was placed, then struck with a hammer to detach the desired blade. The most common tool of the Upper Paleolithic era was a scraper made of flakes or blades (tools with a rounded or ogival edge). Nosed scrapers and steep scrapers also appeared. The latter are high in relation to their active edge, which was made by the technique known as 'bladelet retouch'. Burins (tools with an active edge made either by opposed flake removal or a combination of flake removal and retouch) also became very common and were perhaps used for wood working.

On some Levallois points, bifacial retouch removed the bulbs of percussion on the ventral surface, creating a point that could easily be hafted. This tool was labelled the 'Emireh point' by Miss D.A.E. Garrod and characterizes the end of the Mousterian phase and the beginning of the Upper Paleolithic period. This tool is now known to have existed from the Acheulian through the Upper Paleolithic cultures and therefore cannot serve as a 'guide fossil'. During later stages of the Upper Paleolithic era the Font-Yves point appeared. This is an elongated, pointed blade with special bilateral retouch at the tip. It has also been found in a shorter, more slender form.

The industries assigned to the epi-Paleolithic are characterized by the manufacture of bladelets, by a process which does not differ basically from that of making blades — they are simply shorter and narrower. Microlithic tools were produced from the bladelets. These were minute tools varied in shape by systems of retouch, either semi-abrupt, abrupt or bipolar. The most common types in the earliest industries are obliquely truncated backed bladelets, narrow micropoints, and inversely or alternately retouched bladelets. Before the appearance of the Natufian culture the abrupt and bipolar retouch became most common and the microliths became geometrical in outline: triangles, rectangles, and trapezes. Later, during the Natufian era, crescents appeared. At the same time, grinding tools made of basalt and limestone were commonly used.

The Natufian culture added the bifacial ridge-back (Helwan) retouch to the technology of the period. The manufacture of blades incrased, serving as sickleblades when hafted into bone or wood handles for the purpose of reaping wild or cultivated cereals. Microlithic tools continued to exist and a special method was devised to facilitate their manufacture. This is termed the 'microburin technique'. The primary piece was held diagonally to the edge of an anvil and advanced in a series of abrupt retouching blows to form a notch. The piece was then snapped at the notch, to form an oblique truncation. By this means the detached fragment carried the remains of a dorsal notch and the negative oblique truncation on its ventral side. The remaining bladelet's dorsal face shows the positive of the oblique truncation as well as the remains of the small notch. This technique occurred accidentally in specimens from Upper Paleolithic assemblages and became a deliberate technique only during the Natufian period in Israel.

Grinding tools are frequently found and appear in various forms. They were manufactured by percussion hammering and polishing and were sometimes decorated. A bone industry developed at this time and included many tools with various functions. This new material proved efficient for the fabrication of points, gouges, needles, awls, sickle-hafts, pendants, spatulas and so on.

The pre-Pottery Neolithic A period is characterized by the appearance of a new family of tools — axes, adzes and arrowheads. The axes/adzes were made by bifacial flaking and a transversal blow at their cutting edge. The tools of this period also included knives and sickle-blades as well as arrowheads, which are a possible development of tools that already existed in the latter part of the epi-Paleolithic period. Conventional tools such as scrapers, burins and awls were also used, but the manufacture of blades predominated. During the pre-Pottery Neolithic B period pressure flaking became a common method of modification; retouch by pressure required the brittle qualities of either 'cooked' flint or obsidian as a basic material and is commonly seen on elongated blades and arrowheads. Polishing with the aid of water and sand began with the Natufian methods for bone and grinding tools. It later became the standard Neolithic procedure for sharpening axes and adzes and providing a finish for cult objects. Neolithic grinding tools are shallow and basin-like, and are characterized by querns (handmills) with a step in the middle of the grinding surface.

During the Pottery Neolithic period the manufacture of flakes and blades continued. Blades were used for making knives, sickle-blades and arrowheads, while flakes were used for awls, scrapers, burins and so on. A common type of sickle-blade is heavily denticulated on its active edge. Pressure flaking was the technique most often used and polishing techniques were expanded to include more implements. (*See also* *PREHISTORY*.)

FOOD AND DRINK The diet of primitive man consisted mainly of meat — eaten raw — fish, wild fowl, wild fruit and weeds. It was only later in the Mesolithic period (*Prehistory) that the food-gathering society developed into a food-producing society by

Bearers of food offerings in an Egyptian relief

cultivating plants and domesticating animals. In the Canaanite and Israelite periods the term 'food' included both the produce of the soil and meat, but in the Bible the most frequent term for food is 'bread' (Gen. 3:19; Exod. 2:20, etc.), probably because this was the staple element in the diet.

Bread was made of wheat or barley and sometimes from a mixture of other ingredients. Flour was used both for baking bread and for fried dishes (Lev. 7:12), cakes (2 Sam. 13:8) and wafers mixed with honey, to which the manna of the wilderness is likened in Exodus 16:31. Grain was eaten dried (1 Sam. 17:17) or green (Lev. 23:14). Vegetables were eaten as well — mainly beans, pulses (2 Sam. 17:28) and lentils, from which a soup was made (Gen. 25:34). Other foods mentioned among those to which the Israelites were accustomed in *Egypt are cucumbers, melons, leeks, onions and garlic (Num. 11:5). There is no reason to suppose that these were not grown in Palestine as well; they are all mentioned in the Mishna.

Fruit was abundant. Vines, figs, pomegranates and olives were among the characteristic fruits of the land (Deut. 8:8). Grapes were eaten fresh or pressed into clusters and dried to form raisins (1 Sam. 25:18). Figs were also eaten fresh or pressed into cakes (1 Sam. 30:12), as were dates, no doubt. Although the latter are not mentioned in the Bible the later Jewish literature, as well as the papyri of *Nessana, includes many references to dried and pressed dates. Raisins, figs and dates will keep for years and they were therefore the kind of food taken on long journeys or stored for emergencies. Pips of these dried fruits were found in the *Judean Desert Caves and in the *Negev. Of the wild fruits, that of the sycamore was eaten (Amos 7:14). Olives were abundant; some were eaten pickled, though the greater part of the harvest was used in the production of oil. Most of the oil consumed in Palestine was olive oil (1 Kgs. 17:14) and much olive oil was also exported (2 Kgs. 5:11).

In the absence of sugar, honey was the main sweetener. Although apiculture was known in *Egypt and *Mesopotamia it is not mentioned in the Bible, where all the evidence points to a natural source: wild bees produced honey on the ground (1 Sam. 14:25—7), in rock crevices (Deut. 32:13) and even in the carcass of an animal (Judg. 14:8). However, some scholars believe that much of the honey referred to in the Bible was not bee honey at all, but a sweet syrup produced artificially from the fruit of the carob tree and from dates. Both kinds are still made in the East and are called honey by the Arabs.

The consumption of flesh by the Israelites was restricted by the dietary laws:'...shall ye not eat of them that chew the cud, or of them that divide the hoof' (Lev. 11:4). Even the ritually clean animals were subject to a special method of preparation (Deut. 12:15—24). Certain kinds of fowl were forbidden (Lev. 11:13—19; Deut. 14:11—18) and the same applied to fish (Lev. 11:12; Deut. 14:9—10). Locusts were permitted (Lev. 11:22) and are still eaten by Yemenite and North African Jews, but other 'creeping' creatures were forbidden (Lev. 11:29—31). Meat was probably not eaten every day; it appeared mainly at feasts (1 Sam. 9:12) or to honor distinguished guests (2 Sam. 12:4). Certain parts of the animal were considered more desirable than others, such as the shoulder (1 Sam. 9:24) or the thigh (Ezek. 24:4). In addition to domestic animals, game such as hart, roebuck, fallow deer, wild goat, wild ox and chamois were eaten.

Milk and milk products were consumed as well. As early as the Chalcolithic period pottery vessels of a certain shape were identified as churns and milk was even offered to important personages (Judg. 4:19). The milk came from cows, sheep and goats (Deut. 32:14) and was kept in skins (Judg. 4:19) or in bottles according to the Authorized Version. Butter (Prov. 30:33) and cheese (Job 10:10; 1 Sam. 17:18) were made from milk. Wine was also a staple drink.

Seasoning in the biblical period was limited to salt (Job. 6:6), obtained from the endless supply in the salt hills near the *Dead Sea (Zeph. 2:9) and possibly also thanks to the evaporation of sea water along the Mediterranean coast. It was only in the Hellenistic and early Roman periods that most of the spices now known were brought from Arabia, India and eastern Africa (*Trade). (*See also* *BREAD; *POTTERY; *OIL; *SPICES; *WINE.)

FORTIFICATIONS

NEOLITHIC PERIOD The oldest known fortified city in Palestine is *Jericho. Its first city wall and tower have

A bowl, dry pomegranates, olive and date stones, from the Cave of Letters, Judean desert

been dated by Kathleen Kenyon to 7000 BC, the pre-Pottery Neolithic period (*Prehistory). Three main building phases can be traced. To the first belong a solid, free-standing stone wall $6^1/_2$ feet thick, preserved on the west side to a height of 12 feet. On this side a huge stone tower was found, built against the inside of the wall and still standing to a height of 30 feet. The top could be reached through a passage on the east and up a steep flight of 22 steps. In the next phase the city wall was associated with a rock-cut ditch 27 feet wide and 9 feet deep. When the third wall was built the internal level of the city had risen, so that the wall on its inner side was partly leaning against a hill.

CHALCOLITHIC PERIOD This was a time of open villages without fortifications.

EARLY BRONZE AGE In this period urbanization and fortified towns developed in several places: *Jericho, *Megiddo, *Gezer, *Ai, *Arad, Tell *Sheikh el Areini, Tell el-*Farah (north) and *Beth-Yerah. The fortifications were built of stone, brick or a combination of both, with foundation layers of stones and brick construction above. The fortifications in these places were destroyed and rebuilt several times. Miss Kenyon believes that at *Jericho 17 phases of rebuilding took place, in view of the fact that the walls were made of unbaked mud bricks resting on a foundation of one or more courses or stone. In the early phases the wall was $3^1/_2$ feet thick.

The first wall at *Megiddo belongs to the Early Bronze Age (level XVIII). It was built of stone, about 15 feet thick, and later enlarged to 26 feet. At *Gezer the stone wall was strengthened with buttresses of beaten earth. The structural history of the several stone walls at *Ai is complicated and has not yet been clarified. The city wall at *Arad was erected on bedrock. Between 7 and 8 feet thick, its outer surfaces were of large stones, with a fill of rubble. The fortifications at Tell *Sheikh el-Areini were more complex, consisting of a brick wall with bastions and a glacis.

At *Beth-Yerah the wall had three components: a vertical block in the center and sloping walls on both sides, all constructed of brick. The thickness at the base was about 26 feet. R.de Vaux has discerned three phases in the fortifications at Tell el-*Farah (north). To the first belongs a rampart of crude brick blocking on the west side, $8^1/_2$ to 9 feet thick and rising on a base of three courses of stone. It was strengthened by towers or projecting bastions and an outer wall was added. In the following phase a wall of stones 10 feet thick was added, also set behind an outer wall. Finally, a glacis up to 30 feet thick was constructed against the rampart. To this same phase belongs the new rampart on the north side; this is made of stone, is about 26 feet thick and is strengthened with a glacis.

Many of the city walls were strengthened by semicircular towers, three of which were found at *Arad, two at *Jericho and one at *Ai. Such towers and part of a city wall are depicted on the cosmetic palette of Narmer, King of *Egypt (1st Dynasty), apparently an allusion to that monarch's attack upon a fortified city in Palestine. At *Jericho a rectangular corner tower was also found. The only city gate to be recognized

with certainty is that of Tell el-*Farah (north). It was constructed at the time of the first rampart and consists of two rectangular projecting towers with a passage between. At a later stage this gate was blocked, but it was subsequently reopened.

MIDDLE BRONZE AGE The Middle Bronze Age I is a period of rural and unwalled settlements of semi-nomads who did not reoccupy the abandoned cities of the Early Bronze Age.

To the Middle Bronze Age IIA belongs the angled gate of *Megiddo (level XIII). The gate comprised a tower, an inner and an outer gate and a stepped approach. The inner gate lay parallel to the line of the city wall and led to the outer gate; only after a right-angled turn could the inner gate be entered. Of the adjoining town wall only a short section has been traced.

A complete change in town planning and fortification occurred in the Middle Bronze Age IIB, when the *Hyksos conquered Palestine on their way to *Egypt. The *Hyksos used war chariots and gates were therefore changed from the type with an angled approach to one giving direct access to the interior. The need to accommodate numbers of warriors with their chariots again produced a change in the character of the towns. A camp-like lower town with its own defences grew up alongside the fortified upper town. Two important features were added to the town walls at that time, a sloping glacis and a ditch. Yadin has demonstrated that the purpose of the glacis was to protect the town against battering rams.

On the whole, town fortifications had reached a high standard, though as the sites have been subjected to research of varying intensity, only portions of these typical *Hyksos fortifications can be traced in each. So far they have been found at *Hazor, *Megiddo, *Jericho, *Shechem, *Lachish, *Gezer, Tell el-*Jarisha, Tell el-*Farah (south), Tell el-*Ajjul, Tell en-*Nejileh and Tel *Dan, while gates have been unearthed at *Megiddo, *Hazor, *Shechem, Tell el-*Farah (north), *Beth-Shemesh and *Gezer.

THE GLACIS The cities of this period had been settled for more than 1,000 years, which meant that the remains

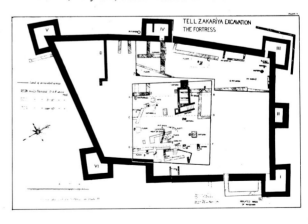

The Israelite fortress at Azekah

*Gate of Megiddo at the end of the
Middle Bronze Age IIB*

of earlier layers of occupation had formed mounds with sloping sides. It is against these slopes that the glacis were constructed. On top of them, at the perimeter of the town, the walls were erected, mostly of brick. Two different methods have been discerned in the construction of the glacis. First came the 'sandwich' method, consisting of separated layers of beaten earth (*terre pisée*), clay, gravel and stones, the outer surface being covered with plaster and smoothed (*Hazor, *Lachish, Tell en-*Nejileh, Tel *Dan). The most complex structure of this type was discovered at Tell el-*Jarisha, where the stone layer of the glacis was strengthened by the addition of layers of bricks. During this period an even better system of defence was introduced, consisting of a battered stone glacis covering the foot of the hill (*Hazor, *Jericho, *Shechem). This was known as the cyclopean wall. Several towns had a ditch below the glacis: *Hazor, Tell el-*Farah (south) and Tell el-*Ajjul. The soil displaced during the excavation of this ditch was used to make the glacis.

Recent excavations have brought to light new variations in the construction of the glacis. At Tel *Dan a wall of stones about 18 feet thick formed the core of a sloping rampart on either side, constructed by the 'sandwich' method. On top of this stone wall rose the brick town wall. At Tell en-Nejileh an embankment of brown earth was laid against the slope of the mound. On the slope a brick wall, $6^1/_2$ feet thick, served as a retaining wall for the glacis, which consisted of layers of crushed limestone, sandstone and brown earth. On

its upper part the town wall proper was built. The most impressive *Hyksos fortifications in Palestine have been found at *Hazor. The lower town's glacis of beaten earth is 765 yd long. At its widest point the base is 100 yd wide across the top and 44 yd at the base.

THE GATE The main feature of the town gates of this period was the direct approach, with a passageway about 50-60 feet long and 10 feet wide. Within were three pairs of pilasters to which three doors could be fixed, thus forming two gate rooms within the passage. Usually there were large towers on either side of the passage, almost certainly multistoried. These towers were subdivided into rooms (Tell el-*Farah [south], *Beth-Shemesh, *Hazor) or had a passage through which they could be entered from the town (*Shechem). The gateway of *Gezer had no towers. At *Hazor the gate was built high on the mound and thus an approach from the outside had to be provided. A path was constructed across the slope, protected by a thick revetment. In front of the gate enough space was left for a chariot to turn.

LATE BRONZE AGE During this period few innovations were made in the system of fortifications. Those from the previous period continued to be in use or were reconstructed on the same lines. To the beginning of this period belongs a new wall at *Gezer (R.A.S. Macalister's outer wall), $11^1/_2$ feet thick, strengthened by a glacis. This was built of huge stones with several rectangular bastions protruding on both sides. A number of them were erected with the wall, while others were added later. The East Gate at *Shechem was built in this period. It had a broad passageway and two pilasters on each side, with two oblong towers behind them. (For fortified temples, *see* *Temples.)

IRON AGE I The last phase of the preceding age saw the collapse or decline of some of the great warfaring eastern empires. For this reason Iron Age I (the period of the Judges and the United Monarchy) was a period of decline in Canaanite fortifications. No fortifications can be attributed to the period of settlement of the tribes of Israel, the first known Israelite fortifications being the casemate walls at Tell en-*Nasbeh, Tell *Beit Mirsim and *Beth-Shemesh, which are attributed to Saul or David. During the reign of Solomon a more elaborate system of fortification was developed. This has been investigated by Yadin, who identified or excavated part of the fortifications of three towns built by Solomon (1 Kgs. 9:15): *Hazor (layer X), *Megiddo (layers Va-IVb) and *Gezer. They comprise three elements: a casemate wall; an inner gate with six chambers formed by three piers on either side and two bastions at the town wall; and an outer gate with two piers built on the slope of the mound. Between these two gates a passageway led into the town. The whole complex was built on the basis of the indirect approach, whereby entry was through a right-angled turn to reach the inner gate. By stratigraphical evidence it has been possible to ascertain that Solomon's gateways were always associated with a casemate wall, and not with a wall of salients and recesses as was first identified at *Megiddo.

IRON AGE II The time of the Divided Monarchy (Israel and Judah) saw great improvements in the fortifications systems in Palestine. At the same time the Assyrians developed the art of siege warfare, especially the technique of the battering ram. This is why Solomon's casemate walls were replaced by a massive wall of salients and recesses in many cities (*Megiddo, *Hazor, *Beth-Shemesh, Tell en-*Nasbeh), while those of lesser strategic importance continued to use the earlier type, the casemate wall, which was improved and repaired. Such a wall was used during Iron Age II at Tell *Beit Mirsim. Apart from the town wall the gate also underwent changes in the period after Solomon, since the depth of the entrance of the inner gate (the part within the town wall) was reduced. This process can best be studied at *Megiddo. The gate of the layer after Solomon (IVa) belongs to Ahab. In the inner gate the number of pilasters was reduced to two on each side. The gate is connected with a massive wall of salients and recesses. A further modification, which took place in layer III, is attributed to Jeroboam II. The gate has one pier on each side behind the town wall, forming a single chamber. In both periods the outer gate with the indirect approach stayed basically the same. Other sites of the Iron Age II have gates of the 'indirect approach' type. Examples are *Megiddo, Tell en-Nasbeh, Tell *Beit Mirsim, Tell el-*Farah (north), *Lachish, Tel *Dan, Tell el-Kheleifeh (*Ezion-Geber) and possibly *Samaria. Some were destroyed during the period and renewed with modifications. The last gate at *Lachish is an elaborate structure, the gateway proper being situated between the inner and outer town walls, the latter being strengthened with recesses and bastions.

ROYAL FORTRESSES These constitute a special type of fortification in the Iron Age and fall into two groups: those which were free-standing structures and those which formed part of the citadel. Of the first group the earliest, excavated at Tell el-Ful, is identified with *Gibeah of Saul (1 Sam. 11:4); it is dated to Iron Age I (more precisely to 1025-950 BC) by pottery evidence. Its plan was rectangular, with four projecting corner towers. There was a gap in occupation until the last decades of Iron Age II, when it was strongly fortified. A special element was the casemate wall of the fortress, the first to be found so late in the Iron Age II. Its basic plan stayed the same—rectangular with four towers. the casemate of the fortress adjoining the tower was 2 feet 6in thick, and the inner wall 1 foot 8in, with a space of 5 feet between them. The outer fortress wall between the towers stood on bedrock and at several places was built against a vertical face cut into the rock. Another new defensive element was a sloping revetment to the east of the casemate wall. It was destroyed in the first campaign of Nebuchadnezzar.

Another fortress, *Mesad Hashavyahu, on the coast half-way between Ashdod and Jaffa, is L-shaped, consisting of two rectangles, the larger containing a courtyard and rooms built against the fortress wall, the smaller with single apartments arranged in three rows with streets between. The fortress wall is 10 feet 6in thick, strengthened by bastions at various points. It was built of bricks on a stone foundation except for the gateway, which was built entirely of stone. The latter has two bastions guarding

ROADWAY & GATE
STRATUM XIII

Gate from Megiddo, Middle Bronze Age IIA

the passageway. This fortress existed for a relatively short period only, about 20 years. It was built by Greek settlers in the last third of the 7th century BC, conquered by Josiah a few years before 609 BC and abandoned in 609 before the advancing Egyptian army.

From the 10th century onwards, mainly in Iron Age II, several fortresses were built in the *Negev in the course of the southward extension of Israelite rule. More than 20 have been found so far during surveys and two have been excavated. The general plan is in fact visible even before excavation. The outer defence is usually a casemate wall with rooms leaning against it and a courtyard in the center. There are three main types. Some fortresses are rectangular, about 130 feet by 160 feet, with projecting towers, as at *Kadesh-Barnea, Khirbet Ghazze and *Arad. They date from the 8th-7th century BC. Another type, which may possibly be dated as early as the 10th century BC, consists of irregularly shaped forts without towers, of about the same size or even larger than the later ones; these are known from *Kadesh-Barnea, Ain Ghadyan on the road to *Elath and elsewhere. The third type was a fort without towers, about 70 feet square. Examples have been discovered on the roads to *Kadesh-Barnea and in the deserts to the south; they are also dated to about the 10th century BC.

The best example of the *Negev fortresses is at *Arad, where six were found (layers XI-VI), covering a period from the 10th to the early 6th century BC. Each of these was built on the ruins of the preceding one. Each was exceptionally strong, and built of well-cut and well-bossed ashlar masonry, but the type of fortification varied from one level to another. The wall of the first fortress was of the casemate type, while that of the second was solid and strengthened with a beaten earth glacis and an outer wall below. This kind of wall existed throughout four successive phases, being additionally strengthened by rooms built against the inside of the wall. The last fortress was again built with a casemate wall. This change of wall type conforms to the development of town fortifications as described above, arising from changes in methods of warfare.

An example of the second group of fortresses, the citadel within a town, was unearthed at *Hazor. Measuring about 70 feet by 84 feet with a wall 6 feet 6in thick, it was built at the western and of the upper town. It was surrounded by Solomon's casemate wall, which was however filled, and turned into a solid wall with bastions. Outside, near the northeastern corner, was a two-chamber watch-tower. This citadel was built in the first half of the 9th century BC and was used throughout the Israelite period.

PERSIAN PERIOD Few settlements of this period have been excavated, so that detailed knowledge of its fortifications is limited. The best example is the Phoenician settlement at Tel *Megadim (*Cartha), where the city was laid out to a rectangular plan and surrounded by a wall, mostly of the casemate type.

HELLENISTIC-ROMAN PERIODS During these periods a city was nearly always surrounded by a stone wall. Excavations of such walls have been undertaken at *Samaria, *Mareshah, *Tiberias, *Jerusalem and *Gerasa. Fortresses have been unearthed at *Beth-Zur, *Arad, *Herodium, *Nessana and other places.

At the beginning of the Hellenistic period in *Samaria the Israelite wall was reused to surround the acropolis, but huge towers were added. In about the 2nd century BC a new wall was built. Little is known of the Hellenistic wall of the lower town, a small section of which was found near the Roman gate to the west. The entire Roman wall was traced, encircling an area of about 170 acres. The gateway was protected by two round towers standing on square bases, most probably the bases of earlier Hellenistic towers. In both periods the masonry was excellent. The outer face of the stones of the Hellenistic tower was carefully smoothed. The Roman wall (apparently built by Herod with additions in the time of Septimius Severus) consisted of stones with heavy projecting bosses with comb-picked margins on all four edges, laid in courses of headers (at right angles to the wall) and stretchers (sideways to the wall). A gate-way with two round towers was also unearthed at *Tiberias, dating most probably to the foundation of the city in the second decade of the 1st century AD. At *Mareshah, which was laid out according to the Hippodamian plan (with streets intersecting at right angles) and was nearly square, the town wall had buttresses and four corner towers. There are two walls, the inner at the edge of the mound and the outer a few feet down. The rough masonry found is apparently part of the foundations. Some of the towers are built on thin brick-like blocks of soft limestone dressed with a broad chisel, often diagonally. On the northeastern and part of the northern side the stones are set in mud with wide joints, roughly flaked and with no distinct dressing. Between the inner and outer wall there was a revetment, in order to strengthen the inner wall, which was built on debris.

The wall at *Gerasa was built or rebuilt under C. Claudius Severus, a legate of Trajan in AD 115, as recorded in an inscription set into the North Gate. The town had four gates and a water sluice defended by two towers, whose inner faces were set at oblique angles to the source so that the water was concentrated in a narrow channel. The wall was built of large stones, headers and stretchers alternating in pairs. Great care was taken when laying them so that no continuous lines were formed by the joints, while rough bosses were left inside a wide marginal drafting. The wall is about 11 feet thick.

Another type of fortification of the Roman period was the military fort, of which a number were built in the late Roman period in the *Negev, in Transjordan and along the Arabah. Several forts also belong to the Byzantine period. An example of a Byzantine city wall was unearthed at *Mampsis, and a fortified citadel at *Oboda.

FURNITURE The furniture of a private house in the biblical period was austere, consisting of a bed, a table and chairs (2 Kgs. 4:10). Most people slept on the floor or on a mud-brick bench, using their garments both as mattress and blanket (1 Sam. 28:23). Only the upper classes could afford real beds. Many beds have been discovered in *Egypt, consisting of four metal legs attached to a flat wooden surface on which a sheet of linen was spread. They were then piled high with cushions and sometimes steps were needed to mount them. The *Egyptians slept with their heads on a raised support; the Assyrians, on the other hand, preferred to lay their heads on a soft pillow. In the Holy Land, too, beds were used by kings and wealthy people (1 Sam. 19:15-16; 2 Sam. 4:7). The same bed was also used as a dining-couch. A nicely made bed (Prov. 7:16-17) or a bed made of ivory (Amos 3:12 and 6:4) were tokens of great riches and luxury. Beds in the Egyptian style have been found in some places in Palestine.

Although tables were a normal item of furniture in the houses of biblical times, a dining table was found in rich houses only. Normally the Israelite would sit on the floor, on which an animal skin, a wooden board or a piece of cloth was laid. Some scholars believe that the table mentioned in the Bible was not a real table but some kind of plate which served both as a table and as a dish for food.

Three types of seating were in use in the ancient Near East. The simplest was a stool without supports, which was used either to sit on or to rest the legs on while sitting on a high stool (Lam. 2:1). To this class belongs a similar folding stool. Both of these originated in Syria, whence they spread into *Egypt in the Middle Kingdom. The second type is a chair with a support for the back sometimes provided with a footstool; this category includes folding chairs with a back-rest. Chairs of the third type have supports both for the back and for the hands. These chairs had elaborate decoration and were used by kings and princes. Solomon's merited special description (1 Kgs. 10:18-20).

Austerity in furnishing also characterizes the Roman period. Furniture at that time consisted of beds, dining-couches in the better homes (a Greek invention to which the Romans added a support for the back), wooden tables and chairs in ordinary houses, and some made of marble or bronze in richer homes. For illumination bronze candelabra were used. (*See also* *LAMPS.)

Clay models of furniture: a bed, a chair and an armchair, Iron Age

G

GABARA; GABATHON According to Josephus (*Life* 123) the third largest city in *Galilee, after *Tiberias and *Sepphoris. During the First Jewish Revolt (AD 66-70) it backed the side of the Zealot, John of Gischala, since Simon, the leader of the city, was a friend of his (Josephus, *Life* 123-5; 203). But under the influence of Josephus it changed sides (*Life* 242 ff.; *War* II, 630), Gabara was the first Galilean city to be conquered by Vespasian, who found it deserted and set it and the surrounding villages on fire (Josephus, *War* III, 132-4).

GADARA *a)* A city south of the River *Yarmuk, identified with the ruins of Umm Keis. In Hellenistic times it was one of the centers of Greek culture in the Transjordan; it was the home town of the poet Meleager, and of Menippus the Cynic (Strabo, XVI, 759). When, under Ptolemaic rule, the Assyrian-Persian provinces were split up, Gadara (Polyb.V, 71) became capital of the biblical district of *Gilead, later called Galaaditis (Josephus, *Antiq.* XII, 330; XIII, 209). After Antiochus III's victory over the Ptolemies at *Paneas it passed to the Seleucids and received additional names, Antiochia and Seleucia (Stephen of Byzantium). The Hasmonean Alexander Jannaeus conquered it in his first campaign (Josephus *Antiq.* XIII, 356). Freed by Pompey (Josephus, *Antiq.* XIV, 75, 91), it was immediately rebuilt and made a member of the *Decapolis (Pliny, *Nat.Hist.* V, 18, 74). On its coinage, from Augustus to Gordian III, the Pompeian era (began 63 BC) is used. Gadara was one of several Greek cities granted to Herod by Augustus (Josephus, *Antiq.* XV, 217; *War* I, 396). At the time of the division of Herod's kingdom it was detached from Archelaus' portion and placed under the proconsul of Syria (Josephus, *Antiq.* XVII, 320). Gadara is mentioned in the gospels as the scene of the healing of the men possessed with devils, though not all scholars agree on its location (*Gergesa) (Matt. 8:28; Authorized Version: 'Gergesenes'; Mark 5:1-2; Luke 8:26-7). According to an inscription of the late Roman period it had the status of a colony, Colonia Valentina Gadara. On the Peutinger map it is shown at a distance of 16 Roman miles from *Tiberias and *Capitolias.

In the north the territory of Gadara extended across the River *Yarmuk (Pliny, *Nat. Hist.* V, 18, 74) to include the famous hot springs of *Hammath-Gader (Eusebius (*Onom.* 74, 10) and in the west as far as the River *Jordan, and possibly to the Sea of *Galilee (Josephus, *Life* 42; Matt. 8:28). In the east the territory reached as far as el-Khureibe, the starting point of the city aqueduct.

In 1886, G. Schumacher produced a plan of the ancient remains of the upper city, whose examination was enlarged and extended to the lower city in 1974 by Ute Lux and E.W. Krueger. Building remains include a colonnaded street in an east-west direction, two theaters, a hippodrome, an agora and a mausoleum.

b) A village northeast of *Jericho, identified with es-Salt near Tell Jadur. Its history before the time of the Hasmonean Alexander Jannaeus is unknown. It is not clear whether his conquest of Gadara, mentioned by Josephus (*Antiq.* XIII, 356), refers to this village, but it was probably here that Alexander was defeated by Obodas I, King of the *Nabateans (Josephus, *Antiq.* XIII, 375). From the 1st century BC it was in Jewish hands. Josephus described it as the metropolis of *Perea, with many wealthy residents (*War*, IV, 413, 415). As a center of resistance it was taken by the Roman army under Vespasian in AD 68 (Josephus, *War* IV, 413 ff.). In Jewish sources of the late Roman period the village is mentioned as Gedor.

GALILEE The northern part of Palestine, also called 'Galilee of the nations' after the Assyrian conquest (Isa. 9:1), possibly because of the many nations which dwelt in that part of the country before the Israelite conquest. Galilee is bordered by the *Jezreel Valley on the south, the Sea of *Galilee on the east, *Lebanon on the north and the Plain of *Acre on the west. It is the highest and coolest region in the country, well watered by the winter rains and with numerous and abundant springs. A deep valley divides the area into two, Upper Galilee rising to a height of more than 3,000 feet above sea level. The main road connecting the Mediterranean coast with the lands to the east of the *Jordan ran through this declivity. Broad valleys, especially in Lower Galilee, provide very fertile soil for agriculture, which was the basis of the rich economy of this region.

When the Israelites conquered the territory Galilee was densely settled with Canaanite city-states, and for a long time the tribes of Asher, Naphtali, Zebulun and Issachar dwelt among them. *Kedesh, 'in Galilee in mount Naphtali', was one of the cities of refuge (Josh. 20:7; 21:32). In the time of Solomon the area comprised four of the administrative divisions of his kingdom (1 Kgs. 4:12, 15-16). The land of *Cabul in Ashur (Josh. 19:27) was ceded by Solomon to Hiram, King of *Tyre, as part payment for his help in building the Temple (1 Kgs. 9:11-12).

In 732 Tiglath-Pileser III conquered the important cities of Galilee: *Ijon, *Abel-Beth-Maachah, Janoah, *Kedesh and *Hazor. The region then became an Assyrian satrapy, known in Assyrian documents as the satrapy of *Megiddo, the seat of its governor. In the Persian period Galilee was outside the Jewish autonomous state. It seems that at that time Galilee and *Samaria were a single district; at any event this was the case in the Seleucid period, when the district, called an eparchy, included also Judea. Under the name of Galila, it is mentioned in one of the Zenon papyri of 259 BC (Zenon visited Palestine from *Egypt in the 3rd century BC). Under the Ptolemies Galilee formed a separate hyparchy. In this period the region was inhabited by many Greeks and *Phoenicians, but there were also some Jewish settlements. In 104-103 BC Galilee was conquered by Aristobulus and added to the Hasmonean kingdom, and when Palestine was conquered by Pompey in 64 BC it remained in Jewish territory. Later it formed part of Herod's kingdom. The capital of the district was *Sepphoris, the other important towns being *Magdala and *Gush-Halav. After Herod's death Galilee became part of the territory of Herod Antipas, who founded the city of *Tiberias, the new capital of Galilee. After his deposition in AD 39 Galilee was given to Agrippa I and after his death it formed part of the kingdom of Agrippa II.

Galilee was the scene of the early ministry of Jesus. He lived in *Nazareth of Galilee (Matt. 21:11; Mark 1:9) and performed his first miracle at *Cana (John 2:1, 11; 4:46). It was while walking beside the Sea of *Galilee that he saw the brothers Simon and Andrew casting nets into the sea and 'called them to become fishers of men' (Mark 1:16 ff.). During the war against the Romans Galilee was fortified by Josephus, and the first battles against the Romans took place there (Josephus, *War, passim*). After the quelling of the revolt it formed part of the Roman province of Judea. Some of the larger cities, such as *Tiberias and *Sepphoris, were made autonomous and their territories enlarged. The area flourished after the period of the Second Jewish Revolt. It was densely populated, with numerous towns and villages, some of which were the seats of the Jewish priestly orders. The great prosperity of the region is evident from the numerous ruins of *synagogues dating to the 3rd, 4th and later centuries.

GALILEE (SEA OF); CHINNERETH; CHINNEROTH These are but a few of the many names by which the freshwater lake in the north of Palestine is known. Some 40,000 acres in area, it is 13 miles long and about $8^{1}/_{2}$ miles across at its widest point, with a maximum depth of 150 feet. Lying 640 feet below sea level, it is surrounded by mountains 1,200-1,500 feet high, rising close to the shore except for short stretches on the south, southwest and northwest. The

The Sea of Galilee

lake is fed from the north by the River *Jordan and by numerous lesser streams, as well as by underwater springs, some of them hot, to which medicinal properties have been attributed. Emerging from the southern end of the lake, the *Jordan carries the outflow to the *Dead Sea.

The great abundance of water and fish, its fertile soil and hot climate turned this region into a real paradise, which attracted settlers as early as prehistoric times. Some of the most important cities in Palestine flourished along its shores, such as *Beth-Yerah in the Canaanite period and *Tiberias in the Roman period. Israelite towns on its shores included *Rakkath, *Chinnereth and *Hammath (Josh. 19:35). The western and southern shores were occupied by the tribe of Naphtali (Josh. 19:35; Deut. 33:23), while the territory of Gad extended from the southeastern shore (Deut. 3:17; Josh. 12:3; 13:27). In the 9th century BC the *Arameans of *Damascus conquered the whole region (1 Kgs. 15:20), but Ahab beat them back (1 Kgs. 20:26-34; Authorized Version: 'Syrians'). In 732 BC the region was taken by Tiglath-Pileser III (2 Kgs. 15:29).

The area was also very prosperous in the Hellenistic, Roman and Byzantine periods. Early on, under the Ptolemies, the fort of Philoteria was built on the site of ancient *Beth-Yerah and served as the capital of a district, developing into a large Jewish city in the Roman period. Later in the same period *Tiberias was founded. The shores of the Sea of Galilee were the scene of the early ministry of Jesus. From *Nazareth he went to preach in the synagogues, some of them in cities close to the sea, such as *Capernaum and *Chorazin. It was from these shores that he called the fishermen, Simon and Andrew, and James and John 'to become fishers of men' (Matt. 4:18-12, etc.), and at the water's edge that he fed the multitude with two loaves and five fishes (Matt. 14:19-20). Tradition places the site of this miracle at *Heptapegon, where the early Church of the Loaves and Fishes was built. Both Jewish and Christian communities flourished along the shores of the lake during the whole of the Roman and Byzantine periods. Excavations made on many sites round the lake, such as *Beth-Yerah, *Tiberias, *Hammath, *Heptapegon and *Capernaum, have revealed much evidence of the splendor and prosperity of the region in all periods.

GALLIM The birthplace of Phalti, son of Laish, the second husband of Michal, Saul's daughter (1 Sam. 25:44); conquered by Sennacherib on his way to *Jerusalem (Isa. 10:30). Eusebius (*Onom.* 72:7) wrote: "And some say that there is some village near *Ekron, named Gallaia". Tentatively identified with Jilya.

GAMES AND TOYS The oldest game boards found during excavations in Palestine come from Tell *Beit Mirsim and *Beth-Shemesh and belong to a layer in the Middle Bronze Age IIB and IIC. The moves were determined by spinning a teetotum, a sort of four-sided top with lettered or numbered sides. This type of game originated in *Mesopotamia and spread all over the East, apparently reaching Palestine under Egyptian influence. The most elaboratate examples of inlaid game boards were found in tombs at *Ur and *Thebes. The game from Tell *Beit Mirsim consisted of a stone slab marked out with three rows of four squares at the top and bottom and 12 squares in the center, and had 10 playing pieces, five conical and four tetrahedral, made of blue faience. The ivory teetotum

Lion and unicorn playing checkers (detail from picture below)

was pierced on four sides and numbered from one to four. This game was much favored in the Late Bronze Age and in the Iron Age. Parts of game boards made of chalk or limestone and teetotums of ivory and limestone have been found at Tell el-*Ajjul, Tell el-*Farah (south). *Gezer and Tell *Jemmeh. An ivory game board with 58 holes was unearthed at *Megiddo and dated by the excavators to 1350-1150 BC. The center was inlaid with gold and blue paste and every fifth hole contained a medallion of gold filled with leaves of blue paste.

Pottery rattles were found in large numbers at *Gezer and in other mounds in Judea. They are thought to have been children's toys, though some seem to be too heavy for a child and were possibly used in religious rites. They were usually box-shaped, closed on all sides, sometimes with small perforations, and filled with small stones or pieces of pottery which made a noise when shaken. Some of them are in the shape of dolls or birds.

Among the ancient Israelites no form of gambling is mentioned, but in the Second Temple period a game played with dice (Hebrew, *kubia*) was adopted by the Jews. Since gambling was popular among the Greeks

A humoristic papyrus from Egypt, 20th-21st Dynasties

and Romans the rabbis strongly condemned it, and the Mishna disqualifies a gambler from testifying before a court of justice. During excavations in the underground part of the Convent of Notre Dame de Sion in *Jerusalem traces of games were found on the flagstones of the court of the Antonia fortress. Christian tradition associates these games with the distribution of Jesus' garments by the Roman soldiers, who cast lots for his seamless robe (John 19:23-4).

GATH; GITTITES *a)* One of the cities of the 'five lords of the Philistines' (Josh. 13:3; 1 Sam. 5:7-10; 6:17), the place where the Anakim remained until they were subdued by Joshua (Josh. 11:22, etc.). Achish, King of Gath, granted refuge to David when he escaped from Saul (1 Sam. 27:2-11). According to one account Gath was conquered in the days of the ministry of Samuel (1 Sam. 7:14), while another indicates that it was taken by David (1 Chr. 18:1). Furthermore, according to 1 Kings (2:39-40), Gath was in the hands of its king, Achish, in the time of Solomon. David had a company of Gittite mercenaries (2 Sam. 15:18). Gath was later one of the cities fortified by Rehoboam (2 Chr. 11:8). Uzziah, King of Judah, broke down its walls (2 Chr. 26:6) and in the time of Amos it was already in ruins (Amos 6:2).

The identification of Gath (which in Hebrew means 'winepress') is not easy. It has been variously identified with some of the larger mounds on the eastern border of the *Plain. One of these was Tell *Sheikh el-Areini, where extensive excavations continued for seven seasons in an effort to establish identification with the Philistine city. But no typical Philistine remains were discovered there, and there was no occupation of the site in the period when the *Philistines were supposed to have inhabited it. Scholars now suggest seeking Gath of the *Philistines at Tell es-*Safi, which would be in line with the towns of *Ekron, *Libnah and *Lachish.

b) A Levitical city of the family of Kohath, in the territory of Manasseh, near *Taanach (Josh. 21:25-6). A place with a similar name is mentioned in the *El Amarna letters, where it is listed with *Shunem. Eusebius (*Onom.* 68:4) also knew a village by this name, 5 miles from *Beth-Gubrin, on the way to *Lod. Not identified.

GATH-RIMMON A Levitical city of the family of Kohath, in the territory of *Dan (Josh. 21:24). It is mentioned in some of the early Egyptian sources, such as the list of Tuthmosis III (*Inscriptions) and the *El Amarna letters. From these it becomes clear that it should be sought near Jaffa. The site is tentatively identified with Tell el-*Jarisha, not far from *Tel Aviv, where remains of a small town have been unearthed. These range in time from the Early Bronze Age to the end of the Early Iron Age. Notable are remains of a formidable glacis, a part of the Hyksos fortifications (18-17th centuries BC).

GAZA A city on the coast of Palestine on the route to *Egypt, the last halt before entering the desert. A caravan point of strategic importance from the earliest times, it was constantly involved in the wars between *Egypt and Palestine, Syria and the Mesopotamian powers, and appears frequently in Egyptian and Assyrian records. Under Tuthmosis III it is mentioned on the Syrian-Egyptian caravan route. In the *El Amarna letters it appears as Azzati. The Hebrew form is Aza, the Greek, Gaza.

The Roman city extended to the seashore, but modern Gaza is about 3 miles from the coast, which agrees with Arrian's account of the siege of Alexander the Great. It seems certain that the medieval and modern city stands on the site of the ancient one, though the evidence of classical authors is not always clear on this point. For about 350 years the city was under Egyptian rule. From the 12th century BC it became one of the five Philistine coastal cities (1 Sam. 6:17) and appears in the story of Samson (Judg. 16). Dagon was worshiped there (Judg. 16:21-30). It was Israelite since the time of David but became Assyrian under Tiglath-Pileser III and Sargon II (around 730 BC). In the 7th century it again came under Egyptian control, but in the Persian period (6th-4th centuries BC) it enjoyed a certain independence and was a flourishing city.

Alexander the Great conquered Gaza in 332 BC after a siege of five months. Belonging at first to the Ptolemaic kingdom, it passed after 200 BC to the

Statue of the Good Shepherd from al-Minah, near Gaza, Byzantine period

Fragment of a chancel screen from the synagogue at Gaza, showing candelabrum (menorah), *ram's horn* (shofar) *and palm branch* (lulab)

Seleucids. In the 1st century BC and the first half of the 1st century AD, it was the Mediterranean port of the *Nabateans, whose caravans arrived there from *Petra or from *Elath on the *Red Sea. In 96 BC the Hasmonean Alexander Jannaeus attacked the city (Josephus, *Antiq.* XIII, 357; *War* I, 87). The inhabitants hoped for help from the Nabatean king, Aretas II (Josephus, *Antiq.* XIII, 360), but when this did not come the city surrendered after a siege of a year. Jannaeus slaughtered the population and destroyed the city (Josephus, *Antiq.* XIII, 364). Under Pompey it was refounded and rebuilt by Gabinius (Josephus, *Antiq.* XIII, 75-6). In the New Testament Gaza is mentioned as being on the caravan route to *Egypt (Acts 8:26). Granted to Herod by Augustus (Josephus, *Antiq.* XV, 217; *War* I, 396), it formed a separate unit within his kingdom, and Cosgabar, the governor of *Idumea, was in charge of its affairs (Josephus, *Antiq.* XV, 254). On the division of Herod's kingdom it was placed under the proconsul of Syria. In the Roman period it was a prosperous city and received grants and attention from several emperors, especially Hadrian. It was adorned with many temples, the main cult being that of Marnas. Other temples were dedicated to Zeus, Helios, Aphrodite, Apollo, Athene and the local Tyche. Shortly after the conversion of its inhabitants to Christianity, under Bishop Porphyrius (AD 396-420), all the temples were destroyed. It then became an important city of the early Christian world and many famous scholars taught at its academy of rhetoric, the best known being Procopius of Gaza (born at the end of the 5th century AD). Gaza's church buildings are important examples of Byzantine architecture. In AD 635 the town was conquered by the Arabs. The Crusaders repeatedly captured and occupied it.

In 1966 remains of a synagogue were found on the sea coast south of Gaza. Near it were living quarters and installations for dyeing. Of the synagogue only the mosaic floor has survived. The building consisted of a nave with two aisles on each side, broader than it was long, and orientated east-west. In the western part of the nave the mosaic floor depicts David as Orpheus, identified by his name in Hebrew letters. Near him were lion cubs, a giraffe and a snake listening to him playing a lyre. In the southern outer aisle a further portion of the mosaic pavement is preserved. The floor was divided by medallions formed by vine leaves, each of which contains an animal: a lioness suckling her cub, a giraffe, peacocks, panthers, bears, a zebra and so on. In one medallion is an inscription naming the floor's donors and the date, AD 508-9. In style the floor is very similar to that of the synagogue at *Maon (Menois) and the church at Shallal (*Mosaics). The same artist most probably worked at all three places.

GEBA *a)* A place on the northern border of Judah in the time of the kingdom of Israel (2 Kgs. 23:8), whence the saying 'from Geba to Beer-Sheba', or, in the days of the Restoration (Zech. 14:10), 'from Geba to Rimmon'. A place named Geba, on the way from *Jerusalem to *Shechem, was also known in the Roman period; according to Eusebius (*Onom.* 74:2), it was situated 5 miles north of *Gophnah. It is identified with Khirbet et-Tell.

b) A place where a Philistine garrison was stationed and where the *Philistines were defeated by Jonathan, son of Saul (1 Sam. 13:3; 14:6-15). The Assyrians camped here on their way to *Jerusalem, before *Ramah and *Gibeah of Saul (Isa. 10:29). Identified with Jeba, north-northeast of Samaria.

GERAR A city and district prominent in the early history of the Hebrew Patriarchs, where Abraham and Isaac enjoyed the hospitality of its king, Abimelech, grazed their flocks and cultivated its lands (Gen. 2-6; 26:1-12). There was constant tension between the Patriarchs and the local herdsmen over the water wells (Gen. 21:25; 26:15-23). In Genesis Gerar is referred to as a Philistine town, but scholars believe that this is an anachronism, because this part of the country did not become Philistine until the 11th century BC. The place is mentioned only once later in the Bible, when Asa, King of Judah, chased Zerah the Ethiopian from *Mareshah to Gerar (2 Chr. 14:12-13). It seems that it does not appear in any of the other ancient sources. In the Byzantine period it was a royal estate known by the name of Saltus Gerariticus, between the domains of *Gaza and *Beer-Sheba. The district is also marked on the *Medaba map. Gerar is identified with one of the four large mounds between *Gaza and *Beer-Sheba: Tell *Jemmeh, Tell Abu Hureira, Tell el-Shariah or Tell et-Tuwail.

GERASA A city in Transjordan, modern Jerash, about 20 miles north of Amman. Situated on an important road (the King's Highway) and on a site with many natural advantages. Remains of the Stone, Bronze and Iron Ages have been found here. These finds, consisting of flint tools and pottery only, do not permit positive conclusions about the importance of the city in Canaanite and Israelite times that is suggested by its position. The Hellenistic-Roman-Byzantine city, whose walls enclose an area of about 200 acres, was one of the largest and most important in this area, and the site was extensively excavated during the years 1928-34 by a joint expedition of Yale University, the British School of Archaeology in Jerusalem and the American School of Oriental Research.

Late tradition (Byzantine) attributes the foundation of the city to Alexander the Great. A Roman inscription refers to the erection of a statue of Perdiccas and it is possible that he was venerated as the founder by the inhabitants. Another inscription mentions Macedonians among the first settlers, which also seems to point to its being an early Hellenistic foundation.

A new chapter in the city's history began after the battle of *Paneas (200 BC), when Palestine and southern Syria passed from Ptolemaic control to the Seleucids. To this period belongs the first of a succession of temples dedicated to Zeus Olympus, which were built on high ground to the south of the forum. The last temple, whose remains are still standing, is dated by an inscription to AD 163. Built on a high podium, it was surrounded by columns of the Corinthian order. Nearby stood a smaller temple that was constructed early in the 1st century BC. The city was conquered by the Hasmonean Alexander Jannaeus (Josephus, *Antiq.* XIII, 395) and freed by Pompey, who made it a member of the *Decapolis. In the First Jewish Revolt (AD 66-70) the city was sacked by the Jews (Josephus, *War* II, 458) and later retaken by order of Vespasian (Josephus, *War* IV, 486-9). On the other hand Josephus mentions the good relations between the Jewish inhabitants and the citizens of Gerasa. Thus the events during that time are not at all clear.

On the whole, little is known of the city's history during the 1st century AD, a period of great expansion and of flourishing caravan trade. During this time, at the latest by AD 75-6, the city adopted the Hippodamian city plan. The streets intersected at right angles, the main street, the *cardo*, being adorned with tetrapylons (shrines built at the intersections of main streets). The forum was built at this period. A small theater within the city was probably built later in the 1st century AD. During the period of the Antonines (second half of the 2nd century AD) the city reached its greatest prosperity and many new monuments were erected: a triumphal arch, public baths, a *nymphaeum*, a *hippodrome and temples, the chief of which was dedicated to Artemis. Built in AD 150-80, it was approached from the east of the *cardo* through a court and a trapezoidal hall. To the west of the *cardo* elaborate *propylaea* (entrances) gave access to two porticoed terraces, on the inner of which stood the temple. The Temple of Zeus was rebuilt during the same period. Outside the city, near the south gate, were the *hippodrome and a triumphal arch dedicated to Hadrian. To the north a theater was erected in the Severan period, connected with a pleasure area and a pool used in the religious festival of the god Maiumaz.

In the 4th century, Gerasa became a center of Christianity, its representatives taking part in church councils as early as AD 359. The religious architecture, a dozen churches and a synagogue later to be converted into a church, attest to the wealth of the inhabitants. The floor *mosaics are of great interest. In AD 634 Gerasa was conquered by the Arabs. It is known that in the 9th century the population was half Greek and half Arab, but by that time the city had long ceased to be important.

A large quantity of inscribed material was found in the excavations. From this a great deal can be gleaned about the religious, administrative, economic and military aspects of life in the city. The earliest inscription honors a Nabatean king. Others are connected with the religious buildings and cults and there are dedicatory inscriptions to emperors, funerary inscriptions, and a number of inscriptions in the churches.

GERGESA A place on the eastern shore of the Sea of *Galilee, between *Susita and *Bethsaida, where Jesus cast out devils (Matt. 8:28 ff). The site was known by the name of Kursi in Jewish sources, the home town of the sage Rabbi Jacob son of Hanilai. Origen and Eusebius (*Onom.* 73:14) mention a village by the name of Gergesai near the Lake of Tiberias, in which the swine drowned. The site is known today by the name of Kursi.

In the years 1970-72 a large monastery and church were excavated on this site on behalf of the Department of Antiquities. The entire complex was surrounded by a strong wall, enclosing an area of 4.5 acres. A road 15 feet wide and 150 feet long, paved with basalt slabs, led to the church (70 feet by 135 feet). In an early stage the atrium had open porticoes on all sides. These were later closer by partition walls to form rooms. Beneath the atrium was a large cistern. The single-apsed basilica was paved with *mosaics decorated with a geometric carpet and medallions containing animals and fowl. The latter were damaged by iconoclasts. A room to the south of the apse had an oval-shaped baptismal font, with a Greek inscription dating to the year AD 585/86. There were service rooms and a chapel along both sides of the basilica. Beneath the chapel was a crypt in which the monks were buried. The construction of the church is dated to the 5th century AD and its destruction to the Persian invasion to Palestine in AD 614.

GERIZIM (MOUNT) A hill rising to 2,849 feet above sea level and commanding, together with Mount *Ebal to the north, the entrance to the narrow valley of Nablus (Neapolis, ancient *Shechem). As this pass gave the only access from east to west into the mountains of Ephraim and was situated on the main road from north to south, it was of strategic importance from earliest times. Abraham entered the Promised Land through *Shechem 'at the oak *Moreh' (Gen 12:16; Authorized Version: 'unto the plain of Moreh'), and the Samaritan tradition places the sacrifice of Isaac on Mount Gerizim (Gen. 22:2), substituting *Moreh for Mount *Moriah in *Jerusalem.

Gerizim and *Ebal were the mountains on whose slopes the tribes of Israel assembled under Joshua, fulfilling Moses' command by hearing the curses and the blessings connected with the observance of the Law (Gerizim being the mount of blessing; *Ebal the mount of cursing) (Deut. 11:29; 27:11-13; Josh. 8:33-4). The Samarian Pentateuch replaces *Ebal with Gerizim in the command to erect an altar (Deut. 27:4). Thus Mount Gerizim has been the spiritual and visible center of the *Samaritans from the beginning of the schism, after the return from Babylon, to the present day. The separation between Jews and *Samaritans was completed by the erection on Gerizim of a rival temple to that in *Jerusalem. Josephus (*Antiq.* XI, 310, XIII, 74) dates this to the time of the conquest of Alexander the Great. The attribution to the time of Sanballat the Honorite, referred to in Nehemiah (13:28), seems too early. Under Antiochus IV Epiphanes the temple was dedicated to Zeus Helios (2 Macc. 6:2; Josephus, *Antiq.* XII, 257 ff.) and it was destroyed by John Hyrcanus in 128 BC (Josephus, *Antiq.* XIII, 255). Although the *Samaritans did not join the Jewish rebellion in AD 67 they had several clashes with the Romans. Shortly before the fall of *Jerusalem Vespasian's general Cerealis surrounded Mount Gerizim and slew there 11,600 *Samaritans (Josephus, *War* III, 307 ff.).

Sources of the 5th and 6th centuries AD record that Hadrian built a temple for Zeus Hypsistos on the mount. This temple is depicted on the imperial coins of Neapolis from the reign of Antonius Pius (AD 130-61) to Volusianus (AD 251-3), when the coinage of this mint ceased. The temple was reached by a monumental stairway, as was mentioned in about AD 330 by the Pilgrim of Bordeaux (587, 3) and by Epiphanius (c. AD 315-403). It is depicted on the coins.

The earliest archaeological remains of Gerizim are those of a temple found on the lower slope belonging to the Middle Bronze Age IIC, consisting of an inner central shrine surrounded by several rooms in a large outer square, nearly identical to the temple at *Rabbath-Ammon.

In excavations in 1964-8 under the direction of R.J. Bull remains of two temples were unearthed on the summit of Tell er-Ras. The upper temple measures 65 feet by 45 feet. On the slope are signs of a staircase leading into the city. The structure stands on a podium which rises above a large stable platform 225 feet by 140 feet and 22 feet high. Erected in the 2nd century AD, it can be identified with the temple to the Most High Zeus dedicated under the emperor Hadrian. Walls of an earlier building and a half cube of unhewn stones, located under the podium of the Roman temple, are identified by the excavator with the Samaritan temple and sacrificial altar, destroyed by John Hyrcanus in 128 BC.

In the Byzantine period there was continuous fighting between the *Samaritans and the Christians. The Emperor Zeno drove the *Samaritans from Mount Gerizim (AD 486) and ordered a church to be built there in honor of Maria Theotokos. When this was later destroyed by the *Samaritans the Emperor Justinian rebuilt it (c. 530) and surrounded it with an enclosure (Procopius, 5, 7). Excavations on the summit brought to light the foundations of an octagonal church with an apse and a narthex to the west, and

part of Justinian's enclosure. After the destruction of this complex during the Arab conquest, and after the breakdown of the Abbasid Khalifate, the *Samaritans regained possession of Mount Gerizim. They still celebrate the feasts of Passover, Pentecost and Tabernacles there every year.

GESHUR A region near the *Bashan (Deut. 3:14) not conquered by Joshua (Josh. 13:13). When the kingdom of Judah was established a small Aramean state was founded at Geshur. David married the daughter of Talmai, King of Geshur (2 Sam. 3:3), and Absalom found refuge there after killing Amnon (2 Sam. 13:37-8). The Geshurite kingdom had ceased to exist by the 9th century BC. Its territory is identified with the area which extends along the eastern shore of the Sea of *Galilee and the northern bank of the River *Yarmuk. There is a possible reference to it in one of the *El Amarna letters.

GETHSEMANE A garden on the Mount of *Olives, on the other side of the River *Kidron (John 18:1; Authorized Version: 'brook of Cedron'). Jesus went there from the place of the Last Supper (Matt. 26:30, 36; Mark 14:26-32). The name derives from the Hebrew *gath sehmanim* ('oil presses'). Tradition places the garden to the east of the Temple Mount.

GEULA (CAVES) These caves, discovered in 1956, are situated on the western slopes of Mount *Carmel, 45 feet above Wadi et-Tin. They are actually remnants of a single large cave which was destroyed by quarrying operations. The remaining niches were dug between 1958 and 1964 by E. Wreschner of Haifa. The site consisted of three layers and assemblages. Layer A, with 6-12in of gray earth, contained many Mousterian implements of Levalloisian facies. Sediment analysis showed that the climate at that time was cold and wet. Layer B1, 12-25in thick, was accumulated during a warm and dry period. Many points, flakes and knives executed by means of the Levalloisian technique were uncovered in this layer. They were dated to 42,000 BC plus or minus 1,700 years by the carbon 14 method. Layer B2 is of blackish-brown earth 20in thick. It contained many large flakes and points of Levalloisian technique as well as 318 bone tools, generally made from the bones of wild oxen. 59 species of animals were discovered in this layer, including gazelle, roe deer, wild boar, wolf, wild ox, hystrix and bats. (*See also* *PREHISTORY; *FLINT TOOLS.).

GEZER The great mount of Gezer is situated on the last ridge of the Judean foothills as they slope down to join the northern *Shephelah, 7 miles southeast of Ramla. It guards the junction of the Via Maris (*Roads) and the trunk road running past Gezer across the Valley of *Ajalon, where Joshua made the moon stand still (Josh. 10:12-13), then up the steep wadi by lower and upper *Beth-Horon and thence through the hills to *Jerusalem and beyond to *Jericho and Transjordan. In addition to the advantages of this strategic position Gezer has a perennial water supply from springs and deep wells at the southeast of the mound. This site of some 30 acres is not only one of the largest in pre-Roman Palestine; throughout the last three millennia BC it was one of the six most important cities in the country.

EXCAVATIONS The Palestine Exploration Fund sponsored excavations from 1902 to 1909 under the direction of R.A.S. Macalister. Macalister's finds were rich, revealing monumental architecture, including four city-wall systems: the 'Middle Wall' (possibly Early Bronze Age); the 'Inner Wall', with a triple gateway (Middle Bronze Age IIC); the 'Outer Wall', belonging mainly to the Late Bronze Age but probably reused in the Israelite and even as late as the Maccabean period; and a casemate wall and typical four-entrance gateway of the Solomonic period (*Fortifications). Other architectural finds were a water tunnel similar to the ones at *Hazor and *Megiddo, 219 feet long, cut through solid rock to an underground spring (*Water supply); the famous 'Gezer High Place', a mortuary shrine of the Middle Bronze Age IIC to Late Bronze Age, with 10 large standing stelae (*Massebot) and numerous domestic installations.

Inscriptions, rare on sites in Palestine, were found here in large numbers. They include the 'Gezer Potsherd' in Proto-Sinaitic script from the early 2nd millennium BC, found by a visitor after the excavation had concluded; cuneiform tablets from the *El Amarna period and the Neo-Assyrian period (7th century BC); the 'Gezer Calendar', from the late 10th century BC - the earliest known Hebrew inscription; 'royal-stamped jar handles, of the 7th-6th centuries BC (*Seals); and nine boundary inscriptions bearing the name 'Gezer' in the vicinity of the mound from the Roman period. Among the small finds were the vessels of the Chalcolithic 'cream ware' of the late 4th millennium BC (*Pottery); important finds from the beginning of the Early Bronze Age; Egyptian imports from the 12th-18th Dynasties; beautiful painted Philistine pottery; silver vessels of the Persian period. A mass of other material emerged from the mound itself and from nearly 300 tombs in the vicinity.

This material is fascinating in itself, but unfortunately it has proved largely useless in reconstructing the history of the city, because of the way in which it was excavated and published (*Archeology, methods of research). It soon becomes clear from the plans of the architecture of the eight so-called 'strata' that, although each conveys the impression of being a completed town plan of the period, it is really a composite plan of several different levels. There are no surveyor's elevations on the plans. The pottery and small objects are described in terms of seven or eight general phases - 'pre-Semitic', 'First Semitic' to 'Fourth Semitic', 'Hellenistic' and 'Roman Byzantine', some covering hundreds of years. Even the trench from which an individual piece comes is often not specified, let alone the *locus*.

It has long since been recognized that new excavations at Gezer would be desirable. In fact a second series was begun in 1934, again under the sponsorship of the Palestine Exploration Fund, this time directed by A. Rowe. However, an unfortunate choice of areas brought these excavations to a halt in six weeks and the plans were abandoned.

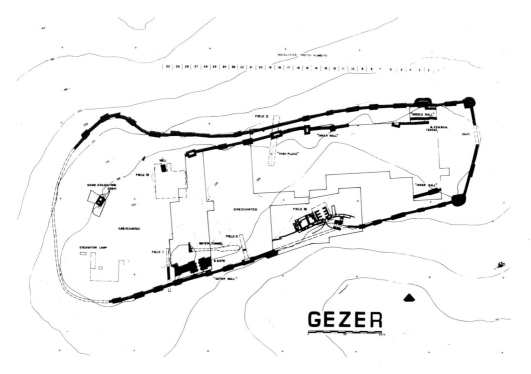

GEZER

Plan of the mound and excavation areas at Gezer

RECENT EXCAVATIONS A 10-year project was begun in 1964 by the Hebrew Union College Biblical and Archaeological School in Jerusalem, in conjunction with the Harvard Semitic Museum. G.E. Wright directed the first season, with subsequent seasons directed by W.G. Dever. J.D. Seger directed the 1972-74 seasons, and Dever returned for a final season in 1984, sponsored by the University of Arizona. In addition to re-excavating the monumental architecture of Macalister with more precise modern methods, the recent Gezer excavations opened up numerous fields in areas previously untouched, yielding a total of twenty-six strata (c. 3000 BC - AD 100). The project also pioneered the interdisciplinary methods of the 'new archaeology' (in vogue since the early 1970's), as well as introducing the concept of the 'field school' and the use of student volunteers instead of hired labor. A projected series of eight volumes (several already are published) will set forth the aims, methods, and results of the Gezer excavations.

In field I the 'Inner Wall' - 50 feet wide and the largest stone structure ever uncovered in Palestine - was dated to c. 1600 BC, in the Middle Bronze Age IIC. A glacis some 25 feet in height and sloping up at an angle of about 45⁰ was added still later in the same period. The gate was the usual triple-entrance type (field IV). This wall was superseded in Late Bronze Age II by the 'Outer Wall', which continued in use throughout the remainder of the history of Gezer. Its rectangular towers of fine ashlar masonry were built in the Solomonic era and the semicircular bastions surrounding these were added in the Maccabean period. In field II the Solomonic casemate wall was excavated. together with a succession of Iron Age strata from the 10th to the early 6th centuries BC. This shed light on the 'gap' postulated by most archaeologists thanks to Macalister's failure to publish much of his Iron Age II material. In field III the 'Maccabean Castle' of Macalister proved to be, as Yadin had already suggested, a partly excavated Solomonic four-entrance gateway nearly identical to those already known from *Megiddo and *Hazor. This discovery sheds interesting light on the Solomonic fortifications mentioned in 1 Kings (9:15-17). Several Iron Age II destructions and repairs were discovered; these had been extensively reused in the 2nd century BC as a two-entrance gateway. The 1984 season in field III added evidence of a well (constructed 10th century BC), a barracks-administrative center, and definite proof of the Solomonic reuse of the Late Bronze Age 'Outer Wall' in connection with the ashlar built lower 'Gatehouse'. This building was rebuilt as a larger palace in the early 8th century BC, after which it was destroyed in the Assyrian conquest, along with the upper gateway.

In addition to clarifying details of the fortifications these initial trenches gave a fairly complete preview of the stratification of the mound. Field I produced some 17 strata in the 25 feet from bedrock to the surface. These began with a Late Chalcolithic occupation and extended through Early Bronze Age I and II, Middle Bronze Age IIB-C, Late Bronze Age I-II, Iron Age I (with Iron Age II missing owing to erosion but known

from field II), Late Hellenistic and Roman of about the beginning of the Christian era. At the extreme southern end of the trench, beyond the 'Outer Wall', a Late Bronze Age burial cave (I 10A) produced 68 interments and a rich assemblage of both local and imported Egyptian objects. Well preserved skeletal materials provided valuable evidence for diet, disease, and longevity at Gezer in the 15th-14th centuries BC.

Field V was devoted to re-excavating the 'Gezer High Place', one of Palestine's most famous monuments from antiquity. This consists of 10 enormous stone stelae (the biblical *massebot, singular massebah), several more than 9 feet high, set in a north-south line in an open plaza on the north side of the mound, just inside the city wall. To the left of the alignment is a large stone basin or perhaps a socle for a now-missing massebah. The whole area is set off by a curb and faced with plaster. The recent excavations have conclusively dated this complex to Middle Bronze Age IIC, which makes it contemporary with the 'Inner Wall' of field I. Field VI, on the 'acropolis' and within a 750 square meter area excavated in 1968-71, provided the largest exposure of domestic architecture from the beginning of the Middle Bronze Age to the early Israelite era (c. 190-1000 BC). The Middle Bronze strata showed densely built-up and continually occupied levels with rather elaborate terraces, courtyards, cisterns, houses, and a beautifully plastered granary. These levels were violently destroyed, along with the 'South Gate' of field IV, in the Egyptian campaigns (c. 1550-1500 BC). During the 'Amarna Age' of the Late Bronze Age (14th century BC), a two-story palace had existed over the ruins, but there remained only hints of the massive plastered walls and its imported Egyptian luxuries. A period of disruption and partial abandonment at the end of the 13th century BC probably points to the destruction claimed by Pharaoh Merneptah (below). Following this period, field VI gave rich evidence of a succession of five Philistine phases and no less than three destructions. A multi-roomed public granary was destroyed twice in the 12th century BC, which was succeeded by two unusually large courtyard houses in the 11th century. Both building phases were accompanied by fine bichrome pottery and other Philistine materials.

Although the domestic sequence in field VI broke off in the 10th century BC, the 10th through the early 6th centuries were well preserved in field VII in the south central portion of the mound, which was excavated in 1972-74. Both the Assyrian and Babylonian destructions were dramatically attested (late 8th and early 6th centuries, respectively). A final, extensive reoccupation belonged to the Maccabean-Hasmonean period (second century BC) when the circular bastions were added to the towers of the 'Outer Wall'.

LITERARY SOURCES Gezer figures prominently in the literary sources, quite apart from written remains found in the mound itself. The site is first mentioned in the accounts of Tuthmosis III and IV in the 15th century BC, whose claims to have destroyed the site seem to be corroborated by the evidence of massive destruction at that period brought to light in the recent excavations. From the *El Amarna period of the following century date ten letters written to the pharaohs from three different kings of Gezer. The famous 'Israel Stele' of Merneptah (c. 1210 BC) (*Inscriptions) lists Gezer with *Ashkelon and Yanoam as major cities captured in Palestine. From the Solomonic period the historical footnotes in 1 Kings (9:15-17) have already been mentioned. In addition Pharaoh Sheshonq's list of conquests mentions Gezer as one of the sites taken in a raid up the coast by another pharaoh in about 918 BC. Evidence for this is again provided by recent excavations.

The first Mesopotamian records to mention the site date from the Assyrian period. An 8th century BC relief from the palace of Tiglath-Pileser III depicts the siege of 'Gazru', apparently Gezer, and the Assyrian and especially the later Babylonian destructions are both reflected in the archaeological finds. After not being mentioned in the sources for a long time Gezer reappears during the Hasmonean uprising. Frequent references in 1 and 2 Maccabees and in Josephus indicate its prominence; for a time it was the residence of Simon Maccabaeus and later the headquarters of John Hyrcanus. The last sources before the modern period are the Gezer boundary inscriptions of the 1st century AD reading in Hebrew 'the boundary of Gezer' and the giving in Greek what is apparently the name of the landlord of the estate, 'Alkios'.

GHASSUL TULEILAT See *TULEILAT GHASSUL.

GIANTS (VALLEY OF THE); REPHAIM A valley to the south of *Jerusalem. One of the landmarks between the territories of Judah and Benjamin (Josh. 15:8; 18:16) through which the *Philistines invaded Judah (2 Sam. 5:18, 22), and where they were beaten by David (2 Sam. 5:25).

GIBBETHON A town in the territory of *Dan, given to the Levites (Josh. 21:23). During the days of the kingdom of Israel it was held by the *Philistines (1 Kgs. 15:27; 16:15). In 712 BC it was conquered by Sargon, King of Assyria. Identified with Tell Melat, north of *Ekron.

GIBEAH; GIBEAH OF SAUL A town on the main road through the hills of Judah and Ephraim (Judg. 19:11-13). The principal town in the territory of Benjamin, it was referred to as 'Gibeah which belongeth to Benjamin' (Judg. 19:14) and was destroyed after the incident of the concubine (Judg. 19-20). The *Philistines conquered the mountains of Benjamin and placed a garrison at Gibeah (1 Sam. 10:5; Authorized Version: 'hill of God'; 13:3; Authorized Version: 'Geba'). Saul's home was there (1 Sam. 10:26; 11:4) and following his victory over the *Philistines he made it his capital and named it after himself (1 Sam. 15:34). Michaiah, the wife of Jeroboam, also came from there (2 Chr. 13:2). It is mentioned for the last time in the Bible in the description of Sennacherib's advance on Judah (Isa. 10:29). It must have existed in the Roman period because a village by the name of Gabath Saul is mentioned by Josephus in his description of Titus' advance to *Jerusalem; he situates it 30 stadia from the city (War v, 51). He also mentions the burial-place of Eleazar the high priest at Gabatha, probably the same as Gibeah (Antiq. v, 119), and says

that Rachel's tomb lay not far from it (Antiq. vi, 56).

Gibeah is identified with Tell el-Ful, situated on a hill 2,500 feet above sea level about 3 miles north of *Jerusalem, on the main road to *Shechem. Excavations on the site were made as early as 1868 by C. Warren on behalf of the Palestine Exploration Fund. More important are the excavations made in 1922-3 and 1933 by W.F. Albright on behalf of the American School of Oriental Research in Jerusalem. Five occupation periods were observed, ranging from the 12th century BC to Roman times. Some potsherds of the Middle Bronze Age were found, but no building remains. The earliest settlement, period I, was in existence in the 12th century BC. This was a small settlement and was probably destroyed by the conquering Benjaminites. At the end of the 11th century BC (period II) a citadel was built on the site. This was a rectangular building, 100 feet by 160 feet, in the form of a courtyard surrounded by a casemate wall strengthened by four towers at the corners (*Fortifications). Some of the rooms in the casemate wall were used as stores. The citadel was attributed by the excavator to Saul, but others think that it was built by the *Philistines and used by Saul after the conquest. In period III (8th-7th centuries BC) a new and smaller citadel was built, more in the nature of a road fort. The outer face of the wall was protected by a slanting stone screen. This fort was destroyed, probably c. 735 BC during the campaign of Rezin, King of Aram, and Pekah, King of Israel, against Ahaz, King of Judah. It was rebuilt, but destroyed again in 597 BC by the *Babylonians. In the second half of the 5th century BC (period IV) it was again rebuilt; a small vine growers' village sprang up on the eastern slope, as is indicated by the evidence of winepresses. This village flourished up to about the early 2nd century BC. The latest settlement (period I) belongs to Herodian times and was probably finally destroyed by Titus on his way to *Jerusalem.

GIBEON; GIBEONITES One of the most ancient Canaanite cities. In the Bible it is referred to as one of the four Hivite cities (Josh. 9:7, 17) and '...a great city, as one of the royal cities,...greater than Ai, and all the men thereof were mighty' (Josh. 10:2). Although the Gibeonites were condemned by Joshua to perpetual bondage (Josh. 9), he nevertheless made an alliance with the city (Josh. 9:17-18). The King of *Jerusalem and his allies were vanquished by Joshua at Gibeon (Josh. 10) and it was on that occasion that Joshua made the sun stand still (Josh. 10:12-13). David 'smote the host of the Philistines' from Gibeon to *Gezer (1 Chr. 14:16; Authorized Version: 'Gazer'). The men of Joab and of Abner fought each other near the pool of Gibeon, at a place called Helkath-Hazzurim (2 Sam. 2:12-17). There was a great high place at Gibeon where Solomon offered a sacrifice and prayed for wisdom (1 Kgs. 3:4 ff.; 2 Chr. 1:3 ff.). Johanan, son of Kareah, fought Ishmael, son of Nethaniah, 'by the great waters that are in Gibeon' (Jer. 41:11-12). After the Restoration the Gibeonites took part in rebuilding the walls of *Jerusalem (Neh. 3:7).

Josephus mentions Gibeon under the name of Gabao, a place where Cestius Gallus camped on his way to *Jerusalem in October of the year AD 66; it lay

The circular rock-cut pool at Gibeon

50 stadia from *Jerusalem (*War* ii, 516, 544). Eusebius recorded that a village of this name still existed in *Ramah, 4 miles west of *Beth-El (*Onom.* 48,9:11).

Gibeon is identified with el-Jib, about 8 miles northwest of *Jerusalem, on the way to *Beth-Horon. In the years 1957, 1959, 1960 and 1962 J.B. Pritchard excavated the site on behalf of the Museum of the University of Pennsylvania. Except for some traces of settlement in the Late Bronze Age all the remains on the site are from the Iron Age and later periods. The main discoveries were the fortifications, a large pool, two water tunnels, wine cellars, some houses and a large amount of epigraphic material which confirms the identification of the site.

The rock-cut pool is 37 feet in diameter and 82 feet deep. A spiral stairway of 79 steps, also cut into the rock, leads down to the bottom. The excavators believe that the pool was used either for storing rainwater or to provide better access to the water-table. It may possibly be identified with the one referred to in 2 Samuel (2:12-17) and Jeremiah (41:12). The two water tunnels lie at a short distance from the pool. At the spot where the large spring of Gibeon gushed out from the mountain a small reservoir in the form of a cave had been excavated below the surface level of the flowing water. The entrance to the cave was provided with a heavy door, so that it could be blocked when necessary. From this reservoir a tunnel was excavated to the source of the spring itself, which is 180 feet inside the mountain. Thus a good supply of water was

ensured in times of war, while water could be drawn from the spring in times of peace. In order to ensure safe access to the spring in emergencies, a second tunnel was excavated from within the city wall. As the difference in height between the entrance of this tunnel and the spring is 60 feet, 93 steps were hewn in the tunnel to provide a safe approach to the pool. The length of the second tunnel is 150 feet. The excavators date this water-supply system to the 10th century BC. The spring is still used today.

The finding of numerous jar handles stamped with the seal of Gibeon led to the discovery of wine cellars, consisting of a number of simple winepresses, each with a treading floor on the rock and a basin to collect the juice. The wine was made in 11 wine cellars. These were simply jar-shaped cisterns hewn in the rock, 7 feet deep with openings 3 feet wide. The openings could be sealed with heavy stone covers. The capacity of some of the wine cellars was up to 5,000 wine jars. The total storage capacity of all of the wine cellars was about 25,000 gallons.

The walls, massively built of large boulders, were exposed in some sections. Two walls were discovered, one dated to the 10th, the other to the 8th century BC.

In the Roman period a new reservoir, 36 feet by 60 feet and 6-8 feet deep, was excavated to the north of the spring. Some of the wine cisterns were used as tombs or, in the Byzantine period, for storing water.

GIHON *a)* One of the four rivers flowing from the Garden of *Eden, 'that encompasseth the whole land of Ethiopia' (Gen. 2:13). It is most probably a legendary river, although some suggest that it should be identified with the *Nile.

b) A spring in the valley of *Kidron, the most important source of water for *Jerusalem in ancient times, today called ed-Darag. As early as the pre-Israelite period an attempt was made to connect the spring by a tunnel with the city, but this was not completed. Later it is related that 'Hezekiah also stopped the upper watercourse of Gihon, and brought it straight down to the west side of the city of David' (2 Chr. 32:30). This ensured a supply of water to the city during the Assyrian siege and at the same time prevented the use of the spring by the enemy (2 Chr. 32:3-4). The tunnel ascribed to Hezekiah can still be seen today; it is about 1,600 feet long and terminates at the Pool of *Siloam. The making of the tunnel is commemorated by the famous *Siloam inscription. b2See also *WATER SUPPLY; *INSCRIPTIONS.)

GILBOA A ridge of mountains southeast of the *Jezreel Valley, rising some 1,500 feet above sea level. Saul fought his last battle with the *Philistines here and the Israelites were defeated (1 Sam. 28:4ff.; 31:1-6; 2 Sam. 1:6-10). On hearing of this disaster David cursed the mountains of Gilboa (2 Sam. 1:21). A village by the name of Gelbous is mentioned by Eusebius, in the "Philistine Mountains", 6 miles from *Beth-Shean (*Onom.* 72:10). The village is identified with Jalbun.

GILEAD; GALAADITIS The central part of the territory east of the *Jordan, which consisted of three regions: the plain, Gilead and the *Bashan (Deut. 3:10). Gileah extends from the Sea of *Galilee in the north to the *Dead Sea in the south. After the Israelite conquest it was divided between the tribes of Reuben and Gad and half of the tribe of Manasseh (Deut. 3:12-13). The name Gilead is sometimes applied to certain portions of this region (cf. Deut. 3:15-16; 1 Kgs. 4:19), which was rich in pasture and was therefore a place for cattle-raising (Num. 32:1, etc.). It was also famous for its balm (Jer. 8:22).

Archaeological surveys have shown that the area was settled as early as the 24th-23rd centuries BC. After a long period of abandonment it was resettled in the 13th century BC, at the time when the kingdoms of *Edom and *Moab were founded in its southern part. Most of Gilead, however, was occupied by the kings of the *Amorites and later conquered by the Israelite tribes (Num. 32:1 ff., etc.). Jephthah the Gileadite fought *Ammon in Gilead (Judg. 11). Later Saul defeated the *Ammonites who attempted to take *Jabesh-Gilead (1 Sam. 11). After the division of the kingdom Gilead was in Israel, but its northern part was soon conquered by the *Arameans (Authorized Version: 'Syrians'. 1 Kgs. 22) and another part was taken by the *Ammonites (Amos 1:13). In 814 BC Hazael captured the whole of Gilead (2 Kgs. 10:32-3), but when Damascus was assailed by the Assyrians it returned to Israel (2 Kgs. 13:25). In 732 BC the country was conquered by Tiglath-Pileser III and many of its inhabitants were deported to Assyria (2 Kgs. 15:29). The southern part of Gilead was then in the hands of the *Ammonites (Josh. 13:24-5; Jer. 49:1), while in the northern part an Assyrian satrapy by the name of Galaza was formed. After the Restoration Gilead was outside Jewish territory.

During the early Hellenistic period it was a separate district under the name of Galaaditis. Later in the same period, under the Seleucids, Jews settled in a few towns in the district. Some of these were conquered later by Judas Maccabaeus (1 Macc. 5:17-45). In two campaigns early in his reign Alexander Jannaeus conquered the whole of Gilead. When the country was conquered by Pompey (in 63 BC) the region was divided into small units and distributed among the larger cities, some of which were members of the *Decapolis. During the reign of Herod and his successors Galaaditis remained outside their kingdoms. After AD 106 it was part of the Provincia Arabia. Eusebius (*Onom.* 64:2) described it as a famous city in Arabia, in the mountains bordering *Phoenicia and *Arabia, touching upon Lebanon, and extending towards *Petra.

GILGAL The last station on the route of the Exodus, west of the *Jordan, where Joshua set up 12 stones to commemorate the crossing of the river (Josh. 4:19-20). Here, in the plain of *Jericho, the Children of Israel were circumcised (Josh. 5:3). Eusebius (*Onom.* 46:18 ff.) stated that the site was located at a distance of 2 miles from *Jericho. It is often mentioned by ancient pilgrims, some of whom 'saw the stone'. On the *Medaba map the 12 stones are shown north of Jericho. According to Arculf (c. AD 680) a church was built above the stones. The latest mention of this church occurs at the beginning of the 12th century. The site has been identified with Khirbet el-Mefjer as well as with other sites in the region of Jericho. (*See also* *MASSEBAH.)

GIMZO One of the towns conquered by the *Philistines in the days of Ahaz (2 Chr. 28:18). Known also in the Roman period, it is identified with Jimzu, southeast of Lydda.

GITTAH-HEPHER; GATH-HEPHER A town in the territory of Zebulun (Josh. 19:13), the birthplace of the prophet Jonas, son of Amittai (2 Kgs. 14:25). Identified with Khirbet ez-Zurra, west of the Sea of *Galilee.

GITTAIM A town in the north of the *Plain where the two captains, Baanah and Rechab, found refuge after the death of Abner, son of Ner, in *Hebron (2 Sam. 4:1-3). At the time of the Restoration it is mentioned as one of the cities of Benjamin (Neh. 11:33). The large number of places in the Holy Land named Gath (of which the plural in Hebrew is Gittaim) makes identification of this site difficult. Some experts believe that it should be identified with Tell Ras Abu-Hamid, near Ramla.

GLASS Obsidian (volcanic glass) was occasionally imported into Palestine, probably from Anatolia or Armenia, during the Neolithic and Chalcolithic periods. Glazed objects were first made in the Near East in the 5th millennium BC, the glaze being applied as a powder on the surface of the object, to become vitrified by the fire or mixed with the materials, to produce a self-glazing process. The first examples of man-made glass, however, seem to date only to the last quarter of the 3rd millennium BC, when glass beads were first made in *Mesopotamia and *Egypt.

A formative era in the history of glass-making is marked by the appearance of the first glass vessels in the middle of the 2nd millennium BC, again in *Mesopotamia and *Egypt. These vessels were made by an ingenious method involving moulding on a core. Since glass-blowing was unknown in this early period a core was made in the shape of the desired vessel from material strong enough to withstand heating and friable enough to be removed from the finished article. Viscous glass was applied to this core. The surface of the vessel was then decorated with threads of colored glass combed into ornamental patterns. The vessel was afterwards rolled on a flat surface and a handle and a base were added. This method required a high degree of skill. The colors of the glass used in this

Small 'Millefiori' bowl, 1st century AD

period indicate that the makers tried to imitate precious stones such as lapis-lazuli and turquoise. The making of glass vessels began almost at the same time in *Egypt and northern *Mesopotamia, but there are indications that the core technique was invented in *Mesopotamia and introduced into *Egypt later. The heyday of *Egypt's glass industry came in the *El Amarna period (first half of 14th century BC).

Glass vessels were rare in Palestine and Syria in the Late Bronze Age, and only princes and the very rich could afford them. Some vessels were dedicated to temples and shrines (e.g. at *Lachish and *Beth-Shean); others were found in tombs (e.g. at Tell el-*Ajjul, *Beth-Shemesh, *Megiddo and *Ugarit). All these vessels seem to have been imported from *Egypt, except for a Mesopotamian conical beaker discovered at Megiddo.

Mould-blown jug of blue glass, signed by Ennion, probably Sidon, 1st century AD

Amphoriskos formed on a core with thread decoration, 6th-5th centuries BC

The process of casting glass in moulds was also invented in the mid-2nd millennium BC. A homogeneous group of blue glass pendants in the shape of a nude female (possibly a fertility goddess) is represented in such widely separated sites as Nuzi (northern *Mesopotamia), Alalakh (Plain of *Antioch), *Beth-Shean, *Megiddo and *Lachish. Others have been found in *Cyprus, in the Aegean and a very few in *Egypt. They originated either in northern *Mesopotamia or in Syria. During the 14-13th centuries BC, a flourishing Mycenaean industry of cast glass jewelry developed as a result of contacts with the north Mesopotamian glass industry. There is no evidence that glass vessels were made in Palestine in the Late Bronze Age.

A decline set in with the end of the New Kingdom in *Egypt and the end of the Middle Assyrian period (end of the 2nd millennium BC). For the subsequent period there is no positive evidence and it is only in the late 8th and 7th centuries BC that glass vessels are found again. The excavations in the palaces of the kings of Assyria at Nimrud revealed glass vessels that are richly moulded and cut. Glass vessels formed around a core also reappear in this period in *Mesopotamia. The moulded and cut glass vessels were apparently made by Phoenician craftsmen. A few moulded and cut cosmetic glass palettes were discovered at Megiddo and near Samaria; fragments of a bowl of this type were uncovered at Aroer. In the 8th century BC Phoenician glassmakers also produced monochrome and mosaic-glass inlays, which were used in making exquisite furniture (mainly banquet-beds) or were inlaid in ivories, also for furniture. Remains of such ivories were also found in the palaces of the kings of Israel at Samaria. Phoenician glass inlays also embellished cosmetic stone palettes, numerous examples of which have been found at Megiddo.

Small *amphoriskoi, aryballoi, alabastra* and juglets were produced on a large scale from the 6th to the 4th centuries BC. The center for this production seems to have been on the island of Rhodes. Vessels of this type, common all over the Mediterranean area, have been found in Palestine at Athlit, *Achzib, *Hazor, *Gibeah, *En-Gedi and at Meqabelein (near *Amman). *Alexandria was apparently the leading center of glass-making in the Hellenistic period but very few of its luxury products have been found in Palestine.

Glass drinking bowls became fashionable in Palestine during the 2nd century and increasingly so in the 1st century BC. Fragments of such bowls have been found in *Ashdod, *Jerusalem, *Samaria, Tel Anafa and other sites. They may originate from a local glass-producing center, possibly somewhere along the Phoenician coast. On the whole, all through the 2nd and 1st millennia BC glass was a highly prized material used for making receptacles for precious ointments and drinking vessels. This is reflected in the equation of glass with gold in Job (28:17).

An epoch-making advance occurred in the 2nd half of the 1st century BC with the discovery of glass-blowing. This quick and inexpensive method of glass-

*Bottle in shape of fish from
El Amarna, late 18th Dynasty*

making seems to have been invented in Syria, probably in *Phoenicia. Remains of a dump of a glassmaking workshop from *c.* the mid-1st century BC were found in the excavations of the Jewish Quarter in the Old City of Jerusalem. Among the finds were fragments of the earliest blown glass vessels yet discovered. In the course of the 1st century AD glass-blowing was introduced into many parts of the Roman Empire. *Alexandria continued to lead in the production of luxury moulded and cut glass until the early 3rd century AD. Syro-Palestinian glass-blowers maintained a high standard in blowing techniques all through the Roman period and their mould-blown vessels of the 1st and 2nd centuries AD have remarkable decorations in relief; they bear Greek inscriptions and were often made in beautiful colors.

The finest mould-blown glass vessels of antiquity are signed by their maker, Ennion, who probably worked in *Sidon in the Tibero-Claudian era. Other glass-makers working in Rome in the 1st century AD signed their names in Greek and Latin (Artas, Philippos, Neikon, Ariston, Eirenaios, Anios) and boasted of their Sidonian origin. In the 3rd and 4th centuries AD glass vessels were the commonest grave goods in Palestine and reveal the large scale on which this industry must have been producing. The end of the Roman period in the West was paralleled by a decline in standards of glass-making in the East, including Palestine. Glass of the 6th century AD is rather poor compared with earlier examples.

GODED (TEL); (JUDEIDEH)(TELL EL-) A mound in the coastal plain more than a mile north of *Beth-Gubrin. Its former identification by many scholars with *Moresheth-Gath, the birthplace of the prophet Micah, is based on Eusebius (*Onom.* 134, 10), but has been rejected. It is now proposed that it should be identified with *Libnah.

The site was excavated by F.J. Bliss and R.A.S. Macalister on behalf of the Palestine Exploration Fund in 1899-1900. It thus became one of the earliest scientific archaeological excavations in Palestine. The ancient city was built on a natural hill, occupying an area about 1,700 feet long. The excavators concentrated their efforts on the higher part of the hillock, where the remains of the citadel were concealed. This part of the city, the acropolis, was surrounded by a wall enclosing an area 750 feet by 300 feet. Of the whole 6-acre site, less than one-eighth of an acre was excavated. Three main occupation periods were observed. These were labelled by the excavators 'pre-Israelite' (now called Bronze Age or Canaanite); 'Jewish' (now called Iron-Age or Israelite); and 'Hellenistic-Roman'.

Of the earliest period only scanty remains were uncovered. The excavators assumed that after the destruction of the city at the end of the Canaanite period it was not inhabited again until the end of the Judean kingdom. The Israelite period was represented by 40 stamped jar handles of the *lamelek* type (*Seals; *Inscriptions).

The city of the Roman period was the subject of the most extensive excavations. The southern part of the hill was occupied at that time by a fort surrounded by a wall 10 feet thick with gates at the four points of the compass, each flanked by two towers inside the fort. Two streets, a *cardo* running north-south and a *decumanus* running east-west, intersected the fort area, in the center of which stood the commander's headquarters, a building 40 feet square with eight rooms round a central court. There were two other houses in the fort, one a villa in the Hellenistic style with an *impluvium* (a decorative shallow pool, which collected the rainwater that fell on the uncovered part of the court). It also included a *prostas,* a porch which rested on two columns, and beyond it an *oikos* or reception hall. This type of house is the typical *andreion* or men's house. The other house, adjoining it on the west, was built in the eastern style, with no outer windows; it served as a *gynnaekeion* or women's quarters. The fort and other buildings were dated by their style to the early Roman period, perhaps the time of Herod.

GOLAN A city of refuge in the *Bashan (Deut. 4:43; Josh. 20:8), and a Levitical city in the territory of half of the tribe of Manasseh (Josh. 21:27). Eusebius (*Onom.* 64:7) mentions a very large village called Golan which existed in the *Bashan in his time. It is tentatively identified with Sahm el-Jalan.

GOLAN; GAULANITIS The name of a district in northeastern Transjordan. In the Persian period it was included in the satrapy of *Karnaim, which encompassed Golan and the *Bashan. In the early Hellenistic period Golan was detached to form a separate district under the name of Gaulanitis. Early in the reign of the Hasmonean Alexander Jannaeus, the cities of Golan, Gamala and Seleucia were conquered. After the conquest of Palestine by Pompey (63 BC) Golan was given to the Itureans, but when Herod the Great came to the throne it was presented to him. It remained part of his descendants' kingdom until the death of Agrippa II. It was then annexed to the Roman Provincia Judea and later in the Roman period it formed part of Palestina Secunda. During the Roman and Byzantine periods Gaulanitis was a rural area with no large towns. The more important large villages were Seleucia, Sogane, *Bethsaida and Gamala.

A large number of sites were recorded and described before World War I by G. Schumacher. Since 1967 surveys and excavations have been carried out in this region. *Prehistoric evidence (Lower, Middle and Upper Paleolithic) comes mostly from the northern part of the region, from Mt *Hermon to Kuneitra. It is only in the Chalcolithic period (beginning of the 4th millennium BC) that sedentary settlement began near the *Yarmuk River. Chalcolithic settlements from the second half of the 4th millennium BC were recently discovered in the high plateau of the central and northern parts of this region. The settlers engaged in *agriculture and stock breeding and placed basalt pillar shaped house gods in their houses and courtyards. Throughout the 3rd and early 2nd millennium BC the population of the Golan was of a nomadic and semi-nomadic nature.

In order to protect the land for grazing and cultivation the settlers constructed enormous enclosures of massive basalt blocks. These enclosures were sometimes placed on mountain spurs overlooking the richer valleys below. The enclosures were subdivided for different uses; one was 450 feet in diameter. These constructions are tentatively dated to the Early Bronze Age II. This form of settlement continued in the following Middle Bronze Age I, to which is also dated a small fortified site, placed at a strategic point to protect similar enclosures around it. The *dolmen fields also belong to these periods. The earliest material found in the dolmens, which are associated with secondary *burial, is of the Middle Bronze Age I. In the Middle Bronze Age II settlement was concentrated mainly in the southern part of the region, especially in the vicinity of the *Sea of Galilee. The copious springs and softer rock enabled the settlers to store water in cisterns. These settlements were protected by small forts placed on hilltops. Very few settlements of the Late Bronze Age were found. In the Iron Age the south flourished most. A lion's head carved on an orthostat, discovered not in situ was dated on stylistic grounds to the 9th century BC. It was probably originally placed at the entrance of a citadel of a local ruler. Remains of this period are still meager and come mainly from sites along the shores of the Sea of Galilee (see *En-Gev).

From the later period were discovered 11 sites of the Hellenistic period, 45 Roman, 50 Roman-Byzantine, 76 Byzantine and a smaller number of Arab and medieval sites. It is noteworthy that in the late Roman-Byzantine period Jewish settlements occupied the heart of the region, as is evidenced by remains of *synagogues, whereas remains of churches were found only on the outskirts of the region or along the shores of the Sea of Galilee.

GOLGOTHA The site of the Crucifixion (Matt. 27:33; Mark 15:22; John 19:17). The name derives from the Aramaic *golgolta* , meaning 'skull' or 'place of a skull'. Early Christian tradition places the site west of Jerusalem. In the 2nd century AD, when Aelia Capitolina (*Jerusalem) was built, a temple of Aphrodite was set up on the site by the Romans. After the Council of Nicaea (AD 325) the Emperor Constantine felt it his duty 'to make the most blessed spot, the

place of the Resurrection, visible to all and given over to veneration'. In AD 330 the remains of the temple of Aphrodite were torn down, the area cleansed and the great Church of the Holy Sepulcher built. It included the last stations on the Way of the Cross, Golgotha and the Holy Sepulcher. The present church, built by the Crusaders, includes extensive remains of Constantine's structure.

GOMORRAH One of the five Canaanite cities (Gen. 10:19) in the *Jordan Valley (Gen. 13:10). Their location is very much disputed. (*See also* *SODOM.)

GOPHNAH A town in northwestern Judea, mentioned only from the Hellenistic period onwards (Josephus, *Antiq.* XIV, 275). In the late Hellenistic period it is referred to as a small town (1 Macc. 11:34). By 47 BC, when it was conquered by Cassius, it was an important city (Josephus, *Antiq.* XIV, 275), and it was freed shortly afterwards by Mark Antony (Josephus, *Antiq.* XIV, 301 ff.). An important stronghold in the time of the war against the Romans in AD 66 (Josephus, *War* II, 566-8), it was subdued by Vespasian in AD 68 (Josephus, *War* IV, 551). Titus concentrated the fugitives from *Jerusalem there (Josephus, *War* VI, 115). In the Talmud it is referred to as Beth-Guphnin. It must have existed in the late Roman and Byzantine periods because it appears on the Peutinger map, at a distance of 16 miles from *Jerusalem. According to Eusebius (*Onom.* 168, 16) it was 15 miles along the road leading from *Jerusalem to *Neapolis (*Shechem). It also appears on the *Medaba map. Gophnah is identified with Jifnah, north of *Jerusalem.

GOSHEN *a)* The name of a place and a region in Judah (Josh. 11:16) in the southern part of the hill country (Josh. 15:51). Tentatively identified with Tell Khuweilifeh, in the southwest of Judea.
b) A region in *Egypt, rich in pasture, where the Children of Israel settled (Gen. 46:34). 'the best of the land' (Gen. 47:6, 11). The Septuagint identifies Goshen with *Pithom, which is identified today with Tell er-Ratabeh in Wadi Thumeilat. The Bible also refers to the land of Goshen as the 'land of Rameses' (Gen. 47:11), which was the later name for Zoan (*Tanis), to the north. Egyptian sources also mention the granting of grazing rights in the region of *Pithom.

GOZAN An Aramean city-state in northwestern *Mesopotamia, on the southern bank of the River Khabur. Assyrian documents of the early 9th century BC state that it was subject to Assyria. In 732 BC Tiglath-Pileser III deported the Reubenites, Gadites and half the tribe of Manasseh to Halah, *Habor, Hara and to the River Gozan (1 Chr. 5:26). The same fate was also suffered by the inhabitants of *Samaria after its conquest in 721 BC (2 Kgs. 17:6). Isaiah knew of the fate that befell Gozan at the hands of the Assyrians (Isa. 37:11-12).

Gozan is identified with Tell Halaf, where remains of a culture of the Chalcolithic period were discovered. The Aramean city was built in the 10th century BC. It occupied an area of about 150 acres and had temples, a palace and other buildings in which very rich finds were made. On the ruins of this city another was built to which the Israelites were deported by the

Assyrians. Documents found in the later city that refer to this period contained Hebrew names, probably of the deportees.

GREECE *See* *JAVAN.

GUSH-HALAV; GISCHALA A small town of the Roman period in Upper *Galilee, mentioned in the Mishna among the walled cities from the time of Joshua, son of Nun (Arach. 9:6). The Zealot John, son of Levi, a native of the town, fortified it at his own expense by order of Josephus when *Galilee was being prepared for the war against the Romans (Josephus, *Antiq.* II, 575).

Surveys made at the end of the 19th and early 20th century revealed the remains of two synagogues. The village church was built over the remains of one, which stands at the highest point on the hill. The other, built of large carefully dressed blocks and in a better state of preservation, is beautifully situated near the village spring, overlooking a green valley. The inner dimensions of the building are 46 feet by 50 feet. It had an inner colonnade on three sides of the hall, of which the stylobate and some bases and column drums still remain in position. The main entrance to the building was on the south, the side facing *Jerusalem, and was decorated with architectural motifs. Lining the long walls were stone benches to seat the congregation. The lintel of the main entrance, on which an eagle was depicted between wreaths, was found in the debris. On one of the column drums was a Hebrew inscription reading: 'Jose son of Tanhum made this shrine. Let him be blessed.' Both buildings are among the early group of synagogues (i.e. they date from the 2nd-3rd centuries AD). The site is identified with el-Jish in Upper *Galilee.

Relief showing a chariot, Tell Halaf (Gozan), 10th century BC

H

HABIRU One of the names by which the Assyrians, Babylonians and some other nations of the 2nd millennium BC referred to the nomads who, either singly or in groups, were seeking new countries in which to settle. The form in which this name appears in the documents of *Ugarit and *Mari is close to the name 'Hebrews'. Once settled, the Habiru served mainly as mercenaries or laborers in their new countries, but they were never considered to be citizens and their status differed from that of the local inhabitants, from whom they usually lived apart in quarters specially assigned to them.

In the first half of the 15th century BC there were numerous Habiru settlers in Palestine and Syria. Many of the *El Amarna letters, written by the rulers of *Gezer, *Shechem, *Megiddo, *Damascus and other city-states, refer to Habiru recruits who took part in the inner struggles of these cities. In the letters the petty kings accuse each other of employing the Habiru as mercenaries, which was a sign of rebellion against Pharaoh under whose protection the whole land of *Canaan lay. Other letters contain complaints about the atrocities committed by the Habiru, who were said to be plundering cities and setting them on fire. In contrast, some letters refer to them as loyal to Pharaoh and protecting his conquests in *Phoenicia and Syria against rebels.

Accadian documents of the late 16th century BC found at Nuzi in upper *Mesopotamia record that the Habiru who migrated from *Accad and Ashur (*Mesopotamia) came under voluntary bondage, doing various jobs. Other documents refer to service for a specified term, after which the servant could either go free or become a slave in perpetuity. This is reflected in the regulations governing slavery among the ancient Hebrews (Exod. 21:2-6; Deut. 15:12-18).

The oldest reference to the Habiru in Egyptian documents comes in a scene from a tomb depicting them as vintners. They also appear among the prisoners in a list of Amenophis II. A battle against them is recorded on a stele of Sethos I, set up in *Beth-Shean. There are several references to them being employed as soldiers in the Egyptian army, in the great expedition of Rameses IV to Wadi Hammamat, for instance. Other illustrations show them engaged in manual labor, such as stone-quarrying or building.

A study of the personal names of the Habiru reveals that they were not composed of a single ethnic element, although the Semitic element was the strongest. On the strength of the similarity between the terms Habiru and Hebrews, many scholars have suggested identifying the Habiru of the 16th-15th centuries BC with the Hebrew conquerors of the 13th century, but this connection has not yet been satisfactorily proved.

HABOR The name of a river, also known as Gozan, where the 10 tribes were settled after their deportation (2 Kgs. 17:6; 18:11, etc.). Identified with the River Khabur, which rises in the Kharga Dag mountains and flows between the *Euphrates and the *Tigris through a fertile plain about 200 miles long before uniting with the *Euphrates. Some of the cities of *Mesopotamia, such as *Gozan, flourished along its banks. In the 16th-14th centuries BC the Horite kingdom of Mitanni held sway along the river, and in the 10th century BC the *Arameans invaded the area and built riverside towns. In the 8th century BC it became an Assyrian satrapy, but the constant uprisings and subsequent deportations of the Aramean population led to the decline of this region, leaving space for the Israelites who were brought there from *Samaria.

HADID; ADIDA A town in the *Plain, close to *Lod and *Ono, where the tribe of Benjamin settled after the Restoration (Ezra 2:33, etc.). In the Hellenistic and Roman periods it was a fortress that had been built by Simon Maccabaeus (1 Macc. 12:38). It was later used to guard the roads connecting *Lod with *Gophnah and *Jerusalem. Josephus knew of a town named Adida at this spot. It also flourished in the late Roman period. Eusebius (*Onom.* 24:24) knew of a village by the name of Adatha east of Lod. Identified with el-Haditheh, east of Lydda.

HADRACH The name of a town and country in Syria, mentioned only once in the Bible (Zech. 9:1). It is heard of for the first time in the inscription of Zachar, King of *Hamath (c. 800 BC), and then reappears in the Assyrian documents of the 8th century BC, which mention a satrapy called Hatarikka. In 738 BC it was conquered by Tiglath-Pileser III. The prophecy of Zechariah seems to refer to the great revolt against Assyria which took place in 720 BC, in which Hadrach joined with Israel, *Hamath and the Phoenician and Philistine cities. Its exact location is not known.

HAIFA A town on the Mediterranean coast at the foot of Mount *Carmel, identified with Haifa al-Atiqa, ancient Haifa. The town flourished in Roman, Byzantine and later periods. Because of its proximity to *Acre it did not develop into an important city. Eusebius (*Onom.* 108, 31) writes: 'There is a town Sycaminus on the way to Ptolemais from Caesarea, also named Hefa.' This identification of Hefa-Haifa with Sycaminum-*Shikmona is of course erroneous. Haifa was mainly settled by Jews and its sages are frequently mentioned in the Talmud and later Jewish sources. The Romans built a fort near the town, which they named Castra; as they settled *Samaritans there it became known as Castra Samaritanorum. There is some evidence that the Jewish community suffered destruction in AD 352, when the last Jewish revolt broke out in *Galilee in the time of Gallus. All the early remains of ancient Haifa have now been built over. During the building operations remains of the Roman period were uncovered.

HALAK (MOUNT) A mountain marking the southern limit of Joshua's conquest (Josh. 11:17; 12:7). Commonly identified with Jebel Halak, in the central *Negev.

HALIF (TEL) Tentatively identified with *Goshen (Tell Khuweilifeh) in southwest Judea. Since 1977 the Lahav Research Project, under the direction of J.D. Seger has been conducting excavations at Tel Halif. Fifteen strata of occupation were distinguished on the site. The earliest level of occupation (15) is of the Early Bronze Age II-III, at which time the mound was fortified by a wall with towers. The wall, made of bricks on a stone foundation, is 10-18 feet wide and its base was protected by a glacis. At the lower part of the glacis was an additional wall 6 feet wide. The city of this period was destroyed by a fierce conflagration. Early Bronze Age III is represented by three strata (14-12). In this period the settlers built houses above the old wall and on the ashes of destruction. Throughout this period the houses were rebuilt several times. During the last phase of the Early Bronze Age and the Middle Bronze Age Tel Halif was deserted. After this long gap a new settlement (11) was built in the Late Bronze Age I. By the end of this phase (10), as is evidenced by the finds, the town established commercial relations with Egypt. Dated to this period is a spacious building, with a large room (18 feet by 19 feet) in its center which contained bronze vessels. The site was also occupied without interruption at the beginning of the Iron Age (9-7). Houses built in the preceding period (10) were continuously occupied and only the floor levels were raised. *Philistine *pottery of the 11th century BC was uncovered. During the 9th and 8th centuries (6B) the town was again *fortified by a casemate wall. To this period belong several tombs; one contained a bronze *lamp which was an imitation of the shape of the standard Iron Age clay lamps. The destruction of this city is attributed to Sennacherib in 701 BC. The site was occupied for a short time in the second half of the 7th century BC (6A). The results of the excavations in strata 5 (Persian), 4 (Hellenistic), 3 (Roman-Byzantine), 2 (Arab) and 1 (modern) have not yet been published.

Chancel screen from the synagogue at Hammath near Tiberias

HAMATH One of the major cities on the Orontes, in northern Syria, the capital of a district and an Aramean-Hittite kingdom under the name of Hamath the Great (Amos 6:2, etc.). It was conquered by David (2 Sam. 8:9) and Solomon built a store city there (2 Chr. 8:4). According to the Assyrian sources Hamath was one of the countries of the 'land of the Hittites' that joined forces with the neighboring states to oppose Assyria in 853 BC and succeeded in halting Shalmaneser III near *Qarqar. At the beginning of the 8th century BC it formed part of a larger country that was a vassal of Assyria. After rebelling again it was conquered in about 740 BC by Tiglath-Pileser III, then finally destroyed by Sargon in 720 BC. The people of Hamath were deported to Israel (2 Kgs. 17:24), and those of *Samaria were taken to Hamath (Isa. 11:11-12). Known today as Hama.

HAMMATH-GADER A Jewish town of the Roman and Byzantine periods, situated to the east of the *Jordan in the Plain of Gader, north of *Gadara, on the right bank of the River *Yarmuk. There are several springs in this plain, to some of which medicinal properties were ascribed. The Hebrew name of the site means 'hot springs of Gader'. Eusebius (*Onom.* 22, 26) refers to a village called Emmata where there were hot springs; according to later sources these were called Eros and Anteros. The Arab name el-Hammeh, by which this place is known, goes back to the Middle Ages. Remains of a Roman temple, Roman baths, a theater and a synagogue have been discovered on the site.

The synagogue was excavated in 1932 by E.L. Sukenik on behalf of the Hebrew University. It is of the basilical type, 40 feet by 50 feet, with a nave about 15 feet wide and an apse at its southern end, facing *Jerusalem. The aisles and most of the nave had mosaic pavements with geometric patterns. The floor close to the apse, where the Torah Shrine stood, is decorated with a medallion flanked by two lions. There are several dedicatory inscriptions in Aramaic and Greek on the pavement, the most important being in the medallion. The inscriptions mention that the synagogue was built with money donated both by the local congregation and by Jews from neighboring towns, such as *Sepphoris, *Capernaum and *Arbel. The names are mostly Greek and Roman. A chancel screen decorated with a *menorah is flanked by a *shofar* (ram's horn) and *lulab* (palm branch). The synagogue is dated to the 5th century AD.

Since 1979 excavations have been carried out in the thermae of Hammath-Gader by Y. Hirshfeld and G. Solar on behalf of the Hebrew University, the Department of Antiquities and the Israel Exploration Society. The thermae are located between the Roman *theater and the *Yarmuk River. The construction of the thermal bathing installations began in the 3rd century AD. On its east side is a large oval bathing room (70 feet by 35 feet) (*caldarium* in the Roman *bath). A channel from the hot springs supplied this hall with hot water. It contained a pool and bath tubs. The oval pool, which held warm water with a high concentration of minerals, was surrounded by a broad walkway. A passage led from the pool to a hall of pillars, in which there was another pool (25 feet by 46 feet), which was originally covered with a huge vault, like the most elaborate thermae in Rome. Another pool is situated north of the oval hall. The latter (40 feet by 90 feet) was decorated with niches. This pool (30 feet by 75 feet) was lavishly decorated and — as is evidenced by numerous Greek inscriptions — it was renovated in the time of the Empress Eudocia and in the Umayyad period.

Dedicatory inscription from the synagogue, Hammath-Gader

HAMMATH; HAMTHA A fortified city in the territory of *Naphtali (Josh. 19:35), probably the same as Hammoth-Dor, a Levitical city (Josh. 21:32). In Roman and Byzantine times it appears in Jewish sources as Hamtha ('hot baths'), or Ammatous in the Greek form. Renowned for its hot springs, to which medicinal properties were ascribed. In the 3rd century AD a synagogue was built nearby, while the Romans erected a temple to Hygiea, the goddess of health. Identified with Hamman Tabariyeh, south of *Tiberias.

In 1921 N. Slouschz, on behalf of the Palestine Exploration Society and the Department of Antiquities, excavated remains of a synagogue situated 500 yd north of the southern wall of the city. It consisted of a basilical hall (36 feet by 36 feet) with two rows of columns. The entrances to the building were on the north side, and a courtyard east of the building communicated with the eastern aisle. At the southern end of the hall was a small bema enclosed by four small columns; behind it probably stood the Ark of the Law. Close by, in the eastern aisle, was the 'seat of Moses' (*cathedra*). The floor was decorated with *mosaics which had been relaid several times. A study of the plan indicated that in its first phase the entrance to the building was on the south side, as in the Galilean *synagogues; this was changed in a later phase, when doors were opened in the opposite wall. This synagogue is dated to the 4th century AD.

A more sumptuous synagogue was excavated at a small distance from the first. The excavations were directed by M. Dothan on behalf of the Department of Antiquities in the years 1961-3. Beneath the synagogue were occupation levels of the 1st century BC, followed by a level of the 1st or the first half of the 2nd century AD. The building measured 180 feet by 120 feet, and contained a central court with rooms around it, which was possibly a gymnasium. Above this building was the earliest synagogue. Of this building little remains, and it is mainly the later synagogue which has been preserved and whose plan can be studied. This is a broad-house (45 feet by 40 feet), orientated southeast-northwest. Three rows of columns divided the building into a nave and three aisles. Originally, the building was entered on the south through a corridor and doors in the southern wall. Changes were introduced in the later phase, when the corridor was divided by partition walls into small rooms and entrances were opened in the northern wall. The Ark of the Law was set in a small niche, one step up. The entire building was decorated with beautiful *mosaics, which are among the finest found in Palestinian *synagogues. The original order of the mosaic pavement was as follows: nine squares flanked by two lions contained dedicatory inscriptions in Greek. Although one of the dedicators, Severus, is described as 'the pupil of the most illustrious patriarchs', the personal names are all Greek. Next comes a rectangular panel with an inscribed circle. In the corners are personifications of the Four Seasons; the outer circle contains the twelve symbols of the *zodiac, each with its name in Hebrew, and in the center is splendid (although partly damaged) Helios riding the heavenly chariot against a background of a dark sky in which the moon and stars are shining. This is followed by the third panel in which an Ark of the Law is standing in a gabled structure, flanked by a *menorah on either side and by an *ethrog* and *lulab*, *shofar* and incense shovel. The earlier phase of the building is dated to the late 3rd-early 4th century AD, and the phase with the mosaic, apparently the earliest mosaic pavement in a synagogue, is dated to the 4th century AD. This synagogue was renovated, the plan was changed, and a simpler mosaic floor was laid. This synagogue still existed after the Moslem conquest of Palestine.

HANNATHON A town in the territory of Zebulun (Josh. 19:14). Mentioned as Hunnatuna in the *El Amarna letters, where it is referred to as an important town in western *Galilee. Also listed among the conquests of Tiglath-Pileser III. Identified with Tell-el-Bedeiwiyeh, southeast of *Acre.

HAR YERUHAM A Middle Bronze Age I site in the central *Negev, about 20 miles south-southeast of Beer-Sheba, extending over an area of about 3 square miles. At its center are some large constructions, enclosed within a stone fence. On a hill nearby a cult place, in the form of a rock altar surrounded by a stone wall, was discovered. Tumuli and more scattered constructions are found on the neighboring hills.

In 1963 excavations were made on this site by M. Kochavi on behalf of several Israeli and American institutions. Two occupation levels were observed, both of the same Middle Bronze Age I. To the upper level belong remains of a poor settlement, with rounded constructions, tumuli and large stone-walled pens. In the lower level a more compact settlement was discovered, in which there were rectangular houses and some artisans' quarters. One was a public building with a large number of rooms. The whole settlement was surrounded by a stone wall, on to which the houses backed. The numerous stone implements and flint sickle-blades found here show that seasonal agriculture was practised. Pottery was produced in a potter's kiln found on the site. The local art is represented by two animal figurines, one of stone, the other of clay, found near the kiln. In one of the houses a score of copper ingots (*Metals) were found, which were either locally smelted or obtained by way of barter (*Money).

Copper bars from Har Yeruham, Middle Bronze Age

The site of Har Yeruham is one of the very few of the Middle Bronze Age I to have been excavated so far. It provides a glimpse into a little-known community of seasonal farmers and hunters who worshipped their gods on mountain tops and, as indicated by the tumuli, also believed in an after-life.

HAROSHETH OF THE GENTILES The place where Sisera, captain of the host of Jabin, King of *Canaan, lived (Judg. 4:2). After the battle of the *Kishon, Barak, son of Ahinoam, pursued Sisera there (Judg. 4:16). It is not certain whether the name refers to a place or a geographical area. The place was unknown in Eusebius' time (*Onom.* 110:12). He calls it Arisoth, and locates it east of the Jordan. Not identified.

HARAN A city in the upper reaches of the Balih Valley, a commercial and cultural center from the 2nd millennium onwards. It lies on an ancient caravan route from *Mesopotamia to Cappadocia, Syria, Palestine and *Egypt. Terah, the father of Abraham, settled here with his family (Gen. 11:31), and it was an important center in the early history of the Hebrew nation. Abraham sent here to find a wife for his son Isaac (Gen. 24:4) and Jacob came here after escaping from Esau (Gen. 28:10).

Haran is mentioned in the *Mari archives as a religious center for the West Semitic tribes, who worshipped at the temple of the moon god, Sin.

From the 15th to the 13th centuries BC Haran was part of the Horite kingdom of Mitanni; with the collapse of the kingdom it was conquered by Assyria (*c.* 1270 BC). It was subsequently held temporarily by the *Arameans and then recaptured by the Assyrians. When *Nineveh was captured by the Medes (*Madai) and the Chaldeans (612 BC), Haran became the capital of the kingdom of *Madai for a brief period. At about this time it is mentioned by Ezekiel as one of the cities trading with *Tyre (Ezek. 27:23). During the whole of this period it was a center for the cult of Sin. Nabonidus, the last Babylonian king, preferred Haran to *Babylon and rebuilt the temple of Sin there. Some of Nabonidus' most important documents, as well as the autobiography of his mother, were found here.

Haran is identified with Sultan Tepe. Excavations made in the vicinity of the town have uncovered an important library of the later Babylonian period.

HAROD; THE WELL OF HAROD A large spring at the foot of Mount *Gilboa, where Gideon and his men camped before the battle with Sisera (Judg. 7:1).

HAURAN; AURANITIS A region in the northeastern part of Transjordan, on the border of the country described by Ezekiel (47:15-18). Conquered by Shalmaneser III in 841 BC and later turned by Tiglath-Pileser III into an Assyrian satrapy under the name of Hauranu, the region became important in the Hellenistic and Roman periods. Early in the Hellenistic period the large Persian satrapy of *Karnaim was divided into smaller districts, one of which was known in Greek as Auranitis. By the end of the 2nd century BC this region formed part of the Iturean kingdom. Augustus gave Hauran to Herod the Great. In this period many Nabatean colonies were established there, one of the more important being the religious center of Seeia. Hauran remained under Jewish domination in the time of Herod's successors, until the death of Agrippa II when, together with the rest of the north of the country, it was annexed to the Provincia Syria. In AD 295, when Diocletian reorganized the provinces, it was part of the Provincia Arabia. Numerous small towns and villages were scattered all over Hauran, the more important of these being Kanatha (*Kanath), a city of the *Decapolis, and Dionysias-Soweida. The region today comprises Jebel ed-Druz and the fertile plain of Nuqra.

HAVILAH According to Genesis (2:11), a country where there was gold and which was bordered by the River *Pison, which flowed out of the Garden of *Eden. The gold was described as good, and there was also bdellium and onyx here (*Precious stones). In one list its sons are mentioned with the sons of Cush and Seba (Gen. 10:7) and in another with the descendants of Shem (Gen. 10:29). The sons of Ishmael dwelt between Havilah and *Shur. Saul vanquished the *Amalekites in the same area (1 Sam. 15:7).

It seems that Havilah should be sought in the northern part of the Arabian peninsula. It is thought by some to represent the country northeast of Sana, the capital of Yemen. Josephus believed that Havilah, where gold came from, was in *India, which played an important part in the international trade of his own day. Eusebius (*Onom.* 82:5) calls the Pison River which surrounds it by the name of Ganges.

HAVOTH-JAIR A group of small towns in the pastureland in the hilly part of Transjordan, along the bank of the River *Yarmuk. The region was seized by Jair, son of Manasseh, from the *Amorites (Deut. 3:14) or in the *Bashan (Josh. 13:30). In the time of Solomon, Argob in the *Bashan was a district under the command of the son of Geber (1 Kgs. 4:13). The region lies south of the *Yarmuk, southeast of the Sea of *Galilee.

HAYONIM (CAVE) On the right back of Nahal Izhar, about 10 miles west of the Sea of *Galilee, this cave has been in course of excavation by O. Bar-Yosef and E. Tchernov since 1965. Under a Byzantine layer (A) containing many ashes, a Natufian layer (B) was uncovered. Although several stages of occupation and burials were observed within this layer, both lithic and bone industries appear to be identical and are characterized by ridge-backed crescents, sickle-blades, scrapers and many burins. Bones and horns were used for manufacturing points, gouges, spatulas, pendants and sickle-hafts. Seven graves containing primary and secondary burials have been excavated, exposing the remains of seventeen skeletons in either flexed or supine postures (*Burial). One female skeleton was adorned with necklace, bracelets and girdle of dentalium shells, and bone pendants (*Jewelry).

At the entrance to the cave the remains of a long Kebaran occupation were found, with many nongeometric microliths, the most common being obliquely truncated bladelets and narrow micropoints. Aurignacian layers, found inside the cave beneath the Natufian layer, provided an assemblage rich in steep and nosed scrapers that can be assiged to the Upper Paleolithic IV period. Excavation of Mousterian lay-

ers continues beneath the Aurignacian. (*See also* *PREHISTORY; FLINT TOOLS.*)

HAZEROTH One of the desert stations on the route of Exodus (Num. 11:35, etc.), where Miriam and Aaron spoke to Moses about the Ethiopian woman whom he had married (Num. 12:1). Identified with Ain Hadra by those who believe that the Israelites took a southerly route on their way from *Egypt. The eastern pilgrims' road to Mt Sinai passed near this place and pilgrims left there hundreds of inscriptions in Greek, Armenian, Aramaic and other languages.

HAZEZON-TAMAR A town of the *Amorites, south of the *Dead Sea, taken by Chedorlaomer and his allies (Gen. 14:7). According to 2 Chronicles (20:2) it is identified with *En-Gedi. If it is the same as *Tamar, as some experts think, then it should be identified with Ain Husb, in the Arabah. Eusebius (*Onom.* 8:8) knew in his time a village by the name of Thamara, one day's march from *Mampsis, where a garrison of Roman soldiers was stationed.

HAZOR a) A large Canaanite and Israelite city in Upper *Galilee, identified with Tell el-Kedah. The earliest mention of Hazor is in the Egyptian *Execration Texts. It also occurs frequently in the archives of *Mari, where it is referred to as a center for the caravans that travelled from Hazor to *Babylon. According to these documents Hazor also took an active part in the tin trade. During the time of the New Kingdom of Egypt it is mentioned in the lists of Tuthmosis III, Amenophis II and Sethos I. In the *El Amarna letters the ruler of Hazor is called 'king' and in his letters to the Egyptian court he expresses loyalty to the Pharaoh of *Egypt. The last reference to the place in the Egyptian sources comes in a document of the time of Rameses II.

In the Bible Hazor features prominently in the account of the conquests of Joshua (Josh. 11:10-13). The ruler of Hazor was one of the thirty-one kings of Canaan vanquished by Joshua (Josh. 12:19) and the town became part of the territory of Naphtali (Josh. 19:36). Later Jabin, King of Hazor, and his captain Sisera, who lived in Hazor, are mentioned in the account of the wars of Deborah (Judg. 4:2). It is also recorded that Solomon built the city together with *Megiddo and *Gezer (1 Kgs. 9:15), but that in 732 BC it was destroyed by Tiglath-Pileser III. After that date there is no further mention of the city in the sources.

In 1928 J. Garstang made trial digs at Hazor. During the years 1955-8 and 1968-70 the James A. Rothschild Expedition, under the direction of Y. Yadin on behalf of the Hebrew University, made extensive excavations on the site. The ancient city of Hazor was found to consist of two distinct parts: the mound, which occupies an area of 30 acres; and a large 'enclosure' of 175 acres, which was identified by the excavators as the lower city of Hazor.

As a result of the excavations 22 strata of occupation were found. The following chronological table will assist in following the description of the various periods of occupation.

THE LOWER CITY The area thought by Garstang to be an 'enclosure' proved to be a large city, surrounded by an earthen rampart on which the city wall was built.

Excavations in several areas give a fairly good picture of its history. The first area to be excavated, situated in the southwestern corner, was named area C. The earliest remains of occupation date back to the middle of the 18th century BC (stratum 4, Middle Bronze Age IIB), when the city was fortified for the first time. In the next phase, of the 17th-16th centuries BC (stratum 3, Middle Bronze Age IIC), the city suffered violent destruction by fire, which the excavator tends to attribute to Amosis of Egypt.

On top of the ashes remaining from this conflagration a new city was built in the 15th century BC (stratum 2, Late Bronze Age I). The flourishing period of Late Bronze Age Hazor was in the 14th century BC (stratum 1b). In this area a shrine was discovered consisting of a broad hall with a niche in its western wall containing small stelae and statues. There were benches for offerings along the walls. Nearby were several large dwellings, in one of which was a potter's workshop. The local and imported pottery found there help to date this city to Late Bronze Age IIA. The latest city in this area, in which the buildings and shrine of the previous period were rebuilt, was of the 13th century BC (stratum 1a). The equipment of the older shrine was reused in the new one. Among the objects found were a statue on which are seen a pair of hands outstretched towards a crescent and a disc, a basalt statuette of a man and a small basalt lion. The latest pottery on this site was of the end of the 13th century BC, when the city was destroyed.

In four other areas excavated in the lower city all the phases of occupation present in area C were represented. Of special interest were burials, in which large quantities of pottery were found. In the stratum of the 17th-16th centuries BC (stratum 3) numerous infant burials in jars were discovered below the floors of houses. Of great interest also was area F, situated between areas D and E. To the earliest occupation in this area, of the 18th-17th centuries BC, belong rock-cut tombs connected with each other by an intricate system of tunnels; these were, however, found to be empty. To the next phase, of the 17th-16th centuries BC, belongs a large temple with thick walls and an elaborate drainage system which made use of the earlier tunnels. In the 15th century BC part of the temple was reconstructed. This area assumed a completely different setting in the 14th century BC, when a large stone altar was built that contained numerous cult objects. Hundreds of pottery vessels of the same period were discovered in a tomb nearby.

Area H is situated at the northern end of the lower city, close to the rampart. Here four superimposed temples were found, the earliest belonging to the city of the 17th-16th centuries BC. This temple consisted of a broad hall with a rectangular niche at its northern end. The roof was supported by two columns and the entrance to the shrine was flanked by two towers. To the south of the hall was a raised platform, to which a broad flight of ashlar steps gave access. The same temple was still in use in the next phase, of the 15th century BC, but the floor level was raised. At this time the open courtyard was enclosed within a wall and another paved court was made in front of it. In the inner court a high place (*bamah*) was discovered around which cult objects and bones from animal sacrifices were found. Among the cult objects was a clay liver, on which evil omens were inscribed (*Witchcraft and divination).

A major change was introduced in the temple of the next phase, of the 14th century BC. This was built on a tripartite plan. It consisted of a porch with two pillars in it, a hall and then the Holy of Holies, with a rectangular niche in its rear wall, which faced north. The roof of the Holy of Holies was probably supported by wooden posts. The interior of the porch and of the Holy of Holies was lined with smooth basalt orthostats which originated in stratum 2 (at the latest). One orthostat in the form of a lion stood at the entrance to the porch. This temple was reused without any material change in the latest phase of the city, of the 13th century BC. Many elements in it, such as the deliberate tripartite division and the two pillars in the porch, have counterparts in the Temple of Solomon in *Jerusalem. Indeed scholars suggest that the Israelite plan may have originated in a northern Late Bronze Age prototype.

One of the gates of the lower city was discovered in area K, at the southwestern corner of the city. Here a series of superimposed gates, representing all phases of occupation of the town, was discovered (*Fortifications), resembling in their plan contemporary gates at

Aerial View of Tel Hazor

upper city	lower city	period	remarks
I		Hellenistic (2nd century BC)	citadel
II		Persian (4th century BC)	citadel and small settlement
III		Assyrian (7th century BC)	citadel
IV		end of 8th century BC)	unfortified Israelite settlement
V		8th century BC	destruction by Tiglath-Pileser III (732 BC)
VI		8th century BC	city of Jeroboam II, destruction by earthquake (c. 760) BC
VII		9th century BC	reconstruction of part of city VIII
VIII		9th century BC	Omrid Dynasty
IX		end of the 10th to beginning of 9th century BC	conflagration (destroyed by Ben-Hadad I?)
X		mid-10th century BC	city of Solomon
XI		11th century BC	limited Israelite settlement
XII		12th century BC	temporary Israelite settlement, semi-nomadic
XIII	1a	13th century BC	destruction in the second half of the 13th century BC by Joshua
XIV	1b	14th century BC (Late Bronze Age IIA)	El Amarna period
XV	2	15th century BC (Late Bronze Age I)	Tuthmosis III-Amenophis II
XVI	3	17th to 16th centuries BC (Middle Bronze Age IIC)	destruction by conflagration (Amosis?)
XVII	4	18th to 17th centuries BC (Middle Bronze Age IIB)	foundation of lower city (c. mid-18th century BC) (MB IIB)
'Pre XVII'		end of 19th century BC (MiddleTexts?) Bronze IIA(?)-IIB)	(Execration Texts?)
XVIII		Middle Bronze Age I	semi-nomadic settlement; destroyed or deserted (c. 1850 BC)
XIX, XX	not yet founded	Early Bronze Age III	Khirbet Kerak ware
XXI		Early Bronze Age II-III	built on bedrock

(Between the upper city column a vertical label "no longer settled" with arrows spans strata I–XII.)

*Megiddo, *Shechem or *Gezer. These consisted of an entry with three pairs of pilasters, which narrowed the passage to 6 feet. There were four towers, a pair on each side, protecting the gateway. The gate of the 17th-16th centuries BC was connected with a casemate wall, the earliest of its kind in Palestine. Another series of superimposed gates was discovered in the northwestern corner of the lower city. The plan of these gates was identical with those of area K.

THE UPPER CITY On the mound itself six areas were excavated: area A, in the center of the mound; area B, on its western edge; area G on the east, area L in the south, area M in the north and area BA, which is situated between areas A and B. In area A the excavators dug a deep trial trench in order to study the full archaeological history of the site. Strata XXI-XIX represented occupation in the Early Bronze Age II and III, dated by the typical pottery. Stratum XVIII was of the Middle Bronze Age I, when semi-nomads lived at Hazor. Strata XVII-XVI were of the Middle Bronze Age IIB-C. The remains here include a large building, probably a palace. To these levels belongs a brick wall on a stone foundation, 23 feet wide, which probably defended the acropolis. Stratum XV, of the Late Bronze Age I, was represented by a section of a brick-built palace. The thick earlier wall was still in use in this period. The same palace was used also in the next period, stratum XIV, of the Late Bronze Age IIA. In stratum XIII, the last of the Late Bronze Age strata, the building was destroyed by fire. Close to this palace a small rectangular shrine, probably the private shrine of the king, was discovered.

Stratum XII, of the 12th century BC, was the earliest of the Iron Age strata. Hazor was then settled by semi-nomads, who lived in tents or huts. The same temporary settlement continued in stratum XI, of the 11th century BC. The first buildings in this area, of stratum X, are attributed to the Solomonic period. This stratum is subdivided into two phases, to the earlier of which belong the city gate of the typical plan of this period and a casemate wall (*Fortifications) like those found at *Megiddo and *Gezer. The excavations on the mound have shown that the Solomonic city extended over the western half of the mound only, while the later Israelite ones were built over the whole mound.

Stratum IX is attributed to the period between Solomon and the House of Omri (end of the 10th to the early 9th centuries BC). Here a decline in the quality of the building was noted. Stratum VIII represents the rule of the House of Omri. To this period belongs a large storehouse, along the center of which ran two rows of massive pillars. The old casemate wall was also used as storage space. The storehouse was still in use in stratum VII, of the later part of the 9th century BC. In stratum VI, attributed to Jeroboam II, a residential quarter was built on the site of the storehouse. Some of the houses were of the typical Israelite four-room type. This city was destroyed by an earthquake and was subsequently rebuilt (stratum V, 8th century BC). It was again destroyed, this time by a fierce conflagration, attributed to the conquest by Tiglath-Pileser III in 732 BC, after which the site remained unfortified and, after some decades, was probably abandoned.

In Area B remains of the semi-nomads were also observed, in the earlier phases of the Israelite period, strata XII-XI. To the 11th century BC belong remains of a small shrine. To strata X-IX belongs the casemate wall, which encircled the whole mound. At the western end of this area remains of a bastion were discovered. Stratum VIII had a large citadel 65 feet by 77 feet, with walls 6 feet thick. The entrance to the citadel was ornamented with two massive proto-Aeolic capitals, of the same type as those found at *Samaria. Around the citadel were administrative buildings. The casemate wall was filled in to form a solid wall. The citadel was built in the first half of the 9th century BC and remained in use until it was finally destroyed by Tiglath-Pileser III.

During the preparations made to meet the Assyrian menace the houses around the citadel were destroyed and a strong wall with salients and recesses was built and connected with the older wall. Two four-room houses were also built in this quarter. But the whole area still suffered complete destruction. To this period belong several short Hebrew inscriptions. To stratum IV (late 8th century BC) belongs an unfortified settlement. The remaining strata, III-I, are represented by a series of Assyrian, Persian and Hellenistic citadels.

WATER SUPPLY One of the greatest enterprises of Israelite Hazor is its water supply system, which was found at the southern end of the mound (area L), where a deep depression in the ground had previously been noted. The system is situated just above the springs that issued from the foot of the mound, and consists of a huge pier, a tunnel and the approach to the pier. The pier was cut through the early strata of occupation, down to bedrock. Its upper part was supported by huge retaining walls, while the lower part was excavated in the soft limestone. The pier measures 40 feet by 55 feet at its upper end and narrows to about 25 feet by 30 feet at the bottom. The tunnel, 15 feet high and 15 feet wide, slopes down in a series of steps over a distance of more than 90 feet. At the outer end of the tunnel is a small pool from which water was drawn. The vertical measurement of the whole system from top to bottom is about 140 feet. An intricate system of approaches, terminating in a monumental gate, leads from the city to the pier. This water system dates from the early 10th century BC, coinciding with the period in which the water-supply systems of *Megiddo and *Gezer, the other Solomonic cities, were constructed.

b) A town on the southern border of Judah (Josh. 15:25), identified with Hezron (Josh. 15:3), which is also Hazar-Addar (Num. 34:4). Tentatively identified with Ain Qedes.

c) Another town on the southern border of Judah (Josh. 15:23). Not identified.

d) A town in the territory of Benjamin, settled after the Restoration (Neh. 11:33). Tentatively identified with Khirbet Hazur, north of *Jerusalem.

HEBRON One of the most ancient cities of Judah, on the way from *Jerusalem to *Beer-Sheba, where roads leading east and west converge; a Levitical city, and a city of refuge (Josh. 21:13). Also named Kirjath-Arba (Gen. 23.2, etc.), possibly after Arba, who was a great man among the Anakim (Josh. 14:15, cf. also 15:13-14); it seems that the real explanation of this name is that the town probably had four suburbs (*arba* meaning four in Hebrew), one of which could have been *Mamreh (Gen. 35:27).

According to Numbers (13:22) Hebron was built seven years before Zoan (*Tanis) in *Egypt. Zoan was founded in about 1720 BC, so Hebron was certainly settled at the beginning of the 18th century BC. It seems that it was in fact of much greater antiquity. It was owned by the sons of Heth (Gen. 23:1-7). Abraham was 'a stranger and a sojourner' with them (Gen. 23:4); he built an altar unto the Lord here (Gen. 13:18) and saw the Lord (Gen. 18:1). From Ephron, the son of Zohar, Abraham bought the cave of *Machpelah, which was on Ephron's land (Gen. 23:9-17). Joshua defeated Hoham, King of Hebron, at Gibeon (Josh. 10:1 ff.), and later the city was allotted to Caleb, who had conquered it (Josh. 15:13; Judg. 1:20). Because of its connections with the Hebrew Patriarchs Hebron has had an important place in national tradition since its conquest by Joshua. After Saul's death David and his two wives dwelt here (2 Sam. 2:1-3); it was here that David was anointed king over the House of Judah (2 Sam. 2:4). David made a covenant with the people and reigned at Hebron for seven years and six months (2 Sam. 5-5; 1 Chr. 3:4). It was also fortified by Rehoboam (2 Chr. 11:10).

After the Restoration Hebron was resettled (Neh. 11:25). In this period the southern region of Judah was settled by *Edomites and was known as *Idumea, a district extending from the southern hills of Judah to *Beer-Sheba. During the first years of the Hasmonean revolt Hebron was conquered (1 Macc. 5:65) and it has remained part of Judea ever since. After the destruction of the Second Temple the town was given to the Legio X Fretensis, who set up a military base there, in the rear of the *Limes Palestinae. During the later Roman period there was a Jewish community there and a synagogue.

The identificaton of Hebron with modern el-Khalil is accepted by all experts, and confirmed by excavations carried out since 1985 by A. Ofer on behalf of the Institute of Archaeology of Tel Aviv University and the Israel Exploration Society. It has been discovered that in the Middle Bronze Age there was a cultic installation on the site — a room filled with ashes and thousands of

Detail from the building above the Cave of Machpelah, Hebron

animal bones. In the fill of this room was found a fragment of a cuneiform tablet, inscribed with a list of animals fit for sacrifice. But the exact location of the Israelite site is disputed. Its continuous occupation in the later periods makes exact identification difficult until excavation is carried out. It is, however, certain that the beautiful wall which surrounds the Cave of *Machpelah belongs to the time of Herod. The area enclosed measures 160 feet by 90 feet. The walls are 8 feet thick and some of stones are as big as 22 feet by 5 feet by 5 feet. The wall is decorated with flat pilasters. The other buildings above the cave incorporate remains of later periods. A short distance west of the Cave of Machpelah is situated Tell er-Rumeideh, which may possibly contain remains of Bronze and Iron Age Hebron.

HELIOPOLIS; BAALBEK A city in the plain at the foot of the Anti-Lebanon, near the source of the Orontes. The ancient name Baalbek indicates a pre-Roman occupation, though no remains have been found and the earliest written sources are Roman. Attempts by various scholars to identify Baalbek with a town in the Old Testament or in the *El Amarna letters have failed.

Little is known of the Hellenistic history of the site. In the 1st century BC it was the religous center of the Iturean tetrachy, after whose dissolution, in about 17 BC, it was incorporated in the territory of Berytus (Beirut). At the time of Pompey's settlement of Syria (64–63BC) the city was controlled by a ruler named Ptolemy, the son of Mennaeus, and he remained in power by paying large sums of money to Pompey. Augustus settled veterans of two legions in Berytus and Heliopolis and Septimius Severus made it into a Roman colony. It remained a great center of pagan cults until, in the 6th century AD all its temples were destroyed and a church was erected. In AD 637 it was conquered by the Arabs.

Heliopolis owes its fame to its extraordinary architectural remains, all dating from the time of the Roman Empire. From inscriptions found elsewhere it is known that the city was the cultic center of the Heliopolitan Triad, Jupiter Heliopolitanus, Mercury and Venus. Under Septimius Severus and Caracalla one of its temples is represented for the first time on coins. Today three temples and a sacred area with a large altar, entered through a *propylaea*, are extant. The dates of construction are obscure. It is known that Trajan consulted the oracle in the Temple of Baal before his Parthian campaign (AD 113–15). It seems that work on the other temples was begun in the 2nd century AD and completed in the 3rd century.

HEPTAPEGON A spring (et-Tabgha, near the Sea of *Galilee) southwest of *Capernaum, whose name means 'seven springs'. The name cannot be traced earlier than the 6th century AD, when Cyril of Scythopolis mentions it (*Vita S. Sabae, 24*). According to other early Christian traditions of the same period Jesus baptized the apostles at this spot, 2 miles from *Magdala; also it was here that he fed the multitude with five loaves and two fishes. From the 6th century onwards many pilgrims to the Holy Land mention Heptapegon. A church built at the site at an early period was destroyed in AD 614,

when the Persians conquered the country. In the early 9th century a monastery is mentioned there. The same sources refer also to a rock. 'the Lord's Table'. According to a 9th century tradition Jesus appeared there before the disciples after the Resurrection; to commemorate this another church was built.

The church of Heptapegon, which was destroyed in AD 614, probably by the Persians, was excavated in 1932 by A.M. Schneider and A.E. Mader on behalf of the Görresgesellschaft. In 1936 remains of a smaller chapel (60 feet by 30 feet) were discovered under the floor of the church. It incorporates a large stone, probably the traditional table. The superimposed church, built after the middle of the 4th century AD, is a basilica with a transept, an apse and a large *atrium*, with numerous rooms around it to provide accommodation for pilgrims. Remains of a beautiful mosaic pavement are preserved in the nave. It is decorated with geometric patterns and scenes of the Nile, including lotus blossoms, papyrus reeds, swans, geese, ducks, cranes and cormorants. These adorn the northern transept. In the southern transept, some buildings are depicted against a background of the Nile, which includes a Nilometer.

HERMON (MOUNT) A mountain range on the northern border of Palestine, marking the limit of the conquests of Moses and Joshua on the east of the *Jordan, and of the Israelite expansion (Deut. 3:8; 4:48; Josh. 11:17, etc.; Judg. 3:3). The Hermon rises above the valley of *Lebanon (Josh. 11:17) and above the land of *Mizpeh (Josh. 11:3–8). The *Amorites called it Shenir, while to the *Sidonians it was known as Sirion (Deut. 3:9), the name by which it is mentioned in the *Execration Texts and in the documents of *Ugarit. In an agreement made between the King of the *Hittites and a Syrian king in about 1330 BC, the gods of Lebanon and Sirion are mentioned as safeguarding the contract. It appears (as Saniru) in documents of Tiglath-Pileser III of Assyria.

It seems that the name Hermon referred only to the southern part of the Anti-Lebanon. The highest peak rises to about 8,500 feet above sea level. The mountain range is about 18 miles long and is separated from the northern Anti-Lebanon by the deep gorge of the River Barada. It is known in Arabic as Jebel esh-Sheik or Jebel et-Talg ('the mountain of snow') because it is snow-covered for most of the year, and is mentioned in the Talmud under a similar name.

Like most of the higher mountains in Palestine Mount Hermon was the seat of the local Baal, Baal-Hermon (Judg. 3:3; 1 Chr. 5:23). In the Roman period a temple was built there.

HERODIAN JERICHO *See* *JERICHO. HERODIAN.

HERODIUM A town and fortress built by Herod on the eastern border of Judea; between the hill country and the desert, identified with Khirbet el-Fureidis, 3 miles southeast of *Bethlehem. The building of the city and the fortress are described by Josephus, (*War* I, 419–20).

The site was visited and described by numerous scholars in the 19th century. In the tears 1962–7 it was excavated by V. Corbo with the financial help of the Department for Cultural Relations of the Govern-

(Right) The fortress of Herodium, aerial view

ment of Italy. In 1968-9 a clearance and additional excavations were made on the site on behalf of the Israel Department of Antiquities and Museums, under the direction of G. Foerster. Three occupation levels were observed: the fortress built by Herod and an occupation in the time of the First Jewish Revolt; the period of the Second Revolt and an occupation by Christian hermits.

Herod's fortified palace was built on a conical hill whose final form was secured by the erection of massive retaining walls and by clearing the slope of rocks and other protuberances. The fortress itself consists of a double circular wall with four towers, three half-round and one round, facing the cardinal points of the compass, the round tower facing east. The outer diameter of the fortress is 180 feet, the inner 150 feet. The whole of the eastern part of the inner space is occupied by a peristyle court with three rows of free-standing columns and one solid wall with attached half-columns. Entrances in the encircling wall lead to the towers, underground chambers and reservoirs. The western half is divided by a cruciform court into two equal parts. On the south of this court is a *triclinium* with some adjoining rooms, while on the east is a typical Roman bath. The capitals used at Herodium were mostly of the Corinthian order, though some Nabatean capitals are also present and the stone-dressing is typically Nabatean. As at *Masada, much use was made of stucco for the finer architectural details. Frescoes imitating multicolored marble were also used freely. In the bath a mosaic pavement was found.

The period of the Second Revolt is represented by numerous coins, graffiti and ostraca and by changes introduced in some of the buildings. The *triclinium* was transformed into an assembly hall, or perhaps a synagogue.

The occupation of the site by Christian hermits is indicated mainly by numerous inscriptions, coins and some traces of dwellings.

HESHBON The capital of Sihon, King of the *Amorites, formerly in the land of *Moab (Num. 21:26). Heshbon was among the cities of Sihon for which the Reubenites and the Gadites asked Moses (Num. 32:3). It was given to Reuben (Num. 32:37). One of the Levitical cities in the territory of Gad (Josh. 21.39), it was presumably taken by Mesha, King of *Moab. Isaiah (15:4; 16:8-9) and Jeremiah (48:2, 34, 45, etc.) prophesied its destruction. Some time after the beginning of the Hasmonean revolt in 129 BC, the town was conquered by Simon Maccabaeus ((Josephus, *Antiq.* XIII, 255-6). It was part of the Hasmonean kingdom in the time of Alexander Jannaeus, but was returned to the *Nabateans by Hyrcanus II. It was conquered again by Herod the Great, who founded a military colony there which he named Esbous ((Josephus, *Antiq.* XV, 294). After the annexation of the Nabatean kingdom it was part of the Provincia Arabia (AD 106). During the late Roma period it became a *polis* under the name of Aurelia Esbous. Eusebius (*Onom.* 84:4) mentions the worship of Zeus Hadad at this place, which he described as 'the celebrated city of Arabia'. Identified with Hesban, 8 miles north of *Medaba.

HESI (TELL EL-) One of the largest mounds in the *Plain, on the southern bank of Wadi Hesi, 15½ miles northeast of *Gaza. The ancient site consists of a mound 11 acres in area and a lower town 23 acres in area. The site was identified with *Lachish by 19th century scholars; they based their identification on Khirbet Umm Laqis, about 3 miles to the northwest of the mound, which, they believed, preserved the ancient name of the site. Contemporary scholars tend to identify Tell el-Hesi with *Eglon, one of the more important cities on the *Plain. Eusebius (*Onom.* 48:18 f) states that Agla is situated 10 miles from *Beth-Gubrin, on the way to *Gaza. In 1970 an American team under the direction of J.E. Worrel resumed excavations at this site. Under different directors the expedition, sponsored by the American School of Oriental Research, was still working in 1983.

To the Chalcolithic period (around 3200 BC) are ascribed the round structures found there. In the Early Bronze Age III (2650-2350 BC) the site grew into a large *fortified town; the strata of the Late Bronze Age and Early Iron Age have not yet been excavated. In the 8th-6th centuries BC, Iron Age IIC (Stratum VII, sub-strata a-d), the area of the acropolis was extended by the construction of a massive podium (*millo*). This city was destroyed by the Babylonians, leaving a thick accumulation of ashes (Stratum VI). The nature of the settlement in the following Persian period (6th-4th centuries BC, Stratum V) is not entirely clear. It is not certain whether the site contained a military stronghold, or whether it was fortified by a casemate wall. To this period are ascribed silos. A large farming establishment is ascribed to the Hellenistic period (4th-1st centuries BC, Stratum IV). The following levels of occupation are late Arab up to recent times. The evidence is still fragmentary and no clear picture of the site is as yet available.

W.M.F. Petrie excavated this site in 1890 and F.J. Bliss in 1891-3, on behalf of the Palestine Exploration Fund. This was the first scientific excavation in which the relationship of the finds, mainly pottery, to the stratigraphy of the site was emphasized. In the course of their work, during which about a third of the site was excavated, eight strata, numbered I-VIII, and an additional three sub-strata (sub-I, sub-II, sub-IV) were discovered, representing 11 cities. The earliest were sub-I and I. Because of the scarcity of building remains this stratum and its sub-stratum did not merit any description, but it is possible now to date it to the Early Bronze Age by the pottery it contained. The excavators attributed a section of the city's fortifications, found in another part of the mound, to the same period, but it is now clear that these are of the Middle Bronze Age, the same era as cities sub-II and II. The fortifications discovered consist of a section of a city wall, a tower and a glacis, typical of the time of the *Hyksos. The pottery of these strata is typical of Middle Bronze Age II and Late Bronze Age I. These cities also had a cemetery, which was discovered on the slope of the lower city. To city III belongs a section of a wall, against which a row of rooms was built. A clay tablet of the *El Amarna type safely dates this city to the 14th century BC. Found in a layer of ashes, this is a letter written by an Egyptian official named Papu, probably a resident of *Lachish, to his superior at Tell el-Hesi. In this letter Papu complains: 'Shipti-Balu and Zimrida have plotted publicly and Shipti-Balu said to Zimrida: 'The prince of Yaramu [i.e. *Jarmuth] wrote to me: Give me six bows, and three daggers and three swords. Verily I am going out against the land of the king, and thou art my ally.' This is valuable additional material, supplementing the *El-Amarna correspondence.

Cities sub-IV and IV contained a fort, 54 feet square, whose brick walls were 6-15 feet thick. The pottery, cylinder and scarab seals date these cities to the last phases of the Late Bronze Age. A fragment of a bowl, on which a short Canaanite inscription was found, helps to date the destruction of this city to the end of the 14th century BC. The abandonment of the Late Bronze Age city was followed by a long gap. The rebuilding of the city was dated correctly by Petrie to the 10th century BC. To city V belongs a building with six rows of stone bases, named by Petrie the 'Pilaster Building'. Because of its likeness to the stables at *Megiddo, the first of which were discovered at that time, he thought that the Tell el-Hesi building might have been a stable as well, but this is very doubtful.

City VI, of the 9th-8th centuries BC, was inadequately published, perhaps because of the bad state of preservation of the remains. The same applies to city VII, which is dated by the pottery to the 8th century BC. This city suffered destruction by fire. The latest city, VIII, was again not adequately described, but probably dates to the end of the period of the First Temple, i.e. the first half of the 6th century BC.

HIDDEKEL This is the Hebrew name for the Tigris, one of the two large rivers of *Mesopotamia which, according to Genesis (2:14), flowed from the Garden of *Eden. It is formed by the confluence of two rivers that draw their waters from the mountains of Armenia. On its way southwards from Lake Van it receives some large tributaries, the most important of which are the Greater and Lesser Zab and the Diyala. In early times the courses of the Tigris and the *Euphrates were separate — their confluence before they flow into the Persian Gulf is quite recent. The Tigris has a greater volume of water than the Euphrates and flows faster, so that no upstream navigation was possible. The prosperous cities of *Nineveh, *Calah and Ashur flourished along its shores. In the Hellenistic and Roman periods, when the river became known as the Tigris, it was united with the Euphrates by irrigation canals and the cities of Seleucia and Ctesiphon flourished in its valley.

HINNOM (VALLEY OF) A valley on the border between the territories of Benjamin and Judah (Josh. 15:8, etc.), to the south and southwest of *Jerusalem; a continuation of the *Kidron Valley. In Jeremiah (7:32) it is called the 'valley of slaughter'. At a later period the Valley of Hinnom, also known as Gehinnom, became synonymous with hell.

HIPPODROME A course for chariot-racing, the prototype of the Roman circus. Like the *stadium, it was long, narrow and elliptical, but straight at the end from which the racing started.

The hippodrome of *Gerasa was excavated in 1931-3. Situated outside the city at some distance to the south, its inside length is 266yd, with an inside width of 56yd at the north end and just under 55yd at the south end. The date of construction is not clear. Some scholars believe that it was built at the end of the second or beginning of the 3rd century AD and never completely finished, while others prefer a date of about AD 70. The hippodrome of *Gerasa is the only one that has been excavated in Palestine and Transjordan. Remains of others were found at *Caesarea, *Kanath, Bostra (*Bozrah), *Beth-Shean and *Gadara. Josephus, (*Life*, 132, 138) mentions the hippodrome of Taricheae. (*See also* *MAGDALA.)

Like all other similar public buildings the hippodrome was an offence to pious Jews and most of the cities referred to above had a primarily Hellenistic population. Only Taricheae had a Jewish population, though the upper class was Hellenized. In similar conditions, Herod had a hippodrome constructed in *Jerusalem ((Josephus, *Antiq.* XVII, 193), probably in the Tyropoeon valley.

HITTITES One of the most powerful peoples of the ancient Near East, who held sway in the northeastern part of Asia Minor. Early in the 2nd millennium BC this region was inhabited by Assyrian merchants. Documents of this period indicate that the Assyrian colonies were subject to local dynasts, but it is not certain whether some of these were Hittites. The earliest Hittite kingdom is of the 16th-15th centuries BC, but knowledge of this period is limited mostly to names of rulers and their respective cities. It was under Suppiluliumas I, first king of the new Hittite kingdom, that it expanded over Babylonia (*Mesopotamia) towards the southeast and the mountains of Lebanon to the south. Among the conquered cities of Syria were *Kedesh-on-the-Orontes and *Qatna, while *Ugarit became his vassal.

The situation in the area at that period is well known from Hittite documents and from the *El Amarna letters. The strong rivalry between the Hittites and the *Egyptians in Syria reached a climax during the reign of Rameses II, in the battle of *Kedesh in about 1285 BC, after which a peace treaty was concluded. Documents referring to this treaty were found engraved on the walls of Egyptian temples, as well as on clay tablets discovered in the Hittite capital of Hattusa (Boghazkoi).

The great Hittite empire came to an end with the invasion of the Sea Peoples (*Philistines). The late Hittite period (950-715 BC) was one of decline. Asia Minor was already lost and it was only in northern Syria that Hittite city-states, many of whose names are known, lived on. Early in the 8th century BC these were gradually conquered by the Assyrians.

Excavations on Hittite sites in Asia Minor and northern Syria since the beginning of the 20th century have produced an enourmous amount of information concerning the literature, religion, art and architecture of the Hittites. The ancient Hittite language, referred to in their own texts as Khattili, is not yet fully understood, though the later Hittite language, Neshili, is much better known.

In the Bible Heth is the son of Canaan (Gen. 10:15), and in Exodus (23:28) the Hittite, together with the Hivite and the Canaanite, is enumerated among the ancient people of Palestine and referred to as occupying the center of the country (Num. 13:29). The Hittites also lived in the hills of *Hebron, and it was from Ephron the Hittite that Abraham bought the Cave of *Machpelah (Gen. 23). Archaeological evidence of the presence of Hittites in the Holy Land at this early period is still missing. They are heard of in the period of the conquest of *Canaan by the Children of Israel, when they occupied part of the hill country (Josh. 11:3); this was possibly called the 'land of the Hittites' (cf. Josh. 1:1-4). Still more is heard of them in the time of David and Solomon: David had Hittites among his men (1 Sam. 26:6; 2 Sam. 11:3, etc.); Hittites were employed by Solomon (1 Kgs. 9:20-1; 2 Chr. 8:7-8); and among Solomon's wives were included Hittite women (1 Kgs. 11:1). Solomon sold the Hittites chariots and horses that he had acquired from the *Egyptians (1 Kgs. 10:29; 2 Chr. 1:17). In the time of Ben-Hadad there was a military pact between Israel and the Hittites.

HIVITES One of the seven nations that inhabited the land of *Canaan before the conquest of Joshua (Gen. 10:17). From certain references in the Bible it is obvious that the Hivites and the *Canaanites were not the same people (2 Sam. 24:7); that the Hivites and the *Amorites were also different (Isa. 17:19 in the Septuagint); and that the Hivites were identified with the *Horites (Gen. 36:2, 20). The *Shechemites are referred to as Hivites (Gen. 34:2). Current belief is that, unlike the *Canaanites, the Hivites were not of Semitic stock but a branch of the *Horites. According to Joshua (11:3) and Judges (3:3) the Hivites dwelt in the north of the country, in the region of *Lebanon.

HOLON a) In 1963-4 T. Yisraeli-Noy excavated an Acheulian site near modern Holon on the coastal plain. The site was in marshy clay between two layers of red loam. During the excavations many flint implements were collected, among them 40 handaxes. Among the animal remains, molars and the tusk of an elephant were found, as well as deer and turtle bones; this indicated that at that time the coastal plain was partly forest and partly swampland, on the banks of which the Acheulians encamped.

On typological grounds this site has been compared with other upper Acheulian assemblages such as those in *Umm Qatafa and et-*Tabun Caves. (*See also* *PREHISTORY; *FLINT TOOLS.)
b) A Levitical city and a city of refuge in the territory of Judah, south of *Hebron (Josh. 15:51; 21:15). Not identified.

Elephant tusk from Holon

HOR (MOUNT) a) The name of a hill on the border between *Canaan and *Edom. One of the stations on the route of the Exodus, where the Israelites camped near a source of water. From here they tried to penetrate the land of *Canaan but were forced to retreat to the desert. Aaron died here (Num. 20:22-9). Eusebius (*Onom.* 176:6f) places it in the region of *Petra, where the rock is shown. Tentatively located to the northeast of *Kadesh-Barnea.
b) A place on the northern border of the land of *Canaan (Num. 34:7). Not identified.

HORITES The Horites probably originated in the hills of Zagrus and Armenia. They are heard of for the first time in a document from the time of Sargon of *Accad (24th century BC), when they already had a kingdom beyond the Tigris (*Hiddekel). From this kingdom they began their slow but steady penetration along the valley of the Mesopotamian rivers southward. Early in the 19th century BC they had already occupied the land north of Ashur (*Mesopotamia). A study of names shows how deeply the Horites penetrated into upper *Mesopotamia. This movement of Horites, who were of non-Semitic stock, coincided with the appearance of the West Semites, the two elements subsequently constituting the bulk of the population in Syria and Palestine. By the 15th century BC the Horites formed the majority of the population in northern Syria. Towards the 14th-13th centuries BC they were an important element in the ruling classes of southern Syria and Palestine.

The exact date of the arrival of the Horites in Palestine and *Egypt is still in dispute. It is thought by some experts to have coincided with the conquest of *Egypt by the *Hyksos in the 18th century BC, but others date it a century later. Both in *Egypt and in Palestine the Horites and the Hyksos made up the ruling nobility, the *maryannu*, who introduced the horse and chariot into warfare (*Weapons and warfare). Together with other elements, such as the nomadic *Habiru, they formed the population which the Israelites, *Arameans and Sea Peoples (*Philistines) had to face when they arrived in the land of *Canaan in the 13th century BC. There is evidence of the presence of the Horites in Palestine in the 15th-14th centuries BC in the *El Amarna correspondence and in the *Taanach tablets; some names mentioned there, both of individuals and of places, are Horite.

The Horites are not mentioned frequently in the Bible. We are told that those living in Mount Seir (*Edom) were defeated by Chedorlaomer (Gen. 14:5-6), but they remained in the region (Gen. 36:20) until they were destroyed by the descendants of Esau (Deut. 2:12, 22; Authorized Version: 'Horim'). Scholars believe that the *Jebusites and the *Hivites, as well as some other ancient peoples mentioned in the Bible, were of Horite descent.

HORMAH A town in the northeastern *Negev, close to *Arad. It was in the south of the land of *Canaan and is connected with the first attempt to penetrate *Canaan (Num. 14:45; Deut. 1:44). At that time it was a Canaanite city-state held by the King of Hormah. It was conquered and destroyed by Judah and Simeon (Judg. 1:17) and appears in the list of 31 kings vanquished by Joshua (Josh. 12:14). It was later included in the territory of Judah (Josh. 13:30) and given to Simeon (Josh. 19:4). Hormah was one of the cities to which David sent presents after his victory over the *Amalekites (1 Sam. 30:30). It does not appear in the later biblical sources, but the possible mention of Hormah in Egyptian inscriptions found in the mines of Sinai (*Sinai; *Metals), and also in the *Execration Texts attests to its antiquity and its importance in early times. Identified with Tell el-Meshash, about 8 miles southeast of *Beer-Sheba.

HOUSES Compared with what is known about public buildings in antiquity, such as fortifications, temples and palaces, the information that is available about private dwellings is relatively limited. There are two reason for this: firstly, in a mound with continuous layers of occupation only the foundations of underlying levels are preserved; and secondly, the excavators tend to concentrate on public architecture. In the later periods, where houses are still standing to the level of the first floor or higher, it is a different matter: here it is possible to form a detailed picture of what private houses looked like (*Sobata; *Mampsis). Another limiting factor is that in the early periods mud bricks were used for all construction, which means that, as at *Jericho, little has survived. By the Middle Bronze Age most buildings were of stone, but there was generally little fine stonework — walls were built of roughly cut stones and filled with rubble. Not until the time of the Israelite monarchy, under Solomon and Ahab, did the quality of masonry become important, as a result of foreign influences.

NEOLITHIC PERIOD The houses of this period represent a transition from primitive shelters to real homes and are round or curvilinear. The surviving parts of the walls incline inwards, indicating that the houses had domed roofs, thus resembling the huts of nomadic peoples. Each had a stepped or downward-sloping entrance, so that the outside level was higher than the

floor of the house. The walls were built of hand-moulded bricks known as plano-convex (with a flat base and a curved top). Such houses were found only in Jericho from the pre-Pottery Neolithic A period. In the following phase (pre-Pottery Neolithic B) a great change took place: a house then consisted of a large rectangular room with a wide doorway, sometimes flanked by timber posts, with small storage chambers adjoining it. Several such houses were built around a courtyard where cooking took place. The bricks in the walls, shaped like flattened cigars, were still made by hand. The floors and part of the walls were covered with hard lime plaster.

CHALCOLITHIC PERIOD At *Beth-Shean two types of construction were found. In the first phase the walls were built of plano-convex bricks, in the later of flat bricks. The houses of the second phase were of the apsidal type, built to a rectangular plan with one rounded end. In this period a considerable variety of houses existed. At *Tuleilat Ghassul, for instance, the houses are irregular in plan, the rooms varying from nearly rectangular to trapezoidal in shape. They are of moderate size and built close together. The walls have a stone foundation with a superstructure of hand-moulded sun-dried bricks. Around *Beer-Sheba four phases of settlement were found, three of which had subterranean dwellings of an irregular shape cut into the soft loess. Several rounded chambers were connected by corridors and bell-shaped silos and fireplaces were cut into the floors. Entrance was from above. In the last phase earlier dwellings were filled in and on top of them rectilinear houses with brick walls were erected on a stone foundation. Each of these houses was constructed around a central hall, an arrangement that had already been used for the subterranean dwellings.

EARLY BRONZE AGE Unbaked bricks were still used at this date but, in contrast to the previous periods, they were moulded in various sizes. The bricks were bonded with a mortar of fresh clay. The houses were now always built on foundations of one or more stone courses. These foundations increased in height and, instead of roughly hewn blocks, dressed stones now began to be used. Houses had one or several rooms. Floors were of beaten earth and the doorways opening to the outside had sills of flat stones or square brick tiles. Ovens were found in the courtyards between the houses. An apsidal house of this period was found at *Megiddo, but this type was replaced at *Beth-Shean by rectangular houses built of rectangular mud bricks on a stone foundation. One house had six wooden posts set in two rows supporting the roof. At Tell el-*Farah (north) and *Ai several houses had wooden supports standing on a paving slab to provide stability. For square rooms one support sufficed, while elongated rooms had several. At *Arad an Early Bronze Age city showing well-developed architecture was found; it had not been disturbed by later building activities. The typical dwelling is of a broadhouse plan, consisting of a large rectangular room, sometimes with a smaller one attached to it, and with entry through one of the long walls. The floor was below ground level and reached by two or three steps.

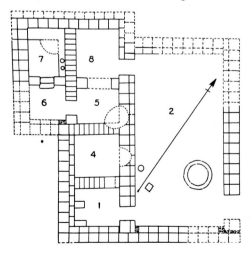

House of an affluent family, Tell Beit Mirsim, Late Bronze Age

MIDDLE BRONZE AGE The first phase of the Middle Bronze Age is a period known mainly through tombs. The people were semi-nomads and this is reflected in their architecture. The best examples of houses are those from the settlement at *Har Yeruham (stratum II) which were all stone constructions consisting of several rooms of different shapes. The roofs were supported by stone pillars made of several cylindrical drums. The pillars were arranged along the main longitudinal axis of the room; a square room would have a single pillar in the center. The floors were bedrock, levelled down or filled with flat stones. Sometimes there were benches along the walls. In the main phase of the Middle Bronze Age, the *Hyksos period, the majority of houses were simple and modest dwellings with small rooms and a courtyard, built closely together. Most probably they had two stories, the ground floor being used for storage and work-rooms while the upper floor provided living accommodation. Food was prepared and cooked in courtyards, where fireplaces have been found. In the ground floors of houses at *Jericho jars full of grain, loom weights, saddle-querns and grinding stones were found, suggesting that they were used for industrial purposes too.

In addition to these simple family homes, houses belonging to the more prosperous inhabitants were also found. At Tell *Beit Mirsin W.F. Albright called such a building a 'patrician house'. This had a large courtyard on the east, entered through a wide doorway, and a plastered basin sunk into the floor. The western part consisted of six rooms. This house certainly had two stories, the lower being used for work and by the servants, the upper for living quarters.

LATE BRONZE AGE Basically the type of habitation did not change, though increasing numbers of larger houses belonging to nobles or important citizens have been unearthed (*Palaces). At *Megiddo the normal house of the period has an inner courtyard with several rooms arranged round it. The houses are not now huddled closely together.

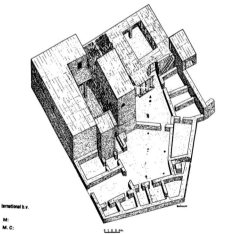

Mampsis. Building XII. Reconstruction of a Nabatean mansion

IRON AGE At the time of the early Israelite kings a new type of dwelling developed known as the four-room house. The plan is nearly square and the inner partition consists of three oblong rooms and another room running along the whole width of the building. The rooms are approximately equal in size. Such houses were found at Tell el-*Farah (north), *Beth-Shemesh, Tell en-*Nasbeh, Tell *Qasileh, *Hazor and so on.

There are several variations of this plan. The middle one of the three oblong rooms was usually a court, containing the fireplace. In some cases this court was shut off from the adjoining rooms by a solid wall; in others one of the rooms was separated from it only by a row of pillars or upright stones somewhat over 3 feet high, either free-standing or incorporated in rubble walls. It is not always possible to ascertain whether these uprights were at least partly sunk into the ground, thus forming solid bases for wooden pillars supporting the roof. At Tell el-*Farah the three oblong rooms were further divided. The excavated area shows houses with an unusually regular layout; they were built side by side and back to back, opening on to parallel streets. The walls were thin, usually one course of stone in width.

The basic plan of the Palestinian house, like others in the Mediterranean area, always consisted of a court with rooms around it, an arrangement imposed by the climate. To provide protection from the heat the buildings were constructed with as few outside windows and doors as possible. Everything was centered around the inner court, where daily life was lived. The roofs were mostly flat and used in the summer for sleeping on. In the Hellenistic, Roman and Byzantine periods this type of house continued to be used, except that the crafts of building and masonry developed. The walls were built of finely cut stones arranged in neat rows. Much decoration was added in the form of carved lintels, attached capitals and doorpost bases. Many houses had their walls covered with white plaster; some had frescoes. The second floor was always carried by arches spanning the room on two sides without doors. On these arches (two, three or four of them according to the size of the room) slabs of stone were laid to form the floor of the next story. The roof was carried in the same way. The houses had their own water reservoirs in the courtyards or in cisterns below any of the ground-floor rooms. (*See also* *BUILDING MATERIALS.)

HUNTING AND FISHING Hunting and fishing were the main source of human sustenance in prehistoric times. Changes in climate and the consequent decrease in afforestation and permanent rivers reduced the hunting grounds and the fish supply considerably. Hunting was not practised to a great extent but it is mentioned in the Bible: Nimrod was famed as a hunter (Gen. 10:9); and so was Esau (Gen. 27:5).

The Jewish dietary laws restricted the kinds of animal that could be eaten as well as the manner in which they might be slaughtered. These limitations may have had an effect on hunting. Some scholars believe that if it was practised at all it was purely for reason of self protection or to prevent damage to fields and other property by wild animals. The trapper's

Snaring birds, in a tomb wall-painting at Thebes, Egypt

methods are nicely portrayed in Job (18:8-10). The implication is that the trap was some kind of a net; a bigger and stronger one would be used for catching larger game and one of finer mesh for birds (cf. also Ezek. 12:13; 17:20; Eccles. 9:12; Amos 3:5). It seems that larger animals could also be caught by the very ancient method of digging a hole in the ground and concealing it with branches (Jer. 48:44).

A hunted animal could be eaten only if it was ritually clean (Deut. 15-16, 22-4) and if the blood had been properly drained from it (Lev. 17:13). Hunting an animal with a bow and arrow, or with a spear as in numerous Assyrian and Egyptian reliefs and wall paintings, was very rare in Palestine (cf. I Sam 17:34-6). On the other hand, Solomon's daily diet included much ritually clean game, which must have been hunted by such methods (1 Kgs. 4:23). In the neighboring countries hunting was an accepted sport and some of the Assyrian monarchs kept large game reserves. It continued to be a very common sport in the Persian, Hellenistic and Roman periods, when it was also used to obtain combat animals, mainly war elephants. In the Roman period hunting also supplied the circuses with wild animals for the popular contests with men.

There is not much evidence of fishing in the Bible and we are told that it was less common than in *Egypt (Num. 11:5; Isa. 19:8). As early as the 11th century BC, fish salted in *Egypt were sold in Palestine and Syria.

The conquest of the coast of Palestine by the Hasmoneans encouraged the Jews to fish. The New Testament (Matt. 4:18-22, etc.) provides evidence of fishing in the Sea of *Galilee in the Roman period, as does the Talmud for a somewhat later period. There was no way of keeping fish fresh for more than a very short time, so it had to be salted and dried if it was to be preserved. One of the major salting centers on the Sea of *Galilee was at Taricheae (*Magdala), a Greek name which means 'fish-salting'. The earlier, Aramaic

name of the same place was Migdal Nunayah — 'Tower of the Fishermen'. Some of the kitchen refuse of ancient towns in the *Negev contains considerable quantities of fishbones from fish that must have been brought from the *Red Sea. This may be taken as evidence that fish was also salted there.

Fishermen in Palestine, as elsewhere, used either a hook and a line or nets (Isa. 19:8); fishing from boats with dragnets was also known (Hab. 1:15; Ezek. 26:5; Luke 5:4). Clay or stone weights were used to make the net sink. Quantities of these were found at Roman *Caesarea and on other sites along the coast.

HUSIFA This name of a Jewish village is mentioned in an elegy found in the Cairo Geniza, and is identified with the village of Isfiye, 7.5 miles southeast of Haifa. In this village graves of the Roman period were found, and the latest coin in a hoard of 4,560 silver coins is of AD 52/53. In the course of road construction in 1930 a *mosaic pavement with a seven-branched menorah was found. The site was excavated in 1933 by M. Avi-Yonah and N. Makhouly on behalf of the Department of Antiquities. Due to the fact that the site is built-over by modern houses, only half of the building was excavated. The building is approximately 30 feet square, with two rows of pillars, facing east. The whole building was paved with *mosaics, and is surrounded by a rich geometric mosaic carpet. At the entrance is a wreath with an inscription in Hebrew: 'Peace on Israel', flanked by two menorahs, a *shofar*, an *ethrog* and an incense shovel. In the nave there are traces of a dedicatory inscription, a geometric carpet, and a *zodiac circle. The synagogue lacked a permanent place for the Torah Shrine. It is dated to the early 6th century AD.

HYKSOS This is the Greek form of the Egyptian name *hku hsht*, which means 'rulers of foreign countries'. Manetho, the Egyptian priest and historian, used this name for the Asiatic princes who invaded *Egypt and founded the 15th Dynasty. According to modern research the Hyksos ruled over *Egypt, Syria and Palestine during the years 1650-1542 BC. Some scholars maintain that they conquered the region in a single assault, while others believe that their penetration into *Egypt was a slow and lengthy process. The origin of the Hyksos is still obscure, but some scholars believe that they began in the Horite movement which in the first half of the 2nd millennium BC expanded over Palestine and Syria (*Horites). The Hyksos' capital was at Avaris in the *Nile Delta. They were finally defeated by Amosis, the founder of the 18th Dynasty.

To the Hyksos is attributed the introduction of the chariot into warfare (*Weapons and warfare) in *Canaan. They are also thought to have made innovations in the method of building fortifications: the construction of huge glacis and the excavations of ditches, such as those found at Tell el-*Yehudiyeh in *Egypt, *Kedesh-on-the-Orontes in Syria and *Hazor, Tell el-*Farah (south) and Tell el-*Jarisha in Palestine. Some of the burial customs of the Hyksos are unusual; the Hyksos cavalryman, for example, was interred together with his mount, his weapons and numerous pottery vessels, including the typical Tell el-*Yehudiyeh type of juglet.

HYRCANIA A fortress 8 miles southeast of Jerusalem, built by Alexander Jannaeus, son of Aristobulus (Josephus, *War* I, 161) and named Hyrcania in honor of his grandfather. The last refuge of the Hasmoneans, it was captured by Gabinius, governor of Syria (Josephus, *War* I, 167). Herod conquered it in 32 BC and turned it into a state prison where executions and secret burials took place (Josephus, *War* I, 364; *Antiq.* XV, 366; XVII, 187). In AD 492 St Sabas founded a monastery called Castellion on the hill. Identified with Khirbet el-Mird. During surveys a double rampart surrounding the flattened summit of the mountain, an aqueduct and ruins from the Roman and Byzantine periods were found.

I

IBLEAM One of the ancient cities of *Canaan named in the list of conquests of Tuthmosis III. It was in the territory of Issachar, but was given to Manasseh (Josh. 17:11-13). In the Israelite conquest of *Canaan it was not taken, but had to pay tribute. In the later Israelite period it is mentioned in conjunction with the flight of Ahaziah, King of Judah (2 Kgs. 9:27). As Bileam it appears as one of the Levitical cities (1 Chr. 6:70). Known as Belemot in the Roman period, Ibleam is identified with Khirbet Belameh, a little over a mile south of Jenin. At the foot of the ancient mound there is a spring whose waters were brought to the city by a tunnel (*See also* *WATER SUPPLY).

IDUMEA The region south of Judea, which in the Persian period was settled by *Edomites. It included the southern hills of Judah, its southern border being north of *Beer-Sheba. In the early Hellenistic period Marissa (*Mareshah) became its capital. During the reign of the Seleucids Idumea was enlarged to include the district of *Ashdod ((Josephus, *Antiq.* XII, 308). After the death of Antiochus VII (129 BC) John Hyrcanus subdued the Idumeans and converted them to Judaism by force. During the reign of Alexander Jannaeus Antipas, grandfather of Herod, was appointed ruler over this district. After the conquest of Palestine by Pompey in 64 BC the western part of Idumea, centered around Marissa, was detached from Judea. Only in 40 BC was it returned to Herod by order of Augustus. After Herod's death the district was in the territory of Archelaus, Herod's eldest son, and from AD 41 it formed part of the kingdom of Agrippa I. After the destruction of the Second Temple it became part of the Provincia Judea and was under the direct control of the Legio X Fretensis. The southern part of that region formed part of the *Limes Palestinae. In AD 200 the whole region of Idumea was given to the newly founded *polis* of Eleutheropolis. (*See also* *BETH-GUBRIN).

IJON A town in the north of the kingdom of Israel, in the territory of *Naphtali, conquered by Ben-Hadad in the time of Baasha, King of Israel (1 Kgs. 15:20). During the reign of Pekah, King of Israel, it was conquered again by Tiglath-Pileser III and its inhabitants were deported to Assyria (2 Kgs. 15:29). Identified with Tell Dibbin in the valley of Merg Ayun, which has preserved the ancient name.

INDIA A country mentioned in the Book of Esther, at the eastern extremity of the Persian Empire (Esther 1:1; 8:9). The northwestern part of the Indian peninsula, along the River Indus and its tributaries, was a Persian satrapy. The links between the west and India that existed in early times were disrupted and not renewed before the neo-Babylonian period (8th-7th centuries BC). Some scholars believe that the 'gold and silver, ivory and apes, and peacocks' mentioned in 1 Kings (10:22) were brought from India. Closer contact with India was established after the passage of Alexander the Great into that region, especially in the Hellenistic and Roman periods, when the great Arabian spice trade flourished.

INSCRIPTIONS Inscriptions mark the boundary between pre-history and proto-history and the beginning of history as such. Inscribed documents have been found in *Mesopotamia and *Egypt in occupation levels dating from as far back as the late 4th millennium BC, while the earliest found in Palestine date back to the 2nd millennium BC. The first scripts were pictographs, such as the Egyptian hieroglyphs and the earliest Sumerian script, which developed into the Mesopotamian cuneiform. As time went on the pictographs lost their primary form and began to represent syllables; the hieroglyphs even included some consonants. In fact they evolved into an alphabetic script.

Since the second half of the 19th century numerous inscriptions have been found in the Middle East whose contents are of great importance in the study of the history of the ancient Near East, including Palestine. The inscriptions are sometimes more important in this respect than classical historical accounts that have come down to us by way of tradition, since later editors very often changed the original texts to suit their views. Even the shortest of such inscriptions are of great importance: each name contained there may be instructive as to ethnic origins; every sentence provides a wealth of evidence for the study of the language in which it was written; sometimes the development of the script itself may also be studied.

BRONZE AGE INSCRIPTIONS Two groups of documents of the 20th-19th centuries BC now known as the *Execration Texts, were found in *Egypt. The *Egyptians were in the habit of writing on clay figurines and bowls

Proto-Sinaitic inscription from Serabit el-Khadem

the names of cities, tribes and rulers hostile to their country. They believed that to break these objects before a military campaign would ensure the victory of Pharaoh over the opponents whose names were so inscribed.

Present knowledge of the history of the New Kingdom of Egypt derives mainly from archaeological finds. In that period the Egyptians conducted numerous campaigns in order to tighten their hold over the Canaanite city-states. Tuthmosis III mentions in his list no less than 119 cities conquered by him in Palestine and Syria, thus providing an indication as to which were the important cities in the 15th century BC. Other such sources were the lists of Pharaohs Amenophis II, Sethos I and Rameses II.

Many details relating to the political situation in *Canaan in the period preceding the Israelite conquest may be ascertained from the letters discovered in the archives of Pharaohs Amenophis III and Amenophis IV (Akhenaten), found at *El Amarna.

From the stele of Pharaoh Merneptah (c. 1220 BC) we learn of the arrival of the Israelites as a unified tribal group. Among other things this stele records: 'Plundered is Canaan with every evil; carried off is Ashkelon; seized upon is Gezer; Yenoam is made as that which does not exist; Israel is laid waste, his seed is not'.

In comparison with the finds in *Egypt and *Mesopotamia those of Palestine are far less numerous, though they also contain material of great importance. The clay tablets found at *Taanach complete the knowledge gained from the *El Amarna letters, and from them it has been possible to glean certain facts concerning social patterns in *Canaan during the 15th century BC. The Canaanite king, appointed by the Egyptian authorities, was assisted by a large body of officials and ministers, and there is also mention of trained servants (cf. Gen. 14:4), the cream of

the army. The names that appear in the tables indicate that the *Horites, among others, were one of the peoples of *Canaan at this period (cf. Gen. 36:20). In addition to the 12 tablets found at *Taanach similar ones, written in cuneiform, were found at *Shechem, *Gezer, *Eglon (Tell el-*Hesi), *Jericho and *Megiddo. The contents of the tablets at *Gezer and Tell el-*Hesi are similar to those found at *El Amarna. At *Megiddo a fragment of the Gilgamesh epic came to light by pure chance.

The rulers of the New Kingdom of Egypt also put up their stelae and statues in the conquered Canaanite cities. At *Beth-Shean two statues put up by Pharaoh Sethos I were unearthed in the course of the excavations. The conquest of *Beth-Shean and the neighboring cities, which formerly belonged to the King of *Pehel and his allies, is described on one of these.

Scores of short hieroglyphic inscriptions have been found on numerous sites in Palestine. These were inscribed on scarabs (*Seals) and cartouches of various Egyptian kings. One clay bowl, the fragments of which were collected from the ashes among the ruins of Canaanite *Lachish, is of the utmost importance in determining the date of the Israelite conquest of that city. It is written in the Hieratic Egyptian script and refers to the 4th year of the reign of an unknown king. If this is assumed to be Merneptah, the latest possible date for the destruction of Canaanite *Lachish would be 1220 BC.

At *Serabit el-Khadem in *Sinai, where an Egyptian mining village flourished in the 2nd millennium BC, stelae and statues bearing inscriptions of a special kind were discovered in 1905. It has been observed that the number of symbols used did not exceed 40, which signifies that they represented not syllables but phonemes. Further study of this script, which became known as proto-Sinaitic, indicated that in the middle of the 2nd millennium BC the Egyptians employed Semitic workers or slaves who spoke a West Semitic language. It is known that they worshipped a goddess called Baalath. The proto-Sinaitic inscriptions are of the utmost importance for the study of the origin of the alphabetic script in which the Phoenician, Hebrew and Aramaic inscriptions were written.

THE ISRAELITE PERIOD (IRON AGE) The Accadian and Egyptian inscriptions of the Israelite period provide numerous details which supplement the information in the Bible. To this group belongs Pharaoh Sheshonq's (biblical Shishak's) list of cities found on the walls of the temple of Karnak, indicating that his campaign in Palestine took place in the fifth year of Rehoboam, King of Judah (1 Kgs. 14:25; 2 Chr. 12:2). According to 2 Chronicles (12:4,7) the Egyptian monarch did not conquer *Jerusalem, but was satisfied with the imposition of a heavy tribute to be paid from the treasures of the Temple and the king's palace. That *Jerusalem was spared is proved also by the list of cities visited by Sheshonq during his campaign; this records that he went from *Gaza to *Gezer, and from there to *Ajalon, *Beth-Horon and *Gibeon (i.e. he passed to the north of *Jerusalem, without touching the city itself) and thence to the cities of the *Jordan Valley.

One of the inscriptions of Shalmaneser III mentions Ahab as one of the chief participants in an anti-Assyrian league. The Assyrian menace, which overshadowed the western countries of the ancient Near East and was felt as early as the middle of the 9th century BC, led to the union of the kings of Palestine and *Aram in a league that attempted to protect the region from the Assyrian onslaught. The King of *Aram-Damascus and Ahab, King of Israel, traditional foes, appear now at the head of the league against Shalmaneser III. In the battle of *Qarqar (853 BC), Ahab mustered 2,000 chariots and a force of foot soldiers 10,000 strong. Jehu is also mentioned — 12 years later — as tributary to Shalmaneser III, King of Assyria.

There is no hint of these events in the Bible but a biblical reference to the campaign of Tiglath-Pileser III in 732 BC (2 Kgs. 15:29) complements the Assyrian epigraphical source. The Assyrian material also refers to the destruction of *Samaria, and especially to Sennacherib's campaign against Judah. Having conquered the Phoenician coastal cities he reached *Joppa, proceeding to capture *Azor, *Bene-Berak, *Beth-Dagon, Eltekeh, *Timnah and *Ekron; he took altogether 46 fortified cities in Judah. The same Assyrian inscription goes on to recount that Sennacherib surrounded Hezekiah like a 'bird in a trap', but does not mention the conquest of *Jerusalem, which withstood the Assyrian onslaught, nor the eloquent speech of Rabshakeh (2 Kgs. 18:19-35). Sennacherib established his headquarters at *Lachish, as we know both from the biblical account and from the Assyrian reliefs in Sennacherib's palace at *Nineveh, his capital, which depict the siege and conquest of *Lachish.

HEBREW INSCRIPTIONS A number of important Hebrew inscriptions of the time of the First Temple have been found. In the excavations at *Gezer a seven-line inscription, written on a plaque of soft limestone measuring 3in by 4in, was discovered. This, known as the *Gezer Calendar, is considered to be the most ancient Hebrew inscription. It dates from about 950-900 BC, i.e. the days of Solomon. Eight agricultural seasons are listed on this calendar. Some of the farming activities extend over a period of two months: harvesting (October-November); sowing (December-January); late sowing (February-March); cutting of flax (April); harvesting of barley (May); harvesting and measuring (June); vintage (July-August); summer fruit (September).

Scholars do not agree on the purpose of the *Gezer Calendar. Some believe that the name Abi, which appears at its foot, denotes a representative of the authorities, and say that he was signing an order concerning the regulation of the agricultural months. Others suggest that this was the name of a schoolboy who scribbled his lesson on a tablet; or that it represents a list of months written by an Israelite farmer. Still others believe that the inscription records a popular song of the time of Solomon. These are only a few of the many suggestions made.

The Book of 2 Kings (3:4) records that 'Mesha king of Moab was a sheepmaster, and rendered unto the king of Israel a 100,000 lambs and a 100,000 rams,

with the wool'. This is the annual tribute which the King of *Moab paid to Omri and Ahab, who overcame him. During Jehoram's reign Mesha revolted against Israel. At the beginning of the punitive expedition Jehoram was successful, but ultimately Mesha defeated him (2 Kgs. 3:27). We have evidence for these events on the stele erected by Mesha in his capital, *Dibon. It was discovered in 1968 and is about 3 feet high by 2 feet wide. In order to secure a higher price it was broken into many fragments, but fortunately a copy of the inscription had been made first. It was afterwards restored and may be seen today in the Louvre in Paris. In this stele the Moabite king, speaking in the first person, gives an account of his breaking of the Israelite yoke, his victories on the battlefield, the prisoners he took and the buildings he erected, and also of the tunnel that he excavated with the labor of 'prisoners of Israel'. Omri, who 'humbled Moab', is mentioned by name, as well as the 'son of Omri' (i.e. Ahab). The victorious battles that are referred to in his inscription are of the same period as those mentioned in 2 Kings (3). The stele of Mesha was written in the Moabite dialect, which is close to biblical Hebrew but differs in some details from the language of the Hebrew inscriptions. Nevertheless the script is similar to the Hebrew one of the 9th century BC. It seems that the Moabites, who were under Israelite influence, adopted the Hebrew script.

In the course of the excavations made at *Samaria (1908-10) 63 ostraca were discovered in the storerooms of the royal palace. These are short texts and consist of a date (the year of the appropriate king's reign), a place name, the name of an individual and a quantity of wine or oil. For example, one text reads: 'In the 9th year, from Ahinoam, of [or to] Jasit, a jar of old wine', or another: 'In the 10th year, from Hazeroth to [or of] Gaddijahu, a jar of fine oil'. These potsherds are invoices or copies of receipts for taxes paid to the king in kind by various villagers in the kingdom of *Samaria, and they tell us something of the system of tax-collection at that time. They are also

Inscription on a Byzantine tomb in Jaffa (Joppa)

Arrow from Bethlehem, beginning of the Iron Age

informative about the language of the Israelites of Mount Ephraim at that period. The excavators ascribed these potsherds to the time of Ahab, but present-day scholars tend to date them to the time of Jehoahaz, son of Jehu, Jeroboam, son of Joash, or Menahem, son of Gadi.

In 1880 an inscription was found on the wall of what is known as Hezekiah's tunnel in *Jerusalem. The tunnel and the inscription are dated to the days of Hezekiah, King of Judah (2 Kgs. 20:20; 2 Chr. 32:30). (*See also* *GIHON, *SILOAM, *WATER SUPPLY .) The *Siloam inscription, as this is called, was not intended to be a stele glorifying the exploits of the king, but is a document in which the excitement and the joy of the laborers is expressed: 'There was heard the voice of a man calling to his fellow'. And the day on which the tunnellers, working from both ends, met in the middle, is referred to as 'the day when the tunnel was driven through'. The inscription records that the length of the tunnel is 1,200 cubits, and that it is 100 cubits below the surface of the ground. This was indeed a magnificent feat of engineering and it is small wonder that the inscription records it with pride.

In the *village of* *Siloam itself three inscriptions were discovered, engraved on façades of tombs of the time of the First Temple. Paleographic research has shown that they should be attributed to the time of Hezekiah. One of them reads: 'This is [the sepulchre of]...yahu who is over the house. There is no gold and silver here but [his bones] and the bones of his slave-wife with him. Cursed be the man who will open this.' The owner of this tomb, 'who is over the house', must have been one of the notables of Jerusalem. The inscription calls to mind the passage in Isaiah (22:15 ff.): 'Go, get thee unto this treasurer, even unto Shebna, which is over the house, and say, What hast thou here, and whom hast thou here, that thou hast hewed thee out a sepulcher on high, and that graveth an habitation for himself in a rock?'

The humid climate in most parts of Palestine caused the decay of organic writing materials such as parchment or papyrus, and mostly only inscriptions written on stone or pottery sherds have survived. Nevertheless, a papyrus was found recently at Wadi Murabbaat, close to the *Dead Sea, which dates back to the 7th century BC (*Judean Desert Caves). As papyrus was a fairly expensive material it was frequently used twice. Such a double inscription is known as a palimpsest. The papyrus found at Wadi Murabbaat is of this kind. The earlier, longer document is part of a letter. There is also evidence that although it was not cheap papyrus was used for official letters and legal documents. About a score of small clay seals were

discovered, each marked with a different impression. On the back of the seals clear traces of the papyrus can still be seen. These seal impressions date from the time of the First Temple, and one bears the legend 'Gedalyahu which is over the house'. A seal belonging to the same man was found at Tell en-*Nasbeh. In addition to papyrus a cheaper material, sherds of broken jars, was used for writing receipts, petitions and letters.

In 1960, during excavations at an ancient fortress now known by the name of *Mesad Hashavyahu, south of *Jabneh on the coast, six ostraca and an inscription on a jar fragment were discovered. Pottery helps to date the fortress to the last third of the 7th century BC. The most important of the ostraca was a letter in Hebrew, of 14 lines, found in the guardroom of the gate of the fortress. The letter opens with the formula: 'Let my lord the governor hear the words of his servant' (cf. 1 Sam. 26:19). A poor reaper then goes on to plead his case: 'Thy servant [behold], thy servant was reaping in Hasar-Asam, and thy servant reaped and finished and there came Hoshayahu son of Shobai, and he took thy servant's garment: And all my brethren will witness on my behalf, they who reap with me in the heat [of the sun], my brethren will witness on my behalf "Verily" I am free of the guilt.' At the end of his letter the reaper begs that his garment be returned to him. The contents of this letter convey a very human picture: the man who was reaping in the king's fields close to the village named Hasar-Asam went to the fortress to plead with the governor, who was in charge of civil as well as military administration. The other man, Hoshayahu, son of Shobai, was the governor's representative, acting as an overseer in the fields. The overseer evidently suspected that the reaper had stopped before his day's work was done, and as a result confiscated his garment. Such an act is referred to in the Bible (Exod. 22:25-7; Deut. 24:1-13). The reaper, on the other hand, attempts to prove that he had finished his reaping before the end of the day. It seems that the confiscated garment was his only one, or as the Bible puts it 'it is his covering only, it is his raiment for his skin' (Exod. 22:27); the biblical injunction is that the garment be given back 'by that the sun goeth down'. The plea of the injured person contained in this letter was therefore supported by biblical injunction. It seems that the reaper came at sunset to the gate of the fortress to see the governor, but when his wish was not granted he had no choice but to dictate his petition to the scribe sitting at the gate. While the opening formula was written by the scribe himself in the third person, the rest of the letter was dictated by the reaper; the phrase 'your servant' occurs no less than seven times in the letter.

At *Tell *Arad,* where remains of an Israelite fortress of the time of the First Temple were discovered, many scores of ostraca were found, most of them fragmentary. The earliest are of the 8th century BC but the most important are of the late 7th or early 6th centuries BC — the eve of the destruction of the Temple. From these documents we learn that a certain man named Eliashib was commander in charge of the military supplies of the region. Numerous messages were directed to him, containing orders or requests to supply wine, oil or wheat. In these the 'Kittim', most probably mercenaries from the countries over the sea, are mentioned. The name Kittim does not refer to the inhabitants of Kition in the narrow sense of the term, but rather to the Sea Peoples (*Philistines) in general; it seems that these were Ionian and Carian mercenaries who were employed in both the Egyptian and Babylonian armies. These short messages are written in abbreviated formulae, intended to be understood only by the sender and the recipient.

The excavations at Tell ed-Duweir, identified with biblical *Lachish, revealed about 20 inscribed sherds in a room close to the city gate. Most of them are letters written to Yaush, the commander of the soldiers who were stationed at Lachish. The sender is his subordinate, Hoshayahu, who was in command of a garrison in one of the smaller towns in the *Plain, situated on the road from *Lachish to *Jerusalem. Hoshayahu writes to his superior in a very humble vein. The usual greetings ('May Yahveh cause my Lord to hear tidings of peace') are sometimes followed by the phrase, 'Who is thy servant [but] a dog?'. This recalls the words spoken by Mephibosheth to David: 'What is thy servant, that thou shouldest look upon such a dead dog as I am?' (2 Sam. 9:8). Five of the letters can be fairly well understood. From them we learn that Yaush accuses Hoshayahu of reading secret letters sent to the commander of *Lachish and of revealing their contents to others. Hoshayahu denies these charges: 'As Yahveh liveth no one hath ever undertaken to read a letter for me; and as for any letter which might have come to me, truly I did not read it at all.'

Part of the epic of Gilgamesh, Late Bronze Age

Other subjects with which these letters deal include the activities of an unnamed prophet who undermines the morale of the warriors: 'The commander of the host, Coniah, son of Elnathan, hath come down in order to go into Egypt; and unto Hodvaiah, son of Ahijah, and his men hath he sent to obtain... from him.' It is possible that the event alluded to was that in which King Jehoiakim and the prophet Urijah from *Kirjath-Jearim were involved (Jer. 26). In one of the letters Hoshayahu informs Yaush that he has fulfilled all the commander's orders and reports on events in his region. The last lines of this letter presumably throw light on the period described in Jeremiah (34:7): 'When the king of Babylon's army fought against Jerusalem, and against all the cities of Judah that were left, against Lachish, and against Azekah: for these defenced cities remained of the cities of Judah.' Hoshayahu's report that they cannot see *Azekah seems to refer to a later stage in the state of affairs described in the book of Jeremiah. Now that *Azekah has fallen as well Hoshayahu is watching for the signals of *Lachish only. These letters are the last in the series of Hebrew documents from the time of the First Temple.

The documents so far described are the most important Hebrew inscriptions of their period, though some shorter ones, no less instructive, have also been found. Sometimes they were written on complete vessels, not just sherds, in which case they were inscribed before the jar was fired. The inscriptions consist mainly of names signifying ownership or responsibility for the capacity of the vessel. To this class belongs a jar found at *Lachish on which the inscription *bath lamelek* ('royal bath', a liquid measure) was engraved. Towards the end of the 7th century BC, when the mass production of these jars began, a preference is noted for making the signs of responsibility on the handles of the jars. About 800 impressions of royal seals were found bearing the inscription *lamelek* and the name of one of three cities: *Hebron, Sochoh (*Socoh) or *Ziph, and the disputed name Mmst, which some interpret as 'of the government'. Similarly, jar-handles were marked with private seals. 80 such impressions were found, representing 30 different seals. It seems that these private seals belonged to officials of the royal court. In addition to the seal impressions 100 of Hebrew seals have been found throughout the country (*Seals).

At *Gibeon 60 graffiti were found inscribed on jar handles, including the name of the town and the names of certain people. It seems that these were associates in the wine trade.

All these inscriptions were written in the Hebrew script, which developed from the proto-Canaanite (including the proto-Sinaitic scripts of Serabit el-Khadem). The proto-Canaanite script was an alphabetic script with about 30 acrophonic pictographic letters, such as a bull's head *(aleph)*, a house *(beth)*, the palm of a hand *(kaph)*, water *(mem)* or an eye *(ain)*. These symbols developed between about 1500 BC and the 11th century BC into linear letters, and finally into the classical Phoenician script. It seems that the Israelites accepted this script in the 12th or 11th century BC, by which time the alphabet did not contain more than 22 letters. By the 9th century BC the Phoenician and Hebrew scripts had developed independently. It seems that the *Arameans adopted the Phoenician script in the 11th or 10th century BC and used it for some 200 years before they began to develop their own independent script in the 8th century BC. This process was very rapid, the reason being that the Assyrians chose Aramaic as the official language, since it was easier to read and write than the Assyrian cuneiform. It thus served as the means of communication between the Assyrian provinces and later became the language of international diplomacy. By the end of the 8th century BC the ministers of Judah could speak *Aramaic, and they assumed that Rabshakeh, Sennacherib's officer, knew it as well (cf. Isa. 36:11; Authorized Version: 'Syrian').

The Moabite script (which as we have seen was identical with the Hebrew one in the 9th century BC) already showed some signs of Aramaic influences in the 8th century, though it retained the elements of the Hebrew script. It seems likely that the *Edomites wrote in a similar script to that of the *Moabites, but the *Ammonites adopted the Aramaic script and limited themselves to this tradition of writing.

SECOND TEMPLE PERIOD The international status of the *Aramaic script* continued in the neo-Babylonian and Persian periods, but the conquests of Alexander the Great resulted in the Aramaic language being replaced by Greek, which was used in Palestine and *Egypt for official documents. Nevertheless, Aramaic was so deeply rooted in Palestine and the neighboring countries that it continued to be used by Jews, *Nabateans and Palmyrenes (*Tadmor), and in large parts of Syria. The talmudic tradition ascribes the introduction of the Aramaic language and the Aramaic (or Assyrian) script to Ezra, who brought it with him on the return of the Jews from the Babylonian exile. It seems that at first the ancient Hebrew script was used for writing Hebrew, while the Aramaic script was confined to Aramaic. After the Restoration the Hebrew script remained in use to a limited extent on seals, on Jewish coins (*Money) and in biblical texts. Pentateuchal fragments written in the ancient Hebrew script have been found at *Khirbet Qumran. Nevertheless, most of the epigraphic finds from the time of the Second Temple are written in the Aramaic script and in the Jewish script developed from it; in the Talmud this is referred to as the Assyrian script (i.e. the square Hebrew script). The most important collection of *Aramaic documents* from the Persian period is that of the Jewish military colony at Yeb (*Elephantine). Similar legal documents were found recently at Wadi Daliyeh, east of *Samaria; they belonged to the Samaritan governor's family, who had fled from the Macedonian conqueror but were intercepted and died in a cave at Wadi Daliyeh. The earliest document of this group is of 375 BC and the latest of 335 BC.

Of special importance are the *yahud* seal impressions stamped on jar-handles of the late 5th and 4th centuries BC and found on various sites in Judea (*Seal). To the same period belong seal impressions with the name Moza inscribed on them.

The tradition of the *yahud* seal impression continued in the Hellenistic period, but at that time the stamps were inscribed in the ancient Hebrew script. Together with impressions of this class, others have been found bearing the name of *Jerusalem in ancient Hebrew, the letters being arranged round a five-pointed star.

The most important of the inscriptions of the time of the Second Temple are the *Dead Sea Scrolls. Apart from these the most important Hebrew and Aramaic epigraphic material consists of epitaphs. One of these, found on Jason's tomb in *Jerusalem, belongs to the end of the Hasmonean period, but all the rest are of the time of the Herodian Dynasty. The epitaphs were written either on the façades of the rock-cut tombs or on the blocking-stones of the *loculi*. To this class, perhaps, belongs the Aramaic inscription which announces: 'Here were brought [to burial] the bones of Uzziah, king of Judah. Not to be opened.' This inscription testifies that in the time of Herod, or somewhat later, the bones of Uzziah, who died of leprosy (2 Chr. 26:23), were removed to a new burial place. This inscription was not found *in situ*; it is now in the Israel Archaeological Museum.

Most of the epitaphs, however, were found on ossuaries (*Burial). There are many Greek inscriptions in this class, but others were written in the Jewish script, either in Hebrew or in Aramaic. These ossuaries have been found in *Jerusalem and on other sites in Judea. Some names occur on them that are known from other sources, for example the name, in Greek, of *Nicanor* 'who made the doors'. This, without doubt, was the burial place of Nicanor, the man who made the gates of the Temple. This fact is mentioned several times in the Talmud. This ossuary was found on Mount *Scopus, in a cave now known as *'Nicanor's Cave'*. The inscriptions on the ossuaries are of importance for the study of Jewish names at the end of the period of the Second Temple. Many are known from biblical and talmudic sources, but Greek names also appear in considerable numbers.

Mention should be made here of the inscriptions found at *Masada. These are also mainly personal names, but some fragments of scrolls, notably one of Ben-Sirah, were found as well. Most of the inscriptions from *Masada belong to the few years after the destruction of the Temple (AD 70-3).

There are numerous inscriptions from the period following the destruction of the Second Temple, some in Hebrew but most in Aramaic, many of them epitaphs. A large group was found in the ancient cemetery of *Joppa, and others come from the large necropolis of *Beth-Shearim. Another important group comprises inscriptions found in synagogues. The texts were either engraved on the building stones of synagogues of the 2nd and 3rd centuries AD or set in the mosaic floors of the later ones, which date to the 6th and 7th centuries AD. These are mostly dedicatory inscriptions, in which the names of donors and blessings for their deeds are recorded.

IRAM The ancient name, confirmed by an inscription, of a Nabatean sanctuary to the goddess Allat, near the spring of Ain Shellaleh in Transjordan. Excavated by

R. Savignac and G. Horsfield in 1934 and later by D. Kirkbride, the temple comprises two phases of construction. The first was a structure surrounded by colonnades, with a shrine 16 feet 6in square that was probably set upon a podium. In the second phase the colonnade was closed on three sides, thus forming a court of about 42 feet by 32 feet around which rooms were constructed. With its square shrine within a rectangular building, it therefore belongs to the well-known class of Nabatean temples.

The temple was dated by the excavators to the reign of Rabel II (AD 70-106) by an inscription found near the spring. On the other hand an inscription of Aretas IV (9 BC-AD 40) found in the ruins of the temple itself helps in dating it to the second half of the 1st century BC, when most of the known Nabatean temples were in fact built.

IRAN The modern name of the region to the east of *Mesopotamia, bordered by the Caspian Sea on the north, the Persian Gulf on the south and *India on the east. The earliest permanent human settlement was discovered at Tell Siyalk, south of Teheran. The lowest occupation level (Siyalk I), of the 5th millennium BC, was of hunters, farmers and herdsmen. They lived at first in tents, but during the same millennium houses of *terre pisée* (beaten earth) were built. At the end of this period copper (*Metals) made its appearance, while numerous clay and stone loom weights give evidence of weaving and beads made of sea shells testify to trade relations with the Persian Gulf. Burials with the bodies placed in a contracted position were found below the floors of the houses.

In Siyalk II, of the 4th millennium BC, houses were built of large mud bricks and their walls were plastered and painted red on the inside. The pottery was made on a wheel and decorated with stylized animals painted in black on red. Tools were of stone and metal. Precious stones such as carnelian and turquoise were also found. The villages were larger than in the previous period. The dog and the horse were now added to the group of domestic animals. To the same millennium belongs Siyalk III. The bricks in this level were moulded in wooden frames, so that larger and better houses could now be built. They had windows, but the doors were narrow and only 3 feet high. An improvement has been noted in the construction of the pottery kilns at this date. Copper was now smelted and numerous figurines found in this level testify to a fertility cult. Remains of the culture of Siyalk III were discovered on other sites in Iran as well, among them Susa (*Shushan). This culture came to a violent end early in the 2nd millennium BC and was replaced by the Susa culture, which was influenced by *Mesopotamia. In this phase an urban culture emerged, that of *Elam, which was organized as a kingdom.

During the 2nd millennium BC Aryan tribes of mounted warriors penetrated Iran. One of these tribes settled in the oasis of Siyalk and turned the village into a fortified town. In the tombs of these warriors weapons and jewelry were found. The pottery of this period is typified by a spouted jug, a design which spread to the neighboring regions. These jugs were decorated with horses and sunbursts, both symbols of the Indo-Aryan tribes. Assyrian reliefs show their towns as surrounded by triple walls and moats. During the 9th and 8th centuries BC Siyalk was under Assyrian rule.

Tumuli were discovered in the region of Luristan, in the district of Kermenshah. These tombs have never been studied scientifically, but iron and bronze vessels and ornaments were found in them and the finds seem to indicate that these were the graves of warriors who used horses and chariots. The origin of this culture, dated to the 8th-7th centuries BC, is not known and the Assyrian documents of the 9th century BC refer to several ancient Iranian tribes. The first of these to found an independent kingdom were the Medes (*Madai), but very little is known of their early history. Herodotus mentions their leader, a man called Phraortes, who unified the tribes and subdued the

Bas-relief at Persepolis. King Darius is shown seated, behind him stands his son and successor Xerxes

Persians who dwelt to the south of Madai in about 670 BC. The capital of the kingdom was *Achmetha (Ecbatana, modern Hamadan) where the treasures of the Median kings were kept. The Medes were frequently at war with the Babylonians and conquered *Nineveh, the Assyrian capital.

The other tribe mentioned in an Assyrian document of about 884 BC was that of the Parsua (Persians), who settled west and southwest of Lake Urmia. In the 8th century BC they wandered southwards and settled in the mountains of Bakhtiari, naming their region Parsumash. Cambyses I, a Persian king, married the daughter of Astyages, King of *Madai. His son, Cyrus II, who was called 'the Great', defeated Astyages in 553 BC and annexed his kingdom. His capital was Parsargadas, in the district of Pars. The city was more like a huge village, with houses scattered through the famous Persian gardens, and its most famous monument was the tomb of Cyrus. The reigns of his heirs represent a golden age for art and architecture.

The organization of the Persian Empire was begun and completed by Darius. The whole empire was divided into a large number of semi-independent satrapies, each ruled by a satrap, with garrisons and officials directly responsible to the royal court. The rich natural resources of the country and the heavy taxes extracted from the satrapies contributed to the development of Persian art and architecture, in which Babylonian, Assyrian, Greek and Egyptian elements are intermingled. Persian art at its best is represented at Persepolis, the residence of the Achaemenid kings. The most famous building was the *apadana*, the audience hall or Hall of a Hundred Pillars. It was begun by Darius I and completed by Xerxes, who built his palace nearby. The whole complex was surrounded by a strong wall. The huge stairway leading up to the audience hall was decorated with beautiful bas-reliefs, the work of foreign artists, depicting scenes from life at the Persian royal court and in the satrapies.

The conquest of the country by Alexander the Great put an end to the Persian Empire. After the king's death the country was ruled by the Seleucids, but in the 3rd century BC the area was overrun by the Parthians, a semi-nomadic people who lived to the southeast of the Caspian Sea, and who ruled the country until AD 226, when the Sassanid Dynasty came to power. In 651 it fell to the Arabs.

IRAQ EL-BAROUD (SEFUNIM) (CAVE)

In 1941 M.Stekelis made the first trial trench in this cave on the left bank of Wadi Misliyeh on Mount *Carmel. The upper layer was subdivided by him into two layers: an upper layer (A1) with Neolithic implements; and a lower one (A2), where he found a Kebaran assemblage characterized by many microliths (*Kebara Cave). Layer B contained numerous curved blades. In layers C and D he recovered steep and nosed scrapers and Font-Yves points. These layers were assigned to the local Aurignacian era (*Flint tools).

In 1965-7 the cave was almost completely excavated by A.Ronen of the University of Tel Aviv. He also dug at the front of the cave, which is not an actual terrace but was formed by the collapse of a portion of the cave roof. Within the cave he identified 13 layers: of the Neolithic, Early Bronze and Arab periods; a very small Natufian assemblage; Kebaran; local Aurignacian; a transitional culture from the Middle to Upper Paleolithic; and a Mousterian deposit directly on the bedrock.

The same general stratigraphy was found on the 'terrace', but the layers dating from before the Neolithic era produced fewer finds than those within the cave. The Mousterian element has been clearly defined. In its uppermost layer a large oval hearth was dug, probably of Aurignacian origin. (*See also* *PREHISTORY, *FLINT TOOLS.)

IRAQ EL-EMIR

A village and a large building near it (the Qasr el-Abd), about 11 miles west of Amman. The building was identified as a fortress constructed by John Hyrcanus, the Tobiad governor of the area from 187-175 BC (Josephus, *Antiq.* XII, 230). According to Josephus it was a palace called Tyros, which is the Greek form of the Aramaic *tura* (mountain). In the papyri of Zenon, who visited Palestine from *Egypt in the 3rd century BC, the Tobiad center is referred to as Birta ('fortress' in Aramaic). Further chronological data were supplied by inscriptions on the rock in the caves above the village, where the name Tobiyah appears twice. This was thought to refer to Tobiah the Ammonite (*Ammon), who lived in the time of Nehemiah, in the 5th century BC (Neh. 2:10, 19). This evidence and its interpretation suggested a continuous occupation of the site under the Tobiah family from before the exile until the 2nd century BC.

Excavations under the direction of P.W. Lapp in 1961-2, on behalf of the American School of Oriental Research, threw new light on the history of this site. The earliest occupation in the village is indicated by Chalcolithic sherds and by an undisturbed Early Bronze Age layer. To Iron Age I belong the foundation walls of a fortress which have been identified by Lapp with the Gadite border village of Ramathmizpeh (Judg. 11:29; Authorized Version: 'Mizpeh of Gilead'), the remains of which were obliterated by John Hyrcanus' building activities. There are further signs of early Roman and Byzantine occupation. Among the Hellenistic structures the so-called Plaster Building is outstanding. Enclosing an area 57 feet by 66 feet is a wall about 3 feet thick with two thin coats of white plaster on its inner surface. In the center of the enclosure are the remains of a building 30 feet by 45 feet with walls about 4 feet thick, its external surface plastered like the surrounding wall and the interior with a thicker red and white plaster. This dates from the time of John Hyrcanus, about 175 BC, and should be identified with one of his two large enclosures, mentioned by Josephus.

The Qasr el-Abd was built during the reign of Hyrcanus but never completed. It is of white stone and decorated with colossal figures of lions in relief, four of which were found still in place and are 9 feet long and 6 feet high. The building stands on a platform and was almost completely surrounded by water. Its outline is rectangular, 13 feet by 57 feet, with four corner rooms, one of which was a staircase tower opening

Inscription of Tobiyah from Iraq-el-Emir

into a gallery and leading to a terrace. The portico is near this tower; then follow the *pronaos* (porch), the *naos* (shrine) and the *hopistodomos* (store at the rear of a temple). The outstanding find from this building was a fountain in the form of a feline creature sculptured in high relief on a block of red and white dolomite. The excavations proved that Qasr el-Abd's identification as a fortress or a mausoleum is not correct: the plan clearly indicates a religious significance, and it was probably a temple. Much evidence has been unearthed which attests to Hyrcanus' building activities and to the accuracy of Josephus' descriptions. As no signs of occupation before the time of Hyrcanus have been traced, Lapp suggests a redating of the inscriptions mentioning Tobiah, since a date before the early 2nd century BC would contradict both Josephus' account and the excavation results. He would also like to revive the suggestion that Tobiah was the Hebrew name of Hyrcanus.

IRQ EL-AHMAR (ROCK SHELTER) This site is on the left bank of Wadi Khareitun, $1^1/_2$ miles south of *Herodium. A large portion of the shelter was excavated by R. Neuville in 1931, and in 1932 with the aid of M. Stekelis. Two sterile layers (I and J) were found above bedrock. The following layer (H) is of black clay gradually thickening towards the exterior and includes an assemblage of flakes and points worked with a Levalloisian technique of which very few specimens show secondary retouch. A brown sterile layer with some stones at its base (G) separated layer H from layers F and E, which consist of an Upper Paleolithic II assemblage characterized by curved backed blades, scrapers on flakes and blades and nosed, carinated and core scrapers. Layer D, a brown loam, included the assemblage that was classified by Neuville as Upper Paleolithic III; this was characterized by the large quantity of Font-Yves points, rounded scrapers, the appearance of nosed scrapers and carinated scrapers that were evolving towards being burins. This layer corresponds to layers E at el-Wad and

*Kebara. Layer C was poor in finds but layer D, a bright brown loam, was rich in gravels and tools — mainly carinated and nosed scrapers with a small number of Font-Yves points. This assemblage is characteristic of the Upper Paleolithic IV period and is comparable to layers D at el-Wad and *Kebara.

Layer A2 shows evidence of Natufian occupants of the rock shelter. They left many and varied flint tools: crescents and sickle-blades executed with Helwan retouch, awls, knives, scrapers and burins, as well as stone implements and bone tools. An intact adult skeleton was found within a burial pit dug into the Paleolithic layers. In the same pit three adult and three child skulls were unearthed. These finds represent an encampment of hunters and food-gatherers. (*See also* *PREHISTORY; *FLINT TOOLS.)

IVORY The earliest recorded use of ivory is in the Neolithic period in *Egypt, where harpoons made of ivory were found. In the early pre-dynastic period ivory was used for making figurines, jewelry and arrowheads. The tusks of hippopotami were used as well as those of elephants, though the early use of ivory in *Egypt may be accounted for by the large numbers of elephants in the region south of the country. Most of the ivory must have come from the Sudan, although elephants were still extant in Syria and the *Lebanon at this date and documents of the 15th century BC mention Egyptians hunting elephants in northern *Mesopotamia, the other important source of ivory. In the 18th-century BC palace of Yamrilim, King of *Alalakh, in northern Syria, a storeroom full of elephant tusks was found; these must have been destined either for local production or for export to *Egypt.

Ivory is mentioned alongside precious metals and stones in the lists of tribute. Thus Sennacherib recounts that he brought to his palace a tribute of silver, precious stones and beds and chairs of ivory, as well as hides and tusks. In Palestine isolated ivory objects were found from as early as the Mesolithic period and they are relatively common in the Chalcolithic period. On sites of the *Beer-Sheba culture and in the *Judean Desert Caves ivory figurines representing men and women, birds and animals were found.

The large ivory collections in Syria and Palestine, *Ugarit and *Megiddo are of the later phases of the Late Bronze Age. At *Ugarit ivories were found in the ruins of the royal palace, whose destruction is attributed to the Sea Peoples (*Philistines) in the second half of the 12th century BC. One room probably served as the artist's workshop. In addition to figurines there was furniture plated with ivory plaques, including a bed and a table. The plaques were about 10in long and 4-5in wide. The carving was in bas-relief in several planes, which gives a three-dimensioned effect. The subjects are either mythological or taken from daily life, examples being a goddess suckling two children and a couple embracing. There are also scenes depicting life at the royal court. As *Ugarit was under the influence both of its northern Hittite neighbor and of the *Canaanites and *Egyptians to the south, the characteristics of all these cultures are discernible, both in the decorative repertoire and in specific details.

Like those of *Ugarit, the ivories of *Megiddo were discovered in a palace whose destruction is attributed to the Sea Peoples. Attached to the palace was a three-room storehouse in which 380 ivories were found. Some of these were carvings that had originally been furniture fittings, while others were objects made entirely of ivory. There is a great diversity of styles: some pieces were made locally by Canaanite artists; others were brought from other centers during the centuries preceding the destruction of the palace. One of the most famous *Megiddo ivories depicts a scene from the royal court, probably a triumphal procession. The king is seen seated on a throne supported by sphinxes, a popular motif in this type of art. He holds a cup and a lotus flower. In front of him a princess or a goddess presents him with another lotus flower and behind her is a girl playing a harp. Then comes a procession headed by a soldier, followed by two captives and a chariot. Behind the king are two cupbearers and a large jar. Other beautiful pieces include a box made entirely of ivory, decorated with lions and sphinxes in very high relief. A large number of plaques are decorated with sphinxes, animals, birds and stylized flowers. Smaller collections of the same period have been found at *Hazor and *Lachish and at Tell el-*Farah (south), where there was also a scene from the royal court. The finds at *Lachish include a scent bottle made in the shape of a woman, similar to one found at *Megiddo.

Ivory was no less common in the Iron Age and is frequently found in *Egypt, as well as at *Nineveh in *Mesopotamia. *Nineveh was the site of the palace of Ashurbanipal III (885-860 BC), renovated by Sargon II (722-705 BC). The other large collection is that of Arslan Tash in northern Syria. The most important collection of the period in Palestine comes from *Samaria and has much in common with that of Arslan Tash; the Samaria ivories are inscribed with Hebrew letters on the back to facilitate their mounting on furniture, while the Arslan Tash one have Phoenician and Aramaic letters. One Phoenician ivory has the name 'Hazael' on it, most probably referring to

the king who ascended the throne of Damascus in 824 BC. It seems that these ivories were part of the booty taken by Adadnirari III of Assyria (810-783 BC). This is also the date given to the Samaria ivories. All are carved in high relief. Much of the decorative repertoire is taken from Egyptian art, examples being the infant Horus, Osiris, Isis and other Egyptian deities. There are numerous winged figurines, sphinxes, animals and stylized plants. It seems that the *Samaria ivories were made by Syrian and Phoenician artists, as were those of Arslan Tash.

There is evidence in the Bible to suggest that the *Phoenicians produced ivory. In a joint enterprise with Hiram, King of *Tyre, Solomon brought ivory from *Tarshish (1 Kgs. 10:22; 2 Chr. 9:21) and used it for his throne (1 Kgs. 10:18; 2 Chr. 9:17). Ahab, King of Israel, an ally of *Sidon, built the ivory house at *Samaria (1 Kgs. 22:39); this was probably the house from which the ivories described above came. Houses of ivory (i.e. inlaid with ivory plaques) and beds of ivory are referred to by Amos (3:15; 6:4). Single ivory carvings of the period have been found elsewhere in Palestine.

Ivory had already found its way to the western countries by the 2nd millennium BC. It was exported from the Near East to Mycenae and re-exported to Syria in the form of finished pieces. Later it was carved in Greece. In the Hellenistic period elephant hunting was a closely guarded state monopoly of the Ptolemies, who exported elephant hides and tusks to Europe. Ivory was also exported from Lybia via Carthage, while *India exported tusks via Persia and Phoenicia. Some idea of the extent of elephant hunting may be obtained from the figure of 600 tusks dedicated by Ptolemy Philadelphus, and 800 by Antiochus Epiphanes, to the temple of Dydima. The ivory trade developed still further in the Roman period. In 188 BC L. Scipio Asiaticus presented the Roman treasury with 1,231 tusks. Ivory was lavishly used for inlaying furniture and was also used by carvers, turners and sculptors, who had previously worked with completely different materials.

Engraving on an ivory knife from Megiddo, Late Bronze Age

J

JAAZER; JAZER An Amorite town east of the River *Jordan, conquered by the Israelites (Num. 21:32). The Gadites settled there, raised cattle (Num. 32:1) and built a city (Num. 32:35), which was one of the cities of refuge (1 Chr. 6:81). It was in the kingdom of David (2 Sam. 24:5). Isaiah (16:8-9) and Jeremiah (48:32) mention it as a Moabite town. At the time of the Second Temple it was Ammonite, but was later conquered by the Hasmoneans (1 Macc. 5:8). Eusebius (*Onom.* 12:3; 10:13) knew it by the name of Iazer, on the 10th mile from Philadelphia (*Rabbath-Ammon) westward, in the *Perea of Palestine and 15 miles from *Heshbon. At that period it was part of the *Perea. Tentatively identified with Khirbet es-Sir.

JABBOK A river east of the *Jordan, the northern border of the kingdom of Sihon, King of the *Amorites (Num. 21:23-4; Josh. 12:2). After the Israelite conquest it was in the territory of Gad. The river rises near *Rabbath-Ammon, flows in a wide curve to the northeast and then turns west, entering the *Jordan near *Adam; it drops from 2,700 feet above sea level to 1,000 feet below sea level in its course from the mountains to the *Jordan Valley, close to the *Jordan it flows through a broad fertile plain, the plain of *Succoth. One important route that followed the course of this valley was taken by Jacob on his way from *Mesopotamia to *Canaan (Gen. 32:22-3). Eusebius (*Onom.* 102:19) states that it flows between *Rabbath-Ammon which is Philadelphia and *Gerasa, at a distance of 4 miles, and it falls into the *Jordan. Today Nahr ez-Zarqa.

JABESH; JABESH-GILEAD A town east of the *Jordan in *Gilead. Because the Jabeshites refused to participate in the war of the Israelites against the Gibeonites all the inhabitants of Jabesh were slain, except for 400 maidens who were given as wives to the Benjaminites (Judg. 21:6-14). In the days of Saul Jabesh was inhabited by Israelites and when it was attacked by the *Ammonites Saul came to their aid (1 Sam. 11:1-13). When Saul was killed and his body exposed on the wall of *Beth-Shean men of Jabesh-Gilead took it down and buried it under a tree at Jabesh (1 Sam. 31:11-13). Eusebius (*Onom.* 110:12) states that in his time it was a village situated on a mountain, on the 6th mile on the way from *Pella to *Gerasa.

JABNEH; JABNEEL; JAMNIA *a)* A town in the northern part of the territory of Judah, close to the Mediterranean coast (Josh. 15:11), and one of the cities of the *Philistines whose walls were breached by Uzziah, King of Judah (2 Chr. 26:6). Known in the Hellenistic period as Iamania, it was at one time the seat of the governor of *Idumea (Josephus, *Antiq.* XII, 308). Used by the Greek Syrians as a base for their operations against the Hasmoneans (1 Macc. 5:58, etc.) it was conquered by Simon Maccabaeus in 147 BC (Josephus, *Antiq.* XIII, 215). It remained part of the Jewish kingdom until the conquest by Pompey in 64 BC, when he made it autonomous and rebuilt it (Strabo, XVI, 2, 40). With the accession of Herod it became part of his kingdom (Josephus, *Antiq.* XII, 308), but it was soon given to Cleopatra, Queen of *Egypt, by Antony as a wedding gift *(Antiq.* XVI, 96). The fall of Antony restored Jabneh to Herod. Some time after his death Jabneh and neighboring *Ashdod became part of the imperial domain *(Antiq.* XVIII, 158).

Regaining its autonomy after the destruction of the Second Temple, Jabneh became a Jewish national center and a seat of numerous sages, the most outstanding being Rabbi Yohanan ben Zakkai and Raban Gamaliel. The Sanhedrin (highest court of justice) of Jabneh was known as the 'Vineyard of Jabneh'. Eusebius (*Onom.* 106:20) states that the small town of Jamnia is situated between *Lod and *Ashdod. In the Byzantine period it was the seat of a bishop and there was also a large Samaritan community there.

Jabneh is identified with the large mound of Yebna, modern Yabneh. No excavations have been made on the site, but potsherds of the Iron Age and the Persian period have been discovered on the surface. There are remains of buildings, tombs and sculpture of the Roman and Byzantine periods. The harbor of Jabneh is identified with Minet Rubin on the coast. This harbor is possibly mentioned in the list of Tuthmosis III under the name of *mahoz,* meaning 'harbor' in the Semitic languages. Trial digs begun at the mound near the harbor in 1959 by J. Kaplan on behalf of the Tel Aviv-Jaffa Museum of Antiquities indicate that the site was inhabited from the Middle Bronze Age throughout all historical periods. Imposing remains of a typical *Hyksos glacis were discovered there.

b) A place on the southern border of the territory of Naphtali (Josh. 19:33), identified in the Talmud with Kefar Yamma (Jer. Megilla I, 1). Josephus mentions a village in *Galilee called Iamneia (*Life,* 187) or Jamnith (*War* II, 573), believed by some to be the same place, but this does not seem likely. The biblical site is in lower *Galilee and is identified with Tell en-Naam, east of Mount *Tabor; the site of the Roman period is identified with Khirbet Banit, at the northern extremity of upper *Galilee.

JAHAZ; JAHAZA A town in *Moab where the Israelites defeated Sihon, King of the *Amorites (Num. 21:23), in the territory of Reuben (Josh. 13:18); a Levitical city (Josh. 21:36). During the time of the Israelite kingdom it was in the hands of *Moab (Isa. 15:4), as is confirmed by the Mesha stele (*Inscriptions). Eusebius (*Onom.* 104:9 ff) says that a place by the name of Iassa, or Iessa, was situated in his time between *Medaba and Debus (possibly *Dibon).Tentatively identified with Khirbet el-Medeiniyeh, southeast of Medda.

JAPHIA; IAFA A town in the territory of Zebulun (Josh. 19:12), mentioned as Yapu in the *El Amarna letters and known as Iafa in the time of the Second Temple. The place was fortified by Josephus when preparing *Galilee for the war against the Romans (*War* II, 573). The Jews of Japhia fought gallantly but could not resist the prolonged Roman siege in AD 67. On July 13, 15,000 of the inhabitants were killed and 2,130 taken captives (*War* III, 289 ff.).

In 1921 L.H. Vincent discovered two decorated lintels reused in the modern village. One was decorated with a menorah, and the other with a wreath flanked by two eagles. This led to the discovery of a *synagogue on the summit of the mountain. It was excavated in 1950 by N. Avigad and E.L. Sukenik, on behalf of the Hebrew University. The partly preserved building was apparently a broad-house, with two rows of columns, placed on pedestals, running from east to west. Its façade apparently faced east. It was decorated with a *mosaic pavement, surviving in a fragmentary state, which depicted wild animals and an eagle standing on a stylized Medusa. The nave was decorated with circles containing symbols of the twelve tribes. The synagogue included elements of the Galilean type (the pedestals, the lintels and the absence of a permanent place for the Torah Shrine) as well as elements of what is considered as the later type of synagogues (such as the mosaic pavement). It was dated to the 3rd-4th century AD.

JARISHA (TELL EL-) The ancient mound, generally identified with *Gath-Rimmon, was extensively excavated between the years 1927 and 1950 by E.L. Sukenik on behalf of the Hebrew University. In the Early Bronze Age a settlement extended over a great part of the mound. After it diminished in size in the Middle Bronze Age I, the site attained its apogee in the Middle Bronze Age II. This is evidenced both by the wealth of the finds as well as by the formidable system of *fortifications defending the city. The defences are based on a glacis, a system used at this period in Egypt and Western Asia. At the upper edge of the mound a wall 9 feet wide and of about the same height was built

of mud-bricks. The natural surface of the slope of the mound was then levelled and covered with alternating layers of dark, beaten earth and sand. This was then overlaid with one or two courses of large mud-bricks, the number of layers increasing close to the wall, to prevent from being undermined. The brick layer was then covered with several layers of beaten earth and sand, covered with crushed sand stone to a thickness of 6-9 feet, making the base of the wall virtually impregnable. Nothing has remained of the upper part of the wall. The pottery found in the fill identifies the *Hyksos as the builders of this fortress at the end of the 18th or beginning of the 17th century BC. By the middle of the 16th century, with the expulsion of the Hyksos from Palestine, the fortress was destroyed. In the following Late Bronze Age a prosperous Canaanite city flourished at the site, stretching over the entire area of the mound. By the 12th century BC the site was abandoned, its destruction caused either by the Israelites or by the *Sea Peoples. Only the upper part of the mound was occupied in the Iron Age. The large quantities of *Philistine *pottery found on the mound identify the new town as Philistine. This city was destroyed by a fierce fire, which is attributed to David. On the ruins of the Philistine town the Levitical town of Gath-Rimmon sprang up and it came to an end either at the end of the United Monarchy, or during Sheshonq's campaign at the end of the 9th century BC.

Further excavations on the site on behalf of the same institution were carried out by S. Geva in 1976. The conclusions reached in that season's work were that the entire fortifications system — glacis and wall — was constructed as a single engineering project in the Middle Bronze Age IIB. Beneath this system were two occupation levels dated to the Middle Bronze Age IIA, as well as occupation levels of the Early Bronze Age. Since 1982 excavations on the site have been carried out by Z. Herzog on behalf of Tel-Aviv University and several American universities, as part of a regional study of the western basin of the *Yarkon River. The strata of the Middle Bronze Age II and the Late Bronze Age were examined. One section of the mound yielded *Philistine *pottery.

JARMUTH *a)* A town in the *Plain (Josh 15:35). It was a Canaanite city-state and appears on one of the Tell el-*Hesi tablets (*Inscriptions) in the form of Ia-ra-muti. Its king, Piram, took part in the war of the kings of the *Amorites against *Gibeon and killed in battle (Josh. 10:3-5). The town was rebuilt after the Restoration (Neh. 11:29) and was still inhabited in the Roman period. Eusebius (*Onom.* 106:9) states that Jerimouth is situated 4 miles from *Beth-Gubrin, in the vicinity of *Eshtaol.

In 1970 excavations were conducted at Tel Jarmuth by A.Ben-Tor on behalf of the Hebrew University. In the northwestern part of the mound two platforms were discovered, the larger of which, 38 feet by 94 feet, is made of retaining walls constructed of large unhewn stones. It is not known what function these platforms served. The pottery found in the fill of the platforms is exclusively Early Bronze Age. To this level is attributed an extremely large building (5000 sq feet) discovered in the southeastern sector of the mound. It is clearly of a public nature and belongs to the beginning of the Byzantine period (Stratum I). The following two strata (II and III) are of the Early Bronze Age III, of which remains of several houses were discovered with *Beth-Yerah ware, which helped to date the lower stratum.

In 1980 excavations were resumed by P.de Miroschedji, on behalf of the French Center for Prehistoric Research in Jerusalem and the Hebrew University. In the excavations it became evident that the mound consisted of an acropolis only, whereas the town itself extended over the lower ground to the southwest. It was a strongly *fortified town in the Early Bronze Age III. Identified with Khirbet Yermuk, northeast of *Zorah.

b) A Levitical city in the territory of Issachar (Josh. 21:29), also called Remeth (Josh. 19:21). Tentatively identified with Kaukab el-Hawa, where the large Crusader castle, Belvoir, is situated. If this identification is correct it might also be the site of Agrippina, where beacons were lit in the time of the Second Temple to announce the new moon.

JATTIR A Levitical city in the south of the territory of Judah (Josh. 15:48; 21:14). It was the birth-place of two of David's mighty men, Ira and Gareb (2 Sam. 23:38; Authorized Version: 'Ithrite') and David sent presents there after his victory over the *Amalekites (1 Sam. 30:27). In the late Roman period it was a large Christian village known to Eusebius (*Onom.* 88:3) by the name of Jethira, a Christian village in his time. It is noteworthy that despite the political difficulties facing Palestinian Jewry in the late Roman and early Byzantine periods, Christianity was able to penetrate the fringes of the Jewish colonization in the south. Identified with Khirbet Attir, about 14 miles northeast of *Beer-Sheba.

JAVAN; GREECE According to the table of nations (Gen. 10:2, 4) Javan was the son of Japhet. The earliest reference in the Bible to Javan mentions the proto-Ionian nations, which spread over the eastern parts of the Mediterranean from about the middle of the 2nd millennium BC onwards. In the later period the land called Javan is also known as Hellas. The Assyrian documents of the 8th-7th centuries BC refer to it as Yaman and state that its people took part in uprisings against the Assyrians. Relations between the ancient Near East and Hellas were not close in the early periods, but became increasingly so in the 6th century BC. Greek pottery, coins and other finds become frequent in many places in Palestine in this century. Ezekiel mentions Javan among the countries with which *Tyre traded (Ezek. 27:13). These connections became still closer in the Hellenistic period (cf. Zech. 9:13; Authorized Version: 'Greece'). It is believed that the 'King of Grecia', mentioned in Daniel (8:21), is the great conqueror Alexander the Great (cf. also Dan. 10:20; 11:2).

JEBUS; JEBUSITES One of the peoples that inhabited *Jerusalem in ancient times. According to Genesis (10:16) the Jebusites were part of *Canaan. They dwelt in *Jerusalem and named their city Jebus (Judg. 19:10-11). During the conquest of *Canaan

Joshua was unable to take the city and the surrounding land (Josh. 15:8; 18:16). In the time of the Judges it was considered to be a 'city of strangers' (Judg. 19:12). The region was still in the hands of the Jebusites in the time of Saul. It was David who conquered it and built an altar to the Lord on the threshing floor of Araunah the Jebusite (2 Sam. 24:16 ff.).

JEHOSHAPHAT (VALLEY OF) The valley where the Last Judgement is to take place (Joel 3:2), also called the 'valley of decision' (Joel 3:14). Early traditions identify it with the Valley of *Kidron, but some scholars think that the Valley of Ziz and Berachah and the Valley of Jehoshaphat are one and the same, and that they should be identified with Wadi el-Arub.

Uncertainty as to the identification of the valley is reflected in Eusebius' writings. Once (*Onom.* 170:10) it is identified with the Valley of *Hinnom, and once (118:18) with a valley between the city and Mount of *Olives. This later identification recurs in pilgrims' descriptions up to the 14th century.

JEHUD A town in the territory of *Dan, in the vicinity of *Bene-Berak and *Gath-Rimmon, east of Japho (*Joppa) (Josh. 19:45). In the Hellenistic period it was named Iudaia, and Judas Maccabaeus fought one of his great battles there (I Macc. 4:15). Identified with el-Yahudiyeh, about 10 miles east of Jaffa.

JEKABZEEL *See* *KABZEEL

JEMMEH (TELL) GAMA (TEL) An ancient mound about 6 miles south of *Gaza, on the southern bank of Wadi Ghaza. The site was excavated by W.F.M. Petrie on behalf of the British School of Archaeology in Egypt in 1926-7, on the assumption that he was excavating biblical *Gerar. This identification has since been rejected and scholars now believe that Tell Jemmeh should be identified with Yerza, an Egyptian town of the New Kingdom known only from Egyptian sources of that period, such as the annals of Tuthmosis III, in which it is related that the city of Iursa was the southernmost city in the land of *Canaan to revolt against the king. It is also mentioned in the *El Amarna letters and still appears in the list of cities conquered by Pharaoh Sheshonq in about 924 BC. It seems that the ancient name was preserved in the form of Iorda/Orda also in Josephus, (*War* 3,51) and on the *Medaba map.

In his excavations Petrie discovered five occupation levels, numbering them JK, GH, EF, CD, AB. He dated the earliest level (JK) to the time of Tuthmosis III and the latest to the Persian period. However, analysis of the finds suggests that this dating was not accurate. The earliest excavated level (there are still earlier levels of occupation that were not excavated by Petrie) is now dated by the typical Philistine pottery to Iron Age I. The second stratum (GH) yielded a few typically Israelite four-room houses. A large furnace was thought by Petrie to indicate an iron foundry, but this is doubtful. The pottery dates this city to the 10th century BC. The third stratum (EF) had a large section of a city with houses made up of oblong rooms and a street running between them. Three additional furnaces belong to this city, which flourished in the first half of the 7th century BC. To the second half of the same century belongs stratum CD. Here Petrie discovered a pit containing what he identified as Assyrian pottery. Later study has shown that, although the stratum itself is later than the previous one, the pit was dug earlier, some time at the end of the 8th or early 7th century BC.

The uppermost city (AB) was excavated over a wider area. A large building with thick walls was identified by Petrie as a fortress, whose construction he attributed to the *Egyptians early in the Persian period. Close to this two additional buildings were discovered. All these were built on the typical Assyrian and Persian plan, which consists of a large central courtyard around which rooms are grouped (*Houses). In addition to local pottery, numerous Greek vessels of the early 6th century came to light, as well as red-figured vessels of the 5th century BC. These finds may be taken as evidence of trade relations with the West at that period. To the same period belong numerous large granaries, which are somewhat later than the buildings; this may be inferred from the damage that was caused to the latter when the granaries were constructed. At the end of the Persian period, in the late 4th century BC, the site was finally abandoned.

Since 1970 excavations have been carried out at the site by G. van Beek on behalf of the Smithsonian Institution, Washington.

The earliest traces of occupation go back to the Middle Bronze Age IIB (1750-1550 BC); in this level were found pottery and *scarabs. Potsherds alone were also found from the Late Bronze Age I (1550-1400 BC). From the Late Bronze Age II (14th/13th century BC) were remains possibly of the *fortifications or a *temple. A granary, already investigated by Petrie, was re-excavated. Two phases of construction were distinguished. To the first phase belongs a round wall 19 feet in diameter made of mud-bricks which was built in a pit. Above this was erected a conical structure, of a type known in Assyria and in Egypt. The granary had two entrances, from which stairs led up to a mud-brick platform. In the second phase the collapsed granary was rebuilt. The date of the con-struction of the granary has not yet been definitely established, though it is certain that it was built after the 6th century BC, probably in the 4th century BC, and its final destruction took place between 200-150 BC.

Another building excavated by this expedition is an Assyrian residence of the 7th century BC. It measures 30 feet by 43 feet and contains six rooms, three of which survived in a good state of preservation. Each is 10 feet long, but of differing widths. The finds in one of the rooms were typically Assyrian. It seems that some of these rooms were partly subterranean and served as storerooms. The lodgings, from which the objects found originated, were on the upper story. Beneath this building was a pavement, possibly of a temple of the Late Bronze Age II. In the northwestern end of the mound were discovered remains of *fortifications. To the Late Bronze Age II belongs a gate, a great part of which has eroded. There are also fortifications of the 12th, 10th, 9th, 8th and 7th centuries BC. The latest is an Assyrian casemate wall (*Fortifications). South of the mound were discovered remains of Roman-Byzantine Orda, among them a church and a ceme-tery.

JERICHO One of the oldest fortified cities in the ancient Near East, long identified with Tell es-Sultan, 6 miles north of the *Dead Sea, about 750 feet below sea level. The plentiful supply of water from nearby Ain es-Sultan turned Jericho into an oasis, and indeed the Bible once refers to it as the 'city of palm trees'. Tell es-Sultan rises 65 feet above the surrounding plain and occupies an area of 10 acres.

After Joshua had sent two spies to Jericho (Josh. 2:1 ff.) the Israelites crossed the *Jordan and camped in the plains of Jericho (Josh. 4:13). The biblical account goes on to relate that, after a siege lasting seven days, the walls of the city fell at the sound of trumpets; the city was burnt and Joshua laid a curse on any man who should arise to build it anew (Josh. 6). But David sent word to his two servants, who were ashamed to return from *Ammon, telling them to interrupt their journey at Jericho until their beards had grown (2 Sam. 10:5). This suggests that the site was inhabited again by that time. The city was rebuilt by Hiel the Bethelite (1 Kgs. 16:34). Later the sons of the prophets were to be found in Jericho. Elijah went there shortly before he was taken up to heaven in a whirlwind (2 Kgs. 2:4-5), while Elisha purified the waters of the town's spring (2 Kgs. 2:18-22). After the Restoration Jericho was resettled and its people took part in the rebuilding of the walls of *Jerusalem (Neh. 3:2; 7:36).

C. Warren, excavating in 1868, found the site unre-warding, but in 1930-6 extensive excavations were made by J. Garstang on behalf of the Institute of Archaeology in the University of Liverpool, and in 1952-8 by K. Kenyon on behalf of the British School of Archaeology in Jerusalem. The combined results are presented here according to the system laid down by Kenyon.

The earliest remains on the site are of the 10th-8th millennia BC, and the material remains are of the Natufian culture (*Prehistory). One construction has been identified as a possible cult place. The dwellings

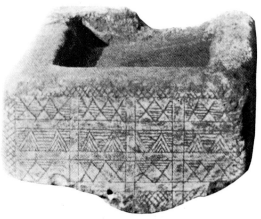

Incense altar, Tell Jemmeh, Persian period

were probably huts or tents of semi-nomads. A settlement flourished here in the early stages of the Neolithic period, when round houes were built. The settlement occupied an area of 10 acres and was surrounded by a wall, preserved in one section to a height of 17 feet. On the west a round tower 25 feet in diameter was built; this is still preserved to a height of 23 feet. A flight of steps led from the city into this massive tower. These are the earliest fortifications of the city of the 8th millennium BC.

The four reconstructions of the walls, and the thickness of the occupation levels, attest to the long life of this city. The houses were built close together and the number of inhabitants at that period is estimated at about 2,000. The prosperity of the early Neolithic city was based on agriculture, and it is possible that these early farmers irrigated their fields by means of channels. This phase of settlement is termed pre-Pottery Neolithic A, and dated to the end of the 9th millennium BC and later.

The city was then abandoned and the site was not resettled for quite a long time. The next phase, dated to between the second half of the 8th millennium and the early 6th millennium BC, is termed pre-Pottery Neolithic B. The houses of this phase are rectangular, each consisting of a large room with a number of smaller ones attached to it. They are of better construction and were built of elongated bricks decorated with a herringbone pattern, while the floors were of beaten earth. At the beginning of this phase the settle-

Earthenware vessel in the shape of a man's head, Late Bronze Age from Jericho

ment was not walled; the old wall was not rebuilt until a later stage. The excavators believe that whereas the culture of the first phase developed locally, that of the second phase came from abroad and reached Jericho in quite an advanced stage of development. The main difference between the two periods (pre-Pottery A and B) is in the stone implements used. Two buildings were identified as cult places; one of them had a round niche while the other had a rectangular room, with a plastered basin in the center and two rounded annexes. A unique cult feature is the large number of skulls on which the features of the human face have been modelled in painted plaster to resemble human flesh. The skulls were found buried beneath the floors of the houses and are believed to be connected with some ancestral cult.

The site was abandoned for a long time, but then traces of the Pottery Neolithic period appear. The settlers, who dwelt in pits, were the first to produce pottery. Three phases are distinguishable in these early vessels, the difference lying mainly in the type of decoration and their location on the site.

The Ghassulian culture (*Tuleilat Ghassul) of the 4th millennium BC is missing at Jericho and settlement did not resume before the end of that millennium. The new settlers buried their dead in rock-cut tombs and produced new forms of pottery, such as bag-shaped jugs and rounded bowls and vessels decorated with linear patterns. This culture is called proto-Urban by Miss Kenyon, because it precedes the urban culture of the Early Bronze Age.

The Early Bronze Age II strata were studied at Jericho in a deep section made on the west of the mound. Here no less than 17 superimposed phases of building and rebuilding of the walls were observed. Of the city itself little has been excavated, but quite enough to show that the houses were large and well built. The tombs of that period were used for mass burial; in one of them about 100 skulls were counted. The Early Bronze Age II terminated abruptly at Jericho and the latest wall, which was hurriedly built, was destroyed shortly afterwards.

The new settlers, of the Middle Bronze Age I, did not build permanent dwellings and were probably nomadic shepherds. Later in this period scattered houses were found but the site was not fortified. The tombs, which were deep and well cut, contained single burials. Despite an overall similarity the tombs do vary, especially in the way the bodies are placed. This is explained by the difference in tribal descent, for the excavators believe that these new tribes were connected with the Amorite migration. In the Middle Bronze Age I the city was still surrounded by a wall built of bricks, as well as the walls of the Early Bronze Age. But most of the buildings crumbled away during the long period of desertion that ensued.

Better preserved were the houses of Middle Bronze Age II. They were small, with small, irregularly shaped rooms. Some contained a large quantity of grain; this was probably intended to be milled on the spot, as more than twenty millstones were dicovered nearby. The fortifications of this period were typical, consisting of a massive retaining wall built of stone and a glacis faced with a layer of hard lime plaster that covered the slope of the mound. The glacis rose 50 feet above the level of the surrounding plain and the wall was built on top. A gentle slope led from the wall to the inside of the town. Three phases were observed in the building of this glacis, the huge retaining wall belonging to the last phase. The burials of this period were again of the mass burial type. Near each body were placed food, drinks, pottery vessels of various kinds and furniture. This city flourished in the *Hyksos period and came to a violent end in about 1560 BC. During most of the 17th and 16th centuries Jericho was not inhabited, and if there were any buildings at this period they must have been washed away by the winter rains.

There was a little pottery of the 14th century BC. It seems that the site was inhabited after the beginning of this century but deserted again by the second half. Nothing remained of the fortifications of this period; their fall, according to the Bible, signalled the conquest of Jericho by Joshua. It is possible, however, that the Late Bronze Age II city of Jericho was conquered by Joshua, and that during the long period that elapsed before its resettlement in the time of Hiel the Bethelite all remains were washed away by the rains. This is not easy to prove and in fact no remains have been found of the city built by Hiel (early 9th century BC). On the eastern slope of the mound one house of the four-room type has, however, been discovered. Little was found of the Persian period, during which the settlement of the time of the Restoration was built. Among the finds of that period were *yahud*-type seals (*Seals). The mound was abandoned shortly afterwards and the Jericho of the Roman period was built at Tulul Abu el-Alaiq.

JERICHO, HERODIAN In the late Hellenistic (Hasmonean) and early Roman (Herodian) periods, Jericho expanded on a large scale, as a garden city alongside a royal estate. This growth was made possible by the construction of a network of well-built water channels which exploited all the water sources in the vicinity (Ain es-Sultan, the springs of Wadi Qelt, Na'aran and Ain Odja).

TULUL ABU EL ALAIQ: Following surveys in the 19th century (at the point of exit of Wadi Qelt from the Judean hills) and soundings by C. Warren (1868) and E. Sellin and C. Watzinger (1910-11), the site of Tulul Abu el Alaiq and its two prominent mounds (one north of the wadi and the other to its south) became known as "Herodian Jericho" — the town of the late Hellenistic-early Roman periods. The excavations of J. Kelso, D. Baramki (1950), J. Pritchard (1951) and E. Netzer of the Hebrew University of Jerusalem (1973-83) revealed clearly that during those periods this site served as a winter palace center for the Judean kings. The palaces developed side by side and simultaneously with a large royal estate of at least $108^1/_2$ acres, in which palm-date trees and *opobalsamum* plants (used in the perfume industry) were probably the major crops.

The Hasmonean palace evolved in stages. The first and main wing (now buried under the northern mound), about 165 feet by 165 feet, surrounded by a moat, was probably built by John Hyrcanus (134-104 BC) in the last quarter of the 2nd century BC. It was first enlarged towards the west, where two swimming pools (each about 26 feet by 30 feet) — were added. The next serious expansion was to the east where an entire complex was built, probably by Alexander Jannaeus (103-76 BC). It included two elaborate swimming pools (each 60 feet by 43 feet), a pavilion surrounded by colonnades in Doric Style, paved areas and gardens. In the last major addition, to the south, two adjacent villas (the Twin Palaces) were built on the same plan. A garden with a small swimming pool lay alongside each villa. The Twin Palaces were probably built by the Queen Salome Alexandra (76-67 BC) to accommodate her two rival sons. The Hasmonean palace also included various bathing installations and many ritual immersion pools — the oldest ones discovered so far. Noteworthy among the finds was an abundance of small plates and a unique drinking horn.

The Hasmonean palace was replaced by three successive palaces built by Herod the Great, which ultimately funtioned as a single unit. The first palace was a rectangular building (282 feet by 150 feet) erected south of Wadi Qelt. It was excavated by Pritchard (and misinterpreted by him as a gymnasium) and probably coexisted with the Hasmonean palace in its last years. The latter seems to have been destroyed during the earthquake of 31 BC, and was followed by Herod's second palace which was constructed above its ruins. The new palace included a structure built on an elevated artificial mound (the northern mound), in which the main building of the Hasmonean palace was buried; a large swimming pool, 105 feet by 60 feet, (combining the two Hasmonean pools east of the mound), and a new extensive wing to the southeast. This wing included a peristyle garden, a swimming pool (originally Hasmonean) and a Roman bathhouse.

The most elaborate of Herod's three palaces dates towards the end of the 1st century BC. It was built as a complex (on an area of $7^1/_4$ acres on both sides of Wadi Qelt. A team of Roman builders took part in its construction and implemented the use of Roman concrete covered with small stones in the *opus reticulatum* and *opus quadratum* methods. To the south of wadi the palace contained an exotic formal garden (the Sunken Garden), a huge pool (295 feet by 130 feet) for swimming and boating, and a round reception hall on a high artificial mound (the southern mound). North of the wadi, the large northern wing was added. It contained a huge reception hall (95 feet by 62 feet) two peristyle courtyards, various rooms, a Roman bathhouse and colonnades overlooking the wadi's southern shore.

A large industrial zone dating to the two periods was exposed close to the palace complex, at the edge of the royal estate. An extensive cemetery of the same period was surveyed and partly excavated by R. Hachlili, northeast of the palaces, at the foot of the Judean Hills. The entire site of Tulul Abu el-Alaiq suffered neglect at the end of the 1st century AD, close to the destruction of the Second Temple in Jerusalem.

TELL EL-SAMARAT: A unique complex, built by Herod, was exposed and studied (1975-6) by E. Netzer on and south of Tell el-Samarat, which is situated between Tell el-Sultan and the winter palaces. The complex combined, on one longitudinal axis: a hippodrome course (about 1033 feet by 280 feet), theater (230 feet wide) and a large building on a high artificial mound behind the theater (about 230 feet by 230 feet). This complex is mentioned in Josephus in the context of political events close to Herod's death and probably functioned in a similar manner to the theaters and hippodromes built by him in Jerusalem and Caesarea.

JERUSALEM

THE CANAANITE AND ISRAELITE CITY

THE SITE The principal remains of biblical Jerusalem have been uncovered on the City of David, the hill overlooking the Gihon Spring (the Virgin's Fountain) in the Kidron Valley. This section of the City of David is bordered on the north by the Temple Mount, on the east by the Kidron Valley, and on the west by the central valley which separates it from the western hill.

In the Canaanite and Israelite periods up to the 10th century BC, the area of the City of David consisted of about 15 acres. In the 10th century BC, the Temple Mount was added in the north enlarging its area to about 37 acres. The area attained its greatest extent — $137^{1}/_{2}$ acres — in the 8th-6th centuries BC with the addition of the western hill.

With the Babylonian conquest of Jerusalem in 586 BC the ancient city's expansion was brought to an end.

HISTORY OF THE ARCHAEOLOGICAL EXCAVATIONS Since the middle of the 19th century numerous archaeologists have excavated in the City of David, around the Temple Mount and on Mount Zion. These include, on behalf of the British Palestine Exploration Fund, C. Warren (1864-7), F.J. Bliss and A.C. Dickie (1884-7), R.A.S. Macalister and J.G. Duncan (1923-5), G.M. FitzGerald and J.W. Crowfoot (1927-8), and K.M. Kenyon (1961-7). A French expedition led by R. Weil excavated in the City of David in 1913-4 and 1923-4.

After 1967, three large-scale Hebrew University expeditions conducted excavations in Jerusalem: the first on the Temple Mount was directed by B. Mazar (1968-78); the second in the Jewish Quarter was directed by N. Avigad (1969-83), and the third in the City of David was directed by Y. Shiloh (1978-85).

The western hill was excavated by M. Broshi (1971-6) and the remains of the citadel near the Jaffa Gate were investigated by various Israeli archaeologists.

THE EXCAVATIONS (the numbering of the strata is based on the findings of the Shiloh Expedition on the eastern slope of the City of David.)

In level 21 a small amount of pottery of the Chalcolithic period was found in the natural cisterns formed in bedrock.

Level 20 dating to the Early Bronze Age I represents the first settlement founded above bedrock. In this level was found a broad-type house which is typical of the architecture of that period. The remains of this building herald the beginning of urbanization in Jer-

Excavations at the City of David

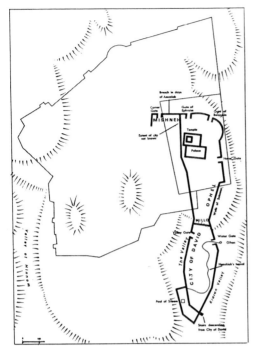

Map of Jerusalem during David's kingship

usalem. The Early Bronze Age (II–III) (level 19) is represented by pottery only. Remains of a Middle Bronze Age IIB city (18th–17th centuries BC) were discoverred in levels 18–17 in area E on the eastern slope of the City of David. Two sections of the city wall erected on bedrock were uncovered by Kenyon above the area of the spring and by Shiloh in area E. Remains of walls of buildings, floors and fills from this period hugged the inner side of the wall.

Remains of the Late Bronze Age II city were uncovered in level 16, mainly in area G on the north side of the hill. Information on the history of the city in the 14th century BC is provided by the El Amarna letters which include six letters sent by Abdi-hiba, King of Jerusalem at that time. In area G solid foundations of retaining walls were uncovered, preserved to a height of 24 feet. These walls were constructed crosswise, and the space in between was filled with stones.

In the Late Bronze Age II this was apparently the site of the Jebusite acropolis and fortress i.e. the Canaanite city. These remains were dated to the 14th–13th centuries BC on the basis of the meager pottery. Very few archaeological finds, mainly pottery and a few poor walls from the 12th–11th centuries BC, were found in level 15 on the eastern slope, in areas D and E, which represent the last phase of the city before its conquest by David in the year 1000 BC.

The Old Testament describes in great detail the planning and construction of the city as the capital of the kingdoms of Israel and Judah. From the 10th century BC — level 14 — Jerusalem served as a royal center. Varous sections of the city were then rebuilt or added to the existing city in order to adapt it to its new role. These included fortifications, the citadel, the palace, the Temple and annexes (1 Kgs. 9:15). Several structures, floors and pottery of the 10th century BC were found in area E on the eastern slope of the City of David, and especially in area G. The remains of the foundations of the Canaanite fortress were apparently covered and sealed by the 'terraced stone structure' constructed during the course of the 10th century BC, and preserved to a height of some 55 feet. It probably served as a solid monumental retaining wall and as the foundation of David's citadel. In the northwestern corner of area G Kenyon uncovered a section of a casemate wall of the 10 century BC, and a proto-Aeolian capital. These finds and the terraced stone structure indicate that this area contained monumental buildings which were constructed in the style customary at other royal centers in Judah and Israel in the 10th–9th centuries BC. This area was apparently included in the southern end of the Israelite acropolis which was built over its predecessor of the Canaanite period and expanded northwards to the Temple Mount. This is apparently the Ophel (Isa. 32:14; 2 Chr. 27:3), the acropolis of the city which is believed to have been situated between the northern end of the lower city to its south and the Temple Mount area, built on the higher part of the hill, to its north. It is possible that the Millo should be sought in the saddle dividing the Temple Mount from the Ophel (2 Sam. 5:9; 1 Kgs. 9:15). B. Mazar uncovered several massive walls in the southeastern corner of his excavations. The 1986–87 excavations in this area, carried out by Eilat Mazar on behalf of the Institute of Archaeology at the Hebrew University, revealed that these walls belonged to a gateway that led into the acropolis, and to adjoining buildings.

Especially rich finds were uncovered in the last three levels of the Israelite city, levels 12–10, from the 8th–6th centuries BC. A section of the city wall, 380 feet long and 15 feet wide and preserved to a height of approximately 9 feet, was uncovered along the eastern slope. This wall added breadth and height to the city wall of the Middle Bronze Age IIB. It also served as the main retaining wall for a system of terraces which stretched along it up the slope. Various buildings were constructed on these terraces in which two building phases can be distinguished: one of the 8th century BC, apparently from the time of King Hezekiah (level 121) and the other from the 7th century BC, the end of the period (levels 11–10).

Today it is clear in the light of Mazar's, and especially Avigad's excavations, that the construction of houses on the western hill began during the 8th century BC. In the days of Hezekiah most of this new area was surrounded by the 'broad wall' which incorporated the city's suburbs — the 'College' and the *Maktesh* (2 Kgs 22:14; Zeph. 1:10–11) — into the fortified area, and then joined the fortification system of the City of David. A stretch of some 190 feet of this wall, which was c. 22 feet wide, was uncovered on the western hill. It probably contained the northern gate of the city, of which an important part was discovered in Avigad's excavations. This strong wall apparently surrounded the entrance to the central valley in the south part of the City of David, as well as the Siloam Pool and Hezekiah's Tunnel (Isa. 22:11) (*See* *IN— SCRIPTIONS). It is evident that the plan for the reconstruction of the city took place in the days of Hezekiah prior to the campaign of Sennacherib who beseiged the city in the year 701 BC (2 Kgs. 18:13; 19). The city was now expanded to $137\frac{1}{2}$ acres and many new suburbs (cf. Zeph. 1:10; Jer. 31:38) were added to its northern part, thus substantially increasing the population of the Judean capital.

The extensive building activity at the end of the Iron Age (level 10) in the time of Josiah is evidenced by several houses uncovered in area E in the City of David, such as 'the house of hewn stones' and 'the house on the lowest terrace', and in area G: 'Achiel's house', 'the burnt room' and the 'bullae house'. In all these structures were found clear signs of the city's destruction by the army of Nebuchadnezzer, King of Babylon, in 586 BC. Similar evidence was also uncovered in the excavations in the Jewish Quarter, mainly near the tower of the northern gate and in the excavations near the Temple Mount. This evidence supplements the wealth of information appearing in the Old Testament on the destruction of Jerusalem by the Babylonians (2 Kgs. 25:8-10; 2 Chr. 36:18-19).

The numerous finds from these structures display most of the typical features of the material culture of this period. Rich pottery assemblages of the 8th-7th centuries and beginning of the 6th century BC, which are typologically similar to other pottery assemblages from Judea, as for example from Beer-Sheba, Stratum II, Lachish, Stratum III, II; Ramat Rahel, Stratum V, En Gedi, Stratum V. The small finds include arrowheads, metal and bone objects, and a large number of fertility figurines. Epigraphic material was also found in large quantities. It includes inscriptions on stone and pottery, and seals and seal impressions. Especially noteworthy is a group of 51 clay bullae which were found in the destruction level of the 'bullae house' named for them.

The bullae include Hebrew names such as 'Benayahu son of Hishayahu' and 'Azaryahu son of Hilkiyahu'; 'Gemaryahu son of Shaphan' who appears among the names may possibly be identical to the scribe who was active in the court of Johoiakim in the fifth year of his reign - 604 BC (Jer. 36:9-12) — about 18 years before the destruction of the city.

The destruction of the city was a total one. In several houses the ruins reached to the ceiling of the first floor. A vivid description of the state of destruction of the City of David is presented by Nehemiah as he found it during his first survey of the city about 140 years later (Neh. 2:13-14). In the beginning of the Persian period the returnees again lived in the restricted area of the City of David as in the days of David and Solomon in the 10th century BC.

THE WATER INSTALLATIONS IN THE CITY OF DAVID The permanent and main source of water of the City of David was the Gihon Spring in the Kidron Valley at the foot of the city's eastern slope. This is an intermittent spring and in order to utilize its waters each flow must be caught as it issues forth and then collected in reservoirs. The only spot topographically suitable for

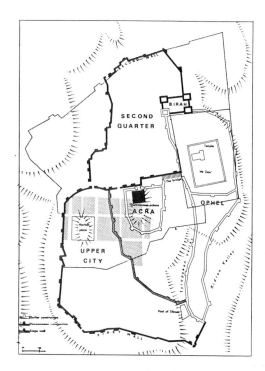

Map of Jerusalem in the Maccabeans' time

this was at the southern end of the City of David. Biblical Jerusalem used three underground water installations during the Iron Age: 'Warren's Shaft', the Siloam Tunnel and Hezekiah's Tunnel.

'Warren's Shaft' was first discovered by C. Warren in 1867, and therefore bears his name. It was discovered anew and cleared in its entirety by the Shiloh expedition. It consists of a 130 foot long tunnel, stepped at the beginning and then continuing horizontally, until at its eastern edge it reached the top of the vertical shaft. The bottom of the shaft is c. 40 feet deep. The water entered it from the Gihon Spring and was drawn from the top of the shaft as from a well by the city's inhabitants who then returned back into the city. A hydrological survey prepared by the Shiloh Expedition revealed that part of the tunnel and the entire vertical shaft are in fact part of natural karstic fissures which were incorporated into the water works during the construction of the royal city in the 10th century BC.

The Siloam Tunnel was partly a rock-cut channel and partly a tunnel. It carried the water directly from the Gihon Spring to reservoirs in the southwest part of the city. Several window-like openings along the tunnel enabled the water to be diverted to irrigation fields in the Kidron Valley. This tunnel was apparently in use in the 10th-9th centuries BC (Isa. 8:6). Hezekiah's Tunnel, named after the king who constructed it at the end of the 8th century BC (2 Kgs. 20:20), is c. 1,700 feet long. It runs along a winding course from the Gihon

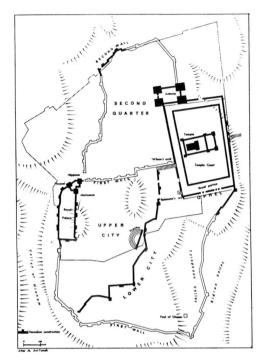

Map of Jerusalem in Herod's time

phical problems of Jerusalem during the Second Temple period. It is now possible to more or less accurately reconstruct the city during this period. The urban develoment of Jerusalem during the Second Temple period is essentially identical with the growth of the city during the First Temple period. In the Persian and Hellenistic periods (6th-2nd centuries BC) the city was confined to the Temple Mount and the area of the City of David to its south. During the Hasmonean period (late 2nd-early 1st centuries BC), the urban center shifted to the western hill. In the Herodian period (late 1st century BC-AD 70) the city's limits expanded farther north to include regions now north of the present Old City.

According to Josephus, Jerusalem was originally built on two hills — the higher and more level western hill on which the Upper City was later built, and the somewhat lower eastern hill forming a long ridge — separated by a central valley (*War* IV, 136-141). The higher northern part, Mount Moriah on which the Temple stood, and below it to the south the traditional City of David together with the valley and the lower eastern slope of Mount Zion formed the Lower City of Jerusalem at that time. Between the two hills lies the central valley — the Cheese-maker's Valley — the Tyropoeon — which extends from the area of the Damascus Gate in the north to the Kidron Valley in the south. North of these two hills Josephus described two others, one was the site of the Akra which is mentioned in connection with the Temple Mount, and the other, which he called Bezetha (*War* IV, 151), should be sought north of the present Old City.

These hills comprised the area of Jerusalem at the end of the Second Temple period. At that time, according to Josephus, the city was defended by three walls and protected on the west and south by the wide and deep Hinnom Valley, and on the east by the steep Kidron Valley. These valleys, together with the massive walls, formed a most effective defense along three sides of the city.

In this period to the time of the Hasmoneans settlement in Jerusalem was limited to the Temple Mount and the City of David alone. Sections of its eastern fortifications which date mainly to the Hellenistic period (2nd century BC) were uncovered in the past along the upper part of the slope. The foundation of the wall had been laid by Nehemiah (Neh. 3) along the earlier wall of the First Temple period outside the city limits. The slope of the hill below the wall contained a series of supporting terraces. On the west side of the City of David a fortified gate identified as the Valley Gate (Neh. 3:13) was rebuilt during the Hasmonean kingdom over earlier foundations.

In the Hasmonean period Jerusalem expanded on to the western hill. This new suburb was subsequently restored by Herod in Hellenistic style and was known as the Upper City of Jerusalem. The king's palace was erected on a raised platform in the northwestern corner of the hill. Its foundations were excavated in the courtyard of David's Citadel next to the Jaffa Gate and it extended farther south to the present Armenian garden. Remains of large private dwellings were recently discovered in the east side of the Jewish

Spring along the foot of the City of David to its southeastern corner, where the Siloam Pool is located at the southern edge of the central valley. Hezekiah's Tunnel replaced the Siloam Channel in its main task of conveying water from the Gihon Spring to the Siloam Pool. But whereas the Siloam Channel and the pool were, until Hezekiah's days, outside the wall of the city, from the time of Hezekiah at the end of the 8th century BC Hezekiah's Tunnel and the Siloam Pool were within the new fortified area of the city. The three water works could have been in use simultaneously, each in its designated role, from the days of Hezekiah until 586 BC. Through 'Warren's Shaft' the inhabitants from the north of the city and the acropolis could reach the spring; Hezekiah's tunnel regularly conveyed the Gihon's water to the reservoirs in the central valley; and the Siloam Tunnel was used, when necessary and in a controlled manner, to divert water for irrigation of the fields along the Kidron Valley.

JERUSALEM DURING THE SECOND TEMPLE PERIOD

Our knowledge of the urban plan and development of Jerusalem during the Second Temple period is based on the numerous sources and increasing archaeological evidence. The main literary source is the famous account in Josephus' *War* V which contains a very detailed description of Jerusalem on the eve of its destruction by the Roman legions in AD 70. The many archaeological excavations in the city during the last 120 years and especially since 1967 have succeeded in resolving most of the important topogra-

Quarter. One was a two-story palatial mansion containing scores of rooms and three terraces around a central courtyard. Several of the rooms were paved with mosaics and the walls were adorned with multicolored frescos, confirming Josephus' description of the beautiful residences in the Upper City belonging to the priests and the wealthy families.

The Upper City was protected by the First Wall, so called by Josephus, the earliest of Jerusalem's three walls. Its foundations date back to the end of the First Temple period (Hezekiah, 8th century BC) and it was reconstructed along the same course in the time of Simeon the Hasmonean and John Hyrcanus (second half of the 2nd century BC, 1 Macc. 16:23-24), probably after the destruction of the Seleucid Akra. The line of the First Wall is described in detail by Josephus: 'Beginning on the north at the Tower called Hippicus it extended to the xystus and then joining the council chamber terminated at the western portico of the Temple'. Beginning at the same point in the other direction westward, it descended past the place called Bethso to the gate of the Essenes and then turned southwards above the fountain of Siloam, thence it again inclined to the east towards Solomon's Pool and after passing a spot which they called Ophlas, finally joined the eastern portico of the Temple (*War* v, 145).

Josephus also mentions that the First Wall contained 60 towers; several long sections of this wall have been excavated. Two sections and a gate have been uncovered in the northwest corner of the Jewish Quarter; a long section still standing to a height of 33 feet with three projecting towers which forms the northwest corner of the wall was discovered in the courtyard of David's Citadel. A huge, impressive tower known by its traditional name, David's Tower, is incorporated in the citadel. It was built of large ashlars and should be identified as the remains of the Hippicus Tower which, together with the Phasael and Miriamne Towers, Herod added to the First Wall north of his palace.

South of David's Citadel a long section of the west side of the First Wall and several towers have been preserved under the foundations of the present Old City wall. The wall skirted Mount Zion and descended along its southern slope towards the Kidron Valley. It was *c.* 18 feet wide and was built of fine ashlars dressed with margins on all four sides. Several massive towers projected from the wall and an outer retaining wall was added by Herod against its foundations on the western side. Varied construction techniques visible in the wall attest to the continual repair of the wall and its towers up to the end of the Second Temple times. In the 1st century BC, the Second Wall was constructed (probably by the Hasmoneans) to enclose the upper part of the Tyropoeon Valley north of the western hill. Josephus' description of this wall is very brief: 'The second wall started from the gate in the first wall which they called Gennath and, enclosing only the northern district of the town, went up as far as Antonia' (*War* v, 146).

Remains of the Gennath Gate were uncovered in the northwest corner of the Jewish Quarter. From here the wall probably extended north above a rock

scarp created by earlier quarries east of the Holy Sepulcher to a gate; the remains of the western octagonal tower of the gate are now buried beneath the present Damascus Gate. The wall then turned south towards the Antonia Fortress, which Herod had attached to the northwest corner of the Temple Mount. In Herod's time the Temple underwent its greatest change since the days of Solomon. The Temple and its surroundings were completely reconstructed, radically altering the shape of Temple Mount. Prior to Herod the sanctuary area was limited to the summit of the hill and this was now included inside the Herodian structure. Herod doubled the area of the Temple Mount. On the northwest side the rock was cut away and on the other side the sloping ground to the southern side was raised by buttress walls, vaults and earth and rubble fill. The northeastern corner was built across the valley. Part of the huge retaining walls of the Temple Mount are perfectly preserved in their Herodian state, especially at the southeastern corner which rises 155 feet above bedrock and the southwestern corner which rises 125 feet. The Temple walls built by Herod have the following dimensions: south, 910 feet; west, 1600 feet; north, 1030 feet, and east, 1540 feet. The area of Temple Mount is 125 sq yards, nearly double the area of the halakhic Temple Mount as given in the Mishna (*Midot* 2, 1). Thus it is clear that Herod's additions on the north and south were not regarded as integral parts of the sacred precinct.

The huge ashlar stones are dressed in typical Herodian manner, a low boss enclosed within a narrow margin. The average height of the stones is 4-5 feet except for the master course, which is 6 feet high and ran beneath the threshold of the southern gate. The stones weigh from 3 to 5 tons. In the southern corners were huge stones weighing scores of tons. The exterior of the walls rising above the Temple Mount were ornamented on their upper part with a row of pilasters like the Herodian structure surrounding the Haram el-Kalil at Hebron. In the southern side of the eastern wall, part of an earlier wall displaying a high boss, was incorporated into the later Herodian construction.

The southern wall contained the two Huldah Gates now known as the double and triple gates. The western Huldah Gate is still preserved with stucco decoration on its ceiling beneath the el-Aksa Mosque. A street 20 feet wide ran along the southern wall towards the Huldah Gates. Near the western Huldah Gate is a monumental stairway 210 feet wide and a much smaller one near the easten gate. They led from the Ophel on the south to the Temple Mount gates. In front of them was a square paved with smooth flagstones which was some 21 feet lower than the street. Remains of the Royal Portico built by Herod on the southern side of the Temple Mount were found outside the Southern Wall. It was decorated with rich geometric and floral patterns. Near the southwestern corner a stone bearing the Hebrew inscription 'to the place of the trumpeting' was found lying on the street. There were four gates in the Western (Wailing) Wall of the Temple Mount. The southern gate stood at the top of a monumental stairway leading from the main street up to the Royal Portico. The remains of this

The exact location of the Temple on the present Temple Mount is a subject of controversy. Many scholars assume that the Rock inside the 'Dome of the Rock' corresponds to the site of the altar for burnt offerings outside the sanctuary, while others assume that it was the site of the Holy of Holies inside the Temple.

In its finished form the Temple made a profound impression on all who saw it. It was built of white stone and gold ornaments which reflected the light of the sun.

The Antonia Fortress was built by Herod in the northwestern corner of the Temple Mount above the remains of Jerusalem's earlier fortress, the Baris, which was constructed after the Restoration. It was rebuilt in Hellenistic times and a letter from Aristeas describes it as located near the Temple and containing a tower garrisoned by 500 men. In the time of the Seleucid occupation of Jerusalem, the Akra fortress was erected, according to the Book of the Maccabees, against the Temple; it was destroyed in 141 BC by Simeon the Hasmonean. The exact location of the Seleucid Akra can only be assumed. The historical and archaeological evidence suggests a location near the Temple Mount, probably to its north on the site of the Baris and the later Antonia Fortress. The latter was built to strengthen the northern defense line of Jerusalem and especially of the Temple Mount. It was later used by Herod and the Roman procurators from which they could observe the Jews approaching the Temple and keep order. It was built on a steep rock 82 feet high. The highest of its four corner towers was on the southeastern side and dominated the entire Temple court. Today only rock cuttings mark the site of this fortress. These remains suggest that it was reconstructed on either side of the Via Dolorosa, adjoining the northwestern corner of the Temple Mount, though it is also possible that it was built as a much smaller fortress on the rock scarp bordering the Temple Mount area and did not extend north of the Via Dolorosa.

*'Tomb of Zechariah', Jerusalem,
period of the Second Temple*

stairway, near the southwestern corner of the Western Wall are known today as 'Robinson's Arch'. It is 47 feet wide and rested upon a large pier projecting 38 feet from the wall. Beneath the arch was a street paved with smooth flagstones that ran southwards along the Western Wall. The other three gates in the wall include: 'Barclay's Gate', located today in the womens' section of the Western Wall; the gate above 'Wilson's Arch' that formed part of a bridge leading to the upper city, and the gate now known as 'Warren's Gate'.

Nothing remains today of the Temple and the other buildings that once stood on the Temple Mount. Porticos extended around the walls of the outer court of the Temple. One complete inscription in Greek and another fragmentary one found outside the Temple Mount originally stood in the inner courtyard of the Temple area, warning the gentiles not to enter the inner courtyard.

The Temple was surrounded by high walls and towers. The main entrance was from the east and led into the square women's court surrounded by porticos and chambers in its corners. The main gate was the famous Nicanor's Gate which was reached by 15 semicircular steps. The gate led to the 'Court of the Priests'; in its southeastern corner was the 'Chamber of Hewn Stone' the seat of the Sanhedrin. Opposite the court stood the high altar of burnt offerings approached by a ramp from the south.

The Temple itself was divided into three main rooms built on an east-west axis. Its east side was wider than the west. The entrance to the porch from the east was covered with a veil. From here a door opened into the hall where the golden candelabrum (menorah) probably stood. At the west end of the hall was a double veil concealing the Holy of Holies; this was an empty room entered only by the high priest on the Day of Atonement.

Following the northern expansion of Jerusalem's population during the 1st century AD, Agrippa (AD 41-44) undertook the construction of the Third Wall to enclose the north side of the city. The wall was completed only after the outbreak of the First Revolt in AD 66: 'The Third Wall began at the tower Hippicus, whence it stretched northwards to the tower Psephinus, and then descending opposite the monument of Helena (Queen of Adiabene and daughter of King Izates), and proceeding past the royal tombs it bent round a corner tower over against the so-called Fuller's Tomb and joining the ancient rampart terminated at the valley called Kidron' (*War* v, 147). The line of the wall contained 90 towers. In the 19th century remains of the northern section of the Third Wall of Jerusalem were uncovered about 1500 feet north of the Damascus Gate. Its remains have been subsequently explored and the full extent of its course is known for over 5/8 mile. Only the foundations of the wall were preserved. It was *c.* 15 feet wide and was built of large ashlars dressed in the typical Herodian manner. Several massive towers, facing north, were also uncovered in the wall. These remains are accepted by most authorities as representing the foundations of Agrippa's Third Wall, though some equate the line of this wall with the present north wall of the Old City.

In the Hellenistic period, public cisterns were cut into bedrock to supply water to Jerusalem's expanding population. Noteworthy examples include the Pool of Towers (Armygdalon), now known as Hezekiah's Pool, and a pool called Struthion which is mentioned in the account of Titus' siege of the Antonia Fortress and identified with the present Twin Pool. Another pool, Bethesda, is located north of the northeastern corner of the Temple Mount inside the Lion's Gate.

In Hasmonean times an aqueduct now known as the lower level aqueduct was built from Wadi Arrub near Hebron to Solomon's Pool, from which it crossed along the mountain's slopes or through tunnels and above 'Wilson's Arch' to the Temple Mount, to fill the many cisterns there.

By the end of the Second Temple period, the necropolis of Jerusalem surrounded the city on all sides and especially on its eastern and northern sides. Thus far about 700 tombs have been surveyed at a distance of 3 miles from the city limits. Outstanding burial monuments mentioned by Josephus in connection with the topography of the city include, among others, Queen Helena's tomb and Herod's family tomb. Most of the monuments around Jerusalem have remained anonymous and are known today by their traditional names such as the 'Sanhedrin Tombs' northwest of the city, or the tomb of Bnei Hezir, *'Absalom's Tomb' and 'Zechariah's Tomb' in the Kidron Valley. These tombs formed part of the vast cemetery encircling ancient Jerusalem and belonged to rich Jewish families who could afford to have monumental tombs cut into the rock. Most of their façades are decorated with reliefs depicting typical floral and geometric motifs common on Jewish tombs at that time. Many of the tombs contained small stone ossuaries used for the secondary burial of the bones.

In the last decades of the Second Temple period, Jerusalem was the focus of numerous opposing tendencies and styles, all expressing the Jewish way of life of that period. The city served as the royal capital and religious center. It was built in Hellenistic style, especially the Upper City and the Temple Mount, the walls and several of the burial monuments. The markets and the Lower City had the aspect of a typical Oriental town. All this was destroyed when the Roman legions conquered the city and razed the Temple in AD 70

JEWELRY Man's propensity for personal adornment expressed itself from earliest times. Prehistoric jewelry consisted of beads and pendants of various shapes made of bone, shells and stone. Simple ornaments of this kind continued to be used throughout all periods alongside the more sophisticated gold and silver jewelry. Great skill is displayed in the ivory, bone and stone jewelry from the Chalcolithic period found at Tell *Abu Matar, which includes pendants and beads of mother-of-pearl, bone, turquoise and ostrich egg-

shell, a bone pin-head representing a young pelican and an ivory amulet in the form of a human head. It is obvious that jewelry had a dual purpose in these cultures: in addition to the desire for ornamentation, the magical power of the amulet as a protector against evil was also significant.

The earliest gold object found in Palestine came to light in an Early Bronze Age II tomb near the Sea of *Galilee. It is a disc-shaped gold plaque with repoussé decoration and a pierced center. Similar pieces have been found at *Gezer, *Byblos, Alaca Huyuk (Anatolia) and Troy. In the Middle and Late Bronze Ages Palestine was politically and culturally under Egyptian influence, as is illustrated by numerous jewelry finds associated with the large city-states. The finds of the Late Bronze Age are especially rich, reflecting the prosperity of the area at that time. Most famous is the unique collection of gold jewelry from Tell el-*Ajjul, now in the Rockefeller Museum in *Jerusalem. The most outstanding of a large number of pieces are a mother-goddess amulet with a female head, a pendant in the form of an eight-pointed star, crescent-shaped earrings with rich granular decoration, gold pendants (used as amulets) in the form of animals, and faience beads depicting animals and flowers. Bracelets of gold and silver are numerous, as are pairs of simple earrings and finger-rings decorated with scarabs.

The rich jewelry hoard of the Early Israelite period from *Beth-Shemesh reflects the Late Bronze Age tradition, while jewelry from the Israelite period as a whole is rare and rather simply made. Phoenician influence is shown in the faience amulets found at *Beth-Shemesh, *Achzib and other sites, representing Egyptian deities such as Isis, Hathor and Bastet, demons, baboons and religious symbols.

From the Persian period onwards the jewelry found in Palestine belongs to types developed in such advanced cultures as those of Greece (*Javan), Asia Minor, *Phoenicia and Persia. The great center of jewelry production during Hellenistic and Roman times were *Alexandria and *Antioch-on-the-Orontes. Gold jewelry is common, much of it connected with religious belief and cult-images such as gods, Eros figures, snakes and dolphins. At a time when international trade flourished much jewelry

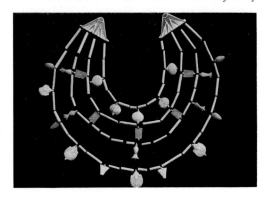

Faience necklace from Lachish

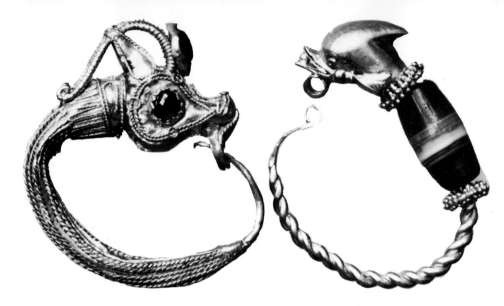

Left: Roman earring with a goat's head. Right: Hellenistic earring with a dolphin's head

came into Palestine from abroad. To the 1st and 2nd centuries AD belongs a large group of gold jewelry from the Nabatean cemetery at *Mampsis. During the Byzantine period Christian symbols were widely used by jewelers. Medallions bearing the head of the emperor were also common. To this period belong some comparatively rare Jewish amulets depicting the menorah flanked by the *shofar* and *lulab*.

JEZREEL *a)* A town in the east of the Hills of Judah (Josh. 15:56), the birth-place of Ahinoam, one of David's wives (1 Sam. 25:43). Not identified.

b) A town on the border of the territory of Issachar, at the foot of Mount *Gilboa (Josh. 19:18, etc.). It was in the fifth district of the kingdom of Solomon (1 Kgs. 4:12) and an important city in the kingdom of Ahab (1 Kgs. 18:45), who had a palace there (1 Kgs. 21:1). The descendants of the House of Ahab were slain at Jezreel (2 Kgs. 10:7, 11). It was finally destroyed by the Assyrians. In the Roman period a large village called Ezdraela flourished there, with a road-station nearby. Eusebius (*Onom.* 108:13) speaks of a very famous village in the Great Valley, between *Scythopolis and *Legio. Identified with Zeriin, west of *Beth-Shean.

c) The Plain of Jezreel, which took its name from one of the most important cities which flourished there in the biblical period, extends across the breadth of the country, between Mount *Carmel, Mount *Gilboa and the hills of lower *Galilee. The River *Kishon flows through its whole length to the Mediterranean. From early times the valley, known later as the Plain of Ezdraelon or the Great Valley, was of the utmost importance to communications between the coast and the countries to the north and east (*Roads). The fortified towns of *Megiddo, *Taanach, *Ibleam and *Beth-Shean were built in order to guard the mountain passes leading into and from the plain. Some of the great battles in biblical history took place there, including the battle between Deborah and Jabin, King of *Hazor (Judg. 4-5); the one between Saul and the *Philistines (1 Sam. 29:1; 31:1 ff.); and between

Josiah and Pharaoh Necho (2 Kgs. 23:29-30). In the Persian period the Plain of Jezreel was part of the satrapy of *Samaria. In the Hellenistic period the Ptolemies had large estates on the fertile plain, and from that time on it was mostly in the personal domain of the rulers. The Plain of Jezreel was conquered by the Maccabees and later formed part of Herod's kingdom. After the Bar-Kochba rebellion the Legio VI Ferrata encamped there and it became known as Campus Maximus Legionis. The Plain of Jezreel was the granary of Palestine in all periods, and became a large malaria-infested swamp only after the Arab conquest in AD 636.

JISR BANAT YACUB This site, found in 1933, is located in the channel of the River *Jordan more than a mile south of the former Lake Hula. It was excavated in 1937 by M. Stekelis, and a series of six layers was exposed to a total depth of 16 feet. Layer I consisted of gravels in which remains of a Mousterian industry were collected. In layer II, a yellow clay, bones of a horse were found together with Micoquian-type handaxes. In the green clay of layer III elephant and rhinoceros bones were uncovered as well as a few handaxes. Layer IV consists of boulders and pebbles in a matrix of black earth with numerous mollusc remains. Abraded Acheulian items were uncovered in this layer. Layer V was the richest in implements and bone remains: in a black soil containing many molluscs an assemblage of handaxes and cleavers made of basalt was uncovered. This represents an assemblage of the Upper Acheulian type, somewhat earlier than that found in layer F of et-*Taban Cave, *Umm-Qatafa Cave and *Ma'ayan Barukh. The unusually large number of cleavers produced by a special technique that is found also in Africa, as well as the fact that most of them were made from basalt, suggests an African source of tradition for the hunters who made them. Layer VI, at the base of layer V, was a gravel bed where Stekelis collected more abraded handaxes and cleavers.

The section of Jisr Banat Yacub illustrates the fluctuations of the ancient Lake Hula, on the shores of which the Acheulian hunters encamped. It seems that the tool-bearing layers belong to the periods of the lake's fullest extension, which was probably contemporaneous with the Ice Age in Europe. (*See also* *PREHISTORY; *FLINT TOOLS.)

JOKNEAM A city whose ruler was among the 31 Canaanite kings defeated by Joshua (Josh. 12:22); one of the Levitical cities of the family of Merari (Josh. 21:34).

One of the most important Canaanite city-states, it appears in the list of conquests made by Tuthmosis III; it was possibly conquered later by Tiglath-Pileser III. The site was also settled in the Roman period, when Eusebius knew it as Kammona, 'a large village in the Great Plain, 6 miles to the north of Legio, on the way to Ptolemais (*Acco)'. Identified with Tel Qaimin, an exceptionally large mound at the entrance to Wadi Milh, one of the important passes leading into the *Jezreel Valley.

Since 1977 excavations have been carried out at Tel Yokneam under the direction of A. Ben-Tor on behalf of the Hebrew University, as part of a regional research project of the western part of the *Jezreel Valley. This mound is outstanding by virtue of its continuous occupation. The following periods were found to be represented at the site: Ottoman, Mameluke, Crusader, early Arab, Byzantine, Roman, Hellenistic, Persian, Iron Age and Late Bronze Age. On the surface were also found potsherds of the Middle Bronze and Early Bronze Ages.

JOPPA A city in the territory of *Dan, on the coast of the Mediterranean (Josh. 19:46), conquered by the *Philistines and not included in Israelite territory. Solomon brought timber to Joppa from the *Lebanon for building his Temple (2 Chr. 2:16) and cedar wood was also brought to the 'sea of Joppa' in the time of the Restoration (Ezra 3:7). Some scholars believe that the port referred to is that of Tell *Qasileh, east of Jaffa. The prophet Jonah sailed from Joppa to *Tarshish (Jonah 1:3).

One of the most ancient ports on the coast of Palestine, Joppa was conquered by Tuthmosis III in about 1468 BC. An ancient story tells that in order to capture it Egyptian soldiers were smuggled into the city in 200 baskets. There was still an Egyptian garrison there in the 14th and 13th centuries BC, when the city is mentioned in the *El Amarna letters. In 701 BC Joppa was conquered by Sennacherib, King of Assyria, who took it from Sidka, King of *Ashkelon. In the Persian period it was given to the Sidonians, where it was known as Japho.

In the days of the Ptolemies Joppa was granted autonomy, with the right to mint coins. In 144 BC the city was conquered by Simon Maccabaeus, who drove out the alien inhabitants and settled his soldiers there so that he could use it as an opening to the sea (1 Macc. 10:76; 12:33-4; 13:11; 14:5). Jewish sovereignty over Joppa was disputed for some time but the Jews held it *de facto*. So important was the city for the economy of the Hasmonean kingdom that Alexander Jannaeus struck a large series of coins with marine symbols to commemorate its conquest. With the decline of the Hasmonean kingdom and the subsequent conquest of Palestine by Pompey in 64 BC Joppa was rebuilt and detached from Judea. This was a great blow to the Judean economy, but in 30 BC Augustus returned it to Herod. Herod conferred the rights of a *polis* on the city, and it became the capital of a small district.

After the destruction of the Second Temple the city was granted autonomy by Vespasian, with the title of Flavia Ioppe. Pliny (*Nat. Hist.* v, 13, 69) relates that the legendary snake Ceto was worshipped at Joppa; according to Greek mythology, it had threatened Andromeda's life until she was rescued by Perseus.

Joppa is mentioned several times in the New Testament. It was here that Tabitha, a disciple of Jesus, died and was revived by Peter (Acts 9:36 ff.) and also here that he saw his vision of the beasts (Acts 10:5 ff.).

After the destruction of the Temple a large Jewish community, including famous scholars, lived in Joppa. It also served as an important commercial center. Tombstones of scholars and merchants, both from Palestine and from the Diaspora, were found in the local cemetery.

Excavations in the ancient mound of Jaffa, which is situated east of the Turkish port, have revealed remains of fortifications and habitations of all periods from the Bronze Age to Byzantine and Arab times. Of great interest are the remains of typical Hyksos fortifications and a gate of the Egyptian town of the Late Bronze Age, on the jamb of which a hieroglyphic inscription was found.

JORDAN (RIVER AND VALLEY) The largest river in Palestine, flowing along the geological Syro-African rift. The river is formed by the confluence of three streams in the foothills of Mount *Hermon, at a height of 250 feet above sea level. As it descends to the Hula region it divides again into several streams. In the next 10 miles before it enters the Sea of *Galilee it descends 850 feet. Along this part of its course the banks are rocky and precipitous, leaving no margin at the water's edge. From the Sea of *Galilee the river winds its way southwards on a meandering course 104 miles long, although the distance to the *Dead Sea is only 65 miles. On its passage southwards the Jordan receives numerous tributaries, mainly from the *Gilead. The plain through which the river flows, referred to in the Bible simply as the *Plain (Josh. 12:1), or the Plain of Jordan (1 Kgs. 7:46), forms two shelves, one above the other. The southern part has different names: Plains of *Moab (Num. 22:1) and Plains of *Jericho (Josh. 4:13). The 'cities of the plain' were located here (Gen. 19:29).

The Jordan Valley is overgrown with thick vegetation and rich in wild life, including boar; lions were also to be seen there in biblical times (Jer. 49:19). The river was not important to the economy of the country, however; its steep banks prevented its waters being used for irrigation, while its winding course, obstructed by rocks in places, was not fit for navigation. It formed a geographical obstacle between the territories on either side of it, since there were few natural crossing places (there were no bridges in biblical times and swimming was kept only for emergencies). Although there were over 20 fords north of the Sea of *Galilee, there were few in the middle reaches and only five closer to the *Dead Sea. For this reason there were frequent struggles at these points. Thus the people of *Jericho attempted to cut off the way of retreat near the ford opposite *Jericho (Josh. 2:7); and after the defeat of Eglon, King of *Moab, the Israelites took the fords of the Jordan towards *Moab (Judg. 3:28). This happened several times (Judg. 7:24; Authorized Version: 'the waters of Beth-Abarah and Jordan'; 12:5-6; Authorized Version: 'passages of Jordan'). In the conquest of the land of *Canaan the Israelites crossed the Jordan, an event considered no less miraculous than the crossing of the *Red Sea (Josh. 3-4). In some places in the Bible the Jordan was considered to be the eastern limit of *Canaan (Num. 13:29; 34:12). After the conquest the river completely separated the tribes on the east from those on the west (Judg. 5:17).

The sanctity of the river goes back to early biblical times. Elijah miraculously divided its waters by smiting them with his mantle, and so did Elisha (2 Kgs. 2:8, 13-14). Naaman, the leprous captain of the host of Syria, dipped seven times in the river, 'and his flesh came again like unto the flesh of a little child, and he was clean' (2 Kgs. 5:14). The holiness of the river was further accentuated when John the Baptist preached and baptized in its waters (Matt. 3:5 ff.; Mark 1:5 ff.), and Jesus himself was baptized by John near *Beth-Abarah (John 1:28-33).

JOTBAH A village in lower *Galilee about 5¹/₂ miles north of *Sepphoris, also called Jodephat. The birthplace of Meshullemeth, daughter of Haruz, the mother of Amon, King of Judah (2 Kgs. 21:19). It is identified with Khirbet Jefat and archaeological surveys made on the site show that it was inhabited as early as the Late Bronze Age. In the Mishna (Arach. 9:6) it is listed among the walled cities dating back to the time of Joshua, son of Nun. Mentioned by Josephus as Jotapata, it was fortified by him when he prepared the defence of *Galilee against the Romans (*War* III, 141-288). After a siege of 47 days Vespasian conquered the fortress in AD 67 (*War* III, 316-38). In the period of the Bar-Kochba rebellion Jotbah was the seat of the priestly family of Miyamin.

JUDEAN DESERT The region extending eastward from the hills of Judah, bordered on the east by the *Dead Sea and on the south by the Plain of Beer-Sheba. It seems that in biblical times this name was applied to a more restricted area (Judg. 1:16). *Arad is situated 20 miles east of *Beer-Sheba and it thus seems that the wilderness of Judah extended to the south of that city. On the other hand, the four geographical regions of Judah are listed in Joshua (15:20-62) as the *Negev, the hills, the plain and the wilderness which has no specific name, but certain regions of it are indicated by the names of the neighboring towns: Wilderness of *Ziph (1 Sam. 23:14); Wilderness of Jeruel (2 Chr. 20:16); Wilderness of *Maon (1 Sam. 23:25); Wilderness of *En-Gedi (1 Sam. 24:1); Wilderness of *Tekoa (2 Chr. 20:20). It was not until the Roman period that the name Wilderness of Judea was applied to the whole region (cf. Matt. 3:1).

The Judean Desert was a place of refuge from early times and David frequently found shelter in various parts of the wilderness when fleeing from Saul (1 Sam. 23; 26). About 2,000 years later the Essenes and the members of the *Dead Sea sect, and later still the combatants in the two revolts against the Romans, also escaped to the Judean Desert (*Khirbet Qumran, Wadi Murabbaat, *Judean Desert Caves). With the rise of Christianity numerous monasteries were founded there.

The eastern slopes of the Judean Hills, which fall steeply towards the *Dead Sea, are almost devoid of vegetation. The meager rainfall and the porous rock of which the hills are composed produce a rugged landscape, and the descent of some 3,000 feet over a distance of less than 15 miles forms deep gorges with precipitous waterfalls, dry for all but a few days in the year. The steep banks of the gorges contain numerous caves that are difficult to reach and are therefore ideal hiding places. Springs are few and small and the only oasis in the whole region is at *En-Gedi, where a copious spring fosters lush vegetation.

JUDEAN DESERT CAVES During the years 1960 and 1961 a cave-to-cave survey was made in the sheer walls of the wadis that drop down to the *Dead Sea, in the region extending from *En-Gedi in the north to *Masada in the south. The survey was carried out by teams from the Hebrew University, the Israel Exploration Society and the Israel Department of Antiquities and Museums, with the help of hundreds of civilian and military volunteers. A great many caves were visited and excavations were made where neces-

Bronze "Crown" found in the Cave of the Treasure, Judean Desert

sary. The caves were numbered, some also being named according to the items found in them. Many yielded remains of the Chalcolithic, Iron Age and Roman periods.

THE CAVES OF NAHAL HEVER (WADI KHABRA) The earliest remains in these caves were dwellings of the Chalcolithic period. Among the finds were pottery, mats and burials, dated by carbon 14 analysis to the middle of the 4th millennium BC. Other remains were of the Roman period. On the rocks above the wadi were the remains of a Roman siege camp, 150 feet square, built in order to prevent the escape of the soldiers of Bar-Kochba and their families, who had found shelter in the caves below. One of these, 250 feet below the camp, was labelled the 'Cave of Horrors'. It contained 40 skeletons of men, women, children and babies, besides numerous household utensils, clothing and small fragments of scrolls that had escaped the notice of the Bedouins who had looted the cave a few years earlier.

THE CAVES OF NAHAL SEELIM (WADI SEIYAL) Here, as well, some remains of the Chalcolithic period were found. There were also traces of an Israelite occupation. On the banks of the wadi small Roman forts were discovered, built in order to block the escape routes. The caves with remains of the Bar-Kochba period are number 31, the 'Cave of Arrows', in which numerous iron arrowheads and wooden shafts were found, and number 34, the 'Cave of Scrolls'. In cave number 34, among written fragments in Hebrew, Aramaic and Greek, were remains of philacteries and a list of names some with the additional title 'brother' (possibly some kind of rank).

NAHAL MISHMAR (WADI MAHRAS) The 'Cave of Letters' was discovered in this section. Its entrance is in the sheer rock face 300 feet below the top of the wadi bank and 600 feet above the river bed. It is about 350 feet long and is divided into three halls. It seems that the fugitive rebels planned to escape and had therefore hidden their belongings and documents in cavities in the rocks. Some, however, did not get away, and their skeletons were found lying in the cave. The finds included a large number of bronze vessels of Italian make, household utensils, clothing and footwear, house keys, glassware, baskets and mats, wool, knitting and cosmetic implements. Documents were also found, among them fragments of books of the Bible (Numbers; Psalms) and the archives of a lady named Babata, daughter of Simon, which included personal documents in Nabatean, Aramaic and Greek. These documents cover the period between AD 93 and 132, the year in which the revolt broke out. There were also 15 letters written by the leader of the revolt, Simeon Bar Cozibah (i.e. Bar-Kochba), to his subordinates in the *Dead Sea region. Both the archives of Babata and the letters of Bar-Kochba provide first-class material for the study of a period in Jewish history that is

Copper vessels from the Cave of the Treasure in the Judean Desert

otherwise little known. (*See also* *DEAD SEA SCROLLS.) The *Treasure Cave was also discovered in this wadi. *Nahal Hemar:* In 1983, in the course of a survey of the Judean Desert, I. el-Toury discovered a cave in Nahal Hemar in the southern part of the desert. It was subsequently excavated by O. Bar-Yosef on behalf of the Hebrew University and D. Alon of the Department of Antiquities. This cave had been used for thousands of years by herdsmen who tended there flocks of goats. The upper two levels yielded *potsherds from the Roman period to the Early Bronze Age. Of most interest, however, are the two lower levels of occupation in which no pottery was found. Organic material analyzed by carbon-14 tests yielded dates of about 9000 BC, i.e. the pre-Pottery Neolithic period. These levels were extremely rich in finds. From everyday life there were wickerwork baskets smeared with bitumen, net baskets, mats, thread, wooden beads painted in green and red, a sickle, flint knives and arrowheads made of flint and wood, *weaving utensils, animal bones and marine shells. Other remains were *cult objects: three stone masks, one painted in red and green with its sides smeared with bitumen, three skulls of adults, one smeared with bitumen, which served as a glueing agent for strips of leather, and three tiny figurines portraying human features painted in red and green and smeared with bitumen. These early discoveries, from the pre-Pottery Neolithic B, are unique.

JUDEIDEH (TELL EL-) *See* *GODED (TEL)

K

KABRI A large tel in the western Galilee, on which small scale excavations were carried out in 1957–58, 1961, 1969 and 1975. In 1986 large-scale excavations were undertaken by the Institute of Archaeology of Tel Aviv University, the Department of Antiquities and the Israel Exploration Society, under the direction of A. Kempinski.

The site was occupied in the Early and Middle Bronze IIa periods, but grew tremendously in the Middle Bronze IIb period, when a 40 m wide glacis was built, surrounding an area of 80 acres. By the end of the Middle Bronze period, the site was already deserted. During the peak period in the life of the city a large, well-built palace, with a multi-colored painted floor in Minoan style, stood in the center of town. The painted floor is a unique feature, never yet encountered in southern Canaan.

KABZEEL; JEKABZEEL A town in the *Negev of Judah, on the border of *Edom (Josh. 15:21), the birthplace of Benaiah, son of Jehoiada, one of David's mighty men (2 Sam. 23:20). Resettled after the Restoration, when it was named Jekabzeel (Neh. 11:25). Tentatively identified with Khirbet Gharreh, 8 miles east of *Beer-Sheba, where an Israelite fortress was discovered.

KADESH-BARNEA An oasis in the Wilderness of *Zin, north of the Wilderness of *Paran, in the northern part of the *Sinai Desert. It was at an important crossroads on the main route leading from *Edom and the *Arabah to *Egypt, called the Way of Shur, and the road leading from *Elath and the central *Negev onwards to *Arad and *Hebron (Num. 13:26). One of the most important stations on the route of the Exodus, with abundant water, where the Children of Israel halted for a considerable period (Deut. 1:46). From here the spies set out for the Land of *Canaan, and here the people complained to Moses and Aaron (Exod. 14) and Miriam died (Num. 20:1). Here also the people begged Moses and Aaron for water (Num. 20:2), so that it became known as the Water of Meribah (Num. 20:13), called by Ezekiel the waters of strife of Kadesh (Ezek. 4:19). It is inferred that the Israelites used Kadesh as a base for their attack on the *Amalekites (*Num. 14:40–5), and on the *Amorites dwelling in the mountain (Deut.

1:44). From Kadesh the Israelites departed for the plain of *Moab after the *Edomites had refused to allow them to pass through their country (Num. 20:16 ff.).

Kadesh-Barnea is identified with Ain el-Qudeirat. On the small tell, near the spring, the remains of an Israelite fortress from the period of the kingdom of Judah have been uncovered, consisting of a casemate wall fortified with towers. Remains of Roman and Byzantine settlements were discovered nearby.

The first archaeological survey on the site was conducted by C.L. Woolley and T.E. Lawrence in 1914 on behalf of the Palestine Exploration Fund. An exploratory excavation was made by M. Dothan on behalf of the Department of Antiquities in 1956. The plan of the fortress prepared by the early investigators was corrected and the chronology was established. The first occupation of the site was dated to the 10th century BC and the construction of the fortress to the subsequent century, perhaps under Jehoshaphat. After its destruction with the end of the kingdom of Judah, there was an additional occupation of the site in the Persian period.

Large scale excavations of the site were carried out in the years 1976–9 by R. Cohen on behalf of the Department of Antiquities. Three separate superimposed fortresses were uncovered. On the natural rock an oval fortress of the casemate type was built in the 10th/9th century BC (Stratum III), with an outer wall 5 feet wide. In plan it resembles other small fortresses discovered in the central Negev. It is believed that the Kadesh-Barnea fortress served as the administrative center for these Judean strongholds of the central *Negev. In the 8th/7th century BC (Stratum II) a completely new fortress was built, according to a different plan. It was a rectangular building 75 feet long, with solid walls 12 feet wide and three projecting towers on each side. Within the citadel were accommodations for the garrison. This fortress was probably erected by Uzziah (781–740 BC), perhaps during preparations for his expedition to the *Red Sea. Its destruction is ascribed to the Assyrians. The latest fortress (Stratum I) is of the 7th/6th century BC. Above the solid wall were constructed casemate walls (183 feet by 125 feet), and it had the same number of towers as its predecessor. The massive northeastern tower (30 feet by 29 feet) still rises to a height of 14 feet. The *pottery found in the fortress consists of the well-known Judean types as well as handmade pottery typical of the Negev. Two Hebrew and three Egyptian ostraca with hieratic symbols were found. The construction of this fortress is ascribed to Josiah, who built it for the protection of the borders of his kingdom. Meager occupation remains of the Persian period were also uncovered.

KANATH; KANATHA A city in the eastern part of the *Bashan, captured by Nobah of the tribe of Manasseh, and renamed Nobah after its conqueror (Num. 32:42). It was a border point after the Restoration and Herod fought the *Nabateans here (Josephus, *Antiq.* I, 336 ff.). In the Roman period Kanatha was the first urban settlement in the *Hauran, and one of the cities of the *Decapolis. According to an inscription found on the site it was raised to the status of a colony by Septimius Severus, when its name became Septimia Kanotha. A surface survey has disclosed many remains of the city's glorious past, such as the Temple of Zeus, a *nymphaeum* and a theater. Eusebius (*Onom.* 112:20) knew it as a village in *Arabia.

KARNAIM; KARNEIN The capital of the *Bashan under Aramean and Assyrian rule, after the decline of neighboring *Ashtaroth, whose name it annexed, being known as Ashtaroth Karnaim. In the Hellenistic period it was called Karnein (2 Macc. 12:21; Authorized Version: 'Carnion'). Identified with Sheikh Saad, northeast of Ashtaroth, where an inscription bearing the name of Rameses II was found. Eusebius (*Onom.* 12:11) states that in his time there was a very large village in *Arabia by the name of Karneia, and that according to tradition Job's house is shown there.

KARTAH A Levitical city in the territory of Zebulun (Josh. 21:34), identified by some with the site of the Crusader castle at Athlit, or with a place a short distance to the east of it. Phoenician tombs have been discovered there. It seems that the territory of Zebulun did not reach so far south and for this reason others identify Kartah with an ancient tell near el-Artiyeh, which may have preserved the ancient name. (*See also* *CARTHA.)

KEBARA CAVE The cave of Kebara, in the southern part of Mount *Carmel about 2 miles from the sea, was found in 1928 by M. Stekelis and first excavated by F. Turville-Petre in 1931.

Beneath layer A, defined as Early Bronze Age to the Arab period, layer B was exposed. This layer belongs to the Natufian culture and is rich in stone implements and bone tools as well as burials. Among the flints many sickle-blades and crescents formed by Helwan retouch are worth noting, as well as a rich assemblage of bone tools including points, bi-points, hooks, harpoons, needles and combs. Four sickle-hafts ornamented with carved animal heads were also found. Layer C consisted of a flint industry characterized by a great quantity of microlithic tools, among which the backed bladelet, obliquely truncated, was the most common. This assemblage became the type site for the Kebaran culture, defined by Neuville as stage XI of the Palestinian Upper Paleolithic era. Layer D, with its two sub-layers, is considered on the basis of its many nosed and steep scrapers to belong to the local Aurignacian or Upper Paleolithic IV era. Layer E belongs to the Upper Paleolithic III era and is characterized by Font-Yves points as well as nosed and steep scrapers.

The excavation was halted by Turville-Petre when he thought he had arrived at the Mousterian level. The dig was renewed in 1951 by M. Stekelis and continued at intervals until 1965. He deepened the excavation to 25 feet under the primary ground level, but still did not reach bedrock. He exposed many Upper and Middle Paleolithic dwelling levels. In 1965, in one of the oldest levels, he found the remains of a two-year-old child. (*See also* *PREHISTORY; *FLINT TOOLS.)

KEDESH *a)* A Canaanite city in *Galilee, in the territory of Naphtali, whose ruler was one of the 31 kings vanquished by Joshua (Josh. 12:22). To distinguish it from other cities with the same name it was also referred to as Kedesh in *Galilee in Mount Naphtali (Josh. 20:7). It was given to the Levites and was a city of refuge (Josh. 21:32). A name which may possibly refer to Kedesh appears in the lists of Tuthmosis III and in the *El Amarna letters. It was conquered by Tiglath-Pileser III, King of Assyria (2 Kgs. 15:29), who deported its inhabitants. In the Hellenistic period it is mentioned in the Zenon papyri. Josephus knew it in a different form as the name of a village in the territory of *Tyre (*Antiq.* II, 459; IV, 104-5). Titus pitched his camp in the vicinity of the village of Cydasa of the *Tyrians, because 'this was a strong inland village of the Tyrians, always at feud and strife with the Galileans' (*War* IV, 104 f). Eusebius (*Onom.* 116:10) calls it 'the city of Kydisos', in the vicinity of *Paneas, some 20 miles from Tyre. A Roman temple and a mausoleum of the same period were discovered there. Identified with Tell Qades, 12 miles north of Safed, where there are two ancient mounds, one of which was occupied from the 3rd millennium BC to the end of the Israelite period.

Since 1981 the Roman *temple has been excavated by a team of Tel Aviv University under the direction of I. Roll. Little of the upper structure of the temple has survived. The entire compound was surrounded by a wall. The temple (60 feet by 54 feet) was built of exquisitely-dressed ashlars. Its eastern facade rose to a height of 33 feet. At the western wall of the shrine is an apse, apparently a later addition which may have held Jupiter's statue. The triple doors of the temple are richly decorated. On the lintels are engraved Jupiter's eagle, a wreath in which was a rosette, bunches of grapes, a vine trellis, acanthus leaves, a deer, and a man's head. According to three Greek inscriptions, the temple was dedicated in AD 117/8 under Hadrian, and repairs were made in AD 214/5 and 280.

b) Kedesh-Naphtali, the seat of Barak, son of Abinoam (Judg. 4:6, 10). This Kedesh is identified with Khirbet Qedish.

c) A place in southeastern Judah, on the border of *Edom (Josh. 15:23). Not identified.

KEDESH-ON-THE-ORONTES One of the most important ancient cities in Syria, identified with Tell Nebi Mend in the plain of Homs, between the

The battle of Kedesh-on-the-Orontes in reliefs from the palace of Tuthmosis III

Lebanon and the Anti-Lebanon. The mound is 100 feet high and stretches for over $^3/_4$ mile along the Nahr el-Asi (Orontes). The site was excavated in 1921-2 by M. Pézard on behalf of the Académie des Inscriptions et Belles Lettres.

Kedesh is mentioned for the first time in connection with the first Asian campaign of Tuthmosis III, in about 1468 BC. In his account of the Battle of *Megiddo the Egyptian Pharaoh refers to Kedesh as the leader of the coalition against which he fought. During his 6th campaign the city was destroyed. During the campaigns of Amenophis II (c. 1447-1421 BC) the ruler of Kedesh took an oath of loyalty to Pharaoh. Among the reliefs of the temple of Sethos I (c. 1318-1301 BC) at Karnak is a scene depicting the war of Sethos against the *Hittites, which took place near Kedesh. The text reads: '...made desolate the land of Kedesh'. The city is mentioned for the last time in the Egyptian sources in connection with the campaign of Rameses II (c. 1301-1234 BC), who fought a Hittite coalition there. In the early 14th century BC, with the rise of the new Hittite empire, Suppiluliumas, King of the *Hittites, led a campaign against the kingdom of

Mitanni in *Mesopotamia, and on his way he fought the city of Kinza (another name for Kedesh) and defeated it. In the second half of the same century, according to the Hittite sources, Kinza revolted twice, but the revolt was put down and a treaty was signed.

In the course of the excavations at Tell Nebi Mend city walls were discovered, built of mud brick. The excavators attributed them to the *'Canaanite' period, but believed that they had been reused by the Seleucids. Important among the single finds from the *'Canaanite' period was the upper part of a stele of Sethos I, in which the Egyptian ruler is seen among the local gods. Four main occupation levels were observed on the site. The lowest level was tentatively identified as Amorite, but the pottery found in it helped to redate it to the Hyksos period. Indeed Kedesh was surrounded at that time with a typical Hyksos glacis. Above it was the Syro-Hittite level, which may be dated by the finds to the Late Bronze Age. Above this was a Syro-Phoenician level, of the Iron Age. The uppermost level was termed Greco-Syrian, but in fact extended well into the Hellenistic and Roman periods.

KEFAR BARAM A village in upper *Galilee about 7 miles northwest of Safed. The site is now known by its Arabic name, Kafr Birim, which most probably preserves the ancient form. Its earliest mention goes back to the 13th century AD, when it was visited by several Jewish pilgrims. They mention seeing two ancient synagogues and say that a Jewish congregation was still living there. The Jews of Kefar Baram continued to be mentioned in the following centuries, but after the middle of the 18th century the site lay in ruins. In 1866 the remains of both synagogues were still visible and were photographed, but by the turn of the century the smaller one had disappeared completely. According to the old photograph the central one of three doors had a lintel that was still *in situ*. On it were two winged Victories supporting a wreath, in which was a rosette.

The other, larger synagogue is in a much better state of preservation. The building is basilical and measures 40 feet by 55 feet, with three colonnades, on the east, west and north. There were three doors on the south, the side facing *Jerusalem. It is built of fine ashlar, laid dry. The whole building is paved with fine slabs of stone. Benches are built against the east and west walls. There is a door in the middle of the east wall, probably leading to a court, and a porch to the south, in front of the three doors, which rested on six columns and was two columns deep. The south facade of the synagogue was found to be in a good state of preservation. The central door again had a lintel decorated with a wreath. The birds or animals that once flanked or supported this wreath have been chiselled off, probably by Jewish iconoclasts (*Synagogues). Above the lintel rose a semicircular arch. The side doors had lintels decorated with rope patterns. Above each door was a rectangular niche crowned with a gable, in the center of which was a rosette. This synagogue is of the Galilean type, of the 3rd-4th centuries AD. Many architectural fragments that most probably belonged to it are built into the walls of modern houses nearby. One has the signs of the zodiac engraved on it, while another depicts a lion's head.

KEFAR NIBORAYA A village of the Roman and Byzantine periods in upper *Galilee, north of Safed, identified with Khirbet en-Nabartain. It is mentioned in the Talmud as the residence of several talmudic sages. In the 19th century remains of a synagogue were discovered there, but the site has not been excavated. The synagogue is basilical in plan, measuring 35 feet by 50 feet, and its single entrance is on the south, facing *Jerusalem. There are remains of two rows of columns on the long sides of the building, and there may possibly have been a third row on the short northern side, as was the normal arrangement (*Kefar Baram). Little of the decoration of the synagogue is visible on the surface, though the door lintel has survived. It is 9 feet 3in long and 2 feet high. The center is decorated with a menorah set within a wreath. Along the full length of the lintel is an inscription dated to the year 494 after the destruction of the Temple (i.e. AD 564). The synagogue itself, however, as well as the style of the lintel, does not permit a date later than the end of the 3rd century AD as with most of the other Galilean synagogues. The only possible explanation of the later date is that the inscription was engraved on an existing lintel when the synagogue was restored in the 6th century AD, a time when many synagogues were built.

In the years 1980-1 the *synagogue was excavated by E. Meyers and others on behalf of Duke University. Three phases in the history of the *synagogue were distinguished: *a)* a broad-house type of building, of AD 135-250; *b)* a basilical building of six columns, which was divided into two sub-phases, of AD 250-306, and AD 306-350/63; and *c)* a basilical building of eight columns, of AD 564-640/700. The earliest building was the smallest (33 feet by 30 feet). It had two platforms at the long, southern wall. An entrance to the building was located in the northeastern corner, and there may have been another one in the southern wall. Except for the southern wall, benches extended along all the walls. The roof of the building was apparently supported by four columns. The building of the second phase (33 feet by 40 feet) had two platforms at the short southern wall, flanking the entrance. On the western platform was found a gable of an *aedicula* (the Torah Shrine), decorated with a conch and two lions. The destruction of this synagogue is dated to the earthquake of AD 306. The latest synagogue (33 feet by 51 feet), of eight columns, is orientated north-south. It had no bema, but there were benches along the eastern and western walls. The floor was paved with large stone blocks. The entrance was in the southern wall, and above it was probably placed the lintel bearing the inscription of AD 564. There may have been an additional entrance to the prayer hall.

KEILAH A fortified town in the *Plain (Josh. 15:44, 1 Sam. 23:7). Mentioned in the *El Amarna letters, where it is related that the King of Keilah cooperated with the *Habiru. David saved the city from the *Philistines (1 Sam. 23:1-8) but was forced to leave it (1 Sam. 23:12-13). In the time of Rehoboam it was conquered by Pharaoh Sheshonq, biblical Shishak. It was divided into two parts at the time of the Restoration, each with its own ruler (Neh. 3:17-18). It was a village in the Roman period and its Greek name was Kela. Eusebius (*Onom.* 88:26; 114:16) locates the village Kela at a distance of 8 miles to the east of *Beth-Gubrin, on the way to *Hebron. Identified with Khirbet Qila, east of *Beth-Gubrin.

KENITES In some of the Semitic languages the name Kenite is the equivalent of 'smith'. This is the implication of 'Tubal-Cain, an instructor of every artificer in brass and iron' (Gen. 4:22). In one place in the Bible the Hebrew *keino* stands for spear, or perhaps metal weapons in general (2 Sam. 21:16; Authorized Version: 'spear'). It seems that Tubal-Cain is to be identified with Tubal, a nation mentioned in the Bible (Ezek. 27:13). It is also known from Assyrian documents, where it is said to produce metal objects and trade in copper in Asia Minor.

According to the Bible Moses' father-in-law was a Kenite (Judg. 1:16). The Kenites were akin to the Midianites and wandered in *Midian, *Edom, *Amalek, *Sinai, the *Negev and northern Palestine. In Balaam's song there is a possible indication that the

Kenites dwelt in the rock (Num. 24:21) not far from *Punon, one of the main sources of copper (*Metals).

After the conquest of *Canaan the Kenites settled in the *Negev (Judg. 1:16; Authorized Version: 'south of Arad'), and part of that region was named after them (1 Sam. 27:10; Hebrew Bible: 'Negeb of the Kenite'; Authorized Version: 'south of the Kenites'). It thus seems that the Kenites, together with some other semi-nomadic tribes, dwelt in the south of the country and held some kind of monopoly of copper mining and the production of copper artifacts. A rare confirmation of their presence in that region is provided by a Hebrew ostracon discovered recently at *Arad, in which a place by the name of Kinah is mentioned, together with another named Ramath-Negeb.

KERIOTH a) A town in Judah (Josh. 15:25). It is possible that Judas Iscariot, meaning 'man of Cariot' (Matt. 10:4, etc.), came from there. Tentatively identified with Khirbet el-Kariathein, north of *Arad.

b) A town in *Moab (Jer. 48:24, 41), mentioned in the stele of Mesha, King of *Moab (*Inscriptions), as a cult place of Chemosh, and identified with el-Qureiyat, northwest of *Dibon.

KEYS AND LOCKS There is evidence that houses were locked in some way in biblical times (cf. S. of S. 5:5; Neh. 3:3), but nowhere in Palestine have keys or locks of the period been found. On the other hand there are numerous examples from the Hellenistic period and even more from the Roman period. In ancient Greece a very simple form of lock existed: a wooden bar set behind the door, which slid into a hole in the doorpost. A more elaborate arrangement involved the bar being pulled across by a strap from the outside; the door could be opened by means of a key which passed through a hole and lifted up the pegs that held the bar in position. Roman locks were more complicated: an iron bolt was shot through the end link of a chain and secured by pins, the ends of which fitted into a series of perforations in the bolt and were kept down by a spring. The bolt was released by a key fitted with teeth corresponding to the perforations; this lifted the pins out of the holes and took their place. The bolt was then drawn aside as the key was moved along a horizontal slot. To accommodate the double movement — first vertical and then horizontal — the keyhole was in the form of a right-angled slit.

KHELEIFEH (TELL EL) Tell el-Kheleifeh is situated in the northern part of the Gulf of Aqabah. It was apparently first discovered during the survey of F. Frank in 1933, and its identification as Ezion-Geber was then suggested. In 1938-40 N. Glueck excavated the site on behalf of the Smithsonian Institution and the American School of Oriental Research. Its identification with the biblical town — where King Solomon built his Tarshish ships — is still accepted, in spite of the fact that no conclusive confirmation for it was found in Glueck's excavations, and some criticism was made of the results and interpretation of the excavations.

The main architectural feature revealed in Stratum I (called Period I by the excavator) is a large (43 feet), almost square, massive building. The inner, partition walls, which are about 3 feet thick, indicate the building was more than one story high, and no doubt dominated the surroundings. The building was surrounded by a casemate wall, in which a gateway was incorporated on the south side. The fortification system helped the excavator to fix the date of its construction to the days of Solomon, in the middle of the 10th century BC, and to relate its destruction to the invasion of the Egyptian king Sheshonq I in the last quarter of that century. As no other buildings were found inside the fortified area, the generally accepted interpretation of the structure is that it served as a storage center, military post or khan.

A drastic change is witnessed in Stratum (Period) II. The main building was reconstructed, and now stood in the corner and not the center of the fortified area. The fortifications underwent a complete change. A double wall, strengthened by two earthern ramparts and a dry moat, replaced the casemate wall of the previous strata and a new, four-chambered gate was added. The excavator dated the construction of this stratum to the first half of the 9th century BC, the days of King Jehoshaphat, and its destruction to the second half of that century, which would explain why after Jehoshaphat's death it is not mentioned again in the Bible. Its destruction should be assigned, according to Glueck, to one of the acts of rebellion of the Edomites against Jehoram, Jehoshaphat's son.

Stratum (Period) III was constructed after a long period of desertion. It is the last Israelite (Judean) settlement on the site. Its establishment is assigned to King Jotham, the sucessor of King Uzziah, in the 8th century BC. On the basis of the appearance of his name on a seal ('belonging to Jotham'). The new site is similar in size and general plan to the previous one. The discovery of houses built close together in this stratum, indicate that in this period the site was more densely populated than in the previous ones, if the stratigraphical assignment of the dwellings to Stratum III is indeed correct.

The next stratum was built by the Edomites. Three different phases of this stratum, extending from the end of the 8th century down to the end of the 6th century BC, indicate a long and intensive settlement under Edomite rule. The site was crowded with buildings and the abundance of Edomite pottery, as well as other finds, such as seals and store jars, seem to indicate that the site served as a trading post. A short South Arabian inscription and some Egyptian objects demonstrate the vast extent of that trade. The Edomite period came to an end with the Babylonian conquest, according to the excavator's interpretation, or with the Assyrian decline a little earlier, as suggested by other authorities.

Stratum (Period) IV belongs to the Persian period, and was dated by Glueck from the late 6th or the early 5th century BC to the late 5th or early 4th century BC. It continued to play a major role in trading activities, as an international trade route passed through that area. A large collection of inscriptions from this stratum testifies to the intensity of that activity. The place was abandoned, probably in the early 5th century BC, and was never rebuilt.

KHIAM TERRACE (EL-) The site is located at the confluence of Wadi el-Khiam and Wadi Khareitun at the foot of a limestone escarpment in the *Judean Desert. R. Neuville excavated two trial trenches here in 1933 and the results were later published by J. Perrot. In 1962 J.G. Echegaray excavated an area of 40sq yd.

The lowest levels, labelled 11 and 12 by Echegaray, include an assemblage assigned by him to the Lower and Middle Aurignacian era, though according to Neuville's classification it is Upper Paleolithic IV. It consists mainly of nosed and carinated scrapers, as well as burins. In layers 9 and 10 the number of burins increases, especially those of the truncated type, and numerous scrapers were found. This denotes an industry characteristic of the end of the local Aurignacian era. Layers 8 to 6 are rich in geometric microliths and are typified by the evolution of crescents. This assemblage was assigned to the Kebaran Culture, but is undoubtedly later than that of the *Kebara Cave.

The assemblage from layers 5 to 4 was labelled as Khiamian by Echegaray, but is considered by Neuville and Perrot to be Natufian. It differs from the usual Natufian assemblage in the development of arrowheads and the almost complete absence of other Natufian elements such as burials and structural remains. Layer 1 contains remains of structures and built-up hearths and a few heavy-duty tools. The finds at el-Khiam indicate an almost continuous occupation of this desert or semi-desert site by groups of hunters. (*See also* *PREHISTORY; *FLINT TOOLS.)

KHIRBET SHEMA *See* *SHEMA (KHIRBET:)

KHIRBET QUMRAN *See* *QUMRAN (KHIRBET).

KHUWEILIFEH (TELL) *See* *HALIF (TEL) *See* *GOSHEN.

KIDRON A valley running between the Temple Mount and the Mount of *Olives and extending through the *Judean Desert to the *Dead Sea. Also referred to in the Bible as 'the brook' (Neh. 2:15) or 'the valley' (2 Chr. 33:14). On the western slope of the valley is the *Gihon, the main permanent water source for *Jerusalem. The eastern slope served as a necropolis in the times of the First and Second Temples (*Jerusalem). By the brook of Kidron Asa, King of Judah, destroyed the idol made by Maachah (1 Kgs. 15:13) and Hilkiah burnt the vessels made for Baal (2 Kgs. 23:4).

KIR-HARASETH; KIR-HARESH; KIR-HERES *See* *KIR MOAB.

KIRJATH-JEARIM A very important town on the northern border of the territory of Judah. Its ancient names were Baale of Judah (2 Sam. 6:2), Baalah (Josh. 15:9) and Mount Baalah (Josh. 15:11), attesting to the cult of Baal at this place. It was one of the cities of the Gibeonites (Josh. 9:17) and later a town on the border of Judah (Josh. 15:9-10, 60), close to the southwestern frontier of Benjamin. It was the last place where the Ark of the Covenant rested before reaching *Jerusalem (2 Sam. 6:2, etc.). The town was resettled after the Restoration (Neh. 7:29). According to Eusebius (*Onom.* 48:22; 114:23) it is situated on the road between Jerusalem and *Lod, 9 miles from Jerusalem.

View of the Kidron Valley from the tomb of the priestly family of Bene Hezir

KIRJATH-SEPHER The ancient name of *Debir (Josh. 15:15; Judg. 1:11).

KIR MOAB The capital of *Moab, a stronghold situated on top of a lofty mountain. Surrounded by a massive wall, it dominated the road from the Gulf of *Elath to *Damascus. In the Bible it is referred to as Kir-Hareseth, Kir-Haresh (Isa. 16:7, 11) and Kir-Heres (Jer. 48:31). Jehoram, son of Ahab, King of Israel, and Jehoshaphat, King of Judah, attacked Kir-Haraseth but could not take it (2 Kgs. 3:1, 25-6). The site is identified with el-Kerak, northeast of *Sodom. In the Roman and Byzantine periods it was in the Provincia Arabia, under the name of Characmoba. In the 2nd century AD it was apparently the center of a district, as may be inferred from the seal impressions of that city found at *Mampsis. The Roman-Byzantine town is mentioned in some of the ancient sources and appears on the *Medaba map.

Clay seal from Mampsis, mentioning the town of Characmoba (Kir Moab)

KISAN (TEL) One of the largest mounds in Israel located in the heart of the Plain of Acco. Its importance is due to the fertility of the region and its proximity to the marshes (providing wild fowl and larger game) and to the ancient port-city of *Acco (Acre), approximately 6 miles away. Kisan was the link between the mountainous region and the coast where the grain from the inland was traded for goods brought by ship to Acco. Attempts have been made to identify it with a biblical site. Kishion, Alammelech, and Mishal have been proposed - and especially Achsaph which is mentioned in Egyptian documents of the 2nd millennium BC and in the Book of Joshua - but all of these suggestions have been rejected. The site was excavated by the English Nielson Expedition in 1935-6, and by the French Ecole Biblique in 1971-80.

The rocky elevation of Kisan served as a shelter in prehistoric times. In the Early Bronze Age a town, extending over an area of 25 acres, and surrounded by a brick wall, was established on the site. The following Middle Bronze Age town was smaller and consisted of 15 acres. It was protected by a Cyclopean wall. A deep well at the foot of the mound reached groundwater. At that time Kisan was a prosperous and powerful city-state which served as a distribution center for goods, arriving from other areas. Egyptian stelae indicate that it was under Egyptian domination at the beginning of the Late Bronze Age. In spite of upheavals, agriculture and trade ensured a continuous settlement from the end of the Bronze Age and through the Iron Age I up to the 1st millennium BC. This was quite remarkable since the beginning of the Iron Age coincides with a period of economic and demographic decline in Palestine.

Kisan very likely served as a refuge during raids of the coast by marauders. In this period the site was invaded by successive waves of the Sea Peoples. Pottery found at the site attests to the harmonious integration of the newcomers with the local Canaanite population. The Plain of Acco then came under the influence of the sea and the Phoenicians. Kisan was coveted by semi-nomads who took control of the hill

region. These nomads were the first waves of Arameans (11th century BC). The region was probably also visited by scattered groups of Hebrews who roamed the country. Kisan was violently destroyed in about 1000 BC. This date marks the end of a prosperity that lasted several thousand years. During the period of the Monarchy, Kisan was, curiously enough, an impoverished town, as is hinted at in 1 Kings 9:11-13 (if the region mentioned is that of Kabul ceded to Tyre by Solomon) by Hiram who declared that the towns ceded to him 'did not please him'. After the fall of Samaria (721 BC), Kisan underwent a period of revival and development under neo-Assyrian control (large quantities of Phoenician pottery were found and signs of close contacts with Cyprus were distinguished). It is quite possible that this revival followed a transfer of population from the Levant.

The town was again sacked between 650 and 600 BC and never again regained its former prosperity. Excavations revealed Persian occupation strata which reflected a period of decline followed by a well populated and active Hellenistic town which, however, revealed no outstanding accomplishments. The site was abandoned in the 2nd century BC, perhaps after a raid by Simon Maccabaeus in 163 BC. Five centuries later the summit of the tell was occupied by a small Christian village built around a church. This last settlement was completely dismantled by Saladin at the time of the siege of Saint-Jean d'Acre (1191) in order to establish his headquarters there.

KISHON A river in the western part of the *Jezreel Valley, which draws its water from the mountains of *Gilboa and *Nazareth. It is perennial only in the last 6 miles of its course. During the Battle of Deborah and Barak, which took place in the winter, the river overflowed its shallow banks, bringing disaster to Sisera's chariots (Judg. 4:7, 13, 5:21). It flows along the foot of Mount *Carmel, where Elijah slew the prophets of Baal (1 Kgs. 18:40). The river mouth served as a harbor in ancient times. Nearby is Tell *Abu Hawam, which is thought to contain the remains of *Libnah or *Zalmon.

L

LACHISH One of the central cities in the *Plain, whose king was one of the five who fought Joshua at *Gibeon and were subdued by the Israelites (Josh. 10:23). Later it became one of the fortified cities in Judah (2 Chr. 11:5, 9). Amaziah, King of Judah, was killed at Lachish, having fled there from the conspirators in *Jerusalem (2 Kgs. 14:19; 2 Chr. 25:27). The town played an important defensive role when Sennacherib made war on Judah, but was taken by him (2 Chr. 32; Isa. 36). A century later it was conquered by Nebuchadnezzar (Jer. 34:7). Lachish also appears in other historical sources: it is mentioned several times in the *El Amarna letters of the 14th century BC; in a contemporary tablet from Tell el-*Hesi; and Assyrian documents refer to the siege of Sennacherib and his conquest of the city, which are also depicted in the reliefs in his palace at *Nineveh.

According to Eusebius (*Onom.* 120:20) Lachish was situated 7 miles from Eleutheropolis (*Beth-Gubrin) on the road leading south. In the 19th century it was identified with Tell el-*Hesi. But as a result of excavations an identification with Tell el-Duweir has been accepted by all scholars. The site was excavated in 1932-8 by J.L. Starkey on behalf of the Wellcome-Marston Research Expedition in the Near East, but the work was halted when its director was murdered by a gang of Arab looters.

In the nearby valley prehistoric remains have been discovered. The caves with which the hill of Lachish is honeycombed were settled for the first time at the end of the Chalcolithic period. This troglodyte settlement continued to flourish in the first two phases of the Early Bronze Age, but in Early Bronze Age III the caves were used for communal burials. The first houses were built on the site in the Middle Bronze Age I. The building remains are scanty, so most of our knowledge derives from 120 rock-cut tombs found in a cemetery southwest of the mound. In the Middle Bronze Age II Lachish became one of the important Hyksos fortresses. Little of this city has been excavated, but there is enough evidence to show that it was protected by a glacis and a moat. In this period, too, reliance must be placed mainly on the rich finds from the tombs.

In the Late Bronze Age Lachish reached the peak of its development. In the moat, which had already gone out of use, three temples were found superimposed one upon another. The earliest was a rectangular building, 30 feet by 15 feet, with some additional rooms adjoining it. Close to the south wall of the main hall was an altar made of mud, which can be dated to the 15th century BC by the numerous pottery vessels discovered nearby. In the Late Bronze Age IIB (14th century BC) a second temple 30 feet square was built. A stone altar stood on the same site as the earlier one. This temple is of the *El Amarna period. A third temple, on the same plan as the previous one, was built in the 13th century BC. Along the walls were brick-built benches on which offering were placed. In the south wall was a niche, probably for a deity. In this temple numerous offerings, such as incense and libation vessels, pottery imported from Cyprus and Mycenae, ivory carvings, clay figurines and scarabs were found. In pits near the temple were large quantities of animal bones, most probably from sacrifices. An inscription on a bowl belonging to the same period helps in dating the destruction of this temple by the Israelite conquerors to about 1220 BC (*Inscriptions). Most of the material relating to Late Bronze Age Lachish comes from these temples and from the tombs. The occupation levels of the period were studied to a limited extent in a section made in the city. The earliest temple is related to stratum VII in the city and the latest one to stratum VI. The last Late Bronze Age stratum yielded some inscriptions, two of them Canaanite of the 13th century BC.

The earliest Iron Age remains date back to the 10th century BC (stratum V). The period between the conquest of Lachish by the Israelites and the 12th century BC is poorly represented. This may well explain the absence of biblical data relating to the period between the conquest and the rebuilding of the city by Rehoboam. The earliest Israelite remains are the foundations of a palace (palace A). It is 100 feet square and is built on the ruins of a Late Bronze Age palace. Its construction is attributed to Rehoboam (928-911 BC). To the time of Asa (908-867 BC, stratum IV) is attributed the building of a city wall, a section of which, 18 feet thick, was discovered in the excavations. To the time of Jehoshaphat (870-846 BC) is attributed the enlargement of the fortified palace, which now extended a further 140 feet towards the south (palace

B). It was subsequently further enlarged (palace C of stratum III). In its final stage the building covered an area of 120 feet by 240 feet. On one of the steps leading to the palace the first five letters of the Hebrew alphabet were found. Close to the palace were numerous stamped jar handles of the *lamelek* type (*Seals).

The city of stratum III was strongly fortified and surrounded by a double wall. The inner wall, 18 feet thick and encircling the summit of the hill, was of bricks. The outer wall, 17 feet high, was built along the middle of the slope on a stone foundation, above which stood the superstructure of bricks. The wall was further strengthened by buttresses and towers. The city gate is on the west. It was protected by a huge bastion measuring 83 feet by 68 feet. On the east of the town a formidable shaft measuring 75 feet by 75 feet by 66 feet was found. It was probably intended to provide the city with a safe water supply, as at *Megiddo and *Hazor, but was never completed. The city of stratum III suffered catastrophic destruction and its remains are buried under a layer of ashes 3 feet thick. Above the remains of this city a new one was built, that of stratum II. The masonry of the houses here is poor. The walls and the gate were rebuilt, but the palace was abandoned. In the gate a series of rooms were added in one of which the famous Lachish letters (*Inscriptions) were found. This city was also destroyed, probably at the time of Nebuchadnezzar's

campaign against Zedekiah in 587 BC. This date is accepted by all scholars, but the cause and date of the destruction of stratum III is much disputed. Some believe that it was the work of Sennacherib in 701 BC. Others, however, tend to attribute it to Nebuchadnezzar's first campaign in 597 BC, basing their conclusion on a comparison of the pottery of strata III and II, which shows only minor variations. Those who hold the latter view believe that the remains of the city that was destroyed by the Assyrians have still to be discovered.

The cemeteries of the Israelite cities yielded numerous finds. One tomb, in a large cave, contained about 2,000 bodies, thrown into the cave through a hole in the roof. Some of them were charred. It is possible that these were the remains of Israelites killed in the war against the Babylonians.

Lachish of the Israelite period yielded much epigraphic material. In addition to the letters, about 300 stamped jar handles were found. There were also 48 private seals, the most interesting being the seal of 'Gedalyhu which is over the house', and numerous inscribed weights. The latest city, that of stratum I, was of the Persian period (mid-5th century BC). On the site of the Israelite palace there now stood a public building measuring 50 feet by 90 feet, consisting of a large court around which halls and rooms were grouped.

The siege of Lachish depicted in one of the reliefs from Sennacherib's palace, Nineveh

In the eastern part of the city a building identified as a Solar Shrine had been excavated. In the years 1966-7 Y. Aharoni conducted further excavation in this temple on behalf of the Hebrew University and Tel Aviv University. Because of Persian pottery found beneath the foundations and Hellenistic pottery found in the foundation trenches, the building was dated to the Hellenistic period. Still deeper, and around this building, were discovered remains of buildings from the Late Bronze and Iron Ages (Strata VI-II). Beneath the interior of the Hellenistic temple were found objects belonging to an Israelite high-place, including a large stone stele (*massebah*), the remains of the trunk of an olive tree which had been intentionally buried (an *asherah*?), and several pits containing broken stone stelae and votive objects. Nearby was a room (12 feet by 16 feet) with plastered benches along its walls and a platform in its western corner. Near the platform were found a horned incense stone altar and a number of clay incense burners, as well as numerous other pottery vessels. This shrine was destroyed in the 10th century BC. Thus, as at *Arad and *Beer-Sheba, the Israelite Iron Age tradition persisted into the later period, at which time Lachish was again inhabited by Jews (cf. Neh. 11:30). This conclusion is also supported by the following evidence: Sennacherib's reliefs show two decorated incense burners; more than 150 small stone incense burners of the Persian period were found at Lachish; and an identical building dating from the Late Bronze Age to the early Hellenistic period was already discovered in the first excavations at a small distance southeast of the Solar Shrine, in which a stone incense altar was also found. Because of these facts Aharoni suggested the possibility that the Jewish cult tradition went back to still earlier times.

In the years 1973-8 excavations at Tel Lachish were resumed by Tel Aviv University under the direction of D. Ussishkin.

On the southwest side of the mound, just outside the city walls, the first excavators had noted that the *fortifications of the city were of exceptional strength, made to meet the topographical weakness in this part of the mound. It seems that the Assyrian army concentrated its assault at this point. At this spot Ussishkin discovered the remains of the Assyrian siege platform, made of unhewn stones bound with mortar. This platform is 165-180 feet wide at its base, narrowing above, and rising to a height of some 18 feet. On the reliefs of Sennacherib's palace at *Nineveh these installations can clearly be seen. This is the earliest known siege ramp in the Middle East. Around the ramp hundreds of arrowheads were found.

The Iron Age Gate. Excavations were renewed in the previously investigated gate. An interesting discovery was made in one of the guardrooms of the last phase of Stratum III (760-701 BC): remains of the bronze fittings of the gate as well as remains of its wooden doors still in the bronze door-hinges. These were made of acacia wood, a tree growing in the *Negev. North and east of the gate were discovered structures belonging to the last phase of Stratum III. One of these (13 feet by 5.5 feet) was apparently a

cellar in which were stored numerous vessels, some of them jars with *lamelek* *seals. The cellar was burnt at the same time as the gate in 701 BC.

The Israelite Fortified *Palace and the Persian Citadel: The excavations in Palace C of Stratum III revealed large quantities of burnt mud bricks, of the final destruction in 701 BC. It was only in the Persian period (and not in the 7th century BC, as Aharoni believed) that the Residence was built. Starkey had dated it on the basis of its pottery to the 5th century BC. The new excavations confirmed this view. It continued in existence until the middle of the 4th century BC. This new structure (150 feet by 109 feet) extended over the entire podium of the Israelite palaces, except for sections on the south and north, which had gone out of use. The old stairway on the northeast was also used in the Persian period. During the earlier excavations three halls, 96 feet long and 18 feet wide, were discovered along the northern end of the podium. These were probably storerooms constructed at the same time that Palace B (9th century BC) was built. A

Fertility goddess from Lachish, Late Bronze Age

similar structure (60 feet by 30 feet) was also discovered to the southeast of the podium, with a triple interior division, which was identified at *Megiddo as 'stables' and at *Beer-Sheba as 'barracks' These too are contemporaneous with Palace B, and suffered the same fate. Excavations were also carried out west of the Palace where a 14 feet wide wall joins the southwestern corner of the Palace and the city-wall. This strong wall was part of a system of walls protecting the palace and separating it from the rest of the town. The excavations indicated that the wall and Palace B are contemporaneous (Stratum IV, 9th/8th centuries BC). When Palace C was built (Stratum III, 8th century BC), the city wall was also repaired.

At its northwestern end the Israelite palace was built above an Egyptian-Canaanite *temple dating to the end of the 14th or beginning of the 13th century BC. It consists of a 40 feet by 18 feet porch (ulam), a 40 feet by 50 feet hall (hechal) and a narrow Holy of Holies (debir). The temple is of an east-west orientation. The Holy of Holies is 4 feet higher than the porch and hall, and the approach to the hall is through seven steps. The hall was paved with mud bricks and its roof was supported by two columns, 3 feet in diameter. Charred cedar wood beams were found in the debris. On the steps were the remains of a pair of wooden supports, apparently of a baldachin with which the Holy of Holies was covered, or, perhaps they were similar to the Jachin and Boaz pillars in the *Temple of Jerusalem. Within the compound were found several graffiti, one portraying the god Resheph, as he is depicted on Egyptian monuments.

LAISH The ancient name of *Dan, before its conquest by the *Danites (Judg. 18:29). It is mentioned as *rws* in the *Execration Texts and in the lists of Tuthmosis III.

LAMPS The lamp, in the form of a small clay bowl in which oil was burned, was the most common form of domestic lighting from very early times. As olive oil was plentiful in Palestine, this was the fuel normally used in lamps (cf. Exod. 27:20; Lev. 24:2); the wick was usually made of flax (Isa. 42:3). According to the Mishna (Shabb. 2:1-3) a much greater variety of oils was used for lighting in the Roman period, including oils extracted from sesame seeds, nuts, horseradish and vegetable resins: naphta (an inflammable oil, obtained by dry distillation of coal, shale, etc.) is also mentioned. The shapes of lamps, and the materials from which they were made, are never specified in the Bible, but clay lamps are among the most common pottery vessels found in the archaeological remains, both in dwellings and in tombs. Since they were very simple and cheap household utensils their shape was not influenced by fashion as much as that of other pottery vessels. They do, however, constitute an important aid to dating. In later periods they are also an important source for the study of art, religious customs and symbols.

The earliest identifiable lamps are those of the Early Bronze Age. These take the form of simple round bowls; in fact it would be quite difficult to distinguish them from other bowls were it not for the blackened spot left by the burning wick. A change in shape

occurred in the Middle Bronze Age I, when the rims were pressed inwards to form four spouts into which the wicks were inserted. The base of these lamps is either flat or rounded. This type did not last long and was replaced in the Middle Bronze Age by a simple bowl with a slightly inward-curving rim, pinched in one place only, and a rounded base. This design became common and there was little change throughout the Late Bronze Age, except that the spout became much more pronounced.

Although the basic principle remains unaltered, there is much more variation in the Iron Age. The lamp of this period has a broad flat rim, a pronounced wick spout and a flat base, which tends to become higher as time goes on until it is even placed on a high stand. Sometimes the lamp and the stand are two separate parts. Less common are lamps with seven wicks, both with and without stands. Somewhat different is the 'cup-and-saucer' type, a vessel consisting of a small bowl with a cup attached. The cup sometimes has one or three small holes through to the bowl, but the identification of this vessel as a lamp is in fact somewhat doubtful, as none has so far been found with a blackened spout on the rims. Bronze lamps were found only rarely.

In the Persian period high-footed lamps disappear completely and the flat bowl lamps become even shallower, preserving the broad Iron Age rim. The base becomes somewhat concave. At this period bronze lamps, similar in shape to their clay prototypes, make their first appearance. From the Hellenistic period onwards, and especially in the Roman period, it is the bronze lamps that influence the design of the clay vessels.

In the 5th century BC, as closer contacts with the western world were established, Greek lamps began to appear. Greek potters had succeeded in producing a closed lamp, thus preventing the oil from spilling. The body of this type of lamp is round, the base concave, the rim slightly incurving, and the nozzle is a separate piece attached to the body. The clay of these lamps is of a far higher quality than that of the local ones and has a lustrous black glaze. A strap handle is attached to the body. In the 5th and 4th centuries BC local imitations of this type were produced in the east; these were inferior in texture and glaze and were sometimes even unglazed.

From its first appearance in the Early Bronze Age up to the late 4th century BC the clay lamp was invariably made on the potter's wheel. In the early Hellenistic period a basic change occurred with the introduction of the mould. This speeded up production and also provided a means of decorating the lamps. In the purely Jewish settlements the bowl lamp was still used, though its shape changed: the flat rim disappeared and the sides were completely pressed together to form a kind of cornucopia. The Greek closed lamp and its local imitations were also in common use during the 4th and 3rd centuries BC. They tended to become deeper, thus providing more lighting hours. Their disc or ring bases ensured a better footing, and some now had a larger handle. Early in the 3rd century BC potters in various Greek centers had already begun to make lamps in moulds. In this process a lamp made of wood, clay or metal served as a matrix from which clay moulds were made. The potter would then press well-powdered clay into the mould. When it had become leather-hard the two parts of the lamp were removed from the moulds, the excess clay was pared off and the filling-hole and the wick-hole were punched out. The two halves were then stuck together and the lamp was ready for firing in the kiln. Another method of preparing a mould was to carve it out of soft limestone. At first moulded lamps imitated those made on the wheel, the decoration consisting of simple geometric or vegetal designs; it was not until the Roman period that this great invention, which turned lamp production into an independent industry, was exploited to the full.

The lamps of the 3rd and 2nd centuries BC have a round or rounded body and a concave disc for the filling-hole, sometimes with additional small holes to ensure that no oil was wasted. The base is flat and the nozzle elongated, terminating either in a sharp triangle or in a bow shape. Many lamps have a large loop handle. Where more light was needed multiple-spouted lamps called *policandelia* were used. These were made either by joining several lamps at the base or by attaching seven spouts to a single larger container, in the form of a seven-pointed star. Towards the 1st century BC lamp production deteriorated and shapes, decoration and glaze (if any) became very austere.

By the middle of the 1st century BC a new type of lamp had made its appearance in Palestine. In contrast to the Hellenistic lamps of the previous centuries and the Roman lamps that appeared in the last quarter of the century it was not moulded but made on the wheel. It is known as 'Herodian', although it in fact made its appearance before Herod's accession and did not disappear until the 2nd century AD. It is made of very finely powdered clay and has a clock-shaped body and a large filling-hole with a ridge around it. The nozzle was made separately and took the form of a splayed arch with a large wick-hole. This type is characterized by the use of a method of knife paring, which made it extremely thin and light. Most of these lamps have no decoration, though some do have incised lines and/or small circles between the nozzle and the body. By the middle of the 1st century AD lamps with more decoration occur, especially when they began to be moulded again. This later type has a loop handle, and by the end of the 1st century is much more lavishly decorated. It seems that the Herodian lamp was mainly used in the region of the Judean Hills, though it was not entirely confined to the use of the Jews, as may be deduced from lamps found in the potter's workshop at *Oboda and certain other Nabatean sites.

In mixed or non-Jewish towns the Roman lamp, known as 'Augustan', is more common. This is round, has a very large disc with a small hole for filling and a triangular or bow-shaped nozzle. As they were made in a mould such lamps could be decorated in a wide variety of ways, mostly on the discs. The decoration ranges from simple rosettes to images of deities,

Clay lamp, Early Roman period

scenes taken from everyday life, animals, birds, fairly coarse erotic scenes, political and religious propaganda and so one. Some lamps of this kind found on sites that were known to be Jewish had their decorative discs broken off, probably in accordance with the prohibition against graven images in the second commandment.

By the middle of the 1st century AD a new type of lamp was being produced in Palestine. This replaced the Herodian lamp completely before the middle of the 2nd century AD and predominated during the next centuries. Lamps of this type are round, flatter than the previous models, and have a large disc, a small filling-hole and a comparatively small round nozzle. Here too there is a wide range of decoration, and deliberately damaged discs have again been observed. During the late Roman period this type became more elongated, with a smaller disc and a larger filling-hole. The decoration, mostly conventional, is limited to the rim and the nozzle, and the handle becomes a mere knob. The nozzle is still rounded, as in the prototype. During the 4th century AD a somewhat smaller lamp evolved, with a more pronounced bow-shaped nozzle. The body is mostly decorated with formal designs, but the space between the nozzle and the body sometimes bears Jewish symbols, such as a menorah, an amphora, a bunch of grapes or an arched façade. In the Byzantine period the most common type of lamp is a development of the late Roman model. It is generally decorated with simple motifs, including certain Christian symbols.

Towards the end of the Byzantine period lamps made on the wheel reappear. They are made of coarse red clay, similar to the material used for cooking pots, and are undecorated. They resemble a boot with a high looped handle and, like Byzantine cooking pots, are ribbed. Alongside these, lamps that developed from those made in a mould are also common; they have similar linear decorations. Among the latter are some decorated with a menorah or a cross and the inscription, 'The light of Jesus shines for everyone'. A large variety of glass and bronze lamps is also found in the Roman and Byzantine periods, the bronze ones being mostly imported from Roman and other provinces.

LEATHER Raw hides and skins were most probably the earliest form of covering for the human body, and the large variety of flint scrapers and burins found in quantities on prehistoric sites were no doubt used to treat hides. To prevent decay they had to be 'cured'. In the earliest periods (and even in primitive societies today) they were tanned merely by being salted and then dried in the sun. It was only later that antiseptics were used. The hide was prepared for tanning by being washed and scraped to remove any dirt, hair and flesh still adhering to it. A tannery has been discovered in *Egypt and this has revealed the materials used in the tanning process. The tanning agents were vegetables, *Acacia arabica willd.* and *Acacia nilotica desf.* Some tomb paintings show that the hide was soaked in a pot, then placed to dry and worked on a wooden tripod. The leather was softened by being soaked in oil and thinned by being beaten with a wooden hammer. It was then ready to be used for making footwear, parts of garments, covers for shields, tents for the army and so on. It could also be dyed.

Skins (Lev. 11:2; 15:17), shoes (Amos 2:6) and the oiling of leather are referred to in the Bible, and Adam and Eve wore coats of skins (Gen. 3:21); but it tells us little about the method used for producing leather. The craft is referred to in the New Testament however: Acts (9:43) records that Peter stayed with Simon the tanner in *Joppa. The Mishna and the Talmud offer a great deal more information about tanning. Here too we are told that the hide was washed, beaten in water to get the dirt off, flayed and soaked in water containing oak-galls or sumach (leaves from a type of shrub).

Hides for making parchment were salted and treated with flour. To make the raw hide supple it was spread out in the street for passers-by to walk on. It was then beaten and treated with dog's dung, washed and thoroughly dried before being cut. In the *Judean Desert Caves sandals, belts and bags made of leather were found. A tanner was not accepted in society because of the stench of the materials that he had to handle and the carcasses that he was forced to touch. The tanner had to collect the dung with his own hands — which would, according to the Jewish Law, give his wife grounds for divorce. The Law also required that a tannery be built well away from the town, on the east, the side away from the prevailing wind.

LEBANON A range of mountains along the northern border of Palestine, 270 miles long and 45 miles wide, with peaks rising to a height of 10,000 feet. The tops of the mountains are covered with snow for most of the year (Jer. 18:14) — hence its name, now identified with a modern state, which in Hebrew means 'white'. It was called *rmm* in Egyptian documents and Labnuna in the Assyrian ones.

The Lebanon became famous for its cedars, cypresses and other splendid trees. In early historic times its timber was already being exported, especially to *Egypt, which had no timber of its own for roofing and shipbuilding. The cedars of Lebanon were used in the building of the First Temple, for Solomon's palace and for the Second Temple in *Jerusalem (Judg. 9:15; 1 Kgs. 5:6; 7:15, etc.). The Assyrian kings cut down trees in Lebanon for their buildings and palaces and used the tall cedars to make masts for their ships (Ezek. 27:5). The area was also noted for its grapes and wine. At the end of the 1st century BC the Romans founded a colony of veteran soldiers at Berytus (Beirut) in order to seize the Lebanon. In one of the higher valleys in the mountain range they built the city of *Heliopolis, which became renowned for the magnificent temples built there during the Roman period. At that time much timber was felled in the Lebanon, chiefly cypresses and firs, for building Roman ships. Little of the former woodland remains today.

LEBANON (VALLEY OF) The valley between the mountains of *Lebanon and the Anti-Lebanon, which extends from Laodicea to Chalcis, the northern limit of the conquests of Joshua (Josh. 11:17). Known today as el-Buqeia, 'the valley'.

LEGIO After the Bar-Kochba Revolt an additional legion, the Legio VI Ferrata, was sent to the province of Judea and stationed at Ceparcotnei (Ptolemy V, 15, 3), the Kefar Otnay of the Mishna (Gittin 2:5; 7:7). The place became known as Legio and is identified

Altar from Legio, Roman period

with the Arab village of Lejjun. The legion's camp received the *Jezreel Valley as an estate. According to Roman law this area thus became *territorium legionis* and belonged to the Roman Empire. In later sources it was called Campus Maximus Legionis (Eusebius *Onom.* 110, 21). The area had been Hasmonean, and also a Herodian royal domain; it had been pillaged by the Roman army during the First Jewish Revolt because it was a center of Jewish activities, but was apparently soon resettled. An altar set up by an officer of the Legio IV Ferrata, found in the vicinity of Legio, belongs to the reign of Elagabalus (AD 218-22). After the legion was withdrawn, in the time of Diocletian, Legio became a city and, according to the Pilgrim of Bordeaux, was renamed Maximinianopolis in honor of Maximianus Herculius, Diocletian's colleague. Eusebius, however, always used the old name (*Onom.* 14, 21). In the Byzantine period the city was the seat of a bishop.

LIBNAH *a)* A Canaanite town in the *Plain conquered by Joshua (Josh. 10:29-30) and given to the priests, also a city of refuge (Josh. 21:13). It resisted the onslaught of Sennacherib (2 Kgs. 19:8). Eusebius (*Onom.* 120:25) mentions a village by the name of Lobana on the border of *Beth-Gubrin. Identified by some scholars with Tell es-*Safi, but others suggest that it should be sought closer to *Lachish. More recently Libnah has been identified with Tell Burna, which was settled in the Early Bronze Age and Iron Age I-II.

b) The 10th station from the *Red Sea along the route of the Exodus (Num. 33:20-1), possibly the same as Laban (Deut. 1:1). It may perhaps be identified with Bir el-Beida, about 20 miles south of *Kadesh-Barnea.

LIMES Roman term for secure and fortified borders. From the time of Augustus (until AD 14), the emperors of Rome had to deal with the momentous task of protecting their approximately 6,000 square mile land border separating their empire which contained a heterogeneous group of peoples, from actual and potential enemies situated beyond this border. These enemies included on the one hand the great Persian power, the Parthians, and on the other, farmers and settled peoples, such as those living in Britain, as well as Arabian nomadic tribes in the East. The prevention of enemy penetration and a guaranteed peaceful and secure existence within the confines of the Roman Empire was one of the greatest compensations granted to the inhabitants of the state in return for the loss of their national autonomy. The *Pax Romana* thus represented an indispensable foundation for the continuation and prosperity of the empire.

Augustus based his system of border defense on legions and auxiliary units (*auxilia*) which were deployed in permanent posts along the border with the barbarians (i.e. non-Roman world) and which were capable of mobile warfare conducted outside their camps. However, during the many centuries of its existence, a great many changes were introduced into this defense system. These include:

Flexible defense system From the time of Augustus to the Flavian period.

Transitional period Flavian period (AD 69-98). From this time the first literary reference to the *limes* as a fortification system has survived (Tacitus, *Agricola* 41, 2).

Static defense system In Hadrian's time (117-138), the strategy of border defense evolved which combined a chain of permanent frontier fortifications, including a network of watchtowers and front-line positions, with well-fortified camps in the rear. In some border regions continuous barriers were erected, such as Hadrian's Wall in Britain and the German and Raetian *Limes*. In deploying the troops there was a tendency to surrender depth for the sake of achieving maximum density.

Reforms of Diocletion and Constantine (284-387). In this period there was a redeployment of forces in depth and a clear distinction was made between the border defense forces (*ripenses*) and the mobile general reserve (*comitatenses*). The regular army units were turned into general reserve forces (*limitanei*) which were allotted state lands on the borders. These farmer-soldiers were freed from the obligation of paying most of the regular taxes and tithes on condition that they served for fixed periods each year and for the duration of any emergency threatening their particular region. This arrangement served the dual purpose of increasing the motivation of the border forces to protect their homes and property, and of easing the burden of paying salaries by compensating the forces with land allotments. At the head of each border unit stood a senior commander (*dux*, e.g. *dux Palaestinae*, *Dux Arabiae*).

Byzantine period. The cities of the border provinces were now included within the permanent chain of frontier defenses. Towards the end of this period (5th century in Europe, 6th-7th centuries in the East), the agricultural border units lost much of their military importance and were turned into regular rural settlements. Furthermore, in this period an increasing number of defensive duties were transferred to friendly tribes who dwelt on the frontiers. They were given the task of assisting the *limitanei* and the regular forces.

Limes Palaestinae. Unlike many of the other frontier zones, Palestine was a highly organized border state for many centuries before the Roman conquest. Due to favorable topographical and climatic conditions it became a flourishing agricultural country on the fringes of the desert. Every ruler who desired to protect this flourishing agriculture from incursions by nomadic desert tribes was compelled to organize a frontier defense system. Due to frequent periods of drought the additional element of the war of survival intensified these raids and was expressed in the desperate need of these tribes to seize cultivated lands essential to their survival. Thus with Rome's conquest of Palestine and Transjordan, it acquired a frontier fortification system which had already been in existence for some 1,000 years.

Politically, the Nabatean kingdom, which included the desert fringes of Transjordan as well as the Negev south of the Beer-Sheba Valley, was an independent vassal state until it was annexed by Trajan in the year

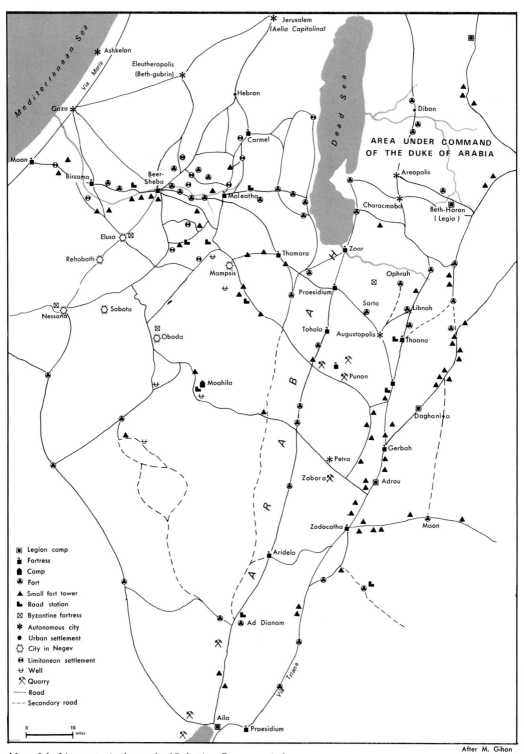

Map of the Limes area in the south of Palestine, Roman period

After M. Gihon

Legend:

- ■ Legion camp
- 🛡 Fortress
- ▲ Camp
- ⦿ Fort
- ▲ Small fort tower
- ⌐ Road station
- ⊠ Byzantine fortress
- ✳ Autonomous city
- ● Urban settlement
- ☼ City in Negev
- ⊖ Limitanean settlement
- ⊍ Well
- ⚒ Quarry
- — Road
- --- Secondary road

Map labels:

Mediterranean Sea, Via Maris, Ashkelon, Jerusalem (Aelia Capitolina), Eleutheropolis (Beth-gubrin), Hebron, Gaza, Carmel, Dead Sea, AREA UNDER COMMAND OF THE DUKE OF ARABIA, Maon, Birsama, Beer-Sheba, Moleatha, Characmoba, Areopolis, Dibon, Beth-Horon (Legio), Elusa, Thamara, Zoar, Rehoboth, Mampsis, Praesidium, Ophrah, Sarta, Libnah, Nessana, Sobota, Tohola, Augustopolis, Thoana, Oboda, Moahila, Punon, Daghaniya, Gerbah, Petra, Zobora, Adrou, Zodocatha, Maon, Aridela, Ad Dianam, Via Traiana, Aila, Praesidium

0   10 miles

AD 105/6 and transformed into the Provincia Arabia. The Nabateans, however, were either incapable of, or unwilling, to create an effective defense system in the Negev to block inroads by the Arabian nomadic Safaitic, Thamudic and other tribes into the cultivated land of Judea.

The survey and excavations conducted by M. Gichon, R. Cohen, A. Negev and others, proved conclusively that the Romans were compelled to take immediate possession of the Herodian frontier defenses stretching along and to the rear of the Besor and Beer-Sheba wadis as well as the chain of forward positions south of these wadis and along the wadi of Malhata to the southern tip of the Dead Sea.

Following the incorporation of the Nabatean kingdom into the Roman Empire there was a weakening of the defenses on the fringes of the desert, i.e. on the border of Judea. The Romans, on the other hand, held the Negev area south of the Beer-Sheba Valley, which was annexed to Provincia Arabia (the defeated Nabatean kingdom), the defense system along the roads of Praesidium-Thamara-Malhata (linking up with the Judean *Limes*), Haseba-Mampsis-Elusa and Moye Awad (Moah?)-Moahila-Oboda, and apparently also the Elusa-Rehoboth-Nessana line. The survey, however, also found traces of the beginnings of agricultural settlements in fortified farmsteads and in settlements along the Judean border from the period of the Severan emperors (193-235). These may have been the forerunners of the *limitanei*, the agricultural militia, which according to the historical sources (*Vita Sev. Alex.* 58, 5), were established by this emperor.

The organization of this defense system was further complicated by the fact that it was necessary to repel penetration not only for a single direction, but from both the Hedjaz and the Sinai as well; the invaders (or raiders), moreover, also made frequent incursions into the province of Judah. The trade routes between Jerusalem and the southern coastal cities and Elath also passed through Arabia. The inhabitants of the western sector were therefore naturally more involved with the Negev while the rulers of Arabia faced further grave dangers from the direction of Wadi Serahan in the northeast part of the province. Conditions assumed a more serious aspect with the accension of the Sassanid Dynasty in Persia. This dynasty in general took a more aggressive stand against Rome and succeeded in mobilizing various frontier Arabs to their side.

In order to improve the organization of the defenses and to make it more efficient, Diocletian in AD 300 incorporated biblical Edom and the entire Negev into Palestine, so that the *dux Palaestinae* was given the unified command over all the southern border zones on both sides of the Arabah.

It is thus possible that many of these frontier posts that were repaired or reestablished in the 4th century may in fact date from Diocletian's time. Tamara was repaired a generation earlier and the fortress at En Boqeq dates from the time of Constantine. Information about the deployment of the Roman forces at the end of the 4th century can be learned from the administrative list preserved in the *Notitia Dignatatum*.

Most authorities are of the opinion that this deployment remained essentially the same until the time of Diocletian.

Deployment in depth and density can be distinguished at that time along the old Flavian *Limes* which girdled the Beer-Sheva Valley as well as along the border of Idumea. These were linked together by the lines of the trans-Negev roads.

The military units — the infantry, cavalry, mixed units and heavy cavalry — were all deployed according to their suitability to the terrain. Thus, for example, the elite cavalry units (*equites*) were placed in charge of the defense of the Beer-Sheba Valley while the camel units patrolled the wadis in the central Negev. The *Legio Fretensis* which constituted the regional reserve units was transferred by Diocletian from Jerusalem to Elath from where it could provide rapid assistance in times of emergency to all locations along the roads spreading fan-like to the north along both sides of the Arabah and to the Arabah itself which was also fortified.

It appears that the incorporation of the south into Palestine could not solve all the problems and in *c.* AD 358 the south was made an independent frontier province known as *Palaestina Salutaris*. In the year 429, when the country's interior was divided into two autonomous provinces, *Palaestina prima* and *Palaestina secunda*, this third province was hereafter named *Palaestina tertia*.

The typical, almost exclusive plan of the larger defensive structures on the *limes* in the Negev and in Idumea was the enclosed courtyard fortress whose interior buildings were all constructed against the curtain walls. In this manner a large square-shaped, all-purpose courtyard was created inside the building. During battles, the soldiers stationed on top of the walls took advantage of the flat roofs which added vital depth. Fortresses have been discovered with corner towers, sometimes projecting, and also without towers. The fortress with projecting towers was known as *quadriburgus*, τετραπυργος in Greek, indicating that the towers were the most important element in the fortifications. *En Boqeq is an example of a site at which a fortress and a watchtower of a small fort were excavated.

From the Flavian period the plan of the fortress underwent no essential change. On the basis of size it is possible to differentiate between Negev fortresses of the types found at Beer-Sheba, Malhata and Tamara, the largest of which are *c.* 16,000 square feet, although most of them do not exceed 5,700 square feet, and between forts which are *c.* 2,000 square feet, and small forts and even smaller towers which are totally different in plan from the enclosed courtyard type.

The larger fortified structures in the Negev and on the border of Transjordan are much smaller than the analogous defenses on the European frontier of the empire. It seems that in Palestine, from the outset, whole units were not stationed together at one base. This is another indicator of the different defense system employed here. In this part of the world, the Romans continued the longstanding strategy which was based on a chain of reciprocal defenses. The enclosed courtyard fortress was especially adapted to archery warfare, which was another characteristic feature of the eastern part of the empire and became common in the West only from the 3rd-4th centuries AD. This fortress plan was common in Palestine from the beginning of the period of the Monarchy and its origin is even earlier. In excavations at Uzza a fortress was uncovered which dated from the First Temple period and which remained in continuous use until its occupation by the Romans. Projecting towers are found in the camp at Oboda which was founded by the Nabateans and subsequently occupied by the Romans as well as in the fort at *Tamara, which was also of Nabatean origin. It is worth noting that the enclosed courtyard type with projecting towers spread gradually from the Palestinian and Syrian *Limes* to all the other borders of the empire. This was the result of the introduction of long-range weapons (bow and arrow, firing machines) into these areas and the transition to a defensive strategy which was similar to that employed in the East.

Changes in the Palestine *Limes* also occurred in the Byzantine period. The fort on the summit of Nessana was repaired during the time of Theodosius II. Her archives reveal that the *limitanei* soldiers stationed at the site were made citizens and in the course of time became full-fledged farmers. Like Nessana, most of the other Negev cities as well were incorporated into the Negev defense system according to the system instituted by Justinian (527-563).

The Persian conquest of Palestine (614-624), the traces of which can be clearly distinguished in the fortresses that have been excavated, paved the way for the final destruction of the Palestinian Limes during the Arab conquest of 632-634.

LOBO-HAMATH A town in the south of the land of *Hamath, at the northern end of the Valley of *Lebanon, near the sources of the *Orontes. According to the Bible it is the northern border of the Promised Land (Num.34:8, etc.; Authorized Version: 'the entrance of Hamath'). Mentioned as Rabah in the Egyptian sources, and as Labu in the Assyrian documents, it is identified with Lebwe.

LOD; LYDDA; DIOSPOLIS A town not mentioned in the Bible until the Restoration (Ezra 2:23, etc.), though its inclusion in a list of Tuthmosis III testifies to its antiquity. In 145 BC it was included in Hasmonean territory. In AD 68 it was conquered by Vespasian, and after the fall of Jerusalem it was the seat of numerous sages. Its main importance, however, lies in its role in Roman and Byzantine times. In the 2nd century AD it was the capital of a district. According to the New Testament the apostle Peter went to Lydda to visit believers who lived there (Acts 9:32). It became a colony, with the title 'Colonia Lucia Septimia Severia Diospolis', in the days of Septimius Severus. In the time of Constantine St George, patron saint of England, was martyred at Lydda, and his shrine was venerated from the 4th century AD. In the period of the Talmud Lod was a center of Jewish learning.

It is again called Lod today and lies 11 miles southeast of Tel Aviv.

LUBIM A people who lived in the north of Africa, west of *Egypt. The Egyptians recruited mercenaries from among them (2 Chr. 12:3, etc.). Some scholars identify the Lubim with the *rbw* of the Sea Peoples (*Philistines), who attempted to invade Egypt in the 13 century BC. According to this view, after their defeat by Rameses III they settled in the area to the west of Egypt, and the country was named after them. By the 10th century BC they had become strong enough to disrupt the rule of the 21st Dynasty and to put Pharaoh Seshonq I, the founder of the 22nd Dynasty, on the throne.

M

MA'AYAN BARUKH This Acheulian site is situated on the northern edges of the Hula region and has been known for many years. The immense collection of tools found in the vicinity of Kibbutz Ma'ayan Barukh came from an area about a mile square. Three main concentrations of tools were located. This collection was studied by M. Stekelis and D. Gilead and was found to contain a very small amount of waste material, which suggests that the Acheulians flaked their tools near the source of the raw material. The tools brought from that source to the site consist mainly of handaxes (85 percent), plus some discs, chopping tools and flake tools. The handaxes, carefully and symmetrically flaked, are generally heart-shaped, disc-shaped, oval or almond-shaped. Some Micoquian handaxes and cleavers, as well as other types, were collected. Among the rest of the assemblage some Levallois cores deserve mention. The lithic industry can be compared with that found at et-*Tabun (layer F) and *Umm Qatafa (layer D2).

Additional field work was carried out by A. Ronen in two trenches where artifacts were buried up to a depth of 6 feet. The dominant tool type is the handaxe; the frequencies of flakes and flake tools are very low and resemble the observations of Stekelis and Gilead.

An attempt to date travertine covered handaxes by the Uranium Series method yielded ages older than 300,000 which are also the limit of this method. (*See also* *PREHISTORY; *FLINT TOOLS.)

MACHPELAH The name of a field and a cave near *Mamreh (Gen. 23:17), which is *Hebron (Gen. 23:19). It was bought by Abraham from Ephron the Hittite. Sarah (Gen. 23:19), Abraham (Gen. 25:9), Isaac, Rebekah and Leah (Gen. 49:31) and Jacob (Gen. 50:13) were buried here. An ancient tradition, which goes back to the time of the Second Temple, sites the Cave of the Machpelah at a place in the Haram el-Khalil at *Hebron, surrounded by a wall built in Herod's times. It is still venerated today.

The present enclosure wall of Haram esh-Sharif goes back to Herod's times. It is 103.5 feet by 203.5 feet, surrounded by a wall 9 feet thick, with offsets and rising to a height of 54-60 feet. It is built of extremely large ashlars, the largest of which is 23 feet by 5 feet. It is the best preserved ancient monument in Palestine. The approach to the enclosure was originally by way

of a monumental staircase and gate on the west. In the 13th century AD, under Sultan Baibars, crenelations were added to the top of the walls. In size the stone paving blocks match the stones of the walls. This compound was erected above a cave, the entrance to which has been forbidden since the Middle Ages by the Moslems. The exact place of the original entrance to the Cave of Machpelah is unknown, and the only present-day opening is the one in the northwestern wall of the church-mosque. Very few people have received permission, or have ventured to enter the inner parts of the cave.

MADAI; MEDES The name of a district and a state in northwestern Persia, whose capital was *Achmetha-Ecbatana. The Medes are mentioned for the first time in Assyrian documents of the 9th century BC, when their country was overrun by the Assyrian kings. At this period the Medes were divided into numerous separate groups under local leaders. Tiglath-Pileser III deported a great number of Medes and annexed their country to the Assyrian kingdom. Frequent rebellions against this state of subjugation culminated at the end of the 8th century BC in the formation of an independent state under the leadership of Diokes, their first king, who built *Achmetha, the capital. The state of war with Assyria continued during the reigns of Sargon II and Esarhaddon. Not until late in the 7th century BC were the Medes strong enough to unite their forces with those of *Babylon and to conquer *Ashur and *Nineveh (612 BC). After these conquests the kingdom of the Medes extended over most of *Iran, northern Assyria, northern *Mesopotamia, Armenia and Cappadocia. During the reign of Cyrus II the Medes were defeated and their kingdom was annexed to Persia (550 BC).

In the Bible the Medes are mentioned as the enemies of *Babylon (Isa. 13). In the Book of Daniel Madai and Persia are referred to as one kingdom, and the prophet foretold that *Babylon would be conquered by the Medes and the Persians (Dan. 5:26-8).

MAGDALA; MIGDAL NUNAYAH; TARICHEAE A town on the western shore of the Sea of *Galilee, about 3 miles north of *Tiberias, the birth-place of Mary Magdalene (Matt. 27:56,61). It is possible that it was visited by Jesus (Mark 8:10; Authorized Version: 'Dalmanutha'). Nero gave it to Agrippa II (Josephus,

Antiq. XX, 159). It was then named Tricheae, meaning 'drying and salting'; the Aramaic form, Migdal Nunayah ('Tower of Fishermen'), has the same connotation. After Josephus had escaped from *Tiberias he made Taricheae a base for his military activities and fortified it (Josephus, *Antiq.* V, 96-7; *Life* 156). It played an important role in the Jewish resistance and was besieged by the Romans. After the death of Agrippa II it became part of the province of Judea. Identified with el-Megdel, the present-day Migdal.

Excavations were carried out in 1971-3 and 1975 under the direction of V. Corbo. Remains of the Roman city with intersecting *cardo* and *decumani* a small synagogue of the Galilean type ($26^1/_2$ feet by $23^1/_2$ feet) and a monastic complex were brought to light.

MAHANAIM A city of *Gilead, on the border between the territories of Gad and Manasseh (Josh. 13:26, 30). This is the place where the angels of God met Jacob (Gen. 32:1-2); one of the Levitical cities; and a place of refuge in the territory of Gad (Josh. 21:38). Abner, son of Ner, enthroned Ishbosheth, son of Saul, at Mahanaim (2 Sam. 2:8), and David fled there when Absalom revolted (2 Sam. 17:24). Solomon appointed Ahinadab, son of Iddo, over the district of which Mahanaim was the center (1 Kgs. 4:14). Identified with Tell edh-Dhahab el—Gharbi, north of the *Jabbok.

MAIUMAS *a)* A harbor of *Gaza, first mentioned in a papyrus of Zenon, assistant to the Ptolemaic minister of finance, of 259 BC. Ptolemy (V, 15, 2) explains the name as denoting a maritime quarter as does Marcus Diaconus (*Vita Porphyrii* 57). It is mentioned in Roman and Byzantine sources. Under Constantine it was renamed Constantia and made an independent city, the inhabitants being converted to Christianity.

b) The harbor of *Ashkelon, referred to by Antonine of Placentia as 'civitas Maiuma Ascalonitis', lying 2 miles from the city.

c) A place in the vicinity of *Caesarea, near springs. Dams were found that diverted the water from these springs into the high-level aqueduct of *Caesarea. There are also remains of a Roman theater. Identified with Mamas.

MAKKEDAH A Canaanite city-state in the northern part of the *Plain (Josh. 15:41), conquered by Joshua (Josh. 10:28). Close to it was the cave in which the corpses of the five Canaanite kings were deposited (Josh. 10:16-29). During the reign of Rehoboam it was conquered by Pharaoh Sheshonq I. Eusebius (*Onom.* 126:22) places it in *Idumea, 8 miles east of *Beth-Gubrin. Identification not certain, but should be sought in the vicinity of *Azekah and *Beth-Gubrin.

MALHATA (TEL) Situated near the richest wells of the biblical Negev, midway between Arad and Beer-Sheba, it was one of the most important settlements in that area during several historical periods. The earliest habitation at the site dates to the Early Bronze Age II, when ancient Arad flourished as the major city of the Negev. Malhata was Arad's 'daughter' located on the northern bank of the wadi bearing the same name. It was a short-lived settlement that came to an end when the 'mother' city ceased to exist, in the 27th century BC.

The second period of settlement at Malhata dates from the Middle Bronze Age. In this period a fortified town was established on the southern bank of the wadi while the deserted Early Bronze Age settlement opposite was resettled as an open suburb beside the fortified town. The date of the founding of this town is uncertain as the excavations stopped before reaching virgin soil. The Middle Bronze Age walled town occupied the eastern, higher part of the existing mound, on an area of about $2^1/_2$ acres only. It existed until the very end of the period and, together with nearby Tel Masos, served as the southeasternmost defense against desert marauders from the settled country lying to its north.

Another long gap of occupation lasted through most of the second half of the second millennium until the tenth century BC. This is the period of the United Kingdom of David and Solomon when a major effort of rebuilding and resettling Malhata took place. On the deserted Middle Bronze Age mound a raised platform was added on the west to form a continuous raised terrain, 15 dunams in area. This area was surrounded by a city-wall $3^1/_2$ feet wide. The first Judean settlement at Malhata was destroyed in the late 10th century BC probably as a result of Pharaoh Sheshonq's invasion of the country. The town was rebuilt after the disaster. Excavations on the western, lower mound exposed a typical Israelite store-house, 48 feet long, in which three phases of repairs and rebuildings were distinguished. On the eastern, higher mound private houses adjoining the city wall were uncovered. Judean Malhata was destroyed at the end of the Iron Age at the time of the Babylonian conquest of Judah. Almost 25 percent of the pottery from the destruction level revealed Edomite affinities, further proof of Edomite involvement in the disturbances in the Negev at this time (Obad. 1). The biblical name of this important Judean stronghold in the Negeb is still unknown. Among its suggested identifications are Hormah, Arad of the House of Yeroham and Baalat-Beer.

The site was known as Molatha in the Roman period when the eastern, higher mound was occupied by a fort. An extensive settlement extended over about 50 acres south of the mound during the Roman-Byzantine period. According to the evidence of the excavations this was not an urban settlement; its buildings were constructed at great distances from each other among gardens and fields. As Molatha was part of the Roman *limes* system (forts guarding the borders of the empire), the settlement adjoining the fort was probably a colony of *limitanei* (garrison troops stationed in the forts). The site was finally abandoned during the early Arab period in the 8th century AD.

MAMPSIS The easternmost town of the central *Negev, 25 miles southeast of *Beer-Sheba. The site is at an ancient road junction where the roads running from *Jerusalem to *Hebron and Aila (*Elath) on the Gulf of Elath, and those from *Gaza and *Beer-Sheba to Aila, converge. It is possible that it was also linked by road with *Oboda. The Arabic name, Kurnub, has no apparent connection with the ancient form. At first the site was identified with biblical *Tamar (Thamara in the Hellenistic and Roman periods), but this identification has been rejected by all scholars. The Hebrew form is Mamshit.

The earliest source in which Mampsis is mentioned is Ptolemy's *Geography* according to whose lists it belonged to *Idumea, west of the Jordan. Eusebius (*Onom.* 8, 8) says that Thamara was situated a day's march from Mampsis, on the road from *Hebron to Aila (*Elath), and that there was a garrison there. The Medaba map shows Mampsis as a walled town, with an arched gate protected by two towers. The town is also mentioned in some other sources of the Byzantine period, as well as in the *Nessana papyri, where it is included in a tax list among towns that paid a moderate sum. Early Arabic inscriptions found at the site indicate that it was occupied by the Arabs for a time after their conquest.

The first European scholar to visit Mampsis was E. Robinson (1838), who did not think it worthwhile to descend the mountain but studied the town from a distance through his binoculars. He describes it as a maze of ruins among which remains of churches or other public buildings were to be seen. E.H. Palmer (1871) paid a short visit to the site, finding very little to say about it. The first comprehensive plan of the town was drawn up by A. Musil (1902), who noted a city wall, two churches and a number of other buildings. C.L. Woolley and T.E. Lawrence (1914) drew a new plan of the town, but theirs was less detailed than Musil's though they did note the water installations in the wadis round the town. During his survey J.H. Illiffe (1934) found Nabatean and early Roman potsherds in the town. The last and best survey was made in 1937 by G.G. Kirk and P.L.O. Guy, on behalf of the Palestine Exploration Fund. They drew a new and much more detailed map, noted some peculiarities in the planning of the town and also discovered two cemeteries. Large-scale excavations were made in 1965-7 on behalf of the Hebrew University of Jerusalem and the National Parks Administration, under the direction of A. Negev: a large part of the town was cleared and two of the cemeteries were investigated.

An analysis of the ancient sources and of the preliminary results of the excavations indicate that Mampsis, like *Sobata and *Ruheiba, belongs to the later group of Nabatean settlements, founded late in the 1st century BC. It seems that at that time an alternative route to *Petra was opened, Mampsis being one of its main stations. Remains of the period lie buried deep under the buildings of the later Nabatean period (late 1st to the middle of the 2nd century AD) which indicates that there was a considerable gap between the two Nabatean settlements. The same gap has been observed at *Oboda. Latin military inscriptions found in one of the cemeteries indicate that Mampsis played an important role when the Nabatean kingdom was annexed to the Provincia Arabia on 22 March in the year AD 106. Units of the Legio III Cyrenaica and cavalrymen of the Cohors I Augusta Thracum, which possibly took part in that operation, were stationed there. The site also flourished long after the annexation, during the reigns of Trajan and Hadrian.

The history of Mampsis in the latter part of the 2nd century and in the 3rd century AD is not very clear. About the end of the 3rd century, when according to Eusebius a garrison was stationed there, the town was surrounded by a wall. There seems to have been no interruption in settlement between the late Roman and the Byzantine periods, as the fortifications built in the late Roman period were kept constantly under repair. Quite early in the Byzantine period, about the end of the 5th century AD, one of the churches was built.

The plan of Mampsis in the Byzantine period was most unusual. Whereas the towns of *Oboda, *Sobata, and apparently also *Nessana, were built completely anew at this period, with complete disregard for earlier buildings, at Mampsis buildings that had been constructed in the early 2nd century AD remained in use throughout the whole of the Byzantine period. This is partly due to the fact that they were extraordinarily well built but it also indicates that from the 2nd century to the 7th the town was never abandoned long enough to allow the houses to fall into a state where they could no longer be repaired. If there were any gaps in the settlement of Mampsis they were considerably shorter than in the other towns of the central *Negev. This factor had its effect on the planning of the Byzantine town. The churches were squeezed into the new plan, sometimes necessitating the sacrifice of parts of an earlier building or a section of the city wall. As the existing wall prevented expansion the planners met the needs of the increasing population by subdividing older habitations or by adding rooms on their outer walls, thus encroaching on streets and public squares.

The exact date of the final destruction of Mampsis is uncertain. It has been accepted among scholars that the Arabs conquered the Byzantine cities of the *Negev between AD 634 and 636. Some, such as *Oboda, were destroyed, while others, such as *Nessana, *Elusa and *Sobata, survived until about AD 800. No coins later than the middle of the 6th century AD have been found at Mampsis, which indicates that the city had already ceased to exist almost a century before the Arab conquest in the 7th century AD. It is therefore possible that, since it was a lone city on the fringe of the central *Negev, it suffered destruction in one of the earlier Arab attacks that preceded the conquest of AD 636. If this is so the Arab conquest of the *Negev must have been a gradual process, with Mampsis the first town to suffer, followed by *Oboda, while the western cities still continued to exist for some time under Arab rule. In any case Mampsis was looted, its churches were destroyed by fire and he conquerors left their imprint in the form of graffiti in the apse of one of the churches. It seems that the Arabs did not hold the city for long, and it was never resettled after the looting.

THE EXCAVATIONS Of the early Nabatean settlement, that of the 1st century AD, it has been possible to trace the ruins of only a few buildings lying deep under later remains. Their dating is, however, certain, thanks to the presence of typical Nabatean and early Roman pottery. More evidence for this phase was discovered in a tomb in the Nabatean cemetery, in which typical pottery and a Nabatean coin of AD 74 were found.

Most of the remains at Mampsis belong to the late Nabatean phase, mostly of the first half of the 2nd century AD. Typical of this period are the excellent masonry, fine stone-dressing showing oblique tooling (*Building materials), Nabatean capitals and other architectural ornaments. The houses were spacious, centered around an inner court, each wing of the house being provided with a stair-well. These stair-wells took the form of a tower, in the center of which stood a heavy pier into which the steps were inserted. One of the buildings had no less than five stair-wells. In the inner courts were balconies supported on pillars. The stair-wells were connected with the balconies, which gave access to rooms on the upper floors. These spacious houses, no matter how large, never had more than one entrance; they thus had a doorless and windowless façade, so that each house was a small self-contained fortress. Another typical feature of two of the houses was their elaborate stables, equalled only in the prosperous town of *Hauran, which is also of the 2nd century. The stables were basilical in form, with a large square court in the middle and two narrow aisles along the sides. Arched doors led to each aisle — the actual stables — while the stone feeding-troughs were placed under similarly arched windows. It seems that breeding Arab thoroughbreds was one of the town's main sources of income.

Mampsis' water supply at this period was again excellently planned. In the deep gorge at the foot of the plateau on which the town was built, and in two of the subsidiary wadis, cross-walls formed large open-air reservoirs big enough to catch large quantities of water during the few hours when the wadis were flooded. From there the water was conveyed in jars to large cisterns hewn in the rock under the houses. The surplus water was stored in a pool roofed over with arches to prevent evaporation. There is very little arable land round the town, so agriculture was one of the least important factors in the local economy.

Some important finds were made in the cemeteries (*Burial). In one of these about 20 undisturbed tombs were found. Each of these once possessed a monument in the form of a solid stepped pyramid on a square base, but all these (except one that had collapsed into the tomb) have disappeared. The pyramids were designed to conceal the tombs from prospective tomb robbers. Below each monument came a filling of large stones closely packed to a depth of 6-8 feet. Beneath this was a stone cavity in which the wooden coffin was placed. Some of the dead were buried with their personal gold jewelry set with semi-precious stones; Mampsis thus offers a unique collection of Nabatean jewellery. In some cases a coin, a dinar of Trajan, was deposited. About 30 clay seal impressions were found in another tomb, one of which was a copy of a coin of Hadrian from AD 130. The other cemetery, probably of the same period, served military personnel at Mampsis. The burial customs practised here were different: the body was first burnt on a pyre, and the ashes alone were deposited under a stepped pyramid or a heap of large stones.

In the late Roman period the town was surrounded by a wall, enclosing an area of about 10 acres. There were two gates, one on the east, facing the main road, the other on the west, leading to the pools in the wadi. In the town itself little was changed in this period. One of the houses, however, was plastered and painted with mythological scenes and geometric designs. In a stair-well close to the painted room a hoard of 10,400 silver coins was found, the latest of which are dated to AD 220. The Mampsis of the 2nd-3rd centuries AD must have fulfilled an important role in guarding the pass that the Romans had constructed about 10 miles to the south of the town, to facilitate traffic travelling to *Petra and Aila (*Elath). It is also possible that it was connected in some way with copper-mining at that time in *Sinai. This may account for the unusually large hoard of coins which was found at Mampsis.

In the Byzantine period the walls were doubled so as to strengthen the fortifications. Two churches were constructed, a large one at the southeastern corner of the town and a smaller one on the southwest. These churches are of the basilical type, with a single apse, a prothesis and a *diakonikon*. The masonry is of a higher standard than was usual in this period, and both churches were decorated with mosaic floors, a feature that is not at all common in the *Negev. The small church to the southwest has a very fine mosaic depicting rich geometric carpets, fruits and birds of various kinds, crosses and peacocks. There are a few dedicatory inscriptions but these do not help much in dating of the church, as they contain no dates at all. The western church was found to be full of ashes from the great fire in which it was destroyed. This is attributed by the excavators to the Arab conquest of the city, which probably occurred in about the middle of the 6th century AD.

MAMREH (PLAIN OF) The Hebrew Bible uses the words *alonei mamreh,* which means 'oaks of Mamreh', to refer to a grove of oaks named after Mamreh the Amorite, who dwelt near *Hebron. Abraham built an altar to the Lord there (Gen. 13:18) and it was there that he learnt of the capture of his brother's son, Lot (Gen. 14:13). The Lord appeared to Abraham there in a vision (Gen. 15:1 ff.) and it seems that the place where Abraham lived was soon sanctified. The Septuagint refers to 'the oak of Mamreh', which would imply that one of the oaks was already being venerated as Abraham's altar.

An early tradition points to *Ramat el-Khalil as the site of Mamreh. Josephus (*Antiq.* I, 186; *War* IV, 533) mentions a large oak there. Herod surrounded it with a beautifully built wall enclosing an area 150 feet by 200 feet in which the altar and the well of Abraham were shown. The site was destroyed during the War against the Romans. Hadrian, during his visit to the East in AD 130 ordered the rebuilding of the compound, which housed one of the three important public markets in Palestine (the other markets being those of *Gaza and *Acco), and dedicated it to Hermes-Mercury. After the crushing of the Bar-Kochba Revolt Jews were sold here as slaves. This market place was still operated in the late Roman and Byzantine periods, and when Constantine I built there one of the first churches in the Holy Land AD 324, Jews were among the merchants who came to trade there. Sozomenus, one of the early Christian biographers, speaks of idols which were placed on Abraham's altar, of libations and incense-burning, as well as sacrifices of oxen, goats, lambs and fowl. Eusebius, who describes the churches built on the site by Constantine, refers to a mosaic pavement on which are portrayed Abraham's guests, among whom is also Christ. This church was already visited by the Pilgrim of Bordeaux (AD 333). It was destroyed by the Persians in AD 614.

MANNA The food eaten by the Children of Israel in the desert (Exod. 16:14-31, etc.), described in the Bible as 'small as the hoar frost... and the taste of it was like wafers made with honey... and the color thereof as the colour of bdellium [i.e. rock-crystal, cf. Num. 11:7-8]. And the people went about and gathered it, and ground it in mills, or beat it in a mortar, and baked it in pans, and made cakes of it; and the taste of it was of fresh oil.'

There have been many theories to explain this phenomenon. According to one of the most recent it is the secretion of certain tamarisk bushes, *Tamarix manifera, Ehr.,* and occurs when the bush is attacked by the *Cocidae,* an insect found in the Sinai desert. The secretion has a rough surface and is white at first, changing later to a yellowish-brown color. It becomes sweet, like honey, when kept for a long time. The local Bedouins call it 'manna of heaven'. They collect it very early in the morning, before the ants wake after the chill of the night, and very quickly, before it melts in the hot morning sun (cf. Exod. 16:21). They store it in tightly closed vessels to protect it from ants and prevent it becoming infested with worms (cf. Exod. 16:20). In the rainy season a Bedouin can collect about 3lbs in one morning. They cook it into a porridge, which keeps for a long time. The preservation of the name *manna* in Arabic may be taken as a proof of the accuracy of this supposition.

MAON; MENOIS *a)* A town in the mountains of Judah (Josh. 15:55), in the vicinity of the desert of Maon where David sought refuge from Saul (I Sam. 23:24); also inhabited in the Roman period. Eusebius (*Onom.* 130:12) mentions it in Daromas (the South), but it was a site of little importance in his day. Identified with Khirbet Main, southeast of *Hebron.

b) A town to the south of *Gaza, of the Roman and Byzantine periods. Eusebius (*Onom.* 130, 7) wrote: 'Medebena [Josh. 15:31; Authorized Version: 'Madmannah'] of the tribe of Judah. And today it is the small town of Menois, close to Gaza.' Hieronymus has the biblical name in its correct form: Medemena. The Medaba map shows 'Medebena, which is today Menois'. According to the *Notitia Dignitatum* (73, 19), a list of Roman military units of the 4th century AD, a unit of Illyrian cavalry was stationed at Menois. The site has been variously identified, one theory being that it lies at Khirbet el-Main, 10 miles south of *Gaza, near Kibbutz Nirim in the northwestern *Negev.

In road-making operations in February 1957 a bulldozer revealed remains of a building with a mosaic pavement. In 1957-8 excavations were made on the site on behalf of the Israel Department of Antiquities and Museums. The whole of the western half of the building had been completely lost, but the remaining part was sufficiently well preserved to permit its identification as a synagogue and to enable its plan and decoration to be reconstructed. The building was basilical, approximately 50 feet by 45 feet, and had an apse facing northwest, in the direction of *Jerusalem. It had three entrances in the southern wall. The aisles and the southern quarter of the nave were paved with slabs of stone. The space between the columns was laid with a mosaic pavement divided into medallions. There were five rows of 11 medallions each, giving a total of 54 in all; the place of the central medallion in the upper row was in fact occupied by the branches of a menorah. Only 37 of these medallions were preserved. At the bottom is an amphora with a vine growing out of it so that its slender branches form the medallions. Small bunches of grapes hang from these branches. The amphora is flanked by two peacocks. The middle row (from bottom to top) depicts a bird of prey, baskets of fruit (pomegranates and grapes), a chalice, a water vessel and a bird in a cage. The remaining medallions are occupied by various animals and birds. Originally these were arranged in pairs, facing each other, with one of the objects of the middle row separating them. The animals include an ibex, a buffalo, a fat-tailed sheep, two hares, a stag, two elephants and a hunting-dog, while among the birds were a flamingo, a pair of doves, a crane, a guineafowl, a pheasant and a goose. The feature that distinguishes this mosaic pavement from its counterpart in the neighboring and contemporary church of Shellal is that the upper part of the pavement, close to the apse which housed the Torah Shrine, has a menorah flanked by two fierce-looking lions. The menorah is made of round yellow discs made to resemble gold and inlaid with mother-of-pearl. On the bar above the seven branches of the menorah stand seven lamps in the shape of glass goblets. Between the lions and the menorah are two *ethrogs* (citrons), a *shofar* (ram's horn) and a *lulab* (palm branch). The scene is flanked by two palm trees, with a pair of birds at the root of each, and the whole panel is surrounded by a border of pomegranate blossoms. Above the border is a dedicatory inscription in Aramaic: '[Remembered] for good be the whole congregation [who have] contributed this mosaic and furthermore Daisin and Thomas and Judah who have donated [the] sum [of] 2 denarii.' On stylistic grounds this mosaic pavement has been dated to the first half of the 6th century AD.

MARAH One of the stations on the route of the Exodus, in the desert of *Shur, where the Israelites found bitter water (Exod. 15:23; Num. 33:8-9; Authorized Version: 'wilderness of Etham'). It is generally identified by those who maintain that the Exodus took a southerly course with the oasis of Ain Hauwarah, a pool of bitter water on the eastern shore of the Gulf of Suez. Those who believe that the Hebrews took a northern course locate it in the region east of the Sirbonian Lake (Sabhat Bardawil). Still others identify it with *Kadesh-Barnea.

MARESHAH; MARISSA A town in the territory of
Judah (Josh. 15:44), identified with Tell Sandahanna. It
is doubtful whether the 'mu-ukh-ra-ash-ti' of the *El
Amarna letters refers to Mareshah; during the excavations no remains ealier than the Iron Age were found.
Rehoboam converted Mareshah into a Judean stronghold, giving it a commander and storing food, oil and
wine there (2 Chr. 11:8, 11). During the first half of the
9th century BC Zerah the Ethiopian attacked Judah, was
defeated by Asa at Mareshah and was pursued as far as
*Gerar (2 Chr. 14:8-15). In the division of Judah into
12 districts (recorded in Joshua [15] but dating to the
time of Jehoshaphat), Mareshah, together with *Keilah,
*Achzib and nine other towns, formed one district.

The town was conquered by Sennacherib in 701 BC.
Although the biblical text describing his campaigns
does not provide a detailed list of towns (2 Kgs. 18:13),
Micah's lamentation over the destruction of the towns
in the *Plain refers to this campaign and does mention
Mareshah (Mic. 1:15). After 586 BC it fell to *Idumea.
In the papyri of Zenon, an Egyptian official of the 3rd
century BC, it is mentioned as a center of the slave trade
with *Egypt. At that time there was a large colony of
Sidonians at Mareshah. Some painted tombs unearthed
during the excavations and dated to about 200 BC con-
tained, besides *Phoenicians, many *Sidonians with
Greek names and certain Apollophanes who was archon
'of the Sidonians at Marisa'. From the books of the
Maccabees and from Josephus' account it is evident
that Marissa was the largest and most important city of
*Idumea. A decline set in after its conquest by
Hyrcanus in the last third of the 2nd century BC
(Josephus, Antiq. X III, 257). Although it was freed by
Pompey in 63 BC (Josephus, Antiq. XIV, 75) and rebuilt
by Gabinius in 57 BC (Josephus, Antiq. XIV, 88) it did
not recover. During its conquest by the Parthians in 40
BC (Josephus, Antiq.a XIV, 364), it was completely
destroyed and was never afterwards resettled, its role
being taken over by *Beth-Gubrin (Eleutheropolis).

The excavations undertaken by F.J. Bliss and R.A.S.
Macalister on behalf of the Palestine Exploration Fund
from 1898 to 1900 revealed the Hellenistic city. Built to
the Hippodamian plan, in which streets intersect at
right angles, the city covers an area 480 feet by 450 feet
and is surrounded by walls and towers. No gates could

be identified. In the western quarter was a complex with
a market and in the eastern quarter a sacred area
(temenos) that was open to the north. It is not clear
whether the building in the northern part of the
temenos was a temple. Of special importance are the
numerous tombs dating from the 2nd century BC, the
largest one adorned with paintings (*Burial). In the area
round Mareshah about 132 columbaria were found
burial caves of the Hellenistic period, and other caves
of the same period some which contained oil presses.

MARI One of the largest cities in Syria, on the right
bank of the *Euphrates, identified with Tell Hariri. The
site has been under excavation since 1933 by a French
expedition under the direction of A. Parrot. Before the
city had been identified, with the help of inscriptions
found during the excavations, Mari was known from
cuneiform texts found at Nippur and Kish, in southern
*Mesopotamia. It is also mentioned in the records of
the campaigns of Sargon (middle of the 3rd millennium
BC) and its capture is recorded in the letters of
Hammurabi (c. 1792-1750 BC). This scanty evidence
from external sources was much enriched by the large
amount of information derived from documents found
in the excavations.

Mari enjoyed two periods of great prosperity: the first
half of the 3rd millennium BC, when her great kings,
Iahdunlim and Zimrilim, restored the city that was later
to be destroyed by Hammurabi, King of *Babylon. To
the first period belong a large palace, the excavation of
which is still in progress, a ziggurat and the temples of
Ishtar, Shamash, Ninhursag, Ishtarat, Ninni-Zara and
Dagan. The second period is represented by the huge
palace of Zimrilim, the town's last king, which extended
over 9 acres and contained more than 300 rooms and
courts. The palace contained numerous statues and wall
paintings, as well as archives. In the time between its
two periods of greatness Mari was a vassal state of the
empires of Agade, the 3rd Dynasty of *Ur, and later of
the Assyrian Empire.

The documents found in the archives of the palace
of Zimrilim are of outstanding importance. They
comprise some 25,000 cuneiform tablets inscribed
with economic, legal and diplomatic texts. The diplomatic texts were letters sent to the Mari court by
officials, neighboring kings, members of the royal

Hunting scene in a wall-painting in a tomb at Mareshah

family and ambassadors. These documents are dated
to the first quarter of the 2nd millennium BC. A
number of the texts refer to the *Habiru, and the tribe
of the Benjaminites also gets special mention. Both
the *Habiru and the Benjaminites are linked by scholars with the early Hebrews. The economic documents
relate mainly to foodstuffs supplied to the court or
distributed by it, hundreds of them dealing with the
daily menus of the king and his retinue. The legal texts
deal mainly with sales and purchases, and loans of
money and grain.

The Mari documents shed light not only on that
flourishing kingdom, but also on the history of the
ancient Near East and of the early Hebrews.

MASADA A natural rock fortress on the western
shore of the *Dead Sea. Josephus (*War* VII, 285) states
that a fortress was built at Masada by 'the high priest
Jonathan'. This could have been either the brother of
Judas Maccabaeus or Alexander Jannaeus, whose
Hebrew name was Jonathan. The place is still referred
to as a fortress when, in 42 BC, it was taken by Malichus, an antagonist of Antipater, Herod's father
(Josephus, *War* I, 237). Herod used Masada as a
safe retreat for his family in 40 BC, before leaving for
Rome (Josephus, *Antiq.* XIV, 280-303; *War* I, 238,
263-6). After his return he built a completely new
fortress on the site. Josephus describes the new fortress in minute detail (*War* VII, 280-300) and it seems
unlikely that he did not visit the site before the Roman
siege, though some scholars believe that he did not.

Little is known of Masada in the years immediately
following Herod's death, but it is most improbable
that it was left unoccupied. What is known with certainty is that at the beginning of the Great Revolt in
AD 66 the fortress was held by a Roman garrison
(Josephus, *War* II, 408, VII, 297). This garrison was
soon expelled by the Zealots, who held Masada until 2
May in the year AD 73, when it was finally conquered
by the Romans. Masada is seldom mentioned by other
classical writers. Strabo (*Geography* XVI, 2, 24) does
describe the region of Masada; and Pliny (*Nat. Hist.* V,
15, 73) refers to the fortress briefly while dwelling at
length on the *Dead Sea region and on the Essenes
who lived there.

The first modern scholar to identify Masada correctly was E. Robinson, who observed it from a
nearby hill in 1838. The first to set foot on it was the
American missionary, S. W. Wolcott, in 1842. Like his
later counterparts, Wolcott climbed the rock from the
west, where the ascent was much easier, wrongly
believing this to be the 'snake', the dangerous path
described by Josephus (*War* VII, 292-3). Wolcott left
the first detailed description of the remains of the
buildings on the rock and of the siege works below
and on the slopes.

In 1848 Masada was visited by an expedition of the
US Navy. They discovered the Roman road leading
from *En-Gedi to Masada, but again mistook the
western approach for the 'snake path'. On the northern slope they observed a round tower, which they
identified as a fort. Three years later the site was
visited by the French archaeologist, F. de Saulcy, who
did not learn of the importance of Masada until after

*Statue of a goddess carrying a jug of water, from the
palace of Zimrilim, Mari (approx. 2040-1870 BC)*

his return. He thought he could distinguish between the earliest remains of Jonathan's fortress, which he believed lay on the northern part of the rock, and that of Herod. In 1858 E.G. Rey paid a visit to Masada. An expert on military affairs, he took greater care in describing the remains of the Roman camps and siege works. He also surveyed and drew the first fairly accurate plan of the remains on the rock, attempting to identify Herod's palace at the northern end. H.B. Tristram, the zoologist, identified some new species of animals when he visited Masada in 1863.

In 1887 a team surveying Western Palestine on behalf of the Palestine Exploration Fund visited Masada. They were the first to climb the rock from the east, discovering sections of the dangerous snake path. They suggested that the large building close to the western gate should be identified as Herod's palace and were able to distinguish correctly between Herod's buildings and those of the Byzantine period.

The first visitor to Masada in the 20th century was Father F.M. Abel, who arrived there in 1909. He believed that most of the stones of Herod's buildings had been hurled down the precipice by the Roman conquerors of Masada, and therefore ascribed the remains on the rock to later periods. But one of the most important surveys at Masada was made by the German archaeologist, A. Schulten, in 1931. Although this was mainly devoted to the Roman military architecture of Masada, he also made a thorough study of the buildings on the rock. Most important, however, was his identification of Herod's palace in the large complex of buildings at the center of the rock, close to the western ascent.

The first systematic archaeological excavations were attempted in 1955-6 by a joint Israeli expedition on behalf of the Hebrew University, the Israel Exploration Society and the Department of Antiquities and Museums. A completely new plan of the remains on the rock was drawn up, special attention being paid to the buildings on the northern part of the rock, which the expedition identified as Herod's palace. They believed that this identification was supported by Josephus' description (*War* VII, 289).

Extensive excavations were made at Masada from 1963 to 1965 by Yigael Yadin, directing a joint expedition of the Hebrew University, the Israel Exploration Society and the Department of Antiquities and Museums. The excavators proposed the following historical terminology: 'pre-Herodian' for buildings or objects preceding Herod; 'Herodian' for building activities undertaken by Herod; 'pre-Revolt' for buildings or objects preceding the Revolt but later than the time of Herod; 'Revolt' for buildings or objects dating from AD 66 to 73; 'garrison' for finds of the Roman period but later than the Revolt; 'Byzantine' for the time of the Byzantine settlement.

Few remains have been discovered of the periods preceding Herod's time. Some potsherds of the Chalcolithic period were found in a cave on the slope and a few Iron Age ones were found on the mountain itself. Following the excavations, it seemed that no building remains of the Hasmonean period had survived on the top of Masada, and only the numerous coins of Alexander Jannaeus were attributed to this period. Since the excavation of the Twin-Palaces at Jericho, which date to the same period (*Jericho Herodian), it seems that the southwestern block of the Western Palace, the small buildings to its east and south (XI, XII and XIII, see below) as well as several other buildings should be attributed to this period. Future excavations only will clarify this theory. However, all the other buildings, excluding the Byzantine ones, belong to the building activities of Herod.

HERODIAN PERIOD The upper plateau of Masada is in the shape of a ship about 2,000 feet long, its maximum width being about 1,000 feet. The whole perimeter of the rock was surrounded by a casemate wall 13 feet wide. There were 110 towers rising above the wall, ranging in height from 20 feet to over 100 feet. The wall and the towers were coated with white plaster. There were three gates: on the east, where the snake path terminated; on the west, not far from the Western Palace, reached by a relatively broad flight of steps; and a water gate, on the northwest, leading to the water reservoirs.

The Northern Palace The Herodian buildings occupy the northern half of the rocky plateau and extend over the northern slope. Those on the northern slope were identified by the excavators as the Northern Palace and the individual buildings were numbered I, II and III. The Northern Palace is made up of three rock terraces. The lower terrace (I) is situated about 100 feet below the top of the rock and was built on the brink of the abyss. The jagged rock was surrounded with huge retaining walls so as to create a platform 54 feet square. On this platform a rectangle of low walls 30 feet by 27 feet was erected. Both the inner and outer walls of the platform had colonnades, which formed porticos all round. Small rooms were attached to the terrace on the east and the west. On the east was a miniature bath, containing all the essential components of a Roman bath, while on the west was a staircase tower leading to the upper terrace. The space between the columns was plastered and painted to resemble multicolored marble.

The middle terrace (II) is 45 feet above the lower one and is again supported by huge retaining walls. It consists of two parallel circular walls with an outer diameter of 46 feet. The circular walls have smooth tops, so that a cover of wood could be placed over them. Both walls probably supported columns, thus forming a *tholos,* or round pavilion. The rock wall to the south of this structure was smoothed, decorated with projecting pilasters, plastered and painted in the same marble patterns as those of the lower terrace. A staircase tower led from this to the upper terrace (III), which included a semicircular platform, 27 feet in diameter, on its northern side and a dwelling to the south. The dwelling had four rooms, arranged round a court. There was probably a portico on the northern side of the court. The rooms were paved with black and white mosaics arranged in very simple geometric patterns.

The Baths A thick sloping wall separated the Northern Palace from the rest of the buildings at Masada. Behind the wall was an open square, to the south of

Masada, aerial view

which stood a public bath (IV). This building is 35 feet by 30 feet in area and contained the normal components of a Roman bath. The largest and most elaborate room was the *caldarium,* about 18 feet by 17 feet with walls 8 feet thick. This room was barrel-vaulted. The *hypocaust* consisted of a thick brick floor on which stood 200 square and round brick colonnettes. The floor above it was laid with *opus sectile* (*Mosaics), while the walls were plastered and painted. To the north of the bath-house was a large court, 56 feet by 25 feet, the floor of which was paved with mosaics. This court probably served as an *apodyterium.* The whole complex was 75 feet by 60 feet in area. (*See also* *BATHS AND BATHING.)

The Storerooms To the east and south of the bath-house extends the huge complex made up of two units of storerooms (V, VI) to which Josephus refers in his descriptions of Masada (*War* VII, 295-6). The southern block (VI) contains 11 oblong halls, each about 80 feet by 12 feet. They all open on to a central corridor that separates the two units. The second unit (V) consists of four storerooms, each 60 feet by 11 feet. Fragments

of numerous storage jars were found in the rooms.

Administrative buildings To the west of the southern unit of storerooms is a building (VII) measuring 90 feet by 75 feet. Its plan is typical of the Herodian buildings at Masada: it has a big open court in the center, with a large number of rooms all round and a double row of rooms on the southern side. Three large storerooms abut on to the building on the south and west. To the south of building VII is building IX, which is about 103 feet by 35 feet. It, too, has a large rectangular open court with living accomodations around it consisting mostly of double rooms with a small forecourt. In the center of the large court was a small building with a small raised platform in front of it. Because of its layout this complex has been identified as a barracks.

The Western Palace To the southwest of building IX is the large complex of building X, which the excavators labelled the Western Palace. The whole complex extends over an area measuring 210 feet by 150 feet. It consists of three units: the southeastern block (100 feet by 75 feet), which served as the residence of the

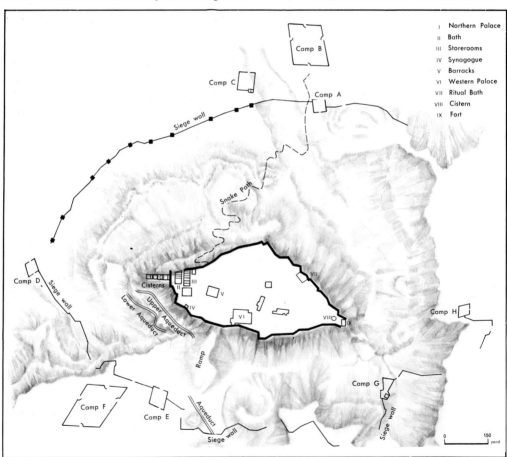

Map of Masada

king himself; the northeastern block (120 feet by 70 feet), which contained workshops and servants' quarters; a complex of storerooms and several additional units (210 feet by 60 feet).

The southeastern block has a central court measuring 36 feet by 32 feet, below which is a large cistern with a capacity of 120 cubic feet. The southern part of the court opens into a large hall with two columns between two *antae* (corner pilasters) on its façade. At the end of this hall stood the king's throne. Rooms led off on three sides of the hall, some with multicolored mosaics arranged in geometric and floral patterns. This complex also included a pool hewn in the rock. Another room contained a bathtub. Three staircases provide evidence of a second story in this part of the palace. The northeastern block contained a central courtyard with rooms all round it. The storerooms in the third complex were similar to those on the north.

Two other small buildings (XI, XII) to the east of the Western Palace were called by the excavators 'Western Small Palace' and 'Eastern Small Palace' respectively.

The synagogue This measures 45 feet by 36 feet and is built against the northwestern section of the wall. It shows two phases of construction. In its original Herodian phase it had two rows of columns, three in each row, supporting the roof, while the entrance was on the east. During the period of the Revolt a room was built into the northwestern corner. Benches were also built along the walls, and in this way two of the columns went out of use. The excavators believe that this structure was originally a synagogue in the Herodian period and that it was certainly used as a prayer house in the time of the Revolt. (*See also* *SYNAGOGUE.)

The water-supply Josephus described the great miracle of the abundance of water at Masada, a place devoid of springs and rain (*War* VII, 290-1). The water-supply system is indeed the most astonishing feature of Herod's fortress. In order to trap the water in the wadi to the north of the rock of Masada a dam was built across it and the water was brought by an aqueduct to 12 large reservoirs, with a total capacity of 40,000 cubic yd, hewn in the rock. From these cisterns the water was conveyed in jars to the various cisterns on the rock itself.

THE PERIOD OF THE REVOLT To this period were attributed numerous small finds, the remains of temporary dwellings in the casemate wall and most of the other buildings at Masada. A number of fragments of scrolls, biblical, apocryphal and sectarian, were also found (*Dead Sea Scrolls). Most important of these was a scroll of some length, of Ben-Sirah, a Hebrew writer of parables. There were also numerous ostraca containing names or referring to tithes. Remains of the period of the Roman garrison, which was stationed at Masada after its conquest by the Romans, are scanty.

THE BYZANTINE PERIOD A small church was built close to the Western Palace, consisting of an atrium and a single nave. In a side room to the north of the nave a multicolored mosaic was discovered decorated with medallions in which were portrayed fruits, an egg-basket and a cross. Remains of Byzantine habitation were also found in the ancient buildings of Masada.

THE ROMAN SIEGE WORKS According to Josephus (*War* VII, 303-19), Silva, the Roman commander, surrounded the whole rock of Masada with a siege wall and also built earth-works on the west, close to the road leading up to the palace, surmounted by a high tower. But the Roman siege works discovered at Masada are far more complicated than those referred to by Josephus. Six camps were built around the rock. Three of these were on the east, to guard the eastern approaches to the fortress: the largest (B) measures 525 feet by 400 feet, while the two others (A and C) are considerably smaller. A fourth camp (D) lay to the north; here a path led up to the general's camp (F), situated on higher ground opposite the northwestern part of the rock. To the south of camp F was camp E. It was thought that this was used to lodge merchants and other camp followers, but it is hardly possible that outsiders would have been allowed to live within the siege works. Two additional camps (G and H) lay on the high ground to the southwest of Masada. All the small camps were built on the line of the wall, while the two larger ones were outside it. The wall was additionally strengthened by numerous towers. The latest finds in a series of trial digs made in some of the camps were of the early 2nd century AD, before the Bar-Kochba revolt, in which Masada played no part.

MASOS (TEL) A site situated 7 miles east of Beer-Sheba, on the bank of the Wadi Beer-Sheba. The site was discovered by Y. Aharoni. Tel Masos includes three different mounds: an Iron Age I site with a few Chalcolithic remains (about $12\frac{1}{2}$ acres in area); an Iron Age II site and a Byzantine monastery (about $1\frac{1}{4}$ acres); and a Middle Bronze Age II site (about $2\frac{1}{2}$ acres). Excavations took place from 1972-5 under the direction of A. Kempinski (Tel Aviv University) and V. Fritz (Mainz University), and in 1979 (under A. Kempinski).

Of the Chalcolithic period pits were found with material almost identical with the Beer-Sheba culture. Two phases of the Middle Bronze Age II were distinguished: an early fortified building, which was destroyed after a short period of existence, and a earthern rampart with an attached building. The north part of the rampart was eroded by the floods of Wadi Beer-Sheba. Both phases were dated by the pottery to the first half of the 18th century BC.

Three strata of the Iron Age I were uncovered in five areas:

Stratum IIIb contained remains of floors, ash-pits and open fire-places which were dated to the end of the 13th century. In Stratum IIIa were found the first Iron Age buildings, one, a three-room house and two public buildings, one of which is fortified. This phase is dated to the end of the 13th and first half of the 12th century BC. Stratum II was the main Iron Age I settlement. The houses were built in a radial belt around the mound. In the southwest corner was an entrance to the settlement (probably the main one), to which were attached public buildings. One, a fortified building, continued from stratum IIIa. This stratum continued from the mid-12th to the first half of the 11th century, as is indicated by the Philistine, Phoenician-Bichrome

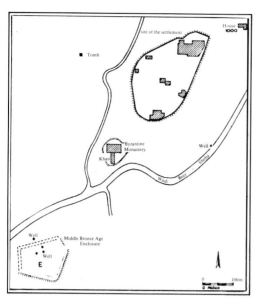

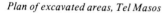

Plan of excavated areas, Tel Masos

The Gezer monuments (massebot), Middle Bronze Age

and 'Midianite' pottery. It was destroyed in an earth-quake, as was revealed in the destruction level of some of the buildings. In stratum I only a few of the buildings of stratum II were reconstructed; a new fortress was erected. This stratum is dated to the end of the 6th century BC. A monastery of the Byzantine period was built in the 6th century and abandoned in the 8th century. It belonged to Nestorian-Syrian monasticism. The church has a square apse, a cistern and burials. Syriac inscriptions were found on stones and plaster.

The site was a station in different periods on the commerical route from Egypt to the Dead Sea and east of the Jordan. It flourished in the Iron Age as a trade center and as the main Israelite settlement in the Beer-Sheba Valley. Tel Masos was identified by Y. Aharoni as biblical Hormah (Num. 14:45; 21:3. Deut. 1:44. Josh. 12:14; 15:30; 19:4. Judg. 1:17. 1 Sam. 30:30. 1 Chr. 4:30).

MASSAH and MERIBAH Names of two places in *Rephidim, so named because it was there that the Children of Israel tempted the Lord, saying, 'Is the Lord among us, or not?' (Exod. 17:7). The cause of the quarrel (*massah* and *meribah* both mean quarrel in Hebrew) was the lack of water at *Rephidim.

MASSEBAH A *massebah* (plural: *massebot*) is a stone (or several stones) arranged in a certain prescribed form to which a cultic meaning was attached, or set up to commemorate an important event. The practice is a very ancient tone, as may be seen from the prehistoric dolmens, menhirs and other forms of commemorative stone structures. The Canaanite and other cults in the Near East made much use of these stone pillars, which would be set up near sacred images or trees and libations would be poured there. The Israelites also

erected *massebot,* but without ascribing divine qualities to them. They used them only as symbols of God, or to recall his appearance at a certain spot. Thus: 'Jacob set up a pillar in the place where he talked with him, even a pillar of stone: and he poured a drink offering thereon, and he poured oil thereon. And Jacob called the name of the place where God spake with him Beth-El' (Gen. 35:14-15). In the same way Moses 'builded an altar under the hill, and 12 pillars, according to the 12 tribes of Israel' (Exod. 24:4). On their arrival in *Canaan, where a cultic significance was attached to such pillars, the Israelites were ordered to break up and destroy all the Canaanite cult places and cult objects (Exod. 23:24; 34:13; Deut. 7:5; Authorized Version: 'images'). Despite this interdiction numerous pillars were set up during the time of the Israelite kingdom (1 Kgs. 14:23; Authorized Version: 'images'). For instance, an image of Baal was set up by Ahab, but this was subsequently destroyed by Jehoram, his son (2 Kgs. 3:2). The setting up of images and their subsequent destruction by pious kings is referred to several times in the Bible. The most elaborate example found in excavations is the row of *massebot* at *Gezer.

Commemorative stones set up for various reasons were more common in Israel. They might commemorate a treaty concluded between two parties, such as the one between Jacob and Laban (Gen. 31:44-8); in such cases the stone also served as a boundary mark and thus constituted a legal document, a practice which originated in *Babylon. The 12 stones set up by Moses belong to this group. Other stones commemorated a victory achieved with the help of God, examples being the one set up after the victory over the *Philistines, called 'Eben-Ezer', the 'stone of help' (1

Sam. 7:12), or the stone (Authorized Version: 'place') that Saul set up at *Carmel after his victory over *Amalek (1 Sam. 15:12). Stones of both types are quite common among archaeological finds and may be grouped with the inscribed stelae set up by different Egyptian kings at places such as *Beth-Shean or *Megiddo. Even more examples of such stelae are to be found in *Mesopotamia and *Egypt. They usually bear a symbolic image of the battle being commemorated and a written description of it.

The group of boundary stones also includes some stone pillars of the Persian period found at *Gezer. The words 'boundary of Gezer' and the name Alkios, a citizen of the city, are inscribed on them in Hebrew and Greek.

MEDABA; MADABA; MEDEBA A town in *Moab, seized by the Israelites from Sihon the Amonite (Num. 21:30); in the territory of Reuben (Josh. 13:16). During the reign of David Joab fought the *Ammorites and the *Amonites there (1 Chr. 19:7 ff.; Authorized Version: 'Syrians'). Mesha, King of *Moab, tells in his stele (*Inscriptions) of Omri's conquest of Medaba and its subsequent liberation by Mesha. In the Hellenistic period it was in the hands of the *Nabateans (1 Macc. 1:9, 31). Alexander Jannaeus siezed the city from them, but it was returned to them by John Hyrcanus II (Josephus, *Antiq.* XIII, 18). Nabatean inscriptions found at Medaba show that it was also in their hands in the Roman period. After the annexation of the *Nabatean kingdom to the Roman empire Medaba became an autonomus city and minted its own *coins. Its rule extended over a large territory, its boundaries extending toward *Heshbon on the north, *Livias on the west, and to the *Arnon River on the south. In the Byzantine period it was an episcopal town and in AD 451 its bishop participated in the Council of Chalcedon. In 1896 a mosaic floor was discovered in a 6th-century church. This depicts a map of the biblical lands, accompanied by appropriate quotations from the Bible. It is known as the Medaba map and is an extremely useful source of information about the topography of the Holy Land. In addition to this church there were numerous other churches at Medaba, some of them richly decorated with mosaics.

MEGADIM (TEL) An ancient mound situated more than a mile to the north of Athlit. The site was partly excavated in 1967 and 1969 by M. Broshi on behalf of the Israel Department of Antiquities and Museums and the Israel Exploration Society. It was occupied in the Early Bronze Age I-II, the Middle Bronze Age II, the Late Bronze Age and the Persian period. The early periods have not yet been thoroughly investigated. The upper strata contained remains of three occupation levels of a Phoenician town of the Persian period. It extended over an area of about 4 acres and was surrounded by a rectangular casemate wall. Inside the town a section of a street was excavated. The dwellings are spacious, one being a four-room house typical of the Iron Age. Some of the houses are believed to have been public buildings. The rooms yielded large quantities of pottery, some typical local pottery of the Persian period and some imported from Greece,

Clay figurine of a Phoenician fertility goddess, Tel Megadim, Persian period

Rhodes and *Cyprus. The finds point to close trade relations with Greece and the islands of the Eastern Mediterranean. The rich soil and the abundance of water helped to create a prosperous agricultural town. Phoenician tombs were discovered nearby, the dead being covered with mounds of sand paved with large potsherds, on top of which were the tombstones. Both cremation and burial of complete bodies were found, cremation being the more typical Phoenician method of disposal.

The lower Early Bronze Age level was reached in trial digs only. The ancient identification of the site remains unknown, but the excavator suggests that it should be identified with *Cartha of the classical sources.

MEGIDDO One of the most important Canaanite cities in the north of Palestine, mentioned for the first time in the annals of Tuthmosis III, who in 1468 BC defeated a Canaanite army near here. The long list of booty is a good indication of the wealth of the city at that time. After this conquest Megiddo became an Egyptian stronghold in the north of the country. Its importance in the 15th and 14th centuries BC is also evident from the *Taanach tablets and the *El Amarna letters. It was still a very strong Canaanite city-state when the Israelites conquered the territory. The 'waters of Megiddo' are mentioned in Deborah's song (Judg. 5:19), though it is listed among the Canaanite cities that were not conquered by the Israelites (Judg. 1:27). Solomon fortified Megiddo together with *Gezer and *Hazor (1 Kgs. 9:15), and it was one of the cities in his fifth division (1 Kgs. 4:12). In 924 BC it was taken by Pharaoh Sheshonq I. Amaziah, King of Judah, died here (2 Kgs. 9:27). In 733-732 BC it was taken by Tiglath-Pileser III of Assyria and became the capital of the Assyrian satrapy of Megiddo. In the 7th century BC it was again part of Judah for a short period, and near it took place the battle between Josiah, King of Judah, and Pharaoh Necho (2 Kgs. 23:29; 2 Kgs. 35:22). After that battle it lost importance as the guardian of the Wadi Ara pass, a role that was taken over by nearby *Legio in the Roman period.

The site of Megiddo has been identified with the large mound of Tell el-Muteselim. It was extensively excavated by J. Schumacher in 1903-5 on behalf of the German Oriental Society, and in 1925-35 by C.S. Fisher, P.L.O. Guy and G. Loud on behalf of the Oriental Institute of the University of Chicago. The first expedition made a trench 60-75 feet wide throughout the whole length of the mound and discovered six strata ranging from the Middle Bronze Age to the Iron Age. To the earlier period belong two large public buildings, beneath which were found some monumental tombs, possibly of the kings of Megiddo of the Late Bronze Age. To the Iron Age, possibly from the time of Solomon, was attributed another large building, identified by the excavators as a 'palace'. Among the small finds the seal of Shema, the servant of Jeroboam (*Seal), is particularly interesting.

The exacavations made by the Oriental Institute were more extensive. The excavators intended to lay bare all the occupation levels from top to bottom, but in fact only the four upper ones were fully excavated, the remaining one being studied in a deep section cut down to the bedrock. First to be excavated was the eastern slope of the mound, where the rubble taken out of the excavation had to be dumped. Here tombs of seven 'stages', all of the Early Bronze Age, were discovered. On the mound itself 20 strata were observed, some of which were further subdivided, the total number of occupation levels being 25. The dating of these strata has now been amended by other scholars and the dates given below are the ones accepted by Israeli archaeologists today.

In the bedrock a small cave was discovered in which were bones and flint tools of the pre-Pottery Neolithic period (*Prehistory). (It is numbered - XX.) Stratum XX (second half of the 4th millennium BC) yielded a few remains of rectangular and apsidal houses built of mud bricks. Stratum XIX is of the earliest phase of the Early Bronze Age (3150/3000-2850 BC). To this period belongs a three-room building, one of whose rooms measures 12 feet by 36 feet, and has been identified as a shrine with an altar against one of its walls (*Temples). Close to it was a court, which probably had more rooms around it. On the stone pavement of the court a hunting scene was scratched. A thick mudbrick wall also belongs to this period, but it could not be identified with certainty as a city wall.

Early Bronze Age II is represented by three strata (XVIII-XVI). To these levels belongs the first city wall, which is 25 feet thick and has a stone foundation that is still standing to a height of 12 feet, though the mud-brick superstructure has disappeared. Close to the early shrine an open-air high place was set up. It is round, 25 feet in diameter and 5 feet high, and built of

small stones, with steps leading up to it on the east. The whole high place is surrounded by a wall. Within the enclosure pottery and bones, probably of sacrificial victims, were discovered. Stratum XV belongs to Early Bronze Age III or IV. The older high place was still in use at this period and close to it three additional temples, identical in plan, were constructed. Each measures 27 feet by 41 feet and consists of one room with a porch in front of it. Facing the entrance, against the back wall, was an altar. The dating of this stratum is in dispute.

The latest city of the Early Bronze Age suffered destruction. Stratum XIV is of the transition period, between Middle Bronze Age I and Middle Bronze Age IIA, when attempts were made to resettle the site. The strong early wall was replaced by a flimsy one and only one of the three temples was used. Inside the large room a smaller one was built, the space between the walls being filled with stones. It is worth noting that the sanctity of this area was preserved in its successive periods.

Stratum XIII, of the Middle Bronze Age IIA, has been subdivided into sub-strata A and B. It contained a new city wall built of mud brick on a stone foundation 5 feet thick. To this wall belongs the earliest city gate, consisting of two narrow entrances standing at right angles to each other, so that it was suitable for pedestrians only (*Fortifications). In the sacred area an open-air high place was maintained.

Strata XII-X are again of the Middle Bronze Age IIA. The earlier city wall was still in use but was now doubled. Set against it were houses that were entered from a street running parallel to the wall. The houses, three of which were unearthed, consisted of a court around which the rooms were built. There must have been a temple in this city but it has not been found. In the city of stratum XI the brick wall was replaced by a stone one 5 feet thick, built in the form of recesses and salients (*Fortifications). This comparatively thin wall was protected by a glacis typical of the *Hyksos period. To this city belongs a palace. It lies quite near the city gate and is similar to the private houses in plan, but more carefully built. A new gate, of the direct-approach type, is also typical of this period. The gateway is built of rough stones faced with ashlar. The 9 foot wide entrance was ample for chariots (*Weapons and warfare).

To the Late Bronze Age I belong strata IX (1550-1468 BC) and VIII (1468-1350/1300 BC, i.e. from the conquest of Tuthmosis III to the *El Amarna period). The palace near the gate was now extended until it was 150 feet in length and was surrounded by wall 6 feet thick. It included a washroom, a complete innovation. Under the floor of one of the rooms a hoard of gold jewelry and carved ivory plaques was found. In the sacred area a new temple was built, consisting one room measuring 35 feet by 30 feet. The entrance to it was protected by two towers with walls 10 feet thick, an arrangement that is typical of the Late Bronze Age (*Temples). No other major changes were made in this period.

Strata VIIB and VIIA are of the Late Bronze Age II. Not many changes in the plan of the city have been observed, though the palace did become a little smaller. In its treasury another hoard of about 200 carved ivories was found, representing Canaanite art at its best. It is dated by the finds to 1140/30 BC. This city suffered violent destruction.

Strata VIB and VIA (1140/20-1020/1000 BC, VB and VA (1020/1000-950 BC, i.e. David's reign and the early part of Solomon's reign), IVB (950-924 BC, i.e. the later part of Solomon's reign down to Pharaoh Sheshonk's campaign) and IVA (924-733/2 BC, i.e. the time of the kings of Israel down to the Assyrian conquest) are all Iron Age strata. The Iron Age at Megiddo begins with a poor city (VIB); it was unfortified but later on (VIA) better houses of the four-room type were built. This city was probably destroyed by the *Philistines. The city of strata VB and VA was insignificant, and it was only later in Solomon's reign (stratum IVB) that it was surrounded by a strong casemate wall with a large direct-approach gate (*Fortifications). To this period belongs the palace discovered by Schumacher. It seems that the construction of the famous stables was begun at this time. In Ahab's day (IVA) two large complexes of stables were built providing stabling for 492 horses. Each unit consisted of a long hall with two rows of pillars down the center to which the horses were tethered. The pillars supported the roof. The gate was rebuilt on a smaller scale and the casemate wall was replaced by a single wall strengthened by salients. The elaborate water supply system was begun in the reign of Solomon and completed by Ahab. It consisted of a shaft 75 feet deep and a tunnel 210 feet long, which ensured safe access to the water.

After the conquest of Tiglath-Pileser III a new city was built (stratum III, of 733/2-630 BC). It was well planned, with spacious houses separated by streets intersecting at right angles. On the sites of the stables, and the palace two large public buildings were erected, each consisting of a large court with rooms around it. Another important building was the large grain store, a circular structure 35 feet in diameter, sunk about 22 feet into the ground and with two flights of steps. This city made use of the earlier city wall and gate.

Stratum II contained a short-lived city of the time of Josiah (630-609 BC). It was not fortified but had a large citadel instead. The latest city, in stratum I, is of the Persian period. It was an unfortified town with no impressive buildings and with it the history of Megiddo came to an end.

In 1960-70 excavations on the site were resumed by Y. Yadin on behalf of the Hebrew University. A section of the city wall in the northeastern part of the mound was investigated. This offset-inset wall had been dated by the excavators to the time of Solomon, but as a result of a comparison of the wall with the Solomonic walls of *Hazor and *Gezer, which were of the casemate type, Yadin was doubtful as to this attribution. In order to establish its date the foundations of the wall were excavated and were found to have been constructed above a fortress or a *palace built partly of ashlars. It also lay partly beneath the foundation of the stable compound. North and west

of this palace were found casemate walls, above which was built the solid offset-inset wall. It thus became evident that the solid wall and the stables were later than this wall, and were thus post-Solomonic, and belonged to stratum IVA — the period of the dynasty of Omri. To Solomon's time (strata VA-IVB) belong the casemate wall and the fortress-palace. This conclusion helped to assign the massive gate of six chambers and two towers to the same casemate *fortification and to correct the dating of the overlying two gates. The investigation of the *water system also showed that it was not of the 13th-12th centuries BC, as the excavators believed, but post-Solomonic and not later than the dynasty of Omri. The buildings of stratum III, according to Yadin, were built under Assyrian influence. Stratum II was an unfortified town possibly from the time of Josiah; its destruction is ascribed to Pharaoh Necho in 609 BC. The town of stratum I dating mainly to the Persian period, was also not fortified.

MEIRON The home-town of Rabbi Simeon Bar Yochai. One of the villages in Upper *Galilee fortified by Josephus Flavius, named by him Mero or Meroth (others, however, identify Meroth with Marun er-Ras farther to the north). Meiron also appears in the list of the priestly courses, and in the Jerusalem Talmud it is renowned for its olive-oil.

Ruins of a *synagogue were observed on the site in the 19th century and in 1868 it was cleared by C. Wilson. The building (app. 82 feet by 40 feet) is oriented to the south. Aside from a section of the facade, part of the cornice and several column bases, little of the building has survived. Three entrances appear in the façade. The doorposts and the lintels were decorated with simple mouldings. There were two rows of eight columns, and an additional possible row of four columns on the northern side. The synagogue is dated to the 3rd-4th century AD.

Excavations at Meiron were conducted in the years 1971-2 and 1974-5 by the American School of Oriental Research under the direction of E.M. Meyers. In these excavations further evidence for dating the synagogue to the late 3rd century AD was found. A block of shops and a spacious private house were also cleared. From the 2nd century AD is a tower still standing to a height of 18 feet. An industrial quarter of the middle and late Roman periods was excavated in the lower town of Meiron. A tomb and charnel house indicate occupation of the town from late Hellenistic to late Roman times. The town was abandoned after the middle of the 4th century AD.

MEMPHIS See *NOPH

MENORAH Candlesticks and clay lamps were used for illumination in biblical times (2 Kgs. 4:10). The golden menorah, a candlestick with seven branches, was one of the most important cult objects connected with the tabernacle (Exod. 25:31-40; 37:17-25) and stood 'without the veil of the testimony, in the tabernacle of the congregation' (Lev.24:3-4). Instead of the one menorah of the tabernacle Solomon ordered 10, also made of gold, for his temple, five to stand on each side in front of the Holy of Holies (1 Kgs. 7:49). The Second Temple also had one golden menorah. After

Coin of Matthias Antigonus depicting a menorah

the destruction of the Temple the menorah was taken to Rome with the other cult objects, to be carried in the triumphal procession. It was portrayed on the Arch of Titus in the Roman Forum. It seems that the base, which according to the arch was ornamented with mythological creatures, must have been made in Rome specially for the procession. Only a few portrayals of the menorah are extant from the time of the Second Temple. It appears on a coin of Matthias Antigonus (*Money), and two candlesticks were scratched on the wall of a tomb of that period in *Jerusalem, which is known as Jason's Tomb. It is also engraved on a limestone measuring-cup of the time of Herod.

Because of its sanctity the menorah was much used in synagogue art, both in Palestine and during the Diaspora, after the destruction of the Temple. It was engraved on capitals and column shafts and was a particularly common motif on the mosaic floors of synagogues of the Byzantine period. A certain development can be traced in these examples, probably corresponding to a change in the actual use of the menorah in the synagogue ritual. In the early synagogues — those of the 2nd-3rd centuries AD — clay lamps were placed directly on top of the branches of the menorah, while in the later ones a bar was laid across the branches and clay or glass lamps were placed on this bar; this probably made the burning lamps more stable. The menorah appears frequently on small objects such as seals, amulets, rings, clay lamps and on tombstones of the 4th-7th centuries AD. It is also seen very often on chancel-screens in synagogues, along with other Jewish symbols.

MEROM; WATER OF MEROM; MERON The place where all the kings of northern *Canaan gathered under the leadership of Jabin, King of *Hazor, and where they were vanquished by Joshua (Josh. 11:5-7). It is apparently mentioned in the list of conquests of Tuthmosis III, and a fortified town in the Galilee by the name of *mrm* is drawn, together with other Galilean cities, on the reliefs of Pharaoh Rameses II. It is also mentioned in a document of Tiglath-Pileser III, referring to his campaign against Galilee in 733/32 BC.

It was known as Meron in the period of the Second Temple but Josephus, who fortified it, refers to it as Meroth (*Antiq.* II, 573). It is still called Meron today. Remains of a synagogue of the 2nd-3rd centuries AD were found here. Unlike most of the synagogues in *Galilee, which were almost square in plan, it was an oblong building, measuring 75 feet by 45 feet. It had a triple colonnade and three entrances on the southern side, facing *Jerusalem. Two of the doorways still have their lintels *in situ*. These and the doorposts were decorated with simple architectural mouldings. The synagogue was approached by a wide flight of four steps. Nothing has remained of its external decoration.

In the years 1971, 1972, 1974 and 1975 excavations were conducted on the site on behalf of the American School of Oriental Research under the direction of E.M. Meyers. It is estimated that the ancient town extended over an area of 37-50 acres. Trial trenches dug around the *synagogue helped in establishing the date of its foundation in the late 3rd century AD. Excavations in various parts of the town revealed that in the Hellenistic period there was a small settlement on the site. The fortifications of the site are not earlier than the 2nd century AD, and nothing was discovered of the period of the War against the Romans. Meiron was abandoned in about AD 360.

MEROZ A town whose inhabitants refused to assist Deborah and Barak, son of Abinoam in the war against Sisera (Judg. 5:23). Eusebius (*Onom.* 128:4-6, 12-13) states that in his time there was a village by the name of Marous, Merrous, 12 miles from *Beth-Shean, near *Dothan, and mistakenly identifies it with *Meiron.

MESAD HASHAVYAHU An Iron Age fortress a mile south of the port of *Jabneh, close to the Mediterranean coast. The site was excavated by J. Naveh in 1960 on behalf of the Israel Department of Antiquities and Museums and the Israel Exploration Society. The L-shaped fortress covered an area of 1½ acres and enclosed a courtyard of 1 acre, with rooms built along its walls, and a smaller space in which three rows of structures were separated by streets. The walls of the fortress were of bricks set on a stone socle and the gate, on the west, was built of dressed stones. In addition to the local Iron Age pottery a large number of Greek imported vessels were found, and these led the excavator to suggest that a Greek colony existed on the site. On the other hand Hebrew documents were also found (*Inscriptions), which would indicate that the fortress was under Judean rule for some time. According to the archaeological data the fortress was founded some time in the last third of the 7th century BC, probably by Greeks who settled on the site. Sometime before 609 BC it was conquered by Josiah, King of Judah, and was abandoned in 609 BC, when the *Egyptians under Pharaoh Necho advanced along the Mediterranean coast. The ancient name of the site is not known.

MESOPOTAMIA 'The land between the rivers', the name first given by Polybius and Strabo exclusively to the lands lying between the Tigris (*Hiddekel) and the *Euphrates, is now applied to various regions. They

Phoenician pottery mask and burnished jugs

Hoard of silver found at En-Gedi

Left page, top: Flint cores and blades; beginning of the Urban Age
Below: Main street at Nabatean Petra

The theater at Shechem; Roman period

Stone chair depicting a dolphin in the Roman theater at Shechem

Interior of tomb of Roman soldiers at Shechem

Egyptian scribe

Sumerian pictographic writing

Above: Commentary of Habakkuk from the Dead Sea Scrolls

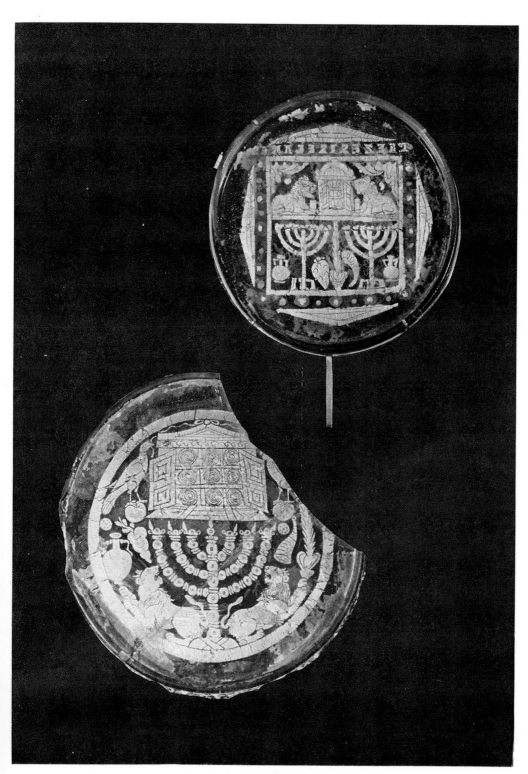

Jewish gilt glass plates, 4th century. Note the cupboards containing scrolls

Back panel of Tutankhamon's throne; 14th century BC

*Votive cup from the Midianite temple at Timnah;
13th century BC*

*Midianite votive serpent from the temple at Timnah;
13th century BC*

Incense burner adorned with snakes; Israelite period

Cultic stand from Taanach

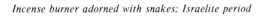

Man playing the flute to his dog; from the mosaic pavement of the monastery at Beth-Shean

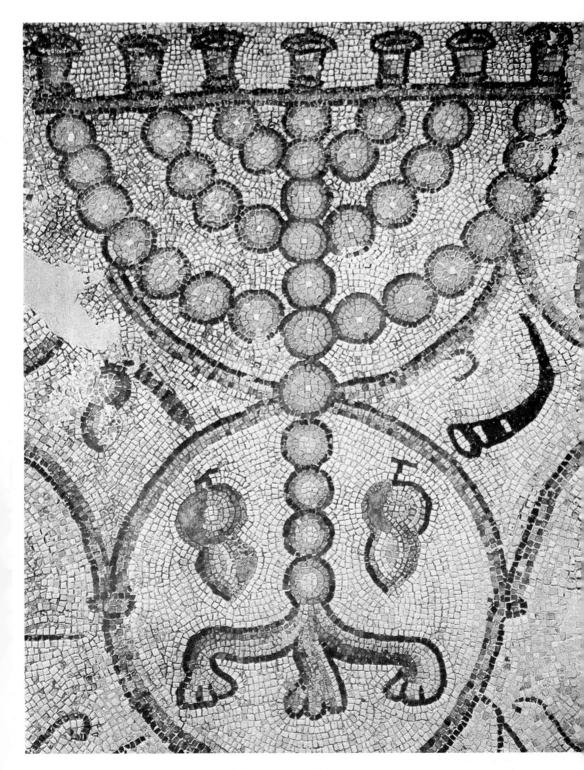

Menorah *depicted on the mosaic pavement of the synagogue at Maon*

A Philistine pottery Krater

Central part of the mosaic pavement at Beth Alpha synagogue: the zodiac wheel with the sun-god in his chariot in the center, the twelve signs, and the four seasons in the corners

Gold bull's head forming part of a lyre from Ur

Daggers and sheaths of Tutankhamon; all of gold except the iron blade of the dagger on the left

Arab jewelry hoard found at Caesarea; AD *969-1171*

are all bordered on the north by the mountains of Kurdistan, to the south by the marshes of the river delta, to the west by the Syrian steppes and deserts and to the east by the mountains of Iran. The northern and southern parts of Mesopotamia differ in many respects — geographically, culturally and in other ways. But they can still be considered as two facets of the same historical entity that can properly be called Mesopotamia throughout its cultural development, which lasts from the beginning of the 3rd millennium BC down to the end of the Persian period. The problems of studying the cultures earlier than the 3rd millennium BC have not yet been fully resolved, since the information available is so scanty.

The oldest known Mesopotamian civilization, at Jarmo in northern Iraq, belongs to the Neolithic period. The subsequent civilizations in the north are those of Hassuna, Samarra and Tell Halaf. In the south the earliest cultures have been unearthed at Tell el-Ubaid. The civilization of Tell el-Ubaid proper flourished in the 4th millennium BC. From then until the emergence of the Assyrian kingdom the hegemony of Mesopotamia was established in the south. Tell el-Ubaid civilization was preceded by the Eridu civilization, the earliest known in southern Mesopotamia; it was succeeded by the Erech civilization, which was to establish the prototypes of the Mesopotamian culture: the appearance of writing, the cylinder seal and the building of ziggurats. This protohistoric era came to an end in about 3000 BC, though its exact date and duration are still a matter of controversy. This period does, however, mark the beginning of a new era that has left behind written testimony — the Sumerian civilization. The early dynastic period of Sumerian civilization lasted about four centuries. Our main sources for its history are a number of lists of kings, together with other documents that assist in identifying them, their dynasties and their deeds, although they provide a far from comprehensive picture of the period.

Extremely interesting and valuable material of the 26th, 25th and 24th centuries BC is to be found in the inscriptions of Lagash, whose kings, called *ensi*, in their struggle for hegemony over Sumer, carried their influence as far as Ashur to the north. It appears that their main efforts were brought to bear against the neighboring town of Umma, thanks to an enmity that was deeply rooted in the historical tradition of the land. Among the kings of Lagash the fame of Urukagina (2378-2371 BC) is outstanding and is based upon the 'restoration of freedom', which he brought about by implementing sweeping economic and social reforms. But Urukagina's rule was a short duration. He was defeated and Lagash was destroyed by his enemy Lugal-Zaggisi, the *ensi* of Umma. The latter retained the hegemony of Sumer for about 25 years, until the advent of Sargon of Agade and the establishment of the Accadian kingdom (2371-2230 BC).

The Accadian kingdom provided the first Semitic interlude in the history of Mesopotamia. Although it was brief and ended in catastrophe, it was considered by later generations to have been the most important because for the first time it gave shape to a great

Head of Hammurabi, Babylonian

empire with a single central authority. It was also to become a source of inspiration for later conquerors who tried to emulate it. The origin of Sargon (2371-2316 BC) is not clear. A legend, of which various versions are known and which is similar to other traditions concerning the birth of the heroes of antiquity, places the beginning of his career at the court of the King of Kish. It seems that Sargon abandoned Kish and moved to Agade, which he had himself founded. From there he set out to conquer the rest of Sumer. He led his campaigns upstream along the *Euphrates and in all likelihood conquered northern Syria, before reaching the Mediterranean coast. If we accept the historical authenticity of a text from the 'omen literature' of Mesopotamia he must even have reached *Cyprus and *Crete. In the east he reached *Elam and captured Susa (*Shushan). Another important member of the Agade Dynasty was Naram Sin (2291-2255 BC), Sargon's grandson, who again ruled over vast territories. Although a number of kings are mentioned as his successors it seems that the decline of the Accadian Empire had begun in his own time with the invasions of barbaric tribes, mainly the Gutians, who came from the Zagros Mountains in the east and ruled over almost the whole of Mesopotamia for about a century. At that time a few cities in the south that had escaped the dominations of the Gutians, *Erech and Lagash especially, enjoyed great prosperity. During the reign of its famous King Gudea, astonishing artistic and literary achievements were made in Lagash.

The Gutians were overcome by the King of *Erech, Utu-Hegal (2120-2114 BC) whose successor, Ur-Nammu of *Ur, founded the celebrated 3rd Dynasty of *Ur. This period, also known as the 'Sumerian renaissance', is extremely well documented by finds from archaeological excavations. The monarchs of this dynasty called themselves 'Kings of Sumer and Accad', a title used from then onwards by all the great kings of Mesopotamia. The fall of the 3rd Dynasty of *Ur was brought about by Semitic tribes who harried it from the west, as well as by invasions from the east and by a chain reaction of internal crises and revolts.

Stele of Hammurabi

Upon the ruins of *Ur sprang up a large number of independent city-states, ruled by kings from the west or from the east. The ruling class was therefore either Amorite or Elamite, as their names prove. They adopted the civilization of the Sumerians, so a cultural continuity was maintained despite the political disintegration and the penetration of foreign elements and influences, mostly Semitic ones. Predominant among these city-states were Isin and Larsa — this is sometimes even called the Isin-Larsa period — and Eshnuna, farther to the north in the Diyala Valley. Eshnuna is known for its codes of law that are essential to a study of Hammurabi's codes. At about the same time Ashuer enjoyed its first period of prosperity and, under the reign of Shamshi-Adad, commanded an empire spreading from the Mediterranean to the mountains of Kurdistan.

Our knowledge of this period is based mainly on the discovery of the archives of *Mari, with thousands of clay tablets containing information about the events that preceded the capture of the town by Hammurabi. They show that during the first years of his reign Hammurabi was the contemporary of the powerful Shamshi-Adad of Ashur, who also controlled *Mari. After the death of Shamshi-Adad and with the succession of his son there was a shift in the balance of power in Mesopotamia. *Mari, under the rule of Zimrilim, succeeded in regaining its independence and thus checked, for the time being, Assyria's ascendancy. There followed a short period during which none of the rulers of the big cities, such as *Mari, *Babylon, Eshnuna and Larsa, was sovereign over the others. Hammurabi eventually succeeded in overshadowing them all and slowly, but with great political shrewdness, founded the Babylonian kingdom that dominated southern and central Mesopotamia and also wielded some kind of influence over Assyria in the north.

Hammurabi's reign (1792-1749 BC) was an era of intense cultural activity and economic prosperity and survived in the memory of the following generations as the 'golden age' of *Babylon. His code of laws, although not the very earliest in Mesopotamia, is the most complete and perfect of them all and became the canon of law studied in the schools of *Babylon. Hammurabi had no successor who was in any way comparable to him and his vast domain was eventually split into a northern and a southern kingdom. This dynasty did, however, contrive to remain on the throne of *Babylon until the *Hittites put an end to it in the year 1595 BC, during the reign of Samsu-Ditana, the last king of the first Babylonian Dynasty.

The invasions of the *Hittites, and the Kassite conquest that followed, brought in their wake a dark age that is characterized by a complete absence of written documents concerning *Babylon. These reappear in the 15th and 14th centuries BC, heralding the Middle Babylonian and Middle Assyrian periods, which were to last until the end of the 2nd millennium BC. During this time Assyria experienced a new ascendancy, which began with the reign of Assur-Ubalit (1364-1329 BC). Its rulers were considered to rank with the pharaohs of *Egypt, the kings of the *Hittites and the kings of *Babylon under the Kassites. These latter kings kept their rank among the great sovereigns of the world despite the fact that *Babylon was in constant political decline throughout this period. Apart from a few revivals it continued to decline until the 8th century BC, when it became merely a part of the Assyrian Empire.

Although politically inferior, Babylonian culture during this Middle Babylonian period exerted a great influence abroad, especially in Assyria, where its scholars were active at the courts. The Babylonian language was an international language and was used far beyond the borders of Mesopotamia.

At the end of the 2nd millennium BC Assyria itself suffered a period of decline and obscurity caused by Aramean invaders and the establishment of their kingdoms on its borders. It emerged from this eclipse only in the days of Ashurdan II (934-912 BC) and Adadnirari (911-891 BC), the founders of the Assyrian Empire. Ashurnasirpal II (883-859 BC) and his son Shalmaneser III (858-824 BC) were mighty conquerors who greatly extended the boundaries of their empire. It was during the reign of Shalmaneser III that the first encounter occurred between a king of Assyria and a king of Israel, at the battle of *Qarqar in northern Syria in the year 853 BC. From that time onwards Assyria, and later *Babylon, were to play a fateful role in the history of the kingdoms of Israel and Judah.

The Assyrian Empire reached its peak during the Sargonid Dynasty founded by Sargon II (720-704 BC). This was the period of its greatest territorial expansion and its richest literary activity. It was now the most powerful empire the world had ever known. Yet its lines of communication were becoming much too long, while the conquered nations were awaiting any opportunity to shake off its yoke. Thus the Babylonians, the Medes (*Medai) and the Scythians united against Assyria in the summer of 612 BC and captured and destroyed *Nineveh, the capital. The ultimate refuge of the Assyrians and of their last king, Ashurubalit II, was *Haran. But that city too was captured in 610 BC and the remainder of the Assyrian army was finally destroyed at *Carchemish on the *Euphrates in 605 BC.

The victor of *Carchemish, Nebuchadnezzar, built the mighty neo-Babylonian Empire, but after his death in 562 BC it quickly declined. Treachery, political and religious conflicts were the rule in *Babylon. This was the situation when Cyrus, King of the Persians, entered world history. He had little difficulty in conquering *Babylon in the year 539 BC: the city surrendered to him without a blow being struck. Although it was not destroyed its capture marks the fall of *Babylon and the decline of the Mesopotamian civilization. The city remained standing for some time but an entirely new era had already dawned, an era marking the end of a civilization that could boast of an uninterrupted tradition lasting over 2,000 years.

Archaeological research in Mesopotamia began in 1625, when the Italian nobleman Pietro della Valle brought back from a journey across Mesopotamia some bricks found at *Ur and *Babylon 'on which were writings in certain unknown characters'. Gradu-

ally academics and monarchs became interested in this new field of investigation and in 1761 the King of Denmark sent a scientific mission out there. The inscriptions copied at Persepolis by its leader, Karsten Niebuhr, were offered to philologists, who began the difficult task of deciphering them. From then on all those who visited the East made a point of exploring the ruins of Mesopotamia, although their activities were confined to surface examinations. It was the French Consul at Mosul, P.E. Botta, who in 1845 started the first archaeological excavations in Mesopotamia at Khorsabad (*Dur Sharrukin) and discovered the Assyrian civilization. He was followed by H. Layard, an Englishman, who dug at Nimrud and *Nineveh. Soon a number of mounds had been excavated, but unfortunately the methods used were far from scientific, the only aim being to find striking museum pieces to send back to Europe.

Scientific methods and scholarly research were introduced into the new discipline by the Germans, mainly by R. Koldewey, who excavated at *Babylon (1899-1917), and by W. Andreae at Ashur (1903-14). Their methods were soon adopted by other archaeologists and the period between the First and Second World Wars was one of brilliant and fruitful archaeological activity. In these years C.L. Woolley dug at *Ur and its famous Royal Cemetery (1922-34), E. Heinrich at Uruk and A. Parrot at *Mari, while the sites of Ubaid, *Nineveh and Kish, to mention only a few, were being explored. After the Second World War work was resumed, and today all the important cities of ancient Mesopotamia and a number of smaller and less famous places have been excavated or are now being excavated. And yet there are still over 6,000 mounds hiding the remains of ancient towns waiting for the explorer's shovel.

METALS From a study of the geological strata of *Egypt, Syria and Asia Minor it is possible to map ancient mines of the Near East. Asia Minor was rich in iron and had some copper. Copper was also mined in northern Syria, in a region known to the authors of the *El Amarna letters as the 'Land of Copper'. More important, however, were the copper mines of *Cyprus, whence copper (Late Latin: *cuprum*) took its name. Some iron and some copper were also found in the *Lebanon. In Palestine the important sources of copper were those of the southern Arabah, *Sinai and *Punon, east of the Arabah, which were exploited at different periods (the attribution of these mines to Solomon now seems very doubtful). Ezekiel knew that the metals used in Palestine were brought by Tyrian merchants from *Tarshish (Ezek. 27:12), and Solomon set up foundries in the *Jordan Valley (1 Kgs. 7:46).

Our knowledge of mining activities in the biblical period is, however, limited. It is certain that surface veins of metal ore were exploited, and the possibility that tunnels were dug in order to reach richer deposits should not be excluded. Job (28:1-7) may have been alluding to such methods. Metals were probably brought to Palestine in bars, from which the finished products were produced locally. Crucibles for founding copper and iron have been discovered in several

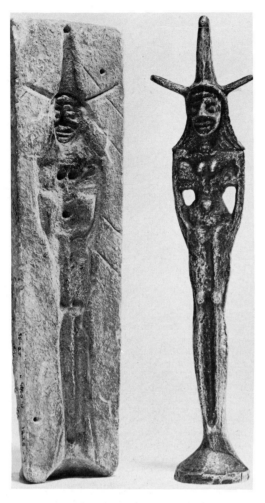

Mould for casting figurines, Nahariya, Middle Bronze Age

GOLD This precious metal was mined in *Egypt in early times. The nuggets containing gold were broken into small pieces with hammers and then ground to dust in mortars. The ground material was then placed on a sloping table and water was poured onto it. The dross was thus washed away while the gold, which was heavier, remained on the table. The laborers to whom this work was entrusted were prisoners and criminals, supervised by overseers who did not know their language. Many gold ingots have been found in Egypt in river-beds. The Bible used many different names for gold, some of which refer to its quality, such as 'pure gold' (Exod. 25:36, etc.); 'refined gold' (1 Chr. 28:18); 'best gold' (a not very good translation of *zahav mufaz* in 1 Kgs. 10:18), 'beaten gold (*zahav shahut*, 1 Kgs. 10:17) and again 'pure gold' (*zahav sagur*, 1 Kgs. 6:20, etc.). Gold is also associated with *Ophir: 'wedge of *Ophir' (Isa. 13:12); 'gold of Ophir' (1 Chr. 29:4) or, in the Hebrew, just 'Ophir' (Job 22:24). The Israelites most probably acquired the goldsmith's art while in *Egypt. According to the Bible many of the vessels used in the tabernacle were made of gold (*Cult objects).

There is no gold in Palestine, so it had to be brought from other countries such as Tarshish, *India or *Arabia. The *Phoenicians brought gold from Havilah (Gen. 2:11), buying it from Arabian merchants (Ezek. 27:22). Solomon sent a fleet to bring gold from Ophir. Gold coins were not minted before the Persian period (*Money); until then payments were made in other metals (cf. Josh. 7:21).

SILVER A precious metal, known in very early times. In Palestine silver vessels have been found in archaeological strata as early as the Middle and Late Bronze Ages. Silver was used for producing cups, bowls, plates and jewelry. The richest silver mines in the ancient world were in Spain. There were also silver mines in the mountains bordering the *Red Sea and large quantities of silver were found in Anatolia, which supplied the needs of *Babylon. In the Hellenistic and Roman periods silver was also mined in Greece.

This metal is rarely found in the pure state. The crude ore, which contains other elements, mainly lead, is refined by a process of smelting. At high temperatures the molten lead and other heavier substances sink, while the lighter silver floats (cf. Jer. 6:28-30; Ezek. 22:17-22). Silver was highly esteemed because of its comparative rarity and because of its chemical and physical properties. Together with gold and copper it was used as payment, in barter (Gen. 20:16, etc.) and for paying taxes (1 Kgs. 15:19; Authorized Version: 'present'). Images of gods were made of silver (Exod. 20:23), as were jewelry and household utensils (Exod. 3:22; 11:2, etc.). Together with gold, silver was much used in the tabernacle (Exod. 26) and in the Temple (2 Chr. 2, etc.). Silver mines are mentioned in Job (28:1) and methods of refining it are often referred to (Prov. 17:3; Zech. 13:9, etc.). Solomon imported silver from Arabia (2 Chr. 9:14) and Tarshish (2 Chr. 9:21; Jer. 10:19, etc.).

In the Hellenistic and Roman periods silver was freely used in everyday life and the art of the silver-

places in Palestine. Some of the installations used in metal-founding are mentioned in the Bible, examples being the iron furnace (Deut. 4:20) and the furnace (Isa. 48:10). The latter was a beehive-shaped construction with air holes at the bottom to create a draft or so that bellows could be used. The metal was smelted in a crucible, which took the form of an earthenware pot. The fuel used was charcoal. Gold and silver were founded in closed crucibles, to prevent the loss of any of the precious metal. The pure metal was cast in moulds, which were made in two halves and provided with holes or small escape channels so that the excess metal could flow out. Moulds for making weapons, figurines and jewelery and later for minting coins have been found in excavations. Precious metals were worked by beating, soldering, engraving and in the filigree technique. A very vivid picture of the metalworker may be found in Isaiah (41:6-7).

smith was soon highly developed. The coinage of most Mediterranean countries was based on silver. During the late Roman period its quality deteriorated greatly, a decline which culminated in the great monetary crisis of the late 3rd century AD.

COPPER The metal referred to by this name in the Bible is not the element *cuprum* but bronze, which is an alloy of copper and tin. Copper in its pure form was rarely used. Bronze was the most useful and most important of metals from as early as the beginning of the 3rd millennium BC down to the 13th century BC, when iron began to supplant it. Weapons, agricultural implements, mining tools, household utensils and jewelry were all made of bronze. It seems that Europe used it before the Near East and indeed the only known sources of tin in the ancient world were in Europe. Some scholars dispute this view and attribute the first appearance of this metal to the East, from where it was introduced into *Egypt and into Europe. The *Egyptians exploited the copper mines of *Sinai, where smelting was also carried out. It was also mined in the Arabah (*Punon) and, early in the Iron Age, at *Timnah, northwest of the Gulf of *Elath. The copper-bearing ore was ground in stone mortars and subsequently smelted in crucibles made of clay. Slag heaps abound in the southern part of *Sinai and along the southern Arabah. According to 1 Kings (7:46) Solomon cast the copper vessels of the Temple between *Succoth and *Zarethan, but no traces of this have as yet been discovered there.

IRON Except for that of meteoritic origin, iron is not found in nature in a pure state. Since it is very hard to separate from its oxides, it was the last of the metals that the ancient world learned to produce, and was not used until about 2,000 years after bronze. The frequent allusions in the Bible to the use of iron in conjunction with copper are considered by many scholars to be anachronistic. The *Egyptians knew the rare meteoritic iron as early as about 3000 BC and used it to produce weapons, but it was not until the 13th century BC that the secrets of separating iron from its oxides was discovered. It seems that the credit for this discovery goes to the *Hittites, from whose territory it was brought by the merchants of *Tyre to Syria and Palestine. The wanderings of the Sea Peoples (*Philistines) brought more iron to the Near East. According to archaeological data the metal was known in Palestine from about the time of their arrival in *Canaan: iron weapons have been found in tombs of Philistine warriors, together with tools and jewelry made of the same metal. According to the Bible, its production was monopolized by the *Philistines (1 Sam. 13:19-20). There was very little iron in Palestine, and it seems that the metal that was used was brought from abroad by Phoenician merchants. Iron ores are mentioned in the *Sinai peninsula, but it is doubtful whether they were in fact exploited (cf. Deut. 4:20; 1 Kgs. 8:51). Iron was also brought from *Tarshish (Ezek. 27:12), and a special kind came from *Javan (Ezek. 27:19). Bolts for gates (Isa. 45:2), nails (1 Chr. 22:3), agricultural implements ((1 Sam. 13:20-1), weapons (Num. 35:16), chains (Ps. 105:18), chariots (Josh. 17:16) and weights (1 Sam. 17:7) were all made of iron. Large numbers of such objects have been found in the corresponding strata of many sites in Palestine.

TIN As we have seen, tin is used in the production of bronze, together with copper. A small amount of it is found in *Egypt but the richest deposits are in Europe. Phoenician merchants brought tin from the Cassiterides Islands, which lay southwest of Cornwall in England, and Spain was another important source, but it is doubtful whether supplies from either were available to the ancient Near East. Bronze was produced there in abundance, but where the tin for it came from remains a mystery. In the Bible it is mentioned in conjunction with copper (Authorized Version: 'brass'), lead and iron (Num. 31:2). According to Ezekiel (22:18-20) it was brought from *Tarshish, together with silver, copper, iron and lead. In the Hellenistic and later periods it was obtained from Europe.

LEAD This metal is rarely found in its pure form. In the Assyrian code of laws it is mentioned even before gold and silver. It was used in the production of figurines, weights for fishermen's nets and in cosmetics. No lead is found in Palestine but there are quite rich deposits in Syria and Asia Minor. The *Phoenicians brought it from *Tarshish (Ezek. 27:12). Although it is rarely found in the strata of the biblical periods its use was known (cf. Exod. 15:10; Amos 7:7). In Assyria lead tablets were used for writing on. During the time of the Second Temple it was used for weights, slingstones, images of gods and as a binding material between stones used for building. It was also very often added to copper and bronze coins. At *Mampsis a 'tongue' of lead weighing 158lb, was found, with the symbols of the foundry and the exact weight stamped on it.

MEVORAH, TEL A small mound in the Sharon Plain, on the southern bank of Nahal Taninim. In recent years a 3rd century AD mausoleum containing several marble sarcophagi was discovered there. Two of the sarcophagi were decorated with scenes of the war between the Greeks and Amazons. A shaft tomb, (*Burial) containing scores of Phoenician and Cypro-Phoenician *pottery, vessels, was accidentally discovered in fields in the vicinity of the mound.

In the years 1973-6 the site was excavated on behalf of the Hebrew University, under the direction of E. Stern. In the Middle Bronze Age IIA a small unfortified settlement was built on a natural hill, and in the Middle Bronze Age IIB the site was fortified by a beaten earth rampart 100 feet square, steep on the outside and sloping down toward the middle to form a crater, strengthened by stone retaining walls. It is dated by a *Hyksos seal impression found on a jar handle. At least on one side of the mound the rampart reached the riverbed which protected it. Within this fort four levels of occupation were distinguished from the Middle Bronze Age IIB and IIC. In the Late Bronze Age the Hyksos *fortifications were covered with a podium made of red-brick material. In the various phases of the period this podium served as the base for a building of a public nature, apparently a sanctuary. It is oriented east-west and measures 30 feet by 15 feet. Five steps on the east lead to a small platform which was possibly covered with a canopy. A bench was built along the eastern wall. The finds included numerous objects which can be identified as cult objects, notably an 8in-long bronze snake, similar to the ones found in the *temples of *Hazor and *Timnah. This wayside sanctuary occupied the entire area of the mound. It is dated to the 15th-13th centuries BC. In the Iron Age a four-room *house dated to the end of the 11th-10th centuries BC occupied the site. It was surrounded by a court and a wall. It possibly served as an administrative center. The upper three levels on the mound belong to the Persian period. They also consist of a single building, apparently an agricultural estate. Scanty remains of the Hellenistic period represent the latest traces of occupation on the mound.

MICHMASH; MICHMAS A town in the territory of Benjamin, in the region of *Beth-El, north of Jerusalem, on the border of the desert. It was apparently founded during the conquest of Canaan by the Israelites. Saul assembled part of his men there (1 Sam. 13:2). It was also on the Assyrian army's route to *Jerusalem (Isa. 10:28). It was resettled after the Restoration (Ezra 2:27). Jonathan the Hasmonean made the town his base after the victory over Bacchides (1 Macc. 9:73). It was a large village in the Roman period. In the Mishna the wheat of Michmash is highly valued. Eusebius (*Onom.* 132:3) states that in his time Michmas was a large village. Identified with Mukhmas, 4 miles southeast of *Beth-El on the border of the *Judean Desert.

MICHVAR; MACHAERUS One of the fortresses built by the Hasmonean, Alexander Jannaeus (Josephus, *Antiq.* III, 417), to the east of the *Dead Sea in the territory conquered earlier by John Hyrcanus. According to Strabo (*Geography* XVI, 40), it was destroyed by Pompey in 64 BC. Pliny (*Nat. Hist.* V, 72) wrote of it as 'Machaerus, at one time the most important fortress in Judea'. This must have referred to the fortress built by Herod, described at some length by Josephus, (*War* VII, 173-7): 'He accordingly enclosed an extensive area with ramparts and towers and founded a city there, from which an ascent led up to the ridge itself. Furthermore, on the top surrounding the actual crest, he built a wall, erecting towers at the corners, each 60 cubits high. In the centre of the enclosure he built a palace with magnificently spacious and beautiful apartments; he further provided numerous cisterns at the most convenient spots to receive the rain-water and furnish an abundant supply, as if he were vying with nature and endeavoring by these artificial defences to surpass the well-nigh impregnable strength which she had bestowed on the site. For, moreover, he stocked it with abundances of weapons and engines, and studied to make every preparation to enable its inmates to defy the largest siege' (Loeb Classics edition).

It was in Herod's palace at Machaerus that John the Baptist was imprisoned and beheaded (Matt. 14; Mark 6, etc.; Josephus, (*Antiq.* XVIII, 116-19). After Herod's death the region of the *Perea, in which Machaerus was situated, passed to Archaelaus.

Machaerus was destroyed by the Romans after a long siege during the Great Revolt, (*War* VII, 190ff.). Under the name of Michvar it is mentioned in the Aramaic translation of Numbers (32:1, 3, 25) instead of Jazer. The mountains of Michvar are mentioned several times in the Talmud.

The site has been identified with Mukawer, which has preserved the ancient name, while the fortress itself was situated on the nearby hill of Qasr el-Misheneq. No excavations have been made but surface surveys have revealed the Roman siege wall, the camps, plus remains of an aqueduct and of the fortress built by Herod.

MIDIAN; MIDIANITES A country in the northwestern part of the Arabian peninsula, along the Gulf of *Elath, bordered by *Edom to the north and the Arabian kingdoms to the south. At times the Midianites controlled parts of the Arabah, the *Negev and *Sinai. It was in *Sinai that Moses met Jethro, the priest of Midian (Exod. 2:15-16). Midian was one of the sons of Abraham born to Keturah and sent by Abraham to live eastward, 'unto the east country' (Gen. 25:2-6). The Midianites, together with the Ishmaelites, were occupied in international trade (Gen. 37:28). In the time of the Judges they were marauding in the settled areas (Judg. 6:1-7). Since they possessed camels (Judg. 6:5), they could pursue their activities as warriors and traders, and indeed they were the chief agents in the trade in gold and incense from *Arabia (Isa. 60:6). In later periods the Midianites are still referred to as nomadic herdsmen (Judith 2:26).

MIGDAL-EDER The place where Jacob sojourned after the death of Rachel (Gen. 35:21; Authorized Version: 'tower of Eder'), known also in the Roman period. In the Septuagint it is located between *Beth-El and Rachel's tomb. In the time of the Mishna the place was still known, and it is there that the Messiah will make himself known. Eusebius (*Onom.* 43:12) and other early Christian sources identify Migdal-Eder with Shepherd's Field $1^1/_2$ miles east of *Bethlehem. Identified with Siyan al-Ghanam, southwest of Jerusalem.

MIGDOL One of the halts on the route of the Exodus (Exod. 14:2), before the crossing of the *Red Sea. Identified with the Migdol fortress of Sethos I and of Merneptah at Tell el-Heir, 13 miles northwest of Qantarah.

MINNITH A town in the land of *Ammon, mentioned among the victories of Jephthah (Judg. 11:32-3). *Tyre exported wheat from here (Ezek. 27:17). Eusebius (*Onom.* 132:2) states that in his time there was a village by the name of Maanith, 4 miles distant from *Heshbon, on the way to *Rabbath-Ammon. Identified by some with Umm el-Khanafish, northeast of *Heshbon.

MISHEAL A Levitical city on the border of the territory of Asher (Josh. 19:26; 21:30; Authorized Version: 'Mishal'). It appears as Msir in the *Execration Texts and in the list of conquests of Tuthmosis III. Identified with Tel Kisan, Tell en-Nahl and Tell *Abd Hawam, all in the Plain of *Acre (*Acco).

MISREPHOTH-MAIM A town on the southern border of *Sidon, where Joshua chased Jabin and the other Canaanite kings after the battle of *Merom (Josh. 11:8). Identified with Khirbet el-Meshrifeh, south of Ras en-Naqura, which was inhabited in all periods.

MIZPAH A town in *Gilead where Jacob and Laban made a covenant (Gen. 31:48-9). It was the home of Jephthah (Judg. 11:11; Authorized Version: 'Mizpeh'). Judas Maccabaeus conquered the town and set it on fire (1 Macc. 5:35; Authorized Version: 'Maspha'). According to Eusebius it was situated 15 miles from *Philadelphia (*Rabbath-Ammon), on the River *Jabbok. It should possibly be identified with er-Ramtha, 8 miles southwest of *Edrei or elsewhere.

MIZPEH A town on the main road from *Jerusalem to *Shechem, on the northern border of Benjamin. In the early Iron Age it was in the territory of Benjamin (Josh. 18:26). The Israelites gathered here to fight against the *Philistines, and it was one of the cities in which Samuel judged the people (1 Sam. 7:5-16). It gained great importance at the end of the First Temple period when it was the seat of Gedalyahu, who was appointed overseer of conquered Judah after the fall of Jerusalem (2 Kgs. 25; Jer. 40-41). After the Restoration it was the capital of the district of Mizpeh (Neh. 3:7). Identified by most scholars with Tell en-*Nasbeh, 8 miles north of *Jerusalem. Others believe that it should be identified with Nebi Samwil, northwest of the city.

MOAB A land east of the *Dead Sea, between *Edom and *Ammon. The King's Way (*Roads), leading from the south to Syria and *Mesopotamia, passed through its eastern part. Its early inhabitants were the Rephaim, Zuzim and Emim (Gen. 14:5). It is possible that Sheth, mentioned in the *Execration Texts, refers to Moab (cf. Num. 24:17).

Archaeological survey has shown that Moab was settled in the Chalcolithic period and more extensively in the Iron Age, from about the 13th century BC, when fortresses were built along its frontiers. To this period date the punitive campaigns of Rameses II against Moab, *Edom and the *Negev. The surrender of Boteret of Moab is depicted in reliefs at Luxor, which also show the fortress of *Dibon. There was constant enmity between Israel and Moab (Num. 22; 2 Kgs. 1:1, 2 Kgs. 3:4 ff.). The Reubenites and the Gadites conquered parts of the country of the *Amorites that had formerly belonged to Moab (Num. 21:25 ff.). There was also a state of war between Israel and Moab in the time of the Judges (Judg. 3:12). Saul fought Moab (1 Sam. 14:47) and David completed its conquest (2 Sam. 8:2), but there were friendly relations between Moab and Israel during Solomon's reign (1 Kgs. 11:1, 7). After the division of the kingdom of Israel Moab regained its independence. Omri then conquered the country, but it was free again in Ahab's time (2 Kgs. 1:1; 3:4 ff.); this is confirmed by the stele of Mesha, King of Moab (*Inscriptions). Sargon II tells in his annals of the conquest of Moab, whose soldiers afterwards helped the Assyrians in their wars against the Arabs. Later it formed part of the Babylonian and Persian kingdoms. In about the 4th or 3rd century BC the Nabateans penetrated Moab after gaining control of *Edom. After AD 106 Moab was part of the Provin-

Stele of Mesha, King of Moab

cia Arabia, whose cities, *Rabbathmoba and Characmoba (*Kir Moab), were administrative centers. The country flourished in the later Roman and Byzantine periods.

MODIIM; MODIIN A village 8 miles to the east of Lydda (*Lod), the birth-place and burial-place of the Maccabean family (1 Macc. 2:1, 15, 23, 70; 9:19; 13:25, 30). Eusebius (*Onom.* 132, 16) says that the monuments built on the tombs of the Maccabees were to be seen in his day, and the site is still marked on the Medaba map, accompanied by the legend: 'Modeim, which today is Moditta, wherefrom were the Maccabees.' Josephus (*Antiq.* XIII, 211) describes the tombs of the Maccabees: 'Simon also built a very great monument of polished white stone, and raising it to a great and conspicuous height, and erected monolithic pillars, a wonderful thing to see. In addition to these he built for his parents and his brothers seven pyramids, one for each, as made to excite wonder by their size and beauty and these have been preserved to this day.'

The site is identified with Khirbet el-Midya. Traces of an Iron Age settlement and some rock-cut tombs were discovered there, but nothing remains of the monuments described by Josephus.

MOLADA A town in the *Negev of Judah (Josh. 15:26) and of Simeon (Josh. 19:2), in the vicinity of *Beer-Sheba. One of the places resettled after the Restoration (Neh. 11:26). The identification of this place is problematic. Some suggest identifying it with Molatha in *Idumea, mentioned by Josephus (18:147), and by Eusebius (*Onom.* 14:3; 88:4; 108:3) as Malaatha and Moleatha, one of the strongholds of the Roman *Limes*, identified with Tell el-Milh east of Beer-Sheba. Others, however, identify it with Khirbet el-Watan, 8 miles southeast of Beer-Sheba.

MONASTERIES Christian monasticism began in *Egypt in the 3rd century AD and spread from there to Palestine, where it took two distinct forms, known as the anchoretic and the cenobitic. The anchorites lived by the *laura* system, in which each monk lived in an individual hermitage, a secluded hut or cave, at first entirely alone and later with others in settlements. They met on feast days for common worship and meals. The cenobites lived a full community life in monasteries made up of living quarters (cells), a din-

ing room (refectory), a kitchen, guest rooms and chapel or church. The work was strictly organized and depended on the area; it included agricultural activities, the cultivation of olives and grapes, production of ropes, baskets and mats, and similar occupations. Communities of cenobites were founded near or in towns and villages and more rarely in desert and the hill country, while the anchorites, seeking complete isolation, went to the dry and unpopulated areas of *Sinai, the *Negev and the *Judean Desert.

The first monastery was founded by St. Hilarion near *Gaza in about AD 330, and at approximately the same time St. Chariton founded a *laura* in a cave of Wadi *Farah, north of *Jerusalem. He also built a church there dedicated to Macarius, Bishop of *Jerusalem (AD 314-33). A short time later he founded the monasteries on the Quarantine and the *laura* of Souka, south of *Bethlehem.

The flourishing period of Palestinian monastic life began in the 5th century AD, under St Euthymius and his pupil St Sabas. St Euthymius established the mon-

The monastery of St Catherine in the Sinai Desert

astery of St Theoctistus in the Wadi Mukelik, east of *Jerusalem, in the *Judean Desert. This monastery and that of Choziba in Wadi Qelt are examples of the two forms of monasticism existing side by side: most of the monks lived in the big monastery but there were also hermits dwelling some distance away and dependent on the abbot of the monastery. In AD 428 St Euthymius set up a *laura* near the monastery of St Theoctistus, identified at Khan el-Ahmar, about 12 miles from *Jericho on the way to *Jerusalem. In 480 the monastery of St Euthymius was built in place of the *laura* and included the saint's tomb. Excavations carried out there in 1929 brought to light the plan of the monastery and the church with the crypt. St Sabas (died 532) founded four *laura* close to each other in the *Judean Desert, the most famous of which, the Great Laura (Mar Saba), is still in existence. This held 150 monks; while the New Laura near it had 120. He also founded four monasteries in the vicinity of the Great Laura, another monastery near Nicopolis (*Emmaus) and the monastery of Scolarios at Muntar.

The monasteries on Mount *Nebo were extensively excavated by S.J. Saller on behalf of the Studium Biblicum Franciscanum. The earliest monks lived in the valleys around the mount in the 4th century AD. The great complex of monastic buildings, consisting of courtyards with rooms around each, dates from the 5th to the 9th centuries AD. A church with mosaic pavements, a refectory and a granary deserve special mention. In the monastery of Mar Saba oil and wine-presses and a bakery were found. The monasteries of Bir el-Qutt and Siyar el-Ghanam, in the vicinity of *Bethlehem, also had oil and winepresses. Monastery farms have been excavated at modern Beth Hashitta (in the *Jezreel Valley) and in the *Negev at *Sobata, *Nessana and *Oboda.

Like the churches, many of the monasteries were decorated with frescoes and mosaic floors. The frescoes at the monastery of St Euthymius, dating from the late 6th century AD, depicted figures of saints with panels of conventional ornamentation beneath them. At *Beth-Shean a monastery with beautiful mosaic floors has been excavated. Irregular in shape, the monastery complex covers an area measuring about 100 feet by 120 feet. It is entered through a large oblong hall paved with mosaics. The hall is surrounded on three sides by rooms, one of which, oblong in shape and paved with mosaics, may have been the refectory, while the adjoining room, with its stone pavement, may have been the kitchen. In the northeast of the complex lies the apsidal chapel, separated from the hall by a narthex. To the south of the chapel is a cluster of rooms; two mosaic inscriptions record that the monastery was founded by a Lady Mary in AD 567. The mosaic floor in the hall has a circle in the center with allegorical figures personifying the 12 months and, in an inner circle, the sun and the moon. The central motifs are surrounded by a carpet of animals and a hunter, framed in octagons, and animals and fruits in squares and rhomboids. The chapel has a pavement with birds set in medallions. In another room a mosaic depicting scenes from rural life is outstanding.

MONEY In prehistoric and early historical times the economy was based on barter — commodities were exchanged for other commodities. At a later stage certain goods, such as hides, cattle and sheep or grain, served as fixed units of value and formed the basis of primitive commercial negotiations. As this method did not prove practicable in all cases, a better one had to be devised. In Palestine the *Canaanites were using a much more progressive system before the arrival of the Hebrews; it was based on rare, and therefore costly, metals. In fact even at this stage there was a double system: in the villages the old method of bartering still prevailed while in the ports and the larger cities metal was used as a token of exchange. When Abraham bought the cave of the field of *Machpelah he weighed out 400 shekels of silver as payment to Ephron the Hittite (Gen. 23:16). It should be noted that the money was weighed, since this was still long before the minting of coins began.

MONEY BY WEIGHT Gold was rarely used in commercial transactions in ancient Palestine; silver, on the other hand, was in common use (cf. Gen. 17:13). The translators of the Bible into English used the word 'money', but in the ancient Hebrew *kesef* meant 'silver'. When the Bible refers to shekels of gold it usually signifies metal by weight in various forms, such as bars, rings or tongues. It is possible that these objects were sometimes used as currency. Only once in the Bible are gold shekels referred to as a monetary unit (1 Chr. 21:25). That silver was used as a unit of value may be inferred from the fact that the payment of fines was calculated in shekels (Exod. 21:22). Half-shekels were paid as ransom for souls of the Children of Israel (Exod. 30:12-13) and as a payment to the seer (1 Sam. 9:8). Wherever a shekel is mentioned in the Bible a unit of weight is meant. It is also known from the Bible that when large sums of money had to be paid scales were always used. But in ordinary commercial intercourse bars of silver, of specific sizes and weights, were used. In 1 Samuel (9:8) the boy had one quarter of a silver shekel. It is possible that the golden tongue mentioned in Joshua (7:21) was also a metal bar of this type. The *agora* of 1 Samuel (2:36) (translated as 'a piece of silver') was probably a unit of small value.

BABYLONIAN SILVER STANDARD In Egypt rings of silver constituted the normal units of payment. It is possible that the golden rings and bracelets of Genesis (24:22) may serve as an example of the influence of the Egyptian monetary system. The Babylonian system of weighing silver on scales, on the other hand, was much more widely used throughout the whole of western Asia. The weighing of silver by Abraham was quite a normal procedure. The *El Amarna letters contain a reference to weighing gold and silver according to the Babylonian practice. This Babylonian standard was in use in Syria, Asia Minor and Palestine in later periods as well. The change from the Babylonian to the Tyrian and Sidonian standard came about when the first Phoenician coins were minted and was used for silver, while for weighing gold the old Babylonian standard was retained. Each of the two monetary systems had in fact two standards, light and heavy, the heavy standard being double the weight of the light one. The weight of the light Babylonian *maneh* was $16^{1}/_{8}$oz or just over 1lb while the heavy one weighed $32^{1}/_{4}$oz or just over 2lbs. The light shekel $^{1}/_{60}$ of the *maneh* — weighed 123 grains or about $^{1}/_{4}$oz, and the heavy one $245^{1}/_{2}$ grains of about $^{1}/_{2}$oz. These weights were valid both for gold and for silver. The ratio between the two metals was $13^{1}/_{2}$, which was much too heavy for the international trade. In order to remedy this the weight of the light shekel was augmented to 168 grains, so that the ratio changed to 1:10. When the Babylonian merchants met their Egyptian counterparts they accepted the Egyptian decimal system, and instead of 60 shekels the *maneh* was reduced to 50, giving 3,000 shekels to the *kikar* (Authorized Version: 'talent') instead of 3,600 (cf. Exod. 38:24-6). This new system was used for transactions in precious metals, while in daily life the old system remained in use. (*See also* *WEIGHTS AND MEASURES.*)

It is not known when the change from the Babylonian silver shekel of 168 grains to the heavy Phoenician shekel of 224 grains occurred, but it may have been at about the time when the Israelites came to Canaan from *Egypt. In weighing gold the Israelites employed the heavy Babylonian shekel of $245^{1}/_{2}$ grains. This silver shekel was used down to the time of the Second Temple, although large sums of money were calculated in *kikars*. The *maneh* is rarely mentioned in the Bible. The commonest unit was the shekel, though sometimes the Bible refers to the sum only without specifying the unit by which it was calculated (the Authorized Version inserts 'shekel': Gen. 37:28; Judg. 17:2-4, etc.).

PHOENICIAN SILVER STANDARD The use of the Phoenician standard referred to above necessitated a change in the value of the Babylonian shekel, because the weight of the Phoenician shekel was two-thirds of the Babylonian shekel (168 grains for the light, 336 grains for the heavy shekel), i.e. 112 grains and 224 grains respectively. Thus 15 Phoenician shekels were equal in value to 10 silver Babylonian shekels or one gold one. The sacred Hebrew shekel was based on the Phoenician heavy shekel of 224 grains. At first money was paid to the Temple by weight, but later coins of a shekel and half a shekel were minted. The new coins were also based on then Phoenician standard. As Judea did not have the right to mint in silver, Phoenician (or rather Tyrian) money was used for legal payment of the sacred shekel until late in the 1st century AD.

PERIOD OF THE RESTORATION The earliest coin bearing Hebrew script is of the middle of the 4th century BC. In this century the local Jewish authorities minted small silver coins bearing the legend *Yahud*, the name of the province of Judea in the Persian period.

HELLENISTIC PERIOD Minting of coins in Palestine did not become regular practice until the beginning of the Hellenistic period. Alexander the Great founded a mint at *Acco (*Acre) that produced gold and silver coins. Under Ptolemy II the Jewish autonomous rule in Jerusalem minted small silver coins in the city inscribed 'Yehuda'. The Ptolemies continued to mint in Acre (Ptolemais) and founded additional mints at

Double shekel of Sidon, Astraton (Abdastart) II 4th century BC

Coin of the Persian province of Judean 'Yahud', 4th century BC

Tetradrachm of Alexander the Great minted in Acco, 4th century BC

Tetradrachm of Seleucus I, 311-281 BC

Coin of John Hyrcanus II, 63-40 BC

Shekel of the Jewish War, AD 66-68

Roman sestertius of Hadrian to commemorate his visit to Judea, AD 130

Tetradrachm of Bar Kochba, AD 132-35

A gold coin of Theodosius I, AD 379-83

Coin of Justin II, AD 518-27

*Joppa, *Ashkelon and *Gaza. The same policy was maintained by the Seleucids. Jewish minting, however, resumed with the Hasmonean dynasty. Permission to mint coins bearing Hebrew inscriptions and Jewish symbols was granted by Antiochus VII Sidetes to Simon the High Priest, but it was probably John Hyrcanus I (135-104 BC) who made use of this privilege, though some scholars now believe that actual minting began with Alexander Jannaeus (103-76 BC). The coins of Alexander bear Hebrew, or Hebrew and Greek, inscriptions, with the king's name and title and that of the High Council of the Jews. Common symbols on these coins are anchors, stars, palm branches, cornucopiae and pomegranate flowers. Some of his later coins also bear dates during his reign. Apart from the name of the monarch there is little difference in the coins of his successors, Judas Aristobulus II (67-63 BC), John Hyrcanus II (63-40 BC) and Matthias Antigonus (40-37 BC), except that the last named depicted the menorah on some of his coins. All Hasmonean coins were bronze with one temporary emission of lead coins under Alexander Jannaeus.

ROMAN PERIOD The next series of coins is that of the Herodian dynasty. Herod the Great (37-4 BC) minted coins bearing Greek legends and pagan and Jewish symbols. Some of Herod's immediate heirs, who inherited parts of their father's territories, used the same range of symbols: palm branches, anchors, bunches of grapes, prows of galleys and so on. Only Philip (4 BC-AD 34), who reigned in the northeastern part of the kingdom beyond the *Jordan, where most of the population was non-Jewish, minted coins with portraits of Roman emperors (Augustus, Tiberius) as well as his own. Herod Agrippa I (AD 37-44) minted coins in which his dependence on the Romans is expressed. For the purely Jewish parts of the kingdom his coins bore symbols that would not offend the Jews. It was he who founded the mint at *Caesarea, which was to last for about 200 years. The same minting policy was observed by Agrippa II (AD 50-100). His coins were minted outside the borders of Judea. After the deposition of Herod Archelaus, Herod's son, in AD 6, Judea was directly ruled by a Roman procurator. The coins of this new province bear the name of the ruling Roman emperor and symbols not unlike those of the Jewish monarchs; they were dated by the number of years for which the emperors had reigned.

Minting by the procurators continued until the First Jewish Revolt (AD 66-70). It was then, for the first time in history, that the Jewish authorities minted coins of large denominations in silver, a privilege previously reserved for the imperial mints. The coins are shekels (tetradrachms) and half-shekels (drachms), both in silver, with smaller denominations in bronze. They bear legends in the ancient, already antiquated, Hebrew script ('Jerusalem the Holy', 'Shekel of Israel', 'The Freedom of Zion' or 'For the Redemption of Zion'), with dates according to the era of the revolt and symbols such as chalices, vine leaves, amphorae, citrons, palm branches and palm trees. When the revolt had been crushed the Emperors Vespasian, Titus and Domitian minted coins to commemorate the great victory over the Jews; these depicted the heads of the emperors, the goddess of victory with trophies, Judea weeping under a palm tree and the inscription '*Judaea capta*'. The last Jewish minting belongs to the time of the Second Revolt under Bar-Kochba (AD 132-5). These coins, of silver and bronze, bear the names of the leaders, Simon and Eleazar, a slogan ('Year one of the Redemption of Israel', 'Year two of the Freedom of Israel', 'For the Freedom of Jerusalem') and such symbols as the façades of the Temple and others that were in use during the First Revolt.

The process of installing mints in all the important cities, which had begun in the Hellenistic period, was accelerated in Roman times. The raising of a town to the rank of *polis, colonia* or *metropolis* is depicted on the coins, which are now known as city-coins. Coins of this class usually bear the effigy of the ruling emperor, a symbol relating to the city or to its cult, and its name. City-coins bear dates according to the local or provincial eras. No coins were minted in Palestine during the Byzantine period, except for one rare case during the Persian siege under Heraclius when the Byzantine emperor issued propaganda coins in AD 614.

MOREH (HILL OF) The place where the *Midianites encamped for their attack on the Israelites, in the days of *Gideon (Judg. 7:1). Identified with Jebel ed-Dehi in the *Jezreel Valley.

MOREH (PLAIN OF) The first halt in the land of *Canaan on Abraham's journey from *Haran (Gen. 12:4), where he saw God and built an altar (Gen. 12:7). Here, near *Gilgal, the blessing and the curse were uttered (Deut. 11:30). The Hebrew Bible has 'alon', which means 'oak', and not 'plain' as in the Authorized Version. It is thus possible that a sacred oak is meant here. This may also apply to the 'plain of the pillar' (Judg. 9:6) and the 'plain of Tabor' (1 Sam. 10:3).

MORESHETH-GATH The birth-place of the prophet Micah, mentioned in connection with the destruction which this and the other towns in this region suffered at the hands of the Assyrians (Jer. 26:6; Mic. 1:1, 14) near *Achzib. Eusebius (*Onom.* 134:10) calls it Morasthei, and states that it is situated east of *Beth-Gubrin. A somewhat later Christian tradition points out Micah's tomb at a distance of 10 stadia from Beth-Gubrin, where a church was built. This is confirmed by evidence from other early Christian sources and by the *Medaba map.

MORIAH; LAND OF MORIAH The land that was designated to be the place of sacrifice of Isaac (Gen. 22:2). It is also the hill where God appeared to David and where the House of God was to be built by Solomon (2 Chr. 3:1). (*See also* *JERUSALEM).

MOSAICS The earliest examples of wall mosaics, dating from the 2nd millennium BC, have been discovered in *Mesopotamia. The *Egyptians and Minoans (*Crete) used mosaic decorations to a much lesser extent and only in minor art. In Greece the first mosaic pavements, using natural pebbles, were no earlier than 400 BC. It was not until the Hellenistic period that pebbles were replaced by cut stones.

The earliest mosaics discovered in Palestine are those in Herod's palaces at *Masada. While the floors in some of the rooms in the upper terrace of the Northern Palace had simple geometric patterns in black and white, those in the Western Palace were multicolored. The designs were still quite simple, the section which has been preserved consisting of a large multipetalled rosette set within a border with a conventional wavy design. At *Masada remains of the artist's workshop also came to light. Here fragments of smoothed slabs of white and black stone were found, as well as oblong chips that were later cut into cubes (*tesserae*) of appropriate size. These would then be arranged in paterns on a mortar floor, which served as a base.

The mosaics of *Masada seem to be quite an exception. Normally the floors of public buildings were paved with large slabs of hard limestone, as in the pagan temples and the synagogues of the 3rd and 4th centuries AD and also in the theater at *Beth-Shean. Alternatively they might be plastered and painted to resemble marble, as in the theater at *Caesarea in its Herodian phases. The explanation may lie in the fact that the ornamentation both of early synagogues and of temples was based on their heavier architectural elements. Thus the exterior was lavishly decorated, while the interior of the building was left quite plain and rather severe. The great change came about in the 4th century AD, the period in which the earliest churches came into being and the new type of synagogue evolved. About the middle of the 3rd century AD rabbinic circles lifted the ban on decorating floors with mosaic pavements.

The earliest known synagogue to be decorated in this way is that of *Hammath, near *Tiberias. This is perhaps the finest mosaic floor in a Jewish religious building in Palestine and was most probably the work of foreign artists, who may have come from *Antioch, where mosaic art was at its height at that time. This floor provides the earliest example of the tripartite division of subjects that was to become common in the next century. In mosaics of this type the whole floor of the nave would be divided into three panels. The first, nearest to the entrance, would include a biblical scene with salvation as its theme. The middle panel would have a circle with Helios in the center, riding in the celestial chariot and accompanied by the sun, the moon and the stars. The outer circle included the 12 signs of the zodiac, with symbols of the four seasons of the year in the corners. The third component, the Torah Shrine, with the menorah and other cultic objects, occupied the third panel, close to the bema (platform) and the niche of the Torah Shrine. At Hammath, however, this part is missing, and instead there are several dedicatory inscriptions. The full range of motifs is found in the 6th-century synagogue at *Gerasa (Noah's Ark), *Naaran (Daniel in the lion's den) and *Beth-Alpha (the sacrifice of Isaac). A new discovery is from a synagogue at *Gaza, in which King David is playing the lyre, and animals listen to the music. Another recent discovery is also quite unusual: in a small prayer hall built in a Jewish home at *Beth-Shean, owned by a man named Leontis, a scene from the Odyssey is depicted.

Side by side with this decorative scheme, others evolved. The synagogue at *Maon (Menois), for instance, has a completely different type of design, consisting of an amphora flanked by two peacocks; out of it grows a stylized vine, the loops of which form medallions framing representations of animals, birds, fruits and scenes of rural life. This kind of decoration was not restricted to synagogues and is still more common in churches. An example is to be seen in the church at Shallal, where the mosaic floor may have been the work of the same artist as the one in the synagogue at *Maon, which is only a short distance away. Only the menorah, flanked by two lions and other Jewish cultic objects, distinguishes the floor of the synagogue from that of the church.

The third type of decoration, quite common in the synagogues of Palestine, consists of purely geometric and conventional designs. Examples of this type are to be seen in the synagogues at *Gadara and *Jericho. Remnants of mosaics in many other synagogues are too scantily formed to determine with any degree of certainty which class they belong to. A new kind of synagogue mosaics are the recent discoveries at *Rehob in the *Beth-Shean Valley and at *En-Gedi. At Rehob there are the usual geometric carpets, but the main decorative element is a 13 feet by 8 feet panel in which there is an inscription of 29 lines in Hebrew. The text is a copy of excerpts from the Talmud, dealing with regions of the country and of cities, fruits and vegetables in connection with tithes and other taxes paid to the Temple. At En-Gedi a different kind of inscription was found. Again, along with a mainly geometric decoration interwoven with some beautifully depicted fowl, the western aisle of the synagogue has five inscriptions in Hebrew and Aramaic. These list the ten generations from Adam to Japheth; the twelve symbols of the *Zodiac; the twelve months of the year; the three Patriarchs and the three friends of Daniel. Then comes a long inscription warning the people of the town to refrain from dissension and forbidding them 'to disclose the secret of the town to gentiles'. The last two inscriptions mention donors.

Little remains of the mosaics of the early churches of the 4th century AD. It seems that in the early period decoration was mostly confined to simple geometric designs. The best preserved mosaic pavement of the early group is that of the Church of the Loaves and Fishes at *Heptapegon, which is more than half a century later than the Constantinian churches of *Jerusalem. Here a completely secular range of subject was depicted and the surviving portion contains a Nile scene with water birds and plants. On the other hand, the somewhat later Church of the Prophets at *Gerasa (AD 464/5) is decorated with purely geometric patterns. Of two churches at *Mampsis that are of about the same date one has a purely geometric design, while the other has an amphora with peacocks, rich carpet patterns, birds and fruit. Scholars believe that the avoidance of human images on floors was more strictly observed by Christians than it was by Jews at that time. The range of subjects becomes richer in the 6th century. The Church of St John the Baptist at Gerasa (AD 531) has images of some of the larger cities

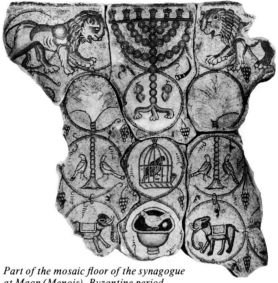

Part of the mosaic floor of the synagogue at Maon (Menois), Byzantine period

of Egypt, while the Church of Sts Cosmas and Damian in the same city (AD 533) has human figures, including saints. Several mosaic floors dating from the second half of the 6th century were discovered at *Beth-Shean. One of these is in a monastery (AD 533) and has numerous human figures, including figures personifying the sun and the moon and the 12 months. To the same period belong the churches of *Medaba and some sites in its vicinity. A church in *Medaba itself contains a mosaic map of the Holy Land, but here the holy figures were later carefully removed by Christian iconoclasts. Another church at *Medaba has images of the apostles, while a church in its vicinity depicts famous churches in the region. These represent only the most outstanding examples, for the number of churches and monasteries discovered in Palestine runs into the hundreds. But the decoration of most of them is very simple, geometric and conventional. Some scholars have attempted to correlate the choice of subjects with certain trends in the attitude of the Christian Church towards figurative art, but their theories are hard to substantiate. It is even difficult to prove that the order of AD 427 prohibiting the use of a cross on the floors of churches was ever observed.

Mosaics were not confined to religious buildings but were also used in private houses. Here, too, most of them have simple geometric designs. Outstanding examples are the mosaics of the villa at *Beth-Gubrin, in which hunting scenes are depicted, and those of the Jewish villa at *Beth-Shean, which have scenes from the *Odyssey*.

It is possible to distinguish between the mosaics of the Roman and the early Byzantine periods in Palestine on technical grounds by the quality of the material and the size of stones. All the colors and shades of the earlier group of mosaics were obtained with stone only, even if certain stones had to be brought from a great distance. In the later period the reds, orange, green and blue were often made of pottery and glass. As to the size of the *tesserae,* the tendency was to use small cubes in the early period and larger ones later. Mosaics were not confined to floors only: remains of wall and dome mosaics have been discovered in the synagogue and in a Christian public building at *Caesarea. The *tesserae* used here were very small, about $^1/_5$in square. Some were made of stone but most were of glass. Many of the glass mosaics were coated with gold, which involved a special technique. The glass was cast in two layers: first a thicker one, on which a thin layer of gold was placed, then a thinner, sealing layer of glass on top.

Another technique used in Palestine, mainly in the Byzantine period, is known as *opus sectile.* In this method squares, rectangles, rhomboids and circles of stones of different colors were laid in different patterns. Remains of floors made in this way have been discovered at *Caesarea, *Bethlehem and the monastery of St Catherine at *Sinai. Far more rare in Palestine was the technique known as *opus reticulatum,* which was very common in Rome and the European provinces. There the entire face of the wall or niche was covered with square-based pyramidal blocks laid with the sides at 45⁰ from the vertical; this produced a net *(reticulum)* pattern, which was then covered with plaster and painted in different colors. Remains of this type were found in Herod's palace at *Jericho.

MOURNING On the death of an important personage (2 Sam. 3:31), when a calamity befell an individual (2 Sam. 12:15-16) or the whole congregation, or when bad tidings were received (Num. 14:1-6), certain prescribed customs, common to the Israelites and to the other peoples of the ancient Near East, were observed. In addition to weeping and wailing, mourning involved rending one's clothes (Gen. 37:29, etc.), walking barefoot and covering one's head (2 Sam. 15:30), girding one's loins with sackcloth (2 Sam. 3:31, etc.) and placing ashes on one's head (2 Sam. 13:19, etc.). The mourner would abstain from washing his feet, trimming his beard, washing his clothes (2 Sam. 19:24) and from anointing himself with oil (2 Sam. 14:2). He might abstain altogether from meat and wine (Dan. 10:3). Mourners would sit on the ground and tremble with grief (Ezek. 26:16), shave their heads and cut their flesh (Jer. 16:6). Some of these mourning signs, such as shaving one's head, shaving a corner of one's beard and cutting the flesh, all of which were very common among the heathen, were forbidden (Lev. 21:5), but it seems that habit was stronger than the Law.

Mourning normally lasted for seven days (Gen. 50:10), but on the death of an important personage it continued for 70 days, the first 40 being the period necesary for the completion of the process of embalming (*Burial) and the last 30 the actual mourning period (Gen. 50:3). Aaron (Num. 20:29) and Moses (Deut. 34:8) were both mourned for 30 days. During the period of mourning people would come to eat with the mourners (2 Sam. 3:35). The funerary meal was observed by the Jews and other peoples in later times as well. To enhance the atmosphere of grief professional women mourners would be invited (Jer. 9:17 ff.,

Clay figurine of a mourner, from Azur

etc.). Egyptian wall paintings in which women are seen standing, weeping and tearing their hair indicate that this was also the practice among other nations in the ancient Near East.

MOZAH A town in the territory of Benjamin (Josh. 18:26), known in the Roman period by the name Ammaous and later as Colonia. This last name was given to the town when Vespasian settled a colony of Roman veterans there. The large local spring was very famous in the Byzantine period. Identified with Qaluniyeh, west of *Jerusalem.

MUNHATA An ancient site extending over many acres in the *Jordan Valley, some 8 miles south of the Sea of *Galilee and about 600 feet below sea level. It was excavated in 1954 by N. Tzori on behalf of the Israel Department of Antiquities and Museums, and in 1962-3 by J. Perrot on behalf of the French Archaeological Mission.

Six occupation levels were distinguished on the site. The lowest was on virgin soil and consisted of stone floors, flint chips, bones and charred organic materials. In the fifth level a mud-brick wall 24 feet long was found, while in the fourth a rectangular building 12 feet by 15 feet was discovered. This was built of field stones and had plastered floors. There was an oven in the middle of the room and on the floor were stone bowls, millstones and numerous flint tools, including sickle-blades and weapons. These three levels belong to the same culture as the pre-Pottery Neolithic B culture of *Jericho and bear a resemblance to it. This settlement marks the beginning of sedentary occupation in Palestine.

Above these levels came the third, a direct continuation of the previous ones, in which a large round building about 60 feet in diameter was discovered. In the center of this was a round court paved with pebbles, which probably had a roof resting on wooden beams. No difference was noted between the flint tools of the earlier level and the ones here, but there were also potsherds, some of which were decorated. The fauna included cattle, goats, sheep and pigs.

Level 2 contained numerous oval storage pits and also large quantities of brightly colored handmade pottery vessels, among them rounded bowls and deep bowls, cups on a high foot, spherical pots and jars. Some of the pottery was burnished red and decorated with painted or incised decoration. There were also some figurines of the *Shaar Hagolan type. The excavators equate this culture with Pottery-Neolithic A and B of *Jericho. The uppermost level contained badly preserved dwellings and gray burnished pottery vessels typical of the end of the 4th millennium BC, when the settlement of Munhata was finally abandoned. (*See also* *PREHISTORY.)

Fertility figurine from Munhata

MUSICAL INSTRUMENTS Since the dawn of civilization man has used musical instruments. Some have been found in excavations while others are known from Assyrian, Egyptian and other wall paintings and reliefs. Numerous musical instruments are mentioned in the Bible, which may indicate that music was important both in religion and in private life in biblical Palestine. Many of these instruments cannot be satisfactorily identified.

BIBLICAL PERIOD

Alamoth (Ps. 46:1) Identification unknown; probably an instrument that produced high soprano sounds.

Gittith (Ps. 8:1; 81:1; 84:1) Identification not certain; possibly named after the town of *Gath or perhaps the name of a group of instruments.

Hazozra (Num. 10:2) An instrument made of metal; a trumpet. The trumpets mentioned in the Bible were made of silver but most trumpets that have been found are made of brass and silver and are sometimes gold-plated. A continuous sound from two trumpets was the signal for the congregation to assemble at the tabernacle, while the sounding of one only marked the gathering of the princes and the chiefs. There were other signals for gathering the congregation and for moving camp in battle. Trumpets were also used in the new moon festivities, on holy days and at the coronation of kings. The trumpet produced a sharp sound. It was made of a metal pipe with a mouthpiece narrower than the body.

Halil (Authorized Version: 'pipe') A wind instrument made of cane, hollowed wood or bone. Its bright sounds were heard in holy day parades (1 Kgs. 1:40; Isa. 5:12), but it could also produce a note of grief (Jer. 48:36). It was used mainly by the common people and never in the Temple service. There were probably several kinds of pipe in use during the biblical period.

Kinnor A stringed instrument; a harp. According to the Bible Jubal was the 'father of all such as handle the harp and organ' (Gen. 4:21). The *kinnor* was much used in the biblical period, in the Temple service (1 Chr. 15:16; 2 Chr. 5:12, etc.), at festivities and banquets (Isa. 5:12, etc.). Prophecies were made to the sound of its strings (1 Chr. 25:1) and it could raise one's spirits in moments of depression (1 Sam. 16:23). The harp was played alone, with string, wind or percussion instruments, or in an orchestra that contained them all. The number of its strings is unknown.

Mahol (Authorized Version: 'dance') Mentioned only in Psalms (150:4), among the many instruments that formed the orchestra of praise. It may belong to the pipe family, but cannot be translated as 'dance', as the Authorized Version and some commentators do.

Menaaneim (Authorized Version: 'cornet') A percussion instrument played together with the timbrels (*See* '*Tof*' below) (2 Sam. 6:5). It was probably made of metal plates that produced a sound when moved, as the Hebrew name implies. It has wrongly been identified with the cornet.

Meziltaim A percussion instrument made of copper; cymbals. The Hebrew name implies a pair of instruments used together to produce a musical sound. They were used by the Levites, with other instruments, in the Temple service (Ezra 3:10, 1 Chr. 15:16, 28, etc.). It

Earthenware figurine of a harp player, Ashdod, Iron Age

Psanterin (Authorized Version: 'psaltery') (Dan. 3:5 ff.) Mentioned once only. The name derives from the Greek *psalter.* Its form is unknown.

Qeren (Authorized Version: 'cornet') A wind instrument made from the horn of an animal (Dan. 3-5 ff.). Some scholars make no distinction between the *qeren* and the *shofar.* Others believe that the difference was that the *shofar* was made only from a ram's horn.

Qitaros A stringed instrument (Dan. 3:5 ff.) The name derives from the Greek *kitharos.* It is translated as 'harp'.

Sabhah (Authorized Version: 'sackbut') (Dan. 3-5 ff.) Not identified. Probably a seven-stringed instrument, as the Aramaic name suggests. Some scholars, however, believe that its name derives from the Roman *sambucus,* a tree whose wood might have been used in its production. The identification with the sackbut or the trombone cannot be substantiated.

Shalishim (Authorized Version: 'instruments of music') (1 Sam. 18:6) Some believe that it was a three-stringed instrument, or a triangular percussion instrument. Either theory can be supported by the Hebrew name.

Sheminith (Ps. 6:1) Thought by some scholars to be an eight-stringed instrument, as the Hebrew name may imply. Others suggest that it was an instrument pitched one octave higher than usual.

Shofar (Authorized Version: 'trumpet') A wind instrument made of a ram's horn, used with stringed instruments (Ps. 150:3), wind instruments (Ps. 98:6) or both (1 Chr. 15:28). It was, and still is, much used in Jewish ritual.

Sumphonia (Authorized Version: 'dulcimer') (Dan. 3:5 ff.) Some scholars believe that it was a bagpipe, while others think that it was not a specific instrument, but a whole orchestra. The identification with the dulcimer is very doubtful.

Tof; timbrel (Authorized Version: 'tabret' or 'timbrel') A percussion instrument with a membrane, or timbrel, mentioned frequently in the Bible (Isa. 5:12; Ps. 81:2, etc.). Timbrels varied in size and were played with the bare hand or with sticks. Large ones were played by two people.

Ugab (Authorized Version: 'organ') (Gen. 4:21) The nature of this instrument is unknown. The commentators describe it as a flute or a stringed instrument. The identification with the organ must be dismissed.

ROMAN PERIOD There is little evidence of musical life in Palestine in the later periods. In the Second Temple the rituals were accompanied by cymbals, harps, lyres and trumpets. An orchestra in the Temple consisted of six psalteries, an unlimited number of harps, one pair of cymbals and two trumpets.

seems that cymbals were used to mark the beginnings, endings and pauses in the chapters sung.

Minnim (Authorized Version: 'stringed instruments') (Ps. 150:4) Although it is certain that this was a musical instrument its identification is not known.

Nebel A stringed instrument, a psaltery, played solo (Ps. 71:22), with the harp (Ps. 150:3) or in a full orchestra (Isa. 5:12; Authorized Version: 'viol'). It was in use in the Temple and in secular life. The number of strings was not fixed but did not exceed ten. A psaltery of ten strings was called *nebel asor* (Ps. 33:2) or simply *asor* (Ps. 92:3), *asor* meaning ten. Some scholars, however, believe that the *nebel* was made of skin, like a bagpipe.

Neginoth A name that occurs in the opening lines of six of the Psalms (4, 6, 54, etc.). Identification not known.

N

NAARAN; NEARA A Jewish village of the Roman and Byzantine periods. The earliest mention of the site is in the account by Josephus (*Antiq.* XVII, 340) of how Archelaus, Herod's son and heir, diverted half the water of Neara in order to irrigate a palm grove near his newly built town of *Archelais. It was known to Eusebius (*Onom.* 136, 24) as a Jewish village about 5 miles from *Jericho, in the territory of Ephraim. At a later period the water of Naaran again became a matter of dispute, this time between the local Jews and those of *Jericho.

In September 1918, when the combined Turco-German forces were shelling the British from their outposts on the other side of the *Jordan, a shell exploding at Ain Duq, the site of Naaran, about $2^1/_2$ miles north of *Jericho, laid bare in an excellent state of preservation the mosaic pavement of a synagogue. The military authorities took the trouble to measure the building and to make a drawing of the pavement. The site was then excavated by Father L.H. Vincent on behalf of the Pontifical Biblical School in Jerusalem. The synagogue consisted of the prayer hall proper, a basilica measuring 46 feet by 40 feet, approached by three entrances on the south, with a narthex on the north and an irregularly shaped courtyard. There was an additional hall attached to the building on the west, linked to the west aisle by a door.

The aisles and the space between the columns were decorated with a multicolored mosaic pavement made up of floral and geometric patterns arranged in larger and smaller carpet-like panels. Facing the main entrance are two gazelles, beautifully portrayed. Then comes a dedicatory inscription: 'Let be remembered for good Halifou, daughter of Rabbi Safra, who donated for this holy place. Amen!' The northern half of the nave is decorated with octagons in which animals, birds in cages and baskets with birds were once depicted. Among the birds were a peacock, a chick and a cockerel, among the animals a bison, a lion and a fox. The birds and animals had been deliberately destroyed but care had been taken not to do any unnecessary damage, so that the cages and the baskets had not been touched at all. It seems that this destruction was done by Jewish iconoclasts at a period of strong religious orthodoxy. Next, on the south, comes a large panel in which the zodiacal circle is depicted with Helios driving the chariot of the sun in the center. Here, too, all the figures had been destroyed, but care had been taken not to touch the names of the signs of the zodiac, which were written in Hebrew. The southern part of the floor is occupied by the Torah Shrine flanked by two seven-branched candlesticks (*Menorah), on the arms of which large lamps are poised. Below the Torah Shrine stood a man, his hands raised, between two lions. This section was also

The aqueduct at Naaran

severely damaged, and were it not for the inscription 'Daniel, shalom' it would be impossible to identify it as Daniel in the lions' den. The area above the candlesticks and the biblical scene is full of dedicatory inscriptions; these show that the synagogue was built with donations from many members of the community.

The excavator dated the synagogue to the 3rd century AD, but this date was not accepted by scholars and it was redated to the 6th century AD. Now, with the discovery of the synagogue of *Hammath, near *Tiberias, an earlier date for this synagogue does seem possible.

NABATEANS A people called 'Nabateoi' and 'Nabatei' in the Greek and Roman sources and 'Nabatu' in their own inscriptions, which are not earlier than the 2nd century BC. The Nabateans left no historical documents and we are thus dependent mainly on Greek and Roman ones, the earliest of which were written no later than the end of the 4th century BC (most are of c. 100 BC-AD 100). These sources are Diodorus Siculus, Strabo, Josephus and Ptolemy, who all refer to the Nabatean Arabs. Some early scholars suggested a connection between Nebajoth, the first-born of Ishmael (Gen. 25:13), or the 'Nabaate' of the Assyrian sources of the 7th century BC, and the Nabateans, but this suggestion was not well founded. Because the Nabatean inscriptions of the 2nd century BC-2nd century AD were all written in the Aramaic language and script (*Inscriptions) it was thought that they might have originated in Aramean stock, but this theory has been decisively rejected. Although no Nabatean inscription earlier than the 2nd century BC has been found, it seems that this people, like the Jews and other nations in the area, simply adopted the Aramaic script and language which was then the *lingua franca* of the region.

The earliest historical record referring to the Nabateans in the former country of the *Moabites is of 312 BC. Diodorus (II, 2, 48) recounts that after the defeat

Nabatean painted pottery bowl, Mampsis

that Demetrius Poliorketes, son of Antigonus, suffered at the hands of Ptolemy I and Seleucus I, Antigonus and his son set out to plunder the country east of the *Jordan. The historian relates that this army penetrated the rock shelters of the Nabateans, who hid their property and families on a 'certain rock' — *petra* in the Greek. It seems that this was the place where the Nabateans later built their capital, giving it the name *Petra, or Raqmu in the Nabatean. They escaped destruction by paying a heavy tribute to the Greeks, a method which bought them their freedom several times in their history.

Archaeological finds also testify to the presence of the Nabateans in southern Transjordan in the 3rd century BC and to their subsequent penetration to the *Negev. At *Petra, *Oboda and *Nessana coins and potsherds of the 4th-3rd centuries BC have been found. Although both pottery and coins are in the main typically Hellenistic, it seems that they should be attributed to the Nabateans. The wide geographical area covered by these finds points to the strong commercial relations of the Nabateans at that early period. Indeed we know from later historical sources that they took a very active part in the Arabian-Indian spice trade, which brought great riches to their country. The caravan trade necessitated the foundation of permanent halts, forts and watering-places along the routes in northern Arabia and in the *Negev. In addition to trading, the Nabateans, like other tribes that originated in the desert, did not refrain from robbery. In this period the Nabateans were tent-dwellers. Remains of a Nabatean encampment of the early Nabatean period were found at *Oboda.

The first Nabatean ruler, Aretas, is not mentioned until 169 BC: Jason, high priest in *Jerusalem, sought refuge in his camp (2 Macc. 5:8). The earliest Nabatean inscription, found at *Elusa, belongs to this period. Relations between the Nabateans and the Hasmoneans were quite friendly at the beginning of the Revolt and later (1 Macc. 5:25; 9:35). At that time the Nabateans had begun the process of expanding their domain in *Moab, and *Medaba was already in their hands. The history of the Nabateans during most of the 2nd century BC is obscure and we know of only one doubtful Nabatean king, Malichus (Josephus, *Antiq.* XIII, 131), who may have reigned in about 145 BC. Towards the end of the 2nd century BC, however, the historical pattern becomes much clearer.

In about 110 BC Erotiums-Aretas II became King of the Nabateans. Whereas their expansion in most of the 2nd century BC had been in desolate regions, they now began to press northwards, towards the fertile region of southern Syria. This move coincided with the period in which John Hyrcanus was completing his conquest of Judea, and his successor, Alexander Jannaeus, extended the Hasmonean kingdom to regions outside Judea proper. A collision of interest inevitably ensued between the two expanding kingdoms. When Alexander Jannaeus was besieging *Gaza (c. 96 BC), the help of Aretas, 'the king of the Arabs', was expected, but it came too late (Josephus, *Antiq.* XIII, 358-60). In the 1st century BC Obodas I became King of the Nabateans (96-87 BC). In his day

Alexander Jannaeus conquered 12 cities in the Nabatean kingdom, most of them in *Moab. In 93 BC a decisive battle was fought between Obodas and Alexander, in which the latter was defeated. This put a stop to Hasmonean expansion in the east (Josephus, *Antiq.* XIII, 382) and opened the road to further Nabatean penetration northwards.

In 87 BC Rabel I, who reigned for less than a year, ascended the Nabatean throne. In that year Antiochus XII Dionysus of *Damascus set out to fight the Nabateans. He marched through Judea, attempting to attack them from the rear. Both the Syrian monarch and the Nabatean king fell in battle, but Nabatea was saved. Aretas III Philhellenos (87-62 BC) conquered northern Trnsjordan and southern Syria (*Hauran) and in 85 BC became ruler of Damascus at the request of its inhabitants (Josephus, *Antiq.* XIII, 392). He subsequently crossed the border of Judea and defeated Alexander Jannaeus near *Hadid. It was to Aretas III that the Nabateans owed their first contacts with Hellenistic culture, the influence of which is strongly marked in every branch of Nabatean art. This is also demonstrated in their first coins, which were struck by Aretas III.

While Aretas was fighting Judea Pompey arrived in the east, conquered Judea and ordered the Nabateans to leave the country. In 62 BC Scaurus, Pompey's general, devastated the region of *Petra, the Nabatean capital, but could not take this natural stronghold, and the Nabateans again bought their freedom by paying tribute (Josephus, *Antiq.* XIV, 80). From that time onwards the Nabatean kingdom was vassal to Rome. The Roman victory was commemorated by a coin in which Aretas is seen kneeling near a harnessed camel.

The history of Nabatea in the time of Malichus I (c. 60 - c. 30 BC) is not well known; nor is the date of his death certain, his dates being known mainly from his coins. Josephus (*Antiq.* XIV, 103-4) mentions a punitive expedition conducted by the Roman general Scaurus against *Petra in 55 BC but does not give the reason for it; nor is the king mentioned. The great struggles in the Roman world took place during the reign of Malichus I. In 47 BC he sent dromedaries to the help of Caesar Augustus in *Egypt. In 40 BC he refused to help Herod, who was then struggling for his throne (Josephus, *Antiq.* XIV, 370 ff.); but at the same time he gave his support to the Parthians, and for this he had to pay tribute to the Romans. When Antony came to *Egypt the Nabatean regions facing the *Dead Sea were given to Cleopatra, Queen of *Egypt. At the end of his reign Malichus was fighting on the losing side; in 32 BC, at the Battle of Actium, he supported the old and weak Hyrcanus II against the victorious Herod.

The image of Obodas II (30-9 BC) is much overshadowed by the stronger figure of Syllaeus, his minister (Josephus, *Antiq.* XVI, 220). There was considerable tension between the Nabateans and the Jews in this period. In recognition of his services Augustus gave Herod Batanea (the *Bashan), Auranitis and Trachonitis (*Hauran) and Gaulanitis (*Golan), parts of which were in the Nabatean domain. After their con-

quest of *Egypt (25 BC) the Romans organized an expedition designed to seize the Nabatean trade routes in *Arabia. The Nabatean minister Syllaeus was appointed chief guide and the Roman general Aelius Gallus marched at the head of 10,000 Roman soldiers, some Nabatean dromedaries and Jewish archers. By treachery, as Strabo puts it, the Nabatean misled the Romans and lost a great part of the army. Those who did not perish of thirst and disease returned to *Egypt without achieving their objective. According to Strabo Syllaeus was put to death in Rome. The last years of Obodas saw a renewal of war between Herod and the Nabateans, in which the later were defeated.

Josephus puts the death of Syllaeus a little later and blames him for the death of Obodas, whom he presumed to have been poisoned by agents of Syllaeus.

After his death Obodas was buried at Oboda, the town named after him. Obodas was deified, and — as evidenced by Nabatean and Greek inscriptions — his cult persisted at Oboda until the 3rd century AD. Without waiting for Augustus' confirmation Aretas IV (9 BC-AD 40), son of Obodas, ascended the throne. In his coins and inscriptions he is known by the title 'he who loved his people'. During his reign the king-

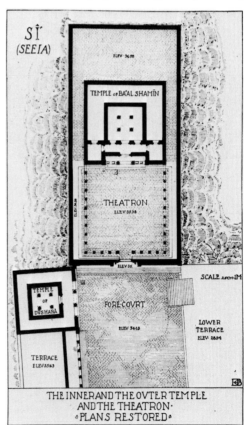

Plan of the Nabatean temple at Seeia, in the Hauran

dom reached its highest point, both economically and in its architecture, sculpture, painting and pottery. Except for the dispatch by Aretas of a military force to quell some riots in Judea after Herod's death in 4 BC (Josephus, *Antiq.* XVII, 287), and a mention of him as ruler of *Damascus in AD 39 (2 Cor. 11:32), there is little about him in the ancient sources. On the other hand an exceedingly large number of inscriptions, dated by the years for which Aretas IV had reigned, have been found in every quarter of the kingdom, from northern *Arabia in the south to southern Syria in the north, and to *Oboda and *Sobata in the west. These testify to the great expansion of the kingdom. The decline set in during the reign of Malichus II (AD 40-70), the first-born son of Aretas IV. First the Nabateans lost *Damascus. In AD 67 Malichus sent an army to help Vespasian in the siege of *Jerusalem (Josephus, *War* III, 68). Otherwise he is little mentioned. It was in his time that the Romans learned to make use of the southwest monsoon. Earlier in the 1st century AD Hippalus had discovered that the monsoon made it possible to sail safely to *India and back and they

Bronze lamp with Nabatean inscription, Oboda

were therefore able to bring spices and aromatics directly from *India to *Alexandria and thence to Rome, dealing a mortal blow to the Nabatean economy. In about AD 50 it seems to have suffered another blow. New tribes migrated from *Arabia to the southern parts of the kingdom and penetrated the *Negev, where they destroyed *Oboda and the forts on the *Petra-Gaza road.

The last Nabatean king, Rabel II (AD 70-106), is never mentioned in external sources, and it is only by means of coins and inscriptions that his history can be followed. The epithet 'he who brought life and deliverance to his people' by which he was known has given rise to a number of hypotheses. Some scholars believe that it was a renewal of some religious or social institution that gave him this title; others think that by some unknown means he succeeded in postponing the annexation of his kingdom to the Roman Empire. Neither of these hypotheses is well supported. The earliest inscription, in which the title figures dates from AD 88, was found at *Oboda and is connected with agriculture. This gives rise to the theory that he earned his title by subjugating the Arab tribes and laying the foundations for dry farming, thus creating a new basis for the economy to replace the international trade that the Nabateans had lost.

In AD 106, possibly after Rabel's death, the Romans annexed the Nabatean kingdom to the newly founded Provincia Arabia, whose capital was initially Petra and later *Bozrah. Although the Nabateans lost their independence, their kingdom flourished under the Roman aegis as it had never done before. Early in the 2nd century Trajan caused a new road to be constructed from the *Red Sea to Syria, with a secondary branch via *Mampsis to the Mediterranean. On the occasion of Hadrian's visit to Arabia in AD 130 *Petra received the new title Hadriana Petra Metropolis. In this period a colonnaded street, a triumphal arch, temples and sumptuous tombs were constructed. But this renewed prosperity was of short duration: in the late Roman period a sharp decline set in and in the Byzantine period *Petra was already an unimportant place.

LANGUAGE AND RELIGION The original language of the Nabateans in the period that preceded their arrival in Transjordan is not known. As we have seen, they acquired the Aramaic language and script early in the 2nd century BC, as did the Palmyrenes (*Tadmor), a tribe of Arabic descent. Nor is enough known about the Nabatean religion. Their chief god was Dushara, a local deity inherited from their predecessors. In the Roman period this god was identified with Dionysus. He was symbolized by a pointed or rounded stele set in a niche and his counterpart was Alat, mother of the gods. She was of Arabic origin, and was later identified by the Nabateans with Atargatis. They also had a dozen or more other gods, known to us only by name.

ARCHITECTURE AND SCULPTURE There is much evidence that the Nabateans' building and sculpture was not confined to their own cities, for the imprint of their hand is to be seen in buildings in Palestine of Herod's time. The earliest Nabatean buildings are not earlier

Silver dinar of Malichus II, 40-70 AD

than the 1st century BC. To this period belong some of their temples, such as those of Seeia Khirbet *Tannur and er-Ram, consisting of a forecourt with benches around the walls — the *teatra* — at the end of which stands the temple proper with the shrine at its center. At Khirbet *Tannur reliefs of gods and goddesses with their attributes (fruit and fishes) were discovered. At er-Ram the walls were plastered and painted. The distinctive features of Nabatean architecture are oblique stone-dressing (although other forms were used as well) and the typical Nabatean capital, which is not seen elsewhere. Unparalleled also are their rock-cut tombs, hundreds of which were found at *Petra; similar ones, apart from those of the Roman temple type, were found in the other important Nabatean center of el-Hegr in northern Arabia. Tombs of other types were also found at *Mampsis.

POTTERY Although Nabatean pottery has its roots in the pottery art of the Hellenistic-Roman world, it has certain individual characteristics, such as a special method of applying the decoration on the finer class of bowls, and the thinness of the ware, which is no thicker than $1/_{10}$ in and is sometimes even thinner. These bowls are reddish-brown or reddish-orange and are decorated with stylized plants, which are sometimes applied on a surface previously decorated with very fine lines. In addition to these fine pieces, eastern sigillata wares and a special type of Nabatean sigillata were produced. The golden age of this ware runs from the last quarter of the 1st century BC to the middle of the 1st century after AD, after which a deterioration is noted.

NAGILA (TEL) The large mound, covering an area of about 10 acres, is situated $17^{1}/_{2}$ miles east of *Gaza, some 20 feet above a natural hill on the bank of Nahal Shiqmah. It is one of the many sites with which *Gath of the Philistines has been identified. However, since no remains of the Iron Age I were found on the site, this identification has been rejected.

Excavations on the site were carried out in 1962 and 1963 by R. Amiran on behalf of the Institute for Mediterranean Studies. Traces of the earliest occupation on the site (Stratum XIV) go back to the Chalcolithic period. Strata XIII-XII date to the Early Bronze Age II-III. To this period belong remains of a rectangular-shaped *house with benches running along its walls. A curved wall might have belonged to an apsidal structure. On the slope was discovered a tomb from the Early Bronze Age II. After a gap of six or seven hundred years the site was reoccupied in the Middle Bronze Age II-III (Strata XI-VIV). From this period were unearthed a residential quarter, and parts of two public buildings, as well as an elaborate system of *fortifications. The entire mound was surrounded by an earth embankment above which was erected a mud brick wall, 7-8 feet wide. At a late stage in this period the fortifications were further strengthened by a glacis made of earth and crushed chalk, which covered the foot of the wall and the entire slope. It is 10 feet thick at its junction with the wall and was still protected by a ditch. A tower was associated with this fortification system. The destruction of these fortifications is attributed to Pharaoh Ahmose in about 1550 BC. The section of the residential quarter reveals two parallel streets (5 feet wide), paved with potsherds and pebbles laid in beaten clay. The houses are rectangular in shape, and consist of one or two small rooms (about 6 feet by 9 feet) and a partly roofed courtyard paved with flagstones. The bases of the walls were built of fieldstones and the superstructures were of bricks. The houses contained clay ovens, stone and clay benches and round silos. The public buildings, only partly excavated, are distinguished by 5 feet thick walls. In the vicinity of the Early Bronze Age tomb was found another tomb of this period which contained remains of some fifty individuals, whose skulls were placed along the walls of the tomb. It contained about 150 local *pottery vessels as well as Cypriote and Egyptian objects. Scantier traces of occupation were uncovered from the Late Bronze Age (Strata VI and V), Iron Age IIB (Stratum IV), and Iron Age IIC (Stratum III). The settlement of this last period also spread to the area outside the mound. Pottery and building remains were also found from the Hellenistic, Roman and Byzantine periods (Stratum II) and the Mameluke period (Stratum I), at which time a khan occupied a third of the area of the mound.

NAHALLAL; NAHALOL A Levitical city in the territory of Zebulum (Josh. 19:15). Zebulum did not in fact conquer it and it remained Canaanite (Judg. 1:30). The Jerusalem Talmud mentions it as Mahalul, which is identified today with the Arab village of Malul in the *Jezreel Valley. Others identify it with Tell en-Nahl, in the southern part of the Plain of *Acre (*Acco).

NAHARIYA A village on the Mediterranean coast, at the mouth of the River Gaathon, inhabited from the Middle Bronze Age onwards. The ancient mound has not yet been excavated, but sherds dating from the Middle Bronze Age down to the Persian period have been discovered in surveys of the site. Along the coast, and on the sandstone ridge that runs parallel to it, houses, mosaic floors, potters' kilns and, notably, cemeteries dating from the Hellenistic period to the Byzantine period, were observed.

The most important site was discovered in a shallow mound about half a mile to the north of the river mouth, 150 feet from the shore. Excavated in 1947 by I. Ben-Dor, and in 1954-6 by M. Dothan on behalf of the Israel Department of Antiquities and Museums, it consists of a temple, an open-air court and a high place. The building is of the broadhouse type, facing east, and consists of a large hall with two smaller rooms, one at either end. The stone bases found along the hall indicate that the roof was supported by wooden posts. South of this temple remains of another, the earliest on this site, were unearthed. Three phases were observed in the development of the local cult place. The earliest temple was a stone building 20 feet by 20 feet, with a small high place nearby. Numerous animal bones, probably remains of offerings, were found in the court between the high place and the temple. In the second, and most important, phase the smaller temple was replaced by a larger one, built to the north of it. The high place was enlarged as well, to a diameter of 45 feet, and had a flight of steps leading to it. In the last phase the level of the high

Flask with neck in the shape of a monkey, Nahariya, Middle Bronze Age

place was raised and its area reduced; the temple also became smaller. In the temple, and especially around the high place, finds of a cultic nature came to light, consisting mostly of miniature offering vessels, bowls with seven cups (*Pottery), hundreds of beads, jewelry and animal figurines. Some of the figurines, mostly of women, were of bronze or silver, hammered or cast. A stone mould, probably of the goddess Sea Astarte, was also found. The offerings were probably intended for her, since she was the chief deity of *Ugarit and also the goddess of Phoenician seafarers and fishermen. The cult of this temple was thus basically Semitic. The temple is dated mainly to the 18th-17th centuries BC, the Hyksos period, and went out of use at the beginning of the New Kingdom of *Egypt (16th century BC).

NAIN; NAIM A village in *Galilee, southeast of *Nazareth, called Naim in the later Jewish sources, where Jesus revived the widow's son (Luke 7:11-14). Eusebius (*Onom.* 140:3) calls in Naeim, 12 miles south of Mt *Tabor, near *Endor. A place of some importance in the Byzantine period, when it was known as Kome Nais, the 'village Nais', it is identified with Nein, about 6 miles southeast of *Nazareth. The ruins of the medieval church found there incorporate some remains of an earlier religious building, the exact nature of which has not been determined. There are rock-cut tombs of the time of the Second Temple around the village.

NAPHTALI *See* *KEDESH

NASBEH (TELL EN-) An ancient mound some 6 miles northwest of *Jerusalem, 1,600 feet above sea level, identified with *Mizpeh. The site was excavated in 1926, 1927, 1929, 1932 and 1935 by F. Bade on behalf of the Palestine Institute of the Pacific School of Religion. Because of his untimely death, however, the work had to be completed and published by other scholars. The earliest traces of occupation go back to the Chalcolithic period and to the early phases of the Early Bronze Age (*c.* 3000 BC). Although no building remains were discovered pottery found in tombs and dwelling caves provides evidence of this settlement. The main occupation of the site was in the Iron Age, but there were also tombs of the Persian, Hellenistic, Roman and Byzantine periods.

The main importance of the excavations at Tell en-Nasbeh lies in the fact that the relatively small size of the mound allowed excavation of the whole site, thus providing a fairly clear idea of what a whole provincial Israelite town looked like. The earliest settlement belongs to the 11th-10th centuries BC, although Philistine sherds found on the site may indicate an occupation in the previous century. To the early Israelite town belongs a rather frail city wall of rubble 3 feet thick. In about 900 BC this wall was replaced by a formidable system of fortifications. The new wall is about ½ mile in circumference, enclosing an area of less than 8 acres.

Crevices in the rock were packed with stones. Above this a huge platform of large boulders serves as a foundation for the wall, which is built of stone blocks set in mortar and plastered on the outside. The base of the wall is protected by a huge retaining wall.

Along it 10 projecting towers were built at irregular intervals. The wall is about 13 feet thick and it still rises to a great height, but it is not known whether there was once a brick superstructure. The city gate is in the northeastern section of the wall. It was of the direct-approach type, had two pairs of jambs and was defended by a massive tower. Inside the town a large number of houses were excavated. Near the gate was one large, better built house, probably an administrative center, constructed on the four-room plan, as are all the houses at Tell en-Nasbeh. These did not abut onto the wall but were separated from it by a broad street, thus providing easy access to the defences. Narrower alleys ran between the other houses. Each court, and every empty space, was honeycombed with hundreds of silos and cisterns (*Stores). Many houses had wine-presses nearby. Some were provided with dye vats (*Dyes and dyeing). Numerous kilns on the site indicate that pottery was produced locally.

Astarte figurines and other cult objects provide information about popular religious beliefs. Important among the small finds are the numerous *lamelek* seals, seals of the *Yahud* type, and a group of *msh* seals (probably an abbreviation of *Mizpeh). Interesting among the private seals is that of 'Yaazanyahu servant of the King' (*Seals).

NAVEH; NEVE Capital of the *Bashan region, east of the River *Jordan. Although not mentioned in the Bible it seems to be a place of remote antiquity, as it figures in the lists of Tuthmosis III. It appears in early Hellenistic documents as Naoun. The town of Naveh is more frequently mentioned in Jewish and other sources of the late Roman and Byzantine periods. Eusebius (*Onom.* 136:2-6) mistakenly names it Nineveh, a town of the Jews at the edge of *Arabia, but Hieronymus corrected it to Neue. It also appears on the Peutinger map. In the 6th century AD Naveh was a Christian town, but a Jewish community continued to flourish there and was still in existence in the Middle Ages.

The site was visited by several scholars in the second half of the 19th century. The last survey was that made by L.A. Mayer and E. Reifenberg on behalf of the Israel Exploration Society in the 1930s. Remains of several buildings were described, one of which was a synagogue. Some of the architectural stones were decorated with the menorah and other Jewish symbols. Lintels belonging to the synagogue and other Jewish public buildings and decorated with the same symbols had been reused in houses of the modern village of Nawa, which has preserved the ancient name. One stone still had part of a dedicatory inscription in Aramaic.

NAZARETH The small town in *Galilee where Jesus spent his childhood and youth, and from which he set forth to visit the towns and villages of *Galilee (Matt. 2:23; Mark 1:9; Luke 1:26; 2:4, 39, 51). The New Testament mentions a synagogue there (Luke 4:16). After the destruction of the Second Temple Jews lived at Nazareth and it was the seat of the priestly family of Pises. Eusebius (*Onom.* 138:24 ff) mentions a village in Galilee called Nazareth, opposite *Legio, near Mt *Tabor. No church was built there until the time of

Constantine and it is not mentioned before AD 570. The first church was destroyed by the Arabs in about AD 636 and rebuilt by the Crusaders under the guidance of Tancred. The modern Church of the Annunciation incorporates remains of the Byzantine basilica.

NEAPOLIS *See* *FLAVIA NEAPOLIS

NEBO *a)* The peak of the mountain of Abarim in *Moab, where the Children of Israel camped (Num. 33:47) and from which Moses beheld the land of *Canaan before his death at Mt Nebo. The Bible locates it in the land of *Moab, opposite *Jericho (Deut. 32:49; 34:1, 4). The location of the mountain is not known exactly. Eusebius (*Onom.* 136:13) states that this mountain 'is shown today' at the 6th mile from *Heshbon westward.

b) One of the cities in *Moab (Num. 32:3) that was rebuilt by the Reubenites, after its conquest from Sihon King of the *Amorites (Num. 21;25, 31; 32:33). According to the stele of Mesha, King of *Moab (*Inscriptions), he destroyed the Israelite cult place there. After the campaign of Tiglath-Pileser III in 733-732 BC Nebo became *Moabite (Isa. 15-16; Jer. 48, etc.). Under *Babylonian rule it became part of the eparchy which in the Hellenistic period was known by the name of Moabitis. Eusebius (*Onom.* 136:9) states that the ruined city was shown in his time 8 miles south of *Heshbon. It is identified today with Khirbet Ayn Musa or Khirbet el-Mukhayet. Pottery of the early Iron Age was found in the latter. To the Byzantine period belongs a church with a beautiful mosaic in which famous churches in Palestine are depicted. *c)* A city in Judah, inhabited after the Restoration (Ezra 2:29). Not identified.

NEGEV; NEGEB A region extending southwards from the border of Judah. The name denotes 'dryness' in Hebrew, but in the Bible it is sometimes used to refer to the south, and the Authorized Version usually has 'south' where the Hebrew Bible has 'negeb' or 'negbah'. Geographically and from the point of view of climate the Plain of *Beer-Sheba forms its northern border, but in the Bible the southern and southwestern foothills of *Hebron were also included in it. It is bounded by the Arabah on the east and by the coastal plain and the wildernesses of *Paran, *Zin and *Shur on the northwest and west. Most of the central and southern parts of the Negev are mountainous. The central part is zigzagged by deep wadis and craters, which form a serious obstacle to transport. For this reason no important international trade routes traversed the Negev from north to south, and the two major international thoroughfares (the Via Maris and the King's Way) that skirted it were linked by a network of secondary roads. The more important of these were the biblical 'Way of the mountains of the Amorites' (Deut. 1:7; Authorized Version: 'journey to the mount of'), which connected *Kadesh-Barnea with the southern Arabah, and 'the Way of Edom', which descended from *Arad to the southern part of the mountains of *Sodom (2 Kgs. 3:20). Although there is no biblical evidence for it there may have been a third road, running between *Gaza, *Gerar, *Beer-Sheba, *Hormah and *Arad. In the Hellenistic, Roman and Byzantine periods a road connected

*Petra, *Oboda and *Elusa with *Gaza, while another ran from Aila (*Elath) along the Arabah to *Mampsis, *Hebron and *Jerusalem. In the Byzantine period the road from Jerusalem to Mount *Sinai, through *Hebron, *Elusa and *Nessana, was much frequented by pilgrims.

The Negev was of little economic importance in biblical times. The northern plain and the banks of the wadis did, however, provide grazing for goats and sheep (1 Sam. 25:2 ff.; 1 Chr. 4:38-41; 2 Chr. 26:10), and archaeological surveys and excavations have shown that in the Chalcolithic period and the Iron Age agriculture was also practised to some extent. Of greater economic importance was the establishment, in the period of the Israelite kingdom, of commercial relations with the South Arabian kingdoms, inaugurated by the visit of the Queen of *Sheba, and the subsequent building of a merchant navy with the assistance of *Tyre (1 Kgs. 9:11; 10:22 ff.). This trade route was still used in the times of Jehoshaphat and Azariah (1 Kgs. 22:48-9; 2 Kgs. 14:21-2).

There are copper mines in the southern part of the Negev, in the vicinity of *Timnah to the northwest of *Elath; the initial working of these was formerly attributed to Solomon, but recent research has shown that this date is approximately two centuries too late (*Metals).

The economic value of the Negev increased in Hellenistic, Roman and Byzantine times. From about the beginning of the 3rd century BC the *Nabateans established a spice trade with southern *Arabia and *India and for this purpose they founded a network of caravanserais along the routes in the Negev. In a later phase, at about the end of the 1st century AD, they began to develop a form of agriculture based on draining the scanty rainwater from large catchment areas to small parcels of land. This system was more fully developed in the Byzantine period, when, according to the Nessana papyri grapes, figs, barley, wheat and vegetables were grown, and wine was produced from the grapes. This information is confirmed by actual archaeological finds.

The Negev was already inhabited in prehistoric times but the nature of this settlement is still obscure. The first permanent settlements are of the Chalcolithic period, when in the second half of the 4th millennium BC a highly developed culture, called the *Beer-Sheba culture, flourished in the valleys of the northern Negev. Remains of this culture have been discovered at *Bir-es-Safadi and other sites in the vicinity of *Beer-Sheba. The Early Bronze Age is poorly represented in the Negev, but there are numerous traces of settlements of the Middle Bronze Age. These settlements are mainly scattered throughout the central mountainous part of the Negev, and one of them, *Har-Yeruham, has recently been excavated. The typical graves of these semi-nomads are tumuli tombs (*Burial) scattered along the mountain crests, found mainly in the central and southern parts of the Negev. This was the age of the Patriarchs, described by Professor Nelson Glueck as the period of *pax Abrahamitica*, and it was at that time that Abraham 'dwelt between Kadesh and Shur, and sojourned in Gerar' (Gen. 12:9; 13:1-3; 20:1). In all these cases the term 'Negev' is rendered as 'south' in the Authorized Version. Isaac also lived there (Gen. 24:62; 26:20-1). In the Late Bronze Age Canaanite city states were established only in the northern and northwestern Negev (*Arad, *Hormah, *Gerar, *Sharuhen). In the 13th century BC the Negev, together with *Moab and *Edom, was the objective of several punitive campaigns by Rameses II. After the conquest of *Canaan it was allotted to Simeon, although it was incorporated into the territory of Judah (Josh. 19:1-9; 1 Chr. 4:28-33). At the beginning of the period of the Judean kingdom the region came to be known as the 'Negev of Judah' (1 Sam. 27:10; 2 Sam. 24:7; Authorized Version: 'south').

The archaeological evidence indicates that during the early period of the Israelite kingdom a line of fortresses was built along a route that led from *Arad and *Hormah to *Kadesh-Barnea. Near some of these fortresses small settlements sprang up. One of these, at *Ramat Matred, has now been excavated. It has been dated by its pottery to the first half of the 10th century BC. It was at this time that the expansion towards the Gulf of *Elath and the fortification of *Ezion-Geber took place (1 Kgs. 9:26). In the fifth year of the reign of Rehoboam (924 BC) Pharaoh Sheshonq I led a campaign against Judah (1 Kgs. 14:25-8; 2 Chr. 12:1-12), and the list of conquered sites found in the temple of Amun at Karnak includes the names of 85 places, all of which are believed to have been in the Negev. During Jehoshaphat's reign the Negev was again in Israelite hands (1 Kgs. 22:49-50; 2 Chr. 20:35-7), a fact that is confirmed by archaeological finds. To the northeast of *Beer-Sheba new fortresses and settlements were built in the 9th and 8th centuries BC and also in the time of Azariah, who conquered *Edom and built *Elath (2 Kgs. 14:22; 2 Chr. 26:2), thus necessitating the building of further fortresses. That of Tell Qudeirat, identified with *Kadesh-Barnea, is attributed to this period. During the Assyrian campaigns against Judah the Negev was lost to the Judean kingdom and *Elath was conquered by the *Edomites (2 Kgs. 16:6; Authorized Version: 'Syria').

There was no permanent settlement in the Negev until late in the 4th and early 3rd centuries BC, when it was occupied by the *Nabateans. Evidence for this is provided by potsherds and coins found at *Oboda and Nessana and by a Nabatean inscription found at *Elusa. No building remains whatsoever of this period were found, and like other nomads the *Nabateans lived in tents. Traces of an early camp were observed at Oboda. During the following centuries the Nabatean settlement expanded over larger areas in the Negev, although some gaps in occupation have been noted. There was one such gap at *Oboda, and perhaps in the other settlements as well, at the beginning of the 1st century BC; this was probably due to the conquest of *Gaza, the main *Nabatean trade outlet, by Alexander Jannaeus. Another gap occurred from the middle of the 1st century AD to later in the same century; this affected at least *Oboda and *Mampsis, possibly as a result of the arrival of new nomadic tribes from *Arabia. This has recently been corroborated by a study of the silver content of Nabatean coins. In AD 50 the silver content dropped from 42.5% to 20%. It remained at this low level until AD 73 when the new king, Rabel II (70-106 AD), apparently overcame the intruders and began to consolidate the Nabatean economy. The Nabatean towns were abandoned before the middle of the 2nd century AD, for reasons that are still obscure.

In the last quarter of the 1st century AD the Nabateans in the Negev and the *Hauran embarked on an *agricultural enterprise, using their ancient knowledge of collecting rainwater in cisterns for irrigating terraced fields. It seems that they first engaged in horse breeding and growing barley, with viticulture and the production of wine forming the last stage in the transition to agriculture of the descendants of the Nabateans in the late Roman-Byzantine period. At the beginning of the 2nd century AD *Mampsis grew into a horse-breeders' town. Stables of this period were also found at *Oboda and *Sobata. By the middle of the 3rd century AD the old Nabatean *temple was rebuilt and rededicated to Zeus-Oboda and Aphrodite, as evidenced by numerous inscriptions in Greek, although the personal names of the dedicators of the temple are all Nabatean. It is possible that this renewed prosperity was partly due to the resumption of turquoise and copper mining in southern *Sinai. The Late Nabatean town at *Elusa has recently been located, as has the town of *Sobata. *Nessana seems to have been deserted in this period. Diocletian's interest in the East, continued on religious grounds by Constantine I, is well evidenced in the Negev. Mampsis was surrounded by a wall and fortresses were built at Oboda and Nessa for the protection of the local population.

From the middle of the 4th century AD onwards numerous churches were erected throughout the region. Winepresses and wine cellars were built on the outskirts of the towns, and the valleys and slopes of mountains were terraced and planted with vines, olives and other fruit trees. The decline was slow. Mampsis was apparently destroyed first at the end of the 5th century AD by pre-Islamic Arab tribes; Oboda was destroyed in AD 636 when the Moslems flooded Palestine. The four other towns were spared and were exploited as sources of income. Taxes of wheat, oil and money which weakened their economies and the loss of customers for Negev wine were the reasons for their abandonment of the Negev between AD 700 and 800.

NESSANA A town in the western part of the central *Negev, one of those whose Arabic name, Auja el-Hafir, has not preserved the ancient form. Were it not for the papyri found there the ancient identification would therefore have been a constant puzzle. The meaning of its early name is not known, but some scholars suggest that it is of Nabatean origin.

The history of Nessana belongs to the early chapters of Nabatean settlement of the central *Negev, when the halts of *Elusa and *Oboda were founded. It lies on one of the major trade routes across the *Negev, connecting *Sinai with *Beer-Sheba, *Hebron and *Jerusalem (*Roads). In the Nabatean period a small fort was built on a low hill that rose above a small wadi, on the banks of which the town was later built. It seems that this fort was used by Nabatean sentries and by merchants alike. Hasmonean coins found there may perhaps be taken as evidence of connections with Judea. According to the pottery finds and coins Nessana shared the prosperity of *Oboda, *Sobata, *Elusa, *Mampsis and numerous other smaller sites in the central *Negev. In AD 106, when the *Nabatean kingdom was annexed to the Provincia *Arabia, the Nabateans abandoned Nessana. It was resettled in the times of Diocletian and Constantine I. It has been generally agreed that the military unit of the 'Most Loyal Theodosians' mentioned in a papyrus found at Nessana, were soldiers of a local unit, stationed at the camp of Nessana. A re-examination of this papyrus shows that it deals with two brothers, natives of the village of Nessana, who served in a unit of this name at Rhinocorura on the coast, on the border between the provinces of Palestine and Egypt, and that it has nothing to do with the Negev.

Nessana is not mentioned in the ancient sources but it is possible that Antonine of Placentia, who made a pilgrimage to *Sinai in AD 570, is referring to it when he recounts that after leaving *Elusa he entered 'the head of the desert', and after a march of 20 miles came to a fortress in which there was a hostel of St George, where hermits and pilgrims found shelter. From there, the pilgrim relates, he entered the inner desert.

The Arab conquest did not affect Nessana immediately. For this there is the valuable evidence of the papyri found on the site, a considerable number of which are bilingual, in Greek and Arabic, and are dated to the second half of the 7th century AD. Nessana's period of greatest prosperity came in the 6th-7th centuries BC, when all the towns of the central *Negev were flourishing, but it seems that by the middle of the 8th century AD it was already in ruins.

Situated on the much-frequented route from *Egypt to Palestine, Nessana was visited by many more scholars than any of the ancient sites in the *Negev. The first account of its ruins is that of E. Robinson (1838 and 1856), who insisted on identifying Auja el-Hafir with *Oboda. A. Musil also visited the site twice (1897 and 1902), making his second visit after the Turks had begun to build a police post there to serve as an administrative center for the Bedouins. These operations began the destruction of Nessana, which continued during the years preceding the First World War, when the Turks and German soldiers built a military base there. The consequent destruction of the ancient remains was deplored by several visitors during this period, but the vandalism, also observed by C.L. Woolley and T.E. Lawrence in 1914, continued throughout the war years. During the war K. Wulzinger made a survey on behalf of the Turco-German Committee for the Preservation of Ancient Monuments. It was then that 'Coptic' sherds were found. These turned out to be the first Nabatean painted pottery pieces ever found in the *Negev.

In 1934, when a severe drought had dried up all the cisterns at *Sobata, the expedition of New York University and the British School of Archaeology in Jerusalem, under the direction of H.D. Colt, had to move to Nessana, where water was drawn from ancient wells. This expedition could not find much of the ancient town but was lucky in finding 150 papyri in Greek, Latin and Arabic, of which further details are given below.

There are two conspicuous elements in the town plan of Nessana: the lower town, situated along the banks of a small wadi; and the acropolis, about 240 feet above sea level. The town is shaped like an irregular triangle and occupies an area of about 45 acres. Early travellers, who saw it before its more recent destruction, refer to a city wall with a gate on the east, from which ran a long street; a triangular pool 80 feet long outside the wall on the east; and embankments along the banks of the wadi. Of these nothing remains. The only extant monument in the lower town is a church, at the eastern end. This has been partly cleared of the debris that overlaid it when the Turks built an inn above its ruins. The church was of the basilical type, with one apse, a prothesis and *diakonikon* with small apses in their eastern walls. The walls of the church were apparently decorated with painted plaster. There were also chapels and a monastery attached to the church.

The acropolis, 165yd long and 45-55yd wide, is situated to the west of the town. The earliest remains on this small hill are those of a fort, which is 45 feet square. The excavators have attributed this to the Hellenistic period (2nd-1st centuries BC) because of the coins and pottery associated with it and the typical Nabatean stone-dressing. But it seems that this dating is too early, and that it was not in fact constructed before the end of the 1st century BC, when the main Nabatean occupation began. Most of the building remains on the acropolis belong, however, to the Byzantine period. They consist of a citadel and two churches. The town is connected with the acropolis by a long winding flight of steps terminating at the citadel, which measures 50yd by 100yd and occupies the greater part of the acropolis hill. It is fortified with square towers and has a large number of small rooms attached to its inner eastern and western walls. The rooms were apparently used by the local garrison, and when it was disbanded they probably served as a caravanserai. In the large court of this citadel the Turks built an inn. The rest of the acropolis is occupied by two churches. The larger one is attached to the citadel on the north and was identified by an inscription as the Church of Sts Sergius and Bacchus. It is a basilica with a single apse and is paved with multicolored marble slabs and surrounded by courts, chapels, a baptisty and other rooms. According to an inscription it was in use as early as AD 464 and is thus the earliest dated church in the central *Negev. It is in one of the rooms of this church that the greater part of the papyri collection was found. The other church lies to the southwest of the citadel and is connected to it by a wall. It is a small basilica with three apses, identified by an inscription as the Church of Mary Mother of God. It is a much simpler structure in plan and decoration and belongs to a later phase in the Byzantine

period. Here, too, considerable numbers of papyri came to light.

The papyri are the most important find on this site. They fall into two classes: a group of literary documents; and a larger group of non-literary documents; and a group of non-literary items. The literary papyri include fragments of a Latin classical text, glossaries to that text and a group of New Testament texts. Of greater importance, however, are the non-literary papyri, which include a soldier's personal records, among them documents dealing with loans, legal matters, marriage certificates, inheritances, divisions of property, bills of sale, taxes and contracts. Another of the archives relates to a church. The third contains the records of a family whose members were active in the economic life of the town. The fourth is the Arab archive, which contains documents written in Greek and Arabic; it comprises 40 items and contains a great deal of information about a period in the colonization of the region that would otherwise be completely unknown.

NETOPHA A town in Judah, close to *Bethlehem, the birth-place of two of David's mighty men (2 Sam. 23:28-9), where families of Levites settled (1 Chr. 9:16). It was also inhabited at the time of the Restoration (Ezra 2:22), when the 'sons of the singers' (Neh. 12:28) lived there, and in the Roman and Byzantine periods. It should possibly be identified with Khirbet Bedd Faluh, between *Bethlehem and *Tekoa.

NILE (THE RIVER) In the Bible the Nile is referred to simply as 'the river' (Gen. 41:1, etc.), a term sometimes used as a synonym for any large river (Isa. 33:21; Authorized Version: 'broad rivers'). It is also called Sihor (Jer. 2:18). The seven cows came up 'the river' in the dream of Joseph (Gen. 41:2) and the infant Moses was found in the ark among the flags along its bank (Exod. 2:3). 'The river' also symbolizes the whole land of *Egypt (Ezek. 29, etc.).

The Nile is the biggest river in Africa, about 3,800 miles long, and the second longest in the world. It rises in the region of the Great Lakes and flows northwards, through northeast Africa. In its upper reaches it is known as the White Nile. Near Khartoum it unites with the Blue Nile, which comes down from *Ethiopia to the Mediterranean, where it spreads into a large delta. Some of the most important cities in *Egypt sprang up along the course of the river and among the branches of its delta. The river is from $\frac{1}{2}$ mile to $\frac{3}{4}$ mile wide and flows through a valley varying from 3 to 18 miles in width. The floodwaters of the Nile, which bring down much rich silt, irrigate the valley from May onwards, reaching their greatest height in September-October. In fact the whole life of *Egypt depended, as it still does, on the waters of the Nile. It also served as a most important artery of communication and as a source of fish, which was one of the main components of the Egyptian diet.

NINEVEH The last capital of the Assyrian Empire, situated on the east bank of the Tigris (*Hiddekel), opposite modern Mosul. The city was probably founded early in the 3rd millennium BC. During the reign of Sargon II it became one of the capitals of the Assyrian kingdom, and it was the sole capital during

Bronze head from Nineveh, thought to be King Sargon II

the reign of Sennacherib. Esarhaddon and Ashurbanipal adorned Nineveh with magnificent palaces. The Assyrian sources do not disclose how it was finally destroyed. Diodorus Siculus recounts that Arabaces the Scythian besieged the city for two years but could not take it. But in the third year the waters of the river rose and destroyed its fortifications; the king and his retinue committed suicide by throwing themselves into the flames and the city fell to the Scythians. According to a chronicle of the Babylonian King Nebopolassar the united forces of the Chaldeans (*Ur) and the Medians (*Madai) destroyed Nineveh in 612 BC. Its destruction is vividly described by Zephania (2:13-15).

The remains of Nineveh are hidden in two mounds on either bank of the Hawsar River. One is Kouyunjik Tepe, where the palaces of Esarhaddon and Ashurbanipal were discovered, and the other, on the south bank, is Nebi Younis (the Prophet Jonah), where the palace of Sennacherib stood. These palaces were unusually large, built upon raised platforms about 75 feet high. At the gates of the palaces stood winged lions with human faces. The walls were lined with alabaster and other beautiful stones. On the walls were reliefs depicting the military campaigns of the kings of Assyria and their hunting expeditions, plus mythological and other scenes. Sennacherib's palace occupied the southeastern quarter of the city. It was

here that the relief portraying the siege and conquest of *Lachish was discovered. The city wall was more than 3 miles long and according to the king's description it had no less than 15 gates. Sennacherib encircled the inner wall with an outer one which, in his words, 'was high like a mountain'. The whole city was surrounded by gardens full of scented plants and irrigated by channels that drew water from the neighboring rivers. The great library of Ashurbanipal, containing 25,000 clay tablets dealing with historical, literary and religious matters, was found in Kouyunjik.

NOB A city of priests founded by the sons of Eli after the destruction of *Shiloh (1 Sam. 21-2). David was given refuge there, and in retaliation Saul ordered the massacre of the priests of Nob, with Goliath's sword which was kept there (1 Sam. 22:19). It was a place from which the Assyrians on their march from the north could view the city of Jerusalem for the first time (Isa. 10-32). During the Restorarion Nob was settled by Benjaminites (Neh. 11:32). Not identified.

NOPH One of the most important cities of ancient *Egypt, at the head of the *Nile Delta. The name Memphis, which means 'white wall' or 'wall', is preserved in the name of the local citadel, Leukos Teichos as it was known to the Greeks. The Egyptian form of the name was *Mn nfrw*, which means 'Pharaoh Phiops is beautiful'. The city was built by Pharaoh Phiops I in the 24th century BC. The pyramids of Giza, dating back to the 4th Dynasty, the most famous of which is that of the Cheops, were found nearby. In the same region are Abusir, with the pyramids of the 5th Dynasty, and Sakkara, where tombs of the pharaohs of the 3rd Dynasty and pyramids of the pharaohs of the 5th, 6th and 7th Dynasties were found. The famous temple of Sarapis, in which the bull Apis was interred, also stood at Sakkara, while the pyramids of the pharaohs of the Old Kingdom and the Middle Kingdom were discovered at Dashur. During the New Kingdom Memphis was the second capital of *Egypt and from the time of Tuthmosis III onwards the pharaohs lived there. It became their official residence at the end of the *El Amarna period. Rameses II moved elsewhere, but shortly afterwards the official residence reverted to Memphis once more. The temple of the god Ptah was rebuilt and ornamented and the palaces of Merneptah and Rameses III, remains of which are still extant, were erected. In 730 BC the city was conquered by the Ethiopians, but was taken by Esarhaddon, King of Assyria, in 671 BC and again by Ashurbanipal in 663 BC. During the wars of the Babylonians against Judah many Jews fled to Noph and Jeremiah directed prophecies against them (Jer. 44:1 ff.).

NYMPHAEUM The term (literally 'temple of the nymphs') applied to a Roman building whose decorative features consist of running water, fountains, flowers and statues. Several *nymphaea* have been identified in surveys in Palestine, though none has yet been excavated; all those so far examined are in Transjordan: *Philadelphia (*Rabbath-Ammon), Bostra (*Bozrah), *Gerasa, *Kanath, *Dionysias and Hippos (*Susita). The earliest *nymphaeum* in Palestine has been identified at *Callirrhoe, a group of hot springs

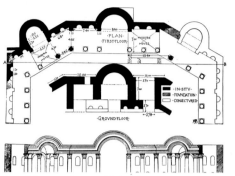

Plan of the nymphaeum, Philadelphia (Rabbath-Ammon)

near the *Dead Sea, where Herod went in search of a cure shortly before his death.

The regular plan of all these buildings is a colonnaded exedra with several small and large niches, their number varying with the size of the whole structure. At Philadelphia the colonnaded exedra is almost 400 feet wide and in front of it is a basin 50 feet deep. This basin could be filled with water from a small rivulet flowing into it, or by the perennial waters of the Wadi Amman, which flowed at the rear of the building. The importance of the *nymphaea* among the public buildings of a city can be deduced from the positions allotted to them within the city. All those mentioned above were found at the city center on the *cardo,* or main street.

O

OBODA; ABDE; AVDAT A town in the central *Negev named after one of the Nabatean kings, possibly Obodas II, who, according to a tradition of the 1st century AD, was deified and buried there. Oboda is mentioned in ancient sources from the 2nd century AD onwards.

According to the archaeological evidence Oboda was settled for the first time at the end of the 4th century or early in the 3rd century BC by the *Nabateans, who established a halt there on the caravan route from *Petra to *Gaza. The conquest of *Gaza by Alexander Jannaeus, the Hasmonean monarch, in about 100 BC put an end to the Nabatean hold on the *Negev. At the end of the 1st century BC, during the reign of Aretas IV, Oboda was rebuilt and enjoyed a period of glory, as is well attested by numerous inscriptions and other archaeological finds. In about the middle of the 1st century AD the city was sacked, probably by newly arrived nomadic tribes from *Arabia, whose rock drawings and graffiti were found on rocks around the site. During the reign of the last of the Nabatean kings, Rabel II, Oboda revived, its economy no longer based on the caravan trade but on dry farming, as is shown by inscriptions engraved on libation altars found near the fields and by actual remains of installations connected with soil preservation and water conservation. The annexation of the *Nabatean kingdom to the Provincia *Arabia had no effect on the fate of Oboda. Following the inauguration of the irrigation system in the last quarter of the first century AD, as attested by Nabatean dedicatory inscriptions found at Oboda, the town embarked on a construction program in the first decades of the 2nd century and the Nabateans of Oboda exchanged their tents for excellently built *houses. These were only recently found on the western slope of the mountain. According to the numismatic evidence this building program continued during the entire 2nd and beginning of the 3rd century AD. A new period of construction began in the second quarter of the same century. Although no change occurred in the population, the Nabateans of Oboda, together with their brethren elsewhere in Nabatea — except for *Sinai — no longer used the Nabatean language, exchanging it for Greek. It is in this language that an epitaph found in a large burial cave was written in AD 232; dedications in Greek from the year AD 267/8 were also found in the *temple to Zeus-Oboda, which occupied the site of the old Nabatean temple. A dedicatory inscription in Greek on a tower in the newly-built quarter to the south of the acropolis dates from AD 295/6.

Oboda's prosperity in the late Roman period was a natural outcome of the intensive development of *agriculture, which was based in its initial stages on horse breeding. Although most evidence for this matter still comes from *Mampsis, two stables were also discovered at Oboda, one in the late Nabatean quarter on the western slope, and another in the northern end of the quarter built in the late Roman period. It is possible that the resumption of turquoise and copper mining in southern *Sinai also contributed toward this prosperity. Security was improved when at the end of the 3rd and the beginning of the 4th century AD, Diocletian and Constantine I included the Negev and

*Bronze statuette of a panther
from Oboda, Early Roman period*

Sinai in the defence system of the empire, and a new citadel was built on the acropolis of Oboda. In the second half of the 4th century the first church — the North Church — was probably erected at Oboda. It was dedicated as a cathedral and a memorial to Elijah and John, and a chapel was added to the citadel. New Oboda was built along the western slope, where scores of houses with caves behind them were excavated. The town in the Byzantine period owed its prosperity to *agriculture, which was based at this time on the cultivation of the wine grape and olive trees. It is possible that the town also benefited to some extent from expanding monasticism and from pilgrims passing on their way to Mount *Sinai. Oboda's prosperity came to an abrupt end when the town was sacked and the churches burnt by the Arabs in AD 636.

The town was rediscovered and correctly identified by E.H. Palmer in 1870. After that it was visited by A. Musil (1902), A. Jaussen, R. Savignac and H. Vincent (1904) and C.L. Woolley and T.E. Lawrence (1912). They all left quite detailed descriptions of the site,

with general maps and detailed plans of various objects. Trial digs were made by the D.H. Colt expedition in 1937. Large-scale excavations on behalf of the Hebrew University and the National Parks Authority have been undertaken by M. Avi-Yonah (1958) and A. Negev (1958-60), and by A. Negev and R. Cohen (Department of Antiquities) in 1975, 1976, 1977.

THE EXCAVATIONS: NABATEAN PERIOD According to an analysis of the archaeological and epigraphical evidence there were three phases of Nabatean occupation at Oboda: 3rd-2nd centuries BC; late 1st century BC to first half of the 1st century AD; and last quarter of the 1st to about the middle of the 2nd centuries AD. Remains of the first phase consisted mainly of datable pottery vessels and coins; no building remains could be attributed to it. Beneath a structure of the 1st century AD in the vicinity of the Nabatean military camp were discovered remains of a campfire, dated by pottery found in it to the 3rd-2nd centuries BC. This was most probably a tent site of the early Nabatean period.

Oboda, aerial view of the city

In the second phase a spur of the rock jutting out of the mountain on which the town was built was surrounded by strong walls to form a podium. From the evidence of inscriptions and architectural remains, mostly in secondary use in buildings of later periods, it may be inferred that a temple was erected on the acropolis at the end of the 1st century BC. The small town occupied part of the plateau to the east and northeast of the acropolis. Here, at the northern extremity of the town, the *Nabateans built a large military camp to house the cavalry units that guarded the caravans. Of special importance is the potter's workshop discovered to the east of the town, which is a unique Nabatean installation. It produced the beautiful Nabatean egg-shell pottery, as well as coarse Nabatean ware and other articles common in Palestine during the early Roman period. Datable pottery types and a large quantity of coins indicate that the pottery workshop, which contained a kiln and other necessary equipment, was active during the first half of the 1st century AD. Also in this period of intensive public construction, the Nabateans still adhered to their old living habits and dwelled in tents. The Nabatean town of this phase was destroyed in a fierce conflagration, as is indicated by the layer of ashes covering the remains of the period in some places. This destruction is attributed by the excavators to the middle of the 1st century AD. The remains of the third phase are found mainly in the agricultural hinterland of the town, where dams and channels for irrigating the fields with the scanty rainwater were discovered. (Rainfall does not exceed 4in in a rainy season of four to five months in this area.) Large inscribed libation altars found near the fields show that the dams must have been built between AD 88 and 98. In the town itself inscriptions were found indicating building activities during the years AD 106/7 and 125/6.

LATE ROMAN PERIOD Inscriptions and architectural remains indicate that the acropolis, including the Nabatean temple, were reused in the 3rd century AD, although the temple was rededicated in AD 267/8 to new deities: Zeus of Oboda (the local Zeus) and Aphrodite. The new town was built to the southeast of the acropolis. It consisted of 20 to 30 houses built of fine ashlar and grouped along short streets, with a central plaza in which the water reservoirs were hewn out of the rock. The latest building in this town, a tower, was dedicated in AD 293/4. According to the evidence of the coins, the town flourished through the entire 4th century AD. At the beginning of the century — again as evidenced by the coins — the Nabatean military camp and some late Nabatean houses were dismantled and a new citadel was built on the eastern part of the acropolis. This must have taken place during the reigns of Diocletian and Constantine (a cross decorates the lintel of one of the citadel gates).

BYZANTINE PERIOD The prosperity of Oboda in the late Roman period continued uninterruptedly throughout the Byzantine period. In the second half of the 4th century the acropolis was completely remodelled. The pagan temple and the other early buildings were dismantled and the stones were reused in the new buildings. A citadel covering an area of 60yd by 40yd and

Lamp showing gladiators from Oboda, Early Roman period

defended by three towers on each side, was built on the acropolis. This was provided with two cisterns to store water drained from the large empty central court and also, by means of channels, from the surrounding area. Except for a small chapel and one room the citadel was completely devoid of buildings of any kind, apparently serving as a protection for the local population rather than as a base for a military garrison. Close to the citadel, to the west, is a large square; at its northern and southern ends are two churches of the usual basilical type and a baptistery. The southern church is identified by an inscription as the 'Martyrion of St Theodore'. The numerous epitaphs found in the church and its atrium range in date from AD 541 to 618. The Byzantine town itself was built on the western slope of the mountain. It consisted of about 400 units, each comprising a hewn cave and in front of it a house built of stone. While the houses served as dwellings the caves provided storage space and shelter from the great heat in the summer; some were used as workshops and wine cellars.

In the private houses wood was used very sparingly. The roofing involved the ample use of stone arches and thin stone slabs were used for the long covering stones. Only in the churches was wood, which was imported at great cost from Syria and northern Palestine, used to any extent. At the foot of the mountain a well 180 feet deep was excavated to supply brackish water for a steam bath. The bathhouse was an excellent structure, with cold, tepid and hot compartments.

On the acropolis, and in the plain to the west of it, three winepresses of a most elaborate type were discovered. They included storage cells, with a slanting window for conveying baskets of grapes to the treading ground, whence channels running under the floor would carry the flowing juice into a series of settling tanks. From these the juice was transferred in jars to the wine cellars for fermentation.

The excavations of Byzantine Oboda revealed that the citadel and the churches were stormed and burnt down. Their destruction was first attributed to the Persians in the years AD 618/20, but renewed investigation indicated that there is no evidence that the Persians ever diverged from the coast on their way to *Egypt. The destruction of Byzantine Oboda is thus attributed to the Arabs in AD 636. Oboda did not share the fate of the other towns in the western part of the central *Negev, such as *Nessana, *Sobata, *Ruheibeh, and *Elusa.

ODEUM A small theater with a roofed auditorium, used for music and recitations. At Philadelphia (*Rabbath-Ammon) the *odeum* was next to the theater and at right angles to it, with a joint colonnade along the front. It was built entirely from ground level. At *Kanath the auditorium was hewn out of the rock; the arena, 63 feet in diameter, is semicircular and the benches are spaced at regular intervals on the gradient without a *praecinctio.* The main entrances were from the sides between the outer wall of the arena and the ends of the seats. In the middle of the stage was a fountain, which used a spring whose water also served the nearby *nymphaeum. (See also* *THEATER.)

Oil-press from Tirat Jehuda

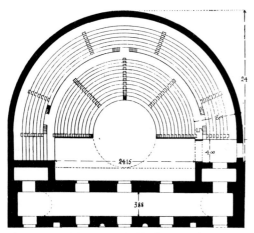

The Odeum, Philadelphia (Rabbath-Ammon), Roman period

OIL Vegetable oil was already known in early periods, but the most common oil in biblical times was extracted from olives. Olives intended for this purpose were left on the tree to ripen fully, until they became black. The fruit was then shaken down with long wooden sticks and conveyed to the olive press in wicker baskets. It was spread on the floor to enable it to ferment; this facilitated the extraction of the oil, which involved either treading them or crushing them carefully in a stone bowl. In early periods the pulp was then placed in water and the floating oil skimmed off. In biblical times the crushed olives were put on a mat or goatskin, tied into a bundle and placed in a deep, narrow, rock-cut channel. Over this a heavy stone was placed; a heavy wooden beam was laid on it, with one

end driven into a hole in the back wall of the installation. This beam was used as a level to press out the oil. Small channels conveyed the oil into a vat, from where it was collected in earthen jars for storage. From the Roman period onwards other methods were used. An upright millstone, turned within a stone receptacle by a plodding beast, crushed the olives, while extraction involved a wooden beampress or a screw press.

Olive oil was a staple food, but it was also used in medicine, for lamps and in cult practices. Other oils were rare in Palestine.

OLIVES (MOUNT OF) A mountain to the east of Jerusalem (Zech. 14:4), on the other side of the *Kidron Valley, rising about 2,500 feet above sea level. It seems to have been sacred from early times (cf. 2 Sam. 15:30, 32; Ezek. 11:23). Solomon built high places there for Ashtoreth, Chemosh and Milcom (2 Kgs. 23:13), but these and the images were broken by Josiah, King of Judah.

The Mount of Olives occupies a special place in early Christian tradition. According to Acts (1:9-12) it was 'a sabbath day's journey' (2,000 cubits) from *Jerusalem, and it was also the place of the Ascension. At the traditional site a Roman lady by the name of Pomenia built a church in about AD 387, but the present chapel dates from no earlier than the Crusader period. To the south of it the Emperor Constantine built the church of Eleona, on the site where Jesus traditionally foretold the destruction of *Jerusalem (Matt. 24:1-3; Mark 13:1-4). The church, of which little remains today, was destroyed by the Persians in AD 614 but was soon rebuilt. Further rebuilding took place in the middle of the 12th century. On the lower slope of the mountain tombs of the time of the Second Temple and remains of additional churches were discovered. Since the Middle Ages this lower slope, facing the Temple Mount, has been used as a Jewish burial-ground.

ONO A town built by families of the tribe of Benjamin in the vicinity of *Lod (1 Chr. 8:12). A site of that name is mentioned in the lists of Tuthmosis III, but it is never again referred to in Egyptian or Assyrian sources, nor does it appear in the early books of the Bible. Ono was inhabited after the Restoration (Ezra. 2:33; Neh. 7:37) by the Benjaminites (Neh. 11:35). In the late Roman period it was the capital of a district and in the talmudic literature it is mentioned once at a distance of 3 miles from *Lod and once at a distance of 5 miles. In the 4th century AD it was an independent town. The site is identified with Kafr Ana, 6 miles northeast of Lydda.

Ostracon (inscribed sherd) from Tell Qasileh, mentioning a consignment of gold from Ophir

OPHIR In the Bible Ophir is referred to as the country from which gold was brought (*Metals). Solomon brought 420 talents of gold from here (1 Kgs. 9:28), but Jehoshaphat failed to acquire any because his ships foundered in a storm at *Ezion-Geber (1 Kgs. 22:48). Ophir gold was considered to be of high quality (Isa. 13:12, 1 Chr. 29:4). It is also mentioned in one of the ostraca from Tell *Qasileh. The location of Ophir is not known with certainty. Josephus, Eusebius and Hieronymus state that it was in *India, while other ancient authorities say that it was an island in the *Red Sea. Today many places are offered as possible candidates, including *Arabia, East Africa and even far-away Sumatra. The coupling of Ophir with other identifiable places (Gen. 10:29; 1 Chr. 1:23) may perhaps point to southern *Arabia.

OPHNI; BETH-GUPHNIN A town in the territory of Benjamin (Josh. 18:24). In the time of the Second Temple its name was changed to Ophnah, or Beth-Guphnin, which was the capital of a toparchy. After the destruction of the Temple the notables of *Jerusalem were sent into exile there. A palace of the Roman period was discovered on the site. Eusebius (*Onom.* 168:16) calls it Gophnah, 15 miles from Jerusalem, on the way to *Neapolis. Identified with Jifneh, near Ramallah.

OPHRAH A town in the territory of Benjamin (Josh. 18:23), prominent in the war between the *Philistines and Israel (1 Sam. 13:17); known in the Roman period as Afairema, or Aifraim. It was in the center of the northern district of Judah from 145 BC until the conquest by Pompey. Identified with et-Taiyibeh.
b) The town of Joash Abi-Ezrite, where the angel of God appeared to Gideon, his son, and where he built an altar (Judg. 6:1-12, 24) and was buried (Judg. 8:32). Eusebius refers to it as a village, 5 miles east of *Bethel. Identified with several places in the *Jezreel Valley, possibly *Affuleh.

P

PALACES Palaces as distinct from houses point to the existence of class groupings within a society. Apart from the 'palace of *Ai', which belongs to the Early Bronze Age, the first palaces unearthed are dated to the Middle Bronze Age IIB and IIC, the period of Hyksos domination. The general plan is like that of the usual oriental dwelling, with rooms arranged round a central court. The buildings had at least two stories, the lower one being used for domestic purposes and the accommodation of servants while the upper story contained the living quarters proper. Excavators very often call a building a palace simply by reason of its size. But the quality of the architecture or a find of some importance — large numbers of scarabs, inscribed material, a hoard of ivory plaques or of gold jewelry — would point to the fact that its inhabitants belonged to a privileged class. The largest palace of the Middle Bronze Age to be

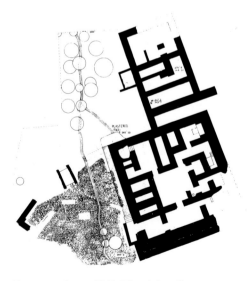

Egyptian palace at Tell el-Farah (south)

unearthed in Palestine was at Tell el-*Ajjul. It occupied half an acre and its exterior wall was about 7 feet wide and built of mud brick on a stone foundation. From the Late Bronze Age onwards several large buildings of this type have been identified. The palace at Tell el-*Farah (south) has a central courtyard, while at *Taanach the courtyard was in the northeast corner and at *Megiddo (stratum VIII), it was on the south.

The most famous palace ever constructed in Palestine was Solomon's royal palace in *Jerusalem. Its several units are described in 1 Kings (7:1–12). As D. Ussishkin pointed out, this palace and the adjoining Temple were built under the influence of northern architecture. It was of a type that originated in Syria in the 2nd millennium BC. The complex is entered through a portico with a single pillar, opening into an entrance hall or 'porch of pillars' (1 Kgs. 7:6) that leads into the throne room or 'porch for the throne' (1 Kgs. 7:7). Then come the living quarters, rooms surrounding 'another court' (1 Kgs. 7:8). The 'great court' (1 Kgs. 7:12) was apparently a huge court in front of the entrance. Built on similar lines, the palace of the Solomonic period at *Megiddo has been identified as being of the same type. Another outstanding palace of the Iron Age was that of Omri and Ahab at *Samaria, which followed the usual plan of rooms grouped round a central court. Its fame derives from the decoration of its furniture with ivory plaques in low or high relief or open-work; hence the reference to 'the ivory house' in 1 Kings (22:39) (*Ivory). A palace of the late Iron Age, the first to be discovered in Judah, was found at *Ramat Rahel and identified by Y. Aharoni with the palace built by Jehoiakim (609–597 BC) and referred to by Jeremiah (22:13–14).

A palace of the Persian period, which was built late in the 5th century BC, has been unearthed at *Lachish. Of the outstanding palace of Roman Palestine, Herod's palace in *Jerusalem, nothing remains, but its splendor can be imagined now that the two palaces at *Masada have been excavated. Palaces of the Herodian period have recently been investigated at *Jericho.

PALEAGAZA The palace south of *Gaza where Ptolemi I defeated Demetrius, son of Antigonus, in 312 BC, according to Diodorus Siculus (19; 80, 5). The name means 'ancient Gaza' and the Greeks believed it to be the forerunner of the Hellenistic city of *Gaza. Identified by some scholars with Tell el-*Ajjul.

PALMYRA *See* *TADMOR

PANEAS; CAESARA PHILIPPI A city on the southern
slope of the *Hermon range, near one of the main
sources of the River *Jordan. The earliest mention of
the city, under the name of Panion, is in Polybius, in his
account of Antiochus III's victory over the Ptolemies
(XVI, 18:2; XXVIII, 1:3). In the time of Zenodorus the
region was called Panias (Pliny, *Nat. Hist.* V, 16:74).
After his death Herod received the city from Augustus
(Josephus, *Antiq.* XV, 359/60; *War* I, 400). His son
Philip made it the capital of his tetrarchy and called it
Caesarea, in honor either of Augustus (Josephus, *Antiq.*
XVIII, 28) or of Tiberius (Josephus, *War* II, 168). To distinguish it from Caesarea Maritima and other cities, it
is often called Caesarea Philippi (Josephus, *War* III,
443, VII, 23). In Matthew (16:13) and Mark (8:27) it is
mentioned as one of the cities visited by Jesus and his
disciples. Agrippa II embellished the city and renamed
it Neronias in honor of Nero (Josephus, *Antiq.* XX, 211).
After his death it was attached to the province of Syria,
and on the division of Syria it passed to *Phoenicia. In
the Talmud it is referred to as Qisariyon, 'Little
Caesarea' (Tos. Sukkah 1:9). In late Roman and Byzantine sources the city appears under its old name,
Paneas, or more rarely as Caesarea-Paneas. It was conquered by the Arabs in the 7th century AD. On the
escarpment north of Paneas is the cave described by
Josephus: 'In the mountains there is a beautiful cave,
and below it the earth slopes steeply to a precipitous
and inaccessible depth, which is filled with still water,
while above it is a very high mountain. Below the cave
rise the sources of the River Jordan' (*Ant.* XV:364).
Nearby is another small cave with a beautiful niche. A
Greek inscription of AD 87 mentions Ecco, the mountain nymph, and Pan. It seems that in this and another
niche statues of Pan were placed. According to another
Greek inscription the cult of Pan persisted here late
into the 3rd century AD. Excavations carried out near
the springs since 1984 unearthed sections of a well-built
public building of the 1st century AD. Directly above
this structure were remains of a Crusader, and then of a
Mameluk private house.

PARAN A desert in the *Sinai peninsula, south of
*Kadesh-Barnea, lying between the land of *Midian and
*Egypt (1 Kgs. 11:18). Ishmael lived here with his
mother, Hagar the Egyptian (Gen. 21:21). One of the
stations of the Israelites on their way from *Egypt to the
Promised Land (Deut. 33:2). Moses sent out men from
there to spy out the land (Num. 13:3) and the Israelites
remained there 40 days (Num. 13:25-6). David found
shelter in the Wilderness of Paran after the death of
Samuel (1 Sam. 25:1).

At quite an early date Christian tradition identified
Paran with the great oasis of Feiran, in the southern
rocky part of the *Sinai peninsula, where Mount *Sinai
is shown at Jebel Musa. In the 2nd and 3rd centuries AD
the *Nabateans venerated two mountains rising above
the oasis, Jebel Moneijah, the lower, and Jebel Serbal,
the higher mountain. The lower mountain served as a
place of pilgrimage, and scores of Nabatean inscriptions, mentioning numerous priests and other religious
functionaries, cover the rocks and flattened blocks of
stone. On the higher mountain a *temple — the resi-

dence of the gods — was built. Early in the Byzantine
period this region became a center of Christian monasticism, and it was there that the monastery of St.
Catherine was built. Throughout the Byzantine period
it attracted numerous pilgrims, who made their way
through the desert under the protection of soldiers stationed in the Byzantine town of *Nessana.

PEHEL; PELLA A city in Transjordan on the slopes of
the *Gilead Heights, about 8 miles southeast of *Beth-
Shean, identified with Khirbet Fahil. The earliest mention of Pella is in the *Execration Texts. In the Late
Bronze Age it appears in other Egyptian texts, such as
the lists of Tuthmosis III and Sethos I. Two of the *El
Amarna letters mention Mut-Balu, ruler of Pella. From
the stele of Sethos I, found at *Bath-Shean, it is known
that the city was in alliance with *Hammath-Gader,
about 10 miles north of *Beth-Shean, against the latter.
The Egyptian Anastasi papyrus mentions Pella,
together with *Rehob, as a center where certain parts of
chariots were made for *Egypt. It is not mentioned in
the Bible and apparently declined in the Late Bronze
Age. Archaeological evidence shows that the site was
occupied in both phases of the Iron Age and it reappears in historical records in the Hellenistic-Roman
period. It was settled by veterans of Alexander the
Great and was given the same name as his birth-place in
Macedonia. Polybius (V, 70) mentions it as one of the
cities taken by Antiochus the Great in 218 BC. By the
time of Alexander Jannaeus it was a center of Hellenistic culture. He made several attempts to conquer it and
succeeded in about 80 BC, when its inhabitants chose to
leave rather than accept the Jewish faith (Josephus,
Antiq. XIII, 397). Pompey passed through the city
(Josephus, *Antiq.* XIV, 49), freed it (Josephus, *War* I,
156) and made it a member of the Decapolis. It was
rebuilt by Gabinius, governor of Syria from 57 BC
onwards (Josephus, *Antiq.* XIV, 75). Pliny mentions it as
being famous for its spring (*Nat. Hist.* V, XVI, 70). It
seems to have been destroyed by the Jews in AD 66, in
revenge for the murder of the Jews of *Caesarea, but
Eusebius (*Eccl. Hist.* III. V, 3) relates that the Christians
of *Jerusalem fled to Pella when Vespasian prepared his
attack. In the later Roman and Byzantine periods it was
one of the centers of the Christian community and its
bishops in the 5th and 6th centuries AD are known.

Excavations of the site were undertaken in 1958 by
H.N. Richardson and R.W. Funk, in 1967 by R.H.
Smith and since 1979 by R.H. Smith, A.W. McNicoll
and J.B. Hennessey. The earliest remains date from the
Neolithic period, while its rapid decline took place in
late Umayyad times. The rich finds, both in architecture and tomb deposits as well as small finds, indicate
that Pella was a prosperous town from the Hellenistic to
the Umayyad periods. Hellenistic and Byzantine civic
buildings, a *theater and three *churches have been
uncovered.

PENUEL; PENIEL A place east of the *Jordan, at a
ford over the River *Jabbok, where Jacob wrestled
with the angel of God and afterwards received the
name of Israel (Gen. 32:22-33). Gideon and his men
crossed the river at this point while chasing Zebah and
Zalmunna, kings of *Midian, and on his way back he
threatened to break down the tower of Penuel (Judg.

8:5-9). Jeroboam built the town anew (1 Kgs. 12:25). Identified with Tell edh-Dhahab esh-Sharqiyeh, on the River *Jabbok. Surveys made here uncovered remains of the Late Bronze Age and Iron Age I and II.

PEOR A high mountain in the land of *Moab, the last of the three to which Balak directed Balaam so that he might curse Israel, and from which instead he proclaimed a blessing (Num. 23:28). Eusebius (*Onom.* 48:3-5) states that a town by this name is located on a mountain with the same name in *Moab near the city called *Livias in his days. Peor is now variously identified with several mountains around *Heshbon.

PEREA A Jewish district east of the River *Jordan, extending along the *Jordan Valley and the northern part of the eastern shores of the *Dead Sea, its name meaning the land 'beyond'. On the east it bordered the city territories of *Gerasa, Philadelphia (*Rabbath-Ammon), *Heshbon and *Medaba, and its main cities were *Gadara, *Abila and Libias (*Bethsaida). In the Persian period this territory was ruled by the Tobiads. After the Hasmonean uprising the Maccabees protected the Jews who settled there from their Arab-Nabatean neighbors. John Hyrcanus I enlarged the territory of the Perea by conquering Nabatean cities (Josephus, *Antiq.* XIII, 225; *War* I, 63). It was part of Herod's domain and its capital was *Gadara. After his death it was ruled by his son Herod Antipas, governor of *Galilee, but its eastern part was restored to the *Nabateans. Later it became part of Agrippa II's realm. During the First Jewish Revolt the cities of the Perea played an active part in the war against the Romans.

PETRA The ruins of the 'rose-red city' of Petra, capital of the Nabatean kingdom, were discovered and identified in 1812 by J.L. Burckhardt. It is generally accepted that 'ha-sela' ('the rock'), the Edomite town (2 Kgs. 14:7; Authorized Version: 'Selah'; 2 Chr. 25:12), should be sought at Umm el-Biyara, one of the highest rocks rising above Wadi Musa. Petra is the Greek form of this Semitic name. The ancient Nabatean name of the town was Rekem, or Rekmu, as it is rendered in a Nabatean inscription. Except for some remains of the Upper Paleolithic period and the Iron Age there is little at Petra that is earlier than the Hellenistic period.

Many scholars believed that the Nabatean tribes arrived from Arabia late in the 6th century BC, when the *Edomites went to settle in the south of Judea, after the destruction of *Jerusalem by the *Babylonians. For this, however, there is no evidence, historical or archaeological. The earliest mention of the *Nabateans at a certain rock goes back to 312 BC, when Antigonus, one of the heirs of Alexander the Great, fought them. But an analysis of the relevant Greek source, Hieronymus of Cardia, whose work has been preserved by Diodorus Siculus, casts doubt on the identification of that rock with Petra, and if the distances mentioned by Hieronymus are taken into account, this rock could be located somewhere in the Nabatean region of the *Negev, perhaps somewhere in the southern part of the western shore of the *Dead Sea. To this period, and to subsequent centuries, belong the earliest pottery and coins found at Petra.

Of this early period hardly any building remains survive. The first Nabatean ruler to be known with certainty, a man called Aretas, is mentioned in conjunction with Jason's flight from *Jerusalem to Petra in 169 BC, but there is no indication of an established Nabatean Dynasty there until the end of that century. From then on Nabatean kings ruled there until its incorporation into the Provincia Arabia in AD 106.

The first flowering of Petra occurred in the reigns of King Obodas II (30-9 BC) and King Aretas IV (9 BC-AD 40), in whose time the great expansion of Nabatean commerce took place (*Trade). Of the history of the city during the reigns of the last two Nabatean kings, Malichus II (AD 40-70) and Rabel II (AD 70-106), less is known, but it is quite certain that the city suffered a decline at that period. After the death of Rabel II the Nabatean kingdom was annexed to Provincia Arabia and Petra became for some time the capital of the province. For the whole of the 2nd century AD and the greater part of the 3rd prosperity returned to Petra, despite the fact that trade was now flowing along other routes to *Egypt and Palmyra (*Tadmor). In AD 131 Hadrian visited Petra; on that occasion the city was raised to the rank of a *metropolis*, with the title Hadriana Petra Metropolis, and coins were struck to commemorate the event. Petra thus continued to be an important administrative center, as it was throughout the Nabatean period. This is clear from some of the later documents found in the *Judean Desert Caves, a number of which were sealed in the Aphrodision of Petra, a temple of Aphrodite, in which the local archives were situated, earlier and later than AD 106, and from seal impressions fround at *Mampsis. Later in the Roman period Petra diminished in importance, though it remained a religious center for some of the cities of southern Syria and *Arabia. In the 4th century AD the Provincia Arabia was subdivided. Bostra (*Bozrah) became the capital of *Arabia, while Petra was the capital of Palestina Tertia, which stretched over the south of Palestine and Nabatea. In the 5th century Christianity penetrated Petra. However, not a single church was discovered on the site, and the only Christian cult place was located in a cave. It is thus possible that the Christians of Petra, as in other parts of the adjoining deserts, were nomads, or semi-nomads, who had bishops of their own. The history of Petra in the first years of the Arab conquest is not known. At the beginning of the 12th century AD it was conquered by Baldwin I; it is last mentioned in conjunction with a visit of Baybars (AD 1260-77).

The first European to set foot in Petra was U.J. Seetzen (1870), who had no idea of its real identity. Thus J.L. Burckhardt, who visited Petra in 1812, is rightly considered to be its discoverer. Throughout the 19th century the site attracted many scholars, painters, poets and globe-trotters, who left scores of descriptions. Scientific research began with the visits of the Reverend Fathers of the École Biblique of Jerusalem, the first being undertaken in 1896. A year later a most important survey was carried out by R. Brünnow and A. von Domaszevski, who surveyed, drew plans of and described about 1,000 monuments at Petra. Their work was soon supplemented by G. Dalman, of the German Evangelical Institute, who investigated the topography of the necropolis and the cult places. During the First World War remains of Roman Petra were investigated by scholars of the Turco-German Committee for the Preservation of Ancient Monuments, which was attached to the German-Turkish headquarters.

The first excavations at Petra were made by G. and A. Horsfield on behalf of the Lord Melchett Expedition in 1929. They excavated some of the dumps, where they found and identified for the first time the beautiful eggshell-painted Nabatean pottery. The same expedition, together with W.F. Albright (1934), later excavated one of the Nabatean high places. Some tombs were excavated at Petra in 1936 by M.A. Murray and J.C. Ellis. From 1955 the Department of Antiquities of Jordan carried out some clearances and restored some monuments under the direction of P.J. Parr. In 1962-3 the Roman theater was excavated by the Theological Seminary of Princeton under the direction of P. Hammond Jr. Since then numerous expeditions of many nations have been working at Petra.

The peculiar topographical formation of the valley of Petra and the surrounding high mountains had attracted the *Nabateans, who found it easy to excavate caves in the soft rock to serve as shelter for their families and their wealth. The valley is about 1,000yd long and 400yd wide and is divided by Wadi Musa into two unequal parts. Above the valley sheer walls of rock rise to a height of about 1000 feet. The rocky mountains on the east are cleft by a deep and narrow gorge, the Siq, which forms the easiest approach to Petra. The sheer mountains are bisected by numerous wadis, whose steep walls are honeycombed with hundreds of burial caves.

EARLY PERIODS Some remains of the Upper Paleolithic and Neolithic periods were found in some places, and especially at el-Beida. Iron Age sherds identified as Edomite were found at Umm el-Biyara.

HELLENISTIC PERIOD For some time only pottery finds and coins could be attributed to this period, as at other early Nabatean sites such as *Oboda, *Nessana and *Elusa. Finally a deep section was cut at Petra so that the stratigraphy of the site could be studied. Deep in the cut remains of houses of primitive construction, built of fieldstones and mud mortar, were found. From the pottery and the coins associated with these remains it was possible to date them to the late 3rd and 2nd centuries BC. The rarity of houses of the Nabatean period at this early stage of their settlement may be accounted for by the nomadic life to which they were accustomed, and by the slowness of their gradual transition to a sedentary life, which was probably completed during the 2nd century BC.

NABATEAN PERIOD (late 1st century BC — early 2nd century AD. Few dwellings of this period have been discovered at Petra. It seems that at the end of the 1st century BC the primitive houses were replaced by better structures displaying the typical features of Nabatean masonry. To prepare the rugged valley for the new buildings a retaining wall 50 feet thick was built along the northern bank of the wadi. Above this the

main east-west road was constructed. The houses were built between the road and the bank of the wadi. The pottery associated with them dates from the late 1st century BC and the 1st century AD. A house discovered in another part of the city shows traces of the typical Nabatean oblique tooling on its outside walls, while on the inside they were plastered and painted.

ROMAN PERIOD (106 BC — 3rd century AD) It seems that after the Roman conquest of Petra, and especially in the second half of the 2nd century AD, most of the older Nabatean houses were demolished and the town assumed a new aspect. This may be inferred from an excavated part where a Roman road was found that had gone out of use. Hadrian's visit to Petra seems to have been considered a good occasion for building new public monuments. The colonnaded street, which ran along the southern bank of the wadi and divided the city into two parts, was probably one of these. It is about 20 feet wide and is provided with pavements along which dwellings were built. At its northern end the street terminated in a triple monumental gate. The street and the gate are not of the same period: the excavators dated the latter to the late 2nd or early 3rd century AD. To the west of the gate stands one of the most beautiful and best-preserved monuments of Petra, the Qasr Bint Farun, the Fort of the Daughter of Pharaoh. A road 200yd long leads to a large enclosure in the middle of which stands a huge building, rising to a height of more than 60 feet. This building, a temple according to the excavators, stands on a large podium measuring 110 feet by 120 feet and originally faced with marble. A broad flight of steps led up to the

Burial cave, rock-cut, Petra

podium and from there to the *pronaos* (porch) (35 feet by 90 feet), with six columns in its façade. A large door led from the *pronaos* to the *naos* (shrine) and from there twelve additional steps led up to the inner shrine. This consisted of the shrine itself and two side rooms. The thick walls of the side rooms conceal stairs leading to the flat roof. This building has been dated by various scholars to the second half of the 2nd century AD; others have suggested that it was built after AD 106. Now, after the discovery of the Nabatean inscription *in situ* in the building's *temenos* (enclosure), it seems quite certain that is should be dated to the end of the 1st century BC.

THE THEATER This monument is situated near the road that leads from the Siq to the city. The seats were cut into a steep mountainside, thus destroying many Nabatean rock-cut tombs, and arranged in three tiers, each divided into six sections. The stage building consisted only of a decorative wall with the usual three openings. The theater was probably built in the 2nd century AD. (*See *also* THEATERS.)

THE NECROPOLIS There were two forms of burial at Petra: shaft graves, sunk into flat rocks; and tombs hewn into the sheer walls of the wadis. The tombs of the second type are much more numerous. There are six types of rock-cut monuments, distinguished by their decoration. For the sake of convenience these are listed in ascending order of elaboration.

Pylon tombs These have a crenellated top and a simple gabled door. The name derives from the pylons standing at the sides of Egyptian temples.

Stepped tombs Here the crenellation is replaced by two large steps, which stand on a cornice of Egyptian type. The doors are plain or gabled.

Proto-Hegr tombs The name comes from el-Hegr, an important Nabatean center in northern *Arabia, where this type of tomb was identified for the first time. In addition to the features already mentioned these tombs have two pilasters on the sides of their façades, adorned with typical Nabatean capitals.

Hegr-type tombs A more elaborate version of the previous type, with an additional entablature and an attic giving greater height.

Arched tombs A relatively small group of monuments, whose tops and doors are arched.

Roman temple-type tombs These have façades like Roman temples, sometimes with a porch resting on columns and two or more stories high. The most famous tomb of this type is Haznet Fira'un, or el-Hazneh, the Treasury of Pharaoh.

There are about 750 monuments of all types at Petra. The various tombs were initially dated to the period from the 4th century BC to the 2nd century AD, but it is now clear that the earlier forms are nor earlier than the second half of the 1st century BC. The more elaborate designs are not necessarily a development of the simple ones and some of them were constructed at the same time. The Roman temple type, however, belongs mainly to the 2nd century AD.

PHARPAR One of the two rivers of *Damascus (2 Kgs. 5:12) rising in the foothills of Mount *Hermon; today possibly the River Barbar, which flows south of *Damascus.

PHASAELIS A city north of *Jericho, founded by Herod the Great in memory of his elder brother Phasaelis (Josephus, *Antiq.* XVI, 145). In this way a formerly wild area was made productive (*Antiq.* XVI, 145); the excellent dates of Phasealis are mentioned by Pliny (*Nat. Hist.* XIII, 4, 44). In his will Herod bequeathed it to his sister Salome (Josephus, *Antiq.* XVII, 189), who at her death bequeathed it to Livia, the wife of Augustus (*Antiq.* XVIII, 31). The city was still standing in the Byzantine period, as is shown by the Medaba map.

The site is identified with Khirbet Fasayil. Many remains can still be discerned on the surface. The city was built according to the Hippodamian plan, with streets intersecting at right angles. Remains of several large buildings have been identified: a palace about 600 feet by 660 feet, a temple and an agora with small shops. Water was supplied to the city and its plantations from the River *Jordan, via an aqueduct $5^1/_2$ miles long. In the vicinity of the city are traces of ruined garden walls built of fieldstones, and many irrigation channels.

PHILADELPHIA See *RABBATH-AMMON

PHILISTINES; SEA PEOPLES The Philistines were a tribe, one of the Sea Peoples, that appeared at the end of the Late Bronze Age in the southeastern sector of the Mediterranean. The Sherden, who are thought to have been one of these peoples, are mentioned in the *El Amarna letters as are the Lukku and the Danuna. The Egyptian sources refer to them as mercenaries in the Egyptian army. In a later period the Sherden took part in the Asiatic campaign of Rameses II, as the king recounts: 'Now then, his majesty had prepared his infantry, and the Sherden...' Somewhat later 'People of the Sea' are listed among those who collaborated with the Libyans in their revolt against *Egypt during the reign of Merneptah. The Philistines, or Purasti (the Egyptian has no 'l'), are mentioned specifically in the time of Rameses III, when the Libyans revolted again. The campaigns of Rameses III against the Philistines are summed up in the Egyptian document known as Papyrus Harris I: 'I have extended all the frontiers of Egypt and overthrew those who have attacked them from their lands. I slew the Denyen in their islands, while the Tjeker and the Purasti [Philistines] were made ashes. The Sherden and the Weshesh of the sea were made non-existent, captured altogether and brought in captivity to Egypt like the sands of the shore. I settled them in strongholds, bounding my name.'

These events are vividly depicted in reliefs, accompanied by inscriptions, in the temple of Rameses III at Medinet Habu in *Thebes. These provide a unique source for the study of the material culture and history of the Philistines and the allied peoples at this early stage. The Philistines are depicted as tall men, shaven and wearing feathered head-dresses secured by chin-straps. The captive Philistines wear a breastplate (or shirt), and in the naval battle they are shown wearing strap-shields. They have broad belts round their waists, and skirts. The Tjekers, on the other hand, are bearded, though otherwise quite similar to the Philistines. According to the inscriptions the great battle between Rameses III and the Sea Peoples took place in the land of Djahi. (*See also* *Phoenicia or *Canaan.)

The army of the Sea People consisted of three main groups: men riding in wagons drawn by oxen; infantry; and cavalry. The cavalry consisted of light chariots drawn by two horses, not unlike the chariots of the Egyptians (*Weapons and warfare). Each chariot was manned by three soldiers, two of whom were armed with two spears each. The infantry fought in small units of four soldiers each. Three of the soldiers were armed with two spears and one straight sword each, while the fourth carried a sword only. All soldiers had round shields, short strap-cuirasses and feathered head-dresses with varied ornamentation. The wagons were manned by men, women and children. Each was drawn by four oxen and all had wheels without spikes. The naval battle took place in the *Nile Delta. Whereas the Egyptian galleys were propelled by oars those of the Sea Peoples had sails only. They were single-masted vessels, each with a crow's nest. Their prows and sterns were raised high, duck-shaped, and were probably used as battering rams. The Egyptians, armed with bows and arrows, were victorious over the Philistines, who had short-range arms only. The different Sea Peoples could be distinguished from each other by variations in apparel.

In a later Egyptian source, that of Amen-em-Opet, of the late 12th or early 11th century BC, three ethnic groups are mentioned among other nations — Sherden, Tjekers and Philistines —and also three towns — *Ashkelon, *Ashdod and *Gaza — all of which were in Philistia. That the Philistines occupied the southern part of the Canaanite coast is also known from the latest Egyptian source, the letter of Wen-Amon of the first half of the 11th century BC, from which we also know that the Tjekers settled in the *Sharon and that *Dor was their capital. Other details help to form a picture of the coastal plain as divided among different princes who formed an alliance and conducted an active maritime trade.

The Egyptian sources give no clue as to the origin of the Philistines and the other Sea Peoples. On the other hand, Genesis (10:14) has: 'and Pathrusin and Casluhim (out of which came Philistim) and Caphtorim'. This is usually understood to mean that the Philistines and the Cheretites were kindred people (Zeph. 2:5; Ezek. 25:16). Moreover, Jeremiah (47:4) and Amos (9:7) both state that the Philistines originated in *Caphtor. It seems from the Bible that *Caphtor and Cheretim were either identical or close to each other.

According to the Bible the Philistines were in the *Negev at the time of the Patriarchs, and their king, Abimelech, dwelt at *Gerar (Gen. 26:1). It seems that this tradition was set down in writing when the Philistines had already settled in *Canaan, in the 12th or 11th century BC. They are very prominent in the Bible in the period of the Judges, when there was an almost constant state of war between them and the expanding Israelites (Judg. 3:31; 15:11, etc.). One of the main issues in dispute between the two peoples was the settlement of the Danites, whose territory bordered that of the Philistines. This serious clash terminated with the resettlement of the Danites in the north of the country (Judg. 13-16). There was a strong and permanent encroachment of the Philistines onto the territory of Judah as well. Open hostilities began at *Eben-Ezer (1 Sam. 4), in the course of which the Ark of God was captured by the enemy (1 Sam. 5). Later, with the conquest of *Beth-Shean, the whole of the Via Maris (*Roads) was in the hands of the Philistines (1 Sam. 31). They established garrisons in Judah and Benjamin (1 Sam. 10:5; 13:3) and took steps to prevent the use of iron weapons (1 Sam. 13). In the latter part of the 11th century BC there was a change of fortune and the Philistines were defeated and driven out of Israelite territory (1 Sam. 13:4; 14:20 ff.) Another clash between the Philistines and the Israelites occurred in the Valley of Elah, where David slew Goliath (1 Sam. 17). This battle was decisive and the decline of the Philistines now began. At that time David was given shelter by Achish, King of *Gath (1 Sam. 21:11-16), who gave him the town of *Ziklag (1 Sam. 27:6). Before the battle of Mount *Gilboa Achish made David 'keeper of his head' (1 Sam. 28:1-2) and in the battle Saul and his sons fell in one of the last clashes in the *Jezreel Valley (1 Sam. 31). It was only after he became King of Israel that David finally defeated the Philistines (2 Sam. 8:18, 25; 8:1; 1 Chr. 18:1), and even used them as mercenaries (2 Sam. 8:18). Uzziah, King of Judah, pushed the Israelite conquest further into Philistine territory, taking *Gath, *Jabneh (Jabneel) and *Ashdod (2 Chr. 26:6-7). During the period of the Assyrian campaigns the Philistines were several times involved in alliances against the Assyrians and on the side of *Egypt. Even up to the time of the Restoration they retained some of their national characteristics, and spoke in the 'speech of Ashdod' (Neh. 13:24).

Philistine jug

The five main Philistine cities are named in the Bible as *Gaza, *Ashkelon, *Ashdod, *Ekron and *Gath, each being the capital of a lordship. Some smaller Philistine towns are also mentioned, such as *Ziklag (1 Sam. 27:6), Timnath (*Timnah) (Judg. 14:1) and the fortified town of *Jabneh (2 Chr. 26:6). It is also recorded that during their expansion further west and north the Philistines established garrisons at *Gibeah (1 Sam. 13:3; Authorized Version: 'Geba') and *Beth-Shean (1 Sam. 31:12). But archaeological finds show that many other towns were also under Philistine influence or direct rule, for Philistine pottery has been found at places such as *Megiddo, Jaffa (*Joppa), *Beth-El and *Beth-Shemesh, and on sites for which there is still no identification, such as Tell *Qasileh.

The Bible contains a great deal of information about the internal organization of the Philistines. At the head of each Philistine kingdom stood a lord (1 Sam. 5:11), or sometimes a king (1 Sam. 27:2), who was probably also the commander-in-chief of the army. At the head of these states was a military aristocracy which, since it was supported by an advanced military organization and superior arms, could impose its rule over a much larger local population. The army consisted of archers (1 Sam. 31), cavalrymen and charioteers (1 Sam.13:5) and was divided into hundreds and thousands (1 Sam. 29:2). In battle the whole army would hold the front line and small units would be sent forward to attack. Another method, alien to the Hebrews, was the use of a champion, such as Goliath (1 Sam. 17), who went into battle clad in a 'helmet of brass' and a 'coat of mail', with 'greaves of brass on his legs and a target of brass between his shoulders', armed with an iron spear and preceded by a shield-bearer. Some of these accoutrements may be seen on the reliefs at Medinet Habu. (*See* *also* WEAPONS AND WARFARE.)

The Philistines carried the images of their gods with them into battle (2 Sam. 5:21). The chief of these was Dagon (Judg. 16:23), and there were temples to him at *Gaza, *Ashdod and *Beth-Shean (1 Chr. 10:10). We are told that a statue of this god stood in the temple at *Ashdod (1 Sam. 5:2-3), while at *Ekron there was an oracle of Baal-Zebub, another Philistine god (2 Kgs. 1:3). The principal goddess was Ashtoreth, whose temple, the house of Ashtaroth, was at *Beth-Shean (1 Sam. 31:10).

Remains of the Philistine material culture have been found in the occupation levels of the 12th and 11th centuries BC on many sites in the coastal plain south of the River *Yarkon. These consist mainly of pottery, the most typical being bowls and jugs with a white wash and painted with a great variety of geometric patterns, birds and fishes. From the similarity of shape and decoration it is obvious that these had their origin in the sphere of the Mycenean culture, though local features and some Egyptian elements are also identifiable.

Peculiar to the Philistines was their disposal of the dead in anthropoid clay coffins. In their cemeteries at *Beth-Shean, *Lachish and Tell el-*Farah (south), as well as in some places in *Egypt, clay coffins of this type were discovered with a cylindrical, elongated body and a cover made in the form of a human head framed by hands. The foreheads of some have decorations that resemble those of the Philistine warriors on the reliefs of Medinet Habu. A Philistine burial would normally contain an anthropoid coffin, numerous pottery vessels and bronze and iron weapons.

No written material of the Philistines has so far been found.

PHOENICIA; PHOENICIANS The name given by the classical authors to the land extending along the coast of the *Lebanon and the northern part of Palestine, and to the peoples living there, extending from *Arvad in the north to *Acco in the south (cf. Herodotus I, 1; II, 44; VII, 89). The name Phoenicia was variously applied to different parts of that area, but at its peak it covered a region extending from *Dora in the south as far as *Ugarit in the north. Some Phoenician settlements were even built south of *Dora.

The natural resources of the country are meager, so that from early times maritime trade played a major part in its economy. Other relatively important elements were fishing and the extraction of purple dye from the murex, a shellfish that abounded on the coast. The earliest traces of human occupation on the Phoenician coast go back to the Paleolithic Age; the men responsible for that culture had reached the same stage of development as in prehistoric Palestine. In the Mesolithic period crops were cultivated and animals domesticated. During the Neolithic period man began to leave his caves and temporary dwellings and to build villages with houses made of mud, their walls set on a stone base. During the last quarter of the 5th millennium BC pottery made its first appearance at *Ugarit and *Byblos. The Chalcolithic culture, characterized by the use of copper weapons (*Metals) and painted pottery, was observed on both of these sites. The houses of this period were apsidal, built of bricks and roofed with timber. By the time of the 3rd-6th Dynasties trade relations were well established and Egyptian alabaster vases bearing the names of some Egyptian pharaohs were found at *Byblos. These relations were, however, disturbed during the period of anarchy that prevailed in *Egypt under the 8th-10th Dynasties, and *Egypt's hold over Phoenicia was therefore interrupted.

The arrival of the *Amorites brought destruction to *Byblos and to other Phoenician centers in the south of the country. *Ugarit, in the north, suffered destruction somewhat later at the hands of the *Horites, who arrived from the northeast. During this period of unrest a new ethnic element, a people skilled in working bronze, arrived in Phoenicia from Anatolia, in the 21st century BC. Both at *Ugarit and at *Byblos weapons and jewelry made of bronze have been found. By the middle of the 20th century BC Phoenicia had come under Egyptian control. Once more *Byblos exported timber to *Egypt and imported alabaster, pottery and furniture. The 19th and a great part of the 18th centuries BC were a period of great prosperity, but this was disrupted by the arrival of the *Hyksos, who ruled over Phoenicia from about 1730 to 1580 BC.

Egyptian rule over Phoenicia was renewed with the rise of the 18th Dynasty. The quelling by Tuthmosis

Phoenician ivory engravings

III of the revolt of the confederacy of Syrian kingdoms, under the leadership of the King of *Kedesh-on-the-Orontes, in the Battle of *Megiddo reduced Syria and Phoenicia to the status of Egyptian provinces. Phoenicia prospered during the reigns of the kings of this dynasty, until the attack launched by Abda-shirts, the Amorite King of Syria, during the reign of Amenophis III. The events of this stormy period are frequently referred to in the *El Amarna letters. The struggle between *Egypt, who supported the kings of some of the Phoenician cities, and those who made alliances with the *Amorites, helped by the *Habiru, continued during the reign of Amenophis IV (Akhenaten). It was Sethos I of the 19th Dynasty who subdued Phoenicia again.

The influence of *Egypt on Phoenicia was great in every field and even Phoenician art included many Egyptian elements. Thus the coffin of Ahiram, King of *Byblos, a contemporary of Rameses II, was fashioned in the Egyptian manner. *Egypt's ascendancy over Phoenicia was disrupted again with the arrival of the Sea Peoples (*Philistines), who together with the *Canaanites were to form the new Phoenician nation. Whereas in the period preceding the 12th century BC the inhabitants of the different city-states had been referred to by the names of their individual cities, from that time onwards they were known as Phoenicians. This period marks the beginning of the golden age of Phoenicia.

During the period between 1150 and 853 BC the Phoenician cities enjoyed independence. *Tyre and *Sidon and some other cities started up their lively maritime trade and Phoenician colonies were founded along the Mediterranean coast, a process which cul-minated in the foundation of Carthage in about 814 BC. At this period the Phoenician alphabetic script found its way to Greece. Trade expanded, and Hiram, King of Tyre, made a treaty with Solomon. Ties were still more closely knit when Ahab, King of Israel, married Jezebel, daughter of Ethbaal, King of *Sidon.

During this period Assyria was gradually expanding towards the Mediterranean. In about 1110 BC Tiglath-Pileser I captured *Arvad and other Phoenician cities, but this conquest did not last long, for Ashurbanipal invaded Phoenicia in 883 BC and imposed a heavy tribute on *Tyre, *Sidon, *Byblos and *Arvad. It was the oppressive Assyrian rule that caused many of the Tyrians to leave their city and go to found their 'New Town' — Kart Hadasha, or Carthage. During the remainder of the 8th and 7th centuries BC Phoenicia paid a heavy tribute to Assyria. Some Phoenician cities attempted from time to time to break the Assyrian yoke. One revolt instigated by a confederacy of Phoenician cities, under the leadership of *Tyre, was severely crushed by Sennacherib. As a result *Sidon was destroyed and its inhabitants were replaced by others who had been brought from far afield. Further revolts by the Phoenician cities were no more successful.

After the defeat of Assyria by the Babylonians and the Medes in 612 BC the Phoenician cities regained their independence, but after the defeat of Pharaoh Necho II, with whom the cities were allied in 605 BC, Phoenicia was brought under direct Babylonian rule. Another revolt, in which Judah and *Tyre took part, resulted in the destruction of *Jerusalem and the capture of *Babylon by Nebuchadnezzar. After the capture of *Babylon by Cyrus in 538 BC Phoenicia became part of a Persian satrapy. At that time *Sidon took the place of *Tyre as its leading city. The large Phoenician navy took part in the wars of Darius and Xerxes against Greece.

Early in the 4th century BC *Tyre, weary of the oppressive rule of the Persian satraps, joined the rebel Greek tyrant of *Cyprus, while Tabnit, King of *Sidon, rebelled later in the same century against the Persians. Artaxerxes III, king of Persia, besieged *Sidon and set the city on fire. Many people, documents and works of art perished. A new city was subsequently built, but only the names of its kings are known.

After the Battle of Issus in 333 BC the way was open for the conquest of Phoenicia by Alexander the Great. Lacking an adequate navy, Alexander conquered the ports of *Arvad, *Byblos and *Sidon by land. *Tyre proclaimed its neutrality and even refused Alexander's request to sacrifice to his patron god Melqart-Heracles. In retaliation Alexander destroyed inland *Tyre (Paleatyros) and used the debris to build a causeway to the fortified island. With the fleets of the conquered cities at his disposal he closed on the island from land and sea, and in 332 BC *Tyre was taken.

During the two decades following Alexander's death Phoenicia was held by different Macedonian armies until 301 BC, when it was conquered by Ptolemy and annexed to *Egypt. In 200 BC Antiochus III defeated Ptolemy V Epiphanes, and Phoenicia remained under Seleucid rule until the dissolution of their kingdom after the death of Antiochus IV Epiphanes. By 112 BC all the Phoenician cities had regained their autonomy. In 64 BC Phoenicia was conquered by the Romans and turned by Pompey into a Roman province, although it retained full autonomy in internal affairs. Under Roman rule Phoenicia enjoyed no less prosperity than in former times. Glass-blowing was invented at *Sidon, and brought additional wealth to the city. The arts and letters flourished both in *Tyre and in *Sidon, and Septimius Severus established a law school at Berytus, modern Beirut. By the middle of the 1st century AD a Christian community was already in existence at *Tyre, a fact which caused much concern to later Romam emperors. During the Byzantine period Phoenicia was one of the richest provinces of the Roman Empire. During Justinian's reign the silkworm was introduced from China and silk production flourished. In AD 614 the country was overrun by the Persians and two decades later it was conquered by the Moslems.

PIRATHON The birth-place and burial-place of the judge Abdon, son of Hillel, in the land of Ephraim, in the mount of the *Amalekites (Judg. 12:14-15); the hometown of Benaiah, one of David's mighty men (2 Sam. 23:30). Identified with the Arab village of Farata, southwest of *Shechem.

PISGAH The highest part of the mountains of *Abarim, close to the northeastern shore of the *Dead Sea (Deut. 3:27, 32:49, 34:1), with a view over the wilderness (Num. 21:20; Authorized Version: 'Jeshimon'). On the field of Zophim, at the top of the Pisgah, Balak met Balaam (Num. 23:14). From the peak of Pisgah, called *Nebo, Moses saw a great part of the land of

*Canaan (Deut. 3:27; 34:1-4). Pisgah was the southern border of the land of Sihon, King of the *Amorites (Josh. 12:2-3). Eusebius (*Onom.* 18,1; 168,28) knew it by the names of Fasgo and Fasga, on the way from *Livias to *Heshbon. It is identified with Ras Siyagha, west of Mount *Nebo.

PISON See *EDEN

PITHOM A city in the land of *Goshen in *Egypt. The meaning of the name is 'the house of the god Atum'. *Goshen was one of the treasure cities built for Pharaoh by the Children of Israel (Exod. 1:11). Herodotus, who visited *Egypt in about 440 BC, mentions Pathomus, a city of *Arabians (II:158). He also speaks of the gods whom they venerae, one of whom is the goddess Alilat. This supports the identification of Pithom with Tell Maskhute, at the western end of Wadi Thumeilat, where a temple of Atum was discovered. In the temple were found three silver bowls on which dedications to Alat were inscribed. One of the names of the father of a dedicator is Abd-amru, which is an Arabian-*Nabatean name. Although inscriptions of the times of the 1st and 6th Dynasties were found there, the city and its fortifications are not earlier than the days of Rameses II, when the Israelites built Pithom. Some of the structures found there were identified by the excavators as storehouses that might have been built by the Israelites. In the Hellenistic period the city was renamed Heronopolis, the 'city of the god Heron'. Other scholars suggest identifying Pithom with Tell er-Retabeh, 10 miles west of Maskhute, where another temple of Atum was discovered.

PLAIN (THE); SHEPHELAH The Plain, *Shephelah* in Hebrew, is one of the geographical regions of Palestine frequently mentioned in the Bible (Deut. 1:7; Josh. 9:1; Authorized Version: 'valleys'; 10:40; Authorized Version: 'vale', etc.). Its Hebrew name implies that it was an intermediate region between the higher mountains to the east and the coastal plain to the west. The Plain is a region of low hills 1,000-1,200 feet high. As a geographical term it is usually applied to the south of the country, adjoining the Judean Hills, bordering on the *Sharon in the north and the *Negev in the south. A distinction is made in the Bible between this and the northern plain: 'the mountain of Israel, and the valley of the same' (Josh. 11:16). The conquest of the cities of the Plain is referred to in Joshua (10). It was an area rich in olives and sycamores (1 Kgs. 10:27; 1 Chr. 27:28). In the Hellenistic and Roman periods the name Sephela was applied to the region between *Lod and *Beth-Gubrin (1 Macc. 12:38).

POTTERY The production of pottery was one of man's great innovations in the later stages of the prehistoric period (*Prehistory), and one of the most important landmarks in the long process of transition from the nomadic life of hunters and food-gatherers towards a settled existence. Pottery is made of clay, a type of soil almost universally available, which with the addition of water acquires plasticity, enabling the potter to shape it as required. Once fired, the shape given to it is retained.

NEOLITHIC PERIOD It was only in the phases of this period that pottery made its appearance. The shapes are coarse, handmade on a mat, which leaves its imprint on the base, but most of these crude pots already show some decoration, incised or painted. The number of shapes is very limited, consisting of jars and bowls only. These vessels were made by building coils of clay one above the other, and smearing the joints with soft clay.

CHALCOLITHIC PERIOD During the transition from the Neolithic to the Chalcolithic period, i.e. from prehistory to protohistory, great changes occurred in the production of pottery, both in repertoire and in decoration. A change was also introduced in the potter's technique, and vessels were now produced in part on a slow potter's wheel. In the Chalcolithic period, likewise, there were several regional cultures in Palestine, each producing its own ware. One of the richest cultural groups in that of *Tuleilat Ghassul. Typical of this culture are V-shaped bowls with a flat base, tapering sides, and a red painted band around the rim. Some of the bowls have rounded sides, while others are closer to a cup in shape. A second very common class consists of cornets; drinking horns, ending in a point. To the same class belongs also the 'egg beaker'. which has a hollow conical base instead of the pointed end of the cornet. Incense bowls form another large group, modelled on basalt prototypes (*Stone implements, *Cult objects). These consist of a broad half-rounded bowl, joined to a fenestrated cylindrical stand. Jars are also plentiful. Some are spherical, with short necks, and numerous pierced lug handles. Some of these are painted with red bands. Common, too, are hole-mouth jars. To this group belong also huge storage vessels, decorated with bands resembling ropes in relief. The large vessels were built up with coils. To the Ghassulian culture, likewise, belong vessels formerly known as 'bird-vases', because of their shape, but now identified as churns. A second important cultural group is that of the *Beer-Sheba culture. The main difference between this and the Ghassulian is the absence of cornets, and the paucity of relief decoration in the former. There are also numerous jars, hole-mouth or with high necks, decorated with red bands, and some provided with spouts. Churns were also common. Vessels of both cultures were found on other Chalcolithic sites in Palestine.

EARLY BRONZE AGE The dating of this one-thousand-year-long period depends on the correlation of its second phase with the period of the 1st Dynasty of Egypt, in the tombs of whose pharaohs were found pottery vessels which originated in Palestine. The end of the Chalcolithic period in Palestine was independently dated to about 3200-3100 BC, and it thus helps to date the beginning of the Early Bronze Age. One of the characteristics of the material culture of this period is the presence of conspicuously different regional cultures in Palestine. The Early Bronze Age I is represented by rich finds in the north of Palestine, mainly at *Tell el-Farah (north) and *Megiddo. The division into groups within this culture is based on the decoration. Typical are jars of the grain-wash or band-slip technique, in which the jars of the grain-wash or band-slip technique, in which the jars were painted with criss-cross bands in dark brown, light brown, red and yellow. Vessels with red slip and bur-

nish form a large group. A third group consists of gray-burnished vessels, typical in their color but differing in shape. Vessels of this class come mainly from Tell el-Farah (north), *Beth-Shean, *Beth-Yerah and other sites in the north. While burnishing is typical of the northern culture, red painted wares are common to the contemporary southern one. The repertoire consists of bowls of different shapes, 'teapots', jars, jugs and juglets, some of which were made in pairs. Pottery of this culture was found at *Ai, *Jericho, *Jerusalem, etc.

Typical of Early Bronze Age II are plates and platters with red slip and burnish, chalices on high feet, spherical juglets with double handles, jugs with high, narrow necks, jars and pithoi. Some of the jars are decorated with combed decoration in criss-cross patterns. Of special interest is the chronologically important group of Abydos ware, i.e. jars from Palestine found in the royal tombs at *Abydos, Egypt. These are mainly jugs with handles attached to the rim, and a typical stump base. To the same group of Abydos ware belong also bottles and jars.

Many of the vessels of the previous phase continue in the Early Bronze Age III, but some new shapes make their appearance, such as the chalice. A completely different type of pottery was observed for the first time at *Beth-Yerah, and was named after that site (also known as Khirbet Kerak ware). To this group belong large bowls, jugs, jars and horseshoe-shaped stands. Later vessels of this type were found at *Beth-Shean, *Megiddo, etc. The pottery is all handmade, and many vessels have a strap loop handle, but most typical is the decoration. The vessels were covered inside and out with a heavy slip, on which oblique lines were incised. The slip was highly burnished, and fired black on the outside and red on the inside. The origin of this group is as yet unknown, but should possibly be sought southwest of the Caspian Sea.

The existence of an Early Bronze Age IV is much disputed, and in consequence no final classification of the pottery of this phase has yet been reached.

MIDDLE BRONZE AGE Pottery pertaining to this period comes mainly from tombs, and only a little from habitation layers. In this period, too, there are distinct cultural groups, a northern and a southern. The vessels of both cultures are spherical or cylindrical in shape, with flat bases, or no base at all. Most vessels lack handles, or are provided with small loop handles. The body of the vessels was handmade, while the necks were turned on the wheel. The decoration is limited to incisions, either simple or in the form of combing in straight or wavy lines. The differences between the two regional cultures are that the northern culture preferred to decorate its vessels in single lines, while the southern preferred combing, and the northern culture had a preference for spherical forms, while cylindrical shapes are more common in the southern.

MIDDLE BRONZE AGE II A-B The main achievement of the potters of this period was the production of the whole vessel on the wheel. This enabled the potter to make more sophisticated shapes, such as the carinated bowl. Bases are flat, or in the form of shallow discs. The decoration consists mainly of red burnishing, while painted decoration is rare. Many vessels are not decorated at all, and show the natural color of the clay. In some the origin in metal prototypes is discernible. Some carinated shapes from Middle Bronze Age II stand on a high hollow foot. Similar to these bowls are chalices on high feet, with carinated or rounded sides. Common also are cups with double loop handles. The crater bowls of this period are either rounded with narrow mouths, or with very wide ones, and some stand on three loop bases. The jars are oval, with or without handles. Some of the jars are decorated with bands or wavy lines in red. Juglets are numerous, and show a large variety of shapes. Some of the piriform (pear-shaped) juglets have trefoil lips, and rare specimens also have animal decoration.

Middle Bronze Age II is the period in which Palestine was ruled by the *Hyksos, and a special type of juglet made its appearance at this time. Most of these

Group of pottery of the Hellenistic period

are piriform, with a double loop handle, burnished black or dark brown, and decorated with finely impressed dots arranged in various patterns, filled in with white pigment. They are known as *Tell el-Yehudiyeh juglets, after the site where they were first identified. In this period close *trade relations were established with the countries of the eastern Mediterranean, mainly with *Cyprus. Thus Cypriot Red-on-Black Ware, and White Painted and White Slip Ware are abundant in Palestine. One of the best known types is the 'milk bowl' with the wishbone handle.

LATE BRONZE AGE I-III Bowls of the earlier phase of this period are typified by the carination, as were the bowls of Middle Bronze Age II. Imitations of the Cypriot White Painted bowls are also common. To the following phase of the Late Bronze Age belong bowls with tapering or rounded sides. Red and black bands on the inside of the bowls are the usual form of decoration. Carinated cups and chalices also continue into this period. Kraters are numerous, and are richly decorated. The decoration is mostly limited to the upper part of the bowl, and consists of metopes in which are geometrical, animal and other designs. These vessels have upright or horizontal bar handles. Typical also are the cooking-pots. The body of the cooking-pots is rounded, without handles. Jars are oval at the beginning of the period, but tend to become more elongated and pointed in the later phases. They all have two massive ear handles placed centrally on the body. Some of the jars have painted bands on the shoulder, in red, brown or white, or a combination of two of these colors. There is a wide range of shapes in jugs and juglets, and of special interest is the group of biconical jugs, decorated with black and red metopes. Some of the most beautiful Late Bronze Age vessels are those in the group known as Bichrome Ware. They include spherical jugs with tall, narrow necks and a large loop handle, painted with bands of different patterns. These are believed to have been produced in the potter's workshop at *Tell el-Ajjul. The body of these jugs is divided by red and black bands into triangular metopes, in which are animals, birds, fishes and geometrical designs. This type of ware is common in Late Bronze Age I, and more rare in Late Bronze Age II.

Another group typical of this period is the 'Chocolate on White', comprising bowls standing on a foot, jugs and kraters. The vessels are covered with a thick white slip, then burnished vertically on the wheel and painted with bands, straight and wavy, and metopes. Still another group consists mainly of kraters and some bowls, with typical decoration of metopes formed by geometrical stripes, in which gazelles are painted standing in front of a palm tree. Birds and crabs are also found. Flasks form a group on their own; these are lentoid, i.e. round bottles, with a narrow neck and two handles attached to the flattened body, which is painted with concentric circles.

In this period, too, imports abound, mainly from Cyprus and Mycenae. From Cyprus come a large number of half-rounded bowls with slip and wishbone handles, a type known as the 'milk bowl'. Bowls of this class were already imported at the end of Middle

Bronze Age IIB and the main difference between these and the later ones lies in the decoration. Another important group of imported pottery is the Base-Ring Ware. Most typical of this group is the jug with the slender oblique neck, standing on a ring. It made of metallic ware, brown-gray-red burnished. The decoration is either painted, or in lines in relief. This type is known as 'bilbil'. Among the Mycenean imports are the kylix, pyxix, flasks, stirrup vase, etc. The decoration is painted, and includes bands, spirals, scales and ivy leaves. Both Cypriot and Mycenean vessels had their local imitations.

IRON AGE The transition from the Bronze to the Iron Age marks a sharp change both in shape and decoration of pottery. The rounded shapes of the Middle and Late Bronze Age become more angular, and the painted decoration is replaced by a variety of burnishing, which is to become the main decorative medium. On the other hand, the long Canaanite tradition of shape and decoration did not die out completely without leaving its mark on the new types. In certain ceramic forms a difference is again noted between the pottery of the north and the south of the country. In bowls the north has an immense range of shapes. Some of these bowls have red and black decoration. The southern group has roughly the same shapes, but in these irregular burnishing is used to decorate the inside of the bowls, and the horizontal handle is more common than in the north. In Iron Age II hand and wheel burnishing becomes the regular procedure in the north. Both techniques are common in this period also in the south, but here some differences in shape are noted, and the horizontal bar handle is very common. In Iron Age III there is some development and the angulation, which in the previous phases was closer to the rim, descends now closer to the middle of the body. In the south regular wheel burnishing becomes the rule. Heavier bowls are provided with four loop handles. The *Samaria bowls constitute a group in themselves. These are shallow, carinated or half-rounded vessels with a typical wheel ring-burnishing. The bowls fall into two classes, thin and thick walled.

Another very common group of Iron Age vessels comprises chalices; bowls on a high hollow base. Few of these have a slip. Craters of this period are also typical, taking the form of a deep heavy bowl with two, four, or multiple loop handles at the rim. Some are decorated with metopes in red on the upper part of the body.

The cooking-pot in the north is angular, with a rounded base, similar to the Canaanite cooking-pot. In the south some angular pots are present, but rounded deep pots are more common. The jars of Iron Age I are mostly a continuation of the Late Bronze Age II oval jar type, but in the later phases other shapes are introduced, such as jars, with angular shoulders, 'sausage jars', and some wider types. Hole-mouth jars are also found. Interesting is the oil jar, with a spherical body, three handles and a bell-shaped spout, on which the dipper juglet could be placed. Numerous jar-handles found in the south were stamped with royal *seals. Exceedingly rich also is the

repertoire of jugs and juglets, suited to every purpose and with every size of opening, wide and narrow, plain and trefoil, some provided with spouts and strainers. One of the most graceful jugs of the Late Iron Age is the decanter, or water jug. It has an angular shoulder, a narrow neck and wider mouth, and one handle. Another common form is the small black burnished juglet, probably for oil, with a spherical body, a narrow neck and one handle. These occur mostly in the south in Iron Age II and III.

The so-called *Philistine pottery is another group on its own. The most common items are the crater, jug and flask. Some of the jugs are provided with a strainer spout, and are thus called 'beer jugs'. Both the shapes and decoration of the Philistine pottery originated in Mycenean prototypes, but Egyptian and local Canaanite influences are also present. The vessels have painted decoration in red and black. The motifs are sometimes purely geometrical, but more typical is the frieze divided into metopes, in which a bird is depicted preening beneath a raised wing, or facing forward. Animals and men are also found. Shape and decoration degenerate with the passage of time.

Some Iron Age pottery types in Palestine were produced under the influence of other cultures. One such is Bichrome Ware, probably produced under *Phoenician influence. Within this group are jugs with spherical bodies and high necks, sometimes with strainer spouts, lentoid flasks and bowls. Red and black circles are the most common form of decora-

Mycenean kylix, 15th century BC

tion. Imported pottery, mainly Cypriot and Cypro-Mycenean, appears alongside the rich local production. The imports include graceful juglets, craters, bowls and jugs. The ware is of excellent quality, with white, black and red surfaces. The decoration consists of concentric and small circles.

PERSIAN PERIOD The destruction of the First Temple left its mark in the field of ceramic art. The repertoire is rather poor and the vessels are mostly devoid of decoration. Some of the earlier shapes persist, but in quite degenerate form. On the other hand some new shapes appear, such as the jar with a pointed base, a shallow angular shoulder and large handles which rise high above the neck. Typical among the bowls is a heavy rimmed vessel on a ring base. Owing to poor firing many of the items are of a pale greenish color.

HELLENISTIC PERIOD The conquest of Palestine by Alexander the Great, and the introduction of the Hellenic culture into the East, made Palestine part of the Hellenistic world. This is apparent also in the pottery. There is a tendency towards uniformity of style throughout the area, and imports from other large pottery-producing centers influenced the local potters to imitate both techniques and shapes.

Locally produced jars of the period are large heavy vessels, cylindrical or bag-shaped, their most typical feature being the collar rim. In the 1st century BC, bell-shaped jars appear, with high necks and ridged rims. In the second half of the same century ovoid jars with ring bases are seen. There is a group of wide-necked jugs with rolled rims, similar to some of the jars. The bodies are round and the bases pressed in. The handles are attached to the lip. In the 1st century BC, narrow-necked jugs, with ribbed bodies, appear. The flasks have a rounded or irregularly bulging body, a narrow neck, and two handles attached below the rim. The juglets of the early phases are spherical, with a narrow neck, widening at the rim, made to hold a stopper. Later types are similar in shape, but have a flat base. Piriform juglets with wider mouths appear at the end of the period.

During the 2nd century BC, a type of very heavy bowl is common, known as a mortarium. The clay from which they are made contains a high percentage of sand. They are rounded, with plain or thickened rim. Among the finer bowls are deep craters with outward curving rims. These appear late in the period. Small bowls are plentiful. They have rounded walls, incurving rims and flat or ring bases. Close to this group are hemispherical bowls, also with flat or ring bases. The vessels are either plain, painted, or glazed. The glaze is mostly of poor quality. There is a large variety of plates, some shallow with flat bases, their rims plain or drooping. Later in the period shallow plates with vertical sides appear. Among cooking-pots, two shapes predominate. Firstly there are spherical pots of different sizes, with two flat loop handles attached to the rim. In the 1st century BC a fine ribbing of the body appears on these. Some of the rims are made to receive a lid. The second group of cooking vessels consists of shallower casseroles, all with lid devices. This type is still rare in the 1st century BC. To the same family belong also frying-pans. These are

large shallow bowls with flat bases and slighty oblique sides. Many of them have a projecting clay cylinder, into which a wooden handle could be fitted. Notable is a group of fusiform vessels, i.e. cigar-shaped, with a bulbous body, thick- or thin-walled, and a thin, tall neck and foot. Produced as containers for precious oils, there are known as unguentaria, and are common both in dwellings and in tombs. By the end of the 1st century BC these are replaced by piriform unguentaria, with slender necks.

There is a group of small deep bowls known as 'Megarian', the term deriving from their point of origin in Greece. These have plain rims, and mostly rounded bases. They were made in moulds and decorated in relief, and all are glazed. The decoration is mostly floral or conventional.

Amongst plates, a well-known type of the Hellenistic period, both imported and produced locally in large quantities in Palestine, is the fish plate. Its characteristics are the shallow body, drooping rim, small cavity at the bottom inside, and a ring or flat base. The bowls range from excellent black glaze on the imported wares, to patchy poor glaze, brownish-red or -gray in the local wares. There are also unglazed, coarse vessels of this class.

From the 2nd century onwards, imports from Greece and the Greek centers also include plates, of different sizes but all with rounded sides, in black and red glazed ware. The earlier examples are black-glazed and decorated on the inside with concentric circles and impressed palmettes, or Isis crowns. From about the middle of the same century bowls of this class were made in Asia Minor, Syria, and probably in Palestine as well, the shapes remaining the same though the black glaze is supplanted by a thick red one.

During the 1st century BC the repertoire expands but the glaze deteriorates, being produced by a different technique. Specimens of the later type, known as Eastern Sigillata A, are more typical of the early Roman period.

ROMAN PERIOD Of this period only the earlier phases, from about 25 BC to AD 70, are well known. In Palestine this period is known as early Roman, or 'Herodian'. Amongst jars, the collared rim disappears and its place is taken by plain, thickened, rolled and ledge rims. The bodies are cylindrical, bag- or bell-shaped. Slight ribbing becomes more common. Cylindrical jars with angular to rounded shoulders, a ring base, and a rim made to receive a lid appear in the middle of the 1st century AD. These jars were used for keeping scrolls, and were found mainly in the *Judean Desert Caves. With minor changes, the Hellenistic shapes continue in jugs and flasks and also globular juglets, but there are also many elongated piriform, and wide-mouthed squat juglets. Mortaria and craters continue with little change. To the category of deep bowls, deep cups are added. In shallow bowls and plates, rounded features give way to upright rims and more angular shapes, in imitation of Roman imported red glazed wares. In cooking-pots, the round Hellenistic form persists, but the angular casserole is more abundant than previously. The fusiform unguentarium disappears, and its place is taken by the slender piriform juglet. The better tableware of this period is in the category of Eastern Sigillata A vessels, which made its appearance at the end of the previous period. From about 20 BC, this class of pottery is much influenced by the finer Roman Arretine Ware, and local workshops produced copies of most undecorated Arretine forms. flat plates, hemispherical bowls, bowls with upright rims, with everted sides, etc. The decoration is simple, consisting of rouletting on the rim, and on the base of the shallow types.

In the south of the country a different class of pottery flourished, the *Nabatean wares, produced in a potter's workshop at *Oboda. The more refined forms appear in plates, bowls, cups and juglets, painted with stylized vegetal and conventional designs in brown-red or black. But this is only one class in a very rich family which includes many scores of shapes to meet every need of the refined taste of the rich Nabatean merchant.

In recent years a breakthrough has occurred in the study of ancient pottery. At the Institute of Archaeol-

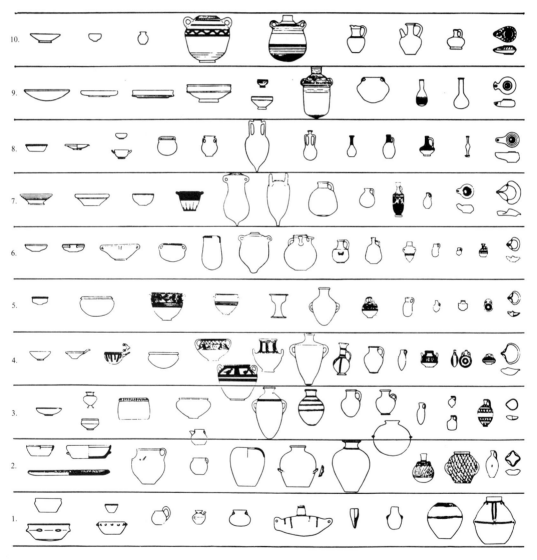

| 1. Chalcolithic period | 3. Middle Bronze Age | 5. Iron Age I | 7. Iron Age III | 9. Roman period |
| 2. Early Bronze Age | 4. Late Bronze Age | 6. Iron Age II | 8. Hellenistic period | 10. Byzantine period |

Characteristic types of pottery of the archaeological periods, as above

Potter's wheel, Hazor, Late Bronze period

ogy of the Hebrew University a laboratory for Neutron Activation Analysis (NAA) was established headed by J. Perlman, J. Yellin and J. Guneweg. Here a number of trace elements found in clays, and hence also in the pottery produced from these clays, are subjected to analysis. Since there is a marked difference in composition between clays of different origin, the source of pottery types can be quite safely determined. In this way it was shown that various types of pottery found in Palestine, covering a wide range of periods, were imported from eastern *Cyprus. Among these types were the so-called Megarian bowls and different types of Eastern Sigillata ware. Another possible pottery source is western Anatolia. These conclusions are far reaching as far as international *trade is concerned. The amount of Eastern Sigillata vessels imported into Palestine from the Hellenistic to the Roman periods is enormous and raises the question whether finished products in the only raw material (i.e., clay) were imported. It is possible that instead of sacks of sand or stones sea-going vessels were packed with baskets of fine clay as ballast, and instead of being thrown into the sea, this clay was sold to potters, thus covering the expenses of sailing to the East.

LATE ROMAN AND BYZANTINE PERIODS The pottery of these periods has received little attention so far. By the 3rd century AD the Eastern Sigillata wares had been replaced by a hard red ware, typical of which are bowls with heavy rims, of various profiles, the bases being flat, or with low rings. From about the 5th century AD, crosses and other Christian symbols, saints, etc., are impressed on the inside of the bases. Cooking utensils do not change much in shape, but the ware becomes brittle, and ribbing is general. Frying-pans are numerous. Jars are normally bag-shaped, though some are cylindrical. All are ribbed, and some have a combed decoration on the shoulder. The flask has a more bulbous body, and the handles are on the shoulder. It can be stated as a general rule that ribbing, combing and brittleness of ware are typical of the Byzantine period. (*See also* *LAMPS; *LIGHTING; *CULT OBJECTS.)

PRECIOUS STONES Man felt a great need to find an outlet for his aesthetic leanings at a very early stage in human culture. One of the ways of fulfilling this need was to acquire rare, gleaming stones. To some of these stones, of unusual shape or color, he would attribute magical or therapeutic qualities or the power of conferring fruitfulness. Much later these beliefs became deeply rooted among the Hebrews and other Semitic peoples, as well as among those of the neighboring countries. The Hebrews' love of precious stones is amply illustrated by many references in the Bible to the extraordinary properties of such stones, and by the large number of stones specifically named.

Very few of the precious stones referred to in the Bible are among the natural resources of Palestine, but in some cases their place of origin is mentioned. The main sources were the rich countries of *Arabia, such as *Havilah (Gen. 2:11-12), where gold and *shoham* (Authorized Version: 'onyx') came from; *Ophir (1 Kgs. 10:11; 2 Chr. 9:10), whence, in addition to precious stones, came gold and precious timber; *Sheba and Raamah (Ezek. 27:22); and Cush (*Ethiopia) (Authorized Version: 'Ethiopia'; Job 28:19). The desire for precious stones was also common among the *Canaanites, and many are mentioned in the *El Amarna letters. In many excavated sites throughout the Middle East precious stones have been found, set into jewelry made of gold, silver and bronze, and into scarabs, weights and seals. The high priest's 'breastplate of judgment' was set with 12 precious stones (Exod. 28:17-20; 39:10-13), and most of these are enumerated by Ezekiel (28:13) among the stones found in the Garden of *Eden. Other stones are mentioned elsewhere (cf. Gen. 2:12; Isa. 54:12; Ezek. 27:16; Job. 28:18; Esther 1:6; 1 Chr. 29:2).

The identification of the precious stones mentioned in the Bible with those known today presents many difficulties. It is only now, with the development of chemistry, mineralogy and crystallography, that the classification of the various stones into groups and their attribution to distinct mineralogical families has become possible. In ancient times they were classified solely on the basis of external characteristics, especially color. Thus stones that are listed in the Bible as belonging to different groups sometimes form a single mineralogical family. The following list includes all the precious stones mentioned in the Bible plus tentative identifications.

AHLAMAH One of the stones of the breastplate of judgment (Authorized Version: 'amethyst', 28:19; 39:12). The identification of this stone is not clear. In the Septuagint it is rendered as 'amethyst', which would mean in Greek 'without being drunk'. The Greeks described it as a stone resembling wine in color and ascribed to it the property of preventing drunkenness. Pliny says that it was crimson, that there were four shades of that color and that it was translucent. Some scholars agree with the Authorized Version's identification of the stone as amethyst, one of the quartzes, which is purple or violet in color. *Ahlamah* is rendered elsewhere in the Authorized Version as 'jasper' (cf. Exod. 28:20; 39:13). This stone is mentioned in the *El Amarna letters and in an inscription of Nabonidus, the last Babylonian king, in which it is referred to as the 'royal stone' out of which Ashurbanipal made the statue of the god Sin. This is identified with jasper, the Greek and Latin *jaspis,* and has been found in excavations in Palestine and in the neighboring countries. Some scholars believe that it should be identified with nephrite, or jade, a green translucent stone found in the Far East and in small quantities in Europe.

BAREQET (Authorized Version: 'emerald', ef. Exod. 28:13) This stone has the same name in the Accadian. The Septuagint calls it *smaragdos,* and the identification with *smaragd,* emerald, is generally accepted. During the Hellenistic period this name was applied to a different stone, the 'false emerald' or malachite, whose greenish shade is close to that of the true emerald. Real emeralds were extremely rare in the ancient world and could not be easily worked. Some scholars believe that *bareqet* should be identified with jasper.

DAR The court of the garden of the Persian king was paved with *dar* (Authorized Version: 'red, blue, white and black marble', Esther 1:6). In Arabic *dar* means pearl, and some scholars believe that it should be identified with mother-of-pearl. Others believe that it was an orange-colored stone.

EQDAH (Authorized Version: 'carbuncle', cf. Isa. 54:12) The Septuagint refers to this as *lithus crystallou,* which would be the equivalent of rock crystal. Some believe that it should be identified with *carbunculus,* the garnet, a red stone.

YAHALOM (Authorized Version: 'diamond', cf. Exod. 28:18; Ezek. 28:13) According to the Midrash this stone is white. Some identify it with anthrax, or carbuncle, which is red, and others with onyx, which has different colors arranged in layers, or even with chalcedony, which was much used for beads and seals. Be this at it may, its identification with the diamond in modern Hebrew should be rejected, as this queen of stones was not known before the Middle Ages.

KADKOD Listed among the precious stones which the Aramean merchants brought to *Tyre (Ezek. 27:16). According to Isaiah (54:12; Authorized Version: 'agate') God will make the windows of the houses of Jerusalem of *kadkod.* In the Septuagint it is rendered

once as *iaspis* and once as *chorchur,* a corruption of *kadkol.* The Arabs give the name *karkund* to a red stone resembling the ruby, identified today with the spinel. Scholars believe that *kadkod* should be identified with hyacinth, the medieval name for a yellow stone with spots of lilac and purple. It may possibly be one of the quartzes that the Greeks and Romans used for jewelry. Pliny says that it was blue and that it came from Gaul. Today, under the name of hyacinth, it is classified among the zircons, stones that range from a colorless quality to green, blue, red and golden yellow.

LESHEM (Authorized Version: 'ligure', cf. Exod. 28:19) The Septuagint has *ligurion,* a corruption of the *lyncurium* of the classical sources, which is a shining yellow color; probably the opal, which is multicolored or a glimmering orange. Other scholars identify it with aventurine, a quartz containing very fine crystals of hematite, limonite or mica, which sparkle when the light catches them. Still others identify it with amber.

NOPHEH (Authorized Version: 'sapphire'; cf. Exod. 28:18; Ezek. 28:13) The Septuagint has *anthrax.* Ancient Greek sources refer to it as a hard red stone, much used by jewelers. Pliny calls the same stone *carbunculus.* Some scholars identify it with turquoise, a sulphate of aluminium, the small percentage of copper it contains giving it its distinctive red color. It was very much used in jewelry.

ODEM (Authorized Version: 'sardius', cf. Exod. 28:17; Ezek. 28:13) Some scholars identify it with the Accadian *samtu,* a red stone. The Septuagint has *sardion,* while Josephus has *sardonyx.* It should probably be identified with the carnelian. Others believe that it was red jasper, an opaque stone found abundantly in Palestine and Egypt. The identification of the *odem* with the ruby cannot be sustained, because this was not known before the 3rd century AD.

PITEDAH (Authorized Version: 'topaz', Exod. 28:17; Ezek. 28:13) The Septuagint gives *topazion.* Most biblical commentators understand this to be a greenish stone. Pliny used the name *topazion* for a stone now known as chrysolithos, or as olivine, but *pitedah* is now identified with plasma, a greenish semi-translucent stone, one of the chalcedonies.

RAMOTH (Authorized Version: 'coral', cf. Ezek. 27:16; Job 28:18) The identification of this stone is not known. Some scholars suggest that it is not a stone at all, but a shell.

SAPIR (Authorized Version: 'sapphire', cf. Exod. 28:18) In the Bible this is referred to among the most precious stones (Job 28:16; Authorized Version: 'sapphire'). Ezekiel's vision of the Garden of *Eden includes the *sapir* (Ezek. 28:13). It is also a symbol of beauty (S. of S. 5:14). The Septuagint has *sapfeiros.* This is not to be mistaken for the sapphire of our day, which is the corundum, a stone that was not known in ancient times. Theophrastos, a Greek scholar, refers to it as blue with gold-white specks, like lapis lazuli.

SHEBO (Authorized Version: 'agate', cf. Exod. 28:19) The Septuagint has *achatis.* The identification with agate is accepted by all scholars. It is believed that the agate of the Bible was not the white stone, but a mixed black and white stone. White-gray agates were found in *Egypt.

SHOHAM (Authorized Version: 'onyx', cf. Exod. 28:20; Ezek. 28:13; Job 28:16). One of the stones brought from *Havilah (Gen. 2:11-12). The Septuagint renders it in various ways: *prasinos* (Gen. 2:12); *herillion* (Exod. 28:20); *sardios* (Exod. 25:7; 35:9); *smaragdos* (Exod. 28:9); *sappheiros* (Ezek. 28:13); *onyx* (Job 28:16) and *soom* (1 Chr. 29:2). It was often engraved. Onyx, the most appropriate identification, comes from the East and has three colors arranged in three stripes: red, blue or brown and black or dark brown.
SOHERET (Authorized Version: 'black marble', cf. Esther 1:6): The identification is not known. Some think it was a black stone used for paving floors.
TARSHISH (Authorized Version: 'beryl', cf. Exod. 28:20) The Septuagint has *chrisolythos*. In the Hellenistic period this name was applied to the topaz, a stone not known in the earlier periods. Now believed to have been identical with mother-of-pearl.

Another stone known in biblical times was the lapis lazuli. There were in fact two qualities of it in the ancient world: natural and artificial. The natural stone was found in *Cyprus and Scythia. Chemically it is a silicate of aluminum and sodium, ultramarine blue in color. The artificial lapis lazuli was produced in *Egypt and was an alkaline silicate in which the blue color came from copper carbonate. It was often set in rings and used for scarabs. Ground lapis lazuli was used as an ultramarine pigment.

PREHISTORY The general division of the prehistoric periods in Palestine has been copied from the system devised for Westen Europe, where research into prehistory originated. This division is of course merely an attempt to classify the evolutionary stages of man's material culture and it cannot establish an absolute chronology for them. There are three basic divisions: Paleolithic, Mesolithic and Neolithic. Each of these is further divided into three substages: Lower, Middle and Upper (the latter term always referring to the most recent layer). Nowadays there is an increasing tendency among archaeologists, particularly in the Holy Land, to discard the chronological division as too schematic and to replace it with a more flexible framework built up from the names of the various cultures that evolved in any given period. These names are generally derived from the name of the locality where the stage of cultural development in questions was first identified.

The assessment is based on the quantity and type of tools or other artifacts found on the site, the stage of development revealed by them, the chronological sequence discovered within the site and, more rarely, the means of subsistence of the people who lived there. Any scientific study of prehistory and any detailed description of prehistoric research and its results must inevitably be full of terms that seem obscure to the layman. But this difficulty can be overcome if he recognizes that all terms other than those relating to chronological periods or geological eras refer to the site (known as the 'type-site') that first provided insight into a particular stage of development in man's history. Such insight will often involve a technique used in the production of an artifact (usually a tool) unearthed at the type-site.

The type-site therefore provides archaeologists both with clues to man's development and with a scientific terminology that enables them to describe the results of their research. For example, the term 'Acheulian' refers to a type-site in France (at Acheule). Such labels (other examples are Olduwan and Aurignacian) can also be qualified as Upper, Middle or Lower, with 'Upper', as in any archaeological context, meaning the topmost or most recent layer. Further classification can be made by the use of the term 'Developed' (for instance, 'Developed Olduwan' denotes an advance in the development of a basic type of artifact first found at Olduwan). Similarly the phrase 'Helwan retouch' with reference to a flint tool denotes a specific type of secondary modification, first observed at Helwan, to a flake struck from a flint core (*See* *FLINT TOOLS).

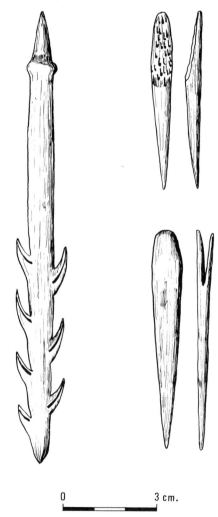

0   3 cm.

Harpoon and spear-points of bone

Many of the type-sites that have provided this terminology are widely separated geographically, but certain Palestinian sites offer a means of defining local stages of development. Thus the finds at *Kebara Cave have given us the term 'Kebaran culture', while Shuqbah Cave in Wadi el-Natuf gives us 'Natufian culture' and so on. Artifacts found at other sites but resembling those found at one of these two type-sites can therefore be labelled 'Kebaran' or 'Natufian'.

The greater part of man's history lies within the last geological era, the Pleistocene era. The subdivisions of this period are based on major geological events such as climatic fluctuations, lava eruptions, faulting and folding (a local example being the Great Rift, which appears in Palestine in the north-south cleft of the *Jordan Valley, the *Dead Sea and the Arabah), with cycles of soil sedimentation and erosion. This era

has not yet been thoroughly investigated in Palestine, since its history is known in a few restricted regions only (e.g. the coastal plain and the *Jordan Valley). Carbon 14 readings for the last 50 millenia are still not able to determine an absolute chronology for the area. The main stages in the evolution of man's material culture are therefore described in the relevant entries without any attempt to define their exact chronological limits.

THE LOWER PALEOLITHIC PERIOD This period ranges from the beginnings of the Pleistocene era to the Upper Pleistocene era and in fact includes the greater part of man's history. At this stage of his evolution Palestinian man lived on the shores of lakes and rivers and it was only towards the end of this era that he began to settle in the caves in the mountainous regions. The earliest traces of this phase are found at *Ubeidiya, where two

Tiny stone tools (microliths) which characterize the Epi-Palaeolithic

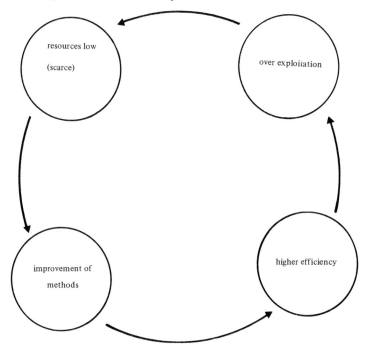

Diagram to show circular relationship between the environment and its exploitation

contemporary cultures, Developed Olduwan and Lower Acheulian, have been found. The first of these cultures shows a predominance of chopping tools or flint pebbles that have been roughly cut and whose cutting edge has been obtained by striking at the two sides alternately.

On the other hand, in the Lower Acheulian period tools known as *coups-de-poing* (a type of pick) are predominant. No examples of Middle Acheulian artifacts have been found in Palestine: the finds in layers E1 and E2 at *Umm Qatafa, although attributed by Neuville to that period, should be properly defined as Upper Acheulian. Other examples of the later period are found at *Jisr Banat Yacub, *Holon, Evron, Baqaa Rephaim, *Ma'ayan Barukh and et-*Tabun (layer F). The lithic industry of the Upper Acheulian period includes chiefly *coups-de-poing* or bifacials (generally cordiform or oval), but amygdaloid (almond-shaped) examples are also found. *Limandes,* straight-edged tools, are also found, particularly at *Jisr Banat Yacub, where most of the examples found are in basalt, whereas flint predominates at other sites. The Tayacian era in Palestine opens with a series of flake industries; sites such as *Umm Qatafa and et-*Tabun show evidence of this. It is generally considered that this culture directly succeeded Upper Olduwan and was contemporary with Upper Acheulian. Chronologically these industries date from the beginning to the end of the Middle Pleistocene era and even continue into the Upper Pleistocene era.

THE MIDDLE PALAEOLITHIC PERIOD This period includes a series of Mousterian cultures, mainly Yabrudian,

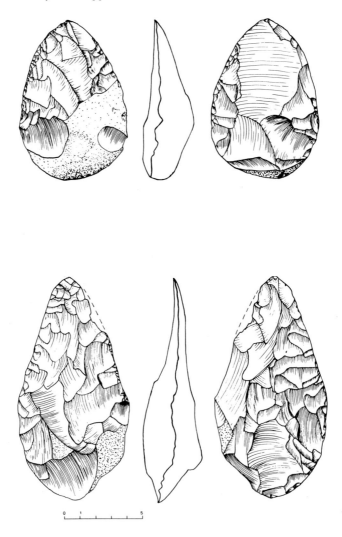

Late Acheulean handaxes

Levalloiso-Mousterian and Mousterian proper.

The Yabrudian culture has been recognized as an eastern variant of the European Mousterian culture of La Quina. It is characterized by a limited use of the Levalloisian technique and the presence of a very large number of racloirs, the majority of which are of the type known as transversal. They are sometimes associated with bifacial implements, which survived into this era ('Acheulo-Yabrudian bifacials'). All these definitions are based on the excavations carried out at the Yabrud I site and it was only in the light of them that Miss Garrod was able to recognize, retrospectively as it were, the same phenomenon at et-*Tabun (layer E).

The culture known as Levalloiso-Mousterian is so called because it bears resemblances to both the Mousterian and Levalloisian cultures, though it cannot be fully identified with either. It was at this period that techniques of cutting flint tools evolved very rapidly and showed much greater refinement. The variety of flint tools used demonstrates this: Levallois points, blades, flakes, borers and scapers. Rich industries have been found at et-*Tabun (B, C and D), es-*Skhul (B), *Kebara cave and *Qafzeh cave.

The Mousterian culture can be recognized by the fact that most of its artifacts have been retouched, but the predominant technique is no longer Levalloisian. The most important finds come from et-*Taban cave, *Umm Naqus, *Qafzeh (F) and, most of all, from *Abu Sif, where a large number of elongated points have been found, some of which resemble knives.

The Middle Paleolithic era is perhaps the most

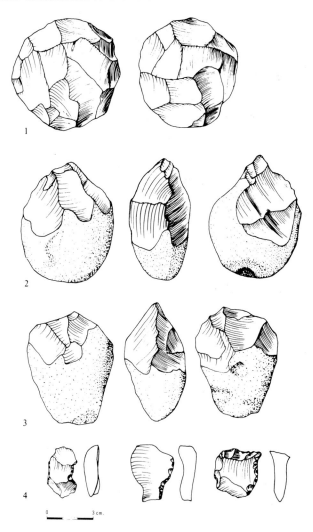

Oldowan tools. 1) spheroid. 2, 3) Chopping-tools. 4) Flake tools

important period in Palestinian prehistory, both because it seems to have lasted for a very long time and because a large number of fossilized human remains have been found (at es-*Skhul, et-*Tabun and the *Wadi Amud caves). To the general surprise of the scientific world, the species of man who lived at this period proved to be an intermediate type between Palaeanthropus (Neanderthal Man) and Neanthropus (*Homo sapiens*). He is known as *Palaeoanthropus Palestiniensis*. Argument about this species of man ranges from his position in relation to the various cultures of the Middle Paleolithic era to his exact origin. Does he represent a specific transitional phase between Neanderthal Man and *Homo sapiens* as known in the Middle East? Or is he the result of interbreeding between populations?

According to the carbon 14 datings obtained from this area, the Middle Paleolithic era ended in about 35000 BC. With it ended an age that had experienced drastic climatic variations, with a rainy phase followed by a cold and dry period, which was followed in its turn by a warm and dry one. It was at this point that large game such as hippopotami, elephants, rhinoceroses and buffaloes disappeared and only medium-sized animals remained in the area. Man now left the shores of lakes and rivers and instead inhabited the Mount Carmel caves or open-air sites on the coastal plain, the the *Jordan Valley or in the arid *Negev.

THE UPPER PALEOLITHIC PERIOD This period has been divided by Neuville into six separate phases. Phase I, known as the Emireh culture, is still open to question, both from the view of typology and from that of

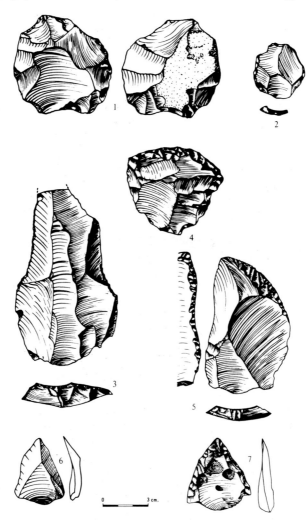

Middle Paleolithic tools. 1 — Levallois core. 2,3 — Levallois flakes. 4, 5 — Scrapers. 6 — Levallois point. 7 — Mousterian point (with cavities produced by heat fractures)

stratigraphy. The name is derived from the presence of Emireh points. Phases II-IV (local Aurignacian) can be recognized by their classic carinated scrapers and their points with a lopped-off cutting edge, and also by the appearance of Font-Yves points (which are no longer present in phase IV). Phase V (Atlitian) shows a further stage of the local Aurignacian culture and has many affinities with the Upper Aurignacian of Europe (though it is in fact the equivalent of a Middle Aurignacian culture). This industry shows evidence of the first microliths. Phase VI (Kebaran) is the first of a series of epi-Paleolithic industries. Although the technological features of the previous stages are still found here, these new industries are typologically different in that microliths predominate strongly (from this point of view the Natufian culture can be classed as epi-Paleolithic).

The Upper Paleolithic period begins in 35000 BC and reaches its peak of coldness and dryness in about 20000-18000 BC. We know little of the Aurignacians of Palestine, since the only human remain that has been found is a single fossilized skull in *Qafzeh cave. At this date the country was mostly covered with forests, which provided abundant game: bison, brown bears, deer and wild boar. This period was followed by an intermediate one (17000-15000 BC) in which microlithic industries predominated. These spread throughout Palestine during phase IV of the Würm glaciation. *Natufian culture* The climatic fluctuations that took place at the end of the the Pleistocene era saw the emergence of the Natufian culture, which began in about 10000 BC. It is characterized by mainly microlithic assemblages: bladelets and points (the most typical being half-moon shaped), crescents or blades in the form of an arc, and pointed burins. Certain large

Neckless, Natufian culture 10000-7500 BC Mugharet el-Wad (Mt Carmel cave)

tools were made of flint (sickle-blades and pick-axes), which point to a very early attempt at agriculture. An abundant bone industry developed along parallel lines, the material being used both for tools and for ornaments. This is also the time when the first signs of an art form appear and naturalistic or schematic animal and human figures are found, some two-

Rock-drawings of hunting, central Negev

Burial, En Gev, Paleolithic period

dimensional, some three-dimensional; incised geometric decoration is found on sickle-hafts.

The Natufians lived in caves or in small complexes made up of a few small houses, generally round and made of unbaked brick. The best-known sites are *Eynon, Oren Terrace, *Jericho and *El-Wad. All these settlements include cemeteries, with burials in single, double or multiple graves. A large number of skeletons were found there, in a variety of postures: lying on the back (supine), on the side, doubled up or in the 'embryo' position. The deceased had generally been buried with all their ornaments, which were placed round their head, round their neck, wrists and chests; this is particularly true of the female skeletons.

THE PRE-POTTERY NEOLITHIC PERIOD The Natufian period ended in about 7500 BC and gave way to the pre-Pottery Neolithic era, which is divided into two phases (A and B). The subdivisions are based on stratigraphy, chronology and cultural changes and the whole period ended in about 6000 BC.

The town of *Jericho with its round tower and its houses built of plano-convex bricks is dated to phase A. The same type of round houses are found in layer 2 at Nahal Oren, except that here they are built of stone specially arranged on terraces. The lithic industries are remarkable for their abundance of axes with a single cutting edge, sickle-blades and knives, together with arrow-heads. The usual tools of previous periods — scrapers, burins and points — are still used.

Pre-Pottery B is not all that different from pre-Pottery A in its lithic industry, except that for technical reasons 'cooked' flint and obsidian was generally used. Obsidian was brought from eastern Anatolia and was only one of the many commodities exchanged at this date between Palestine and the neighboring regions. In the economic field, this period sees the development of early attempts at animal domestication and at practising a type of agriculture that involved the systematic planting of wild cereals. The houses are now rectangular and built of unbaked bricks covered with plaster and, in some cases, with floral decoration (at *Jericho). The same motifs are found at Nahal Oren, but here the houses are built in undressed stone. At *Munhata (layers 3/5), on the other hand, both undressed stone and brick were used. Villages showing similar characteristics have been found at Beidha and at Tell Ramad. Clay statuettes representing human and animal figures and skulls with plaster moulding (at *Jericho) are evidence of a new development in the religious or cultural life of this era.

Pre-Pottery B ended with a dry period which

resulted in a large number of villages being abandoned.

THE POTTERY NEOLITHIC PERIOD This period in Palestine is distinguished by pit and hut dwellings (*Shaar Hagolan, *Munhata (layer 2) and *Jericho (layers VIII/IX)). Not until the end of this period, with the beginning of sedentary life, do we find solidly constructed houses. The pottery of the people who lived in these villages is painted and decorated with herringbone motifs. Clay figurines of women (a type of mother-goddess) and fertility symbols incised on river pebbles represent a new form of art. Sickle-blades, arrowheads in a wide variety of shapes, axes and hatchets, plus the usual lithic assemblages (points, scrapers, burins), abound and show that agriculture was now the main source of subsistence. From the technological point of view the most common method is pressure, though an increasing number of objects were now polished with sand and water. Definite progress in animal domestication can also be observed.

This period ends in about 4000 BC. It is followed by the Chalcolithic period, which takes us out of prehistory and into history.

PRISONS The punitive system of the ancient Near East was based on the *Lex talionis*. It is known that this was common practice in *Babylon and Assyria, and the biblical laws in relation to punishment do not differ from it (Exod. 21:23-5, etc.). The task of the legal authorities was confined to the assessment of guilt; if a man was found to be guilty, the penalty would be automatic.

Imprisonment as a punishment for criminal behavior is never referred to in the Bible or in other ancient legal codes. Nevertheless there are numerous terms in the Bible denoting places of imprisonment. The Hebrew Bible has no less than 11 such names, all rendered as 'prison' in the Authorized Version (2 Kgs. 25-9; Jer. 52-3; 1 Kgs. 22-7, etc.). Other terms used are 'dungeon' (Gen. 40:15; Jer. 37:16) and 'ward' (Num. 15:34). Not until the time of the Restoration is imprisonment specifically mentioned as a punishment (Ezra 7:26). On the other hand it seems that detention before trial sometimes occurred (Num. 15:32-5). Detention on political grounds is also frequently referred to, as for example in the cases of the prophet Micaiah (1 Kgs. 22:26-7); Hoshea, King of Israel (2 Kgs. 17:4); Jehoiachin, King of Judah (2 Kgs. 25-7); Jeremiah (Jer. 37:15-21, etc.); and Zedekiah, who was detained until the day of his death (Jer. 52:11).

It seems that no special place was set aide for detention, the need being met as it arose. Thus Jeremiah was placed in prison in the house of Jonathan the scribe (Jer. 37:15), transferred to the court of *matarah* (Jer. 37:21; Authorized Version: 'court of the prison') and later placed in the dungeon of Malchiah, in the court of the prison (Jer. 38:6 ff.). Joseph was detained in a prison in the house of the captain of the guard (Gen. 39:20-3; 40:1 ff.).

A prisoner would be bound in chains (Jer. 40:1; Isa. 45:4), of brass (Judg. 16:21) or of iron (Ps. 105:18). Sometimes his feet would be placed in stocks (Job. 13:27; Jer. 20:2).

Assyrian relief depicting prisoners of war

In the Roman period, as in biblical times, the law did not recognize imprisonment as a form of punishment. A man could be detained to await trial in order to make him available to the court, but once convicted he was expected to leave Rome and go into exile. It is only in the larger households that a prison for the detention of slaves has been found. In the New Testament we are told that John the Baptist (Matt. 14:3), Peter (Acts 5:18), Paul and Silas (Acts 16:23) were put in the 'common prison', or prison. According to Josephus (*Antiq.* XVIII, 119), John was imprisoned in Herod's palace at Machaerus (*Michvar). The prison referred to in (5) was probably in the Temple, under the custody of the priests. Paul was imprisoned in the Antonia fortress in Jerusalem (Acts 23:10) and also in the palace of Herod at *Caesarea (Acts 23:35). The New Testament also mentions prisoners having their feet put in stocks (Acts 16:24).

PUNON One of the stations on the route of the Exodus, between *Zalmon and Oboth (Num. 33:42-3). Identified with Feinan, 30 miles south of the *Dead Sea, it was known in the Roman period as Finon, or Fainon. The region is comparatively rich in water and arable soil, which contributed to its importance. There are comparatively rich copper mines in the vicinity and these were worked in both early and later historical periods. A regiment of one of the Roman legions once guarded its mines and foundaries. Eusebius states that in his day Finon was an important mining center between *Petra and *Zoar, while Hieronymus refers to it as a village in the desert where prisoners were used as forced labor to mine copper (*Metals). Archaeological surveys have indicated that mining took place there in the Early Bronze Age and the Iron Age, as well as in the Roman and Byzantine periods. Remains of heaps of slag, crucibles and installations connected with mining have been found here

Prisoners on the 'cosmetic palette of the does', from Abydos

Q

QAFZEH (CAVE) The cave of Jebel Qafzeh lies in a deep narrow wadi descending from *Nazareth to the *Jezreel Valley. It was first excavated by R. Neuville and M. Stekelis in 1932. Beneath two historic layers, they found 10 prehistoric levels. Of these layers C, D, and E were assigned to the Upper Paleolithic era, while the lower two layers A and B belonged to the Middle and Lower Paleolithic eras. All three layers contained characteristic Font-Yves points, numerous scrapers on flakes and blades, rare burins, blades with semi-abrupt retouch and an almost complete absence of carinated scrapers. The lithic assemblages were uncovered in brown-red soil which, together with the animal remains, indicated a cold and dry climate which could sometimes become cold and damp.

Layer F was classified as Mousterian on the strength of its many retouched points and racloirs and a diminishing use of the Levallois technique. Layers G to L were labelled Levalloisian, which according to modern terminology would be Mousterian of Levalloisian facies (*Flint tools). In the lowermost level (L) human skeletal remains similar to those at es-*Skhul were found. The Mousterian layers are typified by numerous points while the number of racloirs increases in layer J and decreases in the layers above and below. The quantity of Levallois flakes steadily decreases from the base to the upper layers.

From 1965-1979 B. Vandermeersch conducted 15 seasons of excavations, especially near the cave's entrance. The deposits, truncated by the Bynzantine remains, contains only Mousterian layers. These follow in their initial deposition the bedrock which slopes towards the wadi. The layers labelled in Roman numerals from IV through XXIII contained Mousterian industries. While the upper part of the sequence (IV-XV) was rich in artifacts and broken mammalian bones, the lower part was much poorer, but provided rich microfaunal assemblages and a series of burials. Among these were a joint burial of an adult, in a semi-flexed position with a child at its feet; a burial of a child with fallow deer's antlers across its chest and a semi-flexed burial of an adult. The total number of human remains attains 20 (including those previously exposed by Neuville). All are classified as *Homo sapiens* and their exact age is debatable. While the assemblage of rodents from the lower layers point to a

date in the range of 80-100,000 years ago the lithic industry is considered as of Late Mousterian (40-50,000 years ago) by some scholars (*See also* •PREHISTORY, *FLINT TOOLS).

QARQAR *a)* A site in Wadi Sirhan on the desert route to the land of *Midian, about 150 miles southeast of the point where the River *Jordan enters the *Dead Sea. After defeating the *Midianites near the river (Judg. 7:24), Gideon pursued them along the caravan route to Qarqar (Judg. 8:10-11; Authorized Version: 'Karkor').

b) A site on the Orontes, in northern Syria, where a battle took place between Shalmaneser III, King of Assyria, and a league of kings at whose head stood Ben-Hadad, King of *Damascus, Ahab, King of Israel, and Irhuleni, King of *Hamath-on-the-Orontes. According to Shalmaneser's records he himself was victorious, but as he did not undertake another campaign to the west for four years it seems that his army must have suffered a setback. The Qarqar of this battle is not mentioned in the Bible, but the alliance between Israel and *Aram (1 Kgs. 22:1 ff.) relates to this period.

QASILE (TELL) A mound situated on the northern bank of the Yarkon River, about one mile from the Mediterranean coast. Two Hebrew ostraca found on the surface of the mound led to the systematic excavation of the site which was carried out under the direction of B. Mazar (1949-51, 1956) and continued under A. Mazar (1971-4, 1982-4). The 4-acre site is located on a *kurkar* (sandstone) ridge overlooking the Yarkon River and the coastal plain. A permanent settlement was founded on the site in the mid-12th century BC. The founders were most probably Philistines, the 'Sea Peoples' who settled the southern coastal plain of Palestine during the 12th century BC. Tell Qasile was an important port town since the Yarkon River was ideal for anchoring the small ships of that time. Seafaring and trade were thus basic factors in the economy of the settlers.

Though the ancient name of the Tell Qasile is not known, it is one of the most important sites for studying the material culture of the Philistines during the Iron Age I. Three successive occupation levels of the Philistine town were discovered (strata XII-X), extending over a time span of *c.* 180 years

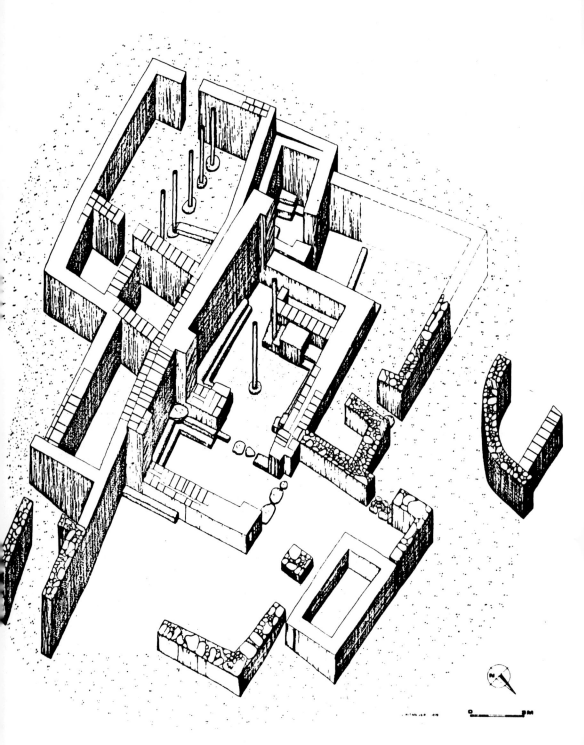

Exonometric view of Area C, stratum X; looking south-west

(1150-980 BC). The town was finally conquered and burnt, most probably during the conquest of the region by David. The transitions between strata XII and XI and between strata XI and X were peaceful, and mark a gradual growth and development of the town.

The buildings of stratum XII are built of mudbricks laid on bedrock with stone foundations. The two most important structures from this earliest occupation level are a temple and a public building. The temple is a small edifice containing one room with benches along the walls and a raised platform. A large courtyard in front of the temple served for ritual ceremonies and sacrifices. The public building, situated south of the temple, contained a large hall with benches along the walls and a freestanding hearth, reminiscent of similar hearths in the Aegean and Anatolian world.

In the following stratum XI, the city was rebuilt, mainly with stone structures. The temple was rebuilt on the remains of the previous ones; it was somewhat larger, the entrance was in the northeast corner and a small chamber inside the main structure, which contained a large collection of cult objects, served as a treasury. In the following stratum X, the temple was enlarged and its plan altered. An entrance chamber with a wide opening led into the main hall, the roof of which was supported by two cedar wood pillars on stone circular bases. Inside the main hall, benches surrounded the walls, a raised platform in the sanctuary served as the Holy of Holies, and a narrow room at the back of the temple was a treasury room. The courtyard of this temple was now surrounded by stone walls; inside the courtyard were auxiliary rooms and a sacrificial altar. In both strata XI and X a small shrine stood on the west side of the main temple. It was a small room with benches along the walls and a raised platform in its corner.

The finds in the successive temples at Tell Qasile are of special importance, as they contained an unparalleled collection of cult objects made of pottery, as well as metal, alabaster and ivory objects. Some of them are unique art objects from the period of the Judges. Both the plans of the temples as well as the cult objects reflect a strong Canaanite influence on the local culture. Similarities to the cultures of Cyprus and the Aegean world point to the origin of the local population, though it can be assumed that the Philistine newcomers were the overlords of the local autochthonous population. This assumption also finds support in the rich pottery assemblages found in the sanctuary. These display a combination of traditions characteristic of the Philistines and of the Canaanite culture.

The residential quarter excavated in the southern part of the mound illustrates the urban planning and the plans of the private dwellings during the 11th century BC at Tell Qasile. The houses are arranged in well-planned blocks. They are square in shape and contain a courtyard divided by a row of pillars. The rich finds uncovered in these houses attest to the wealth of the population on the eve of the Israelite conquest. Trade connections with Phoenicia, Cyprus and Egypt are reflected in the pottery imported from these countries.

A female anthropomorphic vessel

The destruction of Tell Qasile in the time of David did not put an end to the town. During the United Kingdom the town was rebuilt (strata IX-VIII) to a certain extent, though not so densely as in the previous period. The 10th century BC town, which was probably a port town under Israelite control, was destroyed at the end of the century, perhaps during Sheshonq's invasion of the country. A gap in occupation lasted during most of the Iron Age, and only in the late 7th century BC was there a small settlement, which as may have been connected with the Judean expansion to the coast during the time of King Josiah.

A large building at the top of the mound from the Persian period may have served as an administration building. A rock-cut square well supplied water to the site during this time. During the Hellenistic and Roman periods there was a small settlement on the site. Isolated buildings from the Byzantine period, especially a large public bath house uncovered on the mound and a synagogue at the foot of the mound, are evidence that a small town existed in the vicinity of the mound. An isolated estate dated to the Middle Ages (Crusader period?) was found on the summit of the mound.

QATNA A large ancient mound in Syria, 10 miles northeast of Homs, identified with Mishrefeh. The site was excavated in 1927-9 by Mensil du Buisson on behalf of the French Archaeological Expedition.

The earliest traces of settlement on the site are of the prehistoric periods and the earliest building remains date from the early 2nd millennium BC. At this period Qatna was a small fortified town. Owing to its favorable geographical location it developed into a large city during the 2nd millennium BC, and its situation on the Via Maris (*Roads) brought it into trade relations with the neighboring countries. Its earliest contacts with *Ur were established at the time of the 3rd Dynasty (2060-1950 BC). In the 18th-17th centuries BC Qatna had close relations with the Sumerians as well. Jewelry of Sumerian origin was found in the treasure of the temple of Nin-Egal, the 'Lady of Qatna', which was built at this period. The plan of some of the houses also indicates Sumerian influence. The pottery of the early centuries of the 2nd millennium BC is again influenced by styles that came from the *Euphrates valley. On the other hand, there is also evidence of relations with the Syrian coast and the Mediterranean islands.

One of the most formidable systems of fortifications, attributed to the *Hyksos, was discovered at Qatna. It consists of a huge camp surrounded by an embankment $^3/_4$ mile square, of the same type as that at Tell el-*Yehudiyeh. The period of Hyksos rule, and that which followed the expulsion of Hyksos, by the *Egyptians, was one of great prosperity. Documents found in the temple archives refer to donations of precious stones and metals. The temple, which was originally built in the 20th century BC, did not suffer any serious damage until its final destruction in about 1380 BC. This is also true of the royal palace. In about 1468 BC, at the time of the Battle of *Kedesh on the Orontes, Qatna was conquered by Tuthmosis III, and in the period of the *El Amarna letters it suffered greatly. Several letters written by Akizzi, the last known king of Qatna, to Amenophis III are preserved in the *El Amarna correspondence. In these the local ruler asks for Egyptian help against the enemy, the *Hittites, who had invaded Syria and who in the end conquered Qatna and destroyed part of it. The wars with the *Hittites, the subsequent intervention of Mitanni and the failure of *Egypt to assist its allies led to the complete destruction of Qatna. The site was partly inhabited for a short time in the 6th century BC and there was a village on the site in the 2nd century BC.

QUMRAN (KHIRBET) Khirbet Qumran is situated to the northwest of the *Dead Sea, 1,292 feet below sea level, above the left bank of Wadi Qumran. Although the site had been known for more than a century little attention was paid to it until recently, when the *Dead Sea Scrolls were discovered in the nearby *Judean Desert Caves. The site was excavated by Father R. de Vaux, on behalf of the French School of Archaeology in Jerusalem and other institutions, in 1951 and 1953-6. It is situated on a terrace of marl (a soil consisting of clay and carbonate of lime) and is surrounded by precipitous ravines. The earliest remains, of a building of the 8th-6th centuries BC, were incorporated into the building of the later enclosure, which is 250 feet square. The entrance to this enclosure was on the north and was protected by a massive

Inkstand from Khirbet Qumran

tower with three floors, the lower two built of stone and the upper one of bricks. A narrow court leads from the gate to the various parts of the enclosure. Some of the more important rooms lie to the south of the tower. One hall was identified as the *scriptorium*, where the scrolls of the *Dead Sea were copied. The excavators believe that the copying room was above ground level and that access to it was by means of a staircase in a small adjoining court. The *scriptorium* was probably open on one side. To the east of it was another small court, around which were the kitchen, a laundry and some large reservoirs, made watertight with several coats of plaster. South of this complex were an assembly hall measuring 67 feet by 35 feet, a pantry, additional reservoirs and a potter's workshop with two kilns, one for firing small vessels for daily use and the other for larger jars, of the kind in which the scrolls were stored. The western part of this small settlement contained storerooms and workshops, a cornmill, a baker's oven, a forge (?), silos for storing fruit and rooms for storing grain. One hall was a stable with troughs for eight beasts. Here, too, were two large cisterns, one of which was circular. So that water could be obtained a dam was built across Wadi Qumran, from which an acqueduct and numerous channels led to each cistern. To the east of the settlement, separated by a stone wall, was a large cemetery in which no less than 1,100 burials were discovered.

(Right) *General view of the Qumran caves*

The excavators distinguished several occupation levels on the site. The earliest, of the Iron Age II, has already been referred to. This Iron Age construction is tentatively identified with the 'city of Salt' of Joshua (15:62) and its erection is attributed to Uzziah who 'built towers in the desert and digged many wells' (2 Chr. 26:10). The next occupation level is dated to the time of John Hyrcanus I (135-104 BC). The excavators believe that this settlement was established by the Essenes, although other scholars prefer the term the 'Dead Sea sect'. Hardly any buildings of this period are extant and the dating had to rely on coins. In the 2nd phase of the same Hellenistic period the settlement assumed the shape in which it was found. The water supply system was also laid down at this time. The settlement of the 2nd phase was destroyed by a fire and an earthquake, which may have happened on the same day. This earthquake, the excavators believe, is the one of 31 BC referred to by Josephus (*Antiq.* XV, 121-47; *War* I, 370-80). In about 4 BC, during the reign of Archelaus, the place was rebuilt to approximately the same plan as that of the previous period, but in the summer of AD 68, at the time of the First Jewish Revolt, the settlement was destroyed by the Roman (Josephus, *War* IV, 449 ff.). The site was then occupied by a Roman garrison until about AD 90. During the Bar-Kochba Revolt (AD 132-5) fugitives found shelter there, as is indicated by the coins of the Second Revolt that have been found on the site.

AIN FESHKHA The area round Khirbet Qumran is a barren desert, but just a little to the south of it begins a large oasis, irrigated by the waters of Ain Feshkha, an abundant freshwater spring about $1\frac{1}{2}$ miles away. Here (in 1958) Father de Vaux excavated a building which was occupied during exactly the same periods as neighboring Khirbet Qumran. It is obvious that the sectarians, who could not have relied entirely on supplies brought from afar, grew their own food here. Among the ruins several tanks connected by channels were also found. The excavator believes that this installation was a tannery (*Leather) in which the skins used for parchment were prepared.

R

RABBATH-AMMON; PHILADELPHIA The capital of the *Ammonites, on the border of the desert, near the sources of the River *Jabbok; also called Rabbah (Josh. 13:25). Eusebius (*Onom.* 16:15) knew it by the name of Amman, 'known also by the name of Philadelphia, a famous city of Arabia'. It was surrounded by small villages, named daughters of Rabba (Jer. 49:3). It was an important junction for roads leading from the Arabian peninsula in the south to *Damascus in the north, and from the Syrian desert on the east to Palestine and the Mediterranean on the west. The city was built in two parts, the lower one being referred to as the 'city of waters' (2 Sam. 12:27) and the upper as the 'royal city' (2 Sam. 12:26). Joab conquered the city of waters, and waited for David to complete the conquest (2 Sam. 12:27-9). After the division of the United Monarchy, Rabbah became the capital of the independent kingdom of *Ammon. At the beginning of the 6th century BC it was destroyed by 'men of the east', who made it 'a stable for camels' and 'a couchingplace for sheep' (Ezek. 25:4-5). This is possibly a reference to the *Nabateans or an allied *Arabian tribe. In the Persian period it was under the rule of the Tobiads.

Ptolemy II Philadelphus (285-246 BC) rebuilt the city and renamed it Philadelphia. In about 135 BC it was ruled by the tyrant Zenon Cotylas, and from 63 BC, after the Roman conquest, it became part of the *Decapolis and began its own system of dating. In AD 66 the Philadelphians were hostile to the Jews of the *Parea. From AD 106 it formed part of the Provincia Arabia.

Christianity penetrated Rabbath-Ammon in the 4th century AD, when it became the seat of a bishop, subject to *Bostra. Its bishops participated in the Council of Nicaea (AD 325), the Synod of *Antioch and the Council of Chalcedon (AD 451). Under Diocletian Christians of this city were martyred; their relics have been found in local churches. In AD 636 it was conquered by the Arabs who built a citadel on the acropolis.

In 1927 an Italian expedition directed by G. Guidi worked at the site; the excavations continued in 1929-33 under the direction of R. Bartoccini. From 1945 G.L. Harding investigated Amman on behalf of the Department of Antiquities, and in 1966 J.B. Hennessy excavated the Late Bronze Age *temple on behalf of the British School of Archaeology in Jerusalem.

Near the top of the acropolis were discovered tombs of the end of the Middle Bronze Age. Several walls on the acropolis belong to the same period (approximately the 16th century BC). At the site of Amman's airport was discovered a temple 45 feet square. Under walls 6 feet thick, built of unhewn stones, were found foundation offerings, including fowls and animals. Forty gold objects were also deposited as offerings. The temple was built at the end of the 14th century BC and abandoned in the following century. In various parts of the city were found remains of the 9th century BC, including the only known Ammonite *inscriptions. One engraved on a bronze bottle mentions Amminadab son of Hisael son of Amminadab, King of the Ammonites; it dates to the 7th century BC. Several inscribed *seals of Ammonite officals were also found. A number of short inscriptions had been engraved on statues of gods or rulers. In various parts of the city were found *tombs of a type known in Palestine in the 7th and 6th centuries BC. Also from the Ammonite period are the city *fortifications, including a wall and numerous towers.

To the Hellenistic period date a wall constructed of polygonal stone blocks and a subterranean reservoir on the acropolis. Most of the remains are of the Roman period. The *Nabatean remains are few; they include a tomb consisting of two subterranean rooms. The finds in the tomb are important for the dating of Nabatean *pottery. In the Antonine period Philadelphia was a prosperous city. Among the monuments are a *nymphaeum, *odeum and *theater in the lower city, the *propylaea* and steps of the acropolis, and a *temple of Zeus built on the second terrace of the acropolis, above an Ammonite altar. On the summit of the acropolis is another Roman shrine and an agora (160 feet by 120 feet) surrounded by double colonnades. Roman monumental tombs were also uncovered.

RABBATHMOBA; AREOPOLIS It is not known whether the Hebrew form of the name in biblical times (Ar, Ar-Moab, cf. Num. 21:15,28; Isa. 15:1) refers to a place or to a region in the country of *Moab. It was one of the stations of the Israelites on their way from *Elath (Deut. 2:8-9). It is very likely the 'city of Moab'

Seal impression from Mampsis,
depicting the zodiac sign of Libra (scales)
and bearing the name of the town of Rabbathmoba

to which Balaam came (Num. 22:36), which is identified with er-Rabba. It seems to have been built by the *Nabateans, though the first mention of it is in Ptolemy (*Geography* v, 16, 4). As Ptolemy died in about AD 150, this reference may be taken as referring to the late Nabatean period, when Rabbathmoba must have been an administrative center. Of this there is new evidence in the documents discovered in the *Judean Desert Caves, some of which originated in Rabbathmoba and one of which is dated AD 127. The urbanization of Rabbathmoba used to be attributed to Septimius Severus. But it may already have been a *polis* at that time, as indicated by seals of about AD 130, found at *Mampsis, that bear his name.

The town is later mentioned in the Peutinger map. Eusebius (*Onom.* 124, 15-17) gives its new name, Areopolis — the city of Ares — and the effigy of Ares, the war god, does indeed appear both on the coins of Rabbathmoba and on the seals from *Mampsis. According to the *Notitia Dignitatum* Illyrian cavalrymen were stationed there. The later Byzantine sources refer to the town by its older, Semitic name.

No excavations have as yet been made at Rabbathmoba, but surface surveys have revealed remains of a temple built of large, nicely dressed blocks of limestone, on a tripartite plan and measuring 100 feet by 80 feet. It has been identified as Nabatean, but the close resemblance of the architectural decoration to that of later buildings points to a date in the later Roman period.

RABUD (KHIRBET) The largest biblical site in the Judean hill-country south of Jerusalem. It is situated about $7^1/_2$ miles south of Hebron. The meandering Hebron River surrounds the site on three sides, turning it into an excellent strategic point. Khirbet Rabud is identified with the most important city of the southernmost hill-country of Judah — biblical Debir / Kiriath-Sepher (Josh. 15:15), one of the cities of the *Anakims* (Josh. 11:21). Its conquest is attributed to Othniel son of Kenaz (Josh. 15:15-19) and in other passages to Joshua (Josh. 10:38-39; 12:13). Its geogra-

phical location can be ascertained by its position among clearly identified cities of Judah in the hill-country bordering the Negev (Josh. 15:48-51).

Archaeological investigations at Khirbet Rabud and its vicinity have revealed the history of the site and have corroborated its identification with Debir. The site was only sporadically occupied during the 4th and 3rd millennia BC. The first walled city was built during the Late Bronze Age. Four strata of this period, from the 14th and 13th centuries BC, were distinguished. This pre-Israelite city covered an area of about 15 acres. The site was inhabited during the first centuries of the Israelite (Iron Age) period, but a new, more substantial city-wall was erected in the 9th century BC. Israelite Debir was a large city of about $12^1/_2$ acres with an unwalled suburb built sometime during the last centuries of the period and occupying an additional area of about $3^3/_4$ acres. Like many other cities in Judah Debir was destroyed in a conflagration at the end of the 8th century BC, probably at the hands of Sennacherib during his Judean campaign in 701 BC. Like Lachish, the chief Judean city in the Plain, Debir, the most important city in the southern hill-country, was rebuilt after its destruction by Sennacherib. The city wall was nearly doubled in width and new houses and storerooms were built against it. The total destruction of Judah by the Babylonians brought the settlement at Debir to an end. It is never mentioned in post-exilic sources and only scanty occupational remains from the Persian period mark the last phase of its existence.

Through its long history the city of Debir-Khirbet Rabud was wholly dependent on cisterns for its water supply. Two wells that overflow in the springtime, located about 2 miles north of the site and still called *the upper and lower wells*, provide the background for Achsah's demand from her father for the upper and nether springs (Josh. 15:15-19; Judg. 1:11-15).

RAKKATH A fortified town in the territory of Naphtali (Josh. 19:35), situated between *Hammath and the *Sea of Galilee. In the Talmud Rakkath and *Tiberias are considered identical sites. It is identified with Tell Quneitra, $1^1/_2$ miles northwest of Tiberias, where *pottery of the Bronze and Iron Ages has been found. The town dominated the Via Maris (*Roads). In the Roman period Tiberias replaced Rakkath.

RAMAH; RAMATAIM-ZOPHIM; ARIMATHEA A town in the territory of Benjamin (Josh. 18:25; Authorized Version: 'Gaba'), not far from *Geba and *Gibeah of Saul (1 Sam. 22:6). It was fortified by Baasha, King of Israel (1 Kgs. 15:17), 'so that he might not suffer any to go out or come in to Asa King of Judah'. But by command of Asa the stones of Ramah were carried away for use in building *Geba of Benjamin and *Mizpah (1 Kgs. 15:22). Nebu-Zar-Adan assembled the captives of Judah at Ramah before they were taken to *Babylon (Jer. 40:1). It was one of the villages resettled in the time of the Restoration (Neh. 11:33) between *Hazor and *Gittaim. It is apparently situated on the western slopes of the Judean hills, in the vicinity of *Lod. It may have been included in the territory the Seleucids ceded to the Hasmoneans (1 Macc. 10:30,38; 11:34). Eusebius

(*Onom.* 144:28-29) states that it is close to *Lod, the residence of Joseph of Arimathaia, in whose sepulcher the body of Jesus was placed after the Crucifixion (Matt. 27:57 ff.; Mark 15:43; Luke 23:51; John. 19:38). The biblical site has not been identified with certainty. The site of the later periods is identified with Rentis, about 8 miles northeast of Lydda (*Lod).

RAMAT-KHALIL Josephus (*Antiq.* I, 186; *War* IV, 533) mentions an oak named Ogyges, or Terebinthos, near which Abraham lived, not far from the city of the *Hebronites. In another passage he states that the oak was 6 stadia (about 1,100 yd) from *Hebron. According to Hieronymus *(Commentaries to Zech.* 9:2) Hadrian brought the captives of the Bar-Kochba Revolt here so as to sell them into slavery. Jewish sources and pilgrims of the early Christian centuries refer to a market-place at this spot, and early Christian sources also mention a pagan altar there. Thus it is certain that in the Roman period the place served as a marketplace as well as a religious center for the southern part of the country. According to Eusebius (*Life of Constantine* III, 53) the altar was destroyed by order of the emperor, who built a church in its place.

The site is now identified with Ramat el-Khalil, on a mountain 3,000 feet about sea level, about 2 miles north of Hebron. It was visited by the Pilgrim of Bordeaux in AD 333 and Constantine built a magnificent church there. The church was marked on the Medaba mosaic map and was still there to be seen by the pilgrim Arculf in AD 670. But by the 10th century it already lay in ruins.

Excavations were carried out at Ramat el-Khalil in 1926-8 by E. Mader, on behalf of the Archaeological Institute of the Görresgesellschaft in Jerusalem. Some remains of the Middle Bronze Age were found beneath the church enclosure, which was about an acre in area. The earliest building remains on the site were of the 9th-8th centuries BC. In addition to the typical Israelite pottery remains of two towers, perhaps connected with an entrance gate to a sacred enclosure, were discovered. The assumption that the site was already a shrine in the Israelite period is further strengthened by the presence of a pavement in the enclosure court which dates to the time of the Judean kingdom. Then come remains from the Maccabean period (John Hyrcanus conquered the place in about 128 BC). A massive wall which still survives was built of huge blocks of stone with dressing typical of Herod's time and similar to that of the enclosure wall of the Cave of *Machpelah at *Hebron and the wall of the Temple Mount in *Jerusalem. The wall was partly dismantled after the destruction of the Second Temple, but its stones were reused by Hadrian when the new wall was built. The rebuilding of the wall is dated to Hadrian's visit to the East in AD 130. Attached to the east wall a temple was built, the remains of which were later incorporated into the Constantine basilica. Among other remains from Hadrian's time were those of an altar, a stele of Hermes and a head of Dionysus.

The Constantine basilica is the earliest of its kind in Palestine. It is of the broadhouse type and measures 50 feet by 60 feet. In the atrium to the west of the church stood the oak of Abraham, and near it was the well. The church was probably destroyed by the Persians in AD 614, but it was rebuilt immediately. The earliest of the 1,331 coins found in the well date from the Maccabean period, the latest from Crusader times. There are no coins of the period between Vespasian and Hadrian, which confirms that the site was abandoned between AD 70 and 135.

RAMAT MATRED A group of sites in the central *Negev, about 4 miles southwest of *Oboda, situated on a plateau some 2,000 feet above sea level. Archaeological surveys of the plateau have revealed 37 sites of the Middle Bronze Age and 18 of the Iron Age scattered over an area of approximately 2 square miles. Of the Nabatean-Byzantine period only five sites were found. During 1958 and 1959 several Israelite farmhouses were excavated by Y. Aharoni and others, in the course of a study of ancient desert agriculture made by M. Evenari. The farmhouses were of a very simple type: two rooms side-by-side, with walls one stone thick, and a large round court alongside. There were also large livestock enclosures in the vicinity of the village. The fields nearby are situated in small tributary valleys of the large wadis. The whole length of each valley has been dammed with a series of stone walls, to stop the flow of water. One of these settlements consisted of 10 houses, of which one, of the four-room type, was outstanding.

The small settlements of Ramat Matred could not have survived but for four fortresses built on the fringes of the plateau, two to the southeast and two to the southwest, all dominating the main wadis that served as thoroughfares. One of these consisted of a small building with five rooms grouped round a central courtyard. Adjoining it is another large courtyard with a gateway protected by a small tower. Connected to this complex is a larger courtyard, at the corner of which were several rooms; it was probably a caravanserai.

Another complex, more formidable than the first described, occupies the whole extent of a hilltop with precipitous sides, the height of the cliff being 10-16 feet. Elliptical in shape, this fortress is 70 feet long and 38 feet wide at its largest point and is surrounded by a casemate wall. A section of another wall, part of which is single while the rest has casemates, was found on the lower slope of the same hill. The strongest and largest of these fortresses was discovered a short distance from Bir Hafir. It is a rectangular building with a casemate wall to which the *Nabateans later added a large tower and another building. These fortresses were dated by the pottery to the second half of the 10th or the first half of the 9th century BC. The excavators believe that they were built in order to guard a road that ran from Judah to *Kadesh-Barnea, possibly the 'way of the spies' of Numbers (21:1). (*See also* *ROADS.)

RAMAT RAHEL This ancient mound is situated on the southern outskirts of the city of *Jerusalem, halfway between the city and *Bethlehem, about 2,500 feet above sea level. Occupying an area of $2^1/_2$ acres on the broad flat top of the highest hill in the region, it dominates both the *Jerusalem-*Bethlehem road and one of the most important approaches to *Jerusalem

Capital in Proto Aeolian style from Ramat Rahel, end of Iron Age

from the land of the *Philistines. Following the discovery of a Jewish rock-cut tomb in 1931, an excavation of the site was conducted by B. Mazar and M. Stekelis on behalf of the Israel Exploration Society. In the course of this remains of the Iron Age came to light. In 1954, 1956 and 1959-62 extensive excavations were made on the site by Y. Aharoni on behalf of the University of Rome and Israeli institutions. He uncovered five occupation levels ranging from the Late Bronze Age to the early Arab period. In the uppermost level remains of dwellings and pottery of the early Arab period (7th-8th centuries AD) were discovered. Below these were remains of the Byzantine period, in which three building levels were observed.

Most important were remains of a church and of a large monastery attached to it. The church was a basilica with one apse, measuring 60 feet by 40 feet and paved with simple geometric mosaics. It is associated with a well some 500 yd away known as 'Bir Qadismu', a name probably derived from the Greek *kathisma,* meaning 'the Well of the Seat'. A well of this name is mentioned in a source of the 6th century AD which refers to a tradition that Mary and Joseph rested near the well on their way to *Bethlehem. Another source, from later in the same century, states that a church was built in the vicinity of the well. A 12th century traveller knew that the church had been destroyed by pagans. South of the church remains of a bath of the Roman period were discovered. The bricks used for building the hypocaust were stamped with the seal of the Legio X Fretensis, which was stationed in *Jerusalem from the time of the destruction of the Second Temple to about AD 300. During its long

period of use the bath was rebuilt several times. Remains of several houses of the courtyard type belong to the late Roman and Byzantine periods.

The fourth occupation level, in which only remnants of walls were discovered, has been dated, mainly by pottery and coins, to Herodian times, the period of the Second Temple. The fifth level was that of the Hellenistic and Persian periods. The buildings here had been badly damaged by later building activities, but the Persian period is represented by scores of stamped jar handles bearing seals of the following classes: *Yrslm* (Jerusalem); *Ha'ir* (the City); *Yhd* and *Yhwd* and *Phw* (Pahva, the title of the governor) (*Seals). Others had figures of animals and rosettes. the *Phw* group also had names of governors on them: Yehoezer and Ahiyu.

The most important occupation period is the earliest, the late Iron Age, when a royal citadel was built on the site in the 8th-7th centuries BC. At this time the whole mound was surrounded by a wall and the citadel was built on its highest part. The citadel proper is surrounded by a casemate wall measuring 150 feet by 75 feet. The monumental gate, of most beautiful ashlar, is on the east. The gateposts supported two large Proto Aeolian capitals, which were found in the debris. Other decorated stones included crenellations from the tops of the walls and window balustrades. Inside the spacious courts of the citadel, which must have been a royal residence of the kings of Judah, remains of buildings were discovered. The final destruction of the citadel is dated to 587 BC. To this period belong scores of seals of the *lamelek* type; all four names (*Hebron, *Ziph, *Socoh and *mmst*) occur.

Numerous burial caves, mostly of the Herodian and the Roman periods, were investigated by Y. Aharoni on behalf of the Hebrew University, the Department of Antiquities and the Israel Exploration Society. The tombs were rock-cut and some included ossuaries with Jewish names. One tomb was of the *columbarium* type.

RAMESES The name of a town and a district in the eastern half of the *Nile Delta named after Pharaoh Rameses II, where Joseph settled his father and brothers (Gen. 47:11); one of the treasure cities built by the Israelites for Pharaoh (Exod. 1:11). In Egyptian it is known as 'Per-Rameses', 'House of Rameses'. It became the delta residence of the pharaohs from the reign of Rameses II, since it was a more convenient site for their capital while they were concerned with affairs in Syria and Palestine than the former one, further south, at *Zoan (*Tanis). However, some scholars identify Rameses with Tanis, while others prefer an identification with Qantir, about 11 miles to the south, where both Sethos I and Rameses II built palaces. The city of Rameses was much praised for its beauty and luxury.

RAPHIA A city about 20 miles southwest of *Gaza identified with Tell Rafah. Situated on the Via Maris, the road leading from *Egypt through Palestine to the north, it was the southernmost city of Palestine. In the Egyptian sources it is first mentioned in the lists of the campaigns of Sethos I, and in the itinerary of the Egyptian Anastasi papyrus. In Assyrian sources it appears as Rapihu. It was from here that Sargon II, the Egyptian general Sibu and the King of *Gaza deported 9,033 inhabitants and burned the city. This is not however mentioned in the Bible. In the Hellenistic period Diodorus Siculus relates (xx, 74) that the fleet of Demetrius, son of Antigonus, was driven in a storm against the coast of Raphia when he was fighting against Ptolemy I. Polybius (v, 82-6) describes it as the nearest city to *Egypt in Coele-Syria and relates how Ptolemy IV defeated Antiochus the Great there. In 193 BC Ptolemy V married there the daughter of the same Antiochus. The city was conquered by the Hasmonean, Alexander Jannaeus (Josephus, *Antiq.* XIII , 357), freed by Pompey and rebuilt by Gabinius, governor of Syria (Josephus, *Antiq.* XIV, 88). It is mentioned frequently in Byzantine sources.

RED SEA The Hebrew name for this sea is Yam Suf, meaning 'sea of reeds'. Its identification with the Red Sea is an ancient one, and most early translators and commentators of the Bible adopted it. Most biblical references to the Red Sea are directed to its northeastern branch, known as the Gulf of *Elath or Aqabah, although reeds do not grow in these salty waters. The Authorized Version also translates Yam Suf as Red Sea (Num. 14:25; 21:4; Deut. 1:40, etc.). The sea that the Israelites crossed on their way from *Egypt to the land of *Canaan is referred to as the Egyptian Sea (Isa. 11:15) or the Red Sea (Exod. 13:18; 15:4, etc.), and its identification is very much disputed. Some scholars believe that the reference is to the northwestern branch of the Red Sea, known as the Gulf of Suez, but this would have involved a long and unnecessary detour by the Israelites from the land of *Goshen

southwards, with the Egyptian chariots on their heels. Others suggest that it was one of the lakes that lay on the border of *Egypt and *Sinai, between Suez and the Mediterranean, where plenty of reeds still grow. Yet others believe that it should be identified with Lake Sirbonis, which was once a continuation of the eastern arm of the *Nile Delta.

In the Hellenistic period the Red Sea was known as Erithra, or Erithraia Thalassa in Greek and Rubrum Mare in Latin. There is evidence that the ancient *Egyptians, Israelites and Persians were already navigating it. Herodotus knew it as an oblong, comparatively narrow sea. Alexander the Great sent a fleet from Suez to Yemen.

The Ptolemies were the first to establish forts and harbors along its western coast to serve as stations for the elephant hunters in East Africa. The most important of these stations were Berenike, Myos Hormos and Ptolemais Thoron. By the 1st century BC a special *strategos* was appointed to supervise the navigation of the Red Sea. In the early Roman period it became a vital artery in the spice trade with southern *Arabia and *India. The *Nabateans, who played an important role in that trade, built the port of Leuke Kome (the 'white village') on its eastern shore. Better shipbuilding in the Roman period made the navigation of this sea, which is swept by strong northerly and southerly winds, much safer.

REHOB *a)* The name of a place or a geographic region, marking the northern limit of the land of Canaan (Num. 34). It is mentioned in conjunction with the spies sent out by Moses (Num. 13:21). The inhabitants of Beth-Rehob (2 Sam. 10:6) took part in the war of the *Ammonites against David. The identification of site is very doubtful.
b) A town on the northern border of the territory of Asher (Josh. 19:28), given to the Levites of the family of Gershom (1 Chr. 6:75). It was not conquered by the Israelites, and the *Canaanites held it for a long time (Judg. 1:31). Doubtfully identified with Tell el-Balat.
c) Apparently mentioned in the Egyptian *Execration Texts, as well as in the lists of conquests of Pharaoh Rameses II.
d) Eusebius (*Onom.* 142:19) states that it is situated at a distance of 4 miles from *Beth-Shean.

Excavations at the site were conducted in 1974 by F. Vito on behalf of the Department of Antiquities. A *synagogue of the basilical type but without an apse was discovered. The synagogue was adorned with mosaics, of which little remains. In the narthex, however, was discovered the longest mosaic Hebrew inscription in Palestine. It is 13 feet by 8 feet, of 29 lines. It deals with regulations for the use of fruits and vegetables in different regions of the country and the payment of tithes and the *shebiit* (seventh part). These regions include *Beth-Shean, *Susita, *Naveh, *Tyre, *Paneas, *Caesarea and *Sebaste. In some instances this text is more detailed than the Talmud, and hence a source of utmost importance for the study of the geographical history of the Holy Land in the Byzantine period.

REHOBOTH The place in the *Negev where Isaac dug a well (Gen. 26:22). Its identification is not known; Ruheiba in the central *Negev, with which it has been identified, has no remains earlier than the Roman period.

REMETH *See* *JARMUTH

REPHAIM *See* *GIANTS (VALLEY OF THE)

REPHIDIM One of the stations on the route of the Exodus, where Moses smote the rock in order to provide the people with water (Exod. 17:1-7) and where Amalek fought Israel (Exod. 17:8-16). According to Numbers (33:14-15) Rephidim was situated between Alush and the Wilderness of *Sinai. The identification of this site depends on the identification of Mount *Sinai and the wilderness of *Sinai. Those who believe that the Israelites took a northerly route on their way from *Egypt to *Canaan look for Rephidim closer to the Mediterranean coast, between el-Arish and Jebel Hillal, while others suggest that it lies in Wadi Feiran, in the vicinity of Jebel Musa, more to the south.

RIBLAH *a)* A place mentioned in the description of the eastern limits of the land of Canaan (Num. 34:11). Eusebius (*Onom.* 14:18-21) knew this place by the name of Arbela, which is apparently the correct form. Its identification is uncertain.

b) A city in *Aram, near *Antioch-on-the-Orontes. After the decline of the Assyrian Empire Riblah became a political and military center for the armies that ruled Syria. It was there, in 609 BC, that Pharaoh Necho II arrested Jehoahaz, King of Judah (2 Kgs. 23:33-4). After the conquest of *Jerusalem by the Chaldees (586 BC) Zedekiah, King of Judah, his sons and his ministers were brought there to be judged before Nebuchadnezzar (2 Kgs. 25:6, 20-1, etc.). Identified with Ribleh, on the east bank of the Orontes, about 20 miles south of Homs.

RIMMON *a)* A town on the northern border of the territory of Zebulun (Josh. 19:13) given to the Levites (1 Chr. 6:77). It is frequently mentioned in talmudic literature. It is identified with er-Rumane, 6 miles north of *Nazareth.

b) A town in the territory of Zebulun (Josh. 19:13), identified with er-Rumane, north of *Nazareth.

ROADS Many terms are used in the Hebrew Bible to refer to roads. Some are merely synonyms, while others distinguish particular types of road. Thus there are references to a highway in 2 Samuel (20:12-13) and in Isaiah (62:10), where the text specifies a road cleared of stones, with signposts to direct those who used it. Another term in the Hebrew is *maagal* (Isa. 26:7; Prov. 4:26; Ps 140:5), which may be understood to denote a road for wheeled vehicles, but is translated in the Authorized Version as 'path' or 'wayside'. The *orah* of Isaiah (30:11; 33:8) is variously rendered in the Authorized Version as 'path' and 'highway'. The English text thus loses many of the finer distinctions of the Hebrew terms.

Roads, as a means by which hamlets were connected with the fields, villages with central towns, towns with capitals, countries and continents, had their beginnings in remote times. Even the greatest highways began as small, winding paths used only by pedestrians, at the most accompanied by beasts of burden. As transport developed, however, roads became a matter of public concern. For many thousands of years preparing a road consisted solely of clearing the path of boulders, placing them at the side of the road and filling the larger holes. Road construction in the full sense of the term belongs mainly to much later periods. It is possible that some roads, such as those that crossed private property, were fenced in order to prevent trespassing, and this may perhaps explain the passage in Numbers (20:14-19) in which the Israelites ask the King of *Edom for permission to cross his country.

In the Canaanite period, and in the days of Solomon and his successors in the kingdom of Israel, the use of chariots in warfare (*Weapons and warfare) may have created a need for better roads, and even for paved surfaces over marshy ground. There is no evidence in the Bible for this, however. Josephus, writing about the building of the Temple by Solomon, mentions paths paved with black stones leading to *Jerusalem (*Antiq.* VIII, 187), but this must certainly relate to the historian's own time rather than to the time of the First Temple. Evidence concerning road construction in the earlier period is ambiguous. A document of the time of the New Kingdom of *Egypt reports that the dangerous passes near the Nahr el-Kalb, near Beirut, were excavated in order to make the crossing safer. On the other hand another Egyptian source of the 19th Dynasty refers to bad roads that were unfit for use by chariots. Mesha, King of *Moab, records in his stele (*Inscriptions) that he had made a road through the valley of the *Arnon River.

The *Hittites boast of a 'great way to the west', connecting their capital with the Aegean. This should not necessarily be taken to mean a constructed roadway, but may well refer to an ordinary road from which stones had been cleared, possibly with some excavation in the hillier parts in order to facilitate the passage of wagons. The Egyptian pharaohs, notably Tuthmosis III, who made frequent military excursions into Palestine and Syria, may have marked the roads that were used by their large armies in some way. The 'king's highway', which passed over the Transjordanian plateau, was possibly one of these (Num. 20:17-19). 'King's roads' are also referred to in the *El Amarna letters, on one of which a king describes his travels along all the king's roads. On the stretch of road leading from Qantarah to el-Arish (Rhinocorura), one of the most difficult sections of the Via Maris, Sethos I of Egypt established eight halts, each defended by a fort and provided with a water reservoir. No evidence is available in the sources concerning road construction in Palestine itself.

The first constructed roads in Palestine go back to the Persian and Hellenistic periods, when heavier machinery was used in warfare. But the great age of road-building began in the Roman period. Long sections of nicely paved road, protected by curbstones and marked by inscribed milestones, have been discovered throughout Palestine. The inscriptions specify the name of the emperor by whose order the road was constructed, the official in charge of the work and the distance in Roman miles from the capital of the district concerned.

INTERNATIONAL HIGHWAYS From earliest times Palestine was at the crossroads of the main arteries connecting the large empires of the ancient Near East, such as those between *Egypt and the south and Syria, Assyria, *Babylon and Asia Minor in the north and northeast. Most of these roads converged on Aleppo, the point at which the *Euphrates flows closest to the Mediterranean. One of these highways ran from the coast of the Aegean to Aleppo, and from there along the *Euphrates to *Nineveh and *Babylon. A journey from Palestine to *Mesopotamia in early times necessitated travelling as far north as Aleppo, and thence on the road to the east. Only after the domestication of the camel was it possible to take a short cut from *Damascus straight through the Syrian desert to *Mesopotamia, thus avoiding a very long detour. The documents of *Mari, of the 19th century BC, mention a caravan coming from *Qatna in Syria to *Mari on the middle *Euphrates, possibly through *Tadmor, a very important halt for caravans before the desert crossing. At *Tadmor this road joined another one, between *Damascus and the *Euphrates. This route was in use as early as the 2nd millennium BC. Another major international thoroughfare ran from southern Babylonia to *Edom, the Gulf of *Elath, and thence along the western coast of *Arabia down to the Yemen.

ROADS IN PALESTINE Several roads are mentioned in the Bible, some of which were of international importance. One such was the 'way of the sea' (Isa. 9:1), connecting *Egypt with *Babylon. This went through western *Sinai and thence along the coast of the land of the Philistines. A branch of this road passed close to the coast and was known in the Bible as 'the way of the land of the Philistines' (Exod. 13:17); it ran from

*Gaza to *Ashdod and *Joppa. To avoid the marshland of the *Sharon it then turned eastwards from *Joppa to reach *Aphek, and from there followed the foothills to the pass of Wadi Ara, Iron, *Aruboth and *Megiddo.

This road is also known as the Via Maris. From *Megiddo it divided into three: the northern branch went from *Megiddo to *Jokneam, *Acshaph, *Acre, *Tyre, *Sidon and along the Syrian coast to Anatolia; the northeastern branch went to the Sea of *Galilee and via *Ijon and *Kedesh (Naphtali) to Syria and *Mesopotamia; the third branch went from *Megiddo to Jezreel, *Beth-Shean and across the River *Jordan to *Damascus. There were also other roads connecting *Egypt to Palestine. The second major route known from the Bible was, as we have seen, the 'king's highway' (Num. 20:17), which ran from *Arabia up to the head of the Gulf of *Elath and thence northeastwards to *Edom (2 Kgs. 3:8), 'the way through the wilderness of Edom ', and on to *Rabbath-Ammon and *Damascus, where it merged with the 'way of the sea'.

In addition to these international thoroughfares there was a network of secondary roads connecting them. From *Memphis, for instance, at the base of the *Nile Delta, a road crossed the *Sinai desert to touch the heads of the Gulfs of Suez and *Elath. Another secondary road passed through northern *Sinai to *Kadesh-Barnea and the *Negev to join the 'king's highway'.

Many local roads are mentioned by name in the Bible, the names generally referring to their destinations. Some of the more important, from south to north, were: the 'way of the mountain of the Amorites' (Deut. 1:19), a road which traversed the central

The ascent of Beth-Horon

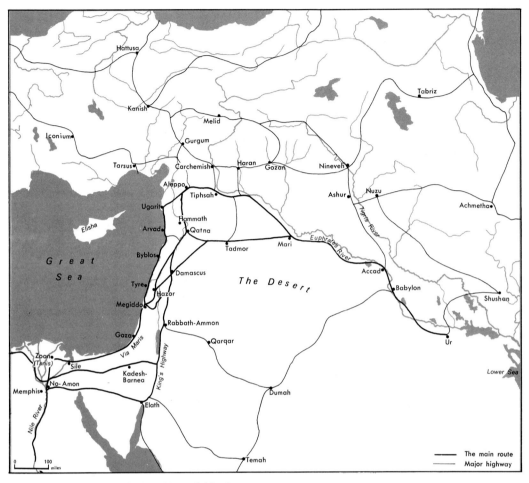

International routes in the Near East in biblical times

part of the *Negev; the 'way of the Red Sea' (Num. 14:25), leading along the Arabah, from *Elath to *Tamar; the 'way of the spies' (Exod. 21:1), leading from *Arad to *Hormah and thence southwards; the 'way of Shur' (Gen. 16:7, etc.), possibly a section of the road going along the northern part of the central *Negev; the 'way through the wilderness of *Edom' (2 Kgs. 3:8), leading from *Arad to the *Dead Sea and southwards; the 'way of Ephrath' (Gen. 35:16), from *Hebron to *Bethlehem, *Jerusalem and northwards to *Samaria; the 'way of *Beth-Shemesh' (1 Sam. 6:9), a road connecting the Via Maris with the 'way of Ephrath'; the 'way of the plain of Meonenim' (Judg. 9:37), the continuation northwards of the 'way of Ephrath'; the 'way of the Jordan' (Josh 2:7) and the 'way of the plain' (2 Sam. 18:23), one following the west bank of the *Jordan while the other ran parallel to it on the east; the 'way up to Beth-Horon' (Josh. 10:10; 1 Sam. 13:18) from Jabneel (*Jabneh) to Gittaim, *Gezer and *Michmash through the ascent of

Lower and Upper *Beth-Horon; the 'way of Beth-Hagan' (2 Kgs. 9:27, Authorized Version: 'the way of the garden house'), along the northern part of the hills of *Samaria.

Few basic changes were introduced into the road system of Palestine in the Roman and Byzantine periods. In the early Roman period two major highways crossed Palestine from south to north. One began at *Alexandria in *Egypt and ran northwards to *Gaza, Ascalon (*Ashkelon), Lydda (*Lod), with a branch to *Joppa and on to Antipatris (*Aphek), *Caesarea, Dora (*Dor), *Acre (*Acco) and *Tyre, and further north to *Antioch on the Orontes, thus coinciding with the biblical Via Maris. The other went from Aila (*Elath) to Philadelphia (*Rabbath-Ammon), Bostra (*Bozrah) and *Damascus. This route was fully paved and had bridges over the rivers; it coincides with the original, 'king's highway'. It was constructed in the years AD 111-14 and renamed the Via Nova Traiana, after the emperor who ordered its construction. There

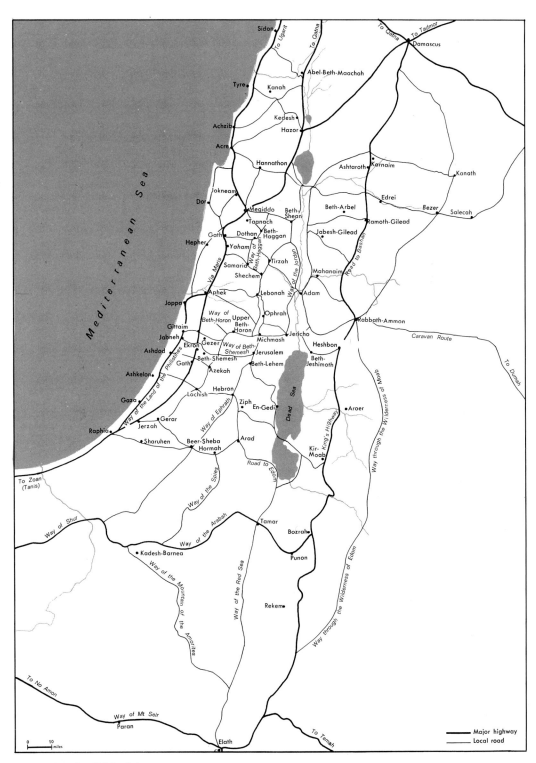

Holyland roads of biblical times

was also a very intricate network of inland roads, the more important being the one that connected *Hebron, *Jerusalem. *Gophnah, Neapolis (*Shechem), *Legio and *Acco, and the one from Neapolis to Scythopolis (*Beth-Shean), and thence to *Damascus. Another road went from *Acco to *Tiberias. The *Negev was intersected by a network of roads constructed by the *Nabateans. One ran from *Petra to *Gaza, via *Oboda and *Elusa, and another from *Elath through the Arabah, *Mampsis and *Beer-Sheba to *Gaza, with a branch from *Mampsis to *Hebron and Jerusalem. Many of the Roman and Byzantine roads were wide, paved, marked with milestones and even provided with road stations.

ROME (EASTERN PROVINCES)

THE PROVINCE OF ASIA In 133 BC Attalus III of Pergamon bequeathed his kingdom to the Roman people, and it was made a *provincia* by M. Aquilius. Asia was a rich country, with its own natural resources, agriculture and industry; it was, furthermore, a center for trade between the Far East and the West. The Romans, their governors and the equestrian tax-collectors exploited this wealth unscrupulously. In consequence the Greek inhabitants allied themselves with Mithridates VI, King of Pontus, in 88-84 BC, and 80,000 Italian residents were killed in one day. It was Sulla who, in 84 BC, reorganized the province and especially the system of taxation. During the civil wars in Rome in the 1st century BC Asia was still subjected to extortion. With the foundation of the principate, order and prosperity returned. Asia became a senatorial province of Rome with a proconsul as governor, who resided at Ephesus and was assisted by three *legates* (ambassadors) and a *quaestor* (treasurer). In the first two centuries of the empire Asia enjoyed great prosperity, signs of which are still visible in the surviving architectural monuments.

Roman milestone on the Jerusalem—Beth-Gubrin (Eleutheropolis) road

Asia consisted of many city territories. Several had been autonomous in the Attalid period and a few held titular freedom under the Romans. Under the authority of the governor the cities were administered by their own magistrates and councils. These were assisted by *logistes*, chosen by the emperor, who controlled the city finances. A General Assembly of the cities (*Commune Asiae*) met every day in a different city to arrange for the official worship of Rome and Augustus and to deal with the organization of games and festivals and the drawing up of petitions for presentation to the emperor on matters of administration. Originally the province consisted of Mysia, Lydia, Ionia and Caria. Phrygia was given to Mithridates VI and not incorporated until after 116 BC.

From 49 BC to AD 297 Asia included all the territory from Tyriaion to the sea, with the adjacent islands. It was bounded on the north by Bythinia, on the south by Lycia and on the east (after 25 BC) by the province of Galatia. In AD 297 Diocletian divided Asia into seven provinces, including areas that had previously been separate provinces. Asia's prosperity declined in the economic retrogression of the 3rd and 4th centuries AD that resulted from civil strife and invasions by border peoples. Its participation in international trade ceased with the interruption of its trade with India and China.

THE PROVINCE OF MESOPOTAMIA For a long period this was the battleground of the Parthian and Roman armies, until it was conquered by Trajan and made a province in AD 114-17. The Romans were never able to hold it for long. After it had been abandoned by Hadrian, the Romans made two further attempts to overrun it, once under Lucius Verus in AD 162-5 and once under Septimius Severus in AD 197-9. But it was never permanently occupied. In AD 284 Diocletian made a pact with Bahram, the Sassanid king, who gave Armenia and *Mesopotamia to the Romans. Diocletian strengthened the border with a *Limes* that included a wall and a chain of forts.

THE PROVINCE OF SYRIA AND JUDEA Syria, once the heart of the Seleucid power, was occupied by Tigranes of Armenis in 83 BC, and on his defeat was made a province by Pompey in 64/63 BC. He restored limited autonomy to a great number of the Hellenistic cities on the coast and inland (*Decapolis) that had been conquered by the Hasmoneans. But they were still subject to the governor of Syria, so that the province comprised these cities, the client kingdoms of Commagene and *Nabatea, the Jewish ethnarchy, the tetrarchy of the Itureans and many small territories in the north. Under the Principate Syria was until AD 70 an important military command with a consular legate and four legions, often held by outstanding men at the end of their career. All the client kingdoms were gradually annexed to the province: Commagene in AD 72; part of Iturea in 24 BC and the remainder with Agrippa II's kingdom in AD 93; Judea became a separate province in AD 70; and the Nabatean kingdom was annexed in AD 106. Judea had been divided on Herod's death between his sons, who ruled as ethnarchs, supervised by procurators. After the fall of *Jerusalem in AD 70, it was made a separate province, under a

Theodosius I, last emperor of the whole Roman empire

praetorian legate who resided at *Caesarea. A legion was withdrawn from Syria and stationed in *Jerusalem, the Legio X Fretensis. A road was constructed between the civil and military headquarters, *Caesarea and *Jerusalem.

After the *Bar-Kochba Revolt (AD 132-4) the province of Judea was added to Syria, which became known as Provincia Syria-Palestina. This province was a predominantly rural area with a comparatively small number of cities, though under the Roman Empire the number of newly founded cities grew. Its exports consisted of agricultural products: wine from the coast (Laodicea, Berytus, *Gaza, Ascalon [Ashkelon]); various fruits and vegetables, such as plums from *Damascus and dates from the *Jericho region, *Phasaelis and *Archelais, and onions from Ascalon. The main industries were linen-weaving (at Laodicea, Scythopolis [*Beth-Shean] and several other Phoenician and north Palestinian towns); wool-weaving at *Damascus; silk at *Tyre; purple dyeing on the Phoenician and Palestinian coast; and glass-blowing at *Sidon. There were iron mines at Germanicia; marble was quarried at *Sidon; bitumen (*Asphalt) came from the *Dead Sea; and there are records concerning soldiers quarrying at Enesh.

Syria-Palestina, being a rural region, was an important recruiting ground for local and other legions and their auxiliary units. After the time of Hadrian the oriental element in the Roman army increased. Information about the legions stationed in Syria can be obtained from a number of historians and from the

'Judaea Capta' coin

military inscriptions found in the area. In AD 23 Tacitus (*Ann.* 4:5) enumerates four legions: Legio III Gallica, Legio VI Ferrata, Legio X Fretensis and Legio XII Fulminata. In AD 66, on the eve of the Jewish Revolt, seven legions were stationed there, the three additional ones being the Legio IV Scythica, Legio V Macedonia and Legio XV Apollonia (Josephus, *War* II, 366ff.) After the destruction of the Temple the Legio X Fretensis was stationed at *Jerusalem; its roof-tile factory was found at Givat Ram (about 3 miles west of the ancient city) and a bath at *Ramat Rahel. Shortly before the Bar-Kochba Revolt, in the suppression of which at least five legions participated, two legions were transferred from *Egypt, the Legio II Triana, which returned afterwards to *Egypt and the Legion XXII Deiotriana, which perished in the war. The Legion XII Fulminata, having suffered severe defeats, was soon transferred to Cappadocia. Units of these legions helped to repair the aqueduct at *Caesarea in the time of Hadrian.

In about AD 200 Septimius Severus divided the province of Syria-Palestina into a northern province with two legions (Coelo-Syria) and a southern part (Syria-*Phoenicia). To this period belongs the evidence of Dio Cassius (LV, 23-5), who mentions four legions in Syria, including Judea, which was then part of Syria-*Phoenicia: the Legio IV Scythica, stationed at Cyrrhus or Zeugma, the Legio XVI Flavia, the Legio VI Ferrata, since Hadrian's time stationed at *Legio, and the Legio X Fretensis at *Jerusalem.

THE PROVINCE OF ARABIA Formed under Trajan, this province consisted mainly of the Nabatean kingdom, including in the north the *Hauran and some cities of the *Decapolis, in the west the *Negev, in the southeast Arabia Petrea and Arabia Felix, and in the center Transjordan. That the annexation took place without conquest can be seen from the evidence of Roman coins carrying the title Arabia *adquisita* ('acquired'), not *capta* ('conquered'). The capital was transferred from Petra to Bostra (*Bozrah), which became the legislative and administrative center. A legion was stationed there, firstly the Legio VI Ferrata but this was replaced under Hadrian by the Legio III Cyrenaica. At the end of the 3rd century AD another legion was added: the X Fretensis was transferred from *Jerusalem to Aila (*Elath). The era of the province began in AD 106, and an internal organization was immediately set up to deal with the provision and conservation of water supplies, land cultivation, the foundation of new cities and assistance for older ones. The greatest undertaking was the construction of a new road, the Via Traiana Nova, whose purpose was as much commercial as strategic, connecting as it did Syria with the *Red Sea; it passed through *Damascus, Bostra (*Bozrah) and Philadelphia (*Rabbath-Ammon).

RUHEIBEH (KHIRBET ER-) A site in the northwestern part of the central *Negev, lying in a gap in the midst of three large sand dunes that stretch from the sea to the *Beer-Sheba-Nessana road. Because of the similarity in name, many scholars have suggested identifying er-Ruheibeh with the *Rehoboth of Isaac, but as no remains of a period earlier than the Roman have been found here this identification cannot be upheld. The ancient name of the site is thus unknown. The *Nessana papyri provide several place-names for which there is no identification, and it is possible that one of these names applies to Ruheibeh. This suggestion is supported by the fact that all the other Nabatean towns of the central *Negev — *Nessana, *Sobata, *Oboda (Eboda in the papyri), *Mampsis and *Elusa — are specifically mentioned.

Lying on the well-trodden track connecting *Jerusalem, *Hebron and *Beer-Sheba, via *Elusa and *Nessana to *Egypt, er-Ruheibeh nearby was visited by every scholar who took this route. The first was E. Robinson (1838), who saw what he identified as a *weli* (sheikh's tomb) at the eastern end of the town. Robinson underestimated the extent of the remains, judging them to cover 10-12 acres. He observed outlines of houses and of streets and recorded that the houses were well built, each having at least one cistern constructed of stones. A large pile of ruins, he thought, represented the site of a church. Because of what he took to be a sheikh's tomb, he assumed that the town had also been settled after the Arab conquest. E.H. Palmer (1870) identified Robinson's *weli* as a wellhouse in view of the deep well that he discovered nearby. This, he suggested, was the well of Sitnah, which Isaac dug near *Gerar (Gen. 26:21). Close to it he saw a large building which he identified as a church. It is now thought to have been a çaravanserai. A. Musil, the best of the early surveyors, could not spare more than a day for er-Ruheibeh (in 1902). He therefore concentrated on drawing plans and describing a single building — the *weli* of Musil, or the 'well-house' of Palmer — which he identified correctly as a bath. There is good reason to be grateful to Musil, because a few years later the Turks destroyed this building in order to erect a police post in its place. Musil refers to er-Ruheibeh as a walled town. N. Schmidt and B.B. Charles, who visited the site a few years later (1905), were lucky to discover the local cemetery, where they found many epitaphs dating from AD 536 to 601. C.L. Woolley and T.E. Lawrence (1914) were of the opinion that the settlement dated to the Byzantine period. They discovered that the town had no wall but that, to compensate for this, the outer walls of the houses and the gardens had been arranged as to form a continuous line, thus affording some protection, as at *Sobata. According to them the town measured 336 yards by 400 yards, which would give an area of some 60 acres — too high an estimate. Of the town itself they said that it was well planned and built. Its roads intersected at right angles, with small squares at the intersections. Close to the bath they discovered a pool measuring 75 feet by 60 feet. They also noted remains of two churches, one in the center of the town and the other to the west. While visiting the site they saw the Turks cleaning the ancient well, which they plumbed to a depth of over 300 feet.

Woolley's and Lawrence's survey was the last to be made at er-Ruheibeh. None of the scholars published any plan of the town, nor was any pottery mentioned. We thus have only a very vague idea of the town and its periods of occupation. During his years of work at

*Mampsis A. Negev visited er-Ruheibeh several times. He found a striking resemblance to the Nabatean buildings of *Mampsis. He believes that the first settlement of this site was in the late Nabatean period, probably after the annexation of the central *Negev to the Provincia Arabia in AD 106. It is also possible that the site was occupied by the Romans, who may have settled army veterans there. No Nabatean pottery has been found on the surface, which may indicate that it was the only town of the central *Negev that was not settled by the *Nabateans in the 1st century BC or the 1st century AD. The quality of the masonry and the stone-dressing are all typical of the late Nabatean period. For the Byzantine period there is evidence of the epitaphs of the 6th century AD. But no evidence has been found of an occupation after the Arab conquest of AD 634-6.

Excavations: In the years 1975-9 the site was excavated by Y. Tzafrir (in the first two seasons with R. Rosenthal) on behalf of the Hebrew University. On the surface lay *Nabatean *pottery of the late 1st century BC-1st century AD. A deep well is ascribed to this period, and possibly also a large open reservoir in the southern slope of the site. It is assumed that Ruheibeh was at that time a caravan halt on a secondary route leading to *Sinai by way of Rhinocorura. In the central part of the city a large building was partly excavated, with a stable of the *Mampsis type. Also found were a bilingual Nabatean-Greek inscription and a 'classic' Nabatean capital. This building, possibly a caravanserai, 90 feet square, had a large central court containing a cistern. It is apparently of the late Nabatean period (2nd century AD). Below the floors of this building was middle Nabatean pottery (1st century AD). The town attained its maximal size in the Byzantine period, extending over an area of 22 acres. The dwellings were spacious but were built close together (unlike *Mampsis). In the center of the town was erected the Central Church, possibly in the late 4th or early 5th century AD. It is a single-apsed basilica, 60 feet by 36 feet. At least in its eastern part the building was supported by vaulted substructures. It was paved with large slabs of marble and the altar was covered by a baldachin. In the fill beneath the south aisle were found decorated building stones, perhaps from a late Roman temple (late Nabatean). Two additional churches were located outside the built-up area, one in the south, in the vicinity of the well, and another — the North Church — in the north. The North Church, a triapsidal building, is one of the largest and most ornate in the Negev. The basilica ($75^1/_2$ feet by 40 feet) is preceded by a spacious atrium. Underneath the place of the altar was a crypt (12 feet by 17 feet), built of ashlars and faced with marble. Around the church were additional chapels and rooms of a monastery, one, an oblong hall, possibly the refectory. Like some of the other large churches of the Negev, it too may have been a center of pilgrimage. An outstanding discovery are small glass plaques decorated with images of saints, which were possibly inlays of a large cross. In the church graveyard and in the large cemetery adjoining it were found numerous Greek inscriptions, the earliest of 488 and the latest of 555.

S

SAFI (TELL ES-) A large mound in the Shephelah (*Plain[The]), halfway between *Gezer and *Lachish, it has been variously identified, the current theory identifying it with *Gath of the *Philistines. (*See also* TELL *SHEIKH EL-AREINI.) The site was excavated in 1898-1900 by F.J. Bliss and R.A.S. Macalister on behalf of the Palestine Exploration Fund. The excavators traced sections of the city wall, the building of which they attributed to the 'Jewish' (Iron Age) period. The wall, 12 feet thick, with a rubble foundation and a mud-brick superstructure, had a series of buttresses projecting 2 feet from it (*Fortifications). On the northwestern part of the mound a trial pit, 80 feet by 60 feet, was excavated down to bedrock, accumulation being about 30 feet thick. In the uppermost level remains of the Crusader castle of Blanche-Garde were discovered. Below this this excavators distinguished three more occupation levels, in two of which were building remains. Using the pottery as a criterion they dated the two earliest levels to a 'pre-Israelite' and a 'Late pre-Israelite' period respectively. The beginning of occupation on the site they dated to the 17th century BC. To the second phase of this period they attributed a 'high place', which was most probably a normal dwelling. The third stratum from below was 'Jewish', 700-550 BC according to their dating. This stratum contained *lamelek*-type seals and also Greek pottery, which they dated to 550-350 BC. The dating of the earliest level was much too high: the 'pre-Israelite' level is now dated to 3000-1800 BC; the 'Late pre-Israelite' one to 1800-1000 BC; and the 'Jewish' one to 1000-587 BC.

SAFIT (TEL) *See* *SAFI (TELL ES-)

SAHBA (CAVE) This cave is in Wadi Djihar, which flows southwards through the *Judean Desert parallel to Wadi Abu Sif. Two Mousterian layers were found during excavations carried out by R. Neuville: they were rich in both straight and curved elongated Mousterian points, which were similar to those found in *Abu Sif Cave. According to the excavator the uppermost layer (B) indicated an evolution of the Abu Sif assemblage. (*See also* *PREHISTORY; *FLINT TOOLS.)

SAIDIYE (TELL ES-) A large mound to the east of the River *Jordan, half-way between the Sea of *Galilee and the *Dead Sea. In 1942 the site was surveyed by N. Glueck, who identified it with biblical *Zare-than. In the years 1964-6 the site was excavated by J. Pritchard on behalf of the University Museum of the University of Pennsylvania. On a low bench of the mound a necropolis was in use during the transitional period between the Late Bronze Age and Iron Age I. One tomb, of a single burial, contained a bronze wine set (laver, bowl, strainer and juglet), a bronze tripod, storage jars, 751 beads of gold and carnelian, two electrum pendants, two electrum toggle pins, five ivory cosmetic containers, a bronze caldron, a bronze lamp and other vessels. Other tombs contained skeletons wrapped in cloth covered with bitumen. On the northern side of the mound was discovered a stairway, originally consisting of 140 stairs, leading down to the water source. On the northwest side of the mound were observed four levels of occupation. Level IV, contained ten houses built of mud brick; one, with an altar table and *cult objects, was probably a shrine. Level III continued the plan of the previous level. In Level II, dated by the pottery to the middle of the 8th century BC, there were twelve houses of identical plan and size, facing two parallel streets, six on each street. Each house consisted of a large, paved room at the front, and a smaller room at the back. In Level I, the latest occupation on the site, the area was covered with threshing floors and numerous storage bins. All the levels of occupation are of the Iron Age. On the acropolis was a palace (65 feet square) from the Persian period. In the Hellenistic period the palace was replaced by a fortress. From the Roman period were found a tower and two plastered water reservoirs.

SALCHAH An important city on the eastern border of the *Bashan, in the former kingdom of Og, which was conquered by Moses (Deut. 3:10; Josh. 12:5; 13:11) and given to half the tribe of Manasseh (Deut. 3:13). It was on the border of the territory of Gad (1 Chr. 5:11). Eusebius (*Onom.* 154:15, 156.2) knew it by the name of Salcha. In the Hellenistic-Roman period a large village under the name of Triakome flourished there. In surface surveys numerous Greek and Nabatean inscriptions were discovered, and also fragments of Nabatean architecture. Much of the ancient city was ruined when the modern Druze village of Salkhad was built.

SALEM; SHALEM *a)* The city of Melchizedek (Gen. 14:18), possibly named after a deity mentioned in documents of *Ugarit and *Mesopotamia. Identified by Jewish tradition with *Jerusalem.

b) A place near *Shechem, where Jacob built an altar to God (Gen. 33:18-20). The Valley of Salem is possibly named after the site (Judith 4:4); the road from *Jerusalem to *Samaria passed through this valley. The name of the site has apparently been preserved in the modern village Salem, some 2 miles east of Tel *Shechem.

SALIM A place in the *Jordan Valley, near Aenon, where John baptized people (John 3:23). Eusebius (*Onom.* 40:3) states that Saleim is situated 8 miles from *Beth-Shean, near the Jordan, in the vicinity of *Aenon. It is marked on the *Medaba map, and was visited by pilgrims in the Byzantine period. Identified with Tell Abu Sus, about 5 miles south of *Beth-Shean. Others still identify Salim, which was located near Aenon, with a large tell east of *Shechem, where architectural remains of the Roman period were found. It is situated at a short distance from the copious springs of Wadi Faria, to which some believe, the 'much water' of John 3:25-30 refers.

SALT The use of salt goes back to early prehistoric times, and it has always been considered to be one of the vital elements of human food. The ancient world valued the savor it gave to food (Job 6:6) and it was consumed in considerable quantities (Ezra 6:9). It was also a necessary ingredient in sacrifices (Lev. 2:13; Ezek. 43:24). In the rituals connected with signing an agreement the consumption of food with salt was an essential part, symbolizing the union between the parties involved; and it was thus referred to as 'salt of the covenant', or 'a covenant of salt forever' (Lev. 2:13; Num. 18:19). A 'land of brimstone and salt' was a barren land (Deut. 29:23,etc.); sowing a city with salt therefore meant its utter destruction (Judg. 9:45). Therapeutic qualities were ascribed to salt. For instance, new-born babies were sprinkled with it (Ezek. 16:4); and Elisha used it to heal the water of the spring of *Jericho (2 Kgs. 2:20ff.).

Salt was one of the main items of international trade. The chief deposits in Palestine were in the *Dead Sea region. Huge quantities of salt were extracted from Mount *Sodom, a mountain 4 miles long and of pure salt (cf. Zeph. 2:9), and collected in the marshes (Ezek. 47:11). It was also obtained by running seawater from the Mediterranean into cavities of the rocks near the coast, and then letting it evaporate.

During the Hellenistic period and later salt was much used, not only as a seasoning but also in the preservation of foods, especially meat and fish. Pickling of fish was much praised along the shores of the Sea of *Galilee, which has excellent fish (*Magdala). Much pickling was also done along the shores of the Mediterranean and in the Gulf of *Elath. This may well explain the presence of the quantities of fish bones found among kitchen refuse on many sites in the *Negev and in Transjordan.

SAMARIA; SHOMRON Samaria, biblical Shomron in Hebrew, was the capital of the ancient kingdom of Israel. Built on a hill about 300 feet above the surrounding fertile agricultural area, the city occupies a strategic point that gives access in three directions: in the west to the coastal plain; in the east to *Shechem (modern Nablus) and from there to the River *Jordan or to *Jerusalem; and in the north to *Megiddo and the *Jezreel Valley.

According to 1 Kings (16:24) the hill was purchased by Omri, King of Israel, from a man named Shemer (hence Shomron) for 2 talents of silver. Omri made it his capital, moving to it from *Tirza. Omri's son Ahab, the next king, put up an altar for Baal in the house of Baal' in Samaria (1 Kgs. 16:32) under the influence of his Phoenician wife Jezebel. Phoenician influence is also indicated in Ahab's 'ivory house' (1 Kgs. 22:39), his palace, where the furniture and perhaps the walls were embellished with ivory plaques. During this period the city was threatened by the *Arameans of *Damascus, who attacked it several times but could not conquer it (1 Kgs. 20:1 ff.; 2 Kgs. 6:24 ff.; Authorized Version: 'Syria'). Omri's dynasty ended with the revolution of Jehu, the founder of the new dynasty, who destroyed Ahab's shrine (2 Kgs. 10:18-28). In the next century another shrine contained the 'calf of Samaria' (Hos.8:5-6). Of the two shrines, no remains have been found during excavations. In the time of Jeroboam II 'houses of ivory' and 'beds of ivory' are again mentioned (Amos 3:15; 6:4). His death brought to an end a period of prosperity for the kingdom of Israel. The Assyrians began to threaten. Samaria withstood the Assyrian attack for three years (725-722 BC) until it was captured and many of its citizens were deported (2 Kgs. 17:6).

According to the Bible, the city fell in the last months of Shalmaneser V (2 kgs. 18:9-10) who died in 722 BC, but Assyrian records show that Sargon II claimed this victory. The city became the center of administration for the Assyrian province of Samerina. New settlers of different origin were brought to the country and the city (2 Kgs. 17:24), each worshiping his own god (2 Kgs. 17:29). Under Persian rule (6th -4th centuries BC) it remained a provincial capital.

After their return from the Babylonian exile, when the Jews began to rebuild the Temple in *Jerusalem, the Samaritans, with their center at *Shechem, offered help. The antagonism that existed between the Jews and the Samaritans in the next centuries (Ezra 4; Neh. 2) originated in the refusal of their offer.

In the second half of the 5th century BC the governor of the province of Samaria was named Sanballat (Neh. 2:10, 19). This same governor and his sons are also known from the papyri of the Jewish community at *Elephantine in *Egypt. During the 4th century BC the Samaritans built their center at Samaria. In 332 BC it was captured by Alexander the Great, who settled Macedonian veterans there. Then in 108 BC it was conquered and utterly destroyed by John Hyrcanus (Josephus, *War* I, 164) and the Hasmoneans imposed Judaism on its Samaritan inhabitants. In 63 BC Pompey annexed Samaria to the Roman province of Syria (Josephus, *War* I, 56). The city underwent considerable reconstruction under Gabinus in 57-55 BC (Josephus, *War* I, 166). Augustus gave it to Herod, who renamed it Sebaste in honor of the emperor, and his building activities made it one of the most magnificent cities in Palestine (Josephus, *Antiq.* XV, 217, 292, 296-7). During the First Jewish Revolt it was destroyed, but was soon afterwards rebuilt. Septimius Severus gave it the status of *colonia* in AD 200. In the late Roman period the city declined and it was no more than an unimportant village in the Byzantine period. A popular Christian tradition placed the tomb of St. John the Baptist at Samaria and several churches were constructed there for this reason, the latest by the Crusaders in the 12th century.

Extensive excavations of the site were conducted in 1908-10 by Harvard University, under the direction of G.A. Reisner and C.S. Fisher, and in 1931-5 a joint expedition with the participation of British institutions, the Hebrew Univeristy and Harvard University. ISRAELITE PERIOD UNTIL THE ASSYRIAN CONQUEST The Israelite settlement consisted of an acropolis and the lower city, each with a separate system of fortifications. While much is known about the acropolis, the lower city remained unexplored and nothing is known about its true extent, though most scholars think that it was no smaller than the area surrounded by the Roman town wall. On the acropolis two walls were found. The first, according to the excavators the 'inner wall', surrounded the summit of the hill, encircling an area extending 194yds from east to west and 106yds from north to south. It was about 5 feet thick and its stones were laid in header-and-stretcher formation. Within this walled area several buildings were discovered. In the west, near the southern wall, was a building thought to have been the palace of the Israelite kings, measuring about 89 feet by 79 feet, with a central court. To the north of the acropolis wall traces of another wall were found. According to the joint expedition this 'outer wall', was also built by Omri. It seems that this system of fortification was not strong enough and that Ahab therefore built new and stronger defences. His was a casemate wall, on the north, west and part of the south side; it extended the walled area on the north and west. On the north the wall is 33 feet wide, the outer side of the casemate being 6 feet thick and the inner about 3 feet. On the west it is 16 feet 16in wide. The southern side of the wall is built on bedrock, only its western part being built of casemates, while the rest is solid. At the southwestern corner a large building was found, and some scholars believe that there was a gateway here. The eastern side of the acropolis wall was not identified. In this area three proto-Aeolic capitals were found, and it is possible that the main entrance to the acropolis was at this spot. In the west, between the 'inner wall' and the casemate wall, was a storehouse measuring 59 feet by 92 feet, and known as the 'House of the Ostracons' because of the ostraca found there. In the northwestern corner a pool measuring 33 feet by $16^{1}/_{2}$ feet was unearthed. On the eastern side of the summit remains of Israelite building, probably the city gate, were discovered.

Six phases of pottery and six periods of building were observed between 876 and 722 BC: layer I (Omri), construction of palace and inner wall of the acropolis; layer II (Ahab), casemate walls, stores and possibly eastern gate; layer III (Jehu and his successors),

casemate walls in continuation, use of existing houses and building of new ones; layer IV (Jeroboam II), repairs to casemate wall, changes in existing buildings and construction of new ones; and layers V-VI, alterations and repairs. A layer of ashes is attributed to the Assyrian conquest in 722 BC.

Opinions differ about the first two periods, which are decisive for the dating of the pottery. Miss Kenyon believes that the sherds of period I, which were found in the buildings of this period, are from vessels brought to Samaria by Omri's builders. Others (W.F. Albright, Y. Aharoni, R. Amiran and G.E. Wright) point out that the pottery from the fill of buildings from periods I and II is earlier than the buildings themselves and, on the basis of typological comparisons with other sites (*Archaeology, methods of research), should be dated to the 10th and beginning of the 9th centuries BC. This would prove that there was a small settlement on the hill when Omri bought it.

Two groups of small finds of this period deserve special mention: the ostraca and the ivory plaques. The ostraca are dated to the reign of Jeroboam II or to that of Menahem and appear to be records of taxes of various kinds, or contributions from the lessees of the royal domain. They are written in the ancient Hebrew

Tower from the Hellenistic period, Samaria

script and follow a regular pattern, giving a date, the name of the official or the owner of the estate and the name of the sender. All the places mentioned seem to be in the vicinity of the city of Samaria. This may indicate a centralized system for collecting contributions from a district, similar to the one organized for the whole country during the reign of Solomon (1 Kgs. 4:7). The ivories point to the wealth of the kingdom and show the influence of foreign cultures on the Israelite upper classes. Their style is Phoenician, but as some are unfinished it is possible that foreign craftsmen executed them in Samaria. Some of the ivories belong to the time of Ahab, but the majority are of the reign of Jeroboam II. Various decorative motifs are used: they include Egyptian themes depicting Horus and other gods; animals, such as the lion; floral decorations of various kinds; and one has a 'woman in the window'.

ASSYRIAN, BABYLONIAN AND PERSIAN PERIODS Little is known of these periods. It seems that Sargon did not destroy the fortifications, and they continued to be used. In the Persian period the summit was covered with agricultural soil that was brought from elsewhere, apparently for the garden of the Persian governor's palace. However, no traces of such a palace were found. A group of papyri discovered by P.W. Lapp in the caves of Wadi Daliyeh in the *Jordan valley, east of Samaria, throws light on the life of the inhabitants during the 4th century BC. Deciphered by F.M. Cross, they date from about 375 to 335 BC and record transactions concerning property and land, loans, broken contracts (including divorce) and the sale, transfer and manumission (freeing) of slaves.

HELLENISTIC AND ROMAN PERIODS In the early Hellenistic period the old walls of the acropolis were still in use, though huge round towers were added, one of which is about 63 feet in diameter and is still standing to a height of about 27 feet. A new wall, enclosing an area of some 250 yards by 130 yards, was built around the acropolis in about the 2nd century BC. About 14 feet thick at its base and strengthened with rectangular towers, this is probably the wall that was destroyed by John Hyrcanus. In the Roman period the whole city was surrounded by a wall, which enclosed about 170 acres. The city gate was on the west and consisted of two massive round towers 46 feet in diameter. These towers stand on square bases of the Hellenistic period. A small part of the Hellenistic city wall has also been unearthed; it encloses an area smaller than that of the Roman period. Additions to the gate were made during the reign of Septimius Severus. Under him the colonnaded street was constructed, running from the

Carved ivory inlays found at Samaria

Basilica from the Roman period, Samaria

west to the east gate: 872 yards long and with 600 columns, it was about 40 feet wide and had shops on either side.

In the western part of the acropolis the residential quarter was found. This was most probably built during the time of Gabinius. Above it rising on the highest part of the hill Herod erected his magnificent temple dedicated to Augustus. The temple measured 115 feet by 79 feet with a spacious court in front; this rested on an artificial platform of 95 yards by 74 yards, supported by vaulted corridors. On the northern side the retaining wall of the platform was 16 feet 6in high. From the court the temple was approached by a wide flight of steps. The temple stood on a podium 14 feet higher than the court. This temple was destroyed, but was rebuilt by Septimius Severus to approximately the same plan. To this phase belongs a new flight of steps, extending the earlier ones, and the altar in the court in front of the temple. To the north of the temple of Augustus the remains of a Hellenistic temple to the goddess Kore were found. It measured about 11 feet by 51 feet and stood within a large *temenos* (enclosure). In its fill architectural fragments from an even earlier temple, of the 3rd century BC, were discovered. In the northeastern part of the lower city was a stadium, but only part of this was excavated. Two phases were observed, one belonging to Herod, the other to the 2nd century AD. On the northeastern slope of the acropolis a theater was excavated that belonged to the early 3rd century AD and was quite well preserved. The forum is situated to the east of the acropolis. It was erected on a platform measuring 139 yards by 74

yards. Adjoining it was a basilica built in the 2nd century AD. Traces of a Gabinian or Herodian basilica were also found. Near the forum are parts of the aqueduct that brought water into the city from the hills to the east. A mausoleum from the Roman period and tombs were found outside the city.

SAMIYA, EIN A vast cemetery extending over an area of about 2 miles between Dhahar Mirzbanah in the north and Khirbet Samiya in the south, on the border of the central mountain range and the Jordan Valley, east of Kfar Malik. The cemetery contains thousands of graves, most of them shaft tombs of the Middle Bronze Age I; others date to the Early Bronze Age and a small number to the Iron Age. These graves were partly damaged by tombs which were hewn among them in the Roman-Byzantine period.

The earliest excavations at the site were conducted by D.G. Lyon at the beginning of the 20th century. In 1963, P.W. Lapp explored the site and further investigations were made by Y. Meshorer in 1968. Excavations were renewed in 1970 by Z. Yeivin, Archaeological Officer, Judea and Samaria. He cleared 44 tombs, most of them dating to the Middle Bronze Age I.

The tombs excavated were found to be of similar plan. They consist of a round shaft, about 3 feet in diameter, which in some cases reached a depth of 20 feet. The descent to the bottom was made possible by cuts in the sides of the shaft. At the base were one or two caves, generally round in shape, from 6-9 feet in diameter. The caves contained more than one burial and numerous funerary objects. The mouths of the caves were blocked by flat circular stones. The shaft was then completely filled with stones and earth up to surface level and the entire tomb was thus tightly sealed.

The dead were laid on their backs, following the shape of the caves, but the head had no fixed orientation. Funerary objects were found alongside the deceased, usually around the head. They included numerous amphoriskoi of the Middle Bronze Age I. Some tombs also contained jugs, hole-mouth jars and small bowls of this period. In almost every tomb there were one or more four-spouted lamps. Some tombs also contained weapons and other metal objects.

In one of the tombs (No. 204) was found a goblet made of silver sheeting (about 1mm thick), in the form of a truncated cone, 3in high and about 2in in diameter. A large number of similar amphoriskoi and some weapons were also found in the tomb.

Frieze of silver cup from a tomb at Ein Samiya

Egyptian Scarab

The goblet was decorated in repoussé and portrays two scenes from the mythological world of Mesopotamia and northern Syria. One scene depicts a twelve-petalled rosette with a human face *en face* in its center. On either side of the rosette are two figures in profile, facing one another. Part of the right-hand figure is missing. The figures wear fringed skirts tied on the shoulder with a strap. They hold a crescent-shaped band under the rosette. Beneath the rosette and between the two figures lies a large twisting serpent. This scene may represent the division of heaven and earth following Marduk's victory over Tiamat.

The main figure in the second scene has a janiform face, hairy neck and human torso. The lower part of its body consists of the two hind parts of oxen. Between its legs is a small eight-petalled rosette. The arms of the central figure are outstretched and raised and hold a plant in each hand. To its right is a dragon standing on its tail. An identical creature was probably set symmetrically to the left of the central figure, but this part of the goblet is missing. The janiform figure may represent Marduk holding poison-repellant plants to counteract the venom-filled monsters set against him by Tiamat.

Phoenician or Hebrew seal Isb'l (Ishbaal)

SARID A town on the southern border of the territory of Zebulun. In some manuscripts of the Septaugint, Shadud, an older form of the name of the place, is mentioned. This supports the identification of Sarid with Tell Shadud, in the northern part of the *Jezreel Valley.

SCOPUS (MOUNT) A hill less than a mile to the north of *Jerusalem where, according to tradition, Alexander the Great was welcomed by the high priest and the inhabitants of *Jerusalem (Josephus, *Antiq.* XI, 329). Josephus states that it was called Saphein, or Zofim, which was translated into Greek as *scopus* ('look-out'), since it was possible to overlook the Temple and the city from this vantage point. According to the Talmud the meeting with Alexander took place at Antipatris (*Aphek), but Josephus' account seems more plausible. Mount Scopus is next mentioned in the account of the First Jewish Revolt against Rome (AD 66-8). It was the site of a camp of Cestius Gallus (Josephus, *War* II, 528) and later Titus approached the city from this point (Josephus, *War* V, 106). It appears frequently in the Talmud as Zofim, a place from which *Jerusalem was visible. In the time of the Second Temple the hill was used as a Jewish burial-place; many ossuaries and ossuary fragments with Hebrew or Greek inscriptions have been found there.

Scarab depicting a fish

SEA (THE) The sea referred to is the Mediterranean, which laps the shores of three continents: Asia, Africa and Europe. It is referred to in various ways in the Bible, firstly as the 'great sea' (Deut. 11:24; Authorized Version: 'uttermost sea'). Off *Joppa it is called the 'sea of Joppa' (Ezra 3:7), while the part bordering the land of the *Philistines, from *Joppa to the border of *Egypt, is referred to as the 'sea of the Philistines' (Exod. 23:31).(*See also* *SHIPS AND NAVIGATION.)

SEALS In ancient times seals were used to denote personal ownership of certain objects, and sealing a document with a personal or public seal confirmed the

Hebrew seal: 'To Šm (Shema) Servant of Jeroboam' found at Megiddo

Phoenician seal Ihzb'l (Iahazbaal)

Aramaic seal Lšm' (to Shema)

Hebrew seal: 'To Jaazaniya Servant of the King'

Two Roman gems: (right) Tyche;
(left) double head

Gnostic amulette

authenticity of the contents. The device was probably first used in *Mesopotamia, where thousands of seals and seal impressions were found. There is ample evidence in the Bible to show that the seal was also in common use in the Holy Land. A document written on a clay tablet would be placed in a clay envelope and sealed, while a document written on papyrus or parchment would be rolled and tied with a string; a ball of soft clay would then be placed on the knot and sealed. The seal would normally be incorporated in a ring, or hung on a string on the chest. Seals brought to Palestine from other countries were either made of steatite or of faience. The ancient Hebrew seals were normally made of semiprecious hard stones, carnelian (brought from Egypt or Arabia), rock-crystal, hematite, amethyst, lapis lazuli and of local hard limestone.

The earliest seals found in Palestine date back to the beginning of the 4th millennium and are of Mesopotamian origin. From the 18th century BC and especially from the arrival of the *Hyksos, the number of seals multiply. These are of the scarab type, many of which originate in Egypt. They are elliptical in shape, and decorated on the back with a beetle — scarabeus — an insect venerated by the Egyptians. The scarabs bear the names of kings, or of members of the royal family, and various incantations, and carry representations of deities, men, animals, plants and geometrical designs.

From the Iron Age, there are many seals inscribed with the owner's name, written in Hebrew, Phoenician or Aramaic. They date mainly to the 8th-6th centuries BC. These were used for sealing documents and letters written on papyrus and parchment (*Writing materials). The Hebrew seals are also scaraboidal in shape, flat at the bottom and convex on top. Some, however, are conical. Many of the Hebrew seals bear only the name of their owner, and have a sub-dividing horizontal line. These are chiefly of the 7th-6th centuries, and are typical mainly of the kingdom of Judah. Some, however, were decorated with various winged mythological creatures, such as the griffin, the sphinx, serpents, beetles, the winged sun, etc. Quite common are seals decorated with lions, oxen, galloping horses, apes, donkeys, snakes, locusts, birds and cocks. Of the plants the most common are the lotus, the papyrus plant, the palmette and the pomegranate.

In the various sites where Iron Age strata have been excavated numerous seals, and still more seal impressions, have been found. The more famous ones are of persons known from the Bible, such as 'the servant of the king' (Shema the Servant of Jeroboam) (2 Kgs. 22:12), 'the governor of the house' (1 Kgs. 18:3), 'which is over the house' (cf. Isa. 22:15), and Gedaliah (2 Kgs. 25:22). Seals of this class are quite numerous, and new ones still come to light from time to time.

Large numbers of seal impressions have been found on jar-handles on many sites in Judea. These seals bear the inscription *lamelek* — 'of the King' — on the upper part of the seal. At the bottom comes one of four names: Hebron, Ziph, Socoh or *mmst*. Between the lines appears a two-or four-winged symbol of the sun. Those with a four-winged sun are of the 8th century; the others are of the 7th-6th centuries BC.

At the beginning of the Persian period the seals resemble the ancient Hebrew ones in shape and script, but gradually the square Aramaic script replaces the older one. The seals are fashioned in the form of a cone with an octagonal base and a perforation at the top. The decoration consists of representations of priests. In some places in Judea, seals carrying the name of *Yahud* were found. This was the official name of the province of Judea in the Persian period. Other seals have *ha'ir*, meaning 'the City', Jerusalem, and still others have the name of Jerusalem inscribed on them in full. It is believed that the jars thus stamped were used for the collection of taxes pertaining to the Temple.

From the Roman period there are two types of seals in Palestine, one found on pottery vessels, the other on documents. The seals of the first group are found on handles of jars, bases of bowls, lamps, etc. These seal impressions originated mainly in the large potteries of Italy (Arretium, Puteoli), Alexandria, Asia Minor and Gaul. In the case of the jars the handles are stamped with official seals bearing the names of Roman consuls. To this class belong also seal impressions on roof tiles and bricks produced in Roman military potteries. Seal impressions of the second type, those stamped on documents, are less common. Of this class two groups were found in Palestine, one from the *Judean Desert Caves, and the other from *Mampsis. The seals from the Judean Desert Caves are anepigraphical, one being decorated with an olive branch, vine leaf and pomegranate, while the other has a bearded man wrestling with a lion. Of greater importance is the group of seals from Mampsis. These are impressions from the official seals of three cities in Arabia: *Petra, Characmoba (*Kir Moab), and *Rabbathmoba. Each of the seals has the name of the respective city. In the center of each is a symbol — in some cases it is the figure of a god or a goddess (Tyche of Arabia, Tyche of *Antioch-on-the Orontes, and Ares), while others have signs of the zodiac with their Hebrew names in Greek form. These seals are of the years AD 106-40 and are especially nicely preserved.

There are large numbers of seals from the Byzantine period, though marking pottery became less common. There are numerous seals set in rings, with Christian monograms, symbols or figures of saints. There is also a class of large clay or wooden seals which were used for marking the Holy Bread, and also seals with Jewish symbols for marking cheese.

SEIR *a*) The name of a mountainous region southeast of the *Dead Sea. The name occurs for the first time in a topographical list of Amenophis III. In the *El Amarna letters the prince of *Jerusalem informs the king of Egypt that war against the king is raging in the mountains of Seir. In the 13th century BC the name appears on an obelisk of Rameses II found in *Tanis: 'A fierce lion spoils the land of Seir'. A papyrus from the time of Rameses III (12th century BC) refers to the destruction of Seir, possibly by nomadic tribes who sojourned there. It was attacked by Ashurbanipal in his ninth campaign against the Arabs. It was formerly inhabited by *Horites (Gen. 14:6), where Esau lived later; identified with *Edom (Gen. 36:8 ff.). Around Mount Seir the Children of Israel 'compassed many days' on their way from *Egypt to the land of Canaan (Deut. 2:1,5).

b) The name of a mountain on the borders of the territory of Judah (Josh. 15:10). Location not known.

SELAH A town in northern *Edom. When Amaziah, King of Judah, conquered the town and slew 10,000 *Edomites he changed its name to Joktheel (2 Kgs. 14:7; 2 Chr. 25:12 ff; Authorized Version: 'rock'). Eusebius (*Onom.* 142,7) mistakenly identifies it with *Petra, a city in *Arabia, which the Syrians (i.e., the *Nabateans) called *Rekem.The name Selah has been preserved in modern es-Sela where a small Edomite-Nabataean fortress has been discovered 5 miles southwest of Tafileh.

SEPHARAD A country in which exiles from Judah settled (Obad. 1:20); identified with Sardis in Asia Minor. The identification of Sepharad with Sardis was made possible by the decipherment of an Aramaic-Lydian inscription, from which it became evident that this was indeed the Aramaic form of the name. This identification is also supported by cuneiform inscriptions of Sargon II, Darius I and Xerxes in old Persian, *Elamite and *Accadian.

SEPHARVAIM Men deported from this country were settled by the King of Assyria in *Samaria, to take the place of the exiled Israelites (2 Kgs. 17:24, etc.). It should probably be identified with Sippar, 14 miles southwest of Baghdad.

SEPPHORIS; DIOCAESAREA A town in Lower *Galilee, mentioned for the first time at the beginning of the reign of the Hasmonean, Alexander Jannaeus, when it was attacked in 103 BC by Ptolemy Latyrus (Josephus, *Antiq.* XIII, 338). Its importance in the Hellenistic period is indicated by the fact that after Pompey's conquest of Palestine in 64 BC it became the capital of one of the five newly proclaimed districts (*Antiq.* XIV , 91). At the beginning of his reign Herod conquered Sepphoris during a snowstorm (*Antiq.* XIV, 413). When disturbances broke out on his death, the royal palace of Sepphoris was pillaged by Judas, son of Ezekiad (*Antiq.* XVII, 271). It then became part of the territory of Herod Antipas, who fortified the city and made it the capital of *Galilee, which it continued to be until the foundation of *Tiberias (*Antiq.* XVIII, 27). During the revolt of AD 66-70 Sepphoris remained loyal to the Romans, but after the destruction of the Temple it became an important Jewish center, and was for some time the seat of the Sanhedrin. Vespasian conferred the status of *polis* on the city, and Hadrian renamed it Diocaesarea (Hier. *Onom.* 17, 14). At that time a temple dedicated to the Capitoline (Jupiter, Juno and Minerva) triad was erected. Hadrian made Diocaesarea an autonomous city and extended its territory. It was a military center early in the 5th century AD. Constantine gave Joseph the Convert permission to build a church there.

In 1931 L. Waterman made excavations on the site, which is identified with Saffuriyeh, on behalf of the University of Michigan. On the acropolis the excavators unearthed a Crusader fort, built of sarcophagi and Roman architectural stones. Below the fort remains of a large, earlier (possibly Roman) building were discovered. To the Byzantine period belong remains of a badly preserved basilica with a mosaic pavement in one of its rooms. To the Roman period belongs a large theater, of which only a section was excavated. This building is of the Roman type, about 110 feet in diameter, and is estimated to have seated between 4,000 and 5,000 spectators. The stage (*scaenae frons*) was about 90 feet long and 18 feet wide. There were no entrances in the stage building, but it had towers at each end. To the same period belong remains of an aqueduct, a tunnel and reservoirs, part of the water-supply system of the city, through which water was brought from a spring miles away.

SERABIT EL-KHADEM A center of turquoise and copper mining in central Sinai in the times of the pharaohs. As early as 1762 an Egyptian sanctuary was observed on the site by C. Niebuhr. Since then it has been visited constantly by numerous scholars. During the British Ordnance Survey of 1872 hieroglyphic inscriptions commemorating Ammenemes IV of the 12th Egyptian Dynasty, as well as an Egyptian shrine, were discovered there. In 1905 excavations were made on the site by W.F.M. Petrie on behalf of the British School of Archaeology in Egypt.

During the excavations an early high place, and a series of temples that replaced it, were revealed within a *temenos* (enclosure), 200 feet by 140 feet in area. The original Egyptian shrine consisted of a cave sacred to Hathor, goddess of the land and of minerals. In front of the cave a portico was constructed, and then a large court; and further shrines were added during the long Egyptian occupation of the site. Within the *temenos* were caves dedicated to other deities, such as the moon-god Thoth.

Mining of turquoise did not begin at Serabit el-Khadem until the time of the 12th Dynasty, although it had already started in early dynastic times at Jebel Mughara, in the same rock massif but further south. Turquoise was essential to the Egyptian jewelry industry, while copper was important for the production of tools and weapons (*Metals). The earliest Egyptian monarch to send an expedition to *Sinai was Sneferu, the first king of the 4th Dynasty. Mining continued with some interruption down to the end of the 6th Dynasty, when both mines were again worked under Ammenemes III of the 12th Dynasty. Stalae set up in the temple record the various mining expeditions, of which no less than seven took place during Ammenemes III's reign.

At first mining was easy, but the surface veins were soon exhausted and one of the stelae found nearby recounts: 'The desert burnt like summer; the mountains burnt like fire; the vein seemed exhausted; the overseer questioned the miners; the skilled workers who knew the mine replied, "There is turquoise to all eternity in the mountain", and at that moment it appeared'. It was at that time that deep shafts were dug so that the underground veins could be reached by means of tunnels, some of which were more than 200 feet long. By the end of the 12th Dynasty mining had ceased. It was resumed only after the expulsion of the *Hyksos from *Egypt and the establishment of the 13th Dynasty. Under the dynasty's founder, Amosis,

mining began again both at Serabit and at Jebel Mughara, to continue in full swing during the reigns of Hatshepsut and Tuthmosis III, and also during the 19th Dynasty. The temple of Serabit el-Khadem had been enlarged repeatedly. Continuing the process, Sethos I, founder of the 19th Dynasty, extended it. Rameses II and Merneptah are also recorded in the temple, as is Rameses III of the 20th Dynasty. At the beginning of the 21st Dynasty the mines of *Sinai went out of use once more.

One of the most important finds at Serabit el-Khadem is a small statue inscribed with letters in a hitherto unknown script. Although this has not yet been fully deciphered it is now recognized to be the earliest Semitic alphabetic script, each letter being represented by a pictograph. Since the initial discovery in 1906, a further 25 statuettes have been found in the mining region. The script is dated today to about 1500 BC.

It seems that the mines in the region were worked again in the Roman period, though the evidence for this is as yet only indirect, in the form of thousands of Nabatean inscriptions, some of which appear at Serabit el-Khadem itself.

The exploitation of turquoise and copper mines was not confined to those in the Jebel Mughara-Serabit el-Khadem region. The discovery by B. Rothenberg of an Egyptian temple at *Timnah, used during the reigns of Sethos I, Rameses II and Rameses III, and subsequently reused by Semites in the 14th-13th centuries BC, links the history of copper and turquoise mining in the southern *Negev with that of southern *Sinai.

SHAALABIM; SHAALABIN A city in the territory of *Dan (Josh. 19:42); also occupied by the *Amorites after the conquest (Judg. 1:35). It was in the second district of Solomon (1 Kgs. 4:9) and within the territory of *Emmaus in the Roman period. A Samaritan synagogue was discovered there. Identified with Salbit.

SHAAR HAGOLAN The site was found on the right bank of the River *Yarmuk in 1943 during a survey for the location of fish ponds at Kibbutz Shaar Hagolan. It is of the Pottery Neolithic period and included rich finds of stone tools and art objects that were later classified as the Yarmukian culture. M. Stekelis spent five seasons of excavations there between 1949 and 1959. His finds, together with those of the survey done by the members of the kibbutz, indicate that the settlement probably consisted of separate huts constructed of some organic material. The flints used by the inhabitants included partly polished axes and adzes, picks and chisels, numerous denticulated sickle-blades and awls and a few scrapers, burins and arrowheads, mainly produced by pressure flaking. The ground stone implements consisted of bowls, grinding stones and cup marks formed in big blocks of basalt. The pottery was handmade and fired in an open fire. The jars were ornamented with red slip, the most characteristic decoration being an incised herring-bone pattern. The whole assemblage indicates the existence of a settlement depending mostly on agriculture, plus some hunting, for its subsistence.

The art objects found on the site represent fertility symbols and may indicate the main features of the spiritual life of its inhabitants. These finds can be divided into three main groups: figurines of women, made of clay or schematically incised on stone pebbles; schematic figures incised on pebbles; and sexual organs of both sexes. The clay figurines represent standing or sitting women, their hands sometimes folded or with a single arm placed across the body holding their breasts. They have protruding, obliquely slanting eyes and an elongated head or headdress with a plait down the back, and possibly represent a mother goddess figure. The little figures incised on river pebbles have straight or slanted eyes with indications of a nose and sexual organs. The third group represents sexual organs exclusively. Other stone pebbles were found with incised linear patterns.

The Yarmukian culture has also been found in *Munhata, with a variant in *Jericho and *Byblos (*See also* *PREHISTORY; FLINT TOOLS*).

SHALIM; LAND OF SHALIM The correct reading of this name is the land of Shaul: 'And the spoilers came out of the camp of the Philistines in three companies: one company turned unto the way that leadeth to Ophrah, unto the land of Shaul' (1 Sam. 13:17). A region in Mount Ephraim is indicated by this name. *Ophrah is identified with et-Tayibeh, situated some 4 miles northeast of *Beth-El. This is identical with the land of Shalim which Saul crossed on his way to find his father's asses (1 Sam. 9:4). This and other regional names in this area apparently derive from the names of families who owned these territories. Not identified.

SHARON The coastal plain between the River *Yarkon on the south and Mount *Carmel on the north, famous for its forests and rich vegetation (Isa. 33:9; S. of S. 2:1). It was rich in pasture and David appointed an overseer for the herds that grazed there (1 Chr. 27:29). The famous route called the Via Maris (*Roads) passed through the Plain of Sharon, connecting *Egypt with Palestine and Syria. The lists of the Egyptian kings who took that road mention many of the cities along it. The name Sharon appears in the list of Amenophis II, who travelled through it on his way to northern Syria. In the Persian and Hellenistic periods Phoenician colonies were built along the coastal strip. In the Roman period it was called *drymos* ('forest'), and some of the most important cities of Palestine were built along the coast at that time.

SHAVEH (VALLEY OF); KING'S DALE A valley in the vicinity of *Jerusalem, where the King of *Sodom went to meet Abraham after vanquishing Chedorlaomer (Gen. 14:17-18); identified with the 'king's dale' (2 Sam. 18:18) where Absalom erected his monument. Location unknown. Josephus puts it at a distance of 2 stadia from *Jerusalem.

SHARUHEN *See* *FARAH, TELL FEL- (SOUTH)

SHEBA A land in the southern, fertile mountainous southwestern part of *Arabia, inhabited in antiquity by the Sabeans (cf. Gen. 10:7, 25-8). In the Bible it was known as an exceedingly rich land, from which the Queen of Sheba brought gold, precious stones and spices (1 Kgs. 10:1 ff.) such as frankincense (Isa. 60:6;

Jer. 6:20; Authorized Version: 'incense'). These were brought to the Mediterranean coast by merchants of *Tyre (Ezek. 27:22). The Sabeans traded in slaves (Joel 3:8) and did not refrain from robbery (Job 1:15; 6:19).

The history of the Sabean kingdom is still not well known. Sheba is mentioned in inscriptions of Tiglath-Pileser III, Sagon and Sennacherib, kings of *Assyria, which refer to luxurious commodities brought by camels from Sheba.

The Romans under Aelius Gallus had already in 25/24 BC equipped an expedition numbering 10,000 Roman, 1,500 *Nabatean, and 500 Jewish soldiers, whose aim was either to gain the friendship of the Arabian peoples, or to conquer a rich country. Although the Romans reached the southern extremeties of the peninsula, neither aim was achieved, nor did it enrich greatly the knowledge of these lands. It is only since about 1950 that more serious archaeological research has been undertaken in this inhospitable area. Of special interest are the American excavations in the temple of the Moon God at Marib, the ancient capital of the Sabean kingdom. The temple was first built in the 8th century BC and was in use until the advent of Islam. From the scanty literary evidence we know that by the beginning of the Christian era most of the Arabian peninsula was ruled by the Sabeans. It was about that time that the Romans attempted to lay their hands on the fabulous riches of Sheba, but without success.

SHECHEM; SICHEM One of the most important Canaanite cities in Mount Ephraim, on the main road from *Jerusalem to the north. The city appears from early times in the Egyptian sources. In the *Execration Texts of the 19th century BC its ruler Absh-Adad is mentioned. Shechem and its ruler Labayu are also frequently referred to in the *El Amarna letters, in which Labayu, one of the strongest Canaanite rulers, annexed a great number of cities and established a strong kingdom with Shechem as its center. It is possible that a reference in the Egyptian Anastasi papyrus of the end of the 13th century BC relates to this city.

Shechem also occupies a prominent place in the early history of the Patriarchs. On arrival in *Canaan, after leaving *Haran, Abraham built an altar to the Lord at Shechem (Gen. 12:6-7). When Jacob came from Padan-Aram he pitched his tent outside the city and bought a parcel of land there (Gen. 33:18-19). The incident concerning his daughter Dinah also took place at Shechem (Gen. 34). After the conquest of *Canaan by the Israelites the border of the territories of Ephraim and Manasseh met at Shechem (Josh. 17:7), which was one of the cities of the Levites (Josh. 21:21). Before his death Joshua gathered the Children of Israel there, and they brought from *Egypt the bones of Joseph, son of Jacob, for burial on the land that his father had bought (Josh. 24). After Gideon's death the Shechemites enthroned Abimelech his son, and gave him 'threescore and ten pieces of silver out of the house of Baalberith' (Judg. 9:1-16); but when they rebelled against him he 'sowed the city with salt' (Judg. 9:45-7). It is in this connection that we hear of the 'tower of Shechem'. It seems that the city retained its special status in the time of the kingdom of Israel, because Rehoboam went there to be enthroned by 'all Israel' (I Kgs. 12:1); and when the tribes of Israel revolted against him Jeroboam, son of Nabat, rebuilt Shechem as his first capital (1 Kgs. 12:25). After the destruction of the kingdom of Israel the King of Assyria brought men from *Babylon, *Cuthah, Ava, *Antioch-on-the-Orontes and *Sepharvaim and placed them in the cities of *Samaria (2 Kgs. 17:24). These were the Samaritans, who made Shechem their religious center and built an altar on top of Mount *Gezirim. The Samaritans, with Sanballat at their head, conspired to hinder Nehemiah in building the walls of *Jerusalem (Neh. 4:1-3). At this period there was also a colony of Sidonians at Shechem (Josephus, *Antiq.* XI, 344).

When Alexander the Great conquered Palestine the Samaritans of Shechem represented themselves as Jews in order to win his favor (*Antiq.* XI, 240); it is in this context that we hear of the Samaritan temple at Shechem (*Antiq.* XI, 346). But in the time of Antiochus Epiphanes the Samaritans, denying any connection with the Jews, describe themselves in a letter directed to that king as 'Sidonians of Shechem' (*Antiq.* XII, 257-64). In 128 BC John Hyrcanus destroyed the Samaritan temple on Mount *Gezirim and the Samaritan city of Shechem as well (*Antiq.* XIII, 256). From that time on it became an insignificant village, and its place was taken by the Roman Flavia Neapolis.

Biblical Shechem is identified with Tell Balatah, to the east of modern Nablus. This location is also identified by Eusebius (*Onom.* 164, 11), the Pilgrim of Bordeaux, the *Medaba map and other Byzantine sources.

The site was first excavated in 1913-4, 1926-8, 1932 and 1934 by E. Sellin, C. Watzinger and others on behalf of the German Society for Scientific Research. The excavators began by unearthing a section of wall 200 feet long on the west of the mound, where a triple-entrance gateway (*Fortifications) was also found. The wall and gate were built of huge blocks of stone, some more than 7 feet wide. In order to study the stratigraphy of the mound they excavated a trench inside the wall. Four strata were observed, but lack of knowledge of the local pottery led to incorrect dating. In the uppermost, 'Greek', level a hoard of 850 bronze and seven iron arrowheads was found in a jar. These were the achievements of the first season. In the subsequent seasons several trenches were sunk in different parts of the mound. Close to the northwestern gate, approached by a ramp leading from it, a 'palace' was discovered. The entrance to it was through a room measuring 33 feet by 20 feet, its roof supported by a single beam. This room led into the main hall, where the roof rested on ten columns. Later rebuildings were observed in this area. Near the palace was another building, measuring 69 feet by 86 feet and identified by the excavators as the house of Baal-Berith. According to the Bible this was destroyed by Abimelech (Judg. 9). These buildings were dated as follows: the eastern wall, the northwestern gate and the palace to *c.* 1700 BC; the eastern wall and a wing added to the palace to *c.* 1500 BC; the temple to *c.* 1300 BC; rebuilding of the

temple to 1150 BC. These dates were later changed several times. Important among the small finds were two cuneiform tablets, one dealing with judicial proceedings, the other a letter written by a teacher to his pupil's father asking for his fee to be paid. In later seasons of excavation the northwestern gate, the large wall and the first phase of the palace were redated to the Late Bronze Age, the *El Amarna period. The results of the excavations were not, however, adequately treated and published.

In the years 1956, 1957, 1962, 1964 and 1966 Shechem was excavated by G.E. Wright on behalf of the Drew-McCormick Archaeological Expedition. The earliest traces of settlement were of the early 4th millennium BC, but the first permanent settlement on the site was in the Hyksos period. The city was then surrounded by an immense glacis about 80 feet wide and 20 feet high, the slope of which was plastered. Above this there had probably been a brick wall. The higher part of the mound, the acropolis, was surrounded by a separate stone wall, to protect a building identified as an early Hyksos shrine, which consisted of a courtyard with several adjoining rooms. There were several building phases in this structure. In the late 18th century BC it had nine rooms, some of which were workrooms. Under the floors burials of babies in jars were found. About half a century later the building was destroyed by fire and rebuilt. The temple of the latest phase had already been excavated by the Germans. To this phase belonged a forecourt with six stone pillars at its northern end and one in the center. This building was finally destroyed in about 1550 BC, when the *Hyksos were expelled by the *Egyptians.

At the end of the Middle Bronze Age the area of the city was enlarged by the addition of an artificial mound held by a huge retaining wall, above which a mud-brick wall was built. Inside the city a thinner parallel wall was joined to it by crosswalls, to form a casemate. The same kind of wall was discovered on the east of the mound. The outer wall was built of huge boulders, thus meriting the term 'Cyclopean'. In the northwest section of this wall was a gate measuring 59 feet by 65 feet, in which three massive piers formed two pairs of rooms. The same gate was rebuilt in the Late Bronze Age. About half a century later a new wall was erected to the same plan and a new gate was built on the east. It consisted of two towers, each 23 feet by 42 feet, containing guard rooms. During the half century of its existence this gate was destroyed and rebuilt three times, before being finally destroyed by the *Egyptians.

To the same Hyksos period belongs the massive fortified temple, built close to the northwestern gate. It served both as a temple and as a fortress. Erected on an earthen platform, it measured 68 feet by 84 feet with walls 17 feet thick. It had a forecourt on the southeast and a wide door leading into a small entrance, which gave access to a large shrine.

The town built after the Egyptian conquest was considerably smaller. The eastern gate was rebuilt on the old plan but the walls were thinner. A paved road led from the gate to an open paved and plastered yard. At the end of the Late Bronze Age the gate was again rebuilt, and it was reused without any change in the Early Iron Age. There is no evidence of destruction at Shechem when the Israelites conquered the country, and the excavators assume that the Shechemites were on friendly terms with the arriving Israelites. A new temple-fortress was built above the first one and this is the one that the excavators believe to be the house of Baal-Berith (Judg.9). On both sides of the entrance, socles for *massebot* were discovered, the pillars themselves lying nearby.

After a period of abandonment Shechem was rebuilt in about 900 BC by the Israelites. Jeroboam I fortified it and made it his first capital (I Kgs. 12:25). To the four strata of the Israelite period belonged several houses in different parts of the mound. Above the temple a four-room house, measuring 50 feet by 60 feet, was erected; this has been identified as a royal granary. The final destruction of Israelite Shechem is attributed to Shalmaneser, who stormed the Israelite kingdom in 724 BC (Cf. Jer. 41:4-5).

The town was abandoned until the 4th century BC, when Alexander the Great made it into a rest camp for his soldiers. It was subsequently occupied by the Samaritans, and this town was probably the Sychar of John (4:5-7; 'Sychem' in the Syriac version), near which was Jacob's well, where Jesus met the woman of *Samaria. During the Hellenistic period Samaritan Shechem was destroyed and rebuilt four times, the last destruction being attributed to John Hyrcanus in 128 BC. During the Roman period the site had already ceased to be occupied.

*See also**FLAVIA NEAPOLIS

SHEIKH EL-AREINI (TELL) One of the most important mounds in the *Plain, about 5 miles northwest of *Lachish. The large mound, extending over an area of about 65 acres, has attracted many scholars, some of whom have suggested that it should be identified with *Libnah because of the white chalk of the surrounding hills (*laban* means 'white' in Hebrew). Later the identification with *Gath of the *Philistines was suggested and it had been accepted by all scholars; at this stage the excavations were carried out. The site was excavated by S. Yeivin on behalf of the Israel Department of Antiquities and Museums and the Oriental Institute of Rome. The excavations failed to produce any appreciable amount of Philistine pottery, however, and the identification with *Gath cannot therefore be sustained. It is now referred to as Tel Erani.

The site consists of an acropolis of 3 acres, with steep sides. On it stands the sheikh's tomb that gave its name to the mound. Around the acropolis is a ledge of 40 acres on which the upper town was built, and below it is another, the extent of which is still unknown. The acropolis was much disturbed by late burials, which penetrated the ancient occupation levels to a depth of about 8 feet. The disturbed strata are mainly of the Persian period. Moreover large storage bins (*Stores) built in the Persian period penetrated and disturbed the underlying Israelite strata of the late 7th and early 6th centuries BC. The city fortifications were discovered on the slope of the acropolis. Here four superimposed casemate walls were found. Of the upper three only the stone foundations remain, but the lowest one still has part of its superstructure of baked bricks, a feature that was most unusual at that time. The date of the fortifications is not certain. Associated with, and not far from, the walls was a large mud glacis.

The combined results of five seasons of excavations show nine occupation levels in the acropolis area: strata I-III are disturbed remains of the Hellenistic and Persian periods; IV probably belongs to the Iron Age IIC, and was disturbed by the Persian buildings. Stratum V was an earlier phase of the same period. The disturbance reaches this stratum, but nevertheless remains of three large buildings were discernible, including *lamelek* seal impressions. Stratum VI was of the same century and had four-room houses. Stratum VII, of the late 8th-early 7th centuries BC, was distinguished by houses of a different plan, with rooms built around a central court. A jar neck with the Hebrew inscription *'l'Yeheza'*, 'belonging to Yeheza', was found in this stratum. Stratum VIII, of the 8th century BC, has houses of the same type. The earliest stratum (IX) contained a lime kiln only, which cannot be safely dated.

Another section of the mound, on the upper shelf this time, revealed occupation levels of the Early Bronze Age II. The houses of these levels were of mud brick on a stone foundation. In the underlying stratum II a round construction was found, identified by

Clay figurine from Tell Sheikh el-Areini, Iron Age

the excavators as an offering table, and the building near it is tentatively identified as a cult place of the first half of the 3rd millennium BC. Stratum II had no less than five phases of building. Stratum III is similar to stratum II. Of great importance is stratum IV, from which came a large number of broken jars containing seeds of wheat, barley and flax. A carbon 14 analysis dated the destruction of this stratum to 2550 BC (plus or minus 250 years), which would give a date in the Early Bronze Age I to this occupation level. To the same period belongs a large house with a court, and rooms on at least two sides. The town of this period extended over quite a large area. Stratum V was also important for dating, because of some pottery imported from *Egypt found in it. The pottery is of the pre-Dynastic period and the first phase of the Dynastic period. Some of the jars are inscribed with an Egyptian name, probably that of King Narmer, the last king of the pre-Dynastic period. Remains of a large public building, some of whose rooms served as stores, belong to this period. This town was surrounded by a strong mud-brick wall. The underlying stratum VI had suffered severe damage. It contained a hitherto unknown type of pottery which bears a resemblance to the Chalcolithic repertoire. To this stratum belongs a large building with many rooms grouped around a spacious court. This building already existed on a somewhat different plan in the earlier stratum VII. In a trial trench remains of additional strata (VIII-IX) were discovered. The debris in this area was about 80 feet thick.

Other parts of the mound were excavated with the object of finding the extent of the ancient site, but these did not alter the picture as described above.

SHEMA (KHIRBET) A ruin situated in the close vicinity of *Meiron in Upper Galilee. Scholars identify it with Tekoa of Galilee, mentioned in Jewish sources in conjunction with its good quality olive oil. The site was excavated in the years 1970-2 under the auspices of the American School of Oriental Research, under the direction of E.M. Meyers. A *synagogue of an unusual type was discovered there. It is a broad-house basilica, with east-west colonnades, and a bema on the southern wall facing Jerusalem. A room decorated with frescoes at the western end probably housed a portable Torah shrine. Steps at the southwestern end of the building apparently led up to a women's gallery. The synagogue was founded in the early 4th century AD and destroyed in a natural catastrophe in the 6th century. Soundings were also made in the town itself. Khirbet Shema seems to have flourished in the 4th and 5th centuries AD.

SHEPHELAH See *PLAIN (THE)

SHERA (TEL) Extensive excavations at Tel Shera (Tell esh-Sharia), identified by some with *Gerar, were directed by E. Oren on behalf of the Ben-Gurion University of the Negev in the years 1972-6. Four areas were excavated on the mound itself, and one area on the southern bank of Nahal Gerar. The earliest traces of occupation on the site are sherds of the Chalcolithic period, Early Bronze Age and Middle Bronze Age I. The history of permanent settlement on the site began in the Late Bronze Age (strata XII-IX),

but only the two later strata have been excavated (14th to early 12th century BC). To this period belongs a heavy walled building, 75 feet long on its excavated side. In the debris were found large charred beams of cedars of Lebanon, which had apparently supported the upper floor. This building is identified as the residence of the Egyptian governor, a conclusion supported by numerous small finds of Egyptian origin found in its rooms. The *cult vessels and numerous animal bones attest to the possibility that a cult function was also associated with this building. Of interest is a group of bowls and plates inscribed with hieratic symbols, possibly offerings brought to the temple by the residents of the town. By the middle of the 12th century BC the residence was utterly destroyed, possibly by an early wave of the *Sea Peoples. After an abandonment of the site for about a century new houses were built. This settlement is attributed to the *Philistines (stratum VIII, 11th century BC). The houses are of the four-room type, which was hitherto believed to be an Israelite innovation. In the 10th century BC (VII) extensive building operations took place in the town. Houses were built of mudbrick placed on foundations of *kurkar* stone, some walls being preserved to a height of 6 feet. The bricks were laid in the header and stretcher method, typical of Israelite building. Among the houses were some of a public nature. This phase of occupation ended abruptly at the beginning of the 9th century BC, possibly destroyed by an earthquake. Building operations resumed in the 7th century BC (VI), and now for the first time the town was fortified. The southwestern and northern approaches to the town were strongly defended by casemate walls. In one area was discovered part of a building containing oblong halls, which was apparently a citadel. Among the finds was a Hebrew ostracon, mentioning a place by the name of Asem (Josh. 19:3), which is located in this region. By the beginning of the 6th century BC, this town too was destroyed, either in one of the Babylonian campaigns against southern Palestine, or by an Egyptian military expedition. Both attributions are supported by Mesopotamian and Egyptian objects found in this stratum. The following, Persian period (V), 5th-4th centuries BC, is represented at Tel Shera—as at numerous other sites of this period in southern Palestine—by a large number of brick-lined silos, the larger of which have a diameter of 15 feet. Among the finds in the silos were Aramaic ostraca and Athenian red-figured pottery. Hellenistic (IV) remains were found in one area only. In the Roman period (III) a massive tower was built on a stone platform at the northern edge of the mound. A spacious villa was also discovered from this period, its walls decorated with painted plaster. Among the *pottery, was *Nabatean ware. In the Byzantine period (I) a large building, apparently a church, occupied the peak of the mound. Mameluke, early Islamic remains, and a late Islamic cemetery were found close to the surface of the mound.

SHIHOR-LIBNATH A stream in the vicinity of Mount *Carmel, in the southwestern sector of the territory of Asher (Josh. 19:26). Eusebius (*Onom.*

122:7, 158:16), following the Septuagint, refers to it as two separate places, Shihor and Libnath. The first denotes in Egyptian the name of the *Nile River or one of its tributaries and hence also denotes a river in general. The identification of the stream Sihor and the town Libnath is much disputed. Some seek it south of *Dor, and others at the lower course of the *Kishon. Now identified as the mouth of the River *Kishon, near Tell *Abu-Hawam.

SHILOH A town in Mount Ephraim. Its location is described in the Bible as 'a place which is on the north side of Beth-El, on the east side of the highway that goeth up from Beth-El to Shechem, and on the south of Lebonah' (Judg. 21:19). Shiloh was a religious center of the tribes and after the conquest of the country by Joshua the tabernacle of the congregation was set up there (Josh. 18:1). It was there also that Joshua distributed allotments to the tribes who had not previously received them (Josh. 18:2-10). The house of God (Judg. 18:31) in which Eli and his sons officiated was at Shiloh, and God appeared there before Samuel (1 Sam. 1:19; 3:1 ff.). When the Israelites were hard-pressed by the *Philistines at *Eben-Ezer the tabernacle was transported from Shiloh to the battlefield, but fell into the hands of the enemy (1 Sam. 4:1-5; 5:1). It seems that after this battle the city was set on fire and was only later rebuilt (Jer. 4:5; 7:12; 26:6,9). Ahijah, who prophesied to Jeroboam, son of Nabat, that he would rule over the ten tribes, came from Shiloh (1 Kgs. 11:29-31). At the time of the Restoration men of Shiloh were among those who returned from the Babylonian exile (Neh. 11:5). The town existed under the same name in the Roman and Byzantine periods. Eusebius (*Onom.* 156, 26) states that it is situated 12 miles from *Shechem.

The site of Shiloh was still known in the Middle Ages and in the 19th century it was correctly identified with Khirbet Seilun, about 20 miles north of *Jerusalem. The mound is about 12 acres in area, and contains the remains of biblical Shiloh. The town of the later periods was situated mainly on the southern slope of the mound.

Trial digs were made there by A. Smith, and in 1926-9 the site was excavated by a Danish expedition under the direction of H. Kjaer. On the earlier periods only scanty remains were discovered, the earliest buildings being of the Middle Bronze Age II. One house was of Iron Age I, and its destruction is attributed to the *Philistines. Thee were also some indications of settlement in Iron Age II and traces of a settlement in the Hellenistic and Roman periods, but most of the remains on the site were of the Byzantine period. Among these were remains of two churches of the 6th-5th centuries BC, one of which was a basilica decorated with geometric mosaics.

Excavations were renewed on the site by J. Finkelstein on behalf of Bar-Ilan University in the years 1981-2. The Israeli expedition continued the earlier work of the Danish expedition in some areas. The earliest remains found on the site were *fortifications of the Middle Bronze Age IIB, which included a glacis. A section of a wall 9-11 feet thick, rising above the glacis, was built of large stones. It still stands in some

places to a height of 7½ feet. The upper part of the walls was levelled off, to hold a brick superstructure, which has not been preserved. The Middle Bronze Age II town occupied an area of about 4 acres. In a small section of the site remains of a Late Bronze occupation were observed. It possibly consisted of a single fortified building. Above the glacis private *houses were built in the Iron Age I; these are attributed to an early Israelite occupation. In the lower levels of the houses were found cellars. This expedition also uncovered buildings of the Byzantine period.

SHIMRON One of the Canaanite city-states that took part in the battle on the waters of *Merom, in the north of the country (Josh. 11:1 ff.); subsequently a city in the territory of Zebulun (Josh. 19:15). As attested by various documents Shim'on was the original form of the name. In this form it is possibly mentioned for the first time in the *Execration Texts of the end of the 19th or early 18th century BC. The name also figures in the list of Palestinian towns of Tuthmosis III. In the *El Amarna letters it is related that its prince joined with the King of *Acco with the aim of robbing a *Babylonian caravan at *Hannaton. In the times of the Mishna and Talmud Shimron was identified with Simonia, and Josephus states that it is a village in the vicinity of *Beth-Shearim (*Life* 24). It is identified with Khirbet Sammuniyeh (Tell Shimron), where remains of the Late Bronze Age were observed.

SHIPS AND NAVIGATION Thousands of years before the first ship sailed in the open sea small boats were plying the large rivers of *Egypt and *Mesopotamia. In Assyrian reliefs soldiers are depicted crossing a river on inflated skins. Later numbers of such skins were joined together, covered with a reed mat and used as rafts. Crafts of this kind could be floated downstream, but once they had reached the desired spot and the merchandise had been unloaded, the air could be pumped out and the skins could be dried, placed on a pack animal and brought back to their owner's home. At the same time boats were also made of reeds covered with skins and smeared with tar, propelled by short, broad oars. Models of vessels of this type were found in the royal cemetery of *Ur (c. 3000 BC).

As early as the middle of the 4th millennium BC the use of the sail was already known in *Mesopotamia, and from about the 3rd millennium BC boats were sailing on the *Nile. Small ships also sailed from *Egypt along the Mediterranean coast as far as *Byblos. In the 1st millennium BC the *Phoenicians began to develop their naval might. At first they did not dare to take their small oar-propelled ships into deep waters, but later, when sails were in use, they made voyages as far as the west coast of Spain, north Africa and even to the southernmost part of England. In the Persian period seafaring became still more common and from the time of Alexander the Great occasional voyages were made to the western coast of *India via the *Red Sea. The Romans greatly improved all aspects of shipping.

According to the Bible the tribe of Zebulun was connected with seafaring activities (Gen. 49:13). In Deborah's song Dan and Asher were also seafarers

(Judg. 5:17). The close commercial relations between Israel and *Tyre, which developed in the time of David, led to advances in Israelite shipping, which increased under Solomon with the foundation of the merchant navy at *Ezion-Geber (1 Kgs. 9:26). These ships were jointly operated by Israelite and Tyrian sailors (2 Chr. 9:21). After that nothing further is said in the Bible about Israelite naval enterprises, but Ezekiel (27:5-9) has a wonderful and detailed description of a Tyrian ship. An Egyptian relief at Medinet Habu, of the 12th century BC, depicts Philistine ships. These were very shallow vessels, with a raised prow and stern to give better protection from the waves. The Philistine ships had one mast but no rudder. No Phoenician drawings of ships have yet come to light but Assyrian reliefs show that their ships, which were built by the *Phoenicians, were tall vessels, with one high mast and an upper and a lower deck, the latter being used by the sailors while the former was reserved for passengers.

In the 6th and 5th centuries BC there were great movements of warships, which went into action frequently. There was also a greatly increased traffic on passenger ships, which carried merchants, pilgrims on their way to important religious centers and athletes travelling to take part in contests.

The conquest of the whole of the inhabited world by Rome and the institution of the *Pax Romana,* which permitted travel throughout the provinces of the Roman Empire, both helped in the development of navigation. Roman colonies were established in many of the provinces, while Syrian colonies were set up in various Italian ports. Against this background it is easy to understand how St. Paul was able to voyage between the different provinces of the Roman Empire. The Jews themselves took an active part in Mediterranean trade, following the conquest of *Joppa by Alexander Jannaeus. Although clear literary evidence is missing drawings of ships on the walls of Jewish tombs in Palestine may serve as possible evidence of their part in navigation in the later Roman period.

The absence of a sextant, or its equivalent, by which the course of a ship could be accurately fixed, was a great disadvantage to ancient navigators. Similarly, the comparatively small size of the earliest ships and the primitive sails and rudders prevented them from undertaking long voyages. At first sea crossings were limited to the summer months (i.e. March to October), when the waters were calm and visibility good. The ships sailed mainly close to the shore from port to port and in emergencies could find shelter in the lee of small promontories. When larger ships were built in the Roman period voyages to *India became safer and more frequent. Sea traffic was no longer limited to the summer months, and instead of following the coastline ships could sail direct from *Alexandria to Italy with cargoes of grain. The Romans also cleared the seas of pirates, thereby contributing greatly to safer voyages. The speed of ships of the Roman period was not great; a freighter making good headway did not exceed 3-4 knots, thus taking eight days between *Alexandria and Puteoli in Italy. This was in fact much faster than the average. In the Hellenistic period, but mainly from the time of Augustus, the eastern shores of the Mediterranean had excellent ports, the best in Judea being *Acre (*Acco), *Caesarea and *Joppa.

There were two types of ship in the Roman period: long, narrow and very fast vessels (*naves longae, triremis and quinqereremis* or longships, triremes and quinqueremes) used mainly in war; and heavy broad craft, used as freighters and passenger ships. The warship could sail in fair weather only; the heavy craft, on the other hand, could sail summer and winter, by day or by night. The freighters were built mainly of wood, with simple prows, and were not provided with battering-rams. The aft was raised high, inclining towards the center of the vessel, and sometimes took the form of a duck's head. The decks were covered and contained cabins. They had fixed masts and travelled mainly under sail, though long oars were also used. The early ships had one square sail close to the prow, but in imperial times two or three triangular sails were used. The capacity of these vessels was about 3 tons. The length of a freighter was up to 140 feet, its breadth 36 feet and its depth 33 feet. In the later Roman period ships were large enough to carry loads up to 59 tons.

SHIQMONA; SYCAMINUM A town on the Phoenician coast, possible referred to in the lists of the 5th century BC attributed to Scylax, a Greek traveller.

Relief from Sennacherib's palace at Nineveh

Strabo (*Geography* XVI. 2, 28) mentions Sycaminopolis, of which nothing but the name remained, while Pliny (*Nat. Hist.* V,75) also states that it was a city in *Phoenicia, of which only the memory had survived. The Pilgrim of Bordeaux states that the Sycaminum is a halting-place near Mount *Carmel, while another pilgrim, Antonine of Placentia (*c.* AD 570), refers to it as a Jewish town, 1 mile from Castra Samaritanorum (*Haifa). It is mentioned in the Talmud as Shikoma. Identified with Tell es-Semaq, south of *Haifa.

Excavations on the site were carried out in the years 1963-8 by J. Elgavish on behalf of the Haifa Municipal Museum of Ancient Art. An underwater survey off the site was conducted in 1969-70.

The earliest traces of occupation on the site go back to the Middle and Late Bronze Ages, as is attested by a tomb of the former period, and a clay bulla with a *seal impression of Sethos I from the latter period. The Iron Age and later strata were more thoroughly investigated. Town A is of the 10th century BC. It was fortified by a casemate wall (*Fortifications). Sections of two streets and four houses were also excavated. Two *houses are a variation of the four-room-house, consisting of two adjoining long halls separated by a row of columns, and a third room perpendicular to them. Another building (33 feet by 45 feet) is a *palace of the open court type, with two rows of rooms along the court. The city wall was destroyed by a conflagration at the end of the century. Many pottery vessels were found in the casemates, one bearing a stamp

Clay figurine from Shikmona, Iron Age

inscribed 'to Malkiel'. Town B is of the 9th century BC. No fortifications have been located. Within the town were discovered three *oil-presses adjoining storerooms. There were large stone mortars and a press in the form of a drum with a diameter of $4\frac{1}{2}$ feet. The local art included clay figurines of horsemen and girl musicians. This town was destroyed at the end of the 9th or the beginning of the 8th century BC. Town C, destroyed in the second half of the 8th century BC, yielded few building remains. Town D represents a sparsely occupied settlement. It was destroyed in the 7th or early 6th century BC. After a gap in the Persian period, the town was resettled (Stratum P) in the early 6th century BC. Two intersecting paved streets were discovered. The houses along the streets consist of three rooms and a paved court entered from the steet. There was an oven for baking bread in the court. A room near the court served as a kitchen and contained an oven and plastered basid. One room, found full of pottery vessels, apparently served as a shop for the sale of perfumes. In the late 4th century BC (Stratum PB) a fortress was hastily built. It consisted of several subterranean storerooms, in one of which were store jars inscribed with official *Phoenician *inscriptions. The houses of this settlement were apparently scattered in the fields around the mound. The fortress was either Persian or *Tyrian. Its destruction is ascribed to the struggle between the heirs of Alexander the Great over supervision of this region. The buildings of this period suffered a violent end. A fortress, only partly excavated, was also built in the Hellenistic period (Stratum H). It too had storerooms with jars stamped with Greek letters. One bore the seal of an *agoranomos* (overseer of markets) of the year 131 BC. This fortress was destroyed in about 130 BC. The latest fortress on the site was built in the Roman period (Stratum R), in the second half of the 1st century AD. It existed until the middle of the 3rd century AD. In the following Byzantine period the town also extended towards the surroundings of the mound. The houses of this period were spacious (extending over 500 square feet), paved with colorful *mosaics with geometric patterns and their walls were decorated with frescoes. There were also shops, artisan's quarters and a church.

SHUNEM A town in the territory of Issachar (Josh. 19:18), near Mount *Gilboa. It is mentioned in a list of Tuthmosis III, and the *El Amarna letters contain a reference to its destruction by Labaya prince of *Shechem. The lands of the destroyed city became Pharaoh's domain. A Philistine army gathered at Shunem before the battle in which Saul was slain (1 Sam. 28:4). It was the birthplace of Abishag (1 Kgs. 1:3). Elisha lived for some time there and revived the son of the Shunemite woman (2 Kgs. 4:8-37). It was a small village in the Roman period. Eusebius (*Onom.* 158,11-12) knew a place in his day by the name of Sulem, about 5 miles south of *Mount Tabor. Identified with a small mound near the village of Solem.

SHUQBAH (CAVE) Situated on the right bank of Wadi en-Natuf, on the western flanks of the Judean Hills, this cave is one of the largest in Palestine. It was excavated by Miss D.A.E. Garrod in 1928. Under the initial layer of historical periods she found a layer (B) with an assemblage previously unknown in Palestine. She called it the Natufian culture, after the name of the wadi. Characteristic of this culture are crescents, other geometric microliths, sickle-blades and heavy duty tools and also a rich bone industry that included abundant points, needles (one with an eye) and a fragment of a plaque decorated with groups of parallel incised lines. Grinding stone implements such as mortars and pestles were uncovered in this layer, as well as many burials.

Underlying the Natufian layer Miss Garrod found layer C to be a redeposition of layer D, containing a rich Mousterian industry of Levalliosian facies. It appears that after the Mousterian cave occupation, a spring spurted forth within the cave that destroyed part of the Mousterian layers and later redeposited them in the cave. (*See also* *PREHISTORY; *FLINT TOOLS*)

SHUR The desert crossed by the Israelites on their way up from the *Red Sea. Shura in Aramaic, and thus also in Hebrew (cf. Gen. 49:22; 2 Sam. 22:30; Ps. 18:30). It is possible that the desert took its name from the moutainous barrier that encloses the central plataeu of *Sinai, which looks like a wall when approached from the west. It is however also possible that the name Shur is connected with the line of Egyptian fortresses which defended Egypt from the onslaughts of nomadic tribes from *Sinai by way of the Bitter Lakes. Pharaoh Ammenemes I, founder of the 12th Dynasty, mentions the 'Walls of the Ruler' destined to arrest the infiltration of the Asians to Egypt and to crush the sand-dwellers (the nomads of Sinai). Hagar the Egyptian found refuge by a fountain on the way to Shur (Gen. 16:17), and the sons of Ishmael dwelt between there and *Havilah (Gen. 25:18). Exodus (15:22) indicates that Shur was close to the *Red Sea. Some scholars look for its location east of the *Red Sea and the Bitter Lakes while others who believe that the Israelites took a more northerly route, seek it closer to the Mediterranean.

SHUSHAN The capital of *Elam; Shushu or Shushun in the Elamite kingdom, Susa in the Hellenistic period, today Shush in southwestern Persia; on the River Karha. The city is mentioned in Babylonian documents of the 3rd millennium BC. Its ruins extend over an area of about 400 acres, but it is estimated that the full extent of the city was about 1,800-2,300 acres. It was subdivided into four districts: a fortified mound which was the acropolis of the Achamaenids; a royal city with the palaces of Darius and his successors; and two quarters for artisans, merchants and others, the last occupying the right bank of the river. In the extensive excavations made at Shushan palaces and temples of the various periods have come to light.

EXPLORATION: The first excavations at Susa were carried out by W.K. Loftus in 1851-2. In 1897 J. de Morgan founded the Scientific Delegation to Persia which excavated continuously until the recent revolution in Iran. The remains of the ancient city of Shushan extend over four mounds. The earliest settlement on the site goes back to the 4th millennium BC, from which time a ziggurat (tower-*temple) erected on an extremely large brick-built platform has survived. The earliest document written in proto-*Elamite also belongs to this period. In the second half of the 3rd millennium Shushan was conquered several times by the kings of *Mesopotamia, conquests which also influenced the language and the religion. At the beginning of the 2nd millennium Shushan developed into a prosperous capital whose palaces and temples were filled with riches which had been plundered by the kings of Elam at *Babylon. The ascendancy of the latter under Nebuchadnezzar I caused Shushan's decline and ended in the destruction of Elam by Ashurbanipal in the years 647-646 BC. Under Cyrus (590-530 BC) and Darius I (522-486 BC) Shushan became one of the four capitals of the *Persian kingdom, and was the political, diplomatic and administrative capital of the empire in which the kings of Persia spent the winters. Three major routes connected Shushan with the other three capitals: *Persepolis, Ahmetha and *Babylon, and it also formed a center of communications for the whole empire. By way of the rivers Ulai, on which Shushan was situated, and the Tigris (*Hiddekel) one could reach the Persian Gulf, a route taken by Alexander the Great. Darius dug a channel connecting the *Red Sea with the *Nile, by which the Mediterranean could be reached. In his detailed inscriptions in Persian, Accadian and Elamite, Darius described the splendor of his palaces. The city of Shushan was fortified by a strong wall and a moat filled with the waters of the river Ulai. In 324 BC Alexander the Great celebrated his victory over Persia in the palaces of Shushan. His heirs founded the Macedonian colony of Seleucia on the Ulai. From the 13th century AD the city was deserted.

SIDON One of the most ancient Phoenician cities, situated in the narrow fertile plain between the mountains of *Lebanon and the Mediterranean. Lying at the northern end of the plain, it was fortified by a strong wall, and had two harbors defended by a few small islands and a breakwater. Sidon is mentioned in the Babylonian sources of the late 3rd millennium. Among the epics found in *Ugarit, there is one dedicated to Keret, King of Sidon.

The independence of Sidon was curtailed when the kings of the 18th and 19th Dynasties of *Egypt conquered Palestine and Syria (16th-13th centuries BC), but the kings of Sidon were left free to administer their realm as long as tribute was paid. In the El Amarna letters Zimrida, King of Sidon is mentioned. It is known from these documents that in the 14th century the Sidonians rebelled. In the middle of the 12th century BC the city was destroyed and its inhabitants fled to *Tyre, where they helped in the development of that city. But Sidon soon recovered from this crisis and it seems that it was at that time that the Sidonians exerted pressure over the Israelites (Judg. 10:12). In Genesis (10:19) Sidon is referred to as the border of *Canaan, and in Joshua (11:8) it is described as great Sidon (Authorized Version: 'Zidon').

With the rise of Assyria Sidon was subdued along with the other Phoenician towns, and was also required to pay tribute. Ashurnasirpal (883-859 BC) recounts how, having conquered the Land of Amurru (*Amorites), he reached the shores of the Great *Sea, dipped his weapons in its waters, sacrificed to all gods and extracted tribute from Sidon and all the other Phoenician cities. Ahab, King of Israel, married Jezebel, daughter of Ethbaal, King of the Sidonians, who introduced her native cults into Israel. Shalmaneser VI, Sennacherib and Esarhaddon conducted numerous campaigns to subdue Sidon. Esarhaddon deported a proportion of its inhabitants and in accordance with Assyrian practice brought new ones from the east; but the newcomers were quickly assimilated and the prosperity of the city restored. Nebuchadnezzar conquered Sidon on his way to Judah: during his siege half the inhabitants of the city died of plague. After the fall of *Babylon Sidon revived, however, and under Persian protection its domain extended over the Plain of Sharon, from Mount *Carmel to *Joppa.

Sidon was the first Phoenician city to send ships on to the open seas, and its navigators could find their way at night by the stars. The Sidonians were the first people to establish contacts with the Greeks; indeed they are mentioned several times by Homer. Sidon was famous at an early period for its artisans, its gold and silver, its coppersmiths and its weavers, who also undertook embroidery and dyeing. In the Hellenistic period it became one of the largest centers of glass production. The Sidonians also founded many commercial colonies along the shores of the Mediterranean.

Sidon was destroyed when it rebelled during the reign of Artaxerxes III (352 BC). When Alexander the Great besieged and conquered *Tyre Sidon willingly opened its gates and benefited greatly from the fall of its rival. After Alexander's death the town was held by the Ptolemies of *Egypt, but in 198 BC it was conquered by the Seleucids of Syria. In 64 BC Sidon was taken by Pompey, who acknowledged its autonomy and granted it the right to mint coins.

Up to the present no excavations have been made at Sidon, but surface surveys have produced many remains from the Middle Bronze Age onwards.

SILOAM This important source of water for *Jerusalem is mentioned once in the Bible as 'the waters of Shiloah' (Isa 8:6) and later as 'the pool of Shiloah' (Neh. 3:15); it is referred to in the New Testament as 'the pool of Siloam' (John 9:7). Except for the indication in Nehemiah (3:15) that the wall of the pool was close to the king's garden, which is known to have been on the south of the city, no hint to its location is given. It seems that 'the waters of Shiloah that go softly' (Isa. 8:6) refers to part of the tunnel that brought the waters of the *Gihon (*Water supply; *Inscriptions) into the city. The reservoir built by Hezekiah (2 Kgs 20:20) is identified with the Pool of Siloam, located at Birket el-Hamrah. Ancient traditions, still widely believed, have ascribed therapeutic properties to the waters of Siloam (cf. John 9:1, 7).

SINAI A large peninsula lying between *Egypt and Palestine. Triangular in shape, bordered by the two arms of the *Red Sea, the Gulf of *Elath on the east and the Gulf of Suez on the west, it was the scene of some of the most important events in the history of the Israelites. The northern part of the peninsula is a sandy plateau with low hills, while the southern part consists of granite mountains, reaching to a height of 8,600 feet. The climate is that of a desert — dry, with an annual rainfall that does not exceed $2\frac{1}{2}$in in the north and $1\frac{1}{2}$in in the south. Some brackish water may be found by digging in the wadis to a depth of 2-3 feet, but springs are few, and the two larger ones produced the oasis of *Kadesh-Barnea (Num. 20:1-14). Sinai was therefore the habitat of nomads who found some pasture in the valleys, though agriculture was never practised there.

In addition to the trade routes that crossed Sinai from very early times, the turquoise mines in the southern mountainous part of the peninsula were also of great importance. The center of these mines lay at *Serabit el-Khadem, in the northwestern part of the rocky region. Copper slag heaps have been observed around Wadi Nasb and Wadi Mughara, in the same region, but the actual mines have not yet been found. The turquoise mines were exploited as early as the 1st Dynasty of *Egypt (early 3rd millennium BC). At Serabit el-Khadem turquoise mines, a miners' village, a temple and numerous hieroglyphic inscriptions were discovered. Mining continued until the middle of the 11th century BC, but flourished mainly in the time of Tuthmosis III, Amenophis III, Rameses II and Rameses III. The ancient port through which the minerals were exported to *Egypt was discovered 5 miles south of Abu Zneima. It seems that the laborers in the mines were captives brought from Palestine and Syria, against which *Egypt directed many campaigns. This much may be inferred from the 'Sinaitic inscriptions', written in an early Semitic alphabetic script (*Inscriptions) called proto-Sinaitic, that were found at Serabit el-Khadem. It belongs to the 15th century BC and not all of its letters have been deciphered.

Sinai is the only land bridge connecting *Egypt with Palestine, Syria and *Mesopotamia. It was traversed by several important routes from east to west, most of which passed through the northern part of the peninsula (*Roads). Another road went along the western coast, turning to the north, to reach *Elath. There was also a short cut from the western coast through Wadi Feran to Dahab, probably biblical Di-Zahab.

In the Bible the name Sinai refers to a specific mountain (Ps. 68:8); to a range of mountains (Deut. 33:2; Judg. 5:5) and to a desert or wilderness (Exod. 19:2). The same mountain is sometimes called Horeb (1 Kgs. 19:8), and Mount Horeb is also referred to as the 'mountain of God' (Exod. 3:1) and sometimes just 'the mountain' (Exod. 19:2-3).

Even in early times the Patriarchs were already crossing Sinai on their way to *Egypt and back to the land of *Canaan. It was in this wilderness that the Israelites sojourned 40 years, and that Moses gave them the Law. The stations on the route of the Exodus are listed in Numbers (33). Only a few of these stations can now be identified, and those very hesitantly. *Kadesh-Barnea, however, can be identified with more certainty, because of the large spring there, which is big enough to supply a great multitude (Deut. 1:46). The identification of Mount Sinai is also doubtful. The early Christian tradition identifies it with

Jebel Musa, 'Mount Moses', on which Justinian I dedicated a monastery to St Catherine of Alexandria in AD 527. If this identification is correct it would imply that the Israelites made a long, difficult and topographically unnecessary detour in the rough southern part of the peninsula. Other scholars prefer a more northerly route, and suggest that Mount Sinai should be identified with Jebel Hillal, about 30 miles west of *Kadesh-Barnea. Yet others seek it in the land of *Midian, on the Asiatic coast.

In the Hellenistic period Sinai was part of the Ptolemaic kingdom. Greek geographers of the 1st century BC refer to *Nabateans living around Sinai. Recent archaeological surveys and excavations have shown that in different stages of the Paleolithic (*Prehistory) period sites were occupied in the northwestern part of the peninsula. In this region as well as in the south, there are also structures built of fieldstones from the Middle Bronze Age I. These are 6-20 feet in diameter, and are preserved to a height of $2^1/_2$ feet. Burials were made in plain tumuli or in a platform above which two tumuli were erected, one at either end. After a very long gap in settlement the whole peninsula was again occupied by *Nabateans. Of the Hellenistic period remains were found in the north only. At Qasrawit a level containing Hellenistic pottery, but not associated with structures of any kind, underlies a Nabatean temple of the late 1st century BC-1st century AD. This site was still occupied in the late Roman period (pottery lamps decorated with menorahs were also found). In the south a Nabatean pilgrimage center was discovered at Jebel Moneijah, and a temple was found at the top of the overhanging Jebel Serbal. On both sites

Jebel Musa in southern Sinai, seen in the distance

numerous Nabatean inscriptions were found, some inscribed by priests and other functionaries of the temple administration. Moreover along the routes leading from Aila (*Elath) to the mining centers, and especially in Wadi Mukatteb, Wadi Feiran and their tributaries, thousands of Nabatean graffiti have been found. Some of these are dated to the 2nd and 3rd centuries AD. There were also some Greek graffiti from soldiers of the Legio III Cyrenaica, whose duty it was to guard the Provincia Arabia. It seems that the exploitation of the ancient mines was renewed at that time, and that the Nabateans took an active part in it.

Some time in the 5th century AD, Sinai began to attract hermits — mainly from *Egypt, where monasticism originated (*Monasteries). The Monastery of St Catherine, one of the most important centers, still exists, and in its library important manuscripts are kept. There are more remains of monastic settlements in the region, and still others are mentioned in early Christian literature.

SKHUL (ES-) (CAVE) During 1931 and 1932 T.D. McCown excavated in the Cave of es-Skhul, in the neighborhood of the *el-Wad Cave, and uncovered three layers. He discovered many human remains, and the cave is thought to have been the burial-place of the people living in the et-*Tabun Cave. Within this cemetery McCown and A. Keith identified ten individuals: three male children aged 4-10; two women between 30 and 40 years old; and five adults about 50 years old. Although some of the skeletons were fragmentary, the good state of preservation of most of the bones facilitated detailed study by anthropologists. Most astonishing was the great variety of mixed morphological features seen among such a small group of skeletons. This type is defined as *Palaeoanthropus palastinensis*. Whether it represents a separate, transitional type of man who evolved in the Near East or was the result of interbreeding between populations of Neanderthals and *Homo sapiens* is a matter of controvesy. (*See also* *PREHISTORY; FLINT TOOLS).

SLAVERY AND WORK Slavery was an accepted social institution in the ancient world, and the early society of Israelites was no exception in this. Joseph was sold by Midianite merchants for 20 pieces of silver to the Ishmaelites, who in turn sold him to *Egypt (Gen. 37:28, 36). The sale of boys and girls is also mentioned (Joel 3:2), and Job states that he did not discriminate against his slaves (31:13 ff.).

Slavery in the ancient world did not necessarily mean servitude for life. A distinction was made in the ancient Jewish Law between Hebrew and alien slaves. The Hebrew slave was not forced to serve for more than six years, but if his wife were given to him by the master she and the children born to him had to remain with the master if the slave chose to go free (Exod. 21:2-4). Babylonian law mentions a period of servitude of only three years, but in fact manumission is never referred to, so that it is doubtful whether it was ever put into practice.

There were a number of ways by which a Hebrew could fall into bondage, the most frequent being his inability to pay a debt (Lev.25:39, 47). Selling children was also legal (Exod. 21:7; 2 Kgs. 4:1, etc.). The six-year term of bondage already referred to implies that this period was considered sufficient to cover any debt. If poverty was the reason for servitude the slave had to be treated not as a bondsman but as a hired servant, and was to serve until the year of the jubilee (Lev. 25:39-40). But when a girl was sold as a maidservant she had to remain with her owner (Exod. 21:7). A thief could be sold to make restitution for the damage he had caused (Exod. 22:3). If a Hebrew were sold to a stranger his brethren had to redeem him (Lev. 25:47-8), and the same applied to Hebrew prisoners of war (Neh. 5:8). The servitude of a Hebrew slave did not bring about any change in his social and personal status; after completing his term he was free to go to his own house. Moreover it was the duty of his master to furnish him liberally from his own flock, and with grain and wine '...and thou shalt remember that thou wast a bondsman in the land of *Egypt, and the Lord thy God redeemed thee' (Deut. 14:14-15). In certain cases where a slave preferred to stay with his master and his wife and children, the servitude did not last longer than the coming jubilee, when he was able to return to his land, which would be released to him (Lev. 25:54).

Some slaves reached positions of great eminence, examples being Eliezer, the slave of Abraham (Gen. 15:2-4; 24:2), and Joseph (Gen. 39:4). In some cases the master's daughter could be given to a slave (1 Chr. 2:34-5). A slave was allowed to acquire possessions of his own, including other slaves (2 Sam. 9:8-9), and to use the income in order to redeem himself (Lev. 25:49-51). A master was allowed to strike a slave, but cruelty was punished (Exod. 21:20, but see verse 21). According to Deuteronomy (23:15) a fugitive slave was not to be handed back to his owner; this custom differed from Babylonian law. The provisions for manumission were different for non-Hebrew slaves, who were mainly prisoners of war or women taken as concubines for their masters or their sons (Gen. 34:29; Num. 31:9; Deut. 21:10-14).

After the conquest of *Canaan by the Israelites a different kind of servitude emerged. Some Israelite tribes paid tribute, in most cases in the form of forced labor, thus Issachar became 'a servant unto tribute' (Gen. 49:14-15). However the references are generally to slaves of other nations (Deut. 20:10-15; Josh. 16:10, etc.). This system of servitude developed still further in the time of Solomon, during whose reign the greatly increased building activities called for enormous numbers of laborers, so that all that was left of the ancient population came under bondage (1 Kgs. 9:21-2); the male Israelites had to serve three months a year as well (1 Kgs. 5:13-14). The term 'servant of Solomon' for this kind of servitude was still in use at the time of the Restoration (Ezra 2:58; Neh. 7:57, 60). Associated with these servants were the *Nethinim*, some kind of public slaves (Ezra 2:58; Neh. 7:57-60; 11:3). Similar were the Gibeonites, who became 'hewers of wood and drawers of water for the house of God' (Josh. 9:23, and cf. also Ezek. 44:7-10).

From Persian to Byzantine times slavery was still legally recognized. The Mishna and the Talmud refer to all foreign slaves as Canaanite bondmen. Slaves who were circumcised enjoyed many of the privileges of Jewish society, but they were not allowed to acquire property. Nor could they intermarry with foreign slaves and maidservants. Many Jews were sold into slavery after the destruction of the Second Temple, but they were quickly freed. A synagogue of Libertines is referred to in Acts (6:9).

SOBOTA A town in the western part of the central *Negev whose Arabic name, Subeita, has preserved the ancient form. Sobata is not mentioned in any of the early sources; nor does the name appear in any of the inscriptions found there, so it is only through the papyri found at neighboring *Nessana that this ancient name is known to us. The archaeological finds and a *Nabatean inscription in which King Aretas IV is mentioned indicate that the first settlers of Sobata were *Nabateans, at the end of the 1st century BC. It is

Male and female slaves, in an Egyptian wall-painting

even possible that the original form of the name of the site was Shubitu, a Nabatean personal name. The early town extended over the northern bank of a wadi. At the northern end of the town was built a large double reservoir, into which rainwater was collected from the gentle slope. In the vicinity of this installation houses containing *stables were partly excavated. Little of this early town has been investigated. It seems that in the late Nabatean period Sobata with *Mampsis and *Oboda shared in the development of early Nabatean *agriculture. In any case, the valleys stretching along the wadis in all directions are full of farms and farmhouses. In the second half of the 4th century AD, when Christianity was already well established at Sobata, a cathedral was built east of the reservoir and another pilgrimage church was built outside of the town, to its north. In AD 636 Sobata was conquered by the Arabs. The high and degrading taxes (the 'dog-tax'), and especially the disruption of the production and export of wine, on which the town thrived in the Byzantine period, caused its abandonment around AD 700. In the 8th-9th centuries AD a small Moslem community lived at Sobata and built a small mosque near the South Church.

The first European scholar to visit Sobata was E.H. Palmer (1870), who suggested identifying it with Zepath, which Simeon conquered, changing its name to *Hormah (Judg. 1:17). This identification has not been accepted. The site was later visited by A. Musil (1902); A. Jaussen, R. Savignac and H. Vincent (1905), who found the first Nabatean and Greek-Byzantine inscriptions; C.L. Woolley and T.E. Lawrence (1914); and T. Wiegand, who visited Sobata at the head of the Committee for the Preservation of Ancient Monuments attached to the Turco-German Headquarters (1916) and thus had the opportunity to correct some of the mistakes made by earlier scholars. In the years 1934-8 an expedition of New York University and the British School of Archaeology in Jerusalem, under the direction of H.D. Colt, made large-scale excavations at Sobata, the results of which have not been published. In the years 1958-9 the Israel National Parks Authority, under the guidance of M. Avi-Yonah, carried out some clearance and restoration of the ancient buildings.

NABATEAN PERIOD Only an inscription mentioning Dushara, the Nabatean national god, and some typical Nabatean pottery were found in one of the dumps. The excavators could not penetrate deeply enough under the foundations of later buildings to discover the location of the more ancient remains.

BYZANTINE PERIOD The Sobata of that time was an agricultural-monastic town. It had no city wall, as had *Mampsis, nor a citadel, like *Oboda and *Nessana, but to compensate for this the private houses and some of its public buildings were arranged in such a way as to present a solid wall to the outside, without openings or windows. The built-up area measures 500 yards by 480 yards, or approximately 40 acres. The streets, which are quite wide, do not run in straight lines and some have dead ends. It would seem that this apparently haphazard arrangement was not the result of inefficient planning, but rather a well-calculated

device to exploit every drop of the scanty rainfall in the area. Streets, roofs and a number of nicely paved public squares served to collect rainwater. Indeed although there is not a single spring in the whole area, the number of reservoirs and cisterns, both public and private and fed by an elaborate system of channels, is very large. The town had three sections, of which the earliest seems to be the southern one; it lies close to a wadi through which large quantities of water flow in the rainy season. Close to this section a large double pool was constructed, with a capacity of about 1,900 cubic yds of water. Each of the three sections centers around a large church. The churches are of the ordinary basilical type. At the beginning, in the 4th century AD, the churches were mono-apsidal, with rectangular rooms flanking the apse. At the end of the 5th century the city suffered damage from a severe earthquake and the two main churches of the city were supported by heavy buttresses, and side apses with small niches were built at the sides of the main apse. These changes were apparently made because of changes in the performance of the cult of saints and martyrs, and perhaps a necessity was felt to bring the relics closer to the people. The North Church, which is the largest, has a monastery attached. Some of the floors and walls were faced with marble. This could be taken to indicate quite a high standard of living or, more probably, to show that the churches were built and supported by the imperial Byzantine authorities.

Three types of stones of varying quality were used for building houses: a very hard limestone for the foundations and the walls of the lower stories; a yellowish medium-hard stone for the middle parts of the walls and the voussoirs of the arches; and a soft chalk for the upper stories and the cover-stones of the roofs. Wood was hardly used in private houses, except for shelves in built-in cupboards. The roofing of the private houses was based on a system of arches and cover-stones, and only in the churches were large quantities of wood used.

As has already been noted, the economy of the town was based to a great extent on dry farming. All the valleys, large and small, were traversed by dams, and an elaborate system of channels collected the rainwater from afar, in a ratio of 1:20 or 1:30 of catchment area per unit of arable field. Experiments in ancient methods of farming and water use are being carried out by M. Evenari of the Hebrew University on a reconstructed farm at Sobata. The presence of a number of wine-presses (described by the excavators as baths of a very economical type) indicates that, as at *Oboda, grapes were probably one of the main crops. The presses are of exactly the same type as those at *Oboda, the only difference being in one of the installations discovered in the monastery at Sobata: it has all components of those at *Oboda, except that the cells in which individual growers kept their baskets of grapes are missing, probably because the monastery vineyards were common property, so that this part of the installation was unnecessary.

Sobata of the Byzantine period is the best-preserved town in Palestine and presents a good picture of a town on the firnge of the desert at that time.

EARLY ARAB PERIOD Hardly any changes were introduced at Sobata after the Arab conquest of AD 636. Except for a small mosque built in one of the side rooms of the South Church, and some early Arab pottery, there is very little which can be attributed to the Arabs.

SOCOH a) A city in the *Plain, in the northern part of the territory of Judah (Josh. 15:35), where the Philistines gathered to fight Israel (1 Sam. 17:1; Authorized Version: 'Shochoh'); and one of the cities fortified by Rehoboam (2 Chr. 11:7). It was taken by Pharaoh Sheshonq (biblical Shishak) of *Egypt, and later restored to Judah. In the days of Ahaz it was conquered by the *Philistines (2 Chr. 28:18; Authorized Version: 'Shochoh') but was again in the hands of Judah in the days of Hezekiah. In his time it was an administrative center, as is indicated by the numerous stamped jar handles with the seal of Socoh (*Seals). Eusebius (*Onom.* 156,18) states that it is situated on the 9th mile, on the way from *Beth-Gubrin to *Jerusalem. Identified with Khirbet Abbad, where *fortification remains of the period of the kings of Judah were found. Nearby Khirbet Shuweikeh, containing remains of the Byzantine period, may have retained the ancient form of the biblical name. Identified with Khirbet Abbad.

b) A town in the mountains, in the southern part of the territory of Judah (Josh. 15:48); the seat of a family of scribes (1 Chr. 2:55; Authorized Version: 'Suchathites'). Identified with Khirbet Shuweikeh.

SODOM The chief city in the *Plain, on which the Lord 'rained brimstone and fire' (Gen. 19:24-5). Sodom and the other cities of the *Plain were on the southern border of the land of Canaan (Gen. 10:19). Lot, Abraham's brother, chose to live in the Plain of the *Jordan and pitched his tent towards Sodom. All efforts to locate the site of Sodom have been fruitless. It has been sought at the southern and northern ends of the *Dead Sea; while other excavators have looked for it in the depths of the sea. The name Sodom, however, has been preserved in the Arab Jebel Usdum, Mount Sodom, a hill of table salt near the southwestern shore of the *Dead Sea.

SOREK The Hebrew Bible has *nahal* 'rivulet'. The place where Delilah dwelt (Judg. 16:4), near *Zorah. The name has been preserved at Khirbet Suraiq. Eusebius (*Onom.* 160, 2-4) states that even in his time there was on the border of *Beth-Gubrin, near Zareah, a village by the name of Sorek.

SPICES AND PERFUMES In the primitive hygienic conditions of the ancient world the use of scents and ointments was very necessary. In private life perfumes and spices were used as ingredients in perfumed oils, ointments and powders, for cosmetic purposes, to protect the skin from the heat of the sun and the dry air and in medicine. No less important was the role that they played in the religious rituals of the ancient Near East. Numerous utensils used for crushing, mixing, storing and applying the perfumes have been found in excavations. In *Mesopotamia, for instance, oils were used for the care of the hair and pigments for painting fingernails and toenails. To preserve their freshness the ointments were kept in containers made of wood,

alabaster, stone, faience or ivory. Cosmetics were applied with the finger, or more frequently with a spatula made of wood, bone or, in the Roman period, bronze. One of the oils mentioned in the Bible in connection with cosmetics was the 'good oil' (Authorized Version: 'precious ointment': Isa. 39:2; Ps. 133:2, etc.). This was made from flowers, aromatic seeds and fruits mixed with olive oil. Others were oil of myrrh (Esther 2:12) and the ointment of the apothecary (Eccles. 10:1). Perfume was made from flowers, seed and fruits soaked in oil or water. The mixture was sometimes heated and the essence was then extracted and strained through a cloth (cf. Exod. 30:34). Many perfumes were produced from resins and used either in powdered form or dissolved in oils and mixed with other substances to form an ointment. The perfumes were prepared by apothecaries, who were either men (Neh. 3:8) or women (Authorized Version: 'confectionaries'; 1 Sam. 8:13) and who in the days of Nehemiah formed a guild.

Pigments for tinting the hair, face and fingernails were used everywhere in the East. In *Egypt a green paint made of malachite was used for painting the eyebrows and the corners of the eyes. Kohl, to give emphasis to the eyes and to protect them from the strong sun, was applied on the eyebrows and eyelashes: in *Egypt it was made from galena (lead sulphide), while in Palestine and the other countries to the north it was produced from stibium. Its use is referred to frequently in the Bible (2 Kgs. 9:30; Jer. 4:30, etc.). In *Mesopotamia yellow, and more rarely red, coloring was added to the kohl. Nails were also painted with henna, a plant that originated in Somaliland.

Aromatic plants in various forms were much used in all the religious cults of the East. They were mixed according to quite complicated formulae and burnt on the altars (Exod. 37:25, etc.) and in Canaanite temples, in censers and incense bowls; they were also puffed through incense ladles, numbers of which have been found in the excavations.

Small cosmetic palette, Iron Age

Spices and aromatics were very important items in the interational trade of the ancient world. The Bible refers to this commerce and mentions the *Midianites and the Ishmaelites in connection with it (Gen. 37:25). Caravans brought perfumes from Somaliland in East Africa and from the southern Arabian kingdoms along the desert routes to Palestine (cf. Isa. 60:6). Similarly, certain spices that grew in Palestine were. exported to *Egypt and Syria (cf. Gen 37:25; 43:11; Ezek. 27:17). Some spices and aromatics must have come great distances from the Far East, but how they found their way to the Near East is still a mystery. From the Hellenistic period onwards this trade grew in importance, and several kingdoms flourished on it, including the *Nabateans, *Petra and *Palmyra (*Tadmor).

Numerous aromatic plants and spices used in private life or in religious cults or in both are referred to in the Bible. Some of the more important ones are mentioned below:

ALOE (*ohalim; ohaloth*) (cf. Ps. 45:8; S. of S. 4:14; Prov. 7:17) This perfume comes from the resin of a tree that grows in northern *India and Malaya. It is still used for cult purposes in Asia today.

BALSAM (*basaam*) (cf. S. of S. 5:1; Authorized Version: 'spices', 13; Authorized Version: 'myrrh', 6:2; Authorized Version: 'spices') The Hebrew name may signify any perfume, but Josephus (*Antiq.* VIII, 6) and the early commentators say that the aromatic resin was extracted from the opobalsamum tree, which grows around Mecca. Its Arabic name is *basm*, which is close to the Hebrew form. The Mishna refers to this tree under the name *balsamon, opobalsamon* and so on. In Jewish, Greek and Roman sources it is much praised for its excellent fragrance; its high price is also mentioned. Large balsam plantations between *Jericho and *En-Gedi in the time of the Second Temple were also well known to the classical writers.

CASSIA (*quinnamon*) One of the ingredients of holy ointment (Exod. 30:23); also used by women (Prov. 7:17; S. of S. 4:14) and in incense in the period of the Second Temple. There are two types, one of which, the real cinnamon, grows in Ceylon and could not have reached the Near East before the Middle Ages. The other is cinnamon-cassia, which grows in China. It is this substance that is in all probability referred to in the Bible. It was one of the most expensive spices: according to Pliny it sold at 1,000 dinars a pound. The spice was produced from the inner bark of the tree.

GALBANUM (*Helbenah*) (Exod. 30:34) One of the four ingredients of the incense burnt in the tabernacle. In the ancient world *galbanum* was also used as a spice and in medicine. Its Greek name is *chalbane*, which is similar to the Hebrew version.

HENNA (*kofer*) (S. of S. 1:14; 4:13; Authorized Version: 'camphire') This is the scented plant *Lawsonia inermis L.,* which according to the Mishna, was grown in Palestine and, according to the classical sources, also grew around Ascalon (*Ashkelon). It is a small tree whose fragrant flowers grow in clusters. The roots and leaves, when ground and dissolved in water, produce a yellowish-red pigment. It was celebrated in the East for its scent and as a dye for hair, nails and teeth. As a

medicine it was used to cure urinary diseases. The Egyptians also painted their mummies with it. It is grown in Palestine today and is much used everywhere for dyeing hair. The identification of this perfume with camphor has to be dismissed.

FRANKINCENSE (*lebonah*) One of the four ingredients of the incense that was burnt in the tabernacle (Exod. 30:34-5); it was also added to other sacrifices (Lev. 2:1; 24:7). Frankincense was very expensive (Isa. 43:23-4) because it had to be brought a great distance from *Sheba (Jer. 6:20). Because of its high price it was kept almost exclusively among the treasures of the Temple (1 Chr. 9:29), where there was a special storeroom for it (Neh. 13:9). Frankincense was also used in the Second Temple. Those condemned to death were given it mixed with wine before their execution, so that they might not feel pain. Under the name *lebonah* it was known in all the other Semitic languages, hence the Greek name *libanos*. The tree from which the spice was produced grew in *India, Somaliland and the southern parts of *Arabia.

KALAMOS (*kaneh*) One of the ingredients of holy ointment (Exod. 30:23-4). It was an expensive spice, brought from afar (Jer. 6:20) and imported by the Tyrians (Ezek. 27:19). It should probably be identified with an Indian plant, *Kalamos aromaticus*. According to the classical sources it also grew in the upper *Jordan Valley.

MYRRH (*mor*) One of the most important perfumes in biblical times, myrrh was used in the preparation of the oil with which kings were anointed (Exod. 30:23-4). It was also a precious gift (Matt. 2:11) and was much used by women (Prov. 7:17; Esther 2:12; S. of S. 4:14). Myrrh is extracted by means of incisions in the bark of a small tree that grows in tropical Africa and in *Arabia. It was sold both in a solid and in a liquid state. It closely resembles gum; in fact since gum was much cheaper myrrh was often mixed with it. The sages of the Mishna knew of this deception and warned against it. The name myrrh comes from the Semitic languages, from which the Greek and Latin *myrrha* is derived.

NARD (*nerd*) An aromatic plant, the perfume of which was mainly used by women (S. of S. 1:12; 4:13-14). It was also an ingredient in the incense of the Second Temple. It was extracted from plants that grew in Nepal and in the Himalayan Mountains and was brought to the Mediterranean countries by way of *India and Persia. Its Sanskrit name, *nadala*, means 'odoriferous'. Nard was extremely costly. In the time of the Second Temple the essence was extracted by soaking the leaves in oil. This type is referred to in the Mishna and the Roman sources as *foliatum*. The other type, produced from the spikes, was called *spicatum* and its price was 100 dinars a pound.

STYRAX (*zori*, Authorized Version: 'balm') It was among the 'best fruits in the land' that Jacob's sons brought to Joseph in *Egypt (Gen. 43:11), and one of the products exported to *Tyre (Ezek. 27:17). It grew in *Gilead (Gen. 37:25) and was used by the local doctors (Jer. 46:11; 51:8). Its identification with styrax is not at all certain. Some scholars believe that it was a mixture of many spices.

SPIES (WAY OF THE) An important route in the central *Negev by which the Israelites went from *Kadesh-Barnea to Mount *Hor (Num. 20:22; 21:1). The Hebrew Bible has *derech ha-atarim*, which is difficult to explain. Some prefer the reading *tarim* instead of *atarim*, meaning 'the way of the merchants'. This road, scholars believe, coincides with one that was much frequented in all periods and is in use even today; it leads northeast from Ain el-Qudeirat (identified with *Kadesh-Barnea) to Tell el-Milh and *Arad. Remains of the Middle Bronze Age and Iron Age have been discovered along this route. (*See also* *ROADS.)

STABLES Stables are mentioned in the Bible in the account of the riches of Solomon, who had 4,000 stalls for horses and chariots (2 Chr. 9:25; but cf. 1 Kgs. 4:26). These were divided among the chariot cities but he retained some at the disposal of the king in *Jerusalem (1 Kgs. 10:26). Stalls for beasts are also listed among the possessions of Hezekiah (2 Chr. 32:28).

Stables, in the sense of special structures set apart for the housing and maintenance of horses, were already known in *Egypt in early times, but the earliest found in Palestine are no earlier than the Iron Age. Stables have been found on several sites, but the most famous are those of *Megiddo. These were in the form of oblong buildings grouped in units of four or six long halls, each big enough to house 24 to 30 horses. The halls were divided into three parts by two rows of stone pillars, which supported the roof. Between each pair of pillars was a large stone trough. The horses stood face to face in the side aisles, tethered to the pillars, each of which had a perforation through which the ropes were tied. In front of each unit of stabling was a court spacious enough for schooling the horses, with a large watering tank in the center. There was also a shed in each court large enough to hold 50 chariots. The 18 stables discovered at *Megiddo could accommodate 450 horses and 150 chariots. The excavators dated these stables to the time of Solomon, but scholars now believe that they should be attributed to Ahab.

Stables, Mampsis, Roman period

Stables of a very elaborate type, of the Roman period, have been discovered in southern Syria and the *Hauran. In Palestine stables of this kind, built by the *Nabateans in the 2nd century AD were found at *Mampsis, *Oboda, *Sobata and *Ruheibeh. A stable of this sort consisted of a rectangular hall divided into three parts by two rows of arched windows opening on to an inner court. The sill of each window contained a stone trough. The horses were tethered in the narrower side aisles, while the larger central space was used for storing fodder. Each of these stables, which formed part of private houses, could accommodate about 20 horses. It seems that the breeding and upkeep of horses in such a dry area was confined to those of high quality.

STADIUM The term applied to a Roman sports arena that was used for running, for chariot-racing and for athletics, and the buildings associated with it. The course itself was usually about 600 feet long, straight on one side and curved in a narrow ellipse on the other, with starting and finishing posts. The stadium at *Samaria, the first phase of which was Herodian, has been partly excavated. It lies in an artificially levelled depression between two spurs at the foot of the acropolis, within the city wall. The building is rectangular, 650 feet by 230 feet with four colonnaded walks opening inwards on to a central space; it is enclosed by a wall. Apparently this stadium did not follow the normal Roman plan, as no racing track has been identified, and it seems rather to have been a sports field. To Herod's time belongs a building of the Doric order, whose walls were decorated with painted plaster. Another building, of the 2nd century AD, was of the Corinthian order. Josephus (*Life* 92) mentions a stadium at *Tiberias, but this has not been identified.

STONE IMPLEMENTS Stone implements are one of the most ancient products of human culture, existing thousands of years before pottery. The earliest ones, made of local hard limestone or imported basalt, are dated to as early as the Mesolithic period, and they become very common in the Neolithic and Chalcolithic periods. Early stone vessels were used mainly for grinding corn. In the Bible several are mentioned, such as 'mills and mortars' (Num. 11:8) and 'mortars and pestles' (Prov. 27:22). The texts do not, however, specify the difference between the various implements and their uses.

The mortar was one of the earliest stone implements. Generally oval in form, it has a small cup-shaped cavity scooped out of the upper part or it may consist of a shallow bowl standing on three legs. The grinding action was achieved with a pestle. Pestle and mortars continued to be used even after the invention of the more efficient millstones, though during the Early Bronze Age these gradually replaced the pestle and mortar almost completely.

Bowls constitute another class of stone implement. They may be small or large and are mostly decorated with a ridge under the rim. It is not at all clear what they were used for. Quite a large group of stone bowls are set on a high funnel-shaped foot and have triangular or rectangular openings. These vessels made their first appearance late in the Chalcolithic period and were used for cultic purposes, probably for burning incense, as were their clay counterparts (*Pottery). Similar vessels are also found in the Iron Age.

Another cult object made of stone is the incense ladle, which was also common in the Iron Age. These ladles are shaped like a small bowl fashioned in the form of a human hand or a lion's head, with a short perforated pipe attached.

Cosmetic implements were also made of stone. They include containers for oils and ointments made of semi-precious stones such as hematite and serpentine. A beautiful example of such a container of the Late Bronze Age was found at *Megiddo. Another stone cosmetic untensil typical of the Iron Age is a small round limestone bowl used for grinding kohl. These are 3 to 4 inches in diameter and have a cavity of about 1 to 2 inches. The large flat rims are incised with geometric decoration.

Stone implements, bowls and containers not unlike those used in the earlier periods were used throughout the Roman and Byzantine periods. The measuring cups of the time of the Second Temple merit special mention: they are cylindrical in form, with one loop handle near the rim. Typical of these measuring cups is the knife-paring on their sides.

STORES Royal and communal buildings for storing grain were common to most cities. The four Hebrew names by which they were known are rendered in the Authorized Version as 'storehouses' (Deut. 28:8; Jer. 50:26), 'garners' and 'barns' (Joel 1:17). Their shapes are known from excavations and from Egyptian reliefs, the earliest depiction of them appearing on a tomb of the 12th Dynasty at Bani Hasan. The usual granary was circular, with openings below the almost flat roof so that the air could circulate. Stairs on the outside formed a kind of ramp up which the grain was carried, before being poured in at the top. Granaries were either built as free-standing structures or hewn into the rock. Such granaries have been unearthed at Tell en-Nasbeh, *Megiddo, *Jericho, Tell *Beit Mirsim, Tell el-*Ajjul, Tell *Qasileh, *Gezer, *Beth-Shemesh and *Beth-Shean. In many of them grains of corn were found. Dating from the Late Bronze Age, they were between 7 and 10 feet in diameter. In the opinion of W.F. Albright, the frequency of granaries in early Israelite settlements provides evidence of the conditions of great insecurity in which the inhabitants lived.

A large number of circular stores of the Persian period were found at Tell *Jemmeh. These ranged from 18 feet to 30 feet in diameter. W.F.M. Petrie reconstructed them with a conical top on the pattern of Assyrian examples. As they were concentrated in one district of the city they are considered to have had some military significance, perhaps supplying the Assyrian army with food before it set out for *Egypt through the desert. According to Petrie's calculation they could have held provisions for 35,000 people for two months. In addition to the circular structures there were also rectangular storehouses. Examples have been found at *Hazor, the 'House of Pillars', and at *Samaria, the 'House of the Ostracons', both from the time of Ahab.

Fortresses and royal palaces of all periods could accommodate a certain quantity of provisions and arms. Herod's palace at *Masada, for instance, included a large complex of oblong storerooms in which a number of storage jars were found during the excavations.

SUCCOTH *a)* The first station on the route of the Exodus, between *Rameses and Etham (Exod. 12:37; 13:20); tentatively identified with a place near Jebel Mariyam, on the west bank of Lake Timsah, 15 miles from Tell el-Maskhute.

b) A city in the territory of Gad, east of the River *Jordan, but not far from it (Josh. 13:27). There is a river-crossing which Jacob took on his way from *Mesopotamia to *Canaan (Gen. 32:22-3; 33:17). Gideon took revenge on the princes and elders of the city for their refusal to forage his army (Judg. 8:5-16). The copper vessels for Solomon's Temple were cast between Succoth and *Zarethan (1 Kgs. 7:46; Authorized Version: 'brass'). Identified with Tell Dair Alla, east of *Shechem, an identification supported by the Talmud.

SULPHUR A chemical substance known to the ancient world as an inflammable material and mentioned in the Bible in descriptions of destruction. Thus 'the Lord rained upon Sodom and upon Gomorrah brimstone and fire' (Gen. 19:24; cf. also Isa. 30:33; Ezek. 38:22, etc.); and a land of brimstone and salt is contrasted with cultivated land (Deut. 29:23) as an example of devastation. There are quite rich deposits of sulphur in Palestine south of *Gaza, but it is not known whether they were exploited in antiquity. Smaller quantities are also found in the southern part of the *Jordan Valley and around the *Dead Sea, where there are some sulphurous springs; the sulphur content adds to their medicinal qualities. Sulphur was used in *Egypt to a very limited extent, mainly for making amulets and other decorative elements. Most of the sulphur found there is of the Roman period and only small pieces can be ascribed to earlier dates. In Palestine small pieces were found, among other places, on a mosaic floor of the synagogue at *Caesarea. These had probably been used to set the synagogue on fire.

SUSSITA; HIPPOS A Greek city on the heights overlooking the Sea of *Galilee, with the lake on the west; surrounded on the north, northeast and south by deep gorges forming a natural fortification, broken only on the southeast by a narrow ridge giving access to a wadi leading to the lake. From this side the city, founded in the Hellenistic period by the Seleucids or the Ptolemies, was protected by specially strong walls. Its Greek name, Hippos, is a translation of the Hebrew *sus,* horse. The Arabic name is Kalat el-Husn. At the beginning of the 1st century BC Sussita was conquered by the Hasmonean, Alexander Jannaeus (Josephus, *Antiq.* XIII, 395), but it was freed by Pompey in 63 BC (Josephus, *Antiq.* XIV, 74) and made a member of the *Decapolis. It used the Pompeian era on its coinage and from Mero to Caracalla it appears as Antiocheia-ad-Hippum. The coins very often bear the city's symbol on the reverse: a horse, or the head of a horse, or Pegasus. In 20 BC Augustus granted the city to Herod

(Josephus, *Antiq.* xv, 217) and at the time of the division of the kingdom it was placed under the proconsul of Syria (Josephus, *Antiq.* xvii, 320). In the First Jewish Revolt (AD 66-70) it was attacked by the Jews (Josephus, *War* ii, 459) and as a reprisal the Greek inhabitants expelled some of its Jewish inhabitants, holding the rest captive (Josephus, *War* ii, 478). The city was sent on fire by Justus of *Tiberias (Josephus, *Life* 42). In the Byzantine period it was the seat of a bishop.

Several surveys and excavations undertaken by the Israel Department of Antiquities and Museums in 1951-5 have given much information about the layout of the city and the main buildings. It was completely surrounded by a wall, strengthened by several round towers. On the west and east it had gates, and the main street, the *cardo*, ran between them. In the center of the *cardo* was a *nymphaeum*, and near it a large subterranean public reservoir. At some distance a bath was found, built in the Byzantine period. Several large public buildings existed, their architectural splendor still proclaimed by the fragments strewn on the surface. In the Byzantine period the city had four churches, one of which, the cathedral, has been excavated.

In the Roman and Byzantine period the city apparently had a harbor. Merchandise was brought across the water from *Tiberias to Sussita and from there to *Damascus, thus shortening the route, as indicated by the Roman road leading from the Sea of *Galilee to Sussita and references in the Talmud to the city's economic activities.

SUSIYA (KHIRBET) This site, situated some 8 miles south of *Hebron, was hitherto known only from archaeological surveys and excavations. It was described by V. Guerin in 1869, who recognized the importance of the site; in 1874 it was visited by a team of the Survey of Western Palestine who described in more detail the excellent quality of the local architecture. In 1937, during their excavations at *Eshtemoa, L.A. Mayer and A. Reifenberg identified the public building at the northern end of the site as a *synagogue. It was rediscovered in 1969 by S. Gutman who together with Z. Yeivin (Department of Antiquities) and E. Netzer (Hebrew Univeristy) excavated it in 1971-2.

The synagogue is of the broadhouse type (27 feet by 48 feet). It is preceded on the east by an atrium surrounded by porticoes. A monumental staircase leads up to a narthex from which three portals lead to the prayer hall. Benches extend along the southern and western walls. At the north wall, facing Jerusalem, is a raised bema with a niche for the Torah Shrine and an additional platform to its east for the reading of the Law. The bema and platform were faced with marble; there was also a beautifully-made marble screen, inscribed with Aramaic dedications and carvings. Additional rooms were built south of the prayer hall. The atrium and the prayer hall were paved with *mosaics, of which two phases were distinguished. The mosaics of the first phase apparently contained the symbols of the zodiac. The mosaics of the second phase were mainly geometric, but at the western end there was a scene which probably depicted Daniel in the lion's den. In front of the platform is a Torah Shrine flanked by two menorahs, a *shofar* and a *lulab* between two animals. Traces of iconoclastic activities, which apparently followed the Arab conquest, are

The lintel of Menorah cave

Dwelling in wine cellar cave

evident. Four dedicatory inscriptions appear in the mosaic pavement, two in Hebrew and two in Aramaic. One inscription contains partially preserved dates, one according to the Sabbatical Years, and the other according to the Creation of the World. The synagogue is tentatively dated to the end of the 4th — beginning of the 7th century AD and was in use as a Jewish prayer house until the 9th century. In the Islamic period a mosque was built in the atrium of the synagogue.

In 1978 Y. Hirshfeld excavated on behalf of the Hebrew University a house on the western hill. It consists of a large court which contains a baking oven, a manger and other installations. To the east of the court are two dwelling rooms, one with a raised platform for a bed, and two shops opening on a street. The roofs of these rooms are supported by arches. The house is dated, on the basis of coins and pottery, to the end of the Byzantine and Umayyad periods.

Large-scale excavations began on the site in 1984, directed by A. Negev on behalf of the Hebrew University. These were continued in 1985 by A. Negev and Z. Yeivin. The initial survey of the site revealed that it consisted of two separate elements, a horseshoe-shaped hill with the rounded side on the south, and the two arms, an eastern and a western, extending to the north. To the west of this hill is a second hill, on which the above-described house is located. The synagogue

is situated at the junction of the two hills. Excavations in various parts of the horse shoe indicated that it was completely surrounded by a solidly-constructed building, consisting of separate units, built one after the other, beginning at the northern end of the eastern arm. Each unit consisted of an antechamber and a hall. Here and there towers were attached to the units. The entire building was constructed of excellent ashlers, some of them decorated with margins and projecting bosses. One tower featured extremely large bossed ashlars, 6 feet long. In one unit was discovered a ritual bath (*mikveh*), with a lintel decorated with two menorahs, and a slot in the door-post for a mezuzah. These units formed the outer face of a court. The walls of the courts were also built of large ashlars. Entrance to this fortified town was through massive gates opening on narrow streets leading to two or four courts along its sides. Within the courts are cisterns with beautifully made, extremely thick openings and caves. The caves are natural but here and there pickwork can be observed, and where necessary, supporting walls were built of hammer-dressed stones.

Two caves were excavated. One, in the vicinity of the synagogue, is entered through a stepped L-shaped vestibule. The entrance to the cave is decorated with a heavy lintel on which a menorah within a wreath is carved. The main hall of the cave is ventilated and illuminated by a large window in the roof and smaller ones in various parts of the hall. An excellently built wall separates the cave and a plastered cistern to the east. At the back of the cave is a small chamber which was locked by several bolts. It may have served to store costly objects.

A second, much larger cave, is situated to the south of this cave. It too is entered through a stepped vestibule, covered with a barrel vault. At the end of the vestibulum, to the north, is a ritual bath. The cave is more than 60 feet long and is ventilated like the 'Menorah Cave'. A short and narrow tunnel only 34 feet high leads into the innermost part of the cave, which has been identified as a *wine-cellar. It is sparingly illuminated by small windows cut in the roof. On the right side of the cave, where the natural rock was not thick enough, isolation of the wine-cellar was achieved by the construction of very heavy retaining walls and by a thick fill of earth and quarry waste between the rock and the wall. This part of the cave was served by another ritual bath, whose entrance was closed at some stage. The short tunnel leading to this part of the cave was tightly sealed with stones when the fermentation of the wine took place. Adjoining the main cave, on the east, is another small cave, also entered through a barrel-vaulted vestibule, which is flanked by a small cistern and a ritual bath. In this small cave grape juice brought from the wine-presses was strained and poured into jars. It was transported into the main cave through a narrow passage at the western side of the small cave.

In the 1985 excavations a large wine press was unearthed in the court of the wine-cellar cave. In addition to the wine-presses, olive presses were also found, attesting to the town's other important source of income. The town is tentatively dated to the 3rd and 4th centuries AD. At some later date the caves were apparently abandoned, and the new western quarter was built. The caves were again occupied in the 12th and 13th centuries AD when Salah ed-Din fought the Crusaders. A. Negev identifies this site as the Jewish Carmel.

SYNAGOGUES It seems that the earliest synagogues — houses of assembly and prayer of Jewish congregations — originated in *Babylonia during the exile of the Jews after the destruction of the First Temple and in the Persian period. In the Hellenistic period there were synagogues in many Jewish centers throughout the Hellenistic world. For this we have the evidence of two inscriptions from *Alexandria, one of the reign of Ptolemy III (246-221 BC) and another of 37 BC, in both of which synagogues are mentioned. The earliest evidence from Palestine is the inscription of Theodotus, son of Vetinus the Priest, of the 1st century AD, which was found in *Jerusalem. The evidence for the early Roman period is more abundant, both in Palestine and in the Diaspora. The earliest remains of buildings that may have been synagogues are two identified by the excavators as such, one at *Masada, the other at *Herodium.

The synagogue, as a well-defined type of building, dates back to the late 2nd century and early 3rd century AD, both in the Diaspora (Miletus, Priene and Sardis) and in Palestine (the Galilean synagogues).

The Palestinian synagogues have been classified, according to their plan and decoration, into three chronological types: early (3rd-4th centuries); transitional (4th-5th centuries), and late (5th-7th centuries). EARLY TYPE Found mostly in *Galilee and in the *Bashan and *Golan, synagogues of the early type follow the mishnaic prescriptions that a synagogue should be built in a prominent part of the town, such as the top of a hill, close to the seashore or near a spring. They were all built of excellently drafted ashlar and the ground plan was either an almost perfect square (the ratio between length and width being approximately 10:11) or a rectangle. The inner arrangement consisted of a triple or a quadruple colonnade; in the former type the side of the building facing the entrance had no columns. The largest synagogue (*Capernaum) had an area of 385 sq feet, while the smaller ones were less than 200 sq feet. Typical of this group was the triple entrance (though some of the smaller ones had a single entrance only) in the richly decorated main façade of the building, facing *Jerusalem, the direction in which the prayers were said. The center one of the three entrances was larger than the two side ones. Above the decorated lintels (the most usual decoration being a wreath bound with a Hercules knot) were arches with small windows, and the whole was crowned by an arched gable known as a 'Syrian gable'. The arches, windows and doors were all richly decorated, and light entered the building from this side only. In some places, at *Kefar Baram, for instance, there was a porch in front of the main façade, while others such as *Capernaum and *Chorazin had a raised platform. Some synagogues had a colonnaded court adjoining the main building.

The style of architectural decoration in the early synagogues did not differ from the one that was in vogue in Syria and the Hauran in pagan buildings of the same period. Hellenistic-Syrian architecture and art included classical elements, such as the Corinthian capital, the Attic base and the frieze decorated with floral and vegetal motifs. Synagogue art also included such pagan motifs as images of Hercules, Nike bearing wreaths, Medusas, griffins, hyppocampi, Dionysiac scenes and so on, plus some apotropaic (protective) symbols such as the pentagram, the 'Seal of Solomon', and the hexagram, the 'Shield of David'. Religious symbols, such as the menorah and the Torah Shrine, were used only rarely in the early synagogues. The inscriptions, mostly in Aramaic and a few in Greek, are generally donors' dedications. In contrast to the richly decorated façades the interiors were almost devoid of decoration, and there was no furniture other than the benches built in along the long walls.

There is still no satisfactory answer to several problems relating to the synagogue ritual. Some scholars suggest that there may have been a balcony for the women above the colonnade, but there is no archaeological evidence of this. Another problem is still more puzzling. Most scholars believe that there was no permanent place for the Torah Shrine in this type of synagogue, and that it was kept in a side room. The order of worship would thus have been: entry and seating of the congregation on the benches; carrying of the Torah Shrine from the side room and its placing before the central door in the façade (the congregation would then be praying in the direction of the shrine); return of the Torah Shrine to its place; departure of the congregation. Other scholars think that the entry was not through the main doors, but by a door in one of the side walls But such doors have been found in only a few of these synagogues. However, excavations in the synagogue of Sardis have shed new light on the problem. There the synagogue, built also in the 3rd century AD, was a beautifully ornamented basilica with two ritual focal points: a permanent place for the Torah Shrine, in front of the central one of the usual three entrances in the wall facing towards *Jerusalem; and, at the other end, a raised bema from which the prescribed weekly portions from the Bible were read and the sermons preached. Thus the congregation, seated on the benches lining the long walls, could face both the shrine and the bema. It is possible that the early Palestinian synagogues had the same arrangement, but with no permanent fixtures for the shrine and the preacher. It is probable that the design of the synagogues originated in the Diaspora and not in Palestine.

TRANSITIONAL TYPE According to the accepted view the arrangement of the early type of synagogue was not satisfactory to congregations. During the late 3rd and 4th centuries AD, attempts were therefore made to separate the place of entry from the direction of prayer. Thus at *Beth-Shearim there were three entrances in the south façade and no fixed place for the shrine; but on the other hand there was a bema close to the opposite wall, as at Sardis. In a second phase the central door was blocked and a permanent place for the Torah Shrine was provided. At *Eshtemoa a different solution was suggested. Here a broadhouse type of building was constructed, with a niche for the Torah Shrine in the wall facing *Jerusalem; the entrance to the building was on one of the short sides, at right angles to the wall facing *Jerusalem. At *Hammath (*Tiberias) a gradual change can be followed. In the earliest synagogue, dated to the first half of the 2nd century AD, the entrance to the building was on the south, the side facing *Jerusalem, and there was no permanent place for the shrine, as was the case in the early type. But instead of architectural decoration there was a mosaic pavement, a typical feature of the synagogues of the late type. The second stage, dated to the late 3rd or early 4th centuries AD, already had a permanent place for the Torah Shrine near the south wall and the entrances had been moved to the northern wall; in the synagogue of this period the whole floor was ornamented with a mosaic pavement of a very advanced type, previously believed to be typical of the synagogues of the 5th-6th centuries.

LATE TYPE The typical features of this type are an apse in the wall opposite the entrance, in which the Torah Shrine stood; an entrance to the building on the side opposite the direction of prayer; floors decorated with mosaic pavements; and the absence of external architectural decoration. The fully developed synagogues of this type had previously been dated to the late 5th

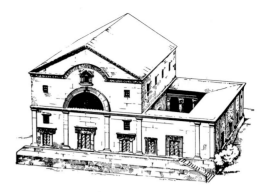

Reconstruction of the synagogue at Capernaum, Late Roman period

century AD, the earliest known example being the synagogue of *Gerasa; it could not have been later than the end of the century, since a church was then built there in its stead. However, the discovery of a synagogue at *Hammath (*Tiberias) now makes this dating doubtful. But by the 5th century there was only one type of synagogue in Palestine: a basilical building, with a court in front of it and a cistern in the middle of the court. The court gave entry to a narthex, from which three doors led into the prayer house proper. The hall was divided by two rows of columns into a nave and two aisles. Close to the wall facing *Jerusalem, opposite the entrance, was a raised bema and behind it an apse in which the Torah Shrine found a permanent place. In the floor of the apse was a place for the *genizah,* in which scrolls that went out of use were kept, or for the community chest. In certain cases this part of the synagogue was separated from the rest of the hall by a decorated marble screen. The synagogue of the late type is thus an almost exact replica of the Christian church of that time.

Methods used for building synagogues of the late type were greatly inferior to those used earlier. Hardly any ashlar was used, for instance, and there was no architectural decoration on the outside of the building; nor was there much inside, save for the column capitals and the screens and their posts. The only ornamentation was on the floor, which was paved with mosaics. Artistically the floors range from work of high quality, such as the mosaic pavement at *Hammath (*Tiberias), which was most probably executed by foreign artists, to those of *Beth-Alpha and *Beth-Shean, made by two local artists, a father and son. They can be classified into several groups, ranging as they do from simple geometric patterns, scenes of rural and animal life, to the most elaborate decoration in which Jewish religious symbols and images appear alongside pagan symbols.

The more elaborate type of decoration has certain constant elements: a dedicatory inscription close to the entrance, flanked by two lions or other animals; a biblical scene, usually symbolizing salvation, such as Noah's Ark (*Gerasa) or the sacrifice of Isaac (*Beth-Alpha) or Daniel in the lions' den (*Naaran); a central panel in which Helius is depicted riding in the celestial chariot; and around this a larger circle in which the 12 signs of the zodiac, each with its name in Hebrew, are depicted. In the corners of the enclosing square are the four seasons of the year, depicted as maidens holding the fruits of the season; the Torah Shrine flanked by two menorahs (*Menorah), accompanied by the other symbols of the religious festivals, the ram's horn, the palm branch, the citron and the incense shovel. Most synagogues have numerous dedicatory inscriptions in Aramiac and Greek; these indicate that they were built with contributions from the whole congregation, and sometimes even with donations from neighboring communities.

In studying synagogue art we may note the fight put up by extremists who attempted to abide by the second commandment: 'Thou shalt not make unto thee any graven image, or any likeness of any thing that is in heaven above, or that is in the earth beneath, or that is in the water under the earth' (Exod. 20:4). Although carvings and reliefs abound in the early type of synagogue, statuary in the round is in fact rare (*Chorazin, *Kefar Niboraya). The obliteration of human faces in the synagogue at *Capernaum is attributed to Jewish iconoclasts, while the careful destruction of all human and animal likeness in the mosaic floor of the synagogue of *Naaran is thought to be the work of a later iconoclastic movement. In any case, the synagogues at *Jericho and at *Hammath-Gader, and the one of the latest phase at *Hammath (*Tiberias) have no human images at all, and the decorative motifs are purely geometric.

Discoveries made in the last decade both enrich our knowledge of the Palestinian synagogues as well as cast serious doubts on their division into types, and especially their dating. The discovery of the rather early synagogue at *Hammath indicates that *mosaics were by no means a typical feature of the late type alone and on the other hand the excavations at *Capernaum revealed that this synagogue, considered a prototype of the early synagogues, was not built before the end of the 4th or beginning of the 5th century AD. An attempt to explain this by assuming that the builders of the late period re-used material of an earlier building does not alter the evidence of its date. In fact, this late dating is also supported by excavations of additional Galilean and Gaulanite synagogues.

The discovery of traces of a zodiac and the portrayal of Daniel in the lions' den at *Khirbet Susiya indicate that these motives were also employed in the south of the country. A unique discovery is the mosaic pavement in a small synagogue at *Beth-Shean in which a scene from the Odyssey is portrayed. The detailed inscriptions found in the synagogues of *Rehob and *En-Gedi demonstrate that the Holy Land still conceals many further surprises in this field as well.

T

TAANACH A fortified Canaanite town at the southern end of the *Jezreel Valley, close to the Wadi Ara pass. The earliest mention of it comes in the account of the conquest of *Megiddo in 1468 BC by Tuthmosis III. It then appears in the *El Amarna letters. The King of Taanach appears in the list of 31 kings vanquished by Joshua (Josh. 12:21), though in other passages we are told that Taanach was not conquered by the Israelites (Josh. 17:11-12; Judg. 1:27). Even when Israel was strong enough to impose tribute on the *Canaanites the town was still not taken (Josh. 17:13; Judg. 1:28); it withstood conquest until the battle of Deborah, which took place 'in Taanach by the waters of *Megiddo' (Judg. 5:19). During the reign of Solomon Taanach was in the same district as *Megiddo and *Beth-Shean. It was destroyed by Pharaoh Sheshonq and is depicted in a relief in his temple at Karnak (*Thebes).

Tanaach is identified with Tell Tiinik, about 5 miles southeast of *Megiddo. The mound covers an area of 16 acres and rises about 160 feet above the valley. It occupies a strategic point at the intersection of important roads coming from *Acco in the north, *Jerusalem in the south and the Mediterranean coast in the west. The site was excavated in 1901-2 by E. Sellin on behalf of the University of Vienna. But the work was carried out without proper attention to the stratification; the excavators were interested only in single finds and did nothing to relate them to the strata in which they were discovered. Nor was the material adequately published. Apart from an Arab fort on the top of the mound, no effort was made to attribute any building to its period (*Archaeology, methods of research).

The earliest period of occupation on the site was the Early Bronze Age II, represented by numerous sherds and one tomb. To the Middle Bronze Age II belong a wall and a glacis, which surrounded the whole mound. To the same period belongs the house of a wealthy citizen on the western part of the mound. Associated with this were child burials in jars under the floor. This building suffered violent destruction at the end of the Middle Bronze Age II. Above the Early Bronze Age tomb a palace was discovered. In the debris above this palace were 40 clay tablets written in Accadian, dating from the middle of the 14th century BC. Some of these mention Amenophis, possibly the second of this name, who after serving as Egyptian governor of *Canaan became Pharaoh of *Egypt. Like the *El Amarna correspondence, these letters are important for a study of administrative, military, economic and social matters in the land of *Canaan. To the Late Bronze Age II belongs another large palace, whose walls were 7 feet thick. A citadel on the west of the mound may possibly be of the same period. A section of a wall and a tower dated to the Iron Age I were also unearthed. Interesting among the single finds is a clay censer (*Cult objects) decorated with two pairs of lions standing on two sphinxes. There were also some remains of Iron Age II, and of the Persian, Roman, Byzantine and Arab periods.

Taanach was re-excavated in 1963, 1966 and 1968 by P.W. Lapp on behalf of the American School of Oriental Research. From these excavations a clearer picture of the occupational history of the site emerged. The main effort of the excavators was concentrated on the fortifications of the city in the various periods. The earliest were of the Early Bronze Age. To this period belong two massive stone walls, one of

One of the Taanach tablets, Late Bronze Age

which is still standing to a height of 7 feet. Another wall, of approximately the same height, was 11 feet thick. To this phase in the same period belongs a massive stone wall protected by a huge glacis, the largest of its kind known. The Middle Bronze Age II is represented by two complexes of glacis. These were all found in sections made on the south of the mound. To the west additional sections of fortifications of the same periods were discovered and remains of houses of the Early Bronze Age city were also found. Another building was of the Late Bronze Age I. To the 12th century BC belong two houses, one of which was destroyed at the end of that century. In the ruins of this a clay tablet written in the Canaanite cuneiform script was found. To Iron Age I belongs a cultic basin, near which a mould for casting Astarte figurines was found, as well as about 140 ankle bones of pigs, which were probably sacrificial victims. The latest building remains discovered on the site were of the Persian and Arab periods.

TABAN (ET-) (CAVE) Lying $1\frac{1}{2}$ miles south of *Abu Sif Cave in the *Judean Desert, this cave was excavated by R. Neuville. Its importance lies in the assemblages of two layers found *in situ* on a rocky ledge. These represent the continuation of original occupation layers that have been destroyed within the cave. The most important finds were Emireh points, which are considered to be typical of the Upper Paleolithic I period. The assemblage also included numerous scrapers on flakes and blades as well as dihedral and polyhedral burins (*See also* *PREHISTORY; *FLINT TOOLS*).

TABERNACLE The portable shrine that the Israelites took with them into the desert, made by Moses according to God's command (Exod. 25:8); also named *ohel moed*, the Tent of Congregation. Its place was outside the camp, where all who sought the Lord could go (Exod. 33:7); there God also spoke to Moses. The Ark of the Covenant was kept in the tabernacle even after the conquest of *Canaan, its permanent place being at *Shiloh (Josh. 18:1).

Fragment of a cornice of the Tabernacle, the synagogue at Capernaum

The tabernacle was built by Bezalel, son of Uri (Exod. 31:1-11), according to a design that was revealed to Moses on Mount *Sinai (Exod. 25:9; 26:30). It consisted of three walls made of boards of shittim wood (acacia), plated with gold (Exod. 26:15-22). Colored curtains, embroidered with cherubim, were hung over the boards. Above the tabernacle were spread 12 plain goatskin curtains and these, in turn, were covered with rams' skins and badgers' skins painted red. The tabernacle was divided into the holy place and the Holy of Holies by a veil (Exod. 26:31-3) suspended on four wooden posts. The tabernacle was 30 cubits long and 10 cubits wide and it stood within a courtyard measuring 100 cubits by 50 cubits (Exod. 27:9-13). This courtyard was divided into two equal parts: in the eastern half stood the tabernacle, while in the western half the vessels used in services were kept. It was surrounded by a fence made of posts from which hangings were suspended. The entrance to the court was on the east, and it was overhung with a veil (Exod. 27:16), like the one at the entrance to the tabernacle. The most important ritual object was the altar of burnt offerings (Exod. 27:1-2), which stood in the center of the eastern half of the court and measured 5 cubits by 5 cubits by 3 cubits. Like most of the furniture in the tabernacle it was made of acacia wood, a tree native to *Sinai, and was plated with copper. It had horns at its four corners. The priests were ordained near the altar (Exod. 29:5-12, 20) and sacrifices were made upon it (Lev. 8:15). Vessels made of copper were kept alongside it (Exod. 30:17-21). The most important pieces of furniture in the tabernacle were the Ark of the Covenant, the golden cherubim, the incense altar and the table for the shewbread, all of which stood in the holy place. At the southern end of the tabernacle stood the golden menorah. (*See also* *CULT OBJECTS*).

TABOR (MOUNT) A mountain at the southern limit of lower *Galilee, 1,700 feet above sea level, 1,200 feet above the *Plain. Its inverted, bowl-like shape attracted attention in ancient times and it was therefore linked with Mount *Hermon and Mount *Carmel (Jer. 46:18; Ps. 89:12). It was a place of worship from very ancient times (Hos. 5:1) and it was the place where the boundaries of the territories of Zebulun, Issachar and *Naphtali met (Josh. 19:23, 34). In the time of Deborah the tribes gathered there to give battle to the *Canaanites (Judg. 4:6, 12, 14). Early in the Hellenistic period the Ptolemies built a royal fortress here. Later it was conquered by the Hasmonean Alexander Jannaeus. Josephus, while fortifying *Galilee against the Romans, built a wall on the mountain (*War* II, 573; IV 54-61). Early Christian tradition placed the scene of the Transfiguration on the mountain, and churches to commemorate the event were built there from an early period.

TABUN (ET-) (CAVE) This cave is situated in a west-facing escarpment of Mount *Carmel, with the coastal plain stretching below it. The same escarpment, bordering the outlet of Wadi Mughara, also contains the caves of el-*Wad and es-*Skhul. It was excavated by Miss D.A.E. Garrod and D.M.A. Bate in 1929 and 1931-4 and found to have the thickest deposits (about

45 feet) so far known in Israel. The lowest layer (G) contained chopping tools, cores, flakes and a few racloirs; it was called Tayacian after a similar culture known in France. Layer F is an Upper Acheulian layer with many tools of which one-third are hand-axes, mostly in the shape of hearts. Many chopping tools and racliors were collected. This layer is considered to be an accumulation from the end of the last Interglacial period, or even from the beginning of the Würm Glacial period. The very thick layer lying above it (E) is more than 24 feet deep and was subdivided by the excavator into four sublayers.

Out of 44,000 artifacts Micoquian handaxes predominate, in addition to the many racloirs and angular racloirs. Much importance was attached to a number of backed blades and the few end-scrapers and burins uncovered, which gave an Upper Paleolithic character to three layers. Unfortunately, owing to the excavation techniques employed, it was impossible to isolate these layers. The entire cultural complex of layer E was originally described by Miss Garrod as Micoquian, reflecting its affinities with the French culture of that name. But it was subsequently relabelled as Acheulo-Yabrudian, as a result of the influence of the excavations at the site of Yabrud.

Layers D, C and B contained a rich Mousterian industry of Levalloisian facies. The lower levels (D and C) were classified as Levallois-Mousterian by Miss Garrod and were typified by the many retouched points and broad flakes. Layer B plus the filling of the chimney, was labelled Upper Levallois-Mousterian; it is characterized by many skillfully made implements on rather thin and delicate flakes. An almost complete skeleton of a woman was found at the base of layer B and intruding into layer C; a separate mandible was also found in layer C. Both of these are ascribed to *Palaeoanthropus Palestinensis*. Two carbon 14 datings acquired from layers C and B gave the dates of 38,950 BC and 37,750 BC respectively.

Excavations at the Tabun Cave were renewed between 1967 and 1972 under the direction of A. Jelinek of the University of Arizona, Tuscon. The application of sophisticated methods of excavation resulted in a much more complex stratigraphical sequence than that described by Garrod. The lithic assemblages ranging from Acheulian to Mousterian were better related to this complex and detailed sequence.

Various prehistoric cultures were identified in layer E (Garrod's). These included Acheulian, Yabrudian, Acheulo-Yabrudian and Amudian.

Jelinek considers these entities as a single cultural tradition which he named 'Mugharan'. According to the results of the lithic analysis the Acheulian layers characterized by high frequencies of bifaces do not differ from the Yabrudian layers characterized by side scrapers, mainly dejete, transversal and convergent types. Furthermore, Jelinek's analysis proved that the 'characteristics' of the Yabrudian assemblages appear in the Acheulian ones and vice versa. He regards the Amudian phenomenon as a facies within the Mugharan tradition. Jelinek views the cultural sequence at Tabun as a cultural continuum, and regards the Mousterian layers as a development from the previous Mugharan tradition. (*See also* *PREHISTORY; *FLINT TOOLS).

TADMOR; PALMYRA An oasis in the Syrian desert on the road from the Mediterranean to the *Euphrates, about half-way between the river and the last two cities to the west, Homs in the north and *Damascus on the southern route.

Tadmor is an ancient Semitic name that appears for the first time at the beginning of the 2nd millennium BC, on tablets found at Kultepe, Cappadocia. During the period of Hammurabi (18th century BC) it appears in two cuneiform letters from *Mari. Then there is silence until it is mentioned in the annals of Tiglath-Pileser I. A proposal that Tadmor should be identified with the *Tamar of 1 Kings (9:18; Authorized Version: 'Tadmor'), built by Solomon, has been rejected. Josephus made the same suggestion (*Antiq.* VIII, 154), pointing out that Tadmor and Palmyra were one and the same, as was further attested by honorary inscriptions. He then adduced the false etymology of Tadmor — Hebrew *tamar* (palm tree) — Latin *palma*. Any identification of settlements earlier than the Hellenistic period must be hypothetical, since no remains whatsoever have been found in the excavations at Tadmor that throw light on the evidence provided by the ancient sources. From the late Hellenistic-Roman periods sound historical sources are available, though their number is somewhat small in relation to the city's importance. Appian (*Civil Wars* v, 9) relates that in 41 BC Antonius set out for Palmyra in order to plunder its riches, planning to profit from the sale of Indian and Arabian goods on the Roman market. Somehow the inhabitants learned of the impending attack and retreated beyond the *Euphrates with their possessions, so that he had to return empty-handed. Pliny (*Nat. Hist.* V, 88) describes the city's greatness and its special position, situated as it was between two great empires, the Parthian and the Roman.

Opinions among scholars are divided as to the date when Palmyra became subject to Rome. Some opt for the time of Tiberius, when Germanicus is alleged to have visited the *Euphrates region. Others date it to

Relief showing the gods of Palmyra (Tadmor)

the beginning of the 2nd century AD, under Trajan. In the light of present knowledge it is quite clear that Rome penetrated gradually, and not by force of conquest into Palmyrene trade activities and civil life, in a manner similar to that in which the Nabatean kingdom was annexed. This process began some time in the 1st century AD; it is known, for instance that Palmyrene archers took part in the First Jewish Revolt, that a road from Palmyra to Sura was constructed in AD 75 and that there was a Claudian tribe at Palmyra. The annexation was complete by the middle of the 2nd century AD, as is shown by the tariff list of Palmyra, drawn up in AD 137 in order to end the disputes between the Roman tax-collectors and the merchants of the city. The city was accorded the title of Palmyra Hadriana when Hadrian went there during his visit to the East in AD 129-30. A cavalry unit that was stationed there at about the same time, the ala Thracum Herculania, was transferred to *Egypt in AD 185 and Palmyrene soldiers, their first unit dating from the reign of Trajan, were stationed in many parts of the empire, including Numidia (Africa) and along the Danubian frontier. Most of them were archers and indeed the city was famed for its archers.

Palmyra was made a Roman colony under Septimius Severus and the great prosperity enjoyed by the Roman Empire during the time of the Severan Dynasty left its mark on the city. Towards the middle of the 3rd century, in the troubled years when the Sassanid Empire threatened the *Roman eastern provinces, Septimius Odaenathus, Prince of Palmyra and of consular rank, became the most important political factor in the East. He took the side of the Romans and inflicted a severe defeat on Shaput, King of Persia, in AD 260. Until 267 he continued to fight against the Persian Empire, having part of the Roman army under his command as well as his own Palmyrene troops. He assumed the title of king, but was murdered, together with his son. The kingdom was then ruled by Zenobia, his second wife, who defeated the Roman army and conquered Syria, Egypt and part of Asia Minor. After she had proclaimed her son 'Augustus' Aurelian marched against her in 271 and destroyed the city in AD 273, leading her as a prisoner to Rome. This was a stroke from which Palmyra was never to recover and it lived on only as a small and unimportant village. Whereas Odaenathus had been content to recognize the nominal sovereignty of the Roman emperor, although he was in fact King of the East, Zenobia's challenge to the Romans led directly to the city's downfall.

Excavations were undertaken by several European institutions and are continuing today by the Syrian Department of Antiquities; work includes restoration and preservation of the ancient remains. The city was enclosed by a wall dating from the time of Zenobia. Inside it were a large number of splendid buildings, of which the colonnaded streets with tetrapyloi, the agora, the senate building, a theater, the sanctuaries of Bel, Baal-Shamin and Nabu and others have been unearthed. Many buildings were found in an excellent state of preservation, since after the city's decline much of it had been covered under sand. The camp

and the baths of Diocletian belong to the last phase of occupation. Much work has been done in the extensive necropolis. Many tombs were adorned with funerary busts of the deceased, and these opened up a whole field of research into the relationship between eastern (i.e. Palmyrene) and Roman art.

The large quantity of inscribed material that came to light in the excavations is also most important. About 1,000 inscriptions in the Palmyrene script and language, some of them bilingual (i.e. with a Greek translation) provide information about the social, civil and political life of the town and about its trade and religion. The most important document is the tariff list, which enumerates the merchandise handled by the town's merchants and thus sheds much light on the development of trade in the East.

TAMAR, TAMARA A town on the southern border of the Land of Israel (Ezek. 47:19; 48:28) whose name is missing from the other lists of the country's borders (Num. 34:3-6; Josh. 15:1-4), where the 'wilderness of Zin' is mentioned as the southern border of the land at that point (and see also 1 Kgs. 9:18 - for Tadmor read Tamar). In 2 Chronicles 20:2 'Hazazon-Tamar is indeed identified with En-Gedi' where Moab and Ammon fought Jehoshaphat: 'There cometh a great multitude...' Late Roman sources mention a place called Tamara. Eusebius (*Onom.* 8,8) locates Hazazon-Tamar in the desert of Kadesh. He also mentions a village called Tamara, one day's journey from Mampsis on the road from Hebron to Aila (*Elath) where there was a garrison in his time. The *Notitia Dignitatum* (34:40), of the 4th century AD, mentions a Palestinian cohort there. Several scholars have suggested that the Tamar referred to in the Roman sources should be identified with Mesad Tamar (Qasr el-Juheiniye), c. 12 miles east of Mampsis, which contains remains of a large castellum. It was excavated in the years 1973-6 by M. Gihon of Tel Aviv Univesity.

The castellum is a square structure (120 feet by 120 feet) with four projecting towers (20 feet by 20 feet) in the corners. All the internal structures lean against the walls of the fortress. Along the northwest and southeast sides of the castellum were barracks, each consisting of six rooms to house two sub-units of Roman soldiers, as well as quarters for officers, and an office or armory. The living quarters of the commander of the fort were located in the southeastern corner from which there was direct access to the headquarters, the regimental shrine and the unit's offices. In the middle of the northeastern side was a gate roofed with a barrel vault; there was a guardroom at the side. A storeroom or a stable was located east of the gate and a bakery with a flour mill to its west. The soldiers' rooms opened onto porticoes with ashlar pillars which provided a shaded area in front of each room.

In the middle of the courtyard was a square pool (30 feet by 30 feet; 12 feet deep). Above it, a flat roof constructed of stone slabs set on wooden beams was supported by eight pillars. The castellum was built in the center of the drainage basin of the surrounding hills and a channel along the base of the southwestern side of the wall conveyed water directly into the pool.

Staircases on either side of the gate led from the courtyard to the flat roofs.

Mesad Tamar was erected in the 1st century AD (?) by the Nabateans and came into Roman possession following their annexation of the Nabatean Kingdom in AD 106. The corner towers may have been added only then, in the time of Trajan. The castellum was abandoned during the days of Hadrian and was seized again by the emperor Aurelian, apparently after his conquest of the Palmyran Empire in AD 271-3.

Although the towers and outer walls remained standing throughout the history of the building and were only repaired occasionally until its destruction in the Moslem conquest in c. 635, the internal structures were built anew on a plan similar to the original one, with minor changes of dimensions.

Four phases can be distinguished in the history of the fortress. In the third phase the garrison soldiers were replaced by militia-farmers and in the last phase, which was apparently rebuilt after the Persian conquest (614-24), the fort also served as a shelter for refugee families from the surrounding area.

The fort's position at the bottom of the valley through which the Roman road passed to the Jordan Valley was of great assistance in blocking this passage. To prevent a surprise attack and to ensure contact with the other posts on the *Limes* through a system of signals, six forts and watchtowers were built in the surrounding hills. The excavation of the tower south of the fortress revealed it to be contemporaneous with the latter.

TANIS; TANIS-ZOAN A city in lower *Egypt, always referred to as Zoan in the Bible, identified as San el-Hagar; in the northeastern part of the *Nile Delta, about 20 miles southeast of Damietta. Because of changes in the course of the river Tanis now lies inland, though it was formerly a harbor on the *Nile. The remote antiquity of Zoan is hinted at in Numbers (13:22), which says, 'Now Hebron was built seven years before Zoan in Egypt.'

Tanis was the main cult-place of the god Seth. A stele set up there during the reign of Pharaoh Horemheb commemorates the 400th anniversary of that cult, in about 1330 BC. Monuments that date back to the 6th Dynasty attest to the city's great age. The *Hyksos built their capital, Avaris, at the same spot (1725-1575 BC). Rameses II also had his capital here, naming it Per-Rameses. The prophets refer to Zoan as an important city (Isa. 19:11-13; 30:4; Ezek. 30:14), and indeed in their time it was a capital once more — this time of the kings of the 26th Dynasty.

TANNUR (KHIRBET) The modern Arabic name for a small Nabatean temple in south central Transjordan. It is located on the nearly flat summit of the high isolated hill of Jebel Tannur, overlooking the confluence of the south-north Wadi el-Aban (Laaban) with the east-west Wadi Hesa (the biblical River Zered) that empties into the southeast end of the *Dead Sea. Less than a mile to the east of it runs the age-old north-south road, extending from *Damascus to Aqabah, known in biblical times as the 'king's highway' (*Roads).

General view of the temple, Khirbet Tannur

*The Dolphin goddess
from Khirbet Tannur*

The small temple, occupying the whole of the top of the hill that rises above the lower part of the steep southern slope of the Wadi Hesa, measures roughly 210 feet by 135 feet and is orientated almost due east. Off the beaten track and not easily accessible, its importance must have been at least regional, if not national. Almost every Nabatean settlement had its own shrine or temple, and Tannur must have served as a high place of pilgrimage for the public at large. The great high place of Zibb Atuf at *Petra has much in common with it in type of location and layout. Both bear similarities to the sanctuary at Hierapolis in Syria. At the tiny Nabatean temple at er-Ram in southernmost Jordan there was a simplified form of the Tannur architecture, consisting of a square *cella* in the center of a walled area. Its antecedents seem to be Parthian and, earlier still, Achaemenian or Persian.

The history of Khirbet Tannur probably extended from the latter part of the 2nd century BC until about the middle of the 2nd century AD. After that there was a tiny squatters' settlement in its ruins during the early Byzantine period, with no subsequent occupation to disturb its remains. It was rediscovered, identified as a Nabatean temple and excavated in 1937 by N. Glueck. He found three clearly distinguishable periods of construction, all of them terminated by earthquakes. It may have replaced an earlier Edomite sacred high place.

Period I lasted for about 100 years, until about the third quarter of the 1st century BC. There was a box-like altar or altar-base in the center of the raised rubble platform of an inner open temple court, with a large sunken forecourt in front of it to the east. It is possible that there were already feasting benches and raised covered platforms facing inward on the north and south sides at this date. This scheme continued in elaborated form in the next two periods. Some of the finest Nabatean pottery found must be assigned to some time before the end of period I.

The beginning of period II can be fixed approximately by a dedicatory Nabatean inscription to the second year of the reign of the Nabatean king, Aretas IV (9 BC-AD 40), i.e. to the equivalent of 8-7 BC. Period III can be dated by its architecture and sculptures to about the first quarter of the 2nd century AD. Its construction probably, although not necessarily, started before AD 106-7, when the Romans annexed the Nabatean kingdom and incorporated it into their Provincia Arabia.

The altar base or podium of period III, on top of which an ornate altar stood, encased that of period II which in turn enclosed that of period I. Staircases on the south and west sides led, in separate periods, to the top of the altar bases of periods III and II. A flight of three steps led up from the west end of the sunken, east forecourt to the gateway of the east façade or pylon of the raised, inner temple court. In the center of this court stood the altar base. A main gateway led through the east pylon of the outer sunken forecourt of period III; two additional side entrances of period II in that wall were now closed up. There was a square altar base in the northeast corner of the sunken outer forecourt of period III, and a smaller one beyond the outer west wall of the raised inner temple court.

To the temple of period III belong stylized sculptures of a complex of Hellenistic-Semitic deities, the Nabatean identity of which is quite clear. Typical of these cultures is a rigid frontal appearance. Among these there is a large relief in which the goddess Atargatis is described as the goddess of vegetation; above the goddess' head is an open-winged eagle. There are also reliefs of Atargatis as the goddess of corn and the goddess of the dolphin. The frieze on which these goddesses appear decorated the pilaster capitals of the façade at the base of the altar. The opposite side had a relief of Zeus-Hadad seated on his throne flanked by two bulls and adorned by a lion-torque and a thunderbolt. There is reason to believe that next to him stood a related figure of Atargatis, also adorned with a torque and enthroned between two lions. Other finds included a relief of Nike supporting a Tyche (*Antioch-on-the-Orontes) surrounded by a circular zodiacal panel, half of whose 'houses' are arranged counterclockwise while the other half run clockwise. There were also small free-standing altars with Greek or Nabatean inscriptions. Related Nabatean sculptures, contemporary with period III of Khirbet Tannur, have been found at *Petra, Qasr Rabbah, Characmoba (*Kir Moab) and Main in *Jordan and at *Mampsis in the *Negev, among other places. Featureless Dushara stones probably characterized period I, with changes occurring in period II, such as crude anthropomorphic forms, some with Nabatean inscriptions, until the appearance of the stylized sculptures of period III.

TARICHAEA *See* *MAGDALA

TARSHISH A place on the shores of the Mediterranean (Isa. 23:6; Jer. 10:9; Ezek. 27:12; Jon. 1:3; 4:2), west of Palestine (cf.Gen. 10:4; 1 Chr. 1:7), but mistakenly located in 2 Chronicles 9:21 on the coast of the *Red Sea. Beaten silver (Jer. 10:9), silver, iron tin, and lead (*Metals) were brought from there by the people of *Tyre (Ezek. 27:12). Tarshish is associated with an island (Isa. 23:6; 66:19) and Jonah went there by ship (Jon. 1:3). Solomon also sent ships there (2 Chr. 9:21). But the identification is not at all clear. Some scholars put forward Tartasus in southern Spain, to which, according to the classical authorities, the *Phoenicians sailed with their ships to obtain silver, iron and tin. Josephus' identification with Tarsus in Cilicia (*Antiq.* I, 127; IX, 208) is accepted by many scholars today. However, there are numerous places along the Mediterranean coast, at which this or that metal was mined, with names similar to Tarshish, so that no identification is firm.

TAXES; TAXATION Both the Canaanite kings and the Egyptian authorities collected taxes from early times, as is well attested by the *El Amarna letters, the *Taanach tablets and also by some allusions in the Bible (1 Sam. 8:11-17). There was no taxation during the period of the conquest of *Canaan by the Israelite tribes, nor during the days of the Judges; but with the establishment of the monarchy taxation became indispensable. At first, during the reign of Saul, it appears to have been limited to bringing gifts to the court (1 Sam. 10:27; 2 Chr. 17:5). That some taxes were paid may be inferred also from Saul's promise to the 'man who should slay Goliath the Philistine, that he would make his house free in Israel' (1 Sam. 17:25).

It seems that regular taxation was introduced by David in the later years of his reign. This necessitated taking a census of the population, a process not favored by the Israelites (2 Sam. 24:1 ff.). Censuses were also taken from time to time by other kings. In order to collect the tribute David appointed a special minister (2 Sam. 20:24). A more detailed list of officials dealing with tax collection is found in 1 Chronicles (27:25-31), where a 'minister over the king's treasures' is mentioned. He was probably responsible for the taxes paid by the people for the upkeep of the court, the collection of booty taken in war and the tribute paid by conquered peoples. Ten other officials were appointed to supervise the revenues from the agricultural economy. This system of taxation was inherited by Solomon, and taxes were paid mainly in kind. To make the system more efficient Solomon subdivided the country into 12 provinces, each of which had to sustain the king's court for one month (1 Kgs. 4:7-9). Surplus produce was exchanged for foreign goods (1 Kgs. 10:15). In Solomon's time the gifts brought by vassal or visiting rulers were an important element in the kingdom's economy (2 Sam. 8:10-12; 1 Kgs. 10:25; 2 Chr. 17:11). Another form of taxation was forced labor, imposed on the conquered peoples as well as on the Israelites (1 Kgs. 9:20-1). Solomon recruited 30,000 of his subjects for the king's work. While one-third of the laborers were working in the Lebanon the remaining two-thirds worked at home, each shift lasting for one month.

In addition to these, 80,000 men hewed stone in the mountains, 70,000 hauled the stone and 3,300 supervised their work (1 Kgs. 5:13-17). The excessive burden of taxation and forced labor was one of the reasons for the division of the kingdom.

A tax order from Beer-Sheba, Byzantine period

During the time of the Restoration the inhabitants of the country supplied the Governor's table with the 'Governor's bread'. In addition to this the people paid 40 silver shekels each day (Neh. 5:14-15). In Ezra (4:13) three additional taxes are mentioned: tribute, a tax paid by the king's subjects in the various provinces; custom, a tax on consumption; and toll, a road tax, or tax on land. (In Accadian documents *ilku* is a tax imposed on those of the king's lands that were leased to his subjects; it was not always paid in kind or in money, but sometimes by forced labor.) All servants of the temple were exempt from such taxes (Ezra 7:24).

There is also evidence in archaeological finds of the payment of taxes in the biblical period. The numerous jar handles stamped with *lamelek* stamps (*Seals), as well as the large number of ostraca found at *Samaria, indicate that payment in kind was well established. It seems that this was the method used by villagers, while city-dwellers paid in silver. In addition to the taxes levied by the kings, half a shekel was paid by each Israelite into the Temple treasury (*Money).

After the destruction of the Second Temple a tax of 2 drachms (*didrachm* — half a shekel), which had previously been paid to the Temple, had to be paid to Jupiter Capitolinus. This money was collected in a special fund, the *Fiscus iudaicus* — 'the Jews' cash'. The tax was levied at least until the 3rd century AD. Another tax was the poll tax on land, which was imposed by Hadrian as a punishment after the Bar-Kochba Revolt. Yet another tax on land was the *demosia* public tax. Excise taxes were paid on most imported goods. From late in the 2nd century AD the *anona militaris* was imposed as a means of extracting supplies for the Roman army. By the end of the 3rd century this became a permanent tax that was levied according to one's income, the basis being reassessed every 15 years. From the middle of the 5th century taxes that had previously been paid to the Jewish religious authorities had to be paid to the Roman emperor.

TEHAPHENEHES A city in lower *Egypt, on the Pelusiac branch of the *Nile Delta, on the caravan route leading to Palestine and *Mesopotamia, known as Daphneh to the classical writers. In this city *Baal-Zephon, the god of seafarers, was worshipped. In the days of Jeremiah it was a strong city (Jer. 2:16; Authorized Version: 'Tahapanes'). Ezekiel prophesied its destruction (Ezek. 30:18).

In the excavations a small fort of the time of Rameses I and II was discovered, but the city itself was built during the reign of Psammetichus I. It was then an important commercial center, inhabited by Greeks and Jews, and it could offer refuge to Jeremiah and those with him (Jer. 43:7, etc.; Authorized Version: 'Tahpanhes'). In the Hellenistic period it became an insignificant village. Identified with Tell Daphneh, about 20 miles south of Pelusium.

TEKOA; TEKOAH A town in Judah, not mentioned in the lists of cities conquered by Joshua but supplemented to Joshua (15:59) in the Septuagint. In the genealogical lists of Judah Ashur was the father of Tekoa (1 Chr. 2:24; 4:5). It was the home of David's

mighty men (2 Sam. 23:26) and a wise woman of Tekoah was sent to David by Joab, son of Zeruiah, to plead for Absalom's return to the court (2 Sam. 14). It was one of the cities fortified by Rehoboam (2 Chr. 11:6) and the birth-place of the prophet Amos (Amos 1:1). After the return from the Babylonian exile the people of Tekoa participated in rebuilding the walls of *Jerusalem (Neh. 3:5), and even repaired 'another piece' (Neh. 3:27); but 'their nobles did not put their necks to the work of their Lord' (Neh. 3:5). In that period Tekoa was the capital of a small district. During the Hasmonean uprising it was fortified by Bacchides (Josephus, *Antiq.* XIII, 15). It was also known in the Roman period. Josephus (*Life* 420) relates that he was sent by Titus to the village of Tekoa to see whether a camp could be pitched there, and it was the scene of some battles during the revolt against the Romans (Josephus, *War* IV, 518). Eusebius (*Onom.* 98, 17, etc.) knew a village under this name, and it is also mentioned in later Byzantine sources. Identified with Khirbet Tequa, about 5 miles south of *Bethlehem.

TEL-ABIB A place in *Babylon, on the river Chebar, inhabited by the exiles from Judah (Ezek. 3:15). There are many places in *Babylon named Tel-Abubi, meaning 'mound of the deluge' (i.e. 'place destroyed by the deluge'). Some believe that this biblical Tel-Abib should be sought in the vicinity of Nippur (*Calneh).

TEL AVIV Tel Aviv, which is one of the youngest cities in the world, has so far yielded about 20 ancient sites, from as early as the Neolithic period down to Hellenistic and Roman times. Most of the ancient remains have been discovered since 1948, during new building activities.

The earliest remains, from the Neolithic and Chalcolithic periods, are scanty and consist mainly of traces of dwelling pits. These are up to 6 feet in diameter and about 5 feet deep; they were probably thatched with some perishable material. They have been dated by the typical pottery, which included Chalcolithic churns, flint tools and animal bones. Burial caves of this period were also found. The whole of the Bronze Age was also represented by some cemeteries found in several locations. Judging by the richness of the finds it seems that ancient Tel Aviv flourished in the Middle Bronze Age II, when the country was dominated by the *Hyksos. Tombs of that time included much pottery, scarabs, weapons and so on. In several places burials of the Iron Age and the Persian period were also found.

Of much interest are the remains of a line of fortifications ascribed to the Hasmonean Alexander Jannaeus. Josephus (*War* I, 99) says: 'Alexander, in alarm, dug a deep dyke to intercept him [Antiochus Dionysus], extending from the mountainside above Antipatris to the coast at Joppa and in the front of the trench erected a high wall with wooden towers inserted, in order to bar the routes where attack was easy.' Remains of this line have been discovered at certain places along the River *Yarkon and at two sites in Tel Aviv itself. One of these was a rectangular tower measuring 40 feet by 27 feet, while the other was octagonal. With both towers Hellenistic pottery and a coin of Alexander Jannaeus were associated. The excavations at Tel Aviv were directed by J. Kaplan on behalf of the Jaffo-Tel Aviv Museum of Antiquities.

TELL A Semitic word for an artificial mound formed by the overlying debris from the settlements and ramparts of ancient cities, each of which has been built on top of the preceding ones. Such mounds are found in many regions of the Middle East. The largest in Palestine are at *Megiddo, *Hazor, *Jericho and *Beth-Shean. Each has about 20 layers of occupation and some of them reach a height of about 60-70 feet. During their excavations at Troy from 1870 onwards H.Schliemann and W. Dorpfeld realized that the mound represented an accumulation of consecutive settlements; but it was not until 1890, when W.F.M. Petrie and later F.J. Bliss worked at Tell el-*Hesi, that the now standard method of arriving at stratigraphical understanding and interpretation was put into practice. (*See also* *ARCHAEOLOGY, METHODS OF RESEARCH*.)

TEMAN A region and a city in *Edom, named after the first-born son of Eliphaz (Gen. 36:11; 1 Chr. 1:36). Husham of the land of Temani was King of *Edom (Gen. 36:34). Ezekiel prophesied the destruction of *Edom from Teman to Dedan (Ezek. 25:13). Eusebius (*Onom.* 96:18) states that a village by the name of Thaiman is located in the region of Gebalitike, about 15 miles from *Petra, but he did not specify the direction. Not identified.

TEMPLES

PRE-CANAANITE AND CANAANITE PERIOD The first temples, shrines consecrated to the service of a god, probably date from as early as man's first settlements. The earliest known temple in Palestine is that at *Jericho (stratum IX), which is of the Neolithic period. It was an oblong structure, with a porch resting on six wooden posts from which an entrance led into a hall; behind this was the inner shrine. This tripartite division of the temple was to become the rule in the later Canaanite and Israelite periods. To the late Chalcolithic period belongs the temple of *Megiddo (stratum XIX or XVIII). This also consists of an oblong hall with a roof supported by wooden posts. Facing the entrance, which was in the long wall, was a mud-brick construction, probably a base for the image of a god and for offerings. A similar temple, of the same period, was discovered at *En-Gedi.

No complete temples of the Early Bronze Age have been found, but there are many of the Middle Bronze Age. One of the most elaborate examples was discovered at *Nahariya. In its earliest phase it was again an oblong building with an east-west orientation, and consisted of an entrance room, a hall and an additional shrine at the back. To the south of the temple was a large stone-built high place, with many offerings around it. The six phases of use observed in this temple demonstrate its long life. That it was consecrated to the worship of the Canaanite-Phoenician goddess Sea Astarte is indicated by a mould for casting images of this divinity that was found on the site. More elaborate still are two temples built to an almost identical plan and discovered in the sacred precinct of Megiddo (stratum XV). These are orientated north-

south and include a forecourt, the roof of which was supported by two columns, and an inner shrine, with a mud-brick structure attached to the wall facing the entrance. A round stone-built high place was constructed at the rear of one of the temples. With minor changes these temples were in use during the whole of the Bronze Age.

The temples of the Late Bronze Age include all three elements: porch, hall and Holy of Holies. Sometimes there is a stone altar in the court in front of the building and the Holy of Holies takes the form of a simple niche in the rear wall of the hall. Whereas the orientation of the Middle Bronze Age temples was mostly east-west, those of the Late Bronze Age were orientated north-south, their entrances facing either south or north. Temples of this period, which are numerous, have been found at places such as *Hazor, *Megiddo, *Beth-Shean, or *Lachish. Some of the larger cities even have more than one. The temple of this period discovered at *Shechem is designed according to the same general plan, but its exceedingly thick walls made it a fortress as well. In Canaanite towns not conquered by the Israelites, such as *Beth-Shean, temples were still being built to the old Canaanite plan in the Iron Age.

TEMPLES OF THE IRON AGE The Canaanite plan was also adopted for the Temple of Solomon in *Jerusalem. Biblical evidence points to the existence of numerous other cult places all over Palestine, in addition to the main Temple of Jerusalem, and such shrines have now been found at *Arad and *Lachish, both of a very

Sanctuary of the Israelite temple at Arad

Sanctuary on a coin from the time of Bar Kochba

thick. The hall measured 40 cubits by 20 cubits, and it was here that most of the priestly ritual was performed. The lighting of the hall was by means of windows, which were wide on the outside and narrow within. The Holy of Holies occupied the back part of the house and in it were the Ark of the Covenant and the cherubim. It measured 20 cubits square and there were probably a few steps leading up to it. Along three sides the Temple was surrounded by a wall. The space between the walls had a gallery, built in three stories (1 Kgs. 6:5, 8-10; Ezek. 41:6-11). Each of the galleries had three rooms, housing the vessels used for the ritual and the treasures of the Temple. (*Cult objects; *Menorah.) The temple of Solomon was looted and burnt to ashes by the Babylonians in 586 BC (2 Kgs. 25:8-17).

THE TEMPLE OF ZERUBBABEL The most important task that faced the people on their return from the Babylonian exile was the building of the new House of God, and this is specifically stated in the declaration of Cyrus (Ezra 1:2-5). But it was Zerubbabel who erected the altar and made the sacrificial offerings (Ezra 3:2, 6). The building of the Temple was completed in the sixth year of Ahasuerus (Ezra 3). One of the important changes introduced into this new building was the addition of an outer court, which surrounded the Temple and inner court. This new court was the Court of Women, to which both men and women were admitted (the inner court, the Court of Israel, was for men only). In the Hellenistic period, with the improvement in economic conditions, some embellishments were added from time to time. The temple was defiled in the days of Antiochus IV (Dan. 9:29, etc.), and was then reconsecrated by the Maccabees. It was completely rebuilt by Herod the Great.

THE TEMPLE OF HEROD Herod begin to build the new temple, always known as the Second Temple, in the 15th or 18th year of his reign. In order to avoid any suspicion he prepared all the necessary materials before the actual building began, 1,000 wagons and 10,000 skilled laborers (1,000 of them priests), half stone-dressers, half carpenters, were engaged in the operation, which lasted for 46 years.

By building huge retaining walls Herod doubled the area of the Temple Mount. On top of this huge podium, most of which is still preserved, he built the Temple proper. All around the Temple Mount beautiful marble porticos were built. Two large bridges connected the Temple with the city on the west. In front of the Temple was the inner court, the Court of Israel, in which were the large altar, measuring 32 cubits square, the laver, the slaughterhouse and the tables on which the offerings were prepared. Around this court were storerooms for the materials necessary to the ritual. To the west of it was the huge Court of the Women, with large rooms at each corner for Nazarites (people who had taken certain vows of abstinence) and lepers, and also for wood and oil.

The Temple itself contained the same three elements as Solomon's Temple: porch, hall and Holy of Holies. The building was orientated to the east. Twelve steps arranged in groups of three, with broad landings, led up from the court to the porch, which

similar plan. A building at *Lachish had been attributed to the Persian period, but it is now quite certain that it belongs to the Hellenistic period. Details of another temple of the Persian period, discovered at *Michmash, north of *Tel Aviv, have not yet been published.

THE TEMPLE OF SOLOMON It was David who conceived the idea of building a house for God in *Jerusalem (2 Sam. 7:2; 1 Kgs. 8:17). He also provided most of the necessary materials, including much gold and silver (1 Chr. 22:1-19; 28 and 29), but the actual work did not begin until the fifth year of Solomon's reign. It lasted seven-and-a-half years. The wood used for its construction, the masons and the carpenters, all came from *Lebanon (1 Kgs. 5:8; 27:8). Like all other temples in the ancient Near East, which were used mainly as the abode of the gods and for the ritual practised by the priests, Solomon's temple was not intended as a place for ordinary people to pray in, but as 'a house unto the name of the Lord' (1 Kgs. 3:2), in which stood the Ark of the Covenant, symbolizing the covenant between God and his chosen people.

No actual remains of the First Temple have come to light, and it is therefore only by the study of the Bible Scriptures and by comparison with other contemporary temples that we can reconstruct the plan. The Temple of Solomon was an oblong building consisting of three parts, one behind the other: the *ulam*, 'porch' (1 Kgs. 6:3; 2 Chr. 3:17; Ezek. 40:48-9); the *hechal*, 'hall' or 'house' (1 Kgs. 6:33; 2 Chr. 3:17; Ezek 41:1-3, 21 ff.); and the *debir,* 'Holy of Holies' (1 Kgs. 6:16; 19-20, 23, 31; 8:6-8; 2 Chr. 3:8, 9, 16; 5:7-9; Ezek. 41:4). The temple was 60 cubits long and 20 wide (all interior measurements — *Weights and measures). The various sources that refer to its height do not agree. The porch, 20 cubits by 10 cubits, separated the profane from the holy. Steps led up from the court to the porch, the front wall of which was embellished by two large pilasters. A gate 10 cubits wide and with doors of cypress wood led into the house, the wall separating the porch from the hall being 6 cubits measured 70 cubits by 11 cubits and had additional rooms on the flanks, making a total breadth of 100 cubits, the same as the height of the building. The back wall of the porch was gold-plated and in it hung a golden lamp. In the center of the façade was the main entrance, over which was suspended a golden bunch of grapes. The only pieces of furniture in the porch were the two tables, one of gold, the other of marble, on which the shewbread was placed. This entrance was not provided with doors and was covered only by a veil. A door led from the porch to the hall, which was 40 cubits square with gold-plated walls. In the hall stood the golden altar, 1 cubit by 1 cubit by 2 cubits, the golden table for the shewbread, on which were two frankincense goblets, and the golden menorah. A double veil separated the hall from the Holy of Holies, to which only the High Priest had access, and then only on the Day of Atonement. There was no furniture at all in this part of the Temple.

The whole complex of Temple and courts was surrounded by a rail and entry to the enclosure was forbidden to Gentiles; two copies of an inscription in Greek to this effect were found near the Temple Mount. The approach to the Temple Mount was by two gates on the south, the Double and the Triple Gates. The king and the priests used the bridges on the west.

In AD 70, on the ninth day of Ab, the Second Temple was destroyed by the Romans.

TEMPLES OF THE HELLENISTIC AND ROMAN PERIODS Apart from the Second Temple, which followed the original plan of its predecessors, there were numerous other temples in Palestine dedicated to pagan deities. To the Hellenistic period, for instance, belongs a building identified as a temple at Marissa (*Mareshah). It consisted of a large court with a small building in it, but nothing of the superstructure has remained. The great age of temple building in Palestine began in the early Roman period, with the dedication by Herod of Temples of Augustus at *Caesarea and *Samaria. Both were exceedingly large and each was set up on a huge podium. Although not much of their superstructures remained, it seems quite certain that they were built on the regular Hellenistic-Roman plan. The one at *Samaria had a large court in front of it, from which the temple was approached by a broad flight of steps, in front of which stood a large altar. At *Caesarea only the podium remained intact, but remains of statuary, made both of local sandstone and of marble, bear witness to its former splendor. Still more temples were built in Palestine during the 2nd and 3rd centuries AD, which was when the temple at *Samaria was rebuilt. Remains of a Roman temple were discovered at *Kedesh (Naphatali), and inscriptions discovered at *Oboda show that there was a temple dedicated to a local Zeus and Aphrodite there. Much more numerous are the temples found in almost every city and village of Transjordan and southern Syria. These

The model of the Second Temple, based on M. Avi-Yonah's reconstruction

range from small, simple shrines to sumptuous peripheral buildings such as those of *Gerasa. Typical in all these temples are the podium and the façade decorated with the 'Syrian gable' (a gable with an arch above the central entrance).

NABATEAN TEMPLES In Palestine traces of a Nabatean temple have been found only at *Oboda. Too little of it remained to give a clear idea of its plan, though the architectural remains incorporated in later buildings show that it was a magnificent building. Many Nabatean temples have been identified to the east of the River *Jordan, dating from the late 1st century BC to the first half of the 1st century AD. Most of them included a number of similar elements. There was usually a large court, called the *teatra* in the Nabatean inscriptions, in which public festivities took place. The court had a colonnade along two of three sides and galleries above it, to which access could be gained by means of staircase towers at the entrances. Also, there was generally a square temple at the back of the court, its facade adorned by two flanking towers with stairs leading to the roof, on which libations were poured and incense burnt. Within the building was an inner shrine, at the corners of which were four columns. There were variations in this basic plan in the different temples, but all were richly decorated, as we can see from the statuary and reliefs discovered in the ruins of the temples at Seeia and Khirbet *Tannur. Early in the 2nd century AD the *Nabateans began to build their temples on the Roman plan, and were it not for the typical Nabatean architectural details such as the Nabatean capital and the Nabatean inscriptions, there would be hardly anything to distinguish them from contemporary Roman ones.

THEATERS More than 20 theaters of antiquity have been identified during surveys in Palestine and Transjordan, and several have been excavated: *Caesarea, *Beth-Shean, Pella (*Pehel), *Gerasa and *Petra.

Those at Bostra (*Bozrah), Philadelphia (*Rabbath-Ammon) and Philipopolis have been extensively surveyed. All those mentioned stood in large and important cities, but there were also theaters in smaller cities, such as Dora (*Dor), *Maiumas near *Caesarea, Hippos (*Sussita), *Dionysias, *Abila, *Gadara and *Flavia Neapolis. All are of the Roman period and the earliest, at *Caesarea, was built under Herod.

The Romans had a different conception of the theater from the Greeks, who built their theaters in sanctuaries, which gave them a religious character, and with equally good seats for all. The Roman theaters, by contrast, were built on any suitable site, and the seats were graded according to social rank, with special accommodation reserved for officials and distinguished visitors. Apart from this there were also architectural differences. While the Greeks constructed their theaters against hillsides, the Romans had to build free-standing structures from ground level. However, on sites where a natural slope was available the auditorium was cut entirely or partly into the rock, as at *Petra, *Philadelphia and *Samaria.

The theater at *Caesarea, first built in the Herodian period, underwent rebuilding and changes until late Roman times. It had two main parts, the semicircular auditorium *(cavea)* and the stage *(pulpitum)*, and the stage building *(scaena)*, all united into a single structure. The auditorium was entered through six radial *vomitoria* (vaulted passageways) connected by a peripheral vaulted corridor. The *cavea* was divided by the *praecinctio* (an open passage) into *ima* and *summa cavea,* the lower and upper tiers of the auditorium. Each *cavea* was divided into *cunei* (blocks of seats). The lower *cavea* had six *cunei* with five passageways of steps, while the upper one had seven *cunei* and a central box for important guests. The lowest row of

The theater, Samaria

The Roman theater at Caesarea

seats surrounded the semicircular *orchestra*, the auditorium where distinguished personages were accommodated in movable chairs. Facing the *orchestra* were the *pulpitum* and the *scaena*, which was as high as the *cavea*. The wall of the stage building that faced the audience, called the *scaenae frons*, was decorated with a large central niche and side niches. In the substructure of the stage building, the *hyposcaenium*, lamps and pottery of the beginning of the 1st century AD were found during the excavations.

This was the essential plan of all Roman theaters though there were many structural variations. The theater at *Samaria was built not earlier than the end of the 2nd century AD. Parts of the lower auditorium and of the stage were found. The theater at *Beth-Shean, the best preserved structure in Palestine, is of Severan date. The main differences from that of *Caesarea is that the auditorium is surrounded by an external peripheral wall with entrances leading to the *vomitoria*. This wall also had stairways leading to the top of the *summa cavea*. The *pulpitum* is enclosed by a *scaenae frons* with no *scaenae* behind it. Remains of the entablature of the *scaenae frons* were found in the debris. It suggests that the theater had been elaborately decorated, for the frieze was adorned with animal and human figures set in medallions of acanthus leaves.

The large city of Gerasa had three theaters, two within the city walls. The third, the one that was excavated, was of Severan date and was outside the city in a semi-sacred area. Near it were a pool and a colonnade and it was used for the religious festival of the *Maiumas, a festival connected with water. The state of preservation in these theaters was such that nothing of the ornamentation, the marble or granite columns, the cornices and friezes was found *in situ*. Only at *Philadephia can remains of columns with Corinthian capitals and part of the entablature still be seen.

THEBES; NO AMON The capital of upper *Egypt, and in certain periods also the capital of the whole country. Although it existed at the time of the Middle Kingdom it flourished mainly during the period of the New Kingdom (18th-20th Dynasties). No Amon meant 'the city of the god Amun' and this is how most of the references to it in the Bible should be understood (cf. Jer. 46:25; Ezek. 30:14; Neh. 3:8). The identification of No Amon with Thebes, the center of the cult of the god Amun, is accepted by all.

The term Thebes refers to both banks of the *Nile. On the east bank the huge temple complexes of modern Karnak and Luxor were erected, while on the west bank lie the necropolis and the funerary temples. The first temple of Amun was built during the First Intermediate Period but is known through inscriptions only. Under the 12th Dynasty the worship of Amun became the central cult of Thebes. Most of these beautiful and elaborate buildings, whose ruins are still impressive, were constructed by the 18th-20th Dynasties. On the east bank of the *Nile, at modern Karnak, were several temples, the largest of which was the Great Temple of Amun. The others were the Temple of Moth, the Temple of Chons and the Temple of the

goddess Mut. South of it, modern Luxor, was another temple of Amun and the heart of the city that comprised the residence of the royal house and local rulers, all surrounded by gardens beyond which stretched the suburbs of the city. The greatest building activities date to the reigns of Hatshepsut, Tuthmosis III and Amenophis III. Amenophis IV (Akhenaten) erected a temple for the sun-god Aton to the east of Karnak. This was, however, soon destroyed.

The large necropolis, or city of the dead, with its beautiful funerary monuments and temples extended along the west bank of the Nile. The largest of these monuments is the complex of Medinet Habu, erected under Hatshepsut, Tuthmosis III and Rameses III. In a wadi neaby, known as the Valley of the Kings, the pharaohs were buried. One of the most famous tombs found here is that of Tutankhamun. To the south of the necropolis Deir el-Medine, a settlement for builders and artisans, developed.

Of great importance are the reliefs found in the tombs and temples, which illustrate the daily life and historic events of their time. In the Ramesseum, the funerary temple of Rameses II on the west bank, the Battle of *Kedesh-on-the-Orontes is depicted. Similarly, a relief in a temple at Karnak depicts Rameses II's conquest of *Ashkelon. Another famous scene, found at Medinet Habu, portrays Rameses III's battle against the Sea Peoples (*Philistines).

Building activities continued at Thebes throughout the period of the Ethiopian Dynasty (25th Dynasty), though on a much smaller scale. In 663 BC the Assyrians sacked the city and carried away the treasures of the large temples. Under the 26th Dynasty the political center was moved to the south and Thebes became a provincial city, but building is recorded until the Ptolemaic period. The Greeks identified the god Amun with Zeus and therefore called the city Diospolis Magna, 'The Great City of Zeus'.

THEBEZ A town in the vicinity of *Shechem, where Abimelech was slain (Judg. 9:50-54; 2 Sam. 11:21). A place of this name also existed in the Roman period. Eusebius (*Onom*. 100:11-14) states that a village with this name still existed in his time on the border of *Neapolis, on the 13th mile on the Neapolis-*Beth-Shean road. This distance fits well the modern village of Tubas, where remains from the Israelite and later periods were found.

TIBERIAS A city on the western shore of the Sea of *Galilee, near hot springs, founded about AD 18 by Herod Antipas and named in honor of the Emperor Tiberius (Josephus, *Antiq*. XVIII, 35-8). Josephus relates that as there had been a burial-ground on the spot it was unclean according to the Jewish Law. Herod solved the problem that this raised of populating his city by admitting poor or landless men, freedmen and soldiers, and even by forcibly bringing settlers from his other domains. He also included well-to-do families without religious or nationalist attachments. The results of this policy can be seen in their subsequent behavior in the First Jewish Revolt (AD 66-70). Contrary to the practice that was common in the Hellenistic period, no city wall was built at the time of the city's foundation. One was not added until

Relief from Tiberias

the time of Septimius Severus. The layout was that of a Hellenistic or Roman city, with streets intersecting at right angles, and Herod adorned it with public buildings, including a stadium on the seashore (Josephus, *War* II, 68), a large synagogue (Josephus, *Life* 277) and a place for himself on a high hill where he set up sculptures and thereby aroused the condemnation of orthodox religious circles (*Life* 65).

Like a Hellenistic city, Tiberias enjoyed a certain degree of autonomy, the head of the city being an elected *archon* (*Life* 271), assisted by a committee of ten men (*Life* 69) and a city council (Josephus, *War* II, 64). The city calculated its era from the day of its foundation and was entitled to mint its own copper coinage.

Tiberias remained the capital of *Galilee until it was given to Agrippa II by Nero in AD 61 (Josephus, *Antiq.* XX, 159) and detached from the district. In the First Jewish Revolt the proletariat was anti-Roman, but the aristocracy was loyal to Agrippa and the Romans. The city therefore surrendered to Vespasian and was spared for the sake of Agrippa (Josephus, *War* III, 446-61).

After the Bar-Kochba Revolt (AD 132-5) the city was paganized by Hadrian, but a little later it became Jewish once more and the seat of a rabbinical school. When Johanan ben Nappaha settled there at the beginning of the 3rd century it became the center of Jewish learning and was the last city in which the Sanhedrin held sittings. It was here that the Mishna, the Talmud and the Massoretic texts assumed their final shape. (*See also* *HAMMATH.) Excavations were carried out in 1973-4 under the direction of G. Foerster. Architectural remains include a colonnaded street, a Byzantine bathhouse, a market place of the early Arab period, a large late Roman building, possibly a basilica, as well as substantial sectors of the city

wall with a gate-way flanked by two round towers (*Fortifications). Rich finds in pottery, metal and glass ware, jewelry and coins attest to the city's prosperity until the 11th century AD.

TIGRIS *See* *HIDDEKEL

TIME

THE DAY The first unit of time was that measured by the alternation of day and night. In *Babylon, *Egypt, Greece and *Rome the day began in the morning and ended in the evening. The conception of the full calendar day varied from one people to another. For those who reckoned according to a lunar calendar, as the ancient Hebrews did, the 24-hour day lasted from evening to evening: 'And God called the light Day and the darkness he called Night. And the evening and the morning were the first day' (Gen. 1:5). For the Egyptians, on the other hand, the day began at dawn. The Babylonians divided day and night into three watches each, while the Egyptians divided the same periods into four watches each, a system that was also accepted by the Greeks and the Romans.

The ancient Hebrews did not have such a rigid system of divisions. Instead the following terms appear: 'rising of the morning' (Neh. 4:21), 'dawning of the day' (Job. 3:9), 'light of the morning' (2 Sam. 23:4), 'morning' (Ps. 55:17), 'noon' (Ps. 55:17) 'noonday' (Job. 5:14), 'twilight' (Prov. 79), 'evening' (Prov. 7:9) and 'dark night' (Prov. 7:9; Gen. 1:5). The time of day could also be fixed by reference to certain activities that normally took place at a certain time, one example being 'the time of the evening, even the time that women go out to draw water' (Gen. 24:11). Thus midday was the 'heat of the day' (Gen. 18:1). The later hours of the afternoon were defined by the long shadows (Jer. 6:4) and the early morning by 'until the day break, and the shadows flee away' (S. of S. 2:17). But the system of dividing the night into watches is not completely missing among the ancient Hebrews, who probably borrowed the practice from the *Babylonians. The first watch was named the 'beginning of the watches' (Lam. 2:19); the second, the 'middle watch' (Judg. 7:19) and the last, the 'morning watch' (1 Sam. 11:11). The *Babylonians divided the day into equal parts by using sundials. The Syrians adopted this division from them. There is no indication in the Bible of such a division, although a time-measuring device, the sundial of Ahaz (Isa. 38:8; 2 Kgs. 20:9), is mentioned. The basic difference between the Babylonian and biblical conception of time is that the first began the day in the morning, it was the other way around with the Hebrews, whose festivals began in the evening of the day preceding the feast (Exod. 12:18, etc.).

THE WEEK This unit of time, consisting of seven days, accords approximately with the moon's orbit. But as the week does not necessarily begin on the day of the new moon, it is not affected by inconsistencies in relation to the positions of the moon during the month. In contrast to this the Babylonian and Assyrian week began on the first day of the month. The week of seven days was thus completely independent of the month, a factor which became more important when the Sabbath took the place of the day of the New Moon as the sacred day.

THE MONTH At first the term 'month' was applied only to the first day of the month, but later the whole period between the first and last days was so called. The Hebrew word *yerah,* 'month', has the same root as the Hebrew word for the moon, which implies that the months mentioned in the Bible are lunar ones. There are three systems of naming months in the Bible: by early Canaanite names; by consecutive numbers; and by Babylonian names. The Canaanite names were in use in Judah and Israel until the time of the Babylonian exile. Of these only four are now known: Abib, the first month (Exod. 13:4); Ziv, the second (1 Kgs. 6:37); Ethanim, the seventh (1 Kgs. 8:2); and Bul, the eighth (1 Kgs. 6:38). The last two are also known from Canaanite sources, in which five additional months are listed. There are notable preferences in the Bible for numerical names rather than Canaanite ones, probably because of the pagan cults that were associated with the latter. The meaning of the name of the first month, Abib, is 'ripening barley', but the meaning of the others remains obscure.

During the Babylonian exile the Jews adopted the local Babylonian calendar. Of the Babylonian names of months seven are known from the Bible, while those of the others may be supplemented from the Mishna and the Talmud. The 12 months are: Nissan (Neh. 2:1); Iyar (R. hash. 3a.); Sivan (Esther 8:9); Tammuz (Shab. 53a); Ab (Taan. 26ab); Elul (Neh. 6:15); Tishrei (R.hash. 1:1); Marheshvan (R. hash, 11b); Kislev (Neh. 1:1); Teveth (Esther 2:16); Shebat (Zech. 1:7); and Adar (Esther 3:7). In certain cases the Bible gives both the name of the month and its numerical order: 'In the first month, that is, the month Nissan' (Esther 3:7); or 'In the third month, that is, the month Sivan.'

In the Roman and Byzantine period the Jews continued to use the Babylonian names for the months, as they still do today. Of this there is ample evidence in documents and inscriptions, notably those in the mosaic floors of some of the later synagogues. These names were also used by the *Nabateans (*Mampsis) and the Palmyrenes (*Tadmor). For official purposes the Macedonian names of the months were used both by the Jews and Gentiles alike. The first month of this calendar was Xanticus, which began on 22 March. Each month lasted 30 days, and five intercalary days, called *epagomenae,* were added after the 12th month. In some places in Palestine there were some local eras which began their year with the eighth month, Dius, on 28 October. In some places in the south of Palestine the Egyptian names for the months were also used. References to the Roman names for the months are found, though not frequently, in certain Byzantine churches.

TIMNAH The Timnah valley lies about 15 miles north of the Gulf of *Elath, enclosed on its south, west and north by a 900-1,200 feet mountain range called the Zuqe Timnah. The area was first explored by J. Petherick (1860), who recognized the metallurgical character of some of the ancient remains. F. Frank (1934) located seven copper smelting camps, dating from the 10th to the 6th centuries BC and published in 1940 by N. Glueck as *King Solomon's Mines.*

In 1959 the Arabah Expedition, led by B. Rothenberg on behalf of Museum Haaretz and Tel Aviv University, began a systematic exploration of the Timnah area and discovered large ancient copper mines at the foot of Zuqe Timnah. Here copper ore, mainly malchite and chalcocite, containing approximately 20% copper, had been extracted during the Chalcolithic period, from the Late Bronze Age to Early Iron Age I and in the Roman-Byzantine period. The excavations revealed a number of sites.

CHALCOLITHIC SMELTING SITE On a low hill 500yd east of the modern Timnah Copper Mines a stone-built copper smelting furnace was found. This is the earliest copper smelting installation to be unearthed anywhere so far, and it has led to the first reconstruction based on factual evidence of the process used when copper production began in the ancient Near East. A small work camp was excavated at the foot of the hill and stone tools, pottery and flint implements were found.

SMELTING CAMP OF EARLY IRON AGE I One of 11 found in the valley, this camp lies to the west of Mount Timnah. Eleven separate areas were excavated, including three copper smelting furnaces and all the metallurgical elements needed for a complete reconstruction of the technological processes in use. The finds include a large number of working tools, rough copper and finished copper implements. The camp is dated by the pottery to the 12th century BC. A small sanctuary of the early Semitic type, as well as a high place, were excavated near the site.

THE HATHOR TEMPLE In 1969 a small hillock measuring 45yd across was excavated at the foot of 'Solomon's Pillars', in the very center of Timnah's ancient copper industry. It turned out to be the site of an Egyptian mining temple dedicated to the Egyptian goddess Hathor. The excavation uncovered four main strata,

The zodiac and the four seasons, mosaic, Beth Alpha

from bedrock upwards. Cut into the red sandstone wadi bed (layer IV) were pits and fireplaces, dated by flint tools and rope-decorated pottery to the Chalcolithic period. Temple I (revealed in layer III) was contained within a court measuring 28 feet by 21 feet; this was formed by a wall of rough red sandstone built against the side of one of 'Solomon's Pillars'. The central chamber, built of white sandstone right against the face of the 'Pillars', enclosed a niche as high as a man that probably housed a large image of Hathor. Temple I was razed to the ground. The site was abandoned for a short period of abandonment, then the temple was reconstructed (layer II). A new floor of white sandstone debris was laid, the court was enlarged until it was 28 feet square and the central shrine was rebuilt. Earlier stelae and ornamental lintels, including square pillars with Hathor faces carved on the sides, were reused in the process. This structure (Temple II) also showed distinct Semitic features: in addition to a stone bench for offerings and a place for the priest, a row of standing stones (*Massebot) stood along the southern wall of the court. Many offerings were found around these *massebot,* including pottery, beads and metal objects. It seems likely that the temple of this phase was covered by a large tent, many parts of which were found along the walls.

The finds from Temple I-II, amounting to several thousands of items, form two main groups. The first consists of Egyptian-made objects, the most important of which bear hieroglyphic inscriptions and royal cartouches dating the temple to the 19th and 20th Dynasties. The list of pharaohs starts with Sethos I and ends with Rameses V, the reconstruction having taken place in the time of Rameses III. The second group of finds consists of locally made objects: handmade primitive pottery, found previously only in the central *Negev and southern Arabah and therefore called 'Negev-type pottery'; bichrome decorated pottery, first found in *Jordan and called 'Edomite pottery', although its origin was most probably in *Midian; and many copper offerings, including a cast figurine of a male god and numerous pieces of jewelry. A beautiful copper snake with a gilded head was found in the central shrine of the temple in its last phase.

Layer I contained a small copper casting furnace, dated to the 2nd-3rd centuries AD, when Roman-Byzantine metalworkers must have dug into the hillock of sand containing the Egyptian mining temple, from which some of the stones that made up the court walls still protruded. Here they built their furnace. In it they melted down copper pellets, collected from the ancient slag heaps of the area, in small crucibles and cast them to form ingots.

The discovery of the temple at Timnah has fundamentally changed the archaeologists' views about the dating and the originators of the copper mines, which were known until recently as 'King Solomon's Mines'. It is now certain that the pharaohs of the 19th-20th Dynasties (14th-12th centuries BC) rather than the kings of Israel and Judah (10th-6th centuries BC) despatched mining expeditions to the Arabah. The Egyptians operated the mines and smelters together with

the indigenous inhabitants; *Midianites-*Kenites and *Amalekites, who possessed metallurgical traditions going back to prehistoric times (cf. Gen. 4:22). It is possible that the hitherto uncertain location of copper mines operated by Rameses III, which are called 'Atika' in an Egyptian papyrus, can now be identified with the 'Arabah' mines. The fact that pottery of the three kinds ('Negev-type', 'Edomite' and Egyptian kitchen-ware) that had been found mixed together in the Early Iron Age I camp was excavated together in stratified layers and mixed with dated Egyptian inscriptions gives certain dates for this Late Bronze to Early Iron Age I pottery. These new dates also apply to many sites over a wide area on both sides of the Arabah and the *Red Sea.

The existence of an Egyptian mining temple in the Arabah in the 14th-12th centuries BC raises many new questions concerning the biblical account of the Exodus. At the same time the numerous finds in the temple may add to our understanding of the cultural and social relationship between the tribes of Israel and the *Midianites-*Kenites, as reflected in the biblical narrative of the relationship between Moses and Jethro, the Midianite priest, father-in-law and adviser to Moses.

ROMAN-BYZANTINE COPPER MINES Copper ore, as well as iron oxide and manganese, were mined in the Timnah Valley during the 2nd and 3rd centuries AD, but no smelting installations of this period have been found there. The ore must therefore have been transported to the large Roman-Byzantine copper smelting plant at Beer Ora, south of Timnah.

TIMNAH

1. A town on the northern border of the territory of Judah, in the Shephelah (Josh. 15:10), enumerated among the cities of Dan (Josh. 19:43). It plays a prominent role in the story of Samson (Judg. 1:1, 2, 5; 15:6). It was conquered by the Philistines in the time of Ahaz (2 Chr. 28:18). The Arab placename Khirbet Tibnah has preserved the ancient form of the name Timnah and it is therefore a natural candidate for its identification. This site is situated 2 miles west-southwest of Beth-Shemesh. The archaeological remains, however, do not confirm this identification and Timnah has thus been identified with Tel Batash on the southern bank of the Sorek Valley, more than 4 miles northwest of Beth-Shemesh. It is situated in the midst of the fertile valley of Sorek and may well provide the background for the biblical story. The fact that it is enumerated once among the cities of Judah, and once of Dan, may be explained as reflecting vicissitudes in the history of the city, once Judean, then Philistine and then Danite. The same Timnah, called Timnath, is apparently mentioned in Genesis 38 in connection with the origins of Judah.

In recent years extensive archaeological excavations have been made at Tel Batash. It was a fortified town in the Middle Bronze Age, when it was defended by an earth embankment. This was followed by an unfortified town in the Late Bronze Age. It was a very flourishing town in the El Amarna period, as is attested by the large quantities of imported pottery. Among the finds was a scarab of Amenophis III. A large building of this period was destroyed in war, and the city declined at the end of the period. In the 12th-11th centuries BC it was an unfortified town inhabited by the Philistines. In addition to typical Philistine pottery a clay impression of a Philistine inscribed seal was also found. In the Iron Age II it was a fortified town containing typical Israelite houses; among its finds were pottery stamped with royal seals and weights inscribed with Hebrew letters. The destruction of this city is ascribed to Sennacherib. The later cities of the Israelite and Persian periods were witnesses to a period of decline.

2. A town in the territory of Judah, in the hill country (Josh. 15:57), listed among a group of towns in the southeastern part of that region (Josh. 15:55-57). Many of the towns listed have been identified: Maon, Carmel, Zif, Juttah, Jokdeam and Cain. Timnah has not yet been identified. (*See also* *BATASH, TEL)

TIRZAH One of the Canaanite city-states conquered by Joshua (Josh. 12:24), though it does not appear in the later lists of places inhabited by the Israelites. On the other hand, Tirzah was the name of one of the daughters of Zelophehad (Num. 26:33; 27:1). Scholars therefore assume that Tirzah, and the other 'daughters' mentioned in these verses, were all towns inhabited by the families of Manasseh. In later times Tirzah was the capital of the kings of Israel until the days of Omri (1 Kgs. 14:17; 15:21; 16:10-18). Omri reigned in Tirzah for six years before he built his new capital at *Samaria (1 Kgs. 16:23-4). It seems that Tirzah was embellished by the kings of Israel who reigned there and so became a symbol of beauty (S. of S. 6:4).

Results of excavations can be found in the entry on Tell el-*Farah (north), which is about 6 miles to the north of Nablus, the site with which Tirzah is identified.

TOB (LAND OF) A region in the northeast of Transjordan, where Jephthah the Gileadite fled from his brothers (Judg. 11:3). In the time of David the people of Tob, together with those of Beth-Rehob and Zobah, went to the assistance of *Ammon (2 Sam. 10:6-8; Authorized Version: 'Ish-tob'). Its location is not certain, but it should perhaps be identified with et-Taiyibeh, southeast of *Ashtaroth.

TOOLS Numerous tools are mentioned in the Bible and still more have been found in archaeological excavations or seen in wall paintings and reliefs in *Egypt, *Mesopotamia and the other countries of the ancient Near East.

TOOLS OF THE SMITH Some tools, and some of the processes by which metal was worked, are described in the Bible. To prepare the metal for forging the smith placed it in the fire, the combustible agent being coal. He held the piece of metal with tongs and worked it with a hammer (Isa. 44:12). Although no anvil is mentioned, no metal, and especially not the harder ones, could have been worked without one. Once the metal had been flattened it could be fastened to wood with nails (Jer. 10:4). There is no mention of bellows in the Bible either, but they must have been known. In early *Egypt bellows in the form of hollow pipes were used. Air was blown through them by the mouth. As early as the middle of the 2nd millennium BC these primitive aids were replaced by bellows operated by the feet. These consisted of two sacks made of animal skins, in the ends of which pipes with clay outlets were inserted. A flat stone was placed on each sack, attached by a string. The pipes were placed in the furnace and the smith's assistant would stamp on one sack, expelling the air through the pipe, at the same time lifting the stone weight on the other sack, thus drawing air in. By alternately stamping and lifting he ensured a strong and continuous draught.

STONE-DRESSERS' TOOLS The implement most frequently mentioned in conjunction with stone-cutting is the hammer (Jer. 23:29). It seems that these hammers were made of stone, for no metal hammers earlier than the Roman period have been found in Palestine. In *Egypt, too, iron hammers were not known until they were introduced by the Greeks. Another tool used by the stone-cutter was the axe (1 Kgs. 6:7; Isa. 10:15). It is difficult to tell from the Bible what its shape was, but it seems that it was not unlike the chisel that is used for dressing stone today. A saw is also mentioned: it was probably used for cutting stones (Isa. 10:15; and cf. also 2 Sam. 12:31; 1 Kgs. 7:9; 1 Chr. 20:3). In *Egypt saws made of bronze were used for this purpose. Their teeth were considerably larger, coarser and more widely spaced than those of saws used for cutting wood.

MASONS' TOOLS These included lines of flax, measuring reeds (Ezek. 40:3 ff.) and measures a cubit long (Josh. 3:4). As they were made of perishable materials there is no means of knowing what they looked like. Another tool used by the mason was the plumbline (Amos 7:7-8). Plumblines have been found in *Egypt from as early as the end of the Old Kingdom and they are shaped just as they are today. Another tool used in building was a wooden form for moulding bricks. This was square or rectangular, without a top or a bottom, and had a wooden handle. Forms of this type have been found in *Egypt from the time of the Middle Kingdom.

CARPENTERS' TOOLS *See* *CARPENTRY

TOOLS USED IN AGRICULTURE The economy of the Holy Land was based mainly on agriculture, which is why so many farmers' tools are mentioned in the Bible. Among these were plowshares, coulters, forks, axes, mattocks and goads (1 Sam. 13:20-1), a sickle (Jer.

Iron knife with curved blade, Athlit, Iron Age

Iron knife and scythe blade, Tell Beit Mirsim, Iron Age

50:16; Joel 3:13), a scythe (Deut. 16:9; Authorized Version: 'sickle'), a threshing instrument (2 Sam. 24:22; Isa. 41:15, etc.), a sieve (Isa. 30:28; Amos 9:9) and a fan (Isa. 30:24; Jer. 15:7). Some of these implements are well known. The plow, for instance, which was probably merely a development of the hoe, was known in the ancient Near East from a very early date. In Egypt it is known from the early 3rd millennium BC. The earliest plows were made of hard wood, to which a flint blade was sometimes attached. They had two handles. Metal blades were used from the second half of the 2nd millennium BC onwards, but as they were made of bronze they snapped easily. It was only after the introduction of iron that metal blades were universally used. Iron plowshares have been found in Palestine from as early as the 11th century BC. The blades had to be sharpened frequently (cf. 1 Sam. 13:20-1). The coulter mentioned in the Authorized Version (1 Sam. 13:20) was not the same as the plowshare, but was an implement for turning the soil by hand; it was made of iron and was about 3-4in wide. Sickles and scythes were used for mowing. In early times, and even in the biblical period, their blades were of flint and their handles of bone or wood. Iron-bladed sickles have also been found on Iron Age sites. It seems that there was no difference between the sickle and the scythe at that time, since the longer scythe does not appear before the Roman period. Forks, most probably a three-pronged variety (cf. 1 Sam. 2:13), were used for gathering the mown corn. The corn was threshed on a threshing floor with a long wooden stick. In the Roman period the stick was replaced by the threshing sledge, which was driven by an animal. The threshed corn was separated from the chaff with a sieve or fan. Very fine sieves, some from the Chalcolithic age and some from the Roman period, have been found at *Jericho and in the *Judean Desert Caves.

In addition to these tools, knives of various shapes and sizes, shaving blades and chisels have been found on many sites in Palestine. In the Roman period the production of tools expanded considerably and covered all trades and professions. It is sometimes even quite difficult to tell a Roman tool from a modern one.

TOR ABU SIF TERRACE The Tor Abu Sif Terrace borders a tributary of the Wadi Abu Sif in the *Judean Desert and was excavated by R. Neuville. Two rich Natufian layers were uncovered here. They yielded crescents that showed abrupt retouch more frequently than the more typical Helwan retouch, plus geometric microliths, microburins, scrapers, burins and awls. The last two tools are considered by the excavator to be unique to this site. (*See also* *PREHISTORY; *FLINT TOOLS.)

TRADE Despite the lack of good natural harbors Palestine played an important part in international trade. Some of the most important trade routes, leading to *Egypt from *Mesopotamia, Syria and *Phoenicia, crossed Palestine (*Roads), and in fact it represented the only approach to *Egypt from the north, except by sea. For this reason the trade routes of Palestine were always thronged with merchants from all parts of the world (Gen. 37:35; 1 Kgs. 10:15, etc.). The tolls collected from them were an important factor in the country's economy at all periods.

Among the finds on sites that were occupied as early as the Neolithic and Chalcolithic periods are objects and materials that certainly did not originate in Palestine, and must therefore have been brought from abroad. Among these were obsidian, precious stones, spices and certain kinds of wood. There is valuable evidence of the existence of a transit trade in the wall painting of Bani Hasan in *Egypt, which depicts a caravan of Semites bringing kohl to *Egypt. Similarly, the *El Amarna letters show that there was extensive trade between *Mesopotamia, *Canaan and *Egypt. The three lists of goods sent by an Egyptian pharaoh to a Babylonian king, and the list of the dowry of a princess who was married to an Egyptian king, contain names of scores of items that were traded in the ancient world. Documents of the middle of the 3rd millennium BC dealing with trade, both local and international, have been found in *Mesopotamia.

The *Phoenicians were intermediaries in the great maritime trade between western Asia and the cities on the Mediterranean coast, as well as in the trade between Syria, *Egypt and the other countries along the shores of the Mediterranean. Early in the 1st millennium BC Greek merchants also took an active

Model of a Roman trade ship

and Persia to *Egypt, the Mediterranean islands and the countries along its shores; and the rise of the Roman Empire. In times of peace merchants would make their way singly or in small groups, with a few beasts of burden. They would travel from village to village buying the local products (Prov. 31:24). Larger companies of traders used camels, the ships of the desert (Gen. 37:25), asses (Gen. 42:26, etc.), mules (1 Chr. 12:40) and servants (2 Kgs. 5:23). During the Persian period armed guards accompanied the caravans (Ezra 8:22).

The chief exports from Palestine in the biblical period were grain, oil and wine. *Tyre bought the products of Palestine in order to resell them in the Mediterranean ports (Ezek. 27:16-7); oil was shipped to *Egypt (Hos. 12:1), along with balm, honey, spices, myrrh, nuts and almonds (Gen. 43:11). *Tyre bought fir trees and cedars for the masts of its ships and the oaks of the *Bashan for its oars (Ezek. 27:5-6), while the Israelites imported cedars and pines from the *Lebanon (1 Kgs. 5:6, 9, etc.).

Few trade regulations are mentioned in the Bible, but certain laws were not calculated to encourage it. A self-contained economic system was the ideal, according to the Bible (Prov. 31:10-27), and 'the laying of usury' was prohibited (Exod. 22:25, etc.). The precept of using a just stone (Authorized Version: 'weight') and a just measure was clearly laid down (Lev. 19:35-6).

It was not until the time of Solomon that the Israelites began to engage in international trade on a large scale. His great building activities, for instance, necessitated the import of timber from the *Lebanon (1 Kgs. 5:6). After the Restoration international trade was mostly in the hands of foreigners, including the men of *Tyre, *Sidon and Greece. Not much is known about the development of trade in the 4th century BC, but the rise of the port of *Alexandria and the granting of permission to Jews to settle there and in the newly founded *Antioch-on-the-Orontes did much for its expansion under the Ptolemaic and Seleucid kingdoms. The conquest of *Joppa by the Hasmoneans provided the Judean kingdom with access to the sea routes; and the opening of this port to Greek

part in this trade. In this way *Egypt imported ivory, ebony, hides and slaves from Nubia (*Ethiopia), and from the countries south of *Egypt. At times ships were also despatched to the spice countries in southern *Arabia, Somaliland and perhaps also further east. On land routes caravans journeyed from *Arabia to Syria and *Egypt.

A number of factors led to the development of international trade: the founding of the Persian Empire, which also ruled over western Asia, *Egypt, the Greek cities of Asia Minor and many of the islands of the Aegean, thus bringing a great part of the inhabited world under one central system; the conquests of Alexander the Great; the subsequent formation of the Hellenistic states and the foundation of many new cities all over the inhabited world; the growth of the Jewish Diaspora, which was dispersed from *Babylon

Caravan of Semite traders from a wall-painting in the Bani Hasan Tomb, Egypt

merchants, who took the place of the Phoenicians, turned it into an international center of commerce.

In the Roman period Judea became part of the huge Roman commercial complex, and its great prosperity in the first centuries AD is due to this connection. The flourishing Nabatean trade flowed through southern Palestine, its countless camel-trains bearing spices, perfumes, herbs, precious wood and gems from the Far East and southern *Arabia. The long trade routes terminated at *Gaza and the ports to the south of it. Other very important routes to Syria, *Phoenicia and *Egypt also passed through Judea, and the tolls collected in the ports and at its borders formed an important part of the country's revenue. But the rise of Palmyra (*Tadmor) in the 2nd century AD led to the diversion of a great part of the international trade to other routes. Another cause of the decline in trade through Palestine was the great expansion in shipbuilding, which permitted direct sailing from the Far East, *Arabia, and East Africa to *Egypt and thence to the ports of Europe.

TRANSPORT Vehicles drawn by animals were not very common in Palestine in the biblical period. The few that are referred to were mainly employed in the service of kings and warriors and should be classed as military equipment rather than as an everyday means of transport. Short journeys would normally be made on foot, but for longer distances, or where the transfer of loads was involved, animals were used.

ASS AND DONKEY The ass was the most common mount in biblical Palestine. Asses were probably domesticated as early as the 4th millennium BC. An Egyptian wall painting of the pre-Dynastic period shows a group of asses arranged in a row. Documents from Cappadocia and *Mari, of the 19th-18th centuries BC, deal with caravans of merchants who used asses in their travels from Anatolia to Syria and *Mesopotamia and asses are also seen carrying burdens in the Egyptian wall painting at Bani Hasan, which shows a caravan of kohl merchants on their way to *Egypt. Bones of asses have been found on many ancient sites in Palestine, while figurines and drawings of asses have been found at *Gezer and *Megiddo. In the Bible there are frequent references to the ass as a

mount (2 Sam. 16:2; 17:23; 1 Kgs. 2:40; 13:13, etc.); in these passages the beast is always saddled. Asses were also ridden by women (Exod. 4:20; Josh. 15:18; Judg. 1:14; 1 Sam. 25:20; 2 Kgs. 4:24), but only in the last reference is a saddle mentioned. They were also used a good deal in the Roman period, both for riding and for carrying loads. Jesus entered *Jerusalem riding on an ass (Matt. 21:2-11).

THE HORSE Horses were most probably introduced into Palestine in the 19th century BC by the *Hyksos, but they were used only in war (*Weapons and warfare). From passages in the Bible in which they are mentioned it does not seem likely that they were ridden in the ordinary way. Even in the post-biblical period they were little used in everyday life. From the late 1st century onwards the *Nabateans in the *Negev and in *Auranitis bred good quality horses, later known as the Arabian horse. These were most probably race horses, but it is possible that horses of inferior quality were used in army service and everyday life.

THE CAMEL The camel (or dromedary) was known in Palestine in early times. Its special qualities enable it to survive the most difficult desert conditions and a good one can travel up to a 100 miles a day, carrying loads weighing up to 500lb. Hence they were much used by caravans that had to make long desert journeys and acquired the epithet 'ship of the desert'. Camels are frequently mentioned in the Bible as early as the time of the Patriarchs (Gen. 12:16; 24:10; 31:17; 32:7). There were also many camels among the neighboring nations that dwelt on the border of the desert, such as the Ishmaelites (Gen. 37:25), *Midianites (Judg. 6:5), *Amalekites (1 Sam. 15:3), *Sheba (1 Kgs. 10:2), *Aram (2 Kgs. 8:9; Authorized Version: 'Syria'), Kedar and *Hazor (Jer. 49:28, 29), Hagarites (1 Chr. 5:20-1), Ethiopians (2 Chr. 14:15) and Egyptians (Exod. 9:3). On their way from the Babylonian exile the Jews used 435 camels and 6,720 asses (Neh. 7:69). Camels were used for riding in peace and war (1 Sam. 30:17; Isa 21:7) and for carrying valuable merchandise (Gen. 37:25) and food (1 Chr. 12:40). There were so many camels in the kingdom of David that a special overseer, Obil the Ishmaelite, was appointed (1 Chr. 27:30).

THE MULE A very strong and hardy animal, the mule was used for tasks that in other countries were allotted to the horse. It was a fast steed (2 Sam. 13:29), a beast of burden (2 Kgs. 5:17; 1 Chr. 12:40) and a mount for a king (1 Kgs. 1:44). On their return from the Babylonian exile the Jews brought 245 mules with them (Ezra 2:66; Neh. 7:68).

THE WAGON The Bible distinguishes between the wagon that was used for transporting men and goods in peace time and the lighter chariot, which was used mainly in time of war, though sometimes by the king and his retinue in peace time. It seems that chariots were used for the first time in Syria and *Egypt in the Middle Bronze Age, when the *Hyksos introduced the horse into this region. Wagons drawn by asses or camels were not uncommon in *Babylon and *Egypt for transporting loads. In the Persian Empire lighter, horse-drawn chariots were used by the royal mail. Normally men did not ride on a loaded wagon but walked beside it. One of the Hittite reliefs shows a flat load wagon with four wheels. Similar wagons were used by the *Philistines in their wanderings, and also in Assyria. A distinction is made in the Bible between a covered wagon, probably used for conveying loads, and a simpler wagon or cart (Num. 7:3; Sam. 6:7). Wagons or carts were used mainly in the plains, where the Jews may have adopted the idea from their neighbors the *Philistines (1 Sam. 6:7 ff.; 2 Sam. 6:3 ff.). An Assyrian relief depicting the retreat of the Jews from *Lachish shows a cart with two wheels and drawn by oxen. It is loaded with bundles, on which two women and children are sitting, while the men walk alongside. Carts with a leather or linen cover are known in *Carchemish and *Ashur and these may well have been the covered wagons of the Bible. Carts, wagons and chariots became increasingly common in post-biblical times, when better roads were constructed.

TRAVEL In ancient times the traveller had to face numerous dangers. He was virtually at the mercy of robbers and the none-too-friendly attitude of the people of the towns and villages through which he would have to pass, far away from the protection of his own folk. People did not travel much, therefore, unless they had to. The Bible gives many examples of the conditions that awaited them when they did. The inhabitants of *Shechem would lie in ambush on the high mountains and rob passers-by of their belongings (Judg. 9:25); anyone who wandered through deserted parts of the country sometimes had to face wild beasts (Isa. 30:6), while for those who journeyed by sea there was the additional danger of stormy waters (Jon. 1:4; Ps. 107:23 ff.). Nowhere in the Bible is there an account of anyone undertaking a journey purely for pleasure. There must always have been a grave reason for any longer expedition, such as the wanderings of Jacob and his sons to *Egypt because of the great famine in the land of *Canaan (Gen. 43 ff.) or the journey undertaken by the young man of *Bethlehem in Judah (Judg. 17:7 ff.).

The main reasons that would force an man to undertake a journey were:

a) Cultic requirements. Already in early times the Israelites were in the habit of travelling considerable distances to central cult places. While still in Egypt, for instance, they asked for permission to make a three-day journey into the desert to sacrifice to God (Exod. 5:3). In the same vein, they were commanded, 'Thrice a year shall all your men children appear before the Lord God' (Exod. 34:23). Both men and women were in the habit of going to a place where an altar was set up in order to sacrifice to God (1 Sam. 1:3, 21; cf. also 2 Kgs. 1:2).

b) Commercial transactions Objects of foreign origin found in settlements dating from as early as the Chalcolithic period indicate that goods were bartered. This inevitably implies long journeys. Such journeys were increasingly undertaken in the Bronze Age, but it was Solomon who brought the Israelites into the orbit of international trade (1 Kgs. 10:28-9). The merchant fleet that he built at *Ezion-Geber took their merchants and sailors to ports on the Arabian and African coasts. Israelite merchants were also frequent visitors to *Damascus and even had 'streets' there (1 Kgs. 20:34).

c) Political and diplomatic missions These were quite common reasons for undertaking journeys. Ehud, for instance, went up to Eglon, King of *Moab, to take him a present (Judg. 3:15 ff.). Later we hear that the king himself and his retinue had to go to foreign countries, to visit the kings to whom they were subject (2 Kgs. 16:10); or that messengers from foreign countries would visit *Jerusalem (Jer. 27:3).

Since these were the three most important reasons for travelling, travellers were usually people of high social standing and ordinary people most probably went away from home very rarely.

Undertaking a journey necessitated careful preparations. For instance, when Nehemiah left the Persian court in order to go to *Jerusalem he was provided with letters of recommendation, written by the kings to the Persian satraps of the provinces through which he would pass. The letters included, among other provisions, orders to supply an armed escort (Neh. 2:7 ff.). Men would rarely go singly and travellers would always prefer to join a caravan. There is evidence of caravans at remote historical periods, showing that they moved along the routes of the Aegean islands, *Cyprus, Asia Minor and *Mesopotamia. Some of these would cross the land of *Canaan on their way to *Egypt. A wall painting from a tomb at Bani Hasan in *Egypt, of the 19th century BC, depicts a caravan coming from *Gilead. The Bible mentions caravans of Ishmaelites and *Midianites (Gen. 37:25-8) going from *Gilead to *Egypt. The movement of caravans is also frequently referred to in the *El Amarna letters, and the Assyrian documents from early in the 1st millennium BC mention caravans moving between the oases of *Arabia, Teima, Dumah and Dedan (cf. also Job. 6:19; Isa. 21:13). The safe transit of caravans depended mainly on the conditions in the territory through which they passed. Interference with the safe movement of caravans is hinted at in the song of Deborah (Judg. 5:6), and is also mentioned in the *El Amarna letters. Even in normal times a heavy road tax had to be paid to local authorities in order to ensure safe conduct (1 Kgs. 10:15).

The traveller in the desert had to carry his provisions with him (Gen. 21:14), as indeed, he sometimes had to even in populated areas. Thus the young man from Mount Ephraim provided fodder for his beast and bread and wine for himself and his servants (Judg. 19:19). When the Gibeonites wished Joshua to believe that they had come from a distant country they took a large quantity of provisions with them (Josh. 9:4-6, 12-14). Wayfarers were sometimes obliged to give undertakings concerning their behavior (Num. 20:17 ff.). There is no reference in the Bible to real caravanserais, and it was only in the Persian period, when the imperial mail was instituted, that these were established, so that it was possible to obtain lodging, though still no food. The Bible does occasionally refer to inns where shelter could be found (Gen. 42:27; 43:21; Josh. 4:3, 8 ['lodging place']; Jer. 9:2; Luke 10:34). It seems that these inns were in out-of-the-way places, never in the towns, and a merchant who travelled in a caravan would have to go to the merchants' quarter to find lodgings. Individuals or companies of travellers who came to a strange city in Israel would enjoy the hospitality of the citizens (2 Sam. 17:27-29; Isa. 21:14-15).

From the foregoing it seems that in the biblical period the traveller was completely at the mercy of the people living in the places through which he travelled. The Bible provides no specific rules concerning hospitality, but Genesis (18:1 ff.; 24:31) and Exodus (2:18 ff.) show how important hospitality was considered to be. And when Job claims to have lived righteously he says: 'The stranger did not lodge in the street: but I opened my doors to the traveller' (Job. 31:32). On the other hand, a passage like that in Judges (19:15) illustrates the fate that could befall a traveller who found the doors closed against him.

But the institution of the Persian royal mail improved conditions considerably. In the Hellenistic and subsequent periods, when many new roads were constructed, more caravanserais were built. Here travellers could find lodging and obtain stabling for their beasts and storage for their merchandise. This fact is well attested by both archaeological finds and literary evidence. Some large caravanserais have been discovered at *Nessana and *Mampsis, for instance. They consisted of large courts surrounded by rooms two stories high. The ones at *Nessana were also mentioned in the papyri found there. Inns where Jews coming from the Diaspora, or from other parts of Palestine, could obtain accommodation were sometimes built next to the synagogues.

TREASURE (CAVE OF THE) One of the *Judean Desert Caves; situated about 150 feet below the bank of Nahal Mishmar (Wadi Mahras) and 750 feet above the river bed. About 600 feet below the cave the water from two springs collects in a small natural reservoir. The cave is natural and measures 42 feet by 36 feet and 3-11 feet high and there are two large natural niches in its walls. There were two occupation levels in the cave. The upper level had remains of the period of the Bar-Kochba rebellion (AD 132-5), among which were household utensils, clothing, footwear, and small fragments of documents in Hebrew and Greek.

Rams' heads on a copper stand from the Cave of Treasure, Judean desert, Chalcolithic period

More important however were the remains of the Chalcolithic period. On the high banks of the wadi were open air enclosures surrounded by field stone walls. These were probably open air cult places. The more important remains of that period were found in the cave itself. These included numerous pottery vessels, stone bowls for grinding, beads, jewelry, textiles, wickerwork baskets and mats, leather footwear, food (wheat, barley, onions, lentils, garlic, olives and dates), animal bones (sheep and goats, gazelle, deer and birds) and a loom of the horizontal type (*Weaving). Most exciting was the treasure which had been intentionally concealed in one of the niches and included 429 implements, all but six made of copper.

Not all the objects found in this cache can be identified with certainty even now. They are of unusually good workmanship, and only very few are paralleled elsewhere. Among the implements were 20 adzes and chisels of different shapes and sizes; 240 mace-heads, varying in shape, size and weight; about 80 sticks, some hollow, others solid, with incised decoration, still others with figurines of birds, animals and a human face; and ten 'crowns', too small to be worn on the head, decorated in the same way as the sticks. There were also five sickle-shaped implements made of hippopotamus bones, each 1 foot long, with numerous perforations. Although the finds in this cave,

which are dated to about 3500-2800 BC, yielded an enormous amount of information about this early period, many questions concerning the origin of these men and the reason why they were forced to abandon their villages, and then their cave shelter, still remain unanswered.

TULEILAT GHASSUL A few small mounds occupying an area of some 7 acres in the *Jordan Valley, about 2 miles northeast of the *Dead Sea, 850 feet below sea level. The sites were excavated in the years 1929-38 by A. Mallon, R. Koppel and R. Neuville on behalf of the Pontifical Biblical Institute in Jerusalem; in 1960 by R. North; and again in 1967-8 by J.B. Hennessy on behalf of the British School of Archaeology in Jerusalem.

From the work of the various expeditions quite a clear picture has emerged of the life of a village that flourished mainly in the Chalcolithic period. Since the site was not fortified, scholars believe that this must have been a period of peace and prosperity. The houses are rectangular, square or trapezoid, built close together, the spaces between being paved with stones. Each house consisted of one large room, with one or more smaller ones attached to it. The walls, 1 foot 6in to 2 feet 8in thick, on a base of stones, were of plastered and whitewashed mud brick, and in some cases were also decorated with multicolored wall

Wall painting depicting a star, Tuleilat Ghassul, Chalcolithic period

paintings. Each house was provided with a large number of mud-brick or stone storage bins of different sizes. Inside the houses large clay jars, ovens and benches built of bricks were sunk into the ground.

Local industry produced pottery, bone, stone and metal implements. The pottery is mostly handmade, for only the upper part of some of the bowls is finished on a primitive potter's wheel. The most typical vessels are bowls decorated with a red band, horn-shaped cups, jars and a jug identified as a churn. This unique group is now classified as 'Ghassulian'. Typical also is the decoration, which consists of painted, moulded and incised patterns. The stone implements found included scrapers, axes and sickle-blades made of flint, together with millstones, mortars, rubbing-stones and pestles made of basalt or limestone. Metal was rare and the few copper implements found included points and two axes. Their importance is that they are the most ancient metal implements yet found in Palestine.

The economy of the village, as shown by the finds, was based to a great extent on agriculture. Of great interest are the wall paintings, the earliest of their period, still unparalleled elsewhere. They include geometric motifs, stars, masks and imaginary and stylized images, which may have been associated with some form of mythology. Most complete is an eight-pointed star measuring about 6 feet across. In other paintings there are birds, or seated figures, all painted in black, white, red and brown.

The site is dated to the second half of the 4th millennium BC. It has given its name to the culture of that period in Palestine, for which parallels have also been found on other sites, and which is now known as the Ghassulian culture.

TYRE; TYRIANS An important Canaanite city in *Phoenicia, its name meaning 'rock'; called Zara or Zaru by the Assyrians and Tyros by the Greeks. The modern Arab town of the same name was built over the ancient site. The oldest part of Tyre was built on the narrow coastal strip and it is this area that was known to the Greeks as *palai Tyros*, 'ancient Tyre'. The city subsequently extended over an island separated from the mainland by straits about ¹/₂ mile wide.

Tyre is mentioned for the first time in the *Execration Texts of the 19th-18th centuries BC. The *El Amarna letters mention that the city suffered badly from the competition of *Sidon and *Arvad, its neighbor. It is mentioned several times in the documents of *Ugarit, which reveal that the king of that city was represented by an agent at Tyre. By the end of the 13th century BC the *Sea Peoples exerted pressure on the whole region and Tyre seems to have suffered destruction. It was refounded at the beginning of the 12th century BC. A century later Tyre prospered greatly. It is also referred to in some of the later Egyptian sources. It was only after the decline of *Egypt that the great prosperity of Tyre set in. It eventually rose to the position of ruler of the sea and was a great commercial and cultural center. After its emancipation from Egyptian influence during the reign of Rameses III it became the most important city in *Phoenicia, founding large commercial colonies along the shores of the

Mediterranean. There was virtually no place in the known world with which Tyre did not have commercial relations.

During the period of the Israelite conquest of *Canaan it was known as the 'strong city of Tyre' and lay on the border of the lot of the tribe of Asher (Josh. 19:29). David sent for cedar trees, carpenters and masons from Tyre in order to build his house (2 Sam.

Silver shekel from Tyre

5:11). Hiram, King of Tyre (969-936 BC), enlarged the Island of Tyre by uniting it with a small island and rebuilt the old temples of Melkart and Astarte. It is possible that the colonies founded by Tyre reached Spain in this period. Solomon renewed his father's pact with Hiram, King of Tyre (1 Kgs. 5:1-3), and enlisted his help in the building of his temple in *Jerusalem. In return for this help Solomon gave Hiram the land of Cabul and 20 cities in *Galilee (1 Kgs. 9:11-13). Israel and Tyre had close relations during the reign of Ahab, who married Jezebel, daughter of Ethbaal, King of the Sidonians (1 Kgs. 16:31). This marriage led to the introduction of idolatry into Israel. It was for this reason that Isaiah (23), Jeremiah (25:22), Ezekiel (26-8), Joel (3:4), Amos (1:9-10) and Zechariah (9:2-4) foretold the destruction of the town and its colonies. After the Restoration, the people of Tyre were again selling on the Sabbath in the markets of *Jerusalem (Neh. 13:16).

Tyre reached its zenith in the 9th century BC, after the foundation of Carthage, which was later to become Rome's bitter enemy. In that period the Assyrians were expanding westwards toward the shores of the Mediterranean. In 701 BC Sennacherib divided the Tyrian kingdom, which extended at that time from *Sidon in the north to *Acco in the south, into two kingdoms, Tyre and *Sidon. When Esarhaddon crushed the revolt of Sidon in 677/6 BC the southern part of Sidon was again annexed to Tyre. This was followed by the strengthening of Tyre's power and the city felt sufficiently secure to form an alliance with Taharqa the Egyptian. The alliance was defeated by Esarhaddon at *Ashkelon. During the reign of Ashurbanipal Tyre revolted twice. In the later decades, at the instigation of the Egyptians, Tyre opposed Assyria, at the twilight of its power, as well as the newly ascendent *Babylonian kingdom. Nebuchadnezzar besieged Tyre for 13 years (585-573 BC), but eventually concluded a pact with it. In the Persian period Tyre planted many colonies on the Palestinian coast, spreading as far south as Ascalon (*Ashkelon). In 332 BC Alexander the Great besieged the town, but he succeeded in taking it only after constructing a causeway between the island and the coast.

The subsequent rise of *Alexandria as a competing commercial power caused the decline of Tyre. It was freed from the Ptolemaic yoke in 273 BC but fell to the Seleucids in 198 BC. It was freed again in 126 BC, when Pompey conquered the city and proclaimed its autonomy. It was known again as an important and flourishing commercial center throughout the Roman period. In AD 638 it was conquered by the Arabs.

U

UBEIDIYA A hill situated 15 miles south of the Sea of *Galilee on the west bank of the River *Jordan, 525-722 feet below sea level. After its discovery M. Stekelis began excavations in 1960. These have continued in conjuction with the work of L. Picard, U. Baida, G. Haas and E. Tchernov, whose field of study is the geological and paleontological succession of what is now termed the Ubeidiya Formation. This consists of a series of deposits accumulated during the advance and retreat of an ancient lake that formerly lay in the central *Jordan Valley. The accumulation of these deposits was halted by further earth movements, which created the minute anticline, with some minor faulting and undulations, of the Ubeidiya Formation. The valley was later filled with an alluvial and gravel formation, which has been called the Naharayim Formation. A subsequent flooding by the Lisan Lake deposited the marly Lisan Formation. The eventual shrinkage of this lake led to the drying out of the *Jordan channel from the Sea of *Galilee down to the *Dead Sea.

Four cycles have been observed inside the Ubeidiya Formation, in which animal remains and prehistoric finds have been unearthed. Numerous animal species (more than 100) include the hippopotamus, giraffe, crocodile, elephant, rhinoceros, deer, gazelle, boars, rodents, bison, bear, wolf, plus many birds. These varied remains indicate that forest, steppe, marsh and lake existed at the same time.

During 1960-74, sixteen field campaigns took place at the site. Over 15,000 man-made artifacts were uncovered from 67 different archaeological horizons originating in different environments of deposition. The dominant tool types encountered are chopping-tools, discoids, polyhedrons, spheroids, handaxes (including picks and trihedrals), heavy duty scrapers, light duty scrapers and varied forms of other retouched flakes. Sample sizes differ drastically from one archaeological horizon to the other. The largest sample sizes derive from the 'living-floors' pavements of unmodified stones, mainly basalt gravels, on which the artifacts and the paleontological remains were found. Another source of large samples are the conglomeratic layers found in the K area (i.e. K-29, K-30).

Differences in the typological composition of different layers were considered by Stekelis to be the result of the coexistence of two distinct cultural traditions at the site: lower Acheulian with over 30% handaxes and Developed Oldowan with smaller frequencies of bifaces (approximately 7%).

A detailed study of all the lithic artifacts was carried out by Goren (1982) in which various typological, technological and stylistic attributes were analyzed. This detailed study demonstrated that the typological variability is due to different sample sizes. It was also demonstrated that the technological properties of all assemblages are similar and do not reflect an existence of two entities. The search for raw material for the production of certain tool types was consistent throughout the stratigraphical sequence of the Ubeidiya Formation. Thus basalt was chosen for the production of bifaces; flint for chopping tools, discoids, polyhedrons, flake tools, and limestone for spheroids. These finds led to the concept that in Ubeidiya a single cultural entity existed throughout the different cycles of deposition — an entity which should be related to the Acheulian Industrial Complex.

Several fragments of a human skull are the only hominid remains found, defined by P.V. Tobias as *Homo.spec.indet.*

The site of Ubeidiya is assigned to the Early Pleistocene era. There are no radiometric dates from the site itself but from related geological formations in the Jordan Valley (Cover Basalt, Yarmuk Basalt). Those combined with the reversal paleomagnetism encountered at the site and the revised study of the big mammalian fossils support an age estimation of *c.* 1.2 million years for the Ubeidiya Formation (*See also* *PREHISTORY; *FLINT TOOLS).

UGARIT An ancient town in northern Syria whose remains have been identified at Ras Shamra; situated near a small harbor named Minet el-Beida ('white harbor'). Excavation of the site began in 1929 under C.F.A. Schaeffer and G. Chenet, on behalf of the French Academy. The site was inhabited as early as the Neolithic period. In the Chalcolithic period it had already developed a relatively rich culture, which shows Mesopotamian influence. It was a key point on the route leading from *Mesopotamia to *Crete and it was by this route that elements of the Mesopotamian culture reached the Mediterranean islands. The arrival of West Semitic settlers in the second half of the

3rd millennium BC brought great prosperity to Ugarit, which then became the great commercial center through which goods originating in Asia Minor, the Aegean island and *Egypt were interchanged.

Politically Ugarit was under Egyptian influence. With the great upheavals of the 18th century BC, which culminated in the formation of the *Hyksos kingdom, a new element, the *Horites, made its appearance in Ugarit. But their efforts to form an anti-Egyptian party failed, the older West Semitic element still prevailing. After the overthrow of the *Hyksos rulers and their expulsion from *Egypt in the second half of the 16th century BC, Egyptian influence revived and the city was even forced to admit an Egyptian garrison. But this did not impair Ugarit's prosperity, and it continued to thrive in the 15th and 14th centuries BC.

The huge fortunes accumulated there had a direct effect on the technical and cultural development of the city, which increased in size and included among its numerous merchants and artists people from the Aegean, *Cyprus and Mycenae. The houses of this period are large and richly furnished, and beneath them are tombs no less magnificent. The city boasted two large temples, one dedicated to Baal, the other to Dagon. In the harbor district large storehouses were

Gold bowl from Ugarit, depicting a hunt in chariots, 14th century BC

Bronze statuettes of Phoenician gods from Ugarit

discovered, with numerous jars still *in situ*. The city's art objects, pottery vessels (local and imported), stone, bone, ivory and metal objects all attest to its great prosperity.

In the middle of the 14th century BC Ugarit was destroyed in a great conflagration. Even before this calamity the *Hittites were pressing it hard, though the *El Amarna letters show that the rulers of Ugarit still remained loyal to *Egypt. But their loyalty was in vain: when the great battle between *Egypt and the *Hittites raged in the early 13th century BC, Ugaritic contingents fought on the site of the *Hittites. When peace was finally restored Ugarit prospered again, without interruption, until the arrival of the Sea Peoples (*Philistines) at the beginning of the 12th century BC. The city never recovered from this conquest and all that remained thereafter was a poor town.

Ugarit is of the utmost importance to research into the development of the Canaanite script and literature, for in addition to the Accadian documents and Horite dictionaries, documents written in a special script have been found there. This is an alphabetic, cuneiform and consonant script, belonging to the Canaanite family but closer to biblical Hebrew. The most important literature in it consists of epic songs in which the deeds of gods and heroes are praised. There is much in common, both in language and in content, between these epics and the biblical literature.

UMM EZ-ZUWEITINA (CAVE) A cave excavated by R. Neuville on the left bank of Wadi Djihar in the *Judean Desert. Only one archaeological layer was found: a Natufian occupation level including a large hearth and a rich flint and bone tool industry. Among the implements were crescents formed by Helwan retouch, sickle-blades and microburins. Of particular interest was a limestone figurine of a kneeling animal (*See also* *PREHISTORY; *FLINT TOOLS.*)*

UMM NAQUS (CAVE) A cave on the right bank of Wadi Khareitun, excavated by R. Neuville. Of the four layers uncovered and labelled A-D only two were found to include prehistoric artifacts. Of these, layer C was typically Mousterian of the Middle Paleolithic period, with short triangular points and racloirs, while layer B presented a small Upper Paleolithic assemblage. (*See also* *PREHISTORY; *FLINT TOOLS.*)*

UMM QATAFA (CAVE) A large cave discovered on the left bank of Wadi Khareitun, south of *Herodium, later excavated by R. Neuville (1928, 1932 and 1949). The cave was formed when water dissolved limestone rocks from the beginning of the Upper Pleistocene epoch, and the lowermost layers, which were accumulated by the action of the water, contained no finds. Above these were layers containing a large number of artifacts, including cores, chopping tools and flakes, some partially retouches. They have been classified as Tayacian, after a similar assemblage in western Europe.

At the end of this period the cave ceiling collapsed and a thick layer of large blocks covered the entire floor. The continously dripping water created stalagmitic crusts on these blocks, so that a new floor was formed. In this layer (E2), and especially in the clay layer (E1) that was accumulating above this floor,

many animal remains were found, as well as an assemblage of handaxes classified by Neuville as Middle Acheulian. Layer D was 7 feet thick and contained several hearths. The excavator divided the lithic assemblage into two groups. The lower one (D2) he called Upper Acheulian. It included many handaxes, which tended to be discoidal as well as elongated, and which he compared to the finds of layer F in et-*Tabun Cave. The upper assemblage (D1) includes many handaxes of less than 4in and others that were still shorter. They had pointed tips and concave side contours. End-scrapers and burins were also found. This type of assemblage is typical of the Micoquian culture as it has been described from western Europe and north African sites. Layers C and B were sterile gravel layers, but some remains of the Ghassulian culture were found (*Tuleilat Ghassul) in layer A.

A study of the micro-fauna reveals that during the entire occupation the cave of Umm Qatafa was on the threshold of the desert, as it is today, and that the lower layers, Tayacian and Middle Acheulian, are part of an interpluvial period. (*See also* *PREHISTORY; *FLINT TOOLS.*)*

UR OF THE CHALDEES A very ancient city in southern *Babylon; identified with Tell Muqayyar, close to the right bank of the *Euphrates, half-way

Silver rein ring from the royal tombs of Ur

between Baghdad and the Persian Gulf. Terah and his sons were born there (Gen. 11:26-8) and set out from there for *Haran (Gen. 11:31).

At the center of the mound of Ur remains of a huge tower were discovered in the middle of the 19th century. This was the temple of the Moon God and excavations have brought to light Babylonian inscriptions which prove that this was Ur. Nabonidus, the last Babylonian king, rebuilt the city in about 550 BC. In ancient times it occupied a great stretch of land along the *Euphrates. The inscriptions record a populous city, inhabited by artisans and merchants, frequented by numerous strangers, since all the important trade routes of the ancient world, running from *Elam, *India and southern *Arabia to the countries in the north and west, converged there.

Ur had a history of about 3,000 years. The Sumerians arrived there in about the 4th millennium BC, driving out a more ancient culture and turning it into a center of their own. The remains of the 1st Dynasty of Ur belong to the 28th century BC. The great richness of this culture is displayed in the royal tombs, where the king, his queen and their attendants and slaves lay amid numerous beautifully made objects fashioned in gold and precious stones. The heyday of Ur, however, came during the 3rd Dynasty (end of 3rd to early 2nd millennium BC), whose influence spread over Ashur and *Haran. The code of laws of Ur-Namm, a copy of which was found in the excavations, probably formed the basis of Hammurabi's code. Remains of this large city were discovered in the excavations.

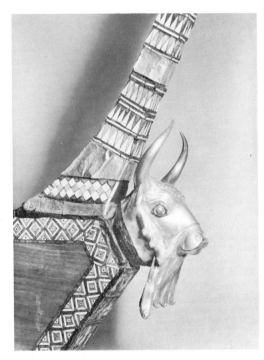

Harp with golden bull's head from Ur

W

WAD, CAVE OF EL The cave of el-Wad is situated in the escarpment of Mount *Carmel facing the sea and near the outlet of Wadi el-Mughara. It was excavated by Miss D.A.E. Garrod in 1929-30. Under layer A, containing remains from the Bronze Age to recent times, the excavator defined two sublayers in which the lithic assemblages are Natufian. Many burials of individuals were found, either singly or in collective graves. The skeletons were in flexed or supine position, a few ornamented with head-bands and necklaces made of dentalium shells and bone pendants (*Jewelry). A wealth of tools reflecting their daily life consisted of pestles and mortars, sickle-hafts (one with blade still *in situ* and another decorated with an incised design of the head of a young deer). Among the flint tools were numerous sickle-blades, crescents and triangles. Bone and horn were used as raw materials for points, awls, gouges and many pendants.

Layer C, beneath the Natufian layer, was characterized by numerous steep scrapers and burins, mainly truncated and polyhedral in shape. This lithic assemblage was considered by the excavator to be a later development of the local Aurignacian culture. Layer D was representative of one of the later stages of this culture, where the main tools were scrapers on blades and flakes, steep and nosed scrapers, and burins. Layer E, referred to as Upper Paleolithic III, is typified by the use of Font-Yves points, steep scrapers, nosed scrapers and burins. Layer F, thought to be the earliest stage of the Upper Paleolithic, contained evidence that spring water had caused the mixture of Mousterian and Aurignacian implements and the accompanying signs of abrasion. As Emireh points were found in this layer, the excavator assigned it to an early culture of the Upper Paleolithic and called it the Emiran culture. The remains of layer G. found as fillings in basins and fissures of the bedrock of the cave, included Mousterian implements of Levalloisian facies. (*See also* *PREHISTORY; *FLINT TOOLS.)

WADI AMUD (CAVES) Wadi Amud descends from the mountains of Upper *Galilee near Safed to the *Jordan Valley and into the Sea of *Galilee. About 5 miles above its entry into the valley the Wadi runs through a limestone gorge 60-90 feet deep. More than a mile from the lower end of the gorge a limestone pillar remains. This pillar (*amud* in Hebrew) is the result of selective erosion and the collapse of big blocks of limestone. In both escarpments of the gorge caves hollowed out by water action were inhabited at various periods, including the prehistoric epochs. In 1925 several of the caves were explored and excavated by F.Turville-Petre; in two of them he found prehistoric remains.

Wadi Amud

EMIREH CAVE The cave is in an isolated cliff near the outlet to the *Jordan Valley and was excavated by Turville-Petre in 1925. Under historic layers at its entrance he found Paleolithic sediment that included an assemblage of flint tools. These were characterized by numerous Mousterian elements (Levallois cores, points and racloirs) and elements of the Upper Paleolithic era (end-scrapers, burins and Font-Yves points). A special tool was found here and later labelled by Miss D.A.E. Garrod as the 'Emireh Point'.

ZUTTIYEH CAVE This cave is in the escarpment on the left bank of the wadi and was excavated by Turville-Petre in 1925 and 1926. Under sediments 6 feet thick he found a broken skull, which he later assigned to *Palaeoanthropus palestinensis*. The lithic assemblage was Mousterian and included Levallois cores, points and racloirs with accentuated Yabrudian characteristics (with high, scale-like retouch and angular in shape). A few handaxes were also found. Miss Garrod compares this assemblage with her finds from et-*Tabun Cave (layer E).

AMUD CAVE A cave beside the pillar on the right bank of the wadi, excavated in 1963-4 by an expedition of the University of Tokyo directed by Suzuki and Watanabe. Although most of the sediments had been disturbed in the early historic periods, a skeleton of the *Palaeoanthropus palestinensis* type was found *in situ* with a Mousterian lithic assemblage.

SHUQBAH CAVE (SHUBABIQ) A cave north of the pillar, on the left bank of the wadi, excavated by S. Binford in 1962. Although most of the layers covering the floor of the cave were disturbed or mixed, an area in the darker part of the cave revealed layers *in situ* under a crust formed by stalagmites. These contained a Mousterian assemblage with Levalloisian facies and two Emireh points. (*See also* *PREHISTORY; *FLINT TOOLS.*)

WATER SUPPLY In prehistoric and early historic times man was very limited in his choice of sites for dwelling places, since he had to be in the immediate vicinity of permanent sources of water such as rivers, springs or freshwater lakes. But he learned at an early date to excavate cisterns in order to store water for

The aqueduct of Caesarea, Roman period

long periods, thus greatly increasing the number of places where he could settle. In the biblical period, however, rivers, lakes and springs were still the most important sources of water, though artificial devices gradually came into use. The device most frequently mentioned in the Bible is the well, called *beer* in Hebrew (Jer. 6:7; Authorized Version: 'fountain', etc.). A well is an artificial shaft by means of which an underground spring, or the underground water level, can be tapped. Of special importance were wells dug in the desert, where hardly any other natural sources of water exist (Gen. 21:17-18). Even today the Bedouins sink their wells in dry river beds. The hole they excavate is about 2 feet deep and 2 feet across. In a short time water accumulates at the bottom of the shaft to a height of about 1 foot. These wells are also called pits, or *geb* in Hebrew (cf. Jer. 14:3). The winter floods silt up these wells and they have to be dug again each spring. The Bible mentions wells being dug and says that enemies sometimes covered them over (Gen. 21:25-31; 26:18-22). In the mountainous regions, where the water level was too far below the surface to be reached by primitive digging techniques, cisterns had to be excavated. Their walls were either lined with stones or hewn in the rock. Cisterns of this kind have been found on numerous sites in Judea, *Samaria and *Galilee. A cistern 60 feet deep and lines with stones has been discovered at *Beth-Shemesh, while another, 120 feet deep and completely hewn in the rock, was discovered at Bir Ayub, near *Jerusalem (probably biblical En-Rogel) (2 Sam. 17:17). The well, or cistern, would normally be covered with a large stone (Gen. 29:3-10) partly to keep the water clean, but mainly to prevent its being used illicitly. In the East it was the duty of the king, the tribe or the extended family to excavate wells, but there were some private wells too (2 Sam. 17:18-19). Along the 'King's Highway' (*Roads) were wells dug by the Egyptian authorities and water was sold to the caravans (Exod. 2:17; 21:22; Deut. 2:6, 28). This was also done in *Mesopotamia.

The first cisterns were dug in the Middle and Late Bronze Age. The rainwater that collected in them during the short rainy season would be enough for at least one dry season. In some parts of Palestine cisterns were the main (sometimes even the only) source of drinking water in peace time as well as in war time. In the early Iron Age the sides of cisterns began to be covered with watertight plaster, which considerably prolonged the time for which water could be stored. It was this important innovation that made it possible to extend the areas of settlement into the mountainous parts of the country.

Cisterns, unlike wells, were usually private property, although it is recorded that Uzziah dug many cisterns in the desert (2 Chr. 26:10; Authorized Version: 'wells'). Innumerable cisterns have been discovered elsewhere. The rocky hill on which *Mizpeh (Tell en-*Nasbeh) was built, for instance, was completely honeycombed with them. The normal cistern was bottle-shaped, with a mouth about 2 feet across hewn into the hard upper layer of rock; the rest was hollowed out in the soft stone below an average depth of 15-20 feet. A pit was dug at the bottom to allow the silt to settle and the walls were covered with plaster containing lime, sand and potsherds, to which ash was sometimes added. The plaster was normally applied in several layers, to ensure that it was waterproof.

Another device for conserving water was a pool hewn in the rock or formed by building a wall across a dry river-bed. The Bible contains references to the famous pools of *Hebron (2 Sam. 4:12), *Gibeon (2 Sam. 2:13). *Samaria (1 Kgs. 22:38) and *Heshbon (S. of S. 7:4). There were also a few pools in *Jerusalem and its vicinity, such as the Upper Pool (2 Kgs. 18:17, etc.), the Lower Pool (Isa. 22:9), the Old Pool (Isa. 22:11), the King's Pool (Neh. 2:14) and the Pool of Siloah (*Siloam) Neh. 3:15). A conduit which brought the water to the pool from the spring is mentioned in conjunction with the Upper Pool.

In the course of the excavations some of the pools mentioned in the Bible have come to light. Most exciting, however, was the discovery of the large pools at *Gibeon. One is a rectangular pool measuring 55 feet by 35 feet, while the other is round, measures 35 feet in diameter and is 60 feet deep. This second one was provided with spiral steps leading down its sides, permitting descent to the level of the water.

The most elaborate feats in ancient water engineering were the tunnels built in order to ensure safe access to a town's vital source of water, which was usually a spring. Tunnels of this sort have been discovered in *Jerusalem and at *Gibeon, *Gezer, Yibleam, *Megiddo and *Hazor. They either brought the water into the towns by gravitation, or provided a safe approach to the source. As the first method necessitated the use of a very long rope by which water was drawn and the second meant a steep descent and a long walk underground, it may be assumed that the tunnels were used only in times of emergency.

The most famous in Palestine are the two tunnels of *Jerusalem. One, known as the 'Warren's Shaft' after its discoverer, brought the water of the *Gihon spring into the city. It was a large arched tunnel, with a flight of steps built into it at the city end, leading to a deep shaft in which the water collected. The spring itself was surrounded by a wall, which formed a large pool from which water could be drawn or conveyed by conduits to gardens around the city. During the time of the Kingdom of Israel the height of the wall was raised, so that a conduit 400yd long could bring the water to a pool to the south of the city. In preparation for the revolt against the Assyrians Hezekiah built a new tunnel, which brought the water of the Gihon right into the city (2 Kgs. 20:20). This tunnel is 1,550 feet long and his great undertaking is commemorated in the celebrated Siloam inscription (*Inscriptions).

The tunnels of *Meggido and *Gezer were very similar, as was the one that has recently been excavated at *Hazor. At *Megiddo and *Hazor large deep shafts were excavated within the city walls and from the bottom of them tunnels led to springs at some distance from the cities, at the foot of the hills on which they stood. At *Gezer and *Gibeon tunnels again led from the towns to the springs.

In the post-biblical periods wells, cisterns, pools and rivers continued to be important sources of water

Water supply tunnel at Megiddo, Iron Age

for drinking and irrigation. But the founding of new large cities with much more sophisticated sanitary installations, among them *Caesarea and *Samaria, necessitated a much more elaborate water-supply system. In Rome, and in many cities throughout the Roman Empire, aqueducts carried on arches and bridges and through tunnels brought water from sources many miles beyond the city's boundaries. The water was then distributed through pipes of clay, stone and lead to public fountains, buildings and baths, and even to private houses two and three stories high. In Palestine Herod set up an elaborate system to supply water to *Caesarea. Here two aqueducts were built: one, on arches, conveyed water to the city from sources at the foot of Mount *Carmel, 8 miles away; the other, a covered channel at ground level, brought water to irrigate the fields from a river 5 miles to the north of the city. At *Samaria a channel that lay partly underground conveyed water to the city from a distant spring.

Also to the Roman period belong some very elaborate devices for water storage built by the *Nabateans at *Mampsis, in the central *Negev. The system consisted of a series of pools formed by dams built across a wadi to trap the flood waters. The water was then transported in jars and stored in the cisterns of private houses, the excess water being stored in a large public pool. Great advances can be noted also in the building of cisterns in the *Negev, and especially in the planning and construction of the collecting channels, so as to conserve as much of the scanty rainfall as possible. It was this system that made possible the great caravan traffic through the desert, and it was not improved upon until the Byzantine period.

WEAPONS AND WARFARE The term 'warfare' as used here includes both battle in open terrain and the besieging of fortified cities, though fortifications are dealt with in a separate entry. Beginning with the first appearance of metal weapons, in the 4th millennium BC, and ending with the destruction of the First Temple in the middle of the 1st millennium BC, we have three main sources of information: excavations, the principal source of weapons (or parts of them) that are made of durable materials; pictorial images such as reliefs, wall paintings and models, which provide information about weapons made of perishable materials and the way they were used in battle; and written documents, thousands of which have been discovered in mounds of the ancient Near East, some dealing specifically with weapons and warfare and telling us the names of weapons, or shedding light on methods of construction, trade, tactics and so on. These three sources naturally complement each other.

EARLY BRONZE AGE

The mace One of the most ancient weapons, the mace probably came into being in the 5th millennium BC and is widely dispersed over the whole of the ancient Near East. There is no basic change in form from its first appearance until it disappears towards the middle of the 2nd millennium BC. Generally it had a wooden handle, one end of which was fitted with the operative part, known as the mace head. The two parts were joined by means of a socket, the wooden handle being inserted into a hole drilled in the mace head. The two most common forms of mace head were those shaped like a pear or like an apple and those that were discoid or saucer-shaped, the latter group being found mainly in *Egypt. The mace head was usually made of stone from the Neolithic period onwards, but from the Chalcolithic period onwards many metal mace heads are found alongside stone ones. The function of the mace was to batter and smash. Thus the development of armor and helmets, especially from the 2nd millennium BC onwards, brought about its gradual decline and eventual disappearance, since it cannot pierce or cut.

The axe This resembles the mace in many respects, the main difference being that while the mace head is

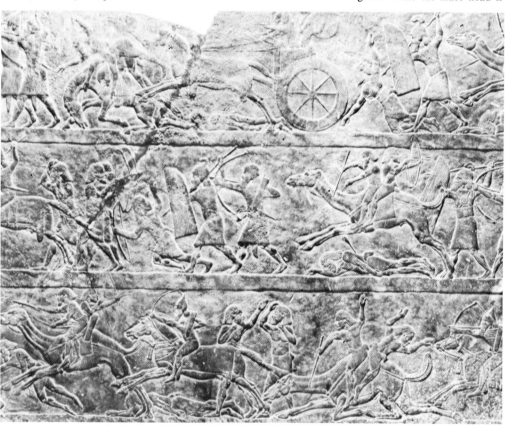

A chariot battle in one of the reliefs from Ashurbanipal's palace in Nineveh

blunt the axe head is sharp, which means that it can cut and pierce. Axes offer a good illustration of the various solutions found by weapon makers to the problem of attaching the operative part to the wooden handle, since some of them have a socket, like the mace, while others have the head inserted into the handle. This method is known as 'tang attachment'. All the axes known from Palestine up to the end of the 3rd millennium BC, except one found in the *Cave of the Treasure in the *Judean Desert, are tang axes. The typical axe found in Palestine during this period is known as the epsilon-shaped tang axe, as its shape resembles the Greek letter E. Three tangs were used, one inserted into the wooden handle while the other two were wound around or laid against it. Several variants of this type, dating from the second half of the 3rd millennium BC, are known from various sites throughout the ancient East.

The sword The Early Bronze Age sword in Palestine is short and straight and sharp at the edges and at the point. In fact such swords should really be defined as daggers. In many cases the blade is thickest along its central axis (known as the spine), which gave it stability and prevented it breaking or bending in action. The blade was always attached to the handle by means of a tang. The daggers of the period have a very short tang secured to the handle by means of several nails.

The spear This was a replica of the javelin in shape, but it was much heavier and was used with a thrusting, forward movement, instead of being thrown. All spear heads known from Palestine during this period are shaped like an elongated leaf; they have a pronounced spine and are fitted to the wooden shaft by means of a tang. Some are barbed, probably so that they would be more difficult to extract.

The chariot The four types of weapon described above are the only ones that have been found in excavations in Palestine from the period preceding the end of the 3rd millennium BC. But paintings and other images found in *Egypt and *Mesopotamia show that various kinds of bows, arrows, helmets and chariots also existed during this period. The earliest known chariots date from the 3rd millennium BC and originated in *Mesopotamia. They include remains of chariots found in excavations, as well as models, portrayals in art and written sources. This is a good example of the type of combined picture that can be derived from the three sources of information mentioned above. So far there is no evidence of the existence of the chariot in *Egypt during this period, and it is also very doubtful whether it was known in Palestine at that time.

Warfare Paintings and drawings found in *Egypt and Mesopotamia depict both battle in open terrain and attacks on fortified towns. Monuments from *Mesopotamia also show close formations of infantry organized in a deep phalanx, as well as chariots. The Egyptian illustrations prove that the battering ram had not yet been introduced, that fortifications were attacked by means of scaling ladders and that gates and walls were breached by means of axes and battering poles.

MIDDLE BRONZE AGE

The axe This presents the most interesting develop-
ment in the repertoire of weapons at this period. In contrast to Early Bronze Age practice, the socket attachment became the most common method of fitting the operative part of the weapon to the wooden handle and shaft and was used for all weapons except swords and daggers. The epsilon-shaped axe developed in the beginning of the Middle Bronze Age into a form known as the 'eye axe'. The 'eyes' were the residual mark of the spaces between the two inward curves of the epsilon tang, but were bound at the rear by the socket. To make this kind of axe a more effective piercing instrument further refinements were soon made: the blade was lengthened and the eyes became smaller. In its new, longer and narrower form this type is known as the 'duck-bill' axe, from its appearance. By the 18th century BC this duck-bill axe had given way to an extremely long and narrow shaft axe, almost resembling a chisel. This type was clearly designed for piercing and penetrating.

The sword This period is marked by the first appearance in Palestine of what is known as the sickle sword. We know from Mesopotamian pictorial images that this striking weapon emerged as early as the second half of the 3rd millennium BC. In its general shape it resembles an axe in which the blade and handle are made in one piece. Short straight daggers were used alongside the sickle sword. At the beginning of this period the dagger was narrow, resembling that of the previous period, but in the second half of the Middle Bronze Age the blade became broader, like an elongated and pointed leaf; this necessitated strengthening the blade with a prominent spine or even several such spines.

The spear and the javelin During the first part of the Middle Bronze Age there appeared in Palestine a type of spear in which the head was fitted to the shaft by means of a long tang, which would be curved at the rear to ensure a firm attachment. The spears and javelins of the period are also characterized by a spike-like metal butt, which was fitted to the shaft in the same manner. These butts allowed them to be stuck into the ground when they were not in use. They could also be used against the enemy in certain circumstances. Such heads and butts are found in great numbers, together with the short daggers mentioned above, all over the northern areas of the biblical lands. They are usually found in graves and during the first part of the Middle Bronze Age probably belonged to the semi-nomadic warriors who poured into Palestine towards the end of the 3rd millennium BC. In the second half of the Middle Bronze Age these tanged heads give way to socketed, leaf-shaped ones.

Other weapons Pictorial images and archaeological finds in countries neighboring on Palestine show that other types of weapons existed during the Middle Bronze Age. One important piece of evidence is the famous wall painting from a tomb at Bani Hasan in *Egypt, which depicts a caravan of Semites (perhaps inhabitants of *Canaan) on their way to *Egypt. The men in this group are holding a duck-bill axe, a double convex bow, spears and hurling sticks. Other images show that shields and slings were also used. Nothing is known about helmets and armor, but the introduction of perfected piercing axes during this period, along with the highly developed armor scales found in the Late Bronze Age, point to the existence of metal helmets and armor at this time. In the Middle Bronze Age the clumsy chariot with two or four solid wheels gave place to a lighter and more advanced model drawn by horses. These were probably brought into *Canaan by the *Hyksos. There is still no evidence of the introduction of the chariot into *Egypt in this period, but written documents and archaeological finds point to their presence in some of the countries bordering on the East Mediterranean, including Palestine, from the second half of the 18th century BC onwards. The introduction of chariots had a visible effect on the planning of city gates (*Fortifications). A fine example is the gates of *Megiddo, dating from the Middle Bronze Age onwards.

Warfare Interesting light is shed on methods of warfare during the Middle Bronze Age by written documents, especially the archives found at *Mari and 'The Story of Sinuhe the Egyptian'. From these it is known that armies were made up of units with a fixed number of soldiers, the smallest unit consisting of ten men. From this period comes the earliest evidence that duels were fought. These were contests between two heroes and the outcome determined the issue between two opposing forces. The battering ram, one of the most important inventions in the history of warfare, was first introduced in the Middle Bronze Age. Egyptian pictorial images of the period depict a primitive kind of battering ram, but direct and indirect references in the archives of *Mari show that it had already become an effective instrument by this period. The massive fortifications typical of the Middle Bronze Age were in fact probably built to counter the threat posed to the defenders of fortified cities once the battering ram came into use. They therefore point — though indirectly — to the decisive role this device played in siege warfare against fortified cities.

LATE BRONZE AGE

The axe Late Bronze Age axes were tanged, in contrast to the socketed axes of the previous period, possibly because Palestine had by now come once more under the rule of *Egypt, where the socket method of attachment was never used. Palestinian tang axes have long, piercing blades and a broad tang one-third the total length of the axe. Alongside these was a group of shaft axes, though they are less common. The back of the socket was sometimes fashioned into ornamental lugs in the shape of fingers or an animal's mane. This kind appears mainly in Western Asia and one found at *Beth-Shean is the only known example in Palestine.

The sword Swords or daggers of the Late Bronze Age are characterized by the fact that the hilt and blade were made in one piece. The hilt was studded, generally with wood, bone or precious metals. The sickle sword was also used and its blade, which in the previous period was comparatively short, became longer. Towards the end of the period a long, straight sword with a narrow blade came into use. It was introduced by the Sea Peoples (*Philistines), some of whom were serving as mercenaries in the Egyptian armies of the 19th Dynasty.

The spear The Late Bronze Age spear resembles that of the previous period. It has a socketed leaf-sheaped head with a protuberant spine.

Other weapons From the Late Bronze Age onwards pictorial images, found in great numbers, plus written documents, constitute the main source of information about both warfare and weapons. Most of these sources are Egyptian and describe not only the Egyptian army but also the armies that the Egyptians met on the field of battle. In addition, they provide the first detailed descriptions of military expeditions to *Canaan. The most noteworthy examples of such images in Palestine are the ivories found at *Megiddo, which tell us that the weapon used by the warriers of Syria and Palestine during the Late Bronze Age was the composite bow, the shaft of the arrow usually being made of reed and the arrowhead of bronze. The arrowhead had a tang, the upper part of which was thickened, and a prominent spine. This ensured that it could penetrate the coat of mail that was widely used in this period, especially for archers and charioteers. The size of the scales varies according to their position on the coat of armor, but they are always rectangular, with a spine on a rounded or pointed base.

Shields too were initially rectangular and were made of reeds or wood covered with leather. But from the 13th century BC onwards round shields appeared alongside the rectangular ones, introduced, as was the long straight sword, under the influence of the Sea Peoples. The helmets are rounded and cap-shaped, designed to protect the forehead and the back of the neck.

The sling is often mentioned in written sources but did not occur as a standard weapon for the regular army until the following period. The chariot appeared in *Egypt for the first time in the Late Bronze Age, probably via *Canaan, but it did not take long for the Egyptians to turn from pupils into teachers. In the beginning of the period the chariot had four-spoked wheels, like the Canaanite one, but from the end of the 15th century BC the Egyptian chariots had six-spoked wheels, which made them more stable and maneuverable than the Canaanite ones.

Warfare It is interesting to note that neither the detailed pictorial images from *Egypt nor the written sources give any hint that the battering ram was used, possibly because the fortifications of the previous period were so massive that they could not be breached by the battering ram as then known. The sources show that a fortified city was most often taken by an enemy who scaled the wall or breached the gate after battering it with axes.

Two important descriptions of warfare in open terrain have come down to us, one of the Egyptian battle against the *Canaanites at *Megiddo and the other of the Egyptians against the *Hittite-*Canaanite coalition at *Kedesh-on-the-Orontes. These give details of the tactical employment of infantry and chariots, the use of the surprise attack and the role played by intelligence reports.

IRON AGE

The axe The Late Bronze Age axe, with tang attachment, was also used at the beginning of the Iron Age.

As time passed socketed piercing axes appeared as well, but as battle tactics were perfected they slowly lost their importance as weapons. Instead, they are often depicted as working tools, used for felling trees or cutting through undergrowth. They were occasionally used for battering gates as well.

The sword Both the daggers of the Late Bronze Age and the long, straight swords that were introduced towards the end of that period continued to be used during the Iron Age. The blade of the sickle sword became longer until, in the late Iron Age, it was almost straight, being curved only slightly at the end.

The spears From the few examples of spear and javelin heads found, spears of both the socketed and the tang type were used; they were leaf-shaped, with a prominent spine.

Other weapons Compared with the previous periods, the Iron Age is the richest in pictorial images and written documents containing material for the study of the weapons and warfare of the period. While most sources at the beginning of the period are Egyptian, those from the 9th century BC onwards are mostly Assyrian, as befits Assyria's increased political importance. Although Egyptian and Assyrian artists mainly describe their own armies and battles, their descriptions also enable us to trace the characteristics of the armies that they faced on the battlefield, including those of Syria and Palestine.

The composite bow, already known from images of the previous period, continued to be used, but arrowheads had a flat spine at the beginning of the period, in contrast to those of the Late Bronze Age. Many iron arrowheads of the Late Iron Age have been found; they are comparatively small and are rhomboid in shape. At the same time socketed arrowheads made their first appearance.

The sling now became a standard weapon of the army. At the beginning of the period David was armed with one (1 Sam. 17:40) and from the 10th century BC onwards whole units of slingmen were introduced, first into the Aramean army and then into the armies of Assyria and Judea. The round shields that appeared towards the end of the previous period became the standard shield, alongside rectangular and convex models. The helmets worn by the warriors of Judea are conical, elongated at the sides to protect the wearer's ears. Coats of mail were also in widespread use and many scales have been found in excavations in Palestine.

At the beginning of the period the chariots of the previous period were still in use. But as time went on they became heavier until, in the 8th century BC, the wheels had eight spokes and were bigger than ever before. They were drawn by four horses and could carry four warriors.

The Assyrian monuments are an ideal source for the study of the battering ram, which became a most effective war machine. Basically it consisted of a wooden, box-like structure whose main function was to protect its operators; it had a turret from the ceiling with a rope hanging from it to which the thrusting beam was tied. The operative end of this wooden beam was made of metal and shaped like an axe head. The whole device moved on wheels. Pictorial images

Egyptian soldiers besieging a fortified town, 20th century BC; note small shields

show that certain variations in detail were introduced from time to time and illustrate the ram's use in battle. The reliefs of the Assyrian kings shed vivid light on the tactics employed for attacking a fortified city, an operation in which the battering ram always played a major role.

Warfare The most important written source for the study of warfare during the Iron Age is, of course, the Bible, while the most noteworthy pictorial images from the beginning of the period are the Egyptian reliefs depicting the battles between the Egyptians and the Sea Peoples (*Philistines). The detailed description of the sea battle should be specially noted, since such accounts are rare. It enables us to study the design and appearance of the warships of both sides and to make a comparison between the weapons and equipment of the two opposing armies.

The biblical accounts of the many battles that took place between the ancient Israelites and their various enemies allow us to find out about systems of recruiting, the structure and organization of the army and various battle tactics. A good example here is the story of the conquest of *Ai, which involved both deliberate deception and ambush (Josh. 8:1-24). Of the numerous battles dated to the period of the Judges the war against Sisera should be specially noted (Judg. 4, 5), since it sheds interesting light on the Israelite militia, which was made up of warriors from the individual tribes. Another interesting feature here is the surprise

attack launched by the Israelites when the *Canaanites could not use their war chariots because of bad weather conditions. The story of Gideon's war against *Midian (Judg. 7, 8) is most instructive in regard to the system of recruiting used, the planning of the campaign and methods of obtaining intelligence information.

Single combat was also practised in the early period of the United Monarchy, as may be seen from the account of the duel between David and Goliath (1 Sam. 17:4-7), especially concerning his 'weaver's beam' javelin, which was probably the typical Aegean loop javelin, so described on account of the loop wound round the shaft, which enabled the weapon to be hurled to a greater distance.

The introduction of chariot squadrons into the Israelite army occurred in the time of Solomon (1 Kgs. 10:26). Their use developed so rapidly that in the 9th century BC, when the great battle between a coalition of the kings of *Aram and Israel against Shalmaneser III took place at *Qarqar, Ahab, King of Israel, brought with him a greater number of chariots than any other member of the coalition. We know this from an inscription of Shalmaneser. (*See also* *MEGIDDO.)

The siege of *Lachish by Sennacherib should be dated to the 8th century BC. The story of this war as related in the Bible (2 Kgs. 18:13-17) is complemented by Sennacherib's own reliefs, which describe the siege, the fortifications, the warriors and the weapons in

Egyptian archers with bows

great detail. The archaeological excavations of *Lachish revealed the city destroyed by the Assyrians, which was covered by a thick layer of ash. Other relics, such as iron arrowheads that tell the story of the battle, were also unearthed.

WEAVING The weaver's craft was known in the ancient Near East from early times. Most of our knowledge of this ancient craft comes from *Egypt, where numerous specimens of cloth, mainly linen, have been preserved thanks to the dry climate. A close study of the techniques employed is therefore possible. Furthermore, wall paintings and clay models found in some tombs show exactly how flax was grown and illustrate the various stages in the process of turning the fibers into yarn and the yarn into cloth. In Palestine it was mainly wool from sheep and goats that was used, as we know from the Bible and from a considerable number of garments of the Roman period that have come to light in the *Judean Desert Caves, permitting an analysis of material and techniques. From the Bible we learn that the wool was spun (Exod. 35:25-6) on a spindle with the help of a distaff (Prov. 31:19). The spindle consisted of a rod about 3 feet long, at the end of which were one or two weights. These weights, hundreds of which have been found on sites inhabited from the Iron Age and later, were made of wood, bone or stone. The method of spinning was quite simple and does not differ essentially from the one used today by Bedouin women. The fibers of wool are placed in a ball on the distaff, which is held under the left arm, and the spindle is held in the left hand. The wool is plucked from the distaff with the right hand and drawn on to the spindle, which is turned at great speed, so producing the yarn. There are variations in the method of using the spindle, however, Woollen yarn was produced in this manner in Greece, as well as in Rome, from the 5th century BC onwards.

The yarn so spun (cf. Exod. 35:25) was washed and cleaned with niter and soap (cf. Jer. 2:22) and was then ready for dyeing (*Dyes and dyeing). The yarn was placed in a pot or basin containing a weak solution of the dyeing pigment and then transferred to another pot, in which the final stage of dyeing took place in a more concentrated solution. The dyed yarn was then rinsed in clean water and subsequently left to dry. It was now ready for weaving. Horizontal hand looms were used; they were placed on the ground and consisted of two parallel rows of pegs driven into the ground, to which the warp threads on which the actual weaving was done were attached. The process is referred to in Judges (16:14): 'and went away with the pin of the beam, and with the web.' The Bedouins spin and weave their yarn by this somewhat primitive method to this day, sometimes producing very considerable lengths of the fabric from which they make their tents.

Another type of loom, much employed in *Egypt and also used in Palestine, was vertical. Two long posts were driven into the ground and a third was placed horizontally on top of them. The warp threads were tied to the horizontal post, each thread being suspended by a weight. Loom weights made of stone

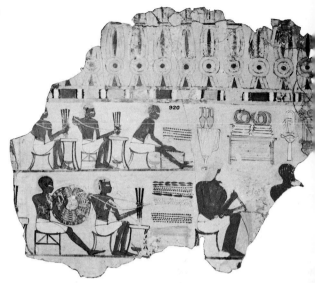

Cloth weaving and dying, in an Egyptian wall-painting

have been found on almost every site in Palestine. The horizontal post of the vertical loom is the 'weaver's beam' referred to in 1 Samuel (17:7). The weaving was done at the upper part of the loom, and the woven fabric was rolled on top of the beam. Initially it was inserted through the warp with the fingers, but later a thin rod, made of wood or bone, was used.

On hand looms such as these either monochrome or polychrome fabrics were produced. Joseph's coat of many colors (Gen. 37:3), or Aaron's 'broidered coat' (Exod. 28:4) may have been of the latter kind, as may the 'prey of diverse colors' of Sisera (Judg. 5:30). If multicolored cloth was to be made groups of fibers of different colors were tied to the horizontal beam. It was not until late in the Roman period that more advanced systems of weaving were introduced.

WEIGHTS AND MEASURES The most ancient standards of weights and measures are those of Egypt and Babylon. The Babylonian six-decimal system is based on a linear unit derived from astronomical calculations. The capacity unit is (the power of three of) the basic linear unit cubed, and the weight of water that such a cube can contain gave the basic unit of weight. The Babylonian system of measures was accepted by all the peoples of the ancient Near East.

In Palestine both the Babylonian system and the Egyptian decimal system were in use. The Hebrews, who had used the Babylonian system, introduced changes into it, as the result of Egyptian influence. Further changes were introduced by the Phoenicians and the Persians, who added some units of their own to the Babylonian system and dropped others. The units of weights and measures referred to in the Bible belong to both these systems, according to the degree of contact with the different cultures at the particular time in question.

LINEAR MEASURES Among primitive peoples the limbs of the human body served as units of length. Thus in the Bible the finger *(esbah)* was the smallest unit (Jer. 52:21); 4 fingers made 1 hand *(tepha)* (1 Kgs. 7:26); 3 hands made 1 span *(zereth)* (Exod. 28:16); and 2 spans made 1 cubit *(amah)*. There were at least two kinds of cubit: the long cubit that was used for sacred matters (Ezek. 40:5); and the ordinary cubit, which was 1 hand shorter than the sacred cubit. The following are the approximate values of the length units:

	long measure	short measure
1 finger	$\frac{9}{10}$in	$\frac{7}{10}$in
1 hand = 4 fingers	$3\frac{3}{5}$ in	3 in
1 span = 3 hands	$10\frac{4}{5}$ in	9 in
1 cubit = 2 spans	1ft $9\frac{3}{5}$ in	1ft 6 in
1 rope = 6 cubits	10ft $9\frac{3}{5}$ in	9ft

Some other measurements are used in the Bible that do not fall within this system, such as the *gomed* (Judg. 3:16); Authorized Version: 'cubit'), which was probably shorter than the normal cubit. The *saad* (2 Sam. 6:13; Authorized Version: 'pace') was probably not a specific measure.

MEASURES OF VOLUME Israelite measures of volume were based on the Babylonian six-decimal system. The smallest unit was the *log* (Lev. 14:10, etc.; Authorized Version: 'deal'), which was used both for dry goods and for liquids. 4 *logs* make 1 *qab* (2 Kgs. 6:25); $1^4/_5$ *qab* make 1 *omer* (Gen. 18:6; 1 Sam. 25:18, etc.; Authorized Version: 'measure'); 5 *ephah* make 1 *leteck* (Hos. 3:2; Authorized Version: 'homer'); 2 *leteck* make 1 *homer* (or *kor*) (Isa. 5:10; Ezek. 45:10-14). By calculating according to the biblical data and using actual measuring vessels found in excavations, scholars have obtained the following approximate values:

1 *log*			$\frac{1}{8}$gall
4 *log* = 1 *qab*			$\frac{1}{2}$gall
$7\frac{1}{5}$ *log* = $1\frac{4}{5}$ *qab* = 1 *omer*			$\frac{7}{8}$gall
24 *log* = 6 *qab* = $3\frac{1}{3}$ *omer*			
= 1 *seah*			2galls 7pts
72 *log* = 18 *qab* = 10 *omer*			
= 3 *seah* = 1 *ephah*			
= (Bath)			8galls 5pts
360 *log* = 90 *qab* = 50 *omer*			
= 15 *seah* = 5 *ephah*			
= 1 *leteck*			
720 *log* = 180 *qab* = 100 *omer*			43galls 2pts
= 30 *seah* = 10 *ephah*			
= 1 *homer* (=*kor*)			86galls 4pts

Except for the *omer*, all the units are multiples or quotients of the six-decimal system.

LIQUID MEASURES *Log* (Lev. 14:10 etc.); *qab* (2 Kgs. 6:25); *hin* (Exod. 29:4); *bath* (1 Kgs. 7:26, 38), equal in capacity to the *ephah*; *kor* (1 Kgs. 4:22; 5:11; Autho-

rized Version: 'measures'), equal to the *homer*. The *mesurah* (Authorized Version: 'meteyard') of Leviticus (19:35, etc.) is not a specific measure, but denotes a small quantity of liquid. In the Talmud the *mesurah* was $^1/_{36}$ *log*. These are the approximate values of the liquid measures:

				litres	
1 *log*				0.54	$\frac{1}{8}$gall
4 *log* =	1 *qab*			2.2	$\frac{1}{2}$gall
12 *log* =	3 *qab* =	1 *hin*		6.6	1gall $3\frac{1}{2}$pts
72 *log* =	18 *qab* =	6 *hin*			
	= 1 *bath*			39.38	8galls $5\frac{1}{2}$pts
720 *log* =	180 *qab* =	60 *hin*			
	= 1 *kor* (= *homer*)			393.8	86galls 4 pts

Except for the *homer,* all the other units are multiples or quotients of the six-decimal system.

WEIGHTS The Israelite weight system was based on the Babylonian standard, although the values of some of the weights were not always identical. The Babylonian values were as follows:

60 shekels = 1 *maneh*
60 *manehs* = 3600 shekels = 1 *kikar*

There were two weight systems, the values of one being double the other. This double standard of weights, which included a light *maneh* (weighing about $15^3/_4$oz), spread over all the ancient Near East.

In addition to the Babylonian system the *Phoeni*-cians and the Greeks developed another system with a heavy shekel weighing 218-224 grains and a light one of 112 grains. In this system the *maneh* contained 50 instead of 60 shekels, and there were 3,000 instead of 3,600 shekels to the *kikar*. The division into 50s probably originated in the Egyptian decimal system. This system, which was used by the Phoenician merchants, was accepted by the Israelites, the Persians, the Greeks and later also by the Romans, who all made some modifications arising from their specific needs. Alongside these systems others were also used at different times and in different places.

Goldsmith weighing gold on scales, Egyptian painting

Weight from Ur

In the excavations in Palestine, especially in the strata of the 7th-6th centuries BC, small stone weights with symbols on them have been found. Some of these symbols represent metrological values, while others are the actual names of the weights. Hundreds of weights have been measured and the results have shown that the same unit could vary considerably. It seems in fact that different values of the same basic units were used for different commodities, as is still done in some places today.

Three groups of weights with names on them have been found in the excavations: the *nesef*, the *pym* and the *beqa*. The Hebrew word *nesef* was unknown and may mean 'half', since *nusf* means 'half' in Arabic. It therefore probably denotes half the sacred shekel. The average weight is 152 grains. A small weight of $42\frac{1}{2}$ grains with the denomination 'quarter *nesef*' has also been found. The average weight of the *pym* is about 120 grains, while that of the *beqa* is about $94\frac{1}{2}$ grains. In addition to these three weights there are others marked by single letters or other symbols. These represented half a *nesef*, half a *pym* and a quarter of a *beqa*.

In the Hebrew Bible a weight is called a stone, indicating the material from which it was made. The Scriptures warn against cheating by using small weights for selling and heavy ones for buying (Deut. 25:15; Amos 8:5, etc.). The merchant would carry the weights on his person (Deut. 25:13, etc.). A weight that had been approved by the authorities was known as the 'king's weight' (2 Sam. 14:26). Commodities were weighed on scales and balances (Lev. 19:36; Isa. 40:12, etc.), the scales consisting of two bowls, equal in size and weight, suspended on three or four strings at the ends of a horizontal cane, which was held by a short rope. Another method involved placing the cane on a fixed base standing on the ground. Many such balances of all periods have been found in excavations.

ISRAELITE WEIGHTS The smallest unit is the *gerah*, or $\frac{1}{2}$ shekel (Exod. 30:13). There were also a $\frac{1}{2}$ shekel (1 Sam. 9:8; Authorized Version: 'fourth part') and a $\frac{1}{3}$ shekel (Neh. 7:71); *beqa*, or $\frac{1}{2}$ shekel (Exod 38:26).

These are all small units. The unit most frequently mentioned in the Bible is the shekel (Exod. 30:23 ff., etc.) and it is not always easy to decide which standard it was related to in any particular passage. It is possible that the shekel referred to in the books of Exodus, Leviticus and 1 Kings was equal to the shekel of Aegina, which weighed about 177 grains. The *maneh* (Exod. 2:69; Neh. 7:71, etc.) belong to the Phoenician standard and was therefore equal to 50 shekels. The *maneh* of the earlier books (1 Kgs. 10:17) was probably the Babylonian one of 50 heavy shekels. The *kikar* (Authorized Version: 'talent') is mentioned frequently in terms of a quantity of silver and sometimes as a weighing unit (Exod. 37:24). The *kikar* of the later books of the Bible is the Phoenician *kikar* of 3,000 shekels, while in the early writings the Babylonian or Syrian unit is referred to.

During the time of the Second Temple the Jews developed a system of weights based on a combination of the Phoenician with the Greek (Attic) and Roman systems. The values of the weights according to this system are:

6 *maoth* (*maah* = *obolos*) = 1 *zuz*	$52\frac{1}{2}$ grains
2 *zuzim* = 1 *shekel* (light)	105 grains
4 *zuzim* = 1 *shekel* (heavy)	210 grains
50 *zuzim* = $\frac{1}{2}$ *maneh*	6oz
100 *zuzim* = 1 *maneh*	12oz
6,000 *zuzim* = 1 *kikar*	720oz

In the non-Jewish cities of Palestine the normal Greek, Roman (and later Byzantine) standards of weights and measures were used.

WINE AND VINEGAR Wine has been known in the East as a beverage since the dawn of history. According to the biblical tradition Noah was the first man to plant a vineyard (Gen. 9:20-2). From the Bible, Egyptian wall paintings and reliefs and the remains of installations found in Palestine that were used in the production of wine, it is possible to reconstruct the methods by which it was made.

The grapes were brought in baskets from the vineyard to the winepress, which in the biblical period was either a natural flat rock or one flattened artificially (Isa. 5:2; 16:10; Jer. 48:33). The grapes were spread out on the rock and trodden, so that the juice flowed through shallow channels to a vat hewn at the foot of the pressing ground. It was left to settle during the night and then collected into jars, which were closed with clay stoppers. The skins of the grapes, which had been left behind after the first pressing, would be pressed again in order to extract the remaining juice. The jars containing the juice were then taken to the wine cellar for fermentation. The cellar might be a natural cave or a hewn cistern, in which the correct temperature for the fermentation process could be maintained. The fermentation of each kind of juice was kept separate, because the juice pressed from the skins would produce a wine that was different in color and taste, as a result of the materials present in the skins. The shoulder of the jar would be perforated, to

Philistine wine-vat and house walls from Gezer

permit the release of the gases that form during the fermentation process (Zech. 9:15). Once the fermentation was completed the hole made in the jar would be sealed and the origin and quality of the wine, plus the name of its owner, would be marked on the seal. Ample evidence of this practice has emerged from the excavations at *Ugarit, where at least three different qualities of wine were produced. Wine used for religious rituals was specially marked.

The Bible has many names for wines: 'blood of the grapes' (Gen. 49:11), 'wine of Lebanon' (Hos. 14:8); 'wine of Helbon' (Ezek. 27:18 — Helbon is also in Lebanon); *mezeg* (S. of S. 7:2; Authorized Version: 'liquor'); *reqah* (S. of S. 5:1; Authorized Version: 'wine'); 'wines on the lees' (Isa. 25:6). Additional names, not all of which are now intelligible, have been found on inscribed jars from the biblical period in Palestine: *themed, semadar*, 'old wine'. Further names are found in the Mishna and other sources, where categories called *Ammonite, Italian, *Sharon and

The vintage and grape-pressing, as depicted in a wall-painting in an Egyptian tomb

white wine are mentioned. A distinction is made in the Mishna between wine that is 40 days, two years and three years old. Wine was also made from dates, pomegranates, apples and other fruit, and from grain. From the New Testament we know that wine was sometimes mixed with other substances such as gall (Matt. 27:34; Authorized Version: 'vinegar'), myrrh (Mark 15:23) or oil for medicinal purposes (Luke 10:34).

There is ample evidence in the Bible that wine played an important role in the religious rituals of the ancient Near East. It was, for instance, used in the daily (Exod. 29:40) and monthly (Num. 28:14) sacrifices and holy days (Num. 15:5 ff.). The Law of the Nazarites forbade the consumption of wine (Num. 6:3; Judg. 13:4) and the Rechabites willingly refrained from it (Jer. 35:2 ff.). The priests officiating in the Tent of Congregation also refrained from drinking wine (Lev. 10:9; Ezek. 44:21).

The wine was a symbol of prosperity and fertility (1 Kgs. 4:25; 2 Kgs. 18:31) and grapes were one of the seven 'fruits' of which the Holy Land boasted (Deut. 7:13). Important personages would be greeted with bread and wine (Gen. 14:18). On the other hand, the Bible does not favor intoxication (Isa. 22:12-13; 28:1; Hos. 3:1; etc.), and abstention was a token of mourning (Dan. 10:3). Wine was given to those who worked hard (2 Chr. 2:10). People on a journey would drink it (Josh. 9:13; Judg. 19:19), as would the weary, those who had lost their way and those who were embittered (2 Sam. 16:2; Prov. 31:6-7). As well as being used in medicine it was an everyday beverage for kings and special ministers were appointed to supply it (Gen. 40:2; Neh. 2:1). The kings of Israel and Judah owned large vineyards and the wine was stored in the royal stores, which were also used to house taxes paid in kind (1 Chr. 12:40; 27:27; 2 Chr. 11:11).

The importance of viticulture in Palestine in biblical times, as well as in the Roman and Byzantine periods, is well attested by the archaeological finds. Many hundreds of winepresses, some of which were most elaborate (*Oboda, *Sobota), have been discovered almost everywhere in the country. It seems that in the late Roman period the vintners in Palestine, mainly those in the high mountains south of *Hebron and the central *Negev, perfected the process of fermentation. Wine-cellars were now made in caves excavated deep in the rock, the lower the level above the sea, the deeper the cave. To avoid as far as possible the penetration of warm air, the approach to the innermost parts of the wine cellar was through long, narrow tunnels, only high and wide enough to allow the safe introduction of the wine jars. Once these were deposited in the cellar, the tunnels were closed by masonry, as were the openings in the roof which supplied light and air during the working season. These were opened only when the wine was ready. There is also ample evidence in the epigraphical sources. Many of the ostraca of *Samaria deal with wine, for instance, while for the later period we have the evidence of the *Nessana papyri. Many reliefs and mosaic pavements in synagogues and churches illustrate the prominence of the vine and wine in Palestine.

Alongside the local wines foreign wines were imported into Palestine, as we can see both in some of the biblical passages referred to above and in evidence from the Hellenistic and Roman periods. Thousands of stamped jar handles from Rhodes, Chios, Cos and other wine-producing islands, as well as from different parts of Italy, attest to this. Pagan cults, in which wine was an important ingredient, were also common in Palestine throughout these periods.

Vinegar is a sour beverage, made from wine or beer before the process of fermentation is complete. Like wine, it was forbidden for the Nazarite (Num. 6:3). It was much used as a flavoring in food.

WITCHCRAFT AND DIVINATION Magic represents an expression of the belief that it is possible for man to exert an influence over his fellow human beings or to change the course of events. Witchcraft, the use of occult or supernatural forces to these ends, was practiced over the whole of the ancient world. Magic could be either 'white' or 'black'. Black magic was alleged to produce malevolent results for the person or people against whom the spell was directed; with white magic the opposite was the case. A magician would pronounce a curse, cast a spell, or break an image made to look like the person or people against whom the magic was directed, or with their name written on it. The *Execration Texts are an example of this. Another method of achieving the same result was for the sorcerer to associate with evil spirits that were alleged to be able to help him. Magicians performed according to specific formulae by which they attempted to influence the gods, the demons or natural forces to act on their behalf.

The Bible contains many references to witchcraft, but is strongly opposed to it. A person who practices this art is called a 'witch' (Deut. 18:10) or a 'magician' (Exod. 7:11, etc.). One of the terms by which the Egyptian magicians are referred to is *hartum* (Gen. 41:24; Exod. 8:3-15 Authorized Version: 'magicians'), the equivalent of the Egyptian *hrtyp*, the name given to the most famous magicians. In Daniel (5:7) Chaldeans are mentioned together with astrologers and soothsayers, the reference being both to an ethnic group and to a class of magicians. Sorcery and witchcraft are also mentioned in the New Testament (Acts 8:9-11, etc.). The 'wise men' (Matt 2:7), *magi* in the Greek, were an ethnic group (the term comes from Medes or *Madai) and, like the Chaldeans, became synonymous with witchcraft.

The biblical view of witchcraft is quite clear: 'There shall not be found among you any one...that useth divination, or an observer of times, or enchanter, or a witch, or a charmer, or a consulter with familiar spirits, or a wizard, or a necromancer' (Deut. 18:10-21). All of these were considered to be sworn enemies of true religious belief, at the center of which stands a belief in one God and adherence to his ways. The true believer will accept whatever God has destined for him and will not make any attempt to change it. In complete opposition to this stands the belief that witchcraft may influence the supernatural. Even the wearing of amulets, a common practice, was condemned by Isaiah (3:18-23; Authorized Version: 'bra-

Charm against the evil eye, Byzantine period

celets'). The attitude towards witches is laconically expressed: 'Thou shalt not suffer a witch to live' (Exod. 22:18). Saul had 'put away those that had familiar spirits', but in the end he had to resort to one himself (1 Sam 28:3, 7-25).

The attitude towards witchcraft expressed in the Bible had one purpose: to put a sharp distinction between Israel and the ways of the *Canaanites, as encountered by the Israelites in the land of Canaan. In practice it seems that this purpose was not always achieved. Jezebel was known for her 'witchcrafts' (2 Kgs. 9:22); Micah (5:12) mentions witchcraft and soothsayers; Manasseh, who 'reared up altars for Baal', also 'observed times, and used enchantments, and dealt with familiar spirits and wizards' (2 Kgs. 21:3, 6); and the methods of a female sorcerer are described by Ezekiel (13:17-23). But these seem to be isolated instances, and when witchcraft is mentioned it is mostly being practiced by other nations, as with the prophecy of Isaiah (47:9-13) on *Babylon. Still more typical is the prophecy of Ezekiel, who saw that 'the king of Babylon he stood at the parting of the way, at the head of the two ways, to use divination: he made his arrows bright, he consulted with images, he looked in the liver. At his right hand was the divination for *Jerusalem...' (21:21-2). This military divination was resorted to by the Romans at a later date.

WITCHCRAFT IN EGYPT The Egyptians resorted to witchcraft in all cases where natural methods were of no avail, using very complicated and exact formulae that involved much study. Witchcraft and religion were closely linked and black magic was hardly used. The welfare both of those in the land of the living and of those who had passed to the nether world was protected by witchcraft. As early as the 3rd millennium BC witchcraft has its special deity: Thot, god of wisdom, and Isis were its patrons. The art of witchcraft as practiced in Egypt was divided into several main classes:

Protective magic This kind of magic was the gift of the sun god, who created the charms by which mankind was protected from certain mischief, such as the bites of snakes, scorpions and wild beasts. It was very close to medicine and in fact Egyptian medicines were administered with certain charms.

Fertility magic This was practiced to ensure fertility, to assist in childbirth and to ensure success in love. It also afforded protection against the effects of storms and bad weather.

Divination People were always anxious to know their future. This type of witchcraft developed first of all in *Mesopotamia and appeared relatively late in *Egypt.

Black magic Generally forbidden in *Egypt; those who practiced it without authority were punished by the state.

Magic connected with the dead This was closely related to the cult of the dead, which was highly developed in *Egypt. It was intended to provide assistance to the deceased, in order to help them to overcome the obstacles that awaited them on their way to the world of the dead.

Performing of miracles The Egyptians left a large number of stories in which the deeds of the wizards are described. One book, ascribed to the four great wizards of *Egypt and dated to about 2700 BC, includes the story of how a crocodile made of wax was brought to life and was subsequently turned into wax again. Another book of the *Hyksos period, tells about animals and birds being revived after their heads had been cut off. These stories were still being related in *Egypt in the 1st century AD.

The Egyptian wizard used certain rituals in which the desired results were imitated. For instance, wax images of one's enemies would be burnt in a fire, which would ensure victory over them. The words of the charms had to be pronounced very carefully and the body must be moved in a strictly prescribed way. This art involved much study. The books that dealt with it were kept in the temples and were accessible only to the priests. The wizard-priest would first invoke the help of the gods, sometimes identifying himself with the bad spirit against whom he was acting, at the same time ordering, threatening, and trying hard to free the afflicted man from the evil spirit. The wizard-priests were trained in the 'House of Life', in which the books were compiled and kept.

Interpretation of dreams This was one of the main preoccupations of Egyptian magicians. In Genesis (41:8) we are told that Pharaoh summoned the magicians and wise men to interpret his dreams. There were also special books in which dreams and their interpretations were recorded. One such book, of the 19th-18th centuries BC, arranges dreams in tabular form, according to the predictions that may be inferred from them. The first list contains dreams that predict good, followed by those that foretell all kinds of calamities. There is a fixed formula: 'If a man did so-and-so in his dream it is a good omen, and such-and-such will happen to him'.

Lekanomancy This term refers to divination by means of a cup (cf. Gen. 44:2, 5, 12). This practice originated in *Babylon (see below).

MAGIC IN MESOPOTAMIA The aims of magic in Assyria and *Babylon were the same as those in Egypt. Here too the practice of magic necessitated much learning. As in *Egypt, it was accompanied by specific rituals, certain movements of the body and prescribed incantations. The following are some of the main types of magic practiced in Mesopotamia.

Protective and curative magic By this kind of magic different illnesses were cured and demons and spirits

were cast out. If the laws of one of the gods had been violated or one of the laws of the moral code transgressed, the magician would read out from a book a list of all possible sins and transgressions and in this way the afflicted man was cured. The effects of an evil spell cast by another magician could also be eradicated by making a wax image of the malign wizard and melting it in the fire, to the accompaniment of an incantation: 'May the wizard melt, as melts this image'.

Divination This was based on the assumption that every event, good or bad, could be foretold by certain signs discernible to the eye of a connoisseur. Such signs were recorded in books, one of which contains no less than 170 clay tablets filled with them. They included such things as a halo round the sun or moon, eclipses, certain constellations of the heavenly bodies, atmospheric phenomena, the flight of birds or insects, births of humans and animals, especially unnatural ones. Hepatoscopy was much used in divination. For this purpose a lamb's liver was used. Lekanoscopy, divination by cups, also belongs to this group. A few drops of oil were added to a cup full of water: the shape that the oil produced on the water enabled the diviner to foretell the future. Predictions could also be made from a cup full of oil on to which water was poured. In the times of the Mishna the Jews of the Roman period used wine instead of oil. (Today coffee is used in the east.)

Interpretation of dreams The library of Ashurbanipal in *Nineveh contained numerous clay tablets referring to this class of literature. Some list incantations for the purification of the effects of bad dreams while others contain no less than 2,000 'signs for the future'. The portents of dreams are grouped under certain items such as 'eat', 'drink' or 'meat', and each line in a table carries a description of a dream.

Malevolent magic As in *Egypt, this type of magic was performed by 'unofficial' magicians, and it was the duty of the official magicians to cure the effects of their spells.

In *Mesopotamia the art of magicians was the special province of a special category of priests, centered round the temples and in the custody of the chief gods Ea and Marduk.

WOOL (*See also* *WEAVING) Sheep's wool was the raw material most commonly used for weaving cloth. When it is mentioned in the Bible the wool of lambs and rams is usually intended (2 Kgs. 3:4). It is also referred to as 'fleece of sheep' (Deut. 18:4) and 'fleece of wool' (Judg 6:37). Being white, it became a symbol of purity (Isa 1:18). Brown or black sheep are also referred to in the Bible (Gen. 30:32 Authorized Version: 'speckled'), but it is doubtful whether their wool was used. Goat hair was also used for weaving, but apparently mainly for producing tents' sheets (Exod. 26:7), and it is thus, probably, that 'all work of goat's hair' (Num. 31:20) should be understood. The natural color of goat hair is black.

WRITING MATERIALS The beginning of writing marks the transition from the prehistoric and protohistoric periods to historical times. The early symbols used for expressing thoughts in writing were very complicated and only a skilled elite was capable of mastering them. Even when the number of symbols had been greatly reduced the art of writing remained in the hands of a limited class of people. The Bible refers to it as 'the writing of God' (Exod. 32:16).

Both the Bible and archaeological finds indicate that many different materials were used. The earliest documents were written on stone, the inscriptions being engraved on large rocks with a hammer and chisel, a stylus (a pointed metal engraving tool) or an iron pen. Many stelae inscribed in this way have been found in *Egypt, *Mesopotamia and Syria (cf. Job 19:23-24). Stones might also be plastered with lime and the writing applied with a brush or a pen dipped into ink (cf. Deut. 27:2-3). Stones could also be chiselled and smoothed, as with the tablets on which the Ten Commandments were written (Exod. 31:18), or the famous stele of Mesha, King of *Moab (*Inscriptions).

Tablets for writing on were in use throughout all periods. Very common in *Mesopotamia, but also found frequently in other countries of the ancient Near East, were clay tablets. A medium-soft lump of clay was taken and shaped into a flat tablet or a prism, on which the writing was engraved by means of a fine stylus. In order to preserve the document so written the clay was then baked by being left in the sun, or sometimes in an oven. Millions of such tablets have come down to us. Sherds of broken jars, called ostraca, with the writing mostly executed by means of ink and a fine brush, or sometimes a pointed tool, were also very common. Scores of these ostraca have been found in *Samaria, *Lachish and *Arad. In *Egypt and in Palestine wooden tablets were also commonly used (Ezek. 37:16), with writing in ink; sometimes they were coated with plaster or waxed, and the writing was done with a pen or stylus.

The commonest writing material in *Egypt was papyrus. The papyrus plant, native to the *Nile, had many uses in Egyptian daily life, the most important of which was in the production of writing paper. The stalks of the plant, which are 10-15 feet high, were dried, split lengthwise, cut to size and glued to form sheets of paper of a convenient size. The writing on papyrus was done with pen and ink. A large number of documents written in this way have also been found in Palestine, but these belong to the Roman and Byzantine periods (*Judean Desert Caves, *Nessana).

Another material frequently used in the Near East, and especially in Palestine, was parchment. This was made from the skins of animals, mostly sheep. The skins would be tanned, cut into sheets and, when necessary, sewn into scrolls. The writing was again done with pen and ink.

Writing on hard materials such as stone, clay and wood, was done with a stylus (Isa. 8:1). On softer materials, such as papyrus and parchment, a pen was used. The pen was made either of cane, sharpened to a fine point, or hard metal (Jer. 17:1; Job 19:24). This instrument permitted more rapid, cursive strokes (Ps. 45:1). The hardest end of the pen was its point (Jer. 17:1). It was sharpened with a penknife, also used for cutting papyrus and parchment (cf. Jer. 36:23).

The main writing pigment was ink. As this was much used in the writing of Jewish documents, the Mishna gives specific formulae for its preparation. Black ink consisted of soot, resin, olive oil and water. Rust in place of soot would produce brown ink, while the addition of a red pigment would give red ink. The ink was a thick sticky substance, so that the scribe could safely carry it in a inkpot in his belt (Ezek. 9:2). To make it ready for writing, water was added. The scribe kept his pens, penknife and inkpot in an inkhorn.

At Khirbet *Qumran tables and inkpots of clay were found in the scribes' rooms. These, together with other scribes' tools found in Palestine, enable us to reconstruct the art of the scribe. His commonest task was to produce books (Gen. 5:1). This term referred to legal documents (Exod. 24:7; Deut. 24:1-3), chronicles (1 Kgs. 14:19, etc.), and official letters (2 Kgs. 5:5). An educated man was one who could read a book (Isa. 29:11-12). Sometimes the word 'scroll' supplants 'book', implying that it was written on a flexible material that could be conveniently rolled (Jer. 36:17-29). Numerous such scrolls were discovered in the *Judean Desert Caves. The term 'letter' is found in the Hebrew only in the later books of the Bible (Neh. 2:7-9). The letter could be a written document or a moral message (2 Chr. 30:6).

Y

YARKON; ME-YARKON The Yarkon or Me-Yarkon ('Waters of Yarkon' in Hebrew) is a river mentioned as being in the territory of *Dan (Josh. 19:46); called el-Auja in Arabic, it is a perennial river rising at the foot of Tell Ras el-Ain. The mound referred to most probably contains the remains of the ancient city of *Aphek (Josh. 12:18; 1 Sam. 29:1), the Herodian Antipatris. The copious waters of the river made its valley ideal for intensive *agriculture. Indeed, along its bank numerous towns and villages sprang up in all periods. It is possible that in ancient times, before the mouth of the river silted, it also served as a safe harbor, and small vessels and rafts could navigate its entire length. Running from the foothills down to the sea the Yarkon River formed a military obstacle. Alexander Jannaeus built a line of fortresses as defense against the Syrians (Josephus, *War* I, 99).

YARMUK Rising from various springs in the *Bashan and the *Hauran, the River Yarmuk is the largest eastern tributary of the *Jordan. Narrow and shallow throughout its course, it widens just before it enters the River *Jordan about 4 miles south of the Sea of *Galilee. It is not mentioned in the Bible. In the Talmud it appears several times as one of the rivers around which Israel was founded. Its Greek and Latin name was Hieromices. Pliny (*Nat. Hist.* V, 16) mentions that it flows near *Gadara.

YEHUDIYEH (TELL EL-); LEONTOPOLIS An ancient mound in lower *Egypt, 20 miles north of *Cairo. The site was excavated at the beginning of this century by W.F.M. Petrie on behalf of the British School of Archaeology in Egypt. The earliest traces of settlement go back to the early period of the Middle Kingdom, but the period of greatest interest is that of the 5th Dynasty, when the site was occupied by the *Hyksos, who left a large fortified camp. The site was also inhabited at the time of the New Kingdom (18th Dynasty) and burials of this period have been found. The 20th Dynasty is represented by remains of a temple of Rameses III. There were also tombs from the time of the Late Kingdom. In the Ptolemaic period a new city, Leontopolis, was built on the site. By permission of Ptolemy VI Philometor, the high priest Onias, built a Jewish temple there; hence the Arabic name for the site, which means 'mound of the Jew'. According to (Josephus, *Antiq.* XIII, 62-73) this temple was built to the same plan as the Temple of Solomon in *Jerusalem. It went out of use at the time of the war between the Romans and the Jews in AD 66.

The Hyksos camp was surrounded by a huge glacis about 1,500 feet square. The width of this embankment is 80 feet by 140 feet at the top, and 130-200 feet at the base. It is made of sand covered with bricks and plastered. The inside of the camp was about 400 yd square and it is estimated that it could have provided shelter for about 40,000 people. On the east side of the camp there was a sloping ascent paved with bricks, about 180 feet long and fortified by two massive towers. This gangway provided a comfortable entry and a quick exit for chariots (*Weapons and warfare).

The temple of Onias was built to the northeast of the Hyksos camp, within a strong stone wall strengthened by a brick revetment on its inner side. It was approached by a very long stairway on the east, which led up from the outside, through the wall and the court, to the temple, of which little has remained.

The cemeteries of Tell el-Yehudiyeh yielded numerous finds from all occupation periods. Of most interest were those of the Hyksos period. In addition to numerous scarabs and bronze weapons a great number of pottery vessels, mostly juglets of a type recognized as typical of the *Hyksos and now termed 'Tell el-Yehudiyeh juglets', were found. These are black or dark brown and decorated with small dots made with a fine point; they form various patterns and are filled with a white pigment.

YERUHAM (MOUNT) An ancient site in the central Negev located on the northeast spur of Mount Yeruham, about $18^1/_2$ miles southeast of Beer-Sheba.

The site was first excavated in 1963 by an expedition headed by M. Kochavi, on behalf of the Department of Antiquities, the Israel Exploration Society, and the Hebrew University. The excavations uncovered remains of a large settlement of the Middle Bronze Age I, of which two levels were distinguished.

The first settlement established on the site (Stratum II) was surrounded, according to Kochavi, by a stone fence, nearly 820 feet long. The settlement was densely built up on an area of c. 1 acre and included square buildings, among which was a public building (Structure 2, 30 feet by 30 feet). Stone pillars, monolithic or made of several cylindrical drums, which supported the roofs, were found in every building. Stone benches ran along some of the walls of the houses. Inside the houses were pebble-lined hearths and cup-marks drilled into the rock. Also uncovered were various installations including a pottery kiln and silos.

The second and last phase of this settlement, was found to contain round structures and large animal pens. In one of these round structures was uncovered a hoard of copper ingots.

In 1973, R. Cohen, carried out three further weeks of excavations at Mt. Yeruham, on behalf of the Hebrew University and the Israel Exploration Society, with the aim of ascertaining whether an earlier settlement had occupied the site prior to the Middle Bronze Age I, and to clarify the relationship between the two strata of settlement. The renewed excavations uncovered no remains prior the Middle Bronze Age I, but the rectangular structures uncovered in the earlier excavations were now attributed to the last phase of the settlement (stratum I) and not the earlier level (stratum II). These structures had been founded on bedrock, and had never been built over. Only in Area C — in the northeastern part of the site — could an earlier settlement phase (stratum II) be distinguished. The 'stone fence' was in fact formed by the outer walls of adjoining, connected buildings. This would account for the absence of this 'stone fence' in certain areas of the settlement — a fact already noted by Kochavi, but which he explained as the result of later rebuilding by the settlers in its last phase.

Remains of two further structures were exposed. A large courtyard was common to both structures and to several other rooms found in the earlier excavations. The rectangular rooms and rooms with rounded walls both belong to the same structure (stratum I). It thus appears that the Middle Bronze Age I settlement at Mt. Yeruham consisted of six or more such structures, all having nearly the same plan, and lying one next to the other.

Z

ZAANANNIM; ZAANANIM A place in the south of the territory of *Naphtali, between Mount *Tabor and the *Jordan (Josh. 19:33). Heber the Kenite 'pitched his tent unto the plain of Zaananim, which is by *Kedesh' (Naphtali) (Judg. 4:11), and Jael killed Sisera there (Judg. 4:21). Not identified.

ZALMON *a)* A high mountain range on which a good deal of snow falls in the winter; also called the 'hill of God' and 'the hill of the Bashan' (Ps. 68:15). In the Roman period it was known as Asalamanos. Should probably be identified with the *Hauran, or Jebel ed-Druz.

b) A mountain in the region of *Shechem, where Abimelech and his men cut down bows from trees with which they set the tower of Shechem on fire (Judg. 9:48). It has been tentatively identified with *Ebal, *Gerizim, or another mountain in the region.

ZANOAH *a)* A place in the north of the *Plain (Josh. 15:34). In the period of the Restoration its inhabitants built the Dung Gate of *Jerusalem (Neh. 3:13). Eusebius (*Onom.* 92:14) mentions a village by the name Zanua located in his time on the border of *Beth-Gubrin, on the way to Jerusalem. Identified with Khirbet Zanu, northeast of *Azekah.

b) A place on the southern border of the territory of Judah, on the edge of the *Negev (Josh. 15:56). Not identified.

ZAPHON A town in the territory of Gad, east of the Jordan, in the valley of *Succoth, formerly a city of Og king of *Bashan (Josh. 13:27). It is possibly mentioned in the *El Amarna letters as well as in the list of conquests of Pharaoh Sheshonq. In the Hellenistic-Roman period it was known as Asafon, in the northern part of the *Perea, where the Hasmonean Alexander Jannaeus was defeated about 108-107 BC in a battle with Ptolemy, King of Cyprus (Josephus, *Antiq.* XIII, 338). Identified with Tell es-*Saidiye.

ZAREPATH An important Sidonian harbor, modern Ras Sarafand, about 6 miles south of *Sidon. It is mentioned for the first time as being situated along the Via Maris (*Roads) in a list of the time of Rameses II. Later it is mentioned among the Phoenician towns taken by Sennacherib in 701 BC. It was at Zarephath that Elijah revived the widow's son (1 Kgs. 17).

ZARETHAN A city in the *Jordan Valley, north of the city of *Adam (Josh. 3:16). According to 1 Kings (7:46) Solomon cast the vessels for the Temple between *Succoth and Zarethan, but the parallel reference in 2 Chronicles (4:17) has Zaredathan. This has led scholars to identify Zarethan with Zaredah, the birthplace of Jeroboam, son of Nebat. On the other hand, it has been pointed out that Zarethan should be sought closer to the River *Jordan. Still others believe that Zarethan is the same as Zererath, to which the *Midianites fled before *Gideon (Judg. 7:22). Several ancient sites, east and west of the *Jordan, have been put forward as probable candidates for identification with Zarethan.

ZEMARAIM A town in the territory of Benjamin (Josh. 18:22), which gave its name to Mount Zemaraim in the mountains of Ephraim. From there Abiah, King of Judah, spoke to the people before the war with Jeroboam (2 Chr. 13:4). The Septuagint and Josephus refer to the mountain as Oros Somoron, possibly Mount *Samaria (Shomron). Zemaraim is mentioned in Pharaoh Sheshonq's list. It is identified with several places, among them Ras el-Tahuneh, north of *Mispah.

ZEROR (TELL) This mound, whose ancient name has not been identified, lies in the Plain of *Sharon, on the Via Maris (*Roads), over which the small town stood guardian. Situated to the east of the modern town of Hederah, it is about 10 acres in area. The site was excavated in 1964-6 by K. Ohata on behalf of the Archaeological Expedition of the Society for Near Eastern Studies in Japan. The earliest remains are of the Middle Bronze Age. This town was surrounded by two walls of sun-dried brick, each about 11 feet thick, one of which possessed a large tower. Five occupation levels were observed in this period, the last of which was destroyed in the middle of the 18th century BC. The city of the Late Bronze Age was unfortified. It expanded over the whole mound and included an industrial quarter, where many ovens and furnaces for smelting copper (*Metals) were discovered, together with crucibles and nozzles for bellows. The large quantities of Cypriot pottery associated with the crucibles may point to the possible source of the metal.

To the early phase of the Iron Age belong poorly built huts, of which hardly any walls remain. The existence of the settlement at this period is mainly proved by the presence of refuse pits. This village suffered destruction by fire, possibly caused by the *Philistines. In about the 11th century BC a small fort was built on part of the mound, but in the 10th and early 9th centuries it was again an unfortified village. In the middle of the 9th century the northern part of the mound was fortified once more. These fortifications consisted of a thin wall strengthened by salients from within the town and by a retaining wall from without. Inside the wall a typical Israelite four-room house was discovered. By the end of the 9th century BC, possibly during the wars between Israel and the *Arameans, this town was finally destroyed. Some remains of the Persian, Hellenistic and early Roman periods have also come to light.

ZIKLAG A town on the southern boundary of Judea, in the lot of Judah (Josh. 15:31). It was given to Simeon (Josh. 19:5), although it seems that it was not in fact conquered by the Israelites, since in the days of Saul it was in the hands of the *Philistines. When David escaped from the wrath of Saul to the land of the *Philistines they gave him Ziklag at his request (1 Sam. 27:1-6). It was burnt down by the *Amalekites, but David recovered the town and took his revenge (1 Sam. 30:1-31). It was there that he learned of the death of Saul (2 Sam. 1:1). The town was resettled after the Restoration.

The identification of Ziklag is not certain. Some scholars identify it with Tell esh-Sharia, about 10 miles northeast of *Beer-Sheba, where remains of the Late Bronze Age to the Roman period have been found. Others believe that it should be identified with Tell Khuweilifeh, 10 miles northeast of *Beer-Sheba.

ZIN The Israelites passed through Zin on their way from *Egypt to *Canaan. It lies between *Kadesh-Barnea and *Akrabbim, and is referred to as the wilderness from which the spies went up to *Canaan (Num. 13:21). It was in this region that the incidents at *Massah and *Meribah took place (Exod. 17:7; Num. 20). It was the southern limit of the territory of Judah (Josh. 15:1-3). Identified as the wilderness lying south of *Kadesh-Barnea.

ZIPH; ZIF *a)* A town in the mountains of Judah (Josh. 15:55), whose inhabitants revealed David's hiding-place to Saul (1 Sam. 23:19 ff.); one of the cities built by Rehoboam for defense (2 Chr. 11:8). Its name appears on stamped jar handles of the time of the First

Seal impression 'To the King, Zif'

Temple (*Seals). It was known in the Roman period as a village called Zif on the main road leading from *Hebron southwards. Eusebius (*Onom.* 92:15) states that Zif is situated in the territory of *Beth-Gubrin, 8 miles east of *Hebron, but he probably mistook south for east. Identified with Tell Zif, southeast of *Hebron.

b) A place in the *Negev (Josh. 15:24). Not identified.

ZOAR The city to which Lot fled from *Sodom and *Gomorrah (Gen. 19:20-3, 30), whose earliest biblical name was Bela (Gen. 14:8); possibly the same as Suhru, mentioned twice in the *El Amarna letters. Zoar is frequently mentioned in the Bible together with the cities of the Valley of *Siddim, and the identification of this valley also determines that of Zoar. Deuteronomy (34:1-3) relates that Moses saw from the top of Mount *Nebo the whole of the country from the land of *Naphtali in the north to Zoar south of *Jericho, the city of palms. According to Isaiah (15:5) the town was situated at the edge of the land of *Moab. It is therefore commonly accepted that it should be sought somewhere south of the *Dead Sea. Josephus knew it in *Arabia (*War* IV, 482, *Antiq.* I, 204) and Eusebius (*Onom.* 42:1) mentions signs of its former fertility. The Talmud refers to 'Zoar the city of palms'. If we accept the theory that puts the Valley of Siddim to the south of the *Dead Sea, then the identification of Zoar with es-Safi, at the foot of the mountains of *Moab, is possible. At that spot there is a large oasis with plenty of water. Other scholars think that the Valley of Siddim should be placed to the northeast of the *Dead Sea, and therefore look for Zoar in that area. In the Roman and Byzantine periods a town called Zoara flourished south of the *Dead Sea.

ZORAH; ZOREAH A town in the *Plain, on the border of the territory of *Dan (Josh. 19:41), always mentioned together with *Eshtaol in this context (Josh. 15:33); the birth-place and burial-place of Samson. From Zorah five men went up to look for a new place for the Danites (Judg. 13:2; 16:31). In the time of Rehoboam it was one of the fortified cities in Judah (2 Chr. 11:10). It was resettled at the time of the Restoration (Neh. 11:29). Eusebius (*Onom.* 156:15) knew a village by this name in the territory of *Beth-Gubrin, 10 miles from that city, on the way to *Emmaus. The ancient name of the site has been preserved in the Arabic Saraa, close to Artuf, where the villagers point out a rock called the Altar of Manoah (cf. Judg. 13:19) and also Samson's tomb.

ZUPH; LAND OF ZUPH A place between Mount Ephraim and *Gibeah, where Saul decided to give up the search for his father's asses (1 Sam. 9:5). Its exact location is not known, but it should be sought in the area round Ramallah.

ZUZIM and EMIM Two peoples mentioned in connection with the war of the kings of Shinar against the kings of the region of the *Dead Sea (Gen. 14:5). According to the Bible Chedorlaomer conquered the Zuzim in Ham and the Emim in Shaveh Kiriathaim. On the other hand (Deut. 2:10-11, 20-1; Authorized Version: 'Zamzummim') the Emim dwelt in the land that was later to be inhabited by the Moabites and the Zuzim (i.e. Zamzummim) in the land of *Ammon.

Glossary

abraded	rubbed or scraped
agora	place of assembly, market-place
agape	love-feast in early Christianity
alabastron, alabastra	perfume bottle made of alabaster
amphora	two-handled vessel of Greece or Rome
amphorisc	a miniature amphora made of glass or pottery
anchorites	hermits
anta	pilaster, usually at a corner, of which base and capital do not conform to architectural style used elsewhere on the building
archon	a member of a body of ten, which administered the Greek polis
aryballos, arybaloy	squat Greek vase
assemblage	collection of implements found in surveys or excavations
lithic assemblage	stone or flint implements, as above (see FLINT TOOLS; STONE IMPLEMENTS; PREHISTORY)
ashlar	square hewn stone, masonry constructed of such stones
atrium	central court of Roman house, covered portico, forecourt of Christian church
basilica	oblong Roman building with double colonnades and semi-circular end; church built to same basic plan
bema	raised platform in church on which the ritual was performed
blades	long narrow flakes of flint at least twice as long as they are wide; (bladelets are smaller versions of these)
bouleuterion	council-chamber
burin	tool used for engraving lines
caravanserai	quadrangular inn with inner court where caravans are put up
carbon-14 dating	see ARCHAEOLOGY, METHOD OF RESEARCH
carinated	ridged
cartouche	scroll ornament, hieroglyphic names and titles of Egyptian king
casemate wall	double wall with partitions (see FORTIFICATIONS)
castellum	rectangular fortress with corner towers
cenobites	members of monastic community
codex	manuscript volume, especially of ancient Bible
colonia	status given to a Roman town
cordiform	heart-shaped
cover-stone	stone covering tomb
cubit	biblical measure of length, equivalent to 18–22ins
diakonikon	sacristy in Byzantine churches
Diaspora	collective term for all Jewish communities outside Palestine
direct-approach	term used to describe fortress or city gates of a special kind (see FORTIFICATIONS)
discoidal	disc-shaped
einkorn	one-grained natural growing corn
enceinte	enclosure in fortifications (see FORTIFICATIONS)
entbulature	upper portion of an architectural column
eparchy	district, administrative division in Hellenistic and Roman times
ethnarchy	country ruled by an ethnarch, 'ruler of the people'
exedra	recess or niche with raised seats
facies	common resemblance among plants, animals, fossils, etc., of any epoch or area
flake	chippings of stone of which implements were sometimes made
glacis	bank sloping down from fort on which attackers are exposed to fire (see FORTIFICATIONS)
graffiti	drawings or writings scratched on rocks, etc.
hamada	flint pebble-covered land
Hippodamian plan	town plan in which the streets intersect at right angles
Holy of Holies	inner chamber of sanctuary in Jewish Temple
hyparchy	administrative unit of country in Hellenistic and Roman times
hypocaust	hollow space beneath floor of Roman buildings in which heat is accumulated, for heating rooms and baths
juglets	small pottery vessel, used as a container for oil, perfume, etc. (see POTTERY)
khirbet	in Arabic, ruin
King's Highway, The	see ROADS
lamelek seals	see SEALS
laura	cave or secluded cell of a hermit
legume	fruits or vegetables of the leguminous family
lithic	see ASSEMBLAGES
loculi	funeral niches in tombs
locus	term used to denote room, court, cave, etc. and any closed unit in archaeological excavation
loess	deposit of fine yellowish-grey loam
lulav	palm branch used in the ritual of the Feast of Tabernacles
martyrium	chapel or church dedicated to a martyr
masoretic	accepted text of Hebrew Bible
massebah, massebot	see MAIN ENTRY
metropolis	title given to chief city of a country or district in Roman times
microlith	small flint or other prehistoric stone implement
Midrash, The	ancient Jewish commentary on the Scriptures
monoapsidal	(church) with single apse
narthex	antenave in Byzantine church from 5th century onwards
Nilometer	graduated pillar, etc., showing height to which Nile rises
orthostate	rectangular polished stone, mainly basalt, used to line the walls of Canaanite temple
ostracon, ostraca (pl.)	inscribed fragment of earthenware
palimpsets	writing material on which original text has been obliterated to make room for second text
peristyle	court surrounded row of columns
phylactery	small leather box containing Hebrew texts on vellum used in prayer
pictograph	pictorial symbol

plano-convex	brick with flat base and curved top	*stadium*	measure of length in ancient Greece, equal to about 202yds
policandelia	pottery or metal lamp with numerous wicks	stele	upright slab or pillar, usually with inscription (*see* MASSEBOT)
polis	Greek style city-state		
potsherd	broken piece of earthenware	stoa	portico in Greek and Roman architecture
propylaea	entrance	stylobate	continuous base supporting row or rows of columns
prothesis	part of church containing eucharistic elements before consecration		
		syncretism	attempt to effect union between differing sects or schools
racloir	*see* FLINT TOOLS		
sabbatical year	7th year in which Israelites were to cease tilling and release debtors and Israelite slaves	talent	ancient weight and money
		tell	*see* MAIN ENTRY
Sanhedrin	highest court of justice and supreme council in ancient Jerusalem, consisting of 71 members	temenos	large court, encircled by a wall, in which temple stood
		tessera	small square or cube used in mosaic
satrapy	provincial governorship in ancient Persian empire	tetrapylon	structure of columns built in the intersections of main streets in a Roman city
scarab	beetle-shaped seal, mainly Egyptian	tetrarch	governor of fourth part of country or province within the Roman empire
scraper	tool used for scraping, shaving smooth, polishing		
		toparchy	district governed by a toparch
shekel	ancient Jewish weight and silver coin	Torah Shrine	structure in which the Scriptures (Torah) are kept
sherd	*see* POTSHERD		
shewbread	12 loaves displayed in Jewish temple and renewed each Sabbath	type-vessel	*see* PREHISTORY
		ventral	lower side of vessel
sickle-haft	shaft made of wood or bone in which sickle inserted	Via Maris	*see* ROADS
		wadi	rocky watercourse that is dry except in rainy season
sigillata	pottery with impressed seal-like patterns		
socle	base or pedestal	tumulus	burial mound, often enclosing masonry
spheroid	rounded	ziggurat	stepped Babylonian temple

Ancient sources used in the compilation of this Encyclopedia

Amenophis II. About 1450–1425 BC. A description of his campaigns to the land of Canaan was found on two stelae in the temples of Memphis and Karnak.

Antonine of Placentia. Otherwise known as Antoninus Martyr. Very little is known about this priest of Placentia, Italy, who made a pilgrimage in the Holy Land at about AD 560–70. His account of the voyage contains important information.

Bible (Old and New Testament).

Cyril of Scythopolis. A Greek monk who lived in the 6th century after Christ, born in Scythopolis. He wrote biographies of Christian saints and martyrs, thus referring to places in the Holy Land in which they lived and acted.

Diodoros Siculus. A native of Sicily who lived in the 1st century BC. Writer of a world history from the earliest times to the conquest of Britain by Caesar in 54 BC. His book is of great importance for the early history of the Nabataeans.

Epic of Gilgamesh. Written in Accadian this epic recounts the creation of the universe and the history of the gods. In many details the Epic of Gilgamesh is parallel to the story of creation and the flood as told in the book of Genesis. A fragment of this epic was found at Megiddo.

Epiphanius. A native of Palestine, lived in the 4th century after Christ. A writer of several church and apologetic books, of which some information concerning the Holy Land in his times may be gained.

Eusebius. A native of Palestine, who lived about AD 260–339. Greek writer of Christian Church history. Among his important writings was the *Onomasticon*. It includes all geographical names of the Holy Land which are found in the Bible and their identification with sites known in the time of writing, and hence its great importance.

Excecration Texts *see* MAIN ENTRY.

Flavius Josephus. A Jewish historian who lived in AD 37–95. His books: *Life, Jewish Antiquities* and *Jewish War* are a primary source for the history and topography of Judaea in the times of the Second Temple.

Herodotus. Lived about 485–425 BC. The Father of History. A Greek, native of Halikarnassus, who wrote the first world history, in which some chapters are dedicated to Palestine.

Hieronymus. Lived AD 348–420. Native of Stridon in Dalmatia. Translator of Eusebius' *Onomasticon* into Latin, adding some information.

'Israel Stele' of Merneptah. Merneptah, King of Egypt, son of Rameses II, left in his mortuary temple at Thebes a hymn glorifying the deeds of the king. In it is referred to also his victory over Israel, and hence the name. The event should have happened in about 1230 BC.

Lachish Letters *see* LACHISH, INSCRIPTIONS.

List of Scylax. Scylax was a Greek sailor who lived in the 5th century BC. A list of Phoenician cities on the coast of Palestine, which was compiled in the 4th century BC was ascribed to him, and hence the name.

Medaba Map *see* MEDABA, MOSAICS.

Marcus Diaconus, Writer of a book on the life of Porphirios, Bishop of Gaza. The exact date of the compilation of the book is not known, possibly in the 6th or 7th centuries after Christ. The book contains a description of the pagan temples at Gaza which were destroyed around AD 300.

Mari Archives *see* MARI.

Mishna. A codex of commentaries to the scriptures. It consists of orders *(sedarim)*, each order containing several treatises *(massektot)*, the further division being into chapters *(perakim)*, and paragraphs *(mishnayot or halakhot)*. The references are made accordingly.

Notitia Dignitatum. A list of the places in the western and eastern Roman empire in which Roman garrisons were stationed, giving the name of each unit. Compiled in the times of emperor Theodosius II (AD 408–50). Of utmost importance for the study of the Roman frontiers in Palestine and the neighbouring countries in the early Byzantine period.

Papyri of Nessana *see* NESSANA.

Papyrus Anastasi I. A collection of Egyptian papyri, named after their collector, now in the British Museum. Some of these papyri have some bearing on the early history of Israel.

Papyrus Haris I. A papyrus originating in Thebes, Egypt, from the times of Rameses III (of about 1164 BC), referring to the battle with the Sea Peoples.

Peutinger Map. A Roman road map of the 4th century after Christ, containing all major roads in the Roman empire, named after its discoverer and first publisher. It includes some of the important roads crossing Palestine, marking the important road stations and the distances from each other in miles.

Pilgrim Arculf. A French bishop who made a pilgrimage in the Holy Land at about AD 670. He stayed nine months in Jerusalem, and on his journey back to Europe he told his story to Adamanus, abbot of a monastery at Iona, an island off the shore of Scotland, who put the story in writing.

Pilgrim of Bordeaux. An anonymous traveller who made a pilgrimage from Bordeaux in France to the Holy Land in AD 333. His account contains his itinerary marking the stations and their distances from each other.

Pliny, Gaius Plinius Secundus ('Pliny the Elder'), lived AD 23–79, died during the eruption of the Vesuvius, which he came to investigate. Writer of *Historia naturalis* — Natural History, being a work of encyclopedic scope, embracing every field of science of his time. Some of the natural phenomena of Palestine are elucidated.

Ptolemy. Claudius Ptolemaeus, died in the middle of the 2nd century after Christ. An Alexandrian mathematician and geographer. One of his major works is his *Geographia*, containing much information on the east.

Sennaherib, Annals of. The annals of Sennaherib (704–681 BC), King of Assyria were written on a clay prism. A pictorial and verbal description of the conquest of several cities in Judaea, like that of Lachish, were found on the walls of his palace at Nineveh, now in the British Museum.

Septuagint Bible. The most important version of the Old Testament, translated under Ptolemy Philadelphus (285–246 BC), in Alexandria. According to tradition the work was done by 72 Jewish scholars, and hence its name. In reality the work is believed to have been done by a large number of scholars, over a longer period of time, terminating at about 132 BC. Except for the books of the accepted Jewish codex, the Septuagint includes also some of the books of the apocryphal literature.

Sethos I, Lists of. Sethos I (about 1318–1304 BC) left a detailed account of his campaigns in Palestine on the walls of the great hall at Karnak, and on a stele discovered at Beth-Shean.

Sheshonq's I List. Pharaoh Sheshonq I (about 945–924 BC) left a list of cities which he conquered in Palestine during a campaign which he conducted there.

Sozomenus, *Historia ecclesiastica*. Sozomenus, a native of Gaza lived in the first half of the 5th century after Christ, and served as a lawyer in Constantinople. He wrote an ecclesiastical history, which refers to holy sites in the Holy Land.

Strabon. Lived about 63 BC–AD 19. Born in Amasia Pontus. A Greek geographer who wrote a *Geographia*, containing much information which derives from earlier writings, as well as some based on his own observations.

Taanach Tablets *see* TAANACH.

Table of Nations. The tenth chapter of Genesis which contains the genealogy of the human race starting with Noah and his three sons.

Talmud, Babylonian and Jerusalem. References to the Talmud, a compilation of commentaries on the Mishna, are made to order, treatise, chapter and page.

Tuthmosis III, Annals of. Tuthmosis III (about 1490–1436 BC), Pharaoh of Egypt left reliefs engraved on the walls of the temple at Karnak, containing both verbal and pictorial descriptions, many of which refer to places in Palestine.

Tiglath-Pileser II, Annals of. Tiglath-Pileser III (745–727 BC), King of Assyria had his annals on his campaigns to Palestine written on clay tablets and on a stone slab found at Calah.

Ugarith Documents *see* UGARITH.

Vitruvius. A Roman architect at the end of the 1st century BC, who compiled a book 'On architecture', the only ancient book on this subject which is extant.

Wen-Amon papyrus. Wen-Amon was an official in the temple of the god Amon at Karnak. In this papyrus, now at Moscow, it is told that he was sent on a mission to Phoenicia, thus mentioning several places, some of which must have been on the Palestinian coast. It dates to the 11th century BC.

Zenon papyri. Zenon, a native of Kaunos in Caria, born at the end of the 3rd century BC, acted as assistant to Apollonius, finance minister of Ptolemy II. In this power Zenon travelled much in the east. In this way some of the accounts of his journeys, written on papyrus sheets, are a first-hand source of knowledge for the history of Palestine at the beginning of the Hellenistic period.

Chronological Tables

The Archaeological Periods in Palestine

Paleolithic (Old Stone Age)	700,000-15,000 BC	Iron Age 2A	1000-900
Epipaleolithic (Middle Stone Age)	15,000-8300	Iron Age 2B	900-800
		Iron Age 2C	800-586
Neolithic (New Stone Age)	8300-4500		
Chalcolithic	4500-3100	*Babylonian and Persian Periods*	586-332
		Hellenistic Period	
Bronze Age		Hellenistic 1	332-152
Early Bronze Age 1	3150-2850	Hellenistic 2 (Hasmonean)	152-37
Early Bronze Age 2	2850-2650		
Early Bronze Age 3	2650-2350	*Roman Period*	
Early Bronze Age 4	2350-2200	Early Roman	37 BC-AD 70
Middle Bronze Age 1	2200-2000	Middle Roman	70-180
Middle Bronze Age 1	2000-1750	Late Roman	180-324
Middle Bronze Age 3	1750-1550		
Late Bronze Age 1	1550-1400	*Byzantine Period*	
Late Bronze Age 2	1400-1300	Byzantine 1	324-451
Late Bronze Age 3	1300-1200	Byzantine 2	451-640
Iron Age		*Early Arab Period*	640-1099
Iron Age 1A	1200-1150		
Iron Age 1B	1150-1000	*Crusader Period*	1099-1291

The Chronology of the Kings of Judah and Israel

The United Kingdom

Saul	*c.*	1020-1004 BC
David		1004-965
Solomon		965-928

Judah		Israel	
Rehoboam	928-911	Jeroboam	928-907
Abijam	911-908	Nadab	907-906
Asa	908-867	Baasha	906-883
Jehoshaphat	867-846	Elah	883-882
Jehoram	846-843	Zimri	882
Ahaziah	843-842	Omri	882-871
Athaliah	842-836	Ahab	871-852
Joash	836-798	Ahaziah	852-851
Amaziah	798-769	Jehoram	851-842
Uzziah	769-733	Jehu	842-814
Jotham	758-743	Jehoahaz	814-800
Ahaz	733-727	Jehoash	800-784
Hezekiah	727-698	Jeroboam	784-748
Manasseh	698-642	Zechariah	748
Amon	641-640	Shallum	748
Josiah	640-609	Menahem	747-737
Jehoahaz	609	Pekahiah	737-735
Jehoiakim	609-598	Pekah	735-733
Jehoiachin	597	Hoshea	733-724
Zedekiah	596-586		

The Herodians

Herod I (the Great)	37-4 BC
Archelaus	4 BC-AD 6
Herod Antipas	4 BC-AD 39
Philip	4 BC-AD 34
Herod Agrippa I	AD 37-44
Agrippa II	AD 53-100(?)

The Procurators

Coponius	*c.* AD 6-9	Cuspius Fadus	41-46
M. Ambibulus	9-12	Tiberius Alexander	46-48
Annius Rufus	12-15	Ventidius Cumanus	48-52
Valerius Gratus	15-26	Antonius Felix	52-60
Pontius Pilatus	26-36	Porcius Festus	60-62
Marcellus	36-37	Albinus	62-64
		Gessius Florus	64-66

The Hasmoneans

Jonathan	152-142 BC	Salome Alexandra	76-67
Simeon	142-134	Aristobulus II	67-63
John Hyrcanus	134-104	Hyrcanus II	63-40
Aristobulus	104-103		
Alexander Jannaeus	103-76	Matthias Antigonus	40-37

Kings of Egypt
(Selected List)

Pre-Dynastic Period			Amenophis IV	1379-1362 BC
4th and 3rd millennia			(Akhenaten)	
Proto-Dynastic Period			Smenkhkare	1364-1361
Ist Dynasty	c. 3100-2890 BC Narmer		Tutankhamun	1361-1352
IInd Dynasty	c. 2890-2686		Ay	1352-1348
IIIrd Dynasty	c. 2686-2613		Horemheb	1348-1320
Old Kingdom			XIXth Dynasty	1320-1200
IVth Dynasty	c. 2613-2494		Rameses I	1320-1318
	Sneferu		Sethos I	1318-1304
	Cheops		Rameses II	1304-1237
	Cheops		Merneptah	1236-1223
Vth Dynasty	c. 2494-2345		Sethos II	1216-1210
VIth Dynasty	c. 2345-2181		XXth Dynasty	1200-1085
	Phiops I		Rameses III	1198-1166
First Intermediate Period			Rameses IV-XI	1166-1085
VIIth Dynasty-Xth Dynasty			*End of New Kingdom*	
Middle Kingdom			XXIst Dynasty	1085-935
XIth Dynasty	c. 2133-1991		XXIInd Dynasty	935-730
XIIth Dynasty	c. 1991-1786		Sheshonq I	935-914
Ammenemes I	1991-1962		Osorkon II	914-874
Sesostris I	1971-1928		XXIIIrd Dynasty	817-740
Ammenemes II	1929-1895		XXIVth Dynasty	730-709
Sesostris II	1897-1878		XXVth Dynasty	750-656
Sesostris III	1878-1843		(Nubian or Ethiopian)	
Ammenemes III	1842-1797		Shabaka	716-695
Ammenemes IV	1798-1970		Taharqa	689-664
Sobkneferu	1789-1786		XXVIth Dynasty	664-525
Second Intermediate Period — the Hyksos Period			Psammetichus I	664-610
XIII-XVIIth Dynasties			Necho II	610-595
New Kingdom			Psammetichus II	595-589
XVIIIth Dynasty	1567-1320		Psammetichus III	526-525
Amosis	1570-1546		XXVIIth Dynasty	505-404
Amenophis I	1546-1526		(Persian)	
Tuthmosis I	1525-1512		Campyses	525-522
Tuthmosis II	c. 1512-1504		Darius I	521-486
Hatshepsut	1503-1482		Xerxes	486-466
Tuthmosis III	1504-1450		Artaxerxes	465-424
Amenophis II	1450-1425		Darius II	424-404
Tuthmosis IV	1425-1417		XXVIIIth-XXXth	
Amenophis III	1417-1379		Dynasties	404-343

Kings of Assyria (Selected List)

Shalmaneser I	1274-1245 BC	Adadnirari III	810-783 BC
Tiglath-Pileser I	1115-1077 BC	Shalmaneser IV	782-772 BC
Ashurnasirpal I	1049-1031 BC	Tiglath-Pileser III	745-727 BC
Shalmaneser II	1030-1019 BC	Shalmaneser V	726-722 BC
Tiglath-Pileser II	966-935 BC	Sargon II	721-705 BC
Adadnirari II	911-891 BC	Sennacherib	704-681 BC
Ashurnasirpal II	883-859 BC	Esarhaddon	680-669 BC
Shalmaneser III	858-824 BC	Ashurbanipal	668-631 BC

Kings of Babylon (Selected List)

Nabopolassar	626-605 BC
Nebuchadnezzer II	605-562 BC
Nabunaid	556-539 BC

Kings of Persia (Selected List)

Cyrus	559-530 BC
Cambyses	530-522 BC
Darius I	522-486 BC
Xerxes	486-464 BC
Artaxerxes I	464-423 BC
Darius II	423-404 BC

Seleucid Kings

Seleucus I Nicator	311-281 BC	Alexander Balas	150-145	Antiochus IX Cyzicenus	115-95
Antiochus I Soter	281-261	Demetrius II Nicator	145-140	Seleucus VI Epiphanes Nicator	96-95
Antiochus II Theos	261-246	Antiochus VI Epiphanes	145-138	Demetrius III Philopator	95-88
Seleucus II Callinicus	246-225	Antiochus VII Sidetes	138-129	Antiochus X Eusebes	95-83
Seleucus III Soter	225-223	Demetrius II Nicator	129-125	Antiochus XI Philadelphus	94
Antiochus III the Great	223-187	Cleopatra Thea	126	Philip I Philadelphus	94-83
Seleucus IV Philopator	187-175	Cleopatra Thea and		Antiochus XII Dionysus	87-84
Antiochus IV Epiphanes	175-164	Antiochus VIII Grypus	125-121	Antiochus XIII	69-64
Antiochus V Eupator	163-162	Seleucus V	125	Philip II	67-65
Demetrius I Soter	162-150	Antiochus VII Grypus	121-96		

The Ptolemies (Selected List)

Ptolemy I Soter	304-282 BC	Ptolemy IX Soter II	116-107 BC
Ptolemy II Philadelphus	285-246	Ptolemy X Alexander I	107-88
Ptolemy III Euergetes	246-221	Ptolemy IX Soter II (restored)	88-81
Ptolemy IV Philopator	221-204	Ptolemy XI Alexander II	80
Ptolemy V Epiphanes	204-180	Ptolemy XII Neos Dionysos	80-51
Ptolemy VI Philometer	180-145	Cleopatra VII Philopator	51-30
Ptolemy VII Neos Philopator	145-144	*overlapping dates usually indicate co-regencies*	
Ptolemy VIII Euergetes II	145-116		

Roman and Byzantine Emperors (Selected List)

Augustus	27 BC-AD 14	Geta	211-212	Constance	353-362
Tiberius	AD 14-37	Macrinus	217-218	Julian the Apostate	361-363
Caligula	37-41	Diadumenianus	218	Valens	364-378
Claudius	41-54	Elagabalus	218-222	Valentinian	364-375
Nero	54-68	Alexander Severus	222-235	Theodosius	379-383
Galba	68-69	Maximian I	235-238	Arcadius	395-408
Vespasian	69-79	Philip the Arab	244-249	Theodosius II	408-450
Titus	79-81	Decius	249-251	Marcian	450-457
Domitian	81-96	Trebonianus Gallus	251-253	Leon I	457-474
Nerva	96-98	Valerian	253-260	Zenon	474-491
Trajan	98-117	Gallienus	253-268	Anastasius I	491-518
Hadrian	117-138	Aurelian	270-275	Justin I	518-527
Antoninus Pius	138-161	Probus	276-282	Justinian I	527-565
Lucius Verus	161-169	Diocletian	284-305	Justin II	565-578
Commodus	180-192	Maximianus	286-305	Tiberius II	578-582
Septimius Severus	193-211	Constantius I	293-306	Focas	602-610
Pescennius Niger	193-194	Galerius	293-311	Heraclius	610-641
Caracalla	211-217	Constantine I	306-337	Constans II	641-668
		Magnentius	337-353		

Acknowledgements

The Publishers wish to express their thanks and appreciation to the following individuals for their help and advice: Inna Pommerantz; Irène Lewitt; Hannah Gafni;

to the following for help in the selection of coins and for permission to photograph their collections: The Department of Antiquities, Israel Ministry for Education and Culture; Teddy Kollek; Ya'akov Meshorer; Arnold Spaer;

to the following for permission to reproduce illustrations: The British Museum (p. 17, 19, 31, 44, 150, 161, 179, 216, 246, 297, 396); Hirmer Fotoarchiv, München (p. 24, 123, 126, 141, 163, 210, 231, 248, 258, 313, 331, 347, 390-392, 403); British School of Archaeology, Jerusalem (p. 189); Galleria del Candelabri, Vatican (p. 28); Nelson Glueck (p. 47, 118, 135, 367, 368); Staatliche Museen zu Berlin (p. 50); The Metropolitan Museum, New York (p. 67, 400); Maritime Museum, Haifa (p. 382); Mission Archéologique Française (p. 311); Hebrew University, Jerusalem, Department of Archaeology (p. 55, 152, 240, 378); Hebrew Union College (p. 96, 97, 103, 113, 155, 165-166); University of Tel Aviv, Department of Archaeology (p. 97, 109, 167); Glass Museum, Tel Aviv (p. 159-161); Antique Art Museum, Haifa (p. 348); The Oriental Institute, University of Chicago (p. 85, 115, 187); Yale University Press (p. 120); Ashmolean Museum (p. 217, 314); Z. Yeivin (p. 337); Louvre Museum (p. 13, 35, 263, 365); Giraudon (p. 73); A. Alon (p. 273, 393, 408); Y. Yadin (p. 14, 169, 233); Pontifical Institute, Jerusalem (p. 386); Y. Aharoni (p. 33, 34, 372); A. Negev (p. 32, 77, 89, 178, 274, 356, 358, 359); M. Broshi (p. 237); E. Anati (p. 139, 140, 242, 311); J. Callaway (p. 20); Palestine Exploration Fund (p. 230); Archaeological Receipts Fund, Ministry of Science, Greece (p. 100, 399); Maurice Chuseville, Vanves (p. 257, 390); A. Mazar (p. 316-317); A. Ronen (p. 306-310); Agora Excavations, Athens (p. 301); E. Stern, Tel Dor Excavations Project (p. 102, 119); Photo Garo / E. Lessing (p. 105, 112, 242); American School of Archaeology (p. 252); City of David Excavations (p. 106, 107, 197); B. Rothenberg (p. 249); Unesco (p. 254); Israel Museum, Jerusalem (p. 43, 78, 86, 104, 107, 109, 111, 142, 185, 241, 243, 247, 249, 266); The Shrine of the Book, Jerusalem (p. 114, 246); Israel Department of Antiquities and Museums (p. 12, 15, 21, 22, 23, 45, 46, 52, 53, 54, 57, 59, 63, 64, 65, 66, 68-71, 76, 92, 93, 100, 102, 133, 147, 151, 176, 183-185, 190, 195, 203, 204, 206, 220, 253, 256, 260, 266, 267, 269-272, 276-278, 285, 287-289, 293, 295, 300, 303, 304, 311, 318, 324, 338-339, 344, 354, 369, 380-381, 385, 405, 412. Items on pp. 12, 15, 45, 46, 64, 92, 93, 176, 185, 220, 250, 251, 260, 270-272, 276-278, 285, 287-289, 295, 300, 303, 304, 324, 385, 405 are on display at the Israel Museum, Jerusalem).

Photographic credits: W. Braun (p. 351); Palphot (p. 395); M. Pan (p. 167); Z. Radovan (p. 84, 97, 98, 99, 104, 105, 106, 108, 119, 244, 270, 373); Brody (p. 274); F. Csasznik (p. 286); Milon (p. 304); Sadeh (p. 382); Burger (p. 142, 295, 300, 330); Lehman (p. 311); Rosen (p. 236); D. Rubinger (p. 41, 82, 149, 173, 207, 264); D. Harris (p. 22, 33, 43, 45, 46, 58, 60, 62, 69-72, 86, 87, 92, 101, 108, 133, 158, 160, 202-204, 206, 213, 220, 240, 266, 267, 269, 271, 272, 276-278, 285, 287, 288, 318, 319, 335, 337-339, 364, 371, 374, 375, 377, 385, 387, 405); A.A. Van der Heyden (p. 99, 105); A. Hai (p. 109); R. Kneller (p. 110); Jerusalem Publishing House (p. 101).

Maps and diagrams p. 198, 199 after M. Avi-Yonah; p. 222 after M. Gihon; p. 234 after Y. Yadin; p. 303 after R. Amiran. Maps by Carta, Jerusalem.

PORTLAND COMMUNITY COLLEGE LRC

3 3019 00239 5680

3